VOICES & VISIONS

VOICES & VISIONS

THE POET IN AMERICA

EDITED BY
HELEN VENDLER

Random House
NEW YORK

PROJECT STAFF—The New York Center for Visual History
Permission Editor: Diane Best
Permission Researcher: Barbara Hale
Caption Editor: Robert Carnevale
Literary Assistant: Robert Clark
Picture Editor: Linda Gutierrez
Picture Researcher: Ellen Tarlow

 Published in the United States by Random House, Inc., New York, and simultaneously in Canada by Random House of Canada Limited, Toronto.

Library of Congress Cataloging in Publication Data

Voices & visions.

T.p. verso.
Published in conjunction with a Public Broadcasting System television series: Voices and visions.
Bibliography: p.
Includes index.
1. American poetry—History and criticism. I. Vendler, Helen Hennessy. II. Voices and visions (Television program)
PS303.V65 1987 811′.009 86-40154
ISBN 0-394-53520-0
ISBN 0-394-37880-6 (pbk.)

Design by Robert Bull and Frederica Templeton

Manufactured in the United States of America

24689753

First Edition

ACKNOWLEDGMENTS

This book is a companion to *Voices & Visions*, a PBS television series and college credit course consisting of thirteen one-hour programs on modern American poetry. *Voices & Visions* is produced by the New York Center for Visual History and presented by the South Carolina ETV Network. It is available as a telecourse through The Annenberg/CPB Project. For further information on the telecourse and on individual videocassettes, call (202) 955-5251, or write The Annenberg/CPB Project, 1111 16th Street, N.W., Washington, D.C. 20036.

Major funding for the *Voices & Visions* series is provided by The Annenberg/CPB Project and the National Endowment for the Humanities. Series funding has also been received from the National Endowment for the Arts and The Arthur Vining Davis Foundations. Program funders include the Corporation for Public Broadcasting, The Pew Memorial Trust, The Geraldine R. Dodge Foundation, Soft Sheen Products, Inc., the New Jersey Committee for the Humanities, The Ohio Humanities Council, Channel 4/United Kingdom, Hartford Insurance Group, The Massachusetts Foundation for Humanities and Public Policy, the Vermont Council on the Humanities and Public Issues, The Witter Bynner Foundation for Poetry, The Rockefeller Foundation, the Connecticut Humanities Council, The George Gund Foundation, the New York Council for the Humanities, and The Seth Sprague Educational and Charitable Foundation. Grateful acknowledgment is made for permission to reprint material by the following authors:

A. R. AMMONS: The lines from *Sphere, The Form of a Motion,* by A. R. Ammons, are reprinted by permission of W. W. Norton & Company, Inc. Copyright © 1974 by A. R. Ammons.

ELIZABETH BISHOP: Excerpts from "The Country Mouse" and "In the Village" from *Collected Prose* by Elizabeth Bishop. Copyright © 1984 by Alice Methfessel. Reprinted by permission of Farrar, Straus and Giroux, Inc.

"Santarém" and excerpts from "At the Fishhouses," "Carusoe in England," "Faustina, or Rock Roses," "The Fish," "In the Waiting Room," "The Man-Moth," "The Map," "The Monument," "The Moose," translation of "Objects & Apparitions" by Octavio Paz, "O Breath," "One Art," "Poem," "Sestina," "Song for the Rainy Season," "Visits to St. Elizabeth's" from *The Complete Poems 1927–1979* by Elizabeth Bishop. Copyright © 1979, 1983 by Elizabeth Bishop. Reprinted by permission of Farrar, Straus and Giroux, Inc.

Excerpts from unpublished material by Elizabeth Bishop from Vassar College Library. Reproduced by permission of the Estate of Elizabeth Bishop.

Excerpts from letters to Robert Lowell. Copyright by the Estate of Elizabeth Bishop, Executrix Alice Methfessel. Reprinted by permission of the Houghton Library and the Estate of Robert Lowell.

ANDRÉ BRETON: Excerpt from "Fata Morgana" by André Breton. Reprinted by permission of Société Nouvelle des Editions Pauvert. English translation reprinted from *A Metapoetics of the Passage* by Mary Ann Caws by permission of University Press of New England. Copyright © 1981 by Trustees of Dartmouth College.

HART CRANE: Excerpts from "The Bridge," "The Broken Tower," "To Brooklyn Bridge," "Chaplinesque," "The Dance," "Eternity," "The Harbor Dawn," "Lachrymae Christi," "For the Marriage of Faustus and Helen," "At Melville's Tomb," "My Grandmother's Love Letters," "Recitative," "The River," "Van Winkle," and "Voyages" reprinted from *The Complete Poems and Selected Letters and Prose of Hart Crane,* edited by Brom Weber, by permission of Liveright Publishing Corporation. Copyright 1933, © 1958, 1966 by Liveright Publishing Corporation.

Excerpts from *The Letters of Hart Crane,* edited by Brom Weber, copyright 1952 by Brom Weber. Reprinted with his permission.

EMILY DICKINSON: Excerpts of poems from *The Complete Poems of Emily Dickinson,* edited by Thomas H. Johnson. Copyright 1914, 1929, 1935, 1942 by Martha Dickinson Bianchi. Copyright © renewed 1957, 1963 by Mary L. Hampson. Reprinted by permission of Little, Brown and Company.

Excerpts from Letters #35, 39, 45, 65, 85, 91, 153, 190, 238, 260, 261, 262, 265, 269, 271, 278, 281, 315, 319, 391, 418, 555, 750, 785, 791, 792, 798. Reprinted by permission of the publishers from *The Letters of Emily Dickinson,* Thomas H. Johnson, ed., Cambridge, Mass.: The Belknap Press of Harvard University Press, copyright © 1958, 1986 by the President and Fellows of Harvard College.

Excerpts reprinted from *The Lyman Letters: New Light on Emily Dickinson and Her Family,* by Richard B. Sewall (Amherst: University of Massachusetts Press, 1965), copyright © 1965 by *The Massachusetts Review.*

Excerpts of poems reprinted by permission of the publishers and the Trustees of Amherst College from *The Poems of Emily Dickinson,* Thomas H. Johnson, ed., Cambridge, Mass.: The Belknap Press of Harvard University Press, copyright 1951, © 1955, 1979, 1983 by the President and Fellows of Harvard College.

Excerpts of letters regarding Emily Dickinson from Thomas Wentworth Higginson to his wife from the Higginson Collection of the Boston Public Library —Ms. AM 1093(34).

T. S. ELIOT: Excerpts from "Choruses from 'The Rock,'" "The Hollow Men," "Journey of the Magi," "The Love Song of J. Alfred Prufrock," "The Waste Land" and other excerpts from *Collected Poems 1909–1962* by T. S. Eliot, copyright 1936 by Harcourt Brace Jovanovich, Inc.; copyright © 1963, 1964 by T. S. Eliot. Reprinted by permission of the publisher and Faber and Faber Ltd.

Excerpts from "The Dry Salvages," "East Coker," and "Little Gidding" from *Four Quartets* by T. S. Eliot, copyright 1943 by T. S. Eliot; copyright © renewed 1971 by Esme Valerie Eliot. Reprinted by permission of Harcourt Brace Jovanovich, Inc., and reprinted by permission of Faber and Faber Ltd. from *Collected Poems 1909–1962.*

Excerpts from "Baudelaire," "Four Elizabethan Dramatists," "Philip Massinger," "The Sacred Wood," "Thoughts After Lambeth," and other excerpts from *Selected Essays,* copyright 1950 by Harcourt Brace Jovanovich, Inc.; copyright © renewed 1978 by Esme Valerie Eliot. Reprinted by permission of the publisher and Faber and Faber Ltd.

Excerpts from a letter to Stephen Spender and the text of a formal toast to Robert Frost from *Uncollected Letters and Writings* by T. S. Eliot, reprinted by permission of Mrs. Valerie Eliot and Faber and Faber Ltd.

ROBERT FROST: Excerpts from letters #47, 225, 321 from *The Letters of Robert Frost to Louis Untermeyer* edited by Louis Untermeyer. Copyright © 1963 by Louis Untermeyer and Holt, Rinehart and Winston. Reprinted by permission of Henry Holt and Company, Inc., Jonathan Cape Ltd. and the Estate of Robert Frost.

Excerpts from "After Apple Picking," "Desert Places," "For Once, Then, Something," "From Iron," "Hyla Brook," "The Most of It," "Mowing," "Neither Out Far nor In Deep," "The Oven Bird," "Pan with Us," "A Servant to Servants," "Take Something Like a Star," "To E.T.," "West Running Brook," and "The Wood-Pile" from *The Poetry of Robert Frost* edited by Edward Connery Lathem. Copyright © 1969 by Holt, Rinehart and Winston, Inc. Copyright © 1962 by Robert Frost. Copyright © 1975 by Lesley Frost Ballantine. Reprinted by permission of Henry Holt and Company, Inc., Jonathan Cape Ltd. and the Estate of Robert Frost.

Excerpts from *Robert Frost: The Later Years, 1938–1963* by Lawrence Thompson and R. H. Winnick. Copyright © 1976 by Holt, Rinehart and Winston. Copyright © 1976 by the Estate of Robert Frost. Reprinted by permission of Henry Holt and Company, Inc.

Excerpts from Letters #20, 79, 80–81, 83–84, 98, 217, 243, 417–419, 565 from *The Selected Letters of Robert Frost* edited by Lawrance Thompson. Copyright © 1964 by Lawrance Thompson and Holt, Rinehart and Winston. Reprinted by permission of Henry Holt and Company, Inc., Jonathan Cape Ltd. and the Estate of Robert Frost.

LANGSTON HUGHES: Excerpts from "Linear Notes: For the Poetically Unhep" from *Ask Your Mama: 12 Moods for Jazz* by Langston Hughes. Copyright © 1959, 1961 by Langston Hughes. Reprinted by permission of Alfred A. Knopf, Inc., and Harold Ober Associates Incorporated.

Excerpts from *The Big Sea* by Langston Hughes. Copyright 1940 by Langston Hughes. Copyright renewed © 1968 by Arna Bontemps and George Houston Bass. Reprinted by permission of Hill and Wang, a division of Farrar, Straus and Giroux, Inc.

Excerpts from "Feet o' Jesus," "Homesick Blues," "Po' Boy Blues," and "Prayer Meeting" from *The Dream Keeper and Other Poems* by Langston Hughes. Copyright 1932 by Alfred A. Knopf, Inc., and copyright © renewed 1960 by Langston Hughes. Reprinted by permission of the publisher and Harold Ober Associates Incorporated.

Excerpts from "Bad Man," "Gals Cry," and "Listen Here Blues" from *Fine Clothes to the Jew* copyright 1927 by Alfred A. Knopf, Inc. Copyright © renewed 1955 by Langston Hughes.

Excerpts from "Afro-American Fragment," "Consider Me," "Desert," "Dream Boogie," "Dream Variations," "End," "Fire," "Genius Child," "Harlem," "I, Too," "Lament Over Love," "Mother to Son," "My People," "Negro," "The Negro Speaks of Rivers," "October 16," "Old Walt," "Song for Billie Holiday," "The Weary Blues," and "When Sue Wears Red" from *Selected Poems of Langston Hughes.* Copyright © 1959 by Langston Hughes. Reprinted by permission of Alfred A. Knopf, Inc., and Harold Ober Associates Incorporated.

Excerpt from "The White Ones" from *The Weary Blues* by Langston Hughes. Copyright 1926 by Alfred A. Knopf, Inc., and renewed 1954 by Langston Hughes. Reprinted by permission of the publisher.

Excerpts from other poems: "Dear Lovely Death," "Fascination of Cities," "Goodbye Christ," "Johannesburg Mines," "Let America Be America Again," "My Loves," "A New Song," "Note on Commercial Theatre," "Play-Toy Land," "A Song of the Soul of Central," and "Tired"—this compilation copyright © 1987 by George Houston Bass. Reprinted by permission of Harold Ober Associates Incorporated.

HUGH KENNER: Excerpt from *The Pound Era,* by Hugh Kenner, p. 471. Reprinted by permission of the University of California Press and Faber and Faber Ltd.

ROBERT LOWELL: Excerpts from *Collected Prose* by Robert Lowell. Copyright © 1987 by Caroline Lowell, Harriet Lowell, and Sheridan Lowell. Reprinted by permission of Farrar, Straus and Giroux, Inc., and Faber and Faber Ltd.

Excerpts from "Epilogue," "Shifting Colors," "To Mother," and "Unwanted" from *Day by Day* by Robert Lowell. Copyright © 1975, 1976, 1977 by Robert Lowell. Reprinted by permission of Farrar, Straus and Giroux, Inc., and Faber and Faber Ltd.

Excerpts from *The Dolphin* by Robert Lowell. Copyright © 1973 by Robert Lowell. Reprinted by permission of Farrar, Straus and Giroux, Inc., and Faber and Faber Ltd.

Excerpts from "Jonathan Edwards in Western Massachusetts," "Night Sweat," "The Old Flame," and "For the Union Dead" *(Relinquunt Omnia Servare Rem Publicam)* from *For the Union Dead* by Robert Lowell. Copyright © 1956, 1960, 1961, 1962, 1963, 1964 by Robert Lowell. Reprinted by permission of Farrar, Straus and Giroux, Inc., and Faber and Faber Ltd.

Excerpts from "Dunbarton," "For Sale," "Man and Wife," "My Last Afternoon with Uncle Devereux Winslow," "91 Revere Street," "Sailing Home from Rapallo," and "Terminal Days at Beverly Farms" from *Life Studies* by Robert Lowell. Reprinted by permission of Farrar, Straus and Giroux, Inc., and Faber and Faber Ltd.

Excerpt from "Mr. Edwards and the Spider," from *Lord Weary's Castle,*

CONTENTS

Walt Whitman.

INTRODUCTION

In 1818, John Keats, attending his dying brother Tom, wrote to his brother George who had emigrated to Kentucky: "If I had a prayer to make for any great good next to Tom's recovery, it should be that one of your children should be the first American Poet. I have a great mind to make a prophecy and they say prophecies work out their own fulfillment." Tom did not recover; and George's "little child / 0' the western wild," as Keats called the expected child in his accompanying poem, did not become a poet. But the earnest hope of Keats for a poetic lineage in America has not been disappointed. The new world produced, in time, a new poetry—one not yet fully understood, not even fully described.

This book takes up some of the major poets who have made that new poetry. They are the writers who knew that a new land, and a new language, needed new rhythms, new genres, "new thresholds, new anatomies," as Hart Crane put it. Keats's England was a long-tamed and agricultural land describable in terms of lambs and robins, apples and swallows. America was different: a wilderness. It exhibited a new flora, a new fauna:

> Deer walk upon our mountains and the quail
> Whistle about us their spontaneous cries;
> Sweet berries ripen in the wilderness:
> And, in the isolation of the sky
> At evening, casual flocks of pigeons make
> Ambiguous undulations as they sink,
> Downward to darkness, on extended wings.

This is Wallace Stevens making Keats American. The English inheritance stood, seductive and forbidding, in the way of American poetry. This book tells, in part, the story of the stand taken by American poets—beginning with Whitman and Dickinson—against English poetry. But it also tells what those poets needed from English poetry in order to do their work. Dickinson needed English hymnody to shape her lyrics. Whitman needed Keats's nightingale to set his own hermit thrush singing. William Cullen Bryant needed the blank verse of Wordsworth to write his indigenous poem of the prairies:

These are the gardens of the Desert, these
The unshorn fields, boundless and beautiful,
For which the speech of England has no name.

All of us writing this book have been conscious of the pull both toward and against those centuries of writing in Europe that preceded our own nineteenth century. We have tried to describe the poetry that has evolved in this country—or that has been claimed by a revolutionary act: poetry that we can genuinely call American. We have been conscious, too, that a poem can be any one of a number of things, from a whimsical couplet to a sublime sequence. A poem, Stevens said, is "an answering look" given back by the poet to life:

Life fixed him, wandering on the stair of glass,
With its attentive eyes . . .
A hatching that stared and demanded an answering look.

That "answering look" can take many forms. Sometimes it is a look back at the landscape; sometimes a look back to another poem; sometimes a look back at a moment of history, past or current. We have all tried to say, in the essays that follow, something about what part of life, history, or art compelled the answering look from our poets. Some writers—Hart Crane and Robert Lowell, for instance—look at their autobiography in their poetry more than do others, like Dickinson and Stevens. Some writers belong to movements: here we have tried to take up, in treating poets like Langston Hughes or Marianne Moore, the cultural ambiance—Harlem Renaissance or Modernist New York—from which they emerged and which they helped shape by raising it to poetic consciousness. Some writers participate in a crucial moment in history: in those cases (as when Whitman gives his answering look to the Civil War, for instance) we have called attention to the historical context. Others participate in an important cultural moment, as Eliot and Pound did when they went to Europe and tried to Europeanize a provincial poetry.

In every case, the passion of the answering look finds its embodiment in the concision of art. Lyric requires of poets that they answer all of life in a moment: they must look back at the Civil War or the Brooklyn Bridge or life in Harlem in a few brief words. Against the demands of brevity in lyric, the sheer boundlessness of America gave our writers their first challenge. How was a nation so amply unrolling to be brought into the maps and forms of art? As usual, Emerson—a writer not included here, but assumed as standing behind each of our poets—said it, in his essay "The Poet," first and best:

The New York Armory Show of 1913 is credited with revolutionizing American art. Less well known is its effect on American poets, such as Marianne Moore and William Carlos Williams.

> Banks and tariffs, the newspaper and caucus, Methodism and Unitarianism, are flat and dull to dull people but rest on the same foundations of wonder as the town of Troy and the temple of Delphi, and are as swiftly passing away. Our log-rolling, our stumps and their politics, our fisheries, our Negroes and Indians, our boats and our repudiations . . . , Oregon and Texas, are yet unsung. Yet America is a poem in our eyes; its ample geography dazzles the imagination, and it will not wait long for metres.

Whitman heard Emerson; Dickinson heard Emerson. The rest is history. American poetry rose, in the twentieth century, to international attention, and claimed equality for the first time with European poetry. It participated in the redefining of poetry that has taken place in the last two centuries—through free verse, surrealism, "found poetry," "concrete poetry," the prose poem, performance art. Whitman was our first avant-garde poet in technique, and American poetry has, since his time, been particularly willing to be surprising, unsettling, and fresh in its intuitions. It is that freshness and originality that we have wanted to show in each of our poets.

Though poets write alone, they arrive in cohorts, thriving on encouragement, competition, and appreciation. Even the most solitary artist—an Emily Dickinson—sends out messages to an unknown audience:

> This is my letter to the World
> That never wrote to Me—
> The simple News that Nature told—
> With tender Majesty
>
> Her Message is committed
> To Hands I cannot see—
> For love of Her—Sweet—countrymen—
> Judge tenderly—of Me

And Whitman wrote, "To have great poems, there must be great audiences too." Most of the poets represented here have had a cluster of friends—fellow writers, artists, editors—who supported their work. The friendships of Eliot and Pound, Frost and Edward Thomas, Moore and Bishop, Allen Tate and Lowell, witness to the need felt by poets to belong to a movement—even if only a movement of two—in order to write. We have tried to recall in these essays those moments of mutual support—often based on the institutional support of a university, a bookstore, a magazine—that enabled the poetry of our twentieth century to be written.

In taking up our poets one by one, we do not mean to underestimate the social and institutional support that enables poetry to flourish. The existence of cities seems to be the first requisite for poetry, and a book of this sort could have been organized around those American cities that have supported poetry: Boston, New York, Chicago, San Francisco. Written poetry has always required a critical mass of readers and a means of publication: these have been found in those cities (Jerusalem, Athens, Alexandria, Vienna, London—to use Eliot's roll call, omitting Paris, where he found his own early ratification) where culture became conscious of itself and self-perpetuating. Even Horace on his Sabine farm was not far from imperial Rome, and Emerson in Concord and Frost in Derry kept literary Boston and Cambridge within reach. But while movements, presses, journals, and cities provide the matrix, individual poets provide the other, greater half of poetry—the genius for imaginative perception, thought, and language; and our essays hope to say something distinctive about each poet's mind and art.

The contributors to this book wrote their pieces while keeping in mind a common set of questions about the poets: what they inherited, what they were fostered by, where they found their language, what they created in the way of forms. The authors notice various matrices for poetry. Frank Kermode suggests how much life in London and the editorship of *The Criterion* meant to Eliot; Richard Poirier presses for recognition of Frost's debt to the pragmatism of Emerson and William James; Richard Sewall emphasizes the survival of Calvinist theology in Dickinson; Vereen Bell knows the poetry of Lowell to be inseparable from European and American history; John Slatin reminds us of those quotations which in Moore represent the textual subsoil from which all new literature grows. Culture and poetry, though indivisible, are not related in any single way: as culture makes poetry, so, in an ongoing symbiosis, does poetry make culture. Each of these essays confronts in some way the pressure that being an American exerted on these poets.

Some of our poets have felt called to address the nation on matters of importance (Whitman, Pound, Frost, Lowell); others have refrained from writing frequently to or about their own country (Dickinson, Bishop). It is of course no accident that the most private of our poets in this respect have been women: women in the past were not encouraged to assume a voice of public exhortation, except in certain restricted (usually church-supported) movements such as Abolition. It is only recently that they have felt able, as private citizens, to urge, criticize, and denounce with the vigor that Pound and Lowell took as their birthright. Nonetheless, whether public or private writers, poets must feel that they belong to a culture. Until the United States developed a sense of national identity, our poetry was feeble

In April 1916 the writers and artists associated with the little magazine Others *gathered at William Carlos Williams's house in Rutherford, New Jersey.* Back row, from left: *Jean Crotti, Marcel Duchamp, Walter Arensberg, Man Ray, R. A. Sanborn, Maxwell Bodenheim.* Front row, from left: *Alanson Hartpence, Alfred Kreymborg, William Carlos Williams, Skipwith Cannell.*

and derivative. The call for an independent American culture, made by Emerson in "The American Scholar" and "The Poet," had to precede the arrival of a flourishing national poetry. It would seem that the mere educated possession of poetic diction —as our early poets possessed English—did not in itself suffice for a national poetry. Until Dickinson began to "think—New Englandly," and Whitman to "hear America singing," American poetry did not come of age.

Emily Dickinson could read, in her 1848 anthology *Poets and Poetry of America* (edited by Rufus Willmot Griswold), the editor's repudiation of English models:

> Too few [of our authors] are free from that vassalage of opinion and style which is produced by a constant study of the Literature of the country from which we inherit our language, our tastes, and our manners.

The old thoughts of the Old World were to be superseded. The art of the New World was to be democratic, not monarchic; free, not feudal; revolutionary, not traditional; America, new in spirit,

The ladies of the Others *group, photographed on the same occasion.* From left: *Helen Slade, Mary Caroline Davis, Yvonne Crotti, Floss Williams, Kitty Cannell, Mrs. Davis (Kitty Cannell's mother), Gertrude Kreymborg, Mrs. Walter Arensberg.*

was to be new in art. (In this respect, American poetry is a child of the French Revolution as much as of British culture.) The political duty of the American poet—to proclaim liberation from cultural, religious, and class oppression—seemed a real and urgent mission to Whitman as it has to many of his successors from E. E. Cummings to Allen Ginsberg.

But the political rhetoric of Griswold's anthology—"Here the free spirit of mankind at length, / Throws its last fetters off" (Bryant)—could scarcely predict that some poets would feel nostalgia for those fetters and represent them, as Eliot does, as forms rather than fetters for the spirit. When Eliot defined himself as a royalist in politics and an Anglo-Catholic in religion, and wrote with piety of East Coker and Little Gidding, he was bringing the American story full circle back to England, embodying that English side—which our poetry can never lose—within a forcibly American modernism. Again, Griswold's anthology had envisaged a new American pastoral: "Ere long thine every stream shall find a tongue / Land of the Many Waters!" (Hoffman); but it did not foresee the coming force of technology that would make Hart Crane invoke the Brooklyn Bridge as an inspiration greater even than the waters of the Mississippi. Nor could the more naive early admirers of American revolutionary history guess that a Robert Lowell, looking back at the extirpation of Indians in New England, could call his Winslow ancestors "Indian-killers," nor that Pound would condemn American capitalistic enterprise as the maker of world wars. In short, though it is true that our history and landscape and character differ from those found in English poetry, American poetry could not become a simple hymn to the difference—to political democracy, unspoiled pastoral wilderness, and republican virtue. Our poets, like other American thinkers, found it "a complex fate" (Henry James) to be American. And that complex fate has engendered a corresponding complexity of poetic language.

We can take up here only some of the more visible aspects of our poetic language. The sensual delicacy and power of Whitman's lines, as Calvin Bedient describes them, are enabled not only by Whitman's democratic and erotic view of the poet's calling, but also by his conviction that the new country required a new idiom and rhythm as original, racy, and loose-limbed as the culture. Marianne Moore, rebelling against British accentual prosody, brought to her French-borrowed syllabics a Puritan rectitude, combined with the critical and creative fastidiousness outlined by John Slatin. Langston Hughes discovered an indigenous American poetry in the black vernacular, opening poetry to those variations in dialect that not only empowered the Harlem Renaissance, as Arnold Rampersad suggests, but proved fertile for white writers like Allen Ginsberg and John Berryman as well. For all these poets—and for subsequent ones—the anterior British rhythm had to be struggled with, and either forsaken or enlivened into formally distinctive American cadence. Marjorie Perloff recounts Williams's stubborn attempts—by new lineation, new placement of words in relation to each other, and an objectivist materiality of language—to make a poem into a genuinely American article. And even where the ghost of English poetry most lingers—in Moore's Herbertian lines, in Eliot's Browningesque and Tennysonian monologues, in Crane's Shelleyan momentum—a remarkable amount of energy has been expended to Americanize the end product. Especially in the youthful poems of our authors, the struggle against the British can be seen—as Bishop works through early imitations of Herbert and Hopkins, as Williams destroys his hundreds of lines of Keatsian couplets, as Plath casts off the example of Auden and Yeats.

One way for the poets to war against the British cadences ever present in the ear was to turn to other languages. This was

W.E.B. DuBois, a cofounder of the National Association for the Advancement of Colored People and a pioneering spokesperson for the new black consciousness of the twenties.

[Later] when I became aware of [the Harlem Renaissance], of Countee Cullen, Langston Hughes, Jessie R. Fauset, Zora Neale Hurston, Wallace Thurman, it seemed to me that what happened . . . was that a great many people carrying degrees of talent . . . left the land, left the South anyway, and came to what was sought as a kind of Mecca. And they made it one. Now, how this happened is very mysterious. How did we get Paul Robeson, for example? How did we get Ethel Waters and the extraordinary Pigmeat Markem and all those people on the Apollo Theater stage. . . . Countee Cullen taught me French . . . in junior high school. I was scared of him but I adored him, adored his poetry, and I tried to write like him. I showed him some of my poetry once, and he said it was too much like Langston Hughes. I never showed him anything again.

—From a *Voices & Visions* interview with James Baldwin

Countee Cullen, one of the other important poets to come out of the Harlem Renaissance.

perhaps the single most successful tactic in finding a new way of writing. Pound's debts to Homer, Anglo-Saxon poetry, and the troubadours as he began the Cantos are retraced here in Hugh Kenner's essay. Eliot, Pound, Stevens, Crane, and others sought out new ironies and new symbolic structures in French modernism (in the poetry of Baudelaire, Rimbaud, Mallarmé, Valéry, Laforgue, for instance). Stevens went so far as to write that "French and English constitute a single language." Frost and Lowell went back to Latin—Frost to Vergil's *Georgics* and

Horace's epistles and Lowell to the *Aeneid* and to Horace's odes. There were even ventures farther afield as Eliot invoked Sanskrit for the conclusion of *The Waste Land*, and Pound put Chinese ideograms into the Cantos. These were all programmatic statements that English literature, and its accompanying cultural biases, did not suffice for the new American consciousness. Even Whitman had looked to pre-Christian bases (in ancient Egypt, in Greece, and in Buddhism) for American culture and had made his elegy for Lincoln out of Egyptian and Greek mourning rituals, at a time when the rest of Lincoln's elegists in the newspapers were emphasizing that Lincoln had died on Good Friday.

In becoming international, American poetry became cosmopolitan. Turning away from its earlier ideological commitment to celebrating American history and American landscape, it began with modernist inwardness (prophesied perhaps in Poe) to take consciousness itself as its chief problem, and, in doing so, to feel itself part of the history of a larger world. American poetry, like America itself, could not, after the First World War, remain isolationist. Pound's gaze took in all of history, from archaic Greece and ancient China to Mussolini's Italy. Eliot, being treated in Switzerland for a nervous collapse, and hearing around him the polyglot voices of Europe, let all his favorite touchstones from ancient and modern literature reverberate as fragments through his international wasteland. Later, Elizabeth Bishop would name her far-voyaging volumes *North & South, Questions of Travel,* and *Geography III,* interrogating her own restless homelessness in Canada, the United States, and Brazil. And even those poets who chiefly stayed at home let their imaginations reach beyond North America. Hart Crane wanted to link his northern epic, *The Bridge*, with a southern epic on the conquistadors. Wallace Stevens's poet-voyager Crispin leaves Europe to visit South America as well as North America (where he decides to settle). Marianne Moore's exotic descriptions come from all over the world; and Robert Lowell's sonnet sequence *History* (beginning in the Garden of Eden) takes in the history of ancient and modern Europe as much as the history of the United States.

We can see in these poets an ever more insistent use of American idiom. William Carlos Williams, though he took his inspiration, as Marjorie Perloff reminds us, from Dada and Surrealism, made his diction American with a vengeance. His example made even formal poets like Lowell, Bishop, and Plath sensitive to the need for an American naturalness of cadence in their lines. Lowell's oscillations between formal and free verse throughout his writing life (charted here by Vereen Bell) can stand as typical of the response of twentieth-century poets to the contrasting variety of available models. All of the poets included in this volume grew up with traditional meters and had internalized the inner rhythms of English prosody; their syllabic verse or free verse is constructed on more regular models—stanzas, pentameter lines—still audible behind many of their experiments. It may be that our most recent poets, who have, on the whole, grown up on free verse rather than on rhymed stanzas, will write a different sort of poetry, whether formal or free.

When we look at the development of American poetry from the publication of the first edition of *Leaves of Grass* in 1855 to the death of Elizabeth Bishop in 1979, we can say that culture seems to be created in gradual steps. First, a terrain is won, a liberty gained: Whitman, for instance, wins for us the right to be nationalistic and free in verse. When that battle no longer needs to be fought, a later poet, like Eliot, can be international and formal. In the same way, Marianne Moore, by writing poems about idiosyncrasy, sophistication, landscape, and art, liberates women from the expectation that they will write about God, children, love, and death, the chief female subjects of the nineteenth century. Once that has been done, a later poet like Plath can indeed return to the domestic—but with a savage difference. Frost, to take another instance, perfects an American colloquial verse written in American "sentence sounds." Then a later poet—say, a James Merrill—can return unselfconsciously to a Byronic or Audenesque conversational idiom. Certainly American poetry could not be international, European, and formal in the twentieth century until it had first, in the nineteenth century, been nationalist, colloquial, and unrhymed. There is no uninterrupted line of development in our poets: each sees an opportunity, a work not yet done, and seizes the chance.

The opportunity seized has to do with a vision of life framed as a technical question. "Impassioned interest in life, that burns its bridges behind it and will not contemplate defeat" is, says Marianne Moore, one of the secrets of creation. "A result which is sensational is implemented by what to the craftsman was private and unsensational" ("Idiosyncrasy and Technique"). The technical questions of a poet's writing are of absorbing interest to other poets; most general readers look first to a poet for the vision of life that radiates through the work. It is this appetite that has drawn women readers, for example, to the work of writers like Bishop and Plath, where they can find twentieth-century life viewed with a surreal intensity (in Plath) and with that tinge of the uncanny (in Bishop) that Helen McNeil remarks in her essays on these poets. Equally, Lowell's vision of a life lived in reckless pursuit of what is to be known, seen,

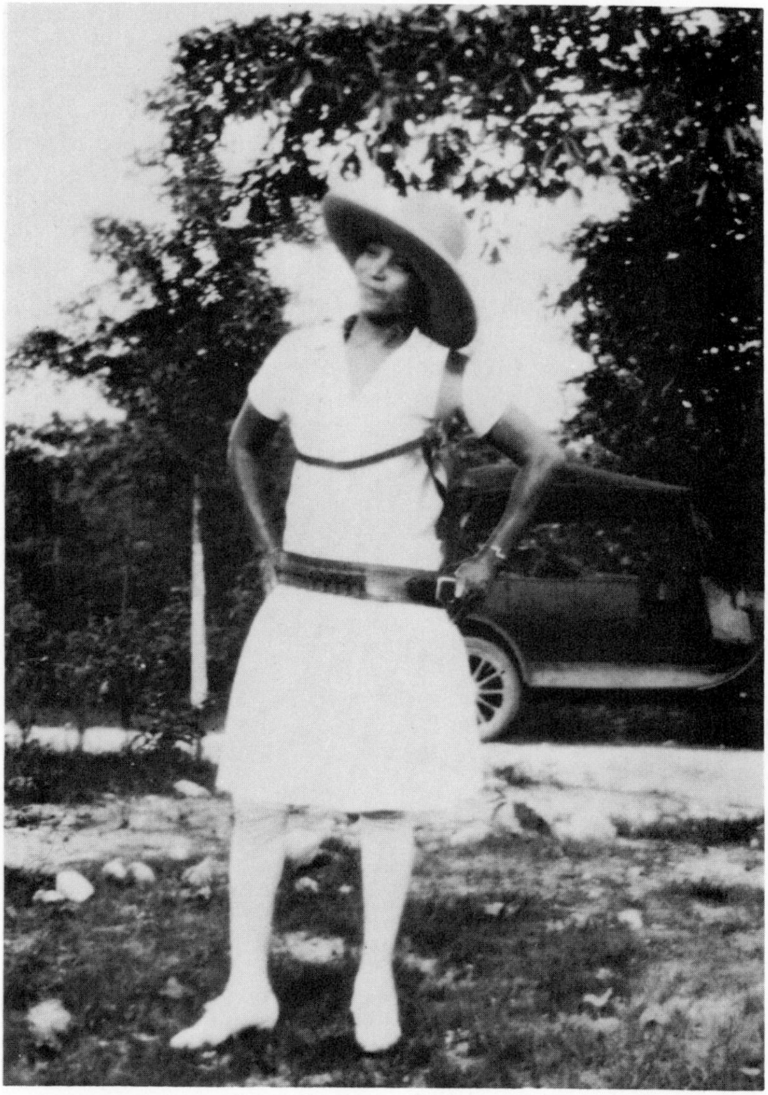

Zora Neale Hurston, fiction writer and folklorist. Like other leading lights of the Harlem Renaissance, she fell on hard times later in life and her work lapsed into obscurity. Today, however, the work is enjoying a well-deserved and substantial revival.

and loved seems to many of us the paradigm of American life —one that has no memory of the contained, regular, familial, and seasonal life of Europe—one that goes beyond national boundaries to a citizenship in the entire world. The critical and celebratory poetry of Langston Hughes offers multiple social perspectives on life that match in complexity his powerful and oppressed dramatis personae. The "wisdom pieces" of Emily Dickinson (as Richard Sewall calls them) have the quality of secular sermons, partly horrible, partly witty, on death, dissolu-

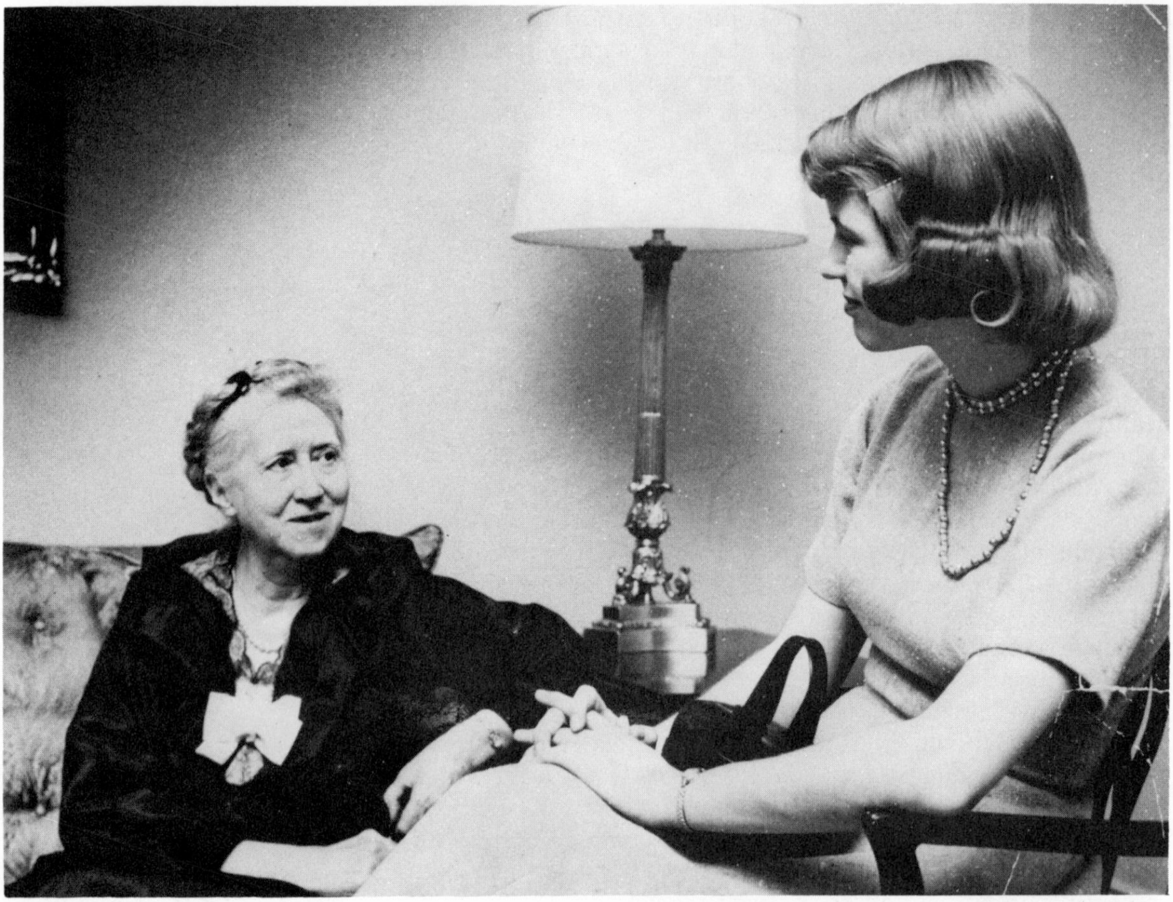

Sylvia Plath with Marianne Moore at the Mount Holyoke College Contest for the Glascock Poetry Prize, 1955.

tion, and the haunted spirit. These visions of life have in common only a powerful idiosyncrasy. Each of them was possible in America; none of them exhausts American possibility. As each of these essays takes up its poet, a vision of life comes into relief. Dickinson reminds us of the majesty of the unsupported mind. Pound urges us to look at all of history. Williams asks us to break up perception and reform it anew. Moore recommends a contradictory combination of creativity and criticism. Plath anatomizes social conditioning. Lowell retells the family romance. In each case, a mind unveils itself to us. It has been our concern in writing these essays to sketch the intensities and amplitudes of those minds.

At the same time, all of these essays are concerned with the reflexive American imagination—what the imagination tells of itself and of its workings. Poets are all engaged in finding ways to envisage reality by projecting it onto an imaginative plane of existence; and they are as interested in the way of projecting as in the reality that they project. Robert Frost, in an early poem ("Pan with Us"), represents himself in the guise of Pan throwing away his archaic pipes, and feeling the exhilaration of a new beginning:

They were pipes of pagan mirth,
And the world had found new terms of worth.
He lay down on the sunburned earth
 And raveled a flower and looked away—
Play? Play? —What should he play?

Many of our poets ask the same question, and find new pipes. When Whitman, at the end of his elegy on Lincoln, passes into that American place, a swamp, to listen to that American bird, the hermit thrush, he has found a way to write about Lincoln's death, but also a way to write about American poetry, its proper locale and its proper voice. When Williams imagines the city Paterson as a man and the falls of the Passaic as the torrent of language he must unravel, he has found a way to write about local reality on an imagined plane. When Stevens places a jar in the Tennessee wilderness (in implicit comparison to Keats's ornamented Hellenic urn in the British Museum), he has found an imaginative plane on which to represent the plight of the American poet with his homemade art. When Moore describes the intimidating and unconceptualizable variety of Mount Rainier, in "An Octopus," she has found a plane on which to project the mind's faltering before immense natural heterogeneity and plenitude.

Whatever the poet knows must be projected imaginatively. And the poets know a great deal, even if intuitively, about the mind of their century. The discoveries of comparative religion (Eliot), of archaeology and philology (Pound), of urban modernism (Moore), of revisionist American history (Pound, Williams, Lowell), of modern philosophy and aesthetics (Stevens), of skepticism (Bishop), of depth-psychology (Plath, Lowell)—these must all be cast by the poets into a new, and imaginatively apprehended, universe. In that world we find Eliot's Buddha and Chapel Perilous, Pound's Greek and Chinese and Renaissance vignettes, Moore's dock rats and Habbakuk, Williams's Sacco and Vanzetti, Stevens's Snow Man and Canon Aspirin, Lowell's Jonathan Edwards and Hawthorne, Crane's Pocahontas and Walt Whitman, Hughes's Harlem gallery. These persons and places, flora and fauna, are now as real as the personal reality from which they were projected.

What we care about in writers is their capacity to *add to*

reality. Plath's poem "Daddy" is now perhaps more real than its human model; and Lowell's Boston, Williams's Paterson, and Pound's Provence are places independent of, if originally dependent on, their historical and geographical sites. Our Civil War has now become Whitman's war, as it is Matthew Brady's: we cannot think of that national crisis without seeing it in part through Brady's photographs and Whitman's elegies for the war dead. These make reality memorable, retard historical oblivion, conceive of how reality is to be constructed, and leave words and images lingering in the culture. Reality does not construct itself: its data are too multiple to be self-forming. Reality is subject to changing social construction, and one part of social construction is literary construction (itself in part socially determined, in that symbiosis mentioned earlier). Reality is, though "uncapturable and vanishing" (in A. R. Ammons's words) subject to being caught in phrases, lines, images, tones of voice, sentence sounds, a "loved Philology" (in Dickinson's words). "Life and the memory of it" (Bishop) is caught—"dim, but how live, how touching in detail." Though the historian also catches the memory of life, and even the touching pathos of its details, the historian does not catch life alive. It is the peculiar gift of art—whether music, painting, or poetry—to catch life in the full immediacy of action or presence. Art bears vivid conviction because it is not a rewording or a recording of life, but a form of life—a living score for experience as explicit as a musical score. If we follow it through, we will have been its melody, have "felt along the line" (Pope). A poem is as polyphonic in its strategies as a piece of instrumental music, as brilliant in its structures as any painted arrangement of line and color.

Our century has wished to understand art as process. We have therefore understood it as experience more fully perhaps than the centuries that saw art as historical record, aesthetic artifact, and vehicle for moral instruction. The radically uncertain philosophical stance of poets since the dissolution of communal belief has helped to give poetry the air of a constant experiment in thinking and feeling. The dissolution of communal belief is commented upon by most of the essayists here, whether they trace a reversion from skepticism to formal faith, as Kermode does in Eliot, or whether they emphasize the nihilism that Bell and McNeil find in later Lowell and Plath. The strategies the poets have displayed in coping with philosophical uncertainty are singled out—Williams's principled attempts, illustrated by Perloff, at the disruption of the teleological sentence-form Stevens's final abdication of certitude in favor of rejoicing in the mind's reformulating energies; Hughes's quest for principles of social justice; Frost's irony of stance. All of

William Carlos Williams and Ezra Pound, Rutherford, New Jersey. At the home of William Carlos Williams, June 30, 1958.

When I was at the University of Pennsylvania, around 1905, I used to argue with Pound. I'd say "bread" and he'd say "caviar." It was a sort of simplification of our positions. Once, in 1912 I think it was, in a letter (we were still carrying on our argument) he wrote, "all right, bread." But I guess he went back to caviar.

—From *Interviews with William Carlos Williams*

Robert Lowell and Elizabeth Bishop, Rio de Janeiro, 1962.

these have their formal counterparts in language and prosody, from Eliot's hesitating rhythms to Stevens's qualified assertions to Williams's broken lineation. Richard Poirier warns us to beware of too superficial and stolid a reading of Frost's deceptively offhand and teasing statements. We can see in Stevens's play of the mind over many perspectives his preference for possibility over a narrow certainty. Crane's passionate hopes show a passion for the unformulable as striking as does Moore's relish for the heterogeneous. Even Dickinson's conclusive definitions almost always, as Sewall shows, concern a mystery "most like Chaos."

In every poet, the probings made by poetic consciousness extend outward as well as inward. They reach out to the "magnificent unconscious scenery" (Whitman) of the world, until an interface between inner consciousness and outer muteness is established—a region where words grope for purchase, sentences eke their existence into being, rhythms knock at the door of the ear, and a form or melody begins to shape itself in the air for the poet. This "final finding of the ear" (Stevens), the coming-into-being of the poem, is, as we know from the testimony of poets and of manuscripts, no simple matter. A poem can begin with no subject and no emotion, for instance, with nothing but a rhythm: "A new rhythm," said Hopkins before writing "The Wreck of the Deutschland," "had long been haunting my ear" —and we may suspect that the same was true of Whitman before the spectacular outburst of "Song of Myself," and of Dickinson as she began to write her poems in phrases between dashes. Or a poem can begin with an event—one that may find no place at all in the final poem, where it has been replaced by symbol—as in so many of Stevens's poems, or Plath's. Or poetry can begin with a strong personal impulse: Moore's impulse to rebuff ignorant and vulgar critics occasions much of her best early poetry. Or it can arise from imitations—giving us Lowell's loose translations from European models or (as McNeil shows in Plath) poems based on certain paintings.

Most of us can hear a poem or see a painting without any need to respond in kind. But the poet utters "counter-love, original response" (Frost)—an answer, a counter-rhythm, a way to render the painting in words. But that is only the beginning. Around the original rhythm and the originating phrases, others have to be permitted to gather, to reverberate, to interact. The rapid scanning, the "innumerable intellectual compositions and decompositions" (Keats) that go into every poetic act are, because they chiefly take place in the mind, only partially visible in manuscripts and in the final text. But every text, as a force-field of language, retains traces of its originating tensions; together with its convergences toward unity, it exhibits contradictions, digressions, speculations, movements which remind us that as it was composed, something was chosen, something rejected, something altered, something added.

As we watch a person becoming a poet we can see that "answering look" in the process of formation. We watch Moore pressed by her own consciousness of eccentricity into the consideration of the uniqueness and specificity and interaction of natural forms. We can see the formally armored young Lowell pressed by psychoanalysis into a loosening of form, an examination of domestic suffering. We can see Whitman's exuberance forced by the Civil War to take stock of tragedy and turn from the personal to the collective in a way no longer erotic. Finding herself in contained England, the well-schooled Plath found it necessary to react with American rage.

Of course, it is not only poets who give "answering looks" to life; prose writers do so too. But when the looks are in verse, they possess a concentration impossible to narration or drama,

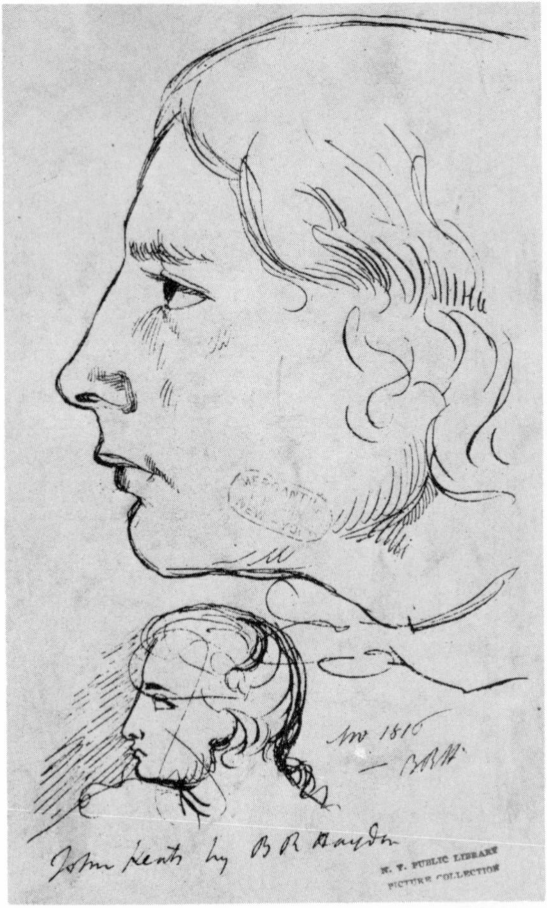

John Keats.

William Shakespeare.

I reckon—when I count at all—
First—Poets—Then the Sun—
Then Summer—Then the Heaven of God—
And then—the List is done—

But, looking back—the First so seems
To Comprehend the Whole—
The Others look a needless Show—
So I write—Poets—All—

Their Summer—lasts a Solid Year—
They can afford a Sun
The East—would deem extravagant—
And if the Further Heaven—

Be Beautiful as they prepare
For Those who worship Them—
It is too difficult a Grace—
To justify the Dream—

—Emily Dickinson

Elizabeth Barrett Browning.

Robert Browning.

a point and finality impossible in a linear or discursive form. Each of these points of concentration, each poem, because it is an answer, secretes within itself its original question or stimulus. Criticism and creation dispute each other in Moore, the proletarian and the educated in Hughes, family horror and family attachment in Lowell, decisiveness and chaos in Dickinson, aspiration and collapse in Crane, the harsh and the tender in Frost, the broken and the integral in Williams, the historical and the contemporary in Pound. There is no interesting poem without such inner strain. "All poets," said Auden, "adore explosions, thunderstorms, tornadoes, conflagrations, ruins, scenes of spectacular carnage." These are only the symbolic forms of the inner strains that poets suffer, tolerate, and exploit. "Vesuvius at home," Dickinson called herself, refusing to confide her "projects pink" to anyone, waiting for the top to blow off and the lava to flow. Poets recognizing that strains of complexity are the material for their art are more willing to entertain them, with that negative capability of which Keats wrote.

The inexhaustible play of poetic language, in which each word has its weight and duration and musical note as surely as in a fugue, ensures that poems give off a different shimmer at different times to the same reader and certainly at the same time to different readers. What is always the same is the intensity, the point, the concentration of the form. Even when the form extends itself—in long poems from "The Song of Myself" through *History*—each segment of the sequence aspires to point, intensity, concentration, and melody. Minor poets exhibit one or two of these: they have point and message but no melody; or melody but no concentration; or intensity without much point. The poets in this book have been admired by other poets for having so often exhibited all the virtues of poetry at one time.

We have hoped by these essays to show these virtues at work, to suggest how much American culture owes to the formulating powers of these poets' minds, how much the American language owes to their preservation of its idiom, how much the world owes to them for representing American consciousness and American beauty in their lines. This book is only one of many that could have been written on our American poets: they could have been differently chosen, differently grouped, differently considered. But each of these essays is one possible "answering look" back at the poet, from the vantage-point of the closing years of the twentieth century. We hope they will provoke more answering looks in their turn.

"The poet's function," said Wallace Stevens, "is not to lead people out of the confusion in which they find themselves. Nor is it, I think, to comfort them . . . His function is to make his imagination theirs . . . ; he fulfills himself only as he sees his imagination become the light in the minds of others. His role, in short, is to help people to live their lives" ("The Noble Rider and the Sound of Words")—"Not to console / Or sanctify, but plainly to propound" ("Notes toward a Supreme Fiction"). The poet propounds so plainly that we see by the light of that third planet (as powerful as sun or moon) the imagination, construing life afresh in believable terms, in the imaginative fictions of art. We cannot forget that even as the text does this intellectual and moral work, it is engaged simultaneously in its work as a dynamic system of verbal signs aiming at aesthetic form. And we value both its functions—its human force and its labyrinth of language, its new combinations and its radiant idiom. Though we cannot do full justice here to the beauty and power of the American imagination and the American language as they are embodied in the poetry of two centuries, we hope that these essays will bring new readers to some poets, will direct some readers to new poems, and will offer for all readers a view of the range and play of the American imagination, a sense of the complication, depth, and grandeur of American poetry.

HELEN VENDLER

VOICES
&
VISIONS

(Poem or passage)

the scenes on the river
~~Pa 6~~ as I cross the
Fulton ferry

Others will see the flow
of the river, also
Others will see on both
sides the city of
New York and the city
of Brooklyn
A hundred years hence others
will see them.
Two hundred years — many
[illegible]

WALT WHITMAN

CALVIN BEDIENT

Americans had at first to invent American art out of the Augustan culture of England—of all cultures the most rational and refined, the least like the sublime barbarousness supposed natural to early America. Native Americans mimicked arts that said "polished" while their forest said, "You have yet to cut the wood." In 1788, Philip Freneau, a propagandist for the American Revolution, wrote:

> Can we never be thought to have learning or grace
> Unless it be brought from that horrible place
> Where tyranny reigns with her impudent face;
> And popes and pretenders . . .
>
> (*NM,* 50)[1]

but it was Pope, not "popes," that Freneau himself was thus bringing over (unsuccessfully) from that horrible place.

Our arts had somehow to dawn (as James Fenimore Cooper observed) out of the afternoon Augustan light, not out of early darkness. This absurdity perplexed both American artists and American critics (the latter brought it up during every postmortem on the former). It also entertained the British, at least one of whom was famously unsympathetic: "But why should the Americans write books, when a six weeks' passage brings them, in their own tongue, our sense, science and genius, in bales and hogsheads? . . . Prairies, steam-boats, gristmills, are their natural objects for centuries to come" (*NM,* 155).

It was the achievement of Walt Whitman (who was born on Long Island in 1819) to create, in the early 1850s, a poetry on a level with prairies and steamboats which yet confirmed Alexis de Tocqueville's view that, precisely because "nothing conceivable is so . . . insipid, . . . so antipoetic, as the life of a man in the United States," democracy would force poets "to search below the external surface . . . to read the inner soul" and find "the plan on which God rules our race." "The principle of equality," the brilliant Tocqueville concluded, renders poetic subjects "less numerous, but more vast" (*NM,* 328–30). Whitman, by a sort of manic tallying, was to refute the aspersion "less numer-

The frontispiece of the first edition of Leaves of Grass *(1855).*

ous," but no poet was ever more consciously avid for amplitude. "The greatest poet," he wrote in the preface to *Leaves of Grass* (1855), dilates "any thing that was before thought small . . . with the grandeur and life of the universe. He is a seer" (*W,* 10). Again: "The known universe has one complete lover and that is the greatest poet. . . . What balks or breaks others is fuel for his burning progress to contact and amorous joy" (*W,* 11–12).

Tocqueville's *Democracy in America* (1840) was first published in Europe as a piece of local fortunetelling, and Whitman himself believed that democracy was unstoppable: the "modern" password (indeed, "the password primeval") of the sacred "Law" that governs and animates the universe. "Law," he wrote in his full-to-bursting essay "Democratic Vistas" (1871), "is the unshakeable order of the universe forever; and the law over all, the law of laws, is the law of successions; that of the superior law, in time, gradually supplanting and overwhelming the inferior one" (*W,* 948). (The word "law" itself was at once Hebraic and scientifically modern.) In self-consciously and cockily and grandly becoming the first American poet, Whitman considered himself, by the same token, the first truly universal poet. He voiced not only the present but the future, he heralded for all human beings—and ants and leaves of grass—their ultimate "rendezvous with God." In that "evolutionist" century, a star-spangled totalizing perspective was as natural to men of genius as opening the front door of a house and taking the night air. Whitman was the first lyricist of a lovingly promotional relation between today and tomorrow, between the least of particles and God.

Whitman looked on the German philosopher Hegel as an ally in announcing that we "tramp a perpetual journey." The convergence of America and Hegel is part of the larger history of the Judeo-Christian belief in a chosen people. The World Spirit, thought the Lutheran Hegel, realizes itself through successions of world-historical cultures. He remarked that while the Orient knew only that *"one is free,"* and the Greeks and Romans that *"some* are free," the Germanic nations, "under the influence of Christianity," know that "man, as man, is free" (*PH,* 18). Whitman was well disposed to Schelling, Hegel, and other German philosophers of the first part of the century (Carlyle helped him to this), but he was as certain that Americans themselves were the God-designated people as the Puritan settlers were, though not for their reasons. They had justified their lonely enterprise by interpreting the Bible as a prophetic historical code. Whitman justified the new country's continuing rawness at a later time by the scientific argument of evolution. When he delightfully says, "Cycles ferried my cradle, rowing and rowing like cheerful boatmen," and of his embryo that "monstrous sauroids transported it in their mouths and deposited it with care," he deepens Hegel's historical view with a still more up-to-date evolutionary perspective that extends "succession" back to "the huge first Nothing, the vapor from the nostrils of death" (*W*, 79–80). Whitman had no fear of science; science was revelation, and supported the view that he who is at the peak of the present—as an American from his very pastlessness tended to be—is the first into the future.

Hegel, however, was the supreme metaphysician and historian of the view that *"the final cause of the World at large"* is *"consciousness* of its own freedom on the part of Spirit" (*PH*, 19), and Whitman was grateful for his "profound horoscope-casting" of the theme (even as his image misleadingly posits Hegel as a dubious reader of the future). At the same time, Whitman believed that what Hegel taught—namely, that "spirit is freedom," and freedom "absolutely perfect Being," and Being absolute freedom, in endless, delicious circularity—could be gleaned, in pioneer American fashion, in "the spirit's hour—religion's hour," when the stars, "thick as heads of wheat in a field," are "the visible suggestion of God in space and time." Such divinations showed that the "Me" and the "Not Me" are infinitely suffused together and far more vastly spread than is even the Milky Way, that "ode of universal vagueness," that "flashing glance of Deity" (*W*, 826).

Even Ralph Waldo Emerson, then and still the chief American sage, had said in his essay "The Poet" (1844) that "the Universe is the externization of the soul" (*EE*, 270) and in his essay "The Over-Soul" (1841) that "the soul's advances are not made by gradation," but "by metamorphosis," as "from the egg to the worm, from the worm to the fly" (*EE*, 194). Yet the soul is over all, an "over-soul." This dissociation of the soul from itself, as both what advances and what awaits our rendezvous—this Hegelian dissociation—required the poet to connect worldly things, for instance, "the factory-village, and the railway" (*EE*, 273) to nature and the All. Beauty is "the creator of the universe," Emerson added, and the poet "the man of beauty" (*EE*, 263–64). On the other hand, America, he said, "is a poem in our eyes; its ample geography dazzles the imagination, and it will not wait long for metres" (*EE*, 287–88). Whitman agreed, even echoing Emerson in his preface to *Leaves of Grass:* "The United States themselves are essentially the greatest poem" (*W*, 5). The American poet need not spring up virtuosically in some poet-shaped interstice between steamboats and the Over-Soul, and consider himself lucky to do so. America itself represents the elusive sublimity of the imagination and the soul. The coun-

There's a lecture that Whitman heard Emerson deliver in New York in the 1840's in which Emerson addresses a question that occupied many people at that time: Is there such a thing as an American literature, an American poetry? Well, Emerson believed that there was no conflict between poetry and democracy, and issued many calls for the emergence of an American poet who would be equal in challenge to the American experience itself. At several points in his lecture, Emerson is practically describing the Whitman who would emerge fifteen years later. Someone who can deal with justice and fairness, with American trade, with American industry, with the commonness, the cheapness and availability of American experience. I imagine that hearing this sort of talk Whitman began to feel awaken in him an ambition which took him a long time to define—to be the poet of America.

—From a *Voices & Visions* interview with Justin Kaplan

try has only to be pursued as the manifold, elusive, evolving thing it is, tracked down to the red caboose lights disappearing into the Rockies. There could not have been a Whitman before the nineteenth century in America, when material progress (power, motion, expansion) and idealism (the soul, freedom, God, Beauty) were for the first and last time in an exuberant accord that seemed to strike hosannahs out of railways and factories as well as stars.

Whitman knew what he had to do: *write up America*. The question was how. Prescient as Emerson was, he had failed to indicate the verse-method for reattaching sex and cider and Negroes and Oregon (his list) to the Whole. And Whitman wanted to be even more polemical at cataloguing, a cross between a hard-pitch salesman of America and a lover never tired of itemizing and caressing its every detail. "Objects gross and the unseen soul are one," he would declare. Therefore "the stumpy bars of pig-iron, the strong clean-shaped T-rail for railroads," and the "loup-lump at the bottom of the melt" (*W*, 360) were the soul, and belonged as intimately to poetry as faeries, yew trees, nightingales, and other English poetic staples. But how fit pig-iron, the T-rail, and the loup-lump in meters without inadvertently mincing and mocking them? Clearly the tired old English aesthetic was out of place here, dripping as it did the after-rain of a thousand English associations. It was tidy, it lacked the necessary sprawl; it sighed about this and that, it lacked divine get up and go.

Emerson had said, it is true, that "it is not metres, but a metre-making argument that makes a poem,—a thought so passionate and alive that like the spirit of a plant or an animal it has an architecture of its own, and adorns nature with a new thing" (*EE*, 266). With his own beautiful talent for and concentration on "the sentence," Emerson showed what such an original "architecture" might be. And why couldn't the same principle be applied to the poetic line? Perhaps Emerson had pointed the way even here in his paratactic brilliance, his continual reapplication of spin to syntax, his balances. What if his model catalogue of the United States in "The Poet" were put into phrase-easy lines, as thus:

Our log-rolling, our stumps and their politics, our fisheries,
Our Negroes and Indians, our boasts and our repudiations,
The wrath of rogues and the pusillanimity of honest men,
The northern trade, the southern planting, the western clearing,
    Oregon and Texas,
Are yet unsung.

(*EE*, 287)

If hardly verse, this might at least furnish a clue, as might Emerson's Americanization of the pentameter line itself in "Bulkeley, Hunt, Willard, Hosmer, Meriam, Flint" and "Hay, corn, roots, hemp, flax, apples, wool and wood" (both in his poem "Hamatreya"). Democratic enumeration of all things as equal-in-the-Whole would create, was creating, out of the God's plenty before it, its own bushel-barrel aesthetic of the concrete discursive manifold and its own log-rolling aesthetic of vigorous, uncheckable cadence and syntax.

But more than a richly detailed rolling catalogue was needed to make Appearance pass into Being, Being into Beauty, Beauty into God. The mere tumble of sounds could be much (though it was not often so in Emerson) and the mere things were much, but quantity whether of cadence or represented material was only half what was wanted. The rest was—well, heroism. A voice like the aurora borealis; projection; amplitude. A Personality. The lyricism of a child of the fire (for, as Emerson had said, "we are not pans and barrows, nor even porters of the fire and torch-bearers, but children of the fire, made of it, and only the same divinity transmuted and at two or three removes, when we know least about it" [*EE,* 262]).

The prescription? A combination and consonance of three things: first, Personality (definite tone, loud declaration, seduction, theatrics); second, a loosened line fit for "orbic works launched forth, . . . to move, self-poised, through the ether," in words from "Democratic Vistas" (expansive rhythms that are laws unto themselves, suggestive of our "momentous spaces," roomy enough for thought, lists, personal "attitude"); third, an American idiom (words live enough for running speech; concrete, racy, factual).

The Personality, if grand and "forbidding" enough, would still the tiresome English objection that the "infant Muse of America" (infant!) had produced nothing "heroic." Whitman himself was stung enough to declare in "Starting from Paumanok": "I will report all heroism from an American point of view" (*W,* 179). This meant recasting the heroic as "the divine average," in a politically aggressive redefinition of the concept. Too, it meant braving the Open (in Rilke's word)—that sacred anticlosure in which Nature itself, as a "successive" thing, subsists. More specifically, it meant being a freedom-fighter, a Union-cannoneer. All in all, Whitman felt entitled to say, and in "As I Ponder'd in Silence" leapt at the chance to say, "I too . . . also sing war, and a longer and greater one than any"—a war whose "field" is "the world," a war waged "For life and death, for the Body and for the eternal Soul . . . I above all promote brave soldiers" (*W,* 165). Yet the new heroism of the average was for the most part casual and lovely: "Was somebody asking to see the soul? / See, your own shape and countenance, persons, substances, beasts, the trees, the running rivers, the rocks and sands" (*W,* 183). Mainly, it was a heroism of insouciance. To make it enticing and stirring, however, Whitman turned his own person into a sort of enlarged-balloon representative of the American, towering and floating with euphoria, bobbing paternally over the country.

Deliberately and with a beautifully just calculation, Whitman spoke and attitudinized on a scale commensurate with "these States" (now with thirty-eight, now forty-four—the number mounted vertiginously with each turn of the kaleidoscope of Manifest Destiny). This buoyant voice-projection, this personality-inflation, was his greatest single imaginative act. Once it occurred to him that he could speak for America, great originality and force lay open to him. Still, he needed a verse-style that was cut to the same X-tra large size as the nationalistic Personality. His love of Italian opera, of stump and pulpit oratory, of newspaper editorial rhetoric (he had practiced it as a newspaperman in Brooklyn for many years) and the Bible—evidently these offered hints. Something full of contagious cadence, not shy of Hebraic parallelism, rapturously erratic, syntactically "open" when not aphoristically fisted—would that do it? Hadn't that intelligent man, Edward Tyrell Channing, in a prose already naturally modern, said in 1816 that American writers could not evade "the rough torrent," however much they might try to allay it with "streams of a softer region"? But what was the rough torrent in the region of rhythm and line, syntax and stanza? "Foreign ornament and manner" were "sickly and unmeaning," as Channing said, "out of their own birth-place" (*NM,* 90)—that was agreed. What, then, was left? Most obviously prose and what one could do with it if one heard it delicately just at the point where it catches the lilt of poetry, imitating its dance, its song, but staying relaxed:

> You must be he I was seeking, or she I was seeking, (it comes to me as of a dream,)
>
> (*W,* 280)

After an iambic beginning such as is traditional in English poetry ("You *must* be *he*"), the line quickens into anapests ("I was *seek*ing, or *she* I was *seek*ing") in a free use of the English rhythm kit. Then the settling return of iambs ("it *comes* to *me* as *of* a *dream*") is a joy like starting over, even as it more than balances the beginning of the line and suggests that the agitation of seeking has passed. No one could say that the line recalls "the sweetness debonair" Whitman objected to in English and

English-influenced verse. Yet it is nothing if not language art. The trembling, grateful rise to the twin pronouns *he* and *she* ("You must be *he* I was seeking, or *she* I was seeking"—Whitman beautifully practiced, and practically invented, the art of accenting accent); the calming cushion-vowel in "comes," which is the next heavily accented vowel after all those teeth-tingling long *e*'s; the way the humming close of "dream" confirms this tranquillity; above all, the internal repetition of the phrase "I was seeking"—all these are products of the ear's love for the music of meaning.

The line could be thought of as a feverishly excited discovery followed by a compensating lapse into soothing regions of dream; and in fact this dialectic between ardor and detachment, pursuit and retreat, is of the essence of Whitman's relations with objects and ends. Not least of his "objects" here is the reader, who to all intents and purposes is the passing stranger thus so intimately addressed. "I have somewhere surely lived a life of joy with you," the poet continues. The reader feels engulfed, loved beyond wildest expectation; yet this love leaves him as anonymous as he secretly suspected he really was. The poet says "You give me the pleasure of your eyes, face, flesh, as we pass, you take of my beard, breast, hands, in return," cataloguing physical riches; yet this intercourse *in passing* is correlative with both chastity and a tenacious fixation of desire:

> I am not to speak to you, I am to think of you when I sit alone
> I am to wait, I do not doubt I am to meet you again,
> I am to see to it that I do not lose you.

Similarly, the rhythm of the line both pursues and retreats from recurrences of sounds and measures. "You must be he I sought" would have sounded finished, even for the ear. But the ear hears "You must be he I was seeking" as unresolved, there must be more to come; there always is in Whitman. Whitman thus urges prose to the erotic chase and medley of meters and the less jingly sorts of rhyme even as he preserves its detachment, a rhythmic marginality. His cadences are free-lance treatments of, raids on, familiar metrical units. They range; he will not fence them in. *He* will not be fenced in either, whether by a lover or a leader. Nor, politically, will the Americans he speaks for. The rhythm must somehow say all this, even as "amorously" it tries to "swallow" the world.

Whitman's rejection of predetermined arrangements of lines (for instance, couplets) was inspired by a related attribution of "self-reliance" to the individual line. (Ornery American independence would later lead William Carlos Williams to de-

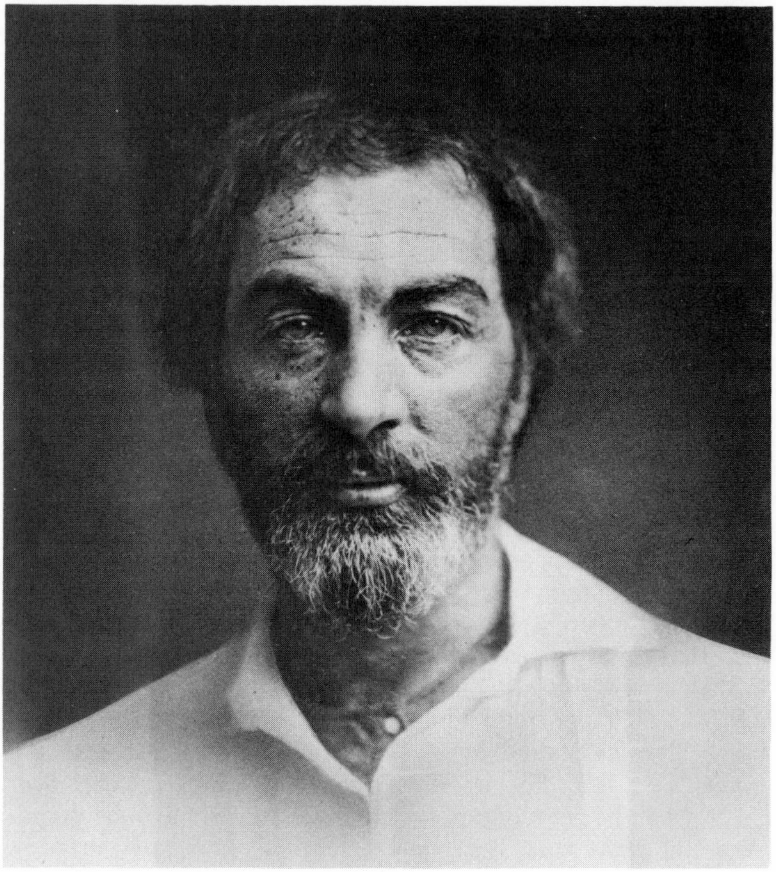

This photograph of Whitman, sometimes called "the Christ portrait," is one that Hart Crane had framed and carried with him in his travels.

nounce the sonnet as fascist.) Further prompting Whitman's composition-by-line, as well as the amplitude of his lines, was his emulation of Nature's "broad handling." Whitman would no more count syllables in a line, or lines in a poem, than he would count the grain in the American prairies, whose "boundless prodigality and amplitude" must, so he said in his prose collection *Specimen Days,* "ever appear in, and in some part form a standard for our poetry and art" (*W,* 866–67).

Besides, a love of *"power,* so important in poetry and war," and equally of motion ("creation's incessant unrest, exfoliation [Darwin's evolution, I suppose]")—these, directed toward America's ample materials, encouraged both positive-sounding lines, or cornucopia pours within the line ("The hairy wild-bee that murmurs and hankers up and down, that gripes the full-grown lady-flower, curves upon her with amorous firm legs, takes his will of her, and holds himself tremulous and tight till he is satisfied" [*W,* 261]), and cornucopia pours of line after line. Verbal power and motion, yet withal, delicacy (for the American land was a "strange mixture of delicacy and power")—these were to keep off, in their New World prominence, the European morbidity, the fainting-sickness of bloody dynasties, the "abnormal beauty" of refinements squeezed from repressions. True poetry is none of this, but the rude health of Homer and the Bible. Tennyson's eloquent, terrible exhaustion ("And ghastly through the drizzling rain / On the bald street breaks the blank day") may be what poetry is in mid-nineteenth-century England, but in mid-nineteenth-century America it is, by rights, a "furious whirling wheel, . . . the centre and axis of the whole" (*W,* 872).

Emerson, divine Emerson, had erred, perhaps, in making many of his lines a bit sharp and thin, brisk and restive. America meant speed, yes, but also power, abundance, amplitude, happiness. *Being* must be here and now, or acknowledged as a fiction. The line, and the poem as a freely organized community of lines, must not be cramped (Nature's own treatment, he observed, was "uncramped"). Whitman's often long, uncrowded lines suggest that he already reposes in the answer (the poet, he said, is the "Answerer") as deliciously as his bones snuggle in his own fat ("I have pried through the strata and analyzed to a hair, / . . . and found no sweeter fat than sticks to my own bones" [*W,* 45]). "Fingers of the organist skipping staccato over the keys of the great organ," he suggested in "Song of the Broad-Axe," in what was to become a familiar modernist strategy, virtually a necessity for an artist starting from "scratch": that of providing within the work itself hints as to how its aesthetic should be viewed. But a skipping staccato was true only of the weird-singing of the opening lines of that poem. "Easily written loosefingered chords! I feel the thrum of their climax and close": this, from "Song of Myself," is more generally apt. Whitman's metal-stringed lines do thrum, his verse-paragraphs enjoy an individual climax and close.

The Bible must have helped Whitman toward breadth, toward eloquence and cadence, toward anaphora and polysyndeton—critics always say so—but Whitman doesn't sound like the Bible any more than he sounds like the best-selling English poet of his day, Martin F. Tupper, whose *Proverbial Philosophy* (1839), with its long, de-metered lines, reads like a complacent paraphrase of Biblical sentiments: "Deep is the sea, and deep is hell, but Pride mineth deeper; / It is coiled as a poisonous worm about the foundations of the soul," and so forth. Whitman sounds only like Whitman. True, like William Blake's, his long lines restore prophecy to verse, but in accents "beyond stint," like one of the American cornfields that he delighted to think would have floored Blake. True, again, that like Hebrew poetry his is pronoun-fermentative, a language of passion with "accents strong and yet light and flowing," to be "uttered with . . . organs yet pliable and vigorous," in words from J. G. von Herder's *The Spirit of Hebrew Poetry* (1833), a book evidently known to Whitman. In both poetries, "the copula is the main thing," for both combine "ideas the most heterogeneous." Grammatical parallelism and "something of the style of command" further link the two, as does the impulse to bind all objects in "sublime choral song." One way of getting away from England —as Channing had indicated—was to go round it "to the very fathers of poetry." At the end of his essay "The Bible as Poetry," Whitman himself says, "Even to our Nineteenth Century here are the fountain heads of song" (*W,* 1143). But in Whitman the old model of "the office of poet" was "adjusted entirely to the modern." He absorbed all his influences into something fresh, wanting the reader to possess above all "the origin of all poems," the poetry before there was verse.

As W. R. Johnson indicated in *The Idea of Lyric: Lyric Modes in Ancient and Modern Poetry* (1982), Whitman resuscitated the ancient choral function of the Greek poets whose happy assumption of sympathetic listeners filled them with a vivid sense of their poetic powers, with living accent, lyric or rhetorical urgency, active formulas such as *I see, I know, I call,* public love, imaginings of the "good community," incitements to will and faith. And just as Whitman's voice must be (as he characterized it) "orotund sweeping and final" to fulfill such a role, so his words must be familiar, of the family:

> Come my children,
> Come my boys and girls, and my women and household and
> intimates,
> Now the performer launches his nerve. . . . he has passed his
> prelude on the reeds within.
>
> Easily written loosefingered chords! I feel the thrum of their
> climax and close.
>
> My head evolves on my neck,
> Music rolls, but not from the organ. . . . folks are around me,
> but they are no household of mine.
>
> (*W,* 75)

Here, as head, priest, and musician of his American household, Whitman comically evolves so fast and far that he hears the hymning (but nonchurchified) spheres themselves and fails to recognize the strange, equally evolved folk around him. His

"Spirit of the Frontier" by John Gast (also known as "Manifest Destiny").

The United States themselves are essentially the greatest poem. . . . Here at last is something in the doings of men that corresponds with the broadcast doings of day and night. . . . Here are the roughs and beards and space and ruggedness and nonchalance that the soul loves.

—From the preface to the 1855 edition of *Leaves of Grass*

words make it easy to follow him, in both senses. *Come, boys and girls, intimates, performer, launches, prelude, chords, thrum, climax, folks*—these are clean-shaped as T-rails, a choral language, the unitary language of the country.

H. L. Mencken in his book *The American Language* noted that "not many specimens of the popular speech ever got into

[Whitman's] writings, either in prose or in verse. He is remembered for few besides *yawp* and *gawk*. His own inventions were mainly cacophonous miscegenations of roots and suffixes . . . and not one of them has ever gained any currency" (*AL*, 81). But Whitman is the quintessential American poet, in part, for being plain American in that hardest of all places, verse, and not for cultivating Americanisms. Incredible that Mencken should sum up his language as "stiff and artificial English." Even if the prose is meant, Whitman's prose (though sometimes choking on itself, as in "Democratic Vistas") is in the 1855 Preface as forceful and natural as any in English or American—for instance, "This is what you shall do: Love the earth and sun and the animals, despise riches, give alms to every one that asks, stand up for the stupid and crazy" (*W*, 11). As for the poetry, Whitman could not, as prophet of the Whole, veer off into regionalism without risking an effect of provinciality. Could he afford to sound like Mencken's favorite, Huck Finn: "We went through the yard so as to see what the hounds would do. They knowed us, and didn't make no more noise than country dogs is always doing when anything comes by in the night"? This is not the language of an express letter to the cosmos, saying, "Arriving soon." Whitman could not afford to be country cute, he had to be in "advance" yet perspicuous as the morning star.

Toward this he was assisted by the surprising unanimity of the American people and their language. As to the first, Cooper observed that "I have never seen a nation so much alike in my life, as the people of the United States" (*NM*, 222); and as to the second, Mencken noted that "in place of the discordant local dialects of nearly all the other major countries, including England, we have a general *Volkssprache*"—but this was an unfortunate way to put it—"for the whole nation"; "Americans use pretty much the same words in the same way" (*AL*, 98). Unlike Melville, with his penchant for a "nervous lofty language" that makes a man "one in a whole nation's census," Whitman had an astonishingly pure feeling for the common idiom, knew how to test-thump its words like melons in the street stalls whose local color he so much delighted in, could tell that each word in

> I resist anything better than my own diversity,
> And breathe the air and leave plenty after me,
> And am not stuck up, and am in my place
>
> (*W*, 43)

would be as good as new after a hundred, or three hundred, years. His "vulgar" colloquialisms, such as (of the air) "It is for my mouth forever" or (of a riverbank in the woods) "I am mad for it to be in contact with me" (but here Emerson had set the precedent in his prose: "In youth we are mad for persons") or "The sounds of the belched words of my voice" were invariably healthy; they could not offend, God himself would smile at them.

But Whitman was not just some miraculous locator of the base line of American English; his genius lay in his imaginative verbal energy and play, his generously enlivening spirit of performance. Though he relished a brisk, crackling language (there was something in him of the Benjamin Franklin who copied his style out of Addison's *Spectator*); though he said "nothing can make up for excess or for the lack of definiteness" and "the art of art . . . is simplicity" (*W,* 13), still he thought that Puritanism had had its day in culture (up against "this vast and varied Commonwealth," he said, its "standards are constipated, narrow, and non-philosophic"). He prized *both* efficiency and color, as in "The brisk short crackle of the steel driven slantingly into the pine, / The butter-color'd chips flying off in great flakes and slivers" (*W,* 333). What was greatest was simplicity plus something lyrical, as in

> I am he that walks with the tender and growing night;
> I call to the earth and sea half-held by the night.
>
> Press close barebosomed night! Press close magnetic nourishing
>   night!
>
> Night of south winds! Night of the large few stars!
> Still nodding night! Mad naked summer night!
>
> Smile O voluptuous coolbreathed earth!
> Earth of the slumbering and liquid trees!
>
> (*W,* 47)

For Whitman, the drama of language was that of living in a cosmos that with human assistance is gradually imagining into being its own freedom, beauty, and joy. This licensed him on the one hand to use the simplest words and on the other to make unexpected figures out of them, to arrange them so that they glowed, since language had an instinct for "perpetual transfers and promotions." So he would refer to his phallus as the "hubb'd sting of myself" (*W,* 261); would say "I know I shall not pass like a child's carlacue cut with a burnt stick at night" (*W,* 46). He caressed language just as he did life ("In me the caresser of life wherever moving" [*W,* 37]) not to indulge himself but to go in for his chances, spend "for vast returns."

American idealism (as George Santayana characterized it in 1920, in *Character and Opinion in the United States*) works on matter, delights in novel attacks on it, clings close to nature. Whitman is the supreme, the glad poet of this idealism. Santayana's sketch of the "universal American" ("of course . . . mythical") effectively outlines Whitman—his adventurous blood, social radicalism, enthusiasm for the future, goodwill, cheerful experimentalism, practical imagination, youth, vitality, nearness to the impulses of nature, and so on. Whitman was in fact so much the universal American that he seemed astonished that others had fallen outside the pattern, with a pipe-stemmed leg dangling there, and here a hand greedily reaching out. Few characterizations of nineteenth-century Americans are chillier than those in "Democratic Vistas," and few scarier than the one in section 42 of "Song of Myself":

> Here and there with dimes on the eyes walking,
> To feed the greed of the belly the brains liberally spooning,
> Tickets buying or taking or selling, but in to the feast never once going;
> Many sweating and ploughing and thrashing, and then the chaff for payment receiving,
> A few idly owning, and they the wheat continually claiming.
>
> (*W,* 75–76)

The initial, unforgiving omissions of human agents at the grammatical level turn metonymy into a terrifying device. Virtue, if only more Americans would see it, is happiness, the adventurous reconciliation of power and altruism, self and other.

"Virtue," Czeslaw Miłosz notes in *Visions from San Francisco Bay,* is "that strength of character from whence arise the qualities indispensable for standing up to the world—courage, resolve, perseverance, control of the constantly changing emotions and impulses" (*V,* 149). And technology is "virtue condensed, consolidated in tangible forms" (*V,* 154). So "Thee for my recitative," Whitman says to a locomotive in winter, "type of the modern—emblem of motion and power—pulse of the continent" (*W,* 583). In "Song of the Exposition" (written for the American Institute's fortieth annual exhibition), he happily installed the Muse "amid the kitchen ware" ("Come Muse . . . / Placard 'Removed' and 'To Let' on the rocks of your snowy Parnassus" [*W,* 342]). The thing poetic about kitchenware or a locomotive (or even a "drainpipe, gasometers, artificial fertilizers") is the evidence that the imagination has successfully gone to work on raw materials, so as to multiply power: "Materials here under your eye shall change their shape as if by magic" (*W,* 345). Power is of all things the most poetic, imagination itself is the power to effect metamorphoses (thus it "excites in the beholder," as Emerson said, "an emotion of joy"), and tech-

Whitman's "Letters from a Travelling Bachelor" (see third column from right) are considered some of his best work as a journalist. His celebration, in this one, of the view of Manhattan's rivers from the high promenade of the Croton Reservoir contains seminal material for his great poem "Crossing Brooklyn Ferry."

Whitman, after being an apprentice printer, and then a working printer, became a working journalist as a reporter or newspaper editor. It may very well be that he was not temperamentally suited to be a journalist; he was too ruminative, too indolent in a receptive way. But what's important about Whitman's journalistic background, I think, is that this, in a sense, is his bank account in experience. This is the way he learns about the city, this is the way he learns what he calls "million-footed Manhattan." This is the way he learns about violence and conflict, this is the way he learns about American society. It's a very direct exposure to experience. There's nothing bookish about Whitman's education.

—Justin Kaplan in the *Voices & Visions* film *Walt Whitman*

nology is the mass poetry of matter. Whitman's own poetic of rumbling hooting lines was patently a power technology. The age of the electromagnet (invented by the American Joseph Henry) was naturally the age of the "unpent" social soul. The soul of America itself is "electric, spiritual," as if to say, elementary, cosmic stuff.

Whitman was consistent in extending the transformative technology of the imagination still further, to the live matter of the senses, the life-drive, as eroticism. "From sex, from the warp and from the woof" (*W,* 249), came his celebration of life, his songs, and he dared to say so, even to speak of "This poem drooping shy and unseen that I always carry, and that all men carry" (*W,* 260). These "lusty lurking masculine poems" were like steam locomotives domiciled in their stations; eroticism too harbored a penetrant rage to be "unpent." Power, through motion, seeks its own apotheosis. As Henry Adams was to note, other Americans "had used sex for sentiment, never for force. Society regarded this victory over sex as its greatest triumph." Whitman objected that "Culture" as "now taught, accepted, and carried out" is "creating a class of supercilious infidels, who believe in nothing." "Shall a man lose himself in countless masses of adjustments," he asked, "and be so shaped with reference to this, that, and the other, that the simply good and healthy and brave parts of him are reduced and clipped away, like the bordering of box in a garden?" (*W,* 962). It was statements like this that grew faun ears on Whitman's most daring

Sunday Dispatch.

VOLUME 4. NO. 52. NEW YORK, SUNDAY MORNING, NOVEMBER 25, 1849. PRICE THREE CENTS.

REVISED BY THE AUTHOR EXPRESSLY FOR THIS PAPER.

THE ADVENTURES OF TOM STAPLETON: OR, NO. 202 BROADWAY.

CHAPTER XVI.

Scarcely had I taken possession of my new retreat than some person was admitted, and the moment after I heard a very distinct and palpable kiss!

"Ho! ho! my lady," thinks I, "That's the way you do business, is it! But what the devil is that to me," I added, as I turned round to pay a little attention to the decanters and trimmings; for I always follow the rule of patronizing "the goods the gods provide us," no matter where or how they may be situated, lest they might take it into their heads that I was treating them with disrespect or ingratitude.

Meanwhile I heard another kiss; then one, two, three; and so on for half a dozen.

"By the Lord," I muttered, "that rascal's in clover, whoever he is," knowing well the while, by the smack of relish and rapture of the demonstrations aforesaid, and by the sympathetic watering of my own mouth that the luxurious stranger was a union of the sex whose prerogative—(a disputed one by the way)—it is to wear small clothes; for I have always remarked that the sound produced by the collision of two ladies' lips, has no true music in it. It is, as it were, the body without the soul—the wine without the flavor—In a word, it is a little better than a libel on the noble art of kissing.

Another smack!

"That's a fellow of taste and courage," I continued, "who must be worth looking at." And accordingly—(the reader will please to remember that I had the lady's permission to do so)—I applied an eye to the key-hole to see what might be seen.

And faith, what I saw was a study for a painter; for there before me stood Mary Anson, radiant and beautiful as the queen of all heaven's houris; while on her left, and with his delirious lips glued to her hand, knelt a gentleman of some forty and odd years, who seemed as if he might be on the point of exploding with intensity of rapture.

[illegible]

...crawling reptile, and may I not return injury for injury? May I not impose a paltry fine on the robber who would plunder me of all that life is worth living for?" She paused for a moment, and then resumed, while her brow lowered and her eye shot forth a flash of resentment. "I shall and will; and think not that I have acted heartlessly; for I feel when he, or such as he, presumes to subject me to the humiliation of their disgusting embraces, that I might be justified for striking them dead at my feet."

"But Miss Anson," said I, "why throw yourself in the way of such insults?"

"The rags and starvation you saw me enduring might answer the question," she replied; "even occasion a wonder how I had escaped the yet lower pitfall! And yet there are reasons paramount to either of these; the first and principal of which is, that having been deceived, I think I have a right to live by deception—that having suffered poverty through my beauty, I now feel justified in making it the medium of earning my daily bread! But no doubt you are curious to know why I have chosen you for my father confessor?"

I answered to the effect that I was, only couched in the most delicate language I was capable of.

"Well," she returned, "there are many and simple. One is, because you revenged me at a time when I was unequal to the task. Another, because you know more about my recent history than any one else; and consequently if I did not tell you what I was, you might suspect me to be worse. A third, that you have me in your power. And a fourth, which makes the last I shall mention, because when I leave the city, (as a matter of course,) and change my name, I want you to take Delauney's place!"

A spasmodic start was the only answer I could give.

"Don't be alarmed," continued Miss Anson, "Your situation will involve neither matrimony nor love, nor even service; but merely the pr...

[illegible]

...that we give what little space we have remaining for this letter to a few lines about the International. Never before has any art exhibition in America contained pieces or work of such high order as this. Long, long half hours have I passed looking at "the Dead Christ," by Ary Scheffer. It has grown into my very soul. The face and breast of the Saviour are exhibited, with the grave clothes raised from them, and the prostrate head of his mother resting on his breast. There are three other female figures, whose faces exhibit different developments of grief. The countenance of the Sacred Corpse is beyond all description; he or she who can look upon it without the deepest emotion must be incapable to the great achievements of art. Yet the painting is entirely free from any strained effect, any daring attempt at wonderful things; it is after the severest forms of simplicity and spirituality. The serene ... great for words, of the female at the left is beautifully expressed—and the bitter wailing of the aged woman more in the background almost touches the ear, but the face of the mother is too intense for depicting, and it is bowed and hidden on the cold bosom of Christ. No tricks of ambitious color, or "warm light," or anything of that sort, mar this great picture.

"The Christian maiden converting her Betrothed," is a large and rich painting by Gendron, and was presented to the International by the French Republic. A young man, seated, is instructed in religious matters by a beautiful female who stands behind him, and pointing over his shoulder, to the open book in front, rests her neck confidingly against his head. The picture is highly finished, and its adjuncts are all complete, and well delineated.

"The Republic," also a donation from France, is a large sized painting—a female figure, emblematical of a Free Government. There is nothing particularly new or striking about it. The attitude of the female, and the expression in her face, are serene and majestical; her ample form is clothed in classically flowing drapery, and her head is surrounded by laurel.

Perhaps the most attractive and popular pictures, however, are "Children leaving School," "The Convalescence," and "The Grandfather's Festival," by Waldmuller. The first named is certainly one of the most remarkable paintings ever produced. Its variety of scene and expression, all comprised in a small compass, and without violent contrasts, is beyond that of any picture I ever saw. A score and more of children are just tumbling out of school, and there they are, with all the vivacity and glee... of their age. One has received a medal, a little girl is laughing in her pleasure at examining it; another is reaching her hand out over the crowd, for her grandfather, who has come after her; one little fellow appears to have the toothache; one is going to strike a young foe, but is restrained by the sister, and so on. It is incomparable! The expression of the old man, in "the Convalescence," is a solemnly beautiful gratitude; he has recovered...

[illegible]

A CHILD ASSAILED BY A FERRET.—A circumstance which might have been fraught with the most fatal consequences happened recently at Framfield, Sussex, on Tuesday last, to an infant, about seven months of age, belonging to a woman named Jones, residing at Tarble Down, in the southern part of this parish. The mother having occasion to visit an adjoining dwelling, left her infant asleep in a basket contiguous to a place allotted to some ferrets. A short time after the exit of the woman, a neighbor became attracted to the spot by the cries of the child, when, shocking to relate, a ferret was discovered fastened on its face, having inflicted very severe injuries on various parts of the neck, nose, and eyes. The poor babe had well nigh exhausted its energies in crying, and endeavoring to ward off its relentless foe, which had apparently continued, without intermission, its murderous attack for some time, the linen having become completely saturated with blood, and it was not until its mother had been severely bitten that the odious animal could be forced to relinquish its hold. For some minutes after the rescue the child continued to wave its little hands as if combating its merciless enemy. It was shortly taken to Mr. Holman, surgeon, of Eastbourne, who pronounced that it had received no vital injury, and it is now, we are happy to state, in a favorable way of recovery. We hope this event may prove a lasting warning to mothers.—*Surrey (Eng.) Standard.*

THE FORMER CONDITION OF ENGLAND.—If we look into England's past history, and compare its present condition with any portion of that history, we shall find that a marked and important change for the better is visible; while the comparison will yield fresh encouragement to the lovers of and believers in progress to continue their labors with redoubled zeal. For instance, some four hundred years ago the people of this country were no better than serfs; political freedom was unknown, and education was confined to the priests; the very nobles of the land, the proudest and the wealthiest, were unable to read or write, and there are numerous records extant which show that they had to substitute a cross or mark for their signature. The books in existence were in the possession of the monks, or chained to the pillars in the churches. In matters of opinion no man was allowed to have a mind of his own; freedom of speech was denied; the man who raised his voice against the errors and abuses of a corrupt religion was hurried to the stake; the faggot and the inquisition were the reward of the reformer. The strong arm ruled; "might was right;" every privilege had to be won by fear and force, and, when obtained, guarded with jealous care against the designs of the monarch and the aristocracy.

CAMPHOR.—Raspail, the celebrated French Socialist, now in prison on account of the June affair, has pointed out one of the powers of camphor, which, in a psychological point of view...

[illegible]

and dazzling pupil, even if he was English—D. H. Lawrence. For his trouble, however, Whitman was reviled. Ladies, it was said, could not read him and even Thoreau grumbled: "It is as if the beasts spoke. I think that men have not been ashamed of themselves without reason." But Whitman seemed radical only because he was "American" enough to want to release power from all its hiding places, send it humming live through all its coils. He was an erotic pioneer.

There was, however, on the unreal plane of logic, a difficulty. Could the body delirious with erotic pleasure also make pig-iron? Where was energy to go, into sex or into factories? The dilemma was not lost on the virtue-sabotaging "flower children" of the 1960s. Everything they stood for could have been taken, and sometimes was, from Whitman's poems. For instance, they opposed stiff dignity with poetry, music, and dance, as Whitman would when he says, "O to have life henceforth a poem of new joys! / To dance, clap hands, exult, shout, skip, leap, roll on, float on!" (*W,* 330). Yet was not this same Whitman the loudest celebrant of American Virtue? No use calling on him to explain the contradiction. He triumphed over it by taking no notice of it—by being himself. Who more shamelessly autoerotic, yet who more bent on promotions, expansions, destiny? To dote on his own flesh, to hymn locomotives—somehow in him it was all one. His locomotive "in the driving storm . . . , the snow" is a hardy emblem of Virtue-as-technology, all right, but no less poetic, musical, and erotic for that, with its "panoply," "measur'd dual throbbing and . . . beat convulsive," twinkling wheels, cars "merrily following," "madly-whistled laughter," and so on. The locomotive was Whitman, and what Whitman himself was, America could also be. He himself contained multitudes, was both "real and ideal," powerful and delicate, transformative and receptive. Then let all Americans be so. "Long enough have you dreamed contemptible dreams," he said, "Now I wash the gum from your eyes" (*W,* 83).

America was then *power in motion. Leaves of Grass* said it, *Moby-Dick* with joy and terror said it, the railroads said it, the Union troops said it. So did Frederick Church's painting *The Great Fall, Niagara.* In a time so bustling with trust in what Whitman called "Nature's amelioration" and expansionist fervor that even still-lifes became noted for "crowded abundance" (as William Gerdts notes in *Portfolio,* September/October 1981), Church's monumental painting, hailed as "Niagara without the roar," was prized as a symbol of America, "a truly great National Work." In the first two weeks of its showing in New

A view of Niblo's Garden Theatre, a New York opera house that Whitman frequented.

I hear the violincello or man's heart's complaint,
And hear the keyed cornet or else the echo of sunset.

I hear the chorus . . . it is a grand-opera . . . this indeed is music!

A tenor large and fresh as the creation fills me,
The orbic flex of his mouth is pouring and filling me full.

I hear the trained soprano . . . she convulses me like the climax of
my love-grip;
The orchestra whirls me wider than Uranus flies,
It wrenches unnamable ardors from my breast,
It throbs me to gulps of the farthest down horror,
It sails me . . . I dab with bare feet . . . they are licked by the
indolent waves,
I am exposed . . . cut by bitter and poisoned hail . . .

—From *Leaves of Grass* (1855 edition)

York City, in 1857, one hundred thousand people viewed it. (Even an English critic dubbed it "the greatest realisation of moving water in the world,") In "The Over-Soul," Emerson had said that "Man is a stream whose source is hidden. Our being is descending into us from we know not whence"—and that was what Church's huge painting, for all its scientific accuracy (Church had made analyses of Niagara's hydraulics), seemed to show: the ethereal water, the "alien energy," from which "the visions come" (*EE,* 189). The painting might equally have illustrated Melville's cry, "O Nature, and O soul of man! how far beyond all utterance are your linked analogies!" Whitman's words on the "unseen moral essence of all the vast materials of America," on the "hidden national will lying in [their] abysms, conceal'd but ever alert," provide still another gloss. Exhaustless the supply and happy the laissez-faire of these rushing waters.

Whitman's *Leaves of Grass* is the poetic twin to Church's *Niagara*—it too strikes a sublime, miraculous accord between "the real and ideal," is tumultuously aflow yet ever self-possessed, and an aesthetic counterpart to the impulsive, expansive politics of Manifest Destiny. Not, of course, that Whitman could compete with the painters (or even with Melville) in visual sublimity, saving an exceptional passage or two. To be a Personality meant to be something other than a painter. Significantly, his own "picture" of Niagara occurs in his catalogue of greatest conscious motion—section 33 of "Song of Myself"—but comes to merely "Under Niagara, the cataract falling like a veil over my countenance" (this at least hintingly aggrandizes the poet as a vital Spirit who wears immense power-motion as a veil). Whitman's poetry, especially "Song of Myself," rivaled *Niagara,* instead, in conveying over the impression of America as a powerful breadth and depth, as epic poise, a past and a future simultaneously contained within a Now. The poem was a point of view in motion, multiple and immense yet instructively directed, amorously submitting to and voicing the elemental laws.

Laid end to end, Whitman's long lines would form their own virtual transcontinental railroad, and the locomotive and cars to boot, and varied sights all along the way. At a time when painters and lithographers were cataloguing America in "genre" studies, Whitman joined in and in one way outdid them all, for he could do a painting a line, and turn to another before the first had begun to dry. On a single page he could be in twenty scenes from Oregon to Florida, drink the wind before him like an Ariel with paintbrush in hand. "I paint myriads of heads," he pointed out, "but paint no head without its nimbus of gold-color'd light"

"Niagara" *by Frederick Church.*

America was then *power in motion. Leaves of Grass* said it, *Moby Dick* with joy and terror said it, the railroads said it, the Union troops said it. So did Frederick Church's painting *The Great Fall, Niagara. . . .* Church's monumental painting, hailed as "Niagara without the roar," was prized as a symbol of America, "a truly great National Work." In the first two weeks of its showing in New York City, in 1857, one hundred thousand people viewed it.

(*W,* 376). From "The negro that drives the huge dray of the stoneyard" and "tosses the slouch of his hat away from his forehead," he could range at will to the butcher boy sharpening "his knife at the stall in the market," or, say, a surgeon ("What is removed drops horribly in a pail"). Among the specialists in American genre studies were Currier and Ives (whose partnership began in 1857), and Whitman matches them almost folio for folio. He too pictures American homesteads, hunters, wagons loaded with hay, clipper ships in rough waters or among icebergs, steamboats wooding up by firelight at night on the Mississippi, firemen, fishermen, mothers with their children, husbands with their wives, locomotives in winter (Whitman's engine, however, importantly in motion, not "Snow Bound"). And if his one- or two-line sketches are often scarcely more than naked namings, they avoid the lithographers' floweriness and overcoloring, they avoid the painters' sentimentality. (Several, it is true, are indebted to specific paintings—for instance, the lines beginning "I saw the marriage of the trapper in the open air in the far-west" to Alfred Jacob Miller's "The Trapper's Bride.") But what mattered was the God's plenty of his sketches and, no less, the motion (both the verse motion and the travel motion) in the course and midst of which each appeared as a quick-stop, the momentary object of the poem's "Deific glance." This poet will "see" America not on horseback ("I but use you a moment and then I resign you stallion"), nor even from a locomotive, but instead in the buoyant "pear-shaped balloon" of his swift fancy: "Swift wind! Space! My Soul! . . . / My ties and ballasts leave me . . . I travel." Resting on the rim of the gondola, how casually his elbows span the continent: "my elbows rest in the sea-gaps" (*W,* 59)! In his catalogues, motion words such as "Over," "Through," "Approaching," and "Hurrying" vie with still-shot words such as "By," "Upon," and "At." He will roll over America as if it were a brink and he Niagara: "I fly the flight of the fluid and swallowing soul" (*W,* 63).

Whether *Moby-Dick* (1851), *Walden* (1854), *Leaves of Grass* (1855), or *Niagara* (1857)—this last a late product of the Hudson River School—great mid-nineteenth-century American art favors a low horizon with plenty of free sky and an open, in-pulling frame and foreground: invitations, all, to adventure, expansion, sublimity. The new aesthetic poised the reader or spectator on the brink of vast space or power. In *Niagara,* Church's "deceptively simple composition," notes Jeremy Adamson in *Portfolio* (November/December 1981), ". . . seemed to draw viewers to the very rim of the Horseshoe Fall. . . . The viewer . . . finds himself suddenly projected into *Niagara*'s pictorial space." The whole immediate spread of the infinitely varied motion of the waters becomes an extended agitation amidst serenity in the viewer's breast. (By contrast, W. J. Bennett's popular 1829 engraving placed two tiny hunters in the foreground below the falls, killing expansionist fantasy.) In *Moby-Dick,* Melville draws a technological, power-driven chase of the "ungraspable phantom" of Power on a canvas of immense horizontal sweep. The book places every reader at the "ever-pitching prow" of the *Pequod* when not in one of its three ever-pitching crows' nests, and is peculiarly open-framed as now a narrative, now a discursive, work. (In this it resembles "Song of Myself.") Thoreau manages to present himself as man in motion even in the one wooded vicinity of Walden Pond, explaining that "we should come home far, from adventures and perils, and discoveries everyday, with new expectations and character."

Walden, too, is horizontally and vertically "open" in form, drawing the "head through atmospheres." Whitman's own sequential poem-plan, whether in "Song of Myself" or the monumental *Leaves of Grass* as a whole, correlates with the open-ended frame and horizontal breadth of *Niagara* and of the "luminist" canvases of the 1860s. In "Song of Myself" the poet offers no orienting groundline except his assurance that "what I assume, you shall assume." You climb into his vehicle and ascend. "These immense meadows, these interminable rivers," the loudspeaker instructs, "you are immense and interminable as they." Separately and together, the expansionist and the evolutionist ethic posited a sublimely open aesthetic. "The Unconscious of man," wrote Thoreau, "is the consciousness of God, the end of the world." And Melville's Father Mapple says, "The world's a ship on its passage out, and not a voyage complete."

"Song of Myself" (strongest in the untitled 1855 version, despite the lack of sectioning) is, to my mind, Whitman's greatest single achievement. Here it was that he made bold to be a Personality—partly out of what seemed a sheer love of performance, but no less to supply America with what it needed, the "image" of a metaphysical democrat, a full-scale American. Just as Church had coaxed Niagara into submission with his brush, so Whitman would "quell" America with his "tongue." The artist-hero, America's hero, he would be that, the first of a new breed. In presenting himself as both the greatest democrat and the greatest poet, as both pioneer and prophet, he would reveal how they are all aspects of the same bold brightness of soul. The poet is only the democrat *with expression,* in keeping with Emerson's accurate idea that "the man is only half himself, the other half is his expression" (*EE,* 263). And just as the pioneer is the prophet of material space, so the prophet is the pioneer of ideal time.

"The most inevitable dramatic conception . . . of the nineteenth century," wrote George Bernard Shaw in *The Perfect Wagnerite,* "is that of a perfectly naive hero upsetting religion, law and order in all directions, and establishing in their place the unfettered action of Humanity doing exactly what it likes, and producing order instead of confusion thereby because it likes to do what is necessary for the good of the race." Change "perfectly naive" to "deliberately, honestly naive" and leave "dramatic conception" intact as appropriate after all to the canny self-presenter of "Song of Myself," and this forms an exact account of Whitman's poem. "What others give as du-

Walt Whitman, c. 1849.

The art of art, the glory of expression and the sunshine of the light of letters is simplicity. . . . I will not have in my writing any elegance or effect of originality to hang in the way between me and the rest like curtains. I will have nothing hang in the way, not the richest curtains.

—From the preface to *Leaves of Grass* (1855 edition)

ties," Whitman said, "I give as living impulses" (*W,* 379). Living impulse became the voice-aesthetic, line-aesthetic, of "Song of Myself," that superb simulation of oral gusto and intimacy, that long, one-man, one-instrument, never-flagging, spectacularly plenteous show. In 1872, Nietzsche was to laud Wagner as a "sublime protagonist" of "the properly metaphysical activity of life," and in "Song of Myself," Whitman, releasing his eroticism like a crowd of birthday balloons over what was then "many-masted Manhattan" and declaring himself magnetic brother to atoms and stars, lyrically lauds *himself* as such. Only the artist, so Nietzsche later hinted in *The Will to Power,* could live resolutely "in the Whole and in the Full." "Song of Myself" showed how this was done, portraying the poet as one who has not lost the scent of life, as one who naturally, superabundantly, affirms, blesses, deifies existence—the "anti-Christian, anti-Buddhist, antinihilist *par excellence.*"

In "Song of Myself" Whitman plays the string of "identity" (yours for you, he explained, and mine for me) and the string of "sympathy" (just those two: but they encompass everything) with so furious a gladness that he fills every syllable and line-corner with their intermixing resonance. He strikes the note of *personal* reality as the joyfullest definiteness against the elusive resonance of everything, and the note of *external* and *universal* reality as a rapturous release from the twangy, hard "I." "The soul," he declared in the 1855 Preface, "has that measureless pride which consists in never acknowledging any lessons but its own. But it has sympathy as measureless" (*W,* 13). The soul, then, is somehow everything, a self and the rest of things, the "Not Me" a "Me" after all.

The back and forth of *being*—now back to the sole "identity," now forth to the world again—means avoiding the opposite extremes of Stoicism and Orphism. Stoicism turns identity rigid, Orphism melts it into everything. The first, so Paul Ricoeur explains in *Freedom and Nature* (1950), reduces the self to "a point of judgment devoid of carnal density" (it treats the body as already corpsed). The second loses identity in a delirium of praise for the Creation: "Orphism tends to a nature worship in which the unique status of the Cogito evaporates in the cycle of the mineral and the animal" (*FN,* 476). In it, the self might be a water-bucket exposed to the elements, drinking rain, thinking stars. In between these reverse ratios of self and other lies "the way of consent": consent, first, to oneself, thence to the Whole as if it were one's further horizon or skin. "Consent gives me to myself and reminds me that no one can absolve me from the act of *yes . . . Yes* to my life, which I have not chosen but which is the condition which makes all choice possible" (*FN,* 476, 479).

In "Song of Myself," this middle way, this keeping the body alive in hope, this keeping off "the nocturnal themes of Orphism," this determined wiping at the always fogging portal of "identity," this trio of self, personal body, and world, is Whitman's province and glory. Whitman is the supreme poet of consent.

Consent happily confuses the Cartesian dichotomy between matter and mental "substance." Its knowing is sportive, infantile, deathless—what Lawrence called knowing in togetherness. Consider Whitman's enchantingly libidinous knowledge of sunrise:

> To behold the daybreak!
> The little light fades the immense and diaphanous shadows,
> The air tastes good to my palate.
>
> Hefts of the moving world at innocent gambols, silently rising,
>   freshly exuding.
> Scooting obliquely high and low.
>
> Something I cannot see puts upward libidinous prongs.
> Seas of bright juice suffuse heaven.
>
> (*W*, 52)

With its authentic tension, such writing is neither subjective nor objective, but what Emerson meant when he said that, because of "the deep power in which we exist, . . . the act of seeing and the thing seen, . . . the subject and the object, are one" (*EE*, 190). It enacts a mutual metamorphosis, of beholder into beheld and vice versa. It does this in the interest of poetry, of "life." For Whitman, the world is the continual metamorphosis of God, and poetry its free-lance changes, racing ahead because excited by the whole adventure, a dog bounding before its master on the beach.

Like the English romantics (only more so) Whitman anticipated process philosophers such as Henri Bergson, Alfred North Whitehead, and Charles Hartshorne, for whom qualities are real and not, as for Descartes, subjective impressions. "We take sentience as the concrete actuality," says Hartshorne, "of which the material properties (spatial characters, motion, and the like) are only abstracted aspects." This sentient universe-in-process is stirringly open and alive. "The creativity of the world," writes Whitehead, "is . . . the flying dart, of which Lucretius speaks, hurled beyond the bounds of the world." "The starting-point for the highly developed human art," Whitehead adds, "is thus to be sought amid the cravings generated by the physiological functions of the body." Whitman indicated the same when he spoke of sex as "the master, the pilot I yield the vessel to, / The general commanding me, commanding all," adding (astonishingly for his age, or any age):

> Sex contains all, bodies, souls,
> Meanings, proofs, purities, delicacies, results, promulgations,
> Songs, commands, health, pride, the maternal mystery, the
>   seminal milk,
> All hopes, benefactions, bestowals, all the passions, loves,
>   beauties, delights of the earth.
>
> (*W*, 258)

Arthur O. Lovejoy summed up romanticism—and, incidentally, the tenets of "Song of Myself"—in the three words *organicism, dynamism,* and *diversitarianism* (the propagation of surprise).

Organic dynamism and diversity are made possible through a mutual modification between the part and the whole. This dialectic provides the plan for "Song of Myself." The plan is incremental, with now "identity" and now "sympathy" returning with redoubled force, thanks to the loving tussle between them. If we could treat the fifty-two cantos as flip pictures (they jerk in any case from one stance to another), we would find Whitman first taking a bow for no more or less a reason than that he exists (1–6); then sweetly gesturing to the Americans, of whom he appoints himself "mate and companion" (7–16); then taking an even deeper bow, now as the bountiful artist, boasting "This is the meal pleasantly set" (17–23); then doting on his body, which surprisingly shades and amorously slips into the body of the world, as in "Landscapes projected masculine full-sized and golden" (24–29); then displaying a now "infinite and omnigenous" capacity for sympathy, including an ascension to the very "orchards of God" (30–37); then posing as a jaunty, best-yet prophet jetting "the stuff of finer republics" (38–45); and finally, in a beautifully extended and mounting valediction, running on before his readers ("I see God") but warmly calling back to them to join him: "Missing me one place search another, / I stop some where waiting for you" (46–52). Laid to its giant breast, a giant ear would hear, in this plan, a heart beating pit-pat, pit-pat, pit-pat, the middle beat really a pitty-pat, thanks to the overlap between pride and sympathy in the celebration of the personal body (sections 24–29). Regular, human readers, however, cannot feel the contagion of rhythms so vast. They read the poem for its superabundance of striking lines and its strongly molded paragraphs (the latter actually indented as such) and its sectional cohesions.

Near-proverbs (a homage to Biblical proverbs), sailing catalogues, metaphoric extravaganzas (again in keeping with Hebraic "metaphors daring beyond account"), the "speech acts" of

THE BUTCHER BOY.

You're educated in a precious school,
Which makes a forward stripling ape the man;
You drink, smoke, talk of women, play the fool,
And act too often on the rowdy plan.

The genus Soaplock claims you for its own,
Nurses you in its evil, fatal ways,
Gives to your blustering oaths its filthy tone,
In vice's shambles murders your young days.

THE VOLUNTEER, OR FIRE ROWDY.

This class of individuals are indigenous to New York. None but a resident citizen can be fully aware of their peculiarities and habits. Their origin is of no great date, at least the origin of the present class of volunteers. house, and as some of them are ever on the watch for an alarm of fire, at the first sound they rush to the house, and oftentimes have their favorite "machine" half way to the fire before a regular fireman can overtake them.

The butcher-boy puts off his killing-clothes or sharpens his knife at the stall in the market,
I loiter enjoying his repartee and his shuffle and breakdown.

Blacksmiths with grimed and hairy chests environ the anvil,
Each has his main-sledge . . . they are all out . . . there is a great heat in the fire.

From the cinder-strewed threshold I follow their movements,
The lithe sheer of their waists plays even with their massive arms,
Overhand the hammers roll—overhand so slow—overhand so sure,
They do not hasten, each man hits in his place.

—From *Leaves of Grass* (1855 edition)

THE LAMPLIGHTER.

When *Casta Diva* cannot shine,
We sing with pleasure in thy praise,
For the important task is thine
To light our dark and crooked ways.

You've got a nice snug **berth, no doubt,**
By the great rush **is made to fill it;**
But don't let too much **oil run out,**
We have to **pay for't when you *spill it*.**

These sketches of New York City laborers were a regular feature of the Aurora*'s front page when Whitman worked there in 1842.*

attestations, commands, and promises, strong but ever-varying cadences, droll melodramatizations, affecting anecdotes: the poem is a veritable carnival of pleasures (discursive, figural, lyrical, narrative, rhetorical, formal). Admirable above all is the unfaltering imaginative and verbal relish—the spirited attack throughout. This gusto underwrites both bold effects, such as the mesmerizing description of the poem itself as "the float and odor of hair," and, at the other extreme, subtle elegances of sound, as in the quivering mobile formed by one of the valedictory lines, "I effuse my flesh in eddies and drift it in lacy jags," which could be rendered thus:

I   ef   fuse
my   flesh   in
     ed   dies
                               and
                  drift
                  it
                  in   lac
                       y   jags

—a line moving in its triumphantly willed but reluctant darts and escapes.

Here Whitman's gusto is one with his relentlessly venturing faith. Of late, the most common error with regard to the poem is to infer from certain passages—among others, the lines "O Christ! My fit is mastering me!" and "Somehow I have been stunned. Stand back!"—a genuine, even awful crisis of doubt. But Whitman goes out of his way, I find, to explain that this is all hamming and shamming (almost reprehensibly so: "Agonies are one of my changes of garments"!). Eventually there emerges the long-prepared-for declaration, "I rise extatic through all, and sweep with the true gravitation, / The whirling and whirling is elemental within me" (*W,* 70). Twentieth-century skepticism must put down its pins before this indomitable balloon of a poem, which is made of a tough nineteenth-century material and won't pop.

As in Whitman's twin heterosexual and homosexual sequences, "Children of Adam" and "Calamus" respectively, the poet here addresses the reader with so much warmth and longing that the latter becomes, in fantasy, a "listener" present before the speaking poet, enabling him to say, for instance, "Undrape. . . . you are not guilty to me, nor stale nor discarded" (*W,* 33), or, wittily, "It is time to explain myself. . . . let us stand up" (*W,* 79). Whitman exploits the erotics of authority (as he plays the mentor) only by turning the latter into the purest kindness: "I lead [you] upon a knoll, / My left hand hooks you round the waist, / My right hand points to landscapes of continents, and a plain public road" (*W,* 82). No other writer in English has addressed the reader so winningly, none has taken so much trouble to validate the reader as a dialogic, indeed ontological, force bearing on composition, on faith itself—a "you" that must be cajoled, playfully taught, made to shiver at sublimity, and so awake.

The beauty of "Song of Myself" is inseparable from its solar erotic glow. Whitman wrote still other masterpieces, however, in which eroticism merely flickers (and the reader is correspondingly merely a reader). Two small instances are "Cavalry

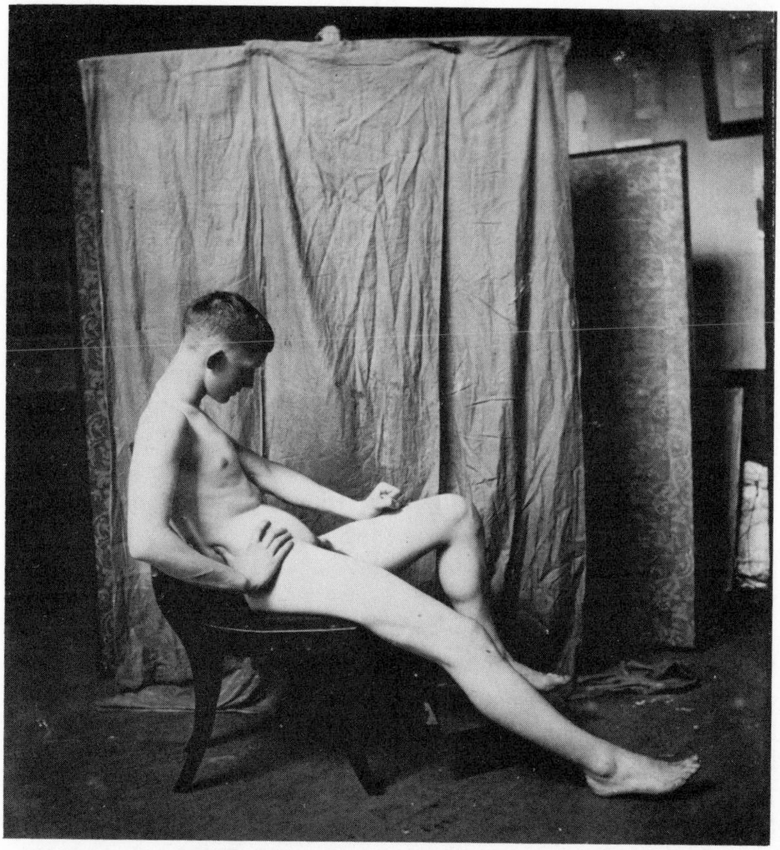

"Nude Model Before Curtain"
by Thomas Eakins.

If I worship any particular thing it shall be some of the spread of
my own body;
Translucent mould of me it shall be you,
Shaded ledges and rests, firm masculine coulter, it shall be you,
Whatever goes to the tilth of me it shall be you,
You my rich blood, your milky stream pale strippings of my life;
Breast that presses against other breasts it shall be you,
My brain it shall be your occult convolutions,
Root of washed sweet-flag, timorous pond-snipe, nest of guarded
duplicate eggs, it shall be you,
Mixed tussled hay of head and beard and brawn it shall be you,
Trickling sap of maple, fibre of manly wheat, it shall be you;
Sun so generous it shall be you,
Vapors lighting and shading my face it shall be you,
You sweaty brooks and dews it shall be you,
Winds whose soft-tickling genitals rub against me it shall be you,
Broad muscular fields, branches of liveoak, loving lounger in my
winding paths, it shall be you,
Hands I have taken, face I have kissed, mortal I have ever touched,
it shall be you.

—From *Leaves of Grass* (1855 edition)

Crossing a Ford" and "Bivouac on the Mountain Side," the two most firmly cinematic, least sentimental of the Civil War poems, two small miracles of negative capability. The first does summon the reader to share in the joy of immediate witness, rising from syntactic passivity to a "hark" and "Behold" that would sanctify the moment, baptize the spectator himself in the water of the natural goodness of life. Still, this is the gentlest of nods of consent; it is the horror of the war that makes this moment of refreshment in the ford almost unbearably unmenaced, sweet. The second poem tilts the horizontal line of the first one precariously, parallel to the precipice of the war. Here, the poet is quelled to a solitary seeing ("I see before me now a traveling army halting"), his angle of vision first sloping down ("Below a fertile valley spread"), then sharply up the "abrupt" mountain, past "the shadowy forms of men and horses, looming, large-sized, flickering" in the numerous campfires, to the sky: "And over all the sky—the sky! far, far out of reach, studded, breaking out, the eternal stars" (*W,* 435). Here the sublime is what man sees, not what he is.

In a third, more sizable masterpiece, "There Was a Child Went Forth" (1855), consent is curiously and almost hypnotically suspended: touchingly, everything has been readied for it, but it fails to take fire. As in a speeded-up yet, withal, oddly lingering motion picture of his gradual mental growth over the years, the poet passes from scenes of his childhood on a farm to his adolescence there, and on to city sights, then to a lonely shore, without ever seeming more than an onlooker. The one apparent exception to this may be the explanation of the rest: a laconic yet toughly concrete indication of stormy interactions with his father: "The father, strong, selfsufficient, manly, mean, angered, unjust, / The blow, the quick loud word, the tight bargain, the crafty lure" (*W,* 139). The interaction implied here is at the same time suppressed—for instance, the recipient of the blow remains subordinate to it, even to the point of being unnamed.

The poet's own manner throughout is mild, recalling "the mother with mild words." The tone itself betrays a preference for the mother, but not one that risks the anger of the father. Frameless and open, the poem is as broadly horizontal and subdued as a "luminist" painting, its conscious subject seeming distributed everywhere and nowhere within it. Here, what Whitman blew up in "Song of Myself"—namely, Personality—lies curiously, if sweetly, low. The poem ends (short of a line or two) by anticipating the low horizon, immobilized time, solitude, silence, and "intimate immensity" (in Gaston Bachelard's phrase) of luminist landscapes:

"Among the Sierra Nevada Mountains, California" by Albert Bierstadt.

Do you take it I would astonish?
Does the daylight astonish? or the early redstart twittering through the woods?
Do I astonish more than they?

—From *Leaves of Grass* (1855 edition)

The strata of colored clouds. . . . the long bar of maroontint away solitary by itself. . . . the spread of purity it lies motionless in,
The horizon's edge, the flying seacrow, the fragrance of saltmarsh and shoremud . . .

The length and syntactic dispersal of each line and the anonymous tone suggest a suppressed son, even as they refer to a diffused sun—a speaker whose being does not contract in the joy of individuality.

Back in the first turbulence of adolescence, doubt as to the reality of individuals arose. And those men and women now left behind in the city—were they real or just "flashes and specks"? Eros and only Eros warmly validates appearances, including those of people, and Eros here is hang-dog, afraid. Whitman will later say, "I cannot answer the question of appearances or that of identity beyond the grave," yet these questions "are curiously answer'd," he nonetheless adds, "by my lovers, my dear friends, / When he whom I love travels with me or sits a long while holding me by the hand" (*W,* 275). Still later, Freud will suggest that only the commingling of two mortal substances (though for Whitman, touch itself is enough, is more than enough) fights off death. In "Children of Adam," "Calamus," and "Song of Myself" Whitman rejects what Herbert Marcuse in *Eros and Civilization* (1955) calls "normal Eros" for "a fuller Eros," one not bound by genital focus, monogamy, the time-efficient work force. The fuller, narcissistic Eros, writes Marcuse, "transforms being: . . . masters cruelty and death through liberation." Its "language is song and [its] work is *play"* (*EC,* 155–56). But in "There Was a Child" the body, hence the horizon too, appears desexualized. There is only the world *out there* where objects petrify ("strata of colored clouds," "a long bar of maroontint"). The poem begins in prosperous remembrance of early lilacs and newborn farm animals and ends in solitary "purity" above a fragrance of damp corruption.

Poetry is here a late and beautiful dissemination of the already garnered. Passivity lies over the poem and its occasion (reminiscence). The reader helplessly, willingly, shares this quietism. Whitman universalizes his state (that of being laden as a honeycomb with the cool, waxy sweetnesses of things received into his impressionable sensibility) by enlisting the reader in the line of reception. The honeycomb is handed over: "These became part of that child who went forth every day, and who now goes and will always go forth every day, / And these become of him or her that peruses them now." ("Become of" fixes the passivity.) In the 1871 version the last line has been lopped off, depriving the poet of his only indicated progeny, if also excising a note of sentimental conscription of the reader. The poet who wrote "The schooner near by sleepily dropping down the tide . . . the little boat slacktowed astern" might prefer to be forever at his mother's side ("clean her cap and gown . . . a wholesome odor falling off her person and clothes as she walks by") but decency forces him on to the ambivalent fragrance of saltmarsh and shoremud. His one consolation is to put everything else in slacktow to his miraculous powers of receptivity; of welcoming, embracing, carrying; of being, in the words of "Song of the Universal," "Love like the light silently wrapping all" (*W,* 370).

Still other masterpieces of the Eros-quashed kind are "The Sleepers," "As I Ebb'd with the Ocean of Life," "When Lilacs

Last in the Dooryard Bloom'd," and "Out of the Cradle Endlessly Rocking." Except for "As I Ebb'd," these are all poems of the nocturnal Orpheus; they attack consent with the Orphic chant (I quote from Freud) that *"The inanimate was there before the animate."*

The most haunting (and sex-troubled) is "The Sleepers"; the most operatically vivid, "Out of the Cradle." Partly because the first is longer and more multiple in scene, I shall add a few words only about the second. Here again the line is something new—not spirited as in "Song of Myself" or equable as in "There Was a Child," but operatically diaphragm-driven—piercing, carrying. Like many New Yorkers of his time, Whitman was an opera buff (Robert D. Faner's book *Walt Whitman and Opera* makes a long bow to the fact). For Whitman, music released pent-up feeling beyond the too-social, well-behaved power of words. Joy, after all, is "madness." Tenors, sopranos, choirs—above all, the contralto Marietta Alboni—whirled the poet "wider than Uranus flies," wrenched from his breast "unnamable ardors" (*W,* 54). "Out of the Cradle" recalls how the "aria" of a mate-bereft mockingbird laid bare the poet's own destiny as a singer of "unsatisfied love." If Whitman spoke truly, the poem translates a cultural moment—the mockingbird, he said, is really a symbol of Alboni—back into a natural one, in keeping with the doctrine that Nature leads out the heart and tells of human destiny (best through bird-language). The poem, however, reads like what it seems, a translation of birdsong into the gorgeous, morbid romanticism familiar in opera.

How the poet prizes swift, cutting access to the "sweet hell within" that his extraordinary empathy with the bird awakened in him when, still a child, he spied all night and many a night on the "lone singer wonderful causing tears" as it perched on the "prong of a moss-scallop'd stake, / Down almost amid the slapping waves":

> Never more shall I escape, never more the reverberations,
> Never more the cries of unsatisfied love be absent from me,
> Never again leave me to be the peaceful child I was before what
>   there in the night,
> By the sea under the yellow and sagging moon,
> The messenger there arous'd, the fire, the sweet hell within,
> The unknown want, the destiny of me.
>
> (*W,* 393)

The pitch and fall of those *Never*'s operatically acts out the stabbing realization of an incurable, yet somehow priceless, deprivation. But what unhappy love can possibly have prepared

And I saw askant the armies,
I saw as in noiseless dreams hundreds of battle-flags,
Borne through the smoke of the battles and pierc'd with missiles I
saw them,
And carried hither and yon through the smoke, and torn and bloody,
And at last but a few shreds left on the staffs, (and all in silence,)
And the staffs all splinter'd and broken.

I saw the battle-corpses, myriads of them,
And the white skeletons of young men, I saw them,
I saw the debris and debris of all the slain soldiers of the war,
But I saw they were not as was thought,
They themselves were fully at rest, they suffer'd not,
The living remain'd and suffer'd, the mother suffer'd,
And the wife and the child and the musing comrade suffer'd.
And the armies that remain'd suffer'd.

—From "When Lilacs Last in the Dooryard Bloom'd"

a mere boy for the perception that life is—opera? What was "the love in the heart long pent, now loose, now at last tumultuously bursting," as again it does in these tumultuous lines?

Psychoanalysis notes that we begin with a ferocious "demand for love." Of this the mother is at once the ministering angel and the frightful denier (no one and nothing could satisfy this absurd, unreasonable demand). Life begins as death-in-life, the too little. Deprivation (somewhere we know this) is destiny. It is also joy. For what is left out is *wonderfully* left behind with the first mother, the immemorial elemental one (figured in the poem as the old crone rocking the oceanic cradle and, in the condition of longing for her lost ones, by the heavy yellow sagging moon). Whole nighttimes of deprivation place us nearer to the missing mother, and mean more joy. By the same logic, death would be the most delicious thing of all, the nothing that is everything. Death is thus the "delicious word" lisped by the old crone, "the word of the sweetest song and all songs"—the key to the "unknown want." Alone again on the shore, inwardly always alone on the verge between life and death, the poet is startlingly explicit about all this, which in its own naive way upsets "religion, law and order in all directions." Here Eros flees down a shore of night. The pleasure principle, Freud said, "seems directly to subserve the death-instincts." The reverse, too, is true, death being delicious. Death is even life, birth in a different, vaster cradle, the one the old crone whispers over. The suffering of love is opera, its final satisfaction a whisper, a care not to waken the regained original sleep.

"What indeed is finally beautiful except death and love?" Whitman asked in "Scented Herbage of My Breast" (*W,* 269). The subversive Eros, the one that loves death and the love that hurts like death, found in him as perfect a singer as did the hardly less subversive "fuller Eros" of the narcissistic personal body, or the genital Eros of "the muscular urge and the blending." Perfection, in the case of "Out of the Cradle," means, among other things, lines of extended virtuosic operatic expenditures of breath, and it means the all-gathering initial period of twenty-two lines, one of the most beautifully sustained and dartingly poised periods in the language. It means, too, the differentiation between the recitative of the poet and the aria of the bird, the latter fittingly simple if ardent (almost tiresomely simple and ardent, given to lines beginning with "O" and ending in exclamations—given indeed to *lines,* spasmodic utterances). Perfection also means those single lines of limpid rhythmic and simple verbal beauty that Whitman seemed able to produce as effortlessly as a bird its nest-learned notes: among others the opening line, "Out of the cradle endlessly rocking" (improved over the original "Out of the rocked cradle," which thumps); "Out of the mocking-bird's throat, the musical shuttle"; "For more than once dimly down to the beach gliding" (the glide originally impeded by a comma after "once" and again after "dimly"—Whitman often deleted commas when revising, usually happily); "The white arms out in the breakers tirelessly tossing": "I, with bare feet, a child, the wind wafting my hair"; and "For I that was a child, my tongue's use sleeping."

The line of "There Was a Child Went Forth" or "Out of the Cradle Endlessly Rocking" is not nationalistic but, in Longfellow's distinction, natural: "Nationality is a good thing to a certain extent, but universality is better. . . . Let us be natural, and we shall be national enough" (*NM,* 304). But in Whitman's case, naturalness followed precisely from a desire to be heroically native, a desire so pressing that it as good as invented American naturalness. Once Whitman had his new liquid-jointed power line he could turn it either to nationalistic themes (though "Song of Myself" goes through and over the nation to be as universal a poem as can be conceived) or to personal themes: growing up by receiving with wonder or pity or love or dread the objects looked upon, and becoming those objects; or the fatal moment when, down almost amid the slapping waters, one knows in a moment what one is for, and awakes. Longfellow had said that "we are very like the English—are, in fact, English under a different sky." But for Whitman, as for Thoreau and Melville, what was under the American sky was different enough to demand new rhythms, a new scale of diction, new forms. His masterpieces were sensitive, individual responses to this perception, variations on a native privilege or plight.

Everything Whitman wrote is sharply interesting, except where he wrote it better before. "Song of Myself" was the apotheosis of the poet-priest in him, and left him gasping ever afterward for something equally important to say. What could he do, in this vein, but repeat himself, and less happily, burdened as he was by the fear that he could not perform the same miracle twice? "I do not suppose," he said, "that I shall ever again have the afflatus I had in writing the first *Leaves of Grass.*"

Fortunately, there were other ways for him to write, to be original. In "Song of Myself" he had pried open the lyric, coaxed it into new depth and breadth, grafted psalm-singing onto it, and catalogues, and freed it from the grip of verbal varnish, of occasions, of conventional themes. He exposed it to the great world of ideas and things, the world of other people, individuals and crowds of them. From here he could move back toward lyrical

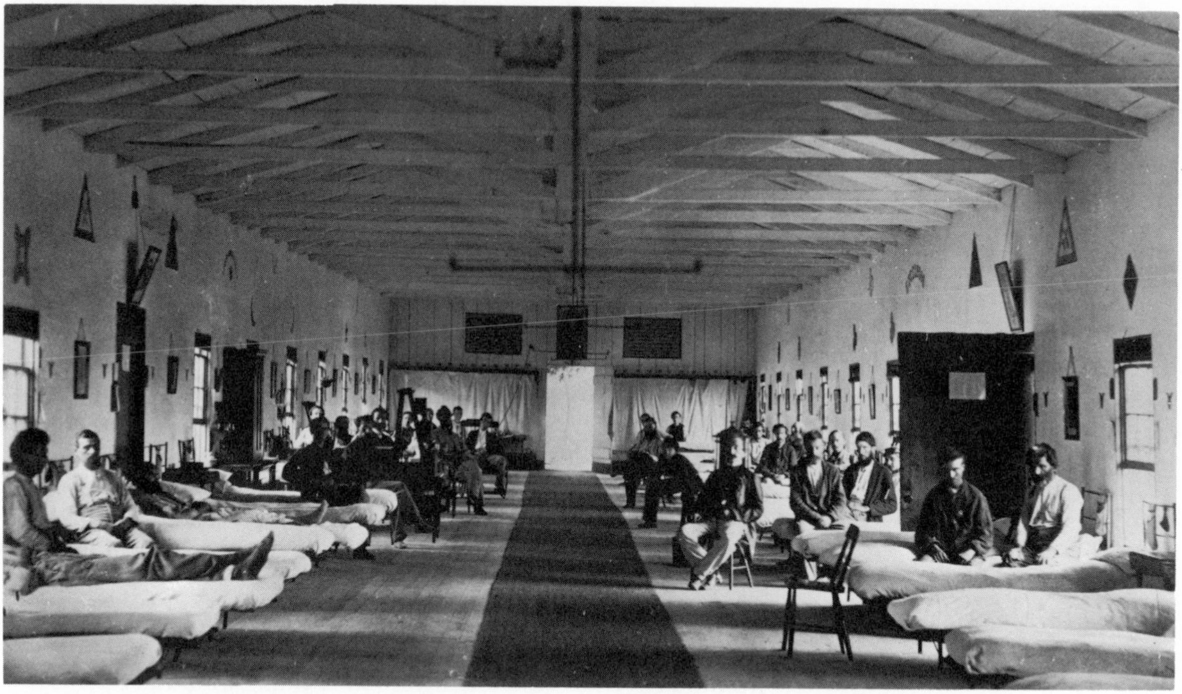

An Army hospital during the Civil War.

I am the man. . . . I suffered. . . . I was there.

The disdain and calmness of martyrs,
The mother condemned for a witch and burnt with dry wood, and
her children gazing on;
The hounded slave that flags in the race and leans by the fence,
blowing and covered with sweat,
The twinges that sting like needles his legs and neck,
The murderous buckshot and the bullets,
All these I feel or am.

I am the hounded slave. . . . I wince at the bite of the dogs,
Hell and despair are upon me . . . crack and again crack the
marksmen,
I clutch the rails of the fence . . . my gore dribs thinned with the
ooze of my skin,
I fall on the weeds and stones,
The riders spur their unwilling horses and haul close,
They taunt my dizzy ears. . . . they beat me violently over the head
with their whip-stocks.

Agonies are one of my change of garments;
I do not ask the wounded person how he feels. . . . I myself become
the wounded person,
My hurt turns livid upon me as I lean on a cane and observe.

—From *Leaves of Grass* (1855 edition)

seclusion, stopping short of the old, stale chambers, or cultivate a talking, public, delicate sort of discourse, even if he was writing about himself: "Beginning my studies the first step pleas'd me so much, / The mere fact consciousness, these forms, the power of motion" (*W,* 171), and so on. Or he could cross the lyrical border into preachiness. There were ways to go on, and he tried them all.

Despite the actual variety of his best poems, Whitman nonetheless repeated himself in his less than best, and *Leaves of Grass* eventually proved a ponderous, labored whole. Ambition to follow Emerson's urging and write a Bible for the New World ("We too must write Bibles," Emerson had said, "to unite again the heaven and the earthly worlds") drove him on through nine editions of his ever-enlarging poetic pasture for the nation, his *Leaves.* The opposite of an author who has only one book in him, Whitman seems to have felt like a book that has only one author to write it all, to make the rounds.

Gradually, if with remissions, his oral quickness and flexibility diminished. C. Carroll Hollis in *Language and Style in Leaves of Grass* (1983) tabulates that his stinging, haughty negatives declined about fifty percent after the 1860 (the third) edition, along with illusions of "speech acts" and vigorous finite verbs. Romance and Latin words, on the other hand, multiplied like mushrooms in clayey soil. Quakerish and literary *thee, thy,* and *thou* often replaced everyday *you* and *your.* All in all, the "word" of the "modern" limped some way back into literary history, even acquiring the affectation of an elided unsounded vowel ("refin'd") that recalled David Humphreys and other early Americans—a practice that, on the transatlantic side, Swift had long ago denounced as uncouth.

Still, outbreaks of exquisitely pure writing continued, as in "On the beach at night, / Stands a child with her father, / Watching the east, the autumn sky," which is followed a few lines later by "And nigh at hand, only a very little above, / Swim the delicate sisters the Pleiades" (*W,* 398–99). All told, Whitman emerges as so great a poet that he really did make good his claim that "the maker of poems settles justice, reality, immortality." Those who come after him (and remorselessly he put them in his charge in "Poets to Come") must tremble at his warning that most poets are merely "one of the singers, . . . eye-singer, ear-singer, head-singer" (*W,* 317), and so on. Few beget. The present-day poet who says of him, "Building on his achievement we may hope to do much better," takes one's breath away.

Ezra Pound's well-known gibe, "It was you that broke the new wood, / Now is a time for carving," blinked Whitman's

From "When Lilacs Last in the Dooryard Bloom'd"

When lilacs last in the dooryard bloom'd,
And the great star early droop'd in the western sky in the night,
I mourn'd, and yet shall mourn with ever-returning spring.

Ever-returning spring, trinity sure to me you bring,
Lilac blooming perennial and drooping star in the west,
And thought of him I love.

masterful carving of the oak of the American idiom, and his form-making. But many American poets would rejoice to say with Pound, "We have one sap and one root— / Let there be commerce between us." There is scarcely a twentieth-century American poet who has not been influenced by Whitman, whether directly, by refraction, or by "aristocratic" repulse. Traced in such books as Diane Middlebrook's *Walt Whitman and Wallace Stevens,* Stephen Tapscott's *American Beauty: William Carlos Williams and the Modernist Whitman,* and Cary Nelson's *Our Last First Poets: Vision and History in Contemporary American Poetry* (which contains a chapter titled "Whitman in Vietnam"), the lines of relationships are legion. They may show up in seemingly small things, for instance, in the prosy praise of power, motion, and glory in Charles Wright's "The cars planing by on the highway, / shooshing their golden plumes," or in a near rudeness of idiom, as in Wallace Stevens's "They will get it straight one day at the Sorbonne," as well as in things easier to spot, such as the long-lined "personalism" (the word was originally Whitman's, then became Frank O'Hara's) of O'Hara, Kenneth Koch, Allen Ginsberg, C. K. Williams, and still others. The immeasurable, international influence (with Whitman epitomizing the repaganized mind of modern man) was summed up by the French critic Marcel Raymond, in *From Baudelaire to Surrealism,* in the words: "a simple aesthetic theory was born from his morality, the morality of a man consubstantial with his poetry, who 'asks for nothing better or more divine than real life' to raise him to a state of perfect euphoria."

We could follow Ezra Pound and T. S. Eliot to London, to watch them unpack the Whitman-related sequential poem, an aesthetic that sparked what little twentieth-century English and Irish long-poem adventurism there has been—for instance, Basil Bunting's *Briggflats,* Thomas Kinsella's "Nightwalker," W. S. Graham's "Malcolm Mooney's Land," and Geoffrey Hill's *Mercian Hymns.* But more recognizable in their commerce with Whitman are the stay-at-home American poets—chiefly Hart Crane, Theodore Roethke, and A. R. Ammons—who have used the Whitman-inaugurated morally aesthetic (as against aesthetically moralizing) long poem much as Whitman himself used it: for a wide sweep of the country, at least in spirit; for spates of what Stevens called the freshness of transformations; and for the gamble, and gambol, of open-ended "evolutionist" faith. These are the poets who conceive that America is still a ship in motion (a legacy of Columbus and the Mayflower) through starry evolutionary space, and that a poet is himself a sailor or even, in Whitman's delightful image, "A ship itself, (see indeed these sails I spread to the sun and air,) / A swift and swelling ship full of rich words, full of joys" (*W,* 330).

Crane's *The Bridge* (1930) images the Brooklyn Bridge as the "Tall Vision-of-the-Voyage," as well as the "Choir, translating time / Into what multitudinous Verb the suns / And synergy of waters ever fuse" and "Love" and "stitch of stars" and "Deity's glittering Pledge"—all figures that Whitman would recognize as words of the modern. (Whitman himself spoke admiringly of the Brooklyn Bridge.) Power and motion ("The nasal whine of power whips a new universe"; "Man hears himself an engine in a cloud") are Crane's wafer and wine. For Crane, power was as awhirl in the dancing Red Indian ("A cyclone . . . [swoops] in eaglefeathers down your back") as it is in the Twentieth Century Limited "whistling down the tracks" or a dynamo "in oil-rinsed circles of blind ecstasy." One way or another, America means fierce "new latitudes" of experience. The Wrights ("windwrestlers") are the Red Indians of space. "Power's script" records man's Lucretian creative process. Thus

> My hand
>   in yours,
>   Walt Whitman—
>   so—

The American junction: "speed / With vast eternity," "Easters of speeding light." (The overstatement was, in part, compensation for Crane's feeling that if America were only "half worthy to be spoken of as Whitman spoke of it fifty years ago [there would be] something left to say.")

Roethke, avoiding the hieratic compression of Crane's pentameters, sounds in "Meditation at Oyster River" (1960) like a fragile, slightly disoriented, fragment-arrested Whitman whose long lines nonetheless argue a love of grand releases:

> And I long for the blast of dynamite,
> The suddenly sucking roar as the culvert loosens its debris of branches and sticks,
> Welter of tin cans, pails, old bird nests, a child's shoe riding a log,
> As the piled ice breaks away from the battered spiles,
> And the whole river begins to move forward, its bridges shaking.

"As when a ship sails with a light wind," Roethke writes elsewhere in the sequence; the national image again; "Our motion continues." Here, also, is the "process" view of a sentient world: "And a drop of rain water hangs at the tip of a leaf / Shifting in the wakening sunlight / Like the eye of a new-caught fish." And the Whitmanic love of the manifold (elsewhere Roethke writes: "Be with me, Whitman, maker of catalogues"). Here, too, the morality of aesthetic joy, the attempt to stand on "the windy cliffs of forever": "Beautiful my desire, and the place of my desire," Roethke writes in words worthy of Whitman. (The Red

Walt Whitman's birthplace on Long Island.

Indian is again evoked, a practice perhaps initiated by Whitman's idealization of himself as "The friendly and flowing savage.")

In *Sphere: The Form of a Motion* (1974), Ammons (perhaps picking up the tender, tentative connecting device of the colon from James Agee's Whitmanic prose work *Let Us Now Praise Famous Men*) tells, in long, unmetered lines which attempt to "force mind from boxes into radiality," of how

> though the surface is crisp with pattern still we know
> that there are generalized underlyings, planes of substratum
> lessening from differentiation: under all life, fly and
>
> dandelion, protozoan, bushmaster, and ladybird, tendon
> and tendril (excluding protocellular organelles) is the same
> cell: and under the cell is water, a widely generalized
>
> condition, and under that energy . . .

From "Out of the Cradle Endlessly Rocking"

Out of the cradle endlessly rocking,
Out of the mocking-bird's throat, the musical shuttle,
Out of the Ninth-month midnight,
Over the sterile sands and the fields beyond, where the child leaving his bed wander'd alone, bareheaded, barefoot,
Down from the shower'd halo,
Up from the mystic play of shadows twining and twisting as if they were alive,
Out from the patches of briers and blackberries,
From the memories of the bird that chanted to me,
From your memories sad brother, from the fitful risings and fallings I heard,
From under that yellow half-moon late-risen and swollen as if with tears,
From those beginning notes of yearning and love there in the mist,
From the thousand responses of my heart never to cease,
From the myriad thence-arous'd words,
From the word stronger and more delicious than any,
From such as now they start the scene revisiting,
As a flock, twittering, rising, or overhead passing,
Borne hither, ere all eludes me, hurriedly,
A man, yet by these tears a little boy again,
Throwing myself on the sand, confronting the waves,
I, chanter of pains and joys, uniter of here and hereafter,
Taking all hints to use them, but swiftly leaping beyond them,
A reminiscence sing.

Energy, the primal stuff of reality, continually moves into clarifications and just as continually runs through and stays all the discretions. With his scientific training and vocabulary ("protocellular organelles"!), Ammons carries on the Whitmanic project of vocalizing "the vastness and splendor and reality with which Scientism has invested man and the universe"; "the best part of science," Ammons declares, is "that it makes mysticism / discussable without a flurry." He is at once "the exact poet of the concrete *par excellence,*" as Whitman might say, and an aspirant to "the high syntheses of overlyings and radiances," and like Whitman he dreams of the "extremes meeting." Chiefly he seeks to "make a home of motion"; he pictures the earth as an "orb" (Whitman much favored the word) that "floats, a blue-green / wonder," and then, via Huckleberry Finn, Americanizes the image of floating in telling of "many rafts to ride" and of how "the tides make a / place to go":

Walt Whitman in Camden near the end of his life.

From *Leaves of Grass* (1855 edition)

I bequeath myself to the dirt to grow from the grass I love,
If you want me again look for me under your bootsoles.

You will hardly know who I am or what I mean,
But I shall be good health to you nevertheless,
And filter and fibre your blood.

Failing to fetch me at first keep encouraged,
Missing me one place search another,
I stop somewhere waiting for you.

motion as a summary of time and space is gliding us: for a
while,
we may ride such forces: then, we must get off: but now this

beats any amusement park by the shore: our Ferris wheel, what
a
wheel: our roller coaster, what mathematics of stoop and climb:
sew
my name on my cap: we're clear: we're ourselves: we're sailing.

Whitman never supposed that the "autochthonic song . . . vital to aspiring Nationality" would coincide with what a hundred years after his "Book" an "evolutionary sense and treatment" (*W*, 1262) would require. On the other hand, "we continue to live in a Whitmanesque age," as Pablo Neruda said, "seeing how new men and new societies rise and grow, despite their birthpangs." Whitman has been as much prized by Latin as by North American poets. "The poetic dream and the historic one coincide in him completely," notes Octavio Paz, and that is what poets in countries awakening to history admire.

With the contrary perspective of a Central European émigré, Miłosz writes that Whitman's work has "suffered a defeat because, though our experience of collective life is still strong, it has now been seasoned with a bitterness which he forbade himself" (*V*, 64). It is indeed tempting to conclude that the nineteenth century was taken in by the democratic dream of a people, even all people, caught in a happy motion together. But, bitterness aside, it may still be too early to pronounce on that. In any case, Whitman's plan was "to display an ideal democrat," as Jorge Luis Borges said, "not to devise a theory." Nor was Whitman wrong to say, "I have all lives, all effects, all hidden invisibly in myself" (an anticipation of a tenet of literary modernism); he took up the elementary things that people have in common, and in this he cannot be superseded. Then, too, the variation he worked on the classic theme of the poet's immortality was brilliant, manipulating it, as he did, so as to derive (again in Borges's words) "a personal relation with each future reader." His democratic goodwill became part of the texture of his poems. Circumventing his own disappearance (*that* defeat), he offers himself in perpetuity to be touched ("touch the palm of your hand to my body as I pass, / Be not afraid of my body" [*W*, 267]), and he suffers others: "O you shunn'd persons, I at least do not shun you" (*W*, 266). With a comic good grace he shouldered "the creativity of the world," even while generously and tauntingly "Expecting the main things from you" (*W*, 175). He was heroic in the stirring extravagance of his trusts and hopes.

My Life had stood - a
Loaded Gun -
In Corners - till a Day
The Owner passed - identified -
And carried Me away -

And now We roam + in
Sovreign Woods -
And now We hunt the Doe -
And every time I speak
for Him
The Mountains straight reply -

And do I smile, such
Cordial light
Opon the Valley glow -
It is as a Vesuvian face
Had let it's pleasure through -

And when at Night - Our
Good Day done -

EMILY DICKINSON

RICHARD B. SEWALL

The Vision—pondered long—
So plausible becomes
That I esteem the fiction—real—
The Real—fictitious seems—

—Poem 646

When Emily Dickinson was nineteen, she wrote a reckless valentine to an Amherst College senior, probably George Gould, a friend of her brother Austin. Valentines were much in fashion, and the young people participated vigorously. On this occasion, she carried the form to new heights. She began with a trumpet blast:

> Magnum bonum, "harum scarum," zounds et zounds, et war alarum, man reformam, mundum changum, all things flarum?

From which it can be gathered that Amherst, Massachusetts, in mid-century—it was February 1850—was hardly the quiet backwater it is sometimes thought to have been nor Emily Dickinson the fragile and retiring young woman that legend would have her. These wild notes, full of her schoolgirl Latin, place her squarely in the flux the world is usually in. She proceeded to show herself as anything but bashful:

> Sir, I desire an interview; meet me at sunrise, or sunset, or the new moon—the place is immaterial. In gold, or in purple, or sackcloth—I look not upon *raiment.* With sword, or with pen, or with plough—the weapons are less than the wielder. In coach, or in wagon, or walking, the *equipage* far from the *man.* With soul, or spirit, or body, they are all alike to me. With host or alone, in sunshine or storm, in heaven or earth, *some* how or *no* how—I propose, sir, to see you.

Then follow several more paragraphs, a glorious mix of sense and nonsense, laying out topics to be discussed in the "interview" and picturing the long and happy association that will result:

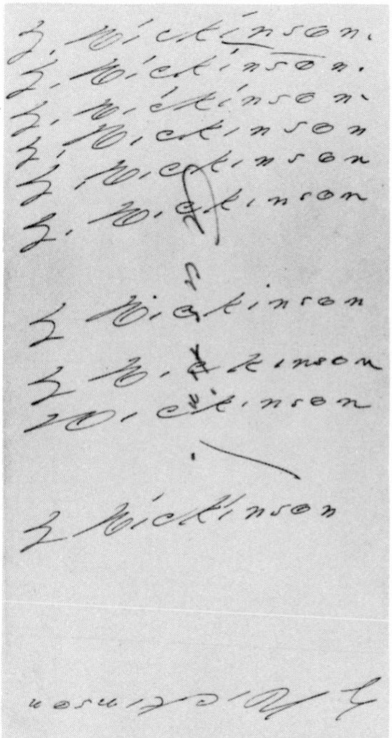

Our friendship sir, shall endure till sun and moon shall wane no more, till stars shall set, and victims rise to grace the final sacrifice. We'll be instant, in season, out of season, minister, take care of, cherish, sooth, watch, wait, doubt, refrain, reform, elevate, instruct. All choice spirits however distant are ours, ours theirs; there is a thrill of sympathy—a circulation of mutuality—cognationem inter nos! I am Judith the heroine of the Apocrypha, and you the orator of Ephesus.

That's what they call a metaphor in our country. Don't be afraid of it, sir, it won't bite. . . .

Style-watchers will note the four rhetorical surges in this paragraph, each rising to a climax like a cresting wave; the diction that would be mere scattershot were it not controlled by a fine sense of rhythm and sound, and the final defiant mini-lecture on metaphor. Clearly, this young woman loved to write—and knew how. The valentine ends with a ringing challenge to her friend to join her in a massive program:

> But the world is sleeping in ignorance and error, sir, and we must be crowing cocks, and singing larks, and a rising sun to awake her; or else we'll pull society up to the roots, and plant it in a different place. We'll build Alms-houses, and transcendental State prisons, and scaffolds—we will blow out the sun, and the moon, and encourage invention. Alpha shall kiss Omega—we will ride up the hill of glory—Hallelujah, all Hail! (*L*, 34)[1]

This is more than mere fooling, good as it is on that level alone. Seen as we now can see it, it is prophetic of what she was to do with her life. Not that she ever became a reformer. Alms-houses and transcendental State prisons (she must have been reading Emerson) were not for her, any more than were the sword and the plough of her second paragraph. The key word there is "pen." She was a writer from the beginning, and she addressed the valentine to a young man in the college who, she hoped, would share her literary ambitions. The most tangible result of her plea was the publication, in a student journal called *The Indicator,* of the entire valentine. George Gould was one of the editors, and either he or one of his colleagues prefaced it with the following comment: "I wish I knew who the author is. I think she must have some spell, by which she quickens the imagination, and causes the high blood 'run frolic through the veins.' "

This is a remarkable comment, an insight that can scarcely be improved upon and, in its own way, also prophetic. It is the best bit of literary criticism to appear in print (perhaps the only one; I know of no other) that Emily Dickinson's writing was to receive for forty years when, four years after she died, a slim volume of her verse was published on November 12, 1890, by Roberts Brothers, Boston, and was reviewed in the press. It is to be noted that the critic in *The Indicator,* ignoring the whimsical substance—the alms-houses and the gallows—went to the heart of the matter: the power of the writer to quicken the imagination and cause the blood to "run frolic through the veins." He called it a "spell." But whatever it was, spell or uncannily good craftsmanship, the world was not to feel its effects until Mabel Loomis Todd, a neighbor of the Dickinsons in Amherst, and Thomas Wentworth Higginson, a man of letters who had known Emily Dickinson's poems since 1862, finally persuaded Roberts

Brothers to take the plunge, which they did, grudgingly. To their surprise—and, no doubt, delight—the little volume of 116 poems (the current complete edition contains 1775) went through eleven editions in two years. The first reviewer, Arlo Bates in the *Boston Courier* (November 23, 1890), echoed *The Indicator,* though in more sedate terms: "There is hardly a line which fails to throw out some gleam of genuine original power, of imagination, and of real emotional thought." Bates found much amiss—"not a stanza," he wrote, "which cannot be objected to upon the score of technical imperfection." But he was willing to forgive, even to judge these "half-barbaric" poems as if they belonged to "a new species of art." It had taken a long time, but Dickinson's career as a published poet had at last begun.

A few samples of the "new species" had, indeed, appeared during the forty-year interval, some dozen of her poems finding their way by hook or by crook (one, she complained, was "robbed of me"—*L,* 316) to various journals, one to an anthology published in 1878 by Roberts Brothers. *The Springfield Daily Republican,* edited by Samuel Bowles, a longtime friend of the Dickinson family, was the most hospitable, starting with another valentine (1852) of the "exuberant" period, this one in seventeen rollicking ballad stanzas (*P,* 3). (This, and another valentine of 1850 in twenty hexameter couplets [*P,* 1], is clear evidence that the style she was soon to adopt as her own—the one that tempted Arlo Bates to form a new category—was not the only one which, had she so chosen, she could have handled with ease.) But these fugitive pieces appeared anonymously, evoked only local notice, and came nowhere near establishing her publicly as a poet. The wonder is that no publisher was sufficiently convinced to take the risk or, if convinced, succeeded in getting a manuscript from Miss Dickinson—at least twice it was she who said no. And yet many times she made her ambitions clear. It is a curious history. We will come closer to understanding it—and in the process much about her and the art she developed—if we look, however briefly, at some of the circumstances that conditioned it, all in interaction with that elusive, paradoxical, still mysterious personality at the center.

Emily Dickinson was born into a family that did everything for her but understand her. Their literary interests were, to say the least, peripheral. Her grandfather, Samuel Fowler Dickinson, had been a leading lawyer in the town, a pillar of the church, and a founder of Amherst College, the purpose of which was to provide the young men of the region with a sounder, more orthodox education than could be had to the east. Edward,

The Dickinson Homestead.

her father, was also a lawyer, for twenty years treasurer of the College, and, though late to conversion, a loyal churchman. A few remarks of Emily's tell much about his influence on her formative years. "He buys me many Books—but begs me not to read them—because he fears they joggle the Mind" (*L,* 261). He was particularly hard on novels, not allowing them in the house. Emily and her brother Austin, three years her senior, saw to that. They smuggled in what they wanted. "Father is too busy with his Briefs," wrote Emily, "to notice what we do" (*L,* 261). Save for Austin, the distance gradually widened between Emily and her family, and even Austin had no ear for her poetry—if he had, he would have done something about it.

It was not only that the family did not understand what she wrote (whether they even knew how much, or how much it meant to her, is a question), she found it difficult to talk with them on matters above the ordinary. "My mother does not care for thought" (*L,* 261), she wrote. "My father seems to me often the oldest and oddest sort of a foreigner. Sometimes I say something and he stares in a curious sort of bewilderment, though I speak a thought quite as old as his daughter" (*LL,* 70). Even her devoted sister Lavinia, two years her junior, was not much help. During her early thirties, Emily wrote a friend: "And Vinnie, Joseph [Lyman], if we had come up for the first time from two wells where we had hitherto been bred her astonishment would not be greater at some of the things I say" (*LL,* 70). To give Vinnie credit, she seems to have understood the anomaly of Emily's position in the family and was content in later years to act as Emily's protector, the guardian at the gate. After Emily died, Vinnie wrote: "She had to think—she was the only one of us who had that to do" (*H,* 414).

It is no wonder, then, that Emily retreated more and more to her second-story room where she could converse with herself. In the early, exuberant days, she had fun, at least, with Austin, who shared her sense of humor. But when he left to teach school in Boston, or to study law in Cambridge, or (in 1856) to get married, he took even that with him. She wrote him in Boston:

> We don't *have* many jokes tho' *now,* it is pretty much all sobriety, and we do not have much poetry, father having made up his mind that its pretty much all *real life.* Fathers real life and *mine* sometimes come into collision, but as yet, escape unhurt! (*L,* 65)

If Emily withdrew from the family center, it was not for lack of love and loyalty. Simply, like Thoreau, she had other business to transact. As for her mother, "the Affection came" later, as Emily put it (*L,* 792); and the loving regard, amounting to a kind of awe, in which she held her father came out movingly in a letter she wrote after his death:

> The last Afternoon that my Father lived, though with no premonition—I preferred to be with him, and invented an absence for Mother, Vinnie being asleep. He seemed peculiarly pleased as I oftenest stayed with myself, and remarked as the Afternoon withdrew, he "would like it to not end."

And then her remarkable summing up:

> His Heart was pure and terrible and I think no other like it exists. (*L,* 418)

It is a tribute to the family that they seem to have taken

Emily's reclusive tendencies quite in stride—at least, I find no record of their irritation over it, or their anxiety. It was Emily's way, and that was the end of it. Vinnie is reported as saying that they all lived "like friendly and absolute monarchs, each in his own domain" (*H,* 413). Emily's domain became increasingly her garden, her conservatory, the kitchen (where she baked bread for her father), but especially her room where, often far into the night when the others were asleep, she could explore her own "real life" and write her poems in peace.

It would be interesting to know just what it was in Emily's talk that so bewildered her father and Vinnie. Even Austin was not exempt: "You say you dont comprehend me," she wrote. "You want a simpler style. *Gratitude* indeed for all my fine philosophy!" (*L,* 45) This was about one of her letters to him in which, apparently, she had taken some lofty flights. Was it the content or the style that bewildered? Austin was a thoughtful young man; his early letters show him probing matters temporal and spiritual in some depth. He was three years older and not one to be outdone. Her fine philosophy couldn't have left him that far behind. It may have been her growing fondness for metaphor, for telling it "slant." A letter of about the same time to one of her confidantes, Jane Humphrey, centers around a sustained metaphor involving a gold thread, "a long, big shining fibre which hides the others"—and leaves Jane to figure it out for herself: "What do you weave from all these threads . . . ?" (*L,* 35) Perhaps Austin refused to put up with such mystification. Emily enjoyed riddles and puns—the "wiles of Words," as she once put it (*L,* 555), and in these early years, she enjoyed her power with them. The problem here may have been stylistic—an excess of wile. Years later she wrote a poem on a small scrap of paper:

> The Riddle we can guess
> We speedily despise—
> Not anything is stale so long
> As Yesterday's surprise—
>
> No. 1222, c. 1870

She was not one to be "despised" by her elder brother. They enjoyed matching wits, and this time, perhaps, she had successfully "riddled" him. Indeed, riddle became a frequent literary way with her, a device like metaphor by which she could take the reader "slant" into her meaning, provided the reader had the wits to follow. Here is her most famous "guess what I mean" poem:

The First Congregational Church of Amherst.

A Route of Evanescence
With a revolving Wheel—
A Resonance of Emerald—
A Rush of Cochineal—
And every Blossom on the Bush
Adjusts it's tumbled Head—
The mail from Tunis, probably,
An easy Morning's Ride—

No. 1463, c. 1879

Answer: Hummingbird

With the others in the family—and with the Amherst community—the problem may have been more substantial. There are signs that, at an early age, Emily began to withdraw from the piety that pervaded the Homestead as it did every staunch late-Puritan New England household. There was a Bible (presumably) on every bed table. (In the Dickinson Collection in the Houghton Library, Harvard, there are nineteen Bibles.) When

Praise to God.

61 Our God, our help in ages past.

"Let the beauty of the Lord our God be upon us."

C. M. D. **Norwich ("Old 137th.")**

ISAAC WATTS, 1719. JOHN DAYE'S PSALTER, 1562.

1. OUR God, our help in a - ges past, Our hope for years to come, Our shel - ter from the
storm - y blast, And our e - ter - nal home, Un - der the shad - ow of Thy throne, Thy

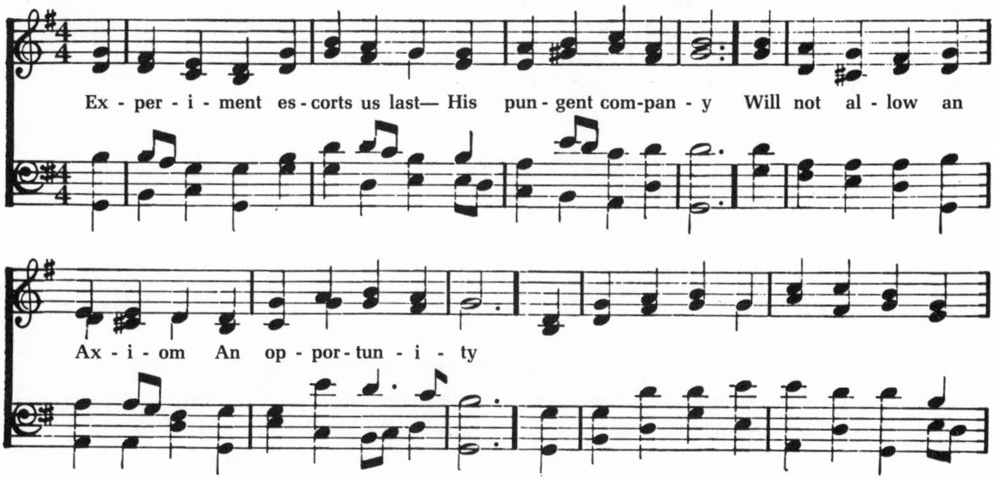
Ex - per - i - ment es - corts us last— His pun - gent com - pan - y Will not al - low an
Ax - i - om An op - por - tun - i - ty

It's interesting that so many of Emily Dickinson's poems are written in this seemingly tight, unprepossessing form of the hymn meter. . . . Why she used it is hard to tell except that she was, of course, familiar with it in the hymns that she sang in church, while she was [still] going to church . . .

—Richard B. Sewall in a *Voices & Visions* interview

Father led prayers every morning for the family and the servants, Emily smiled at what she called his "militant Accent" (*L,* 432) as he read Scripture and, apparently, thought her own thoughts. Later, she made fun of the family devotions in a letter to Thomas Wentworth Higginson, who had inquired about her life: "They are all religious—except me—and address an Eclipse, every morning—whom they call their 'Father' " (*L,* 261). The problem here is the high ironic style. I doubt that she could have gotten away with it with Father, Mother, or Vinnie, and the hope is that Higginson didn't take it literally. The bent and tone of her entire career belie that remark: she was the most religious of them all and never lost her reverence, even when her rhetoric was most playful. What she meant was that the family piety, and much of the pulpit doctrine they seemed to have swallowed whole, were not for her. A remark to her understanding friend, Mrs. Holland of Springfield, shows how far she had gone from at least one of those doctrines: "While the Clergyman tells Father and Vinnie that 'this Corruptible shall put on Incorruption' —it has already done so and they go defrauded" (*L,* 391). Years earlier, she had put it in a poem it is just as well the family did not see:

"Sown in dishonor"!
Ah! Indeed!
May *this* "dishonor" be?
If I were half so fine myself
I'd notice nobody!

"Sown in corruption"!
Not so fast!
Apostle is askew!
Corinthians I.15. narrates
A Circumstance or two!

No. 62, c. 1859

Unacceptable doctrine (especially original sin, which she felt demeaned the human race) was one of the reasons, surely, why she stopped going to church by the time she was thirty and never formally joined it—a fact that did not go unnoticed in Amherst. Another reason was her growing distaste for what she called "august assemblies" (*L,* 91). Even as a student in Mount Holyoke (she entered at sixteen and stayed one academic year) she "enjoyed the solitude finely" (*Life,* 288) when, one day, the other students went off on an outing. She began an early poem:

Some—keep the Sabbath—going to church—
I—keep it—staying at Home— . . .

No. 324, c. 1860

where, she concluded, a "noted Clergyman"—God—preaches, and "the sermon is never long." But more than love of solitude or doctrinal differences, what set her apart from the local piety was her refusal to give herself to what her mind and heart could not wholly accept. She admired and even envied those who claimed to have found spiritual peace. But (to quote Vinnie again) Emily "had to think—she was the only one of us who had that to do." And that meant, for her, a certain amount of withdrawal, a good deal of solitude—and no compromise. If her heterodox opinions shocked and bewildered people, better not bring them up at all.

So it was that she drifted away from the corporate center of both her family and her community. The pattern was repeated with her friendships, which in the early years were many and warm. But one by one her intimates married, left Amherst, or died. Her letters, at first chatty and buoyant and full of confidences, get shorter and cooler. To Abiah Root, long one of her dearest friends, she wrote a kind of ultimatum: "We are growing away from each other, and talk even now like strangers" (*L,* 39). Of Abby Wood, their mutual friend, she wrote Abiah: "We take different views of life, our thoughts would not dwell together as they used to when we were young" (*L,* 39). One of her most important losses was Benjamin Franklin Newton, law student in her father's office during her late teens, who married, removed to Worcester, and died in 1853. He "was much in our family," she wrote. "I was then but a child, yet I was old enough to admire the strength, and grace, of an intellect far surpassing my own. . . . Mr. Newton became to me a gentle, yet grave Preceptor, teaching me what to read, what authors to admire, what was most grand and beautiful in nature, and that sublimer lesson, a faith in things unseen, and in a life again, nobler, and much more blessed—" (*L,* 153) (a lesson, apparently, she did not learn from family prayers). Newton has the distinction of being the first on record to recognize her promise as a poet. "My dying Tutor," she wrote Higginson in 1862, "told me that he would like to live till I had been a poet . . ." (*L,* 265). One wonders why there weren't others, but the annals of those early years reveal none. After Newton left her life, she was pretty much on her own. "For several years," she wrote Higginson, "my Lexicon—was my only companion—" (*L,* 261).

Not strictly true. Although her circle was getting smaller, she still received visitors and was still going out. It was later that she complained of having "lost the run of the roads." She had books—"the strongest friends of the soul" (*LL,* 76), as she later described them to Joseph Lyman—and a few people, at least, to discuss them with. Her insistence on her Lexicon as her only

"The Soul selects her own Society" has always been understood as a covert declaration of love. And it might be that. I suspect myself that it is not. It has to do, certainly, with the affinities one has with a very few people and how the soul, or anybody, makes exclusions and inclusions that are quite arbitrary; but I think this is meant to parallel the question of the Elect of God. So the soul in choosing its friends does very much what the deity does in discriminating between the saved and the damned. There is something very frightening about that; when we think of how ruthless we are about who our friends and enemies might be, at least inwardly, we are performing . . . the same act that God performs when he cuts us off from all hope of salvation. The poem, I think, hovers on the brink of those curious mysteries which are interior and psychological, but are also exterior and theological.

—Anthony Hecht in the *Voices & Visions* film *Emily Dickinson*

companion is whimsical but perhaps important. Her canon of 1775 poems is dotted with "definition poems"—"Exultation is . . . ," "Love is . . . ," "Hope is . . . ," "Despair is . . . ," and dozens of others. Perhaps she was suggesting to Higginson that she used these years to clarify, or accommodate to her own experience, the great abstractions we live with daily and for the most part unheedingly. It is as if she were getting her bearings as a poet, testing words for their full meaning, finding out what she could do with them when she could work in peace and solitude. A poem that cannot be dated even approximately may describe what she was going through and what she was discovering about herself. (To the pious folk of Amherst and to her family the absence of any suggestion of Christian grace or revelation would have been disturbing, even shocking.)

There is a solitude of space
A solitude of sea
A solitude of death, but these
Society shall be
Compared with that profounder site
That polar privacy
A soul admitted to itself—
Finite infinity.

No. 1695

Clearly, by the time (whenever it was) she had written this poem, she had chosen her own way. The camaraderie of the early valentine seems light-years away. Twice, in the meantime, she had made efforts to bring her poetry to the attention of the

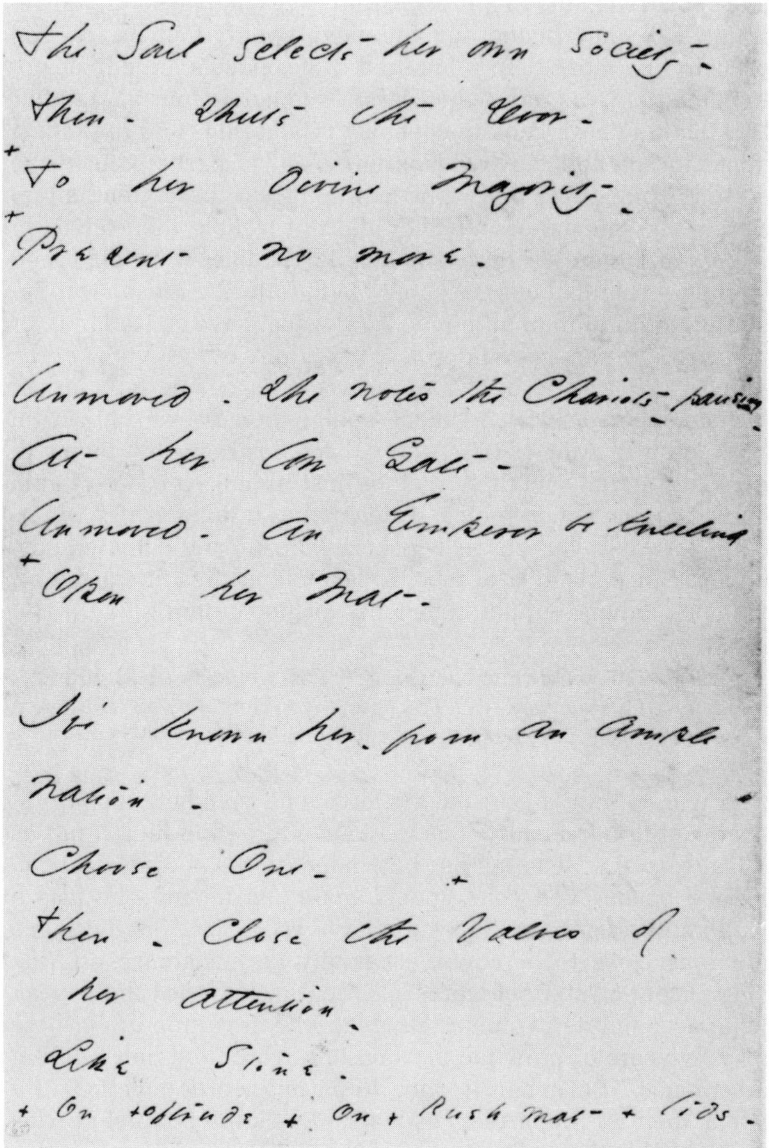
The Soul selects - her own Society -
Then - shuts the Door -
+ To her divine Majority -
+ Present - no more -

Unmoved - she notes the Chariots - pausing
At - her low Gate -
Unmoved - an Emperor be kneeling
+ Opon her Mat -

I've known her - from an ample
nation -
Choose One - +
then - Close the Valves of
her attention -
Like Stone -
+ On + obtrude + On + Rush mat - + lids -

literary world, first to Samuel Bowles of the *Republican,* to whom she sent nearly forty poems in thirty letters, and then to Higginson, whose *Atlantic Monthly* article in April 1862, "Advice to a Young Contributor," led her to send him four of her best, with a hesitant request for an opinion. Over the years, Bowles, or his colleague Dr. Josiah Holland, saw to it that some five appeared in the *Republican;* and Higginson, despite a correspondence that lasted for the next twenty-four years and brought him more than a hundred of her poems, urged her not to publish. It was only when Mrs. Todd, some four years after Dickinson's death, took the poems to Cambridge and read them aloud to him that he was finally moved to participate in the editing. This makes one wonder: was it that these men had no ear for the poems, or that they did not trouble themselves to understand them, or that, like Arlo Bates, they were disturbed by their "technical imperfection"? Whatever the reason (probably a combination of all three), Emily must have sensed in their response the same bewilderment her family felt at "some of the things I say" and perhaps the kind of estrangement that marked the end of her early friendships. A poignant remark to Higginson (in a letter of August 1862) generalizes this recurrent theme of personal estrangement to include just about everybody—and here the issue is her poetry, which makes it important. (Apparently, for whatever reason, Higginson had had difficulty with the poems. Since his side of the correspondence has not survived, we must depend on her comments for its content.)

> You say "Beyond your knowledge." You would not jest with me, because I believe you—but Preceptor—you cannot mean it? All men say "What" to me, but I thought it a fashion—(*L,* 271)

A word about Higginson, the advice he gave her, and why it is crucial in this history. She may have turned to him, if not as a last resort, at least as her best hope. In the *Atlantic* article, he had encouraged young poets, male and female—he was a well-known feminist. She must have recognized many of his ideas as close to her own, especially his insistence on "the magnificent mystery of words": "Oftentimes a word shall speak what accumulated volumes have labored in vain to utter: there may be years of crowded passion in a word, and half a life in a sentence." But when it came to putting words together in a poem, their views parted. His taste, like that of Samuel Bowles (to judge by the poets, many of them women, whom Bowles encouraged in the *Republican*), was for the smooth-flowing, mellifluous, sub-Tennysonian verse of the day (often, to our ears, prolix and sentimental). His criteria were "form, simplicity, thoroughness." He was no man for what Arlo Bates called those "half-barbaric" poems, the "new species of art." Higginson found the Dickinson poems "spasmodic," "uncontrolled," "wayward." He once wrote of Whitman what he might have said of Dickinson: "Art has its law; and eccentricity, though often promising as a mere trait of youth, is only a disfigurement to maturer years." And added: "It is no discredit to Walt Whitman that he wrote 'Leaves of Grass,' only that he did not burn it afterwards and reserve himself for something better" (*Life*, 574). His other literary opinions are all of a piece: he ignored Melville, found Henry James "involved and often puzzling," and considered his friend Helen Hunt Jackson the model for the woman poet in America. No wonder he failed to rally to Dickinson's cause. And with this failure, she seems to have concluded that whatever hopes she might have for publication and fame went glimmering.

In what may have been an ingenuous attempt at saving face, she wrote him the following:

> I smile when you suggest that I delay "to publish"—that being foreign to my thought as Firmament to Fin—
>
> If fame belonged to me, I could not escape her—if she did not, the longest day would pass me on the chase—and the approbation of my Dog, would forsake me—then—My Barefoot Rank is better—(*L*, 265)

This is as far from the truth as her telling Higginson that she was the only one in her family not religious. There is ample evidence that she had thought of publication. In her mid-twenties she had confided her ambition to her cousin Louise Norcross: "It's a great thing to be 'great,' Loo . . . What if we learn, ourselves, some day!" (*L*, 199) To her sister-in-law she wrote: "Could I make you and Austin—proud—sometime—a great way off—'twould give me taller feet—" (*L*, 238). She had bombarded Samuel Bowles with her poems; and then, when "Two Editors of Journals" (*L*, 261) had asked her (a few months before the appearance of the *Atlantic* article) for her poems, she did not reject them—she wrote Higginson for another opinion. When it turned out to be unfavorable, she retreated behind what she called her "vail" (*L*, 107) and chose her "Barefoot Rank" (*L*, 265). In the course of her career, she wrote a dozen poems on fame, a good half of them during this period; one of them describes what she meant by her barefoot rank:

> Fame of Myself, to justify,
> All other Plaudit be
> Superfluous—An Incense
> Beyond Necessity—
>
> Fame of Myself to lack—Although
> My Name be else Supreme—
> This were an Honor honorless—
> A futile Diadem—
>
> No. 713, c. 1863

Susan Gilbert Dickinson, the wife of Emily's brother Austin.

The extent of Sue's help with Emily's poetry is impossible to document, except for the one instance of the poem "Safe in Their Alabaster Chambers." She praised the poem with reservations:

> I am not suited dear Emily with the second verse—It is remarkable as the chain lightening that blinds us hot nights in the Southern sky but it does not go with the ghostly shimmer of the first verse as well as the other one—It just occurs to me that the first verse is complete in itself it needs no other, and can't be coupled—Strange things always go alone—as there is only one Gabriel and one Sun—You never made a peer for that verse, and I *guess* you[r] kingdom doesn't hold one—I always go to the fire and get warm after thinking of it, but I never *can* again—. . .

The note, besides being remarkably perceptive criticism, shows Sue as a mentor of some standing. In reply, Emily composed two alternates for the second stanza, chose one, and sent it to Sue with the question, "Is *this frostier?*"

—From *The Life of Emily Dickinson* by Richard B. Sewall

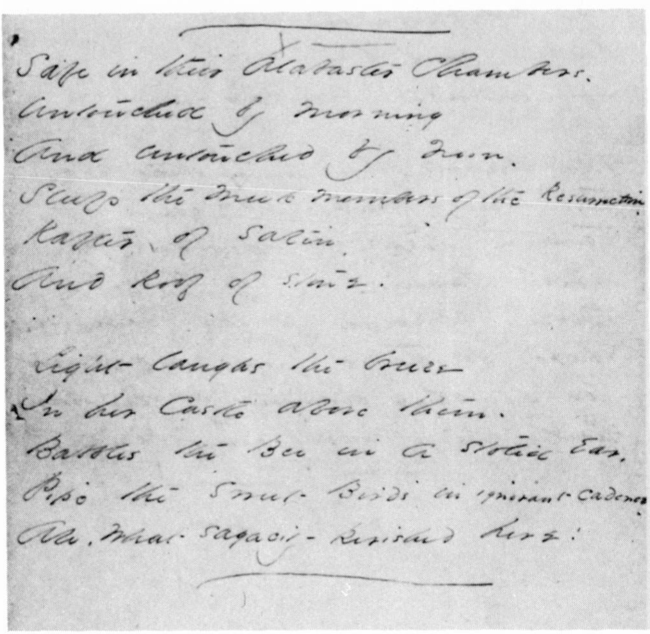

Safe in their Alabaster Chambers.
Untouched by morning
And untouched by noon.
Sleep the meek members of the Resurrection
Rafter of Satin
And Roof of Stone.

Light laughs the breeze
In her Castle above them.
Babbles the Bee in a stolid Ear,
Pipe the sweet Birds in ignorant cadence
Ah, what sagacity perished here!

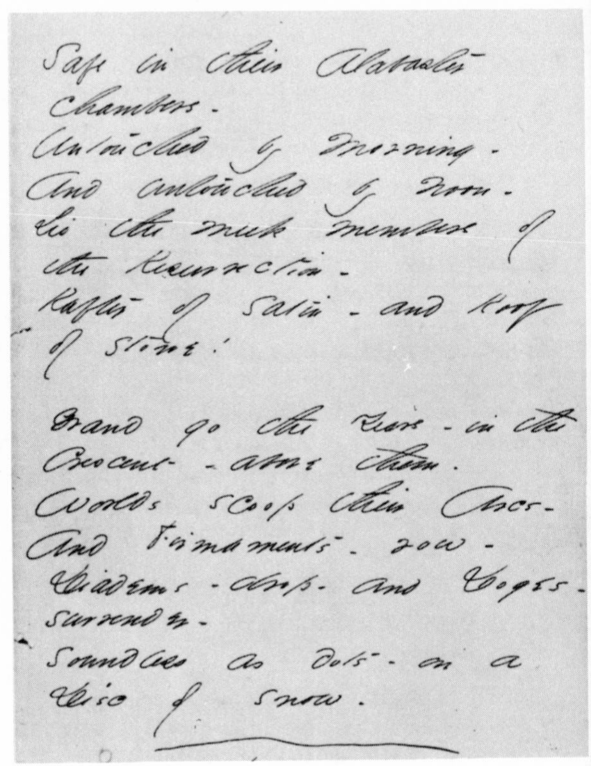

Safe in their Alabaster
Chambers -
Untouched by Morning -
And untouched by Noon -
Lie the meek members of
the Resurrection -
Rafter of Satin - and Roof
of Stone!

Grand go the Years - in the
Crescent - above them -
Worlds scoop their Arcs -
And Firmaments - row -
Diadems - drop - and Doges -
surrender -
Soundless as dots - on a
Disc of Snow.

This brief declaration of independence is one of many about this time, all indicating a conscious choice of a way of life, a dedication to her own way of pursuing the truth, or truths (great and small) that she would crystallize in her art. As if to exorcise, once and for all, the notion of publication from her mind, she wrote a truculent poem reducing the whole procedure to a debasing financial transaction. She did not send the poem to Higginson.

Publication—is the Auction
Of the Mind of Man—
Poverty—be justifying
For so foul a thing

Possibly—but We—would rather
From Our Garret go
White—Unto the White Creator—
Than invest—Our Snow—

Thought belong to Him who gave it—
Then—to Him Who bear
It's Corporeal illustration—Sell
The Royal Air

In the Parcel—Be the Merchant
Of the Heavenly Grace—
But reduce no Human Spirit
To Disgrace of Price—

No. 709, c. 1863

A poem which she did send to Higginson was more polite, indirect, metaphoric; but the theme was the same: "I will not write on your terms." The thrust of his criticism, clearly, had been toward smoother rhythms, more sustained thought, perfect rhymes, simpler figures, less colloquial diction (e.g., change "heft" to "weight"). She would have none of it and sent him this poem in a letter of August 1862:

I cannot dance upon my Toes—
No Man instructed me—
But oftentimes, among my mind,
A Glee possesseth me,

That had I Ballet knowledge—
Would put itself abroad
In Pirouette to blanch a Troupe—
Or lay a Prima, mad,

And though I had no Gown of Gauze—
No Ringlet, to my Hair,
Nor hopped for Audiences—like Birds,
One Claw upon the Air,

Nor tossed my shape in Eider Balls,
Nor rolled on wheels of snow
Till I was out of sight, in sound,
The House encore me so—

Nor any know I know the Art
I mention—easy—Here—
Nor any Placard boast me—
It's full as Opera—

No. 326, c. 1862

"Yes," she seems to be saying, "with a little instruction I could write the way you want me to. It's all here, in my mind. I could be famous. But I cannot pirouette or hop to please audiences." The "cannot" might as well have been "will not." The style she had developed by then, spasmodic, uncontrolled, wayward as it might be, was her own. Curiously, she continued to ask Higginson for instruction, calling him "Preceptor" and signing herself, often, "Your Scholar"—and never followed it.

It is tempting to update another poem of the period into the Higginson era in her life. The "Signor" of the next-to-last line seems very pointed. Or she may have had Bowles in mind, whose *Republican* was promoting many inferior poets to early, if local, fame. Here the metaphor for her poetry is song, from the birds of the first stanza to the Vespers and Matins of the second:

I shall keep singing!
Birds will pass me
On their way to Yellower Climes—
Each—with a Robin's expectation—
I—with my Redbreast—
And my Rhymes—

Late—when I take my place in summer—
But—I shall bring a fuller tune—
Vespers—are sweeter than Matins—Signor—
Morning—only the seed of Noon—

No. 250, c. 1861

The message is clear—and prophetic.

What is emerging here—probably slowly, over the years—is a mature vision of herself and her function. The exchange with Higginson was her first real brush with the professional literary world—Bowles, after all, was a friend of the family and very dear to her—and it may have had the catalytic effect she needed after those years with her lexicon and her growing reclusiveness. Even while asking for his "instruction" in almost obsequious terms, promising "Obedience" and "every gratitude I know," she all but threw down the gauntlet to him in a letter of

Mr Higginson,

Are you too deeply occupied to say if my Verse is alive?
The mind is so near itself—it cannot see, distinctly—and I have none to ask—
Should you think it breathed—and you had the leisure to tell me,
I should feel quick gratitude—
If I make this mistake—that you dared tell me—would give me sincerer honor—toward you—
I enclose my name—asking you, if you please—Sir—to tell me what is true?
That you will not betray me—is needless to ask—since Honor is its own pawn—

—A letter from Dickinson to Thomas Wentworth Higginson, April 15, 1862

July 1862: "Perhaps you smile at me. I could not stop for that—My Business is Circumference—" About the same time, in a letter to her friends the Hollands, she added two more "businesses" (did she pick up the term from Luke 2:49—or from Thoreau?), this time refusing to "stop" even if "the whole United States are laughing at me": *"My* business is to love" and (comparing herself to a bird in her garden who sings though nobody listens) *"My* business is to *sing"*—(*L,* 269). A few years later, she put the matter more soberly to Joseph Lyman in a statement that has an air of command and a new sense of freedom (also, it makes sufficiently clear, I think, that odd word she used to Higginson, "Circumference"): "So I conclude that space and time are things of the body and have little or nothing to do with ourselves. My Country is Truth . . . I like Truth—it is a free Democracy" (*LL,* 71). Such was the "Vision—pondered long—" . . .

So here she was, free by her own choice from publishers, editors, public, and critics, free even (at least figuratively) from the limitations of space and time, free to explore the country she called Truth. The climactic poems of the period show her quite conscious of what she was getting into and what it would cost. One, written about 1861, shows her on the brink—and brings up a problem of metaphor central to many of her poems at this point and later:

One Life of so much Consequence!
Yet I—for it—would pay—
My Soul's *entire income*—
In ceaseless—salary—

One Pearl—to me—so signal—
That I would instant dive—
Although—I *knew*—to *take* it—
Would *cost* me—*just a life!*

The Sea is full—I know it!
That—does not blur *my* Gem!
It burns—distinct from all the row—
Intact—in Diadem!

The life is thick—I know it!
Yet—not so dense a crowd—
But *Monarchs*—are *perceptible*—
Far down the dustiest Road!

No. 270, c. 1861

Does this poem show her on the brink of a decision to devote herself to poetry? The diadem is the same figure she used in "Fame of Myself, to justify" and the monarchs perceptible "Far down the dusty Road" recall the bird of "I shall keep singing!" who, however late, will one day take its place in summer. And yet the "soul" of line three, "One Pearl" of line five, the gem, the Diadem—all have strong religious resonance. Or, out of context, the poem could be read as a love poem—it has been well remarked (by David Porter) that in many of Dickinson's poems there is "an undefined convergence of earthly and divine love." The question is, Which is the vehicle and which the tenor? Is she using religious metaphors to describe a romantic love? or romantic imagery to describe her longing for religious fulfillment? Or do both converge on her literary ambition?

A note on her reading during these formative years (I like to think of her "Lexicon" as an inclusive term for it) may help with this problem of referents. The Bible was always at hand and much in her mind; Shakespeare loosened her spirit as little else could (Higginson quoted her as saying, "Why is any other book needed?" [*L,* 342b]); and she followed the course of literary women—the Brontës, George Eliot, Elizabeth Barrett Browning—with great interest. Their cause was hers. But she was not constituted, like them, to enter the public arena, and no one stepped forward to help her. During these "Lexicon" years, what might have given her, or confirmed in her, a sense of direction and a discipline was a book we know she read carefully and, it would seem, earnestly: Thomas à Kempis, *Of the Imitation of Christ.* In the Houghton Library's Dickinson Collection, there is an 1857 edition with her name on the title page, in her sister-in-law's handwriting. Many passages are marked, probably by Emily. Here are some of the Saint's injunctions: "Fly the tumultuousness of the world as much as thou canst." "Take refuge within the closet of thine heart. . . . The more thou visitest thy chamber, the more thou wilt like it . . . [for it is here that one may] set in order both the outward and the inward man. . . . Both of them are of importance to our progress in godliness." Emily Dickinson had only to change the last two words to read "toward being a poet." At any rate, here was a way of life that perfectly suited her temperament, her talent, and the conditions of her social and domestic life. Far from being an admission of defeat at the hands of an uncomprehending world, her choice of life may represent the discipline, altered to her own tastes and requirements, urged by St. Thomas. Whatever her motivation might have been—religious, literary, or, as many have insisted, neurotic—this is what she did, and the chamber she visited became more and more the center of her creative life. I think she came to regard the dedicated life of the poet as of much the same order as the dedicated life of the religious. Once she wrote to her bereaved cousins: "Let Emily sing for you because she cannot pray" (*L*, 278)—that is, "My poem will be my prayer." So it is not surprising to find a convergence in her poetry of the earthly and divine. The poem *"One Life* of so much Consequence" makes sense both ways. The "Monarchs... perceptible / Far down the dustiest Road" may indeed be a figure for the religious dream of the longed-for beatific vision. But, since we know that the poem was written at a time when her literary ambitions were at their most intense, we may well compare it with other "poet-poems" of the period and see it as a figure for literary success, with the "Pearl" and the "Gem" as figures for her God-given talent, and the "thick life" and the "dense crowd" of the last stanza having the same significance as the birds (of "I shall keep singing!") who "will pass me / On their way to Yellower Climes," the lesser poets who crowded her off the pages, say, of the *Republican*.

Another poem of the period uses figures of various orders—religious, domestic, regal—to develop the same theme of assertive choice. Again we may ask, choice of what? A lover? Christ as her Savior? Or, as the poet-poems suggest, the life dedicated to art?

I'm ceded—I've stopped being Their's—
The name They dropped upon my face
With water, in the country church
Is finished using, now,
And They can put it with my Dolls,
My childhood, and the string of spools,
I've finished threading—too—

Baptized, before, without the choice,
But this time, consciously, of Grace—
Unto supremest name—
Called to my Full—The Crescent dropped—
Existence's whole Arc, filled up,
With one small Diadem.

My second Rank—too small the first—
Crowned—Crowing—on my Father's breast—
A half unconscious Queen—
But this time—Adequate—Erect,
With Will to choose, or to reject,
And I choose, just a Crown—

No. 508, early 1862

Her most famous "choice" poem—firmer, less cluttered, finely chiseled—presents for us many of the same questions. It could be regarded as an expansion of the poem discussed above, "There is a solitude of space," that little meditation on the solitude, the "finite infinity," of a soul "admitted to itself." Here the focus is on the moment when the soul makes its choice:

The Soul selects her own Society—
Then—shuts the Door—
On her divine Majority—
Obtrude no more—

Unmoved—she notes the Chariots—pausing—
At her low Gate—
Unmoved—an Emperor be kneeling
Upon her Mat—

I've known her—from an ample nation—
Choose One—
Then—close the Valves of Her attention—
Like Stone—

No. 303, c. 1862

(An early meaning of "valves" is the two halves of a double door; the line simply dramatizes further the action of line two.) Here again, the poem has been read as a love poem (who was the "chosen one" of the last stanza?) and as a religious poem: the Soul dedicating itself to the spiritual life. And of course those Chariots at her Gate and the Emperor kneeling on her mat have been thought to refer to the two editors who, early in 1862, "asked me [as she wrote Higginson] for my Mind." But she is willfully imprecise about the referent of those metaphors, and we are left guessing.

The great point to keep in mind—and a major point of this essay—is that the experience of guessing need not be frustrating, provided we are clear about certain matters central to her art. Her early turn to metaphor, from that reckless valentine on ("Don't be afraid of it, sir, it won't bite"), gave her freedom to say what she wanted without inviting open confrontations. Years later (about 1868) she formulated her views in a poem from which I have several times borrowed the key word, "slant":

Tell all the Truth but tell it slant—
Success in Circuit lies
Too bright for our infirm Delight
The Truth's superb surprise

As Lightning to the Children eased
With explanation kind
The Truth must dazzle gradually
Or every man be blind—

No. 1129

The "Truth" here, of course, goes far beyond the "truth" of the referents in "The Soul selects" (whom did she have in mind as that "Emperor"? who was the "chosen one"?, etc.), but the prin-

It partakes of the imagery of being twice-born, or . . . confirmed, and if this poem had been written by Christina Rosetti, who was a devout Christian, I would be inclined to give more weight to a theological reading. But it was written by Emily Dickinson, who used the Christian metaphor far more than she let it use her. This is a poem of great pride, not pridefulness, but self-confirmation . . . a poem of movement from childhood to womanhood, of transcending the patriarchal condition of bearing her father's name and crowing on her father's breast. . . . There were numerous revivals going on in the New England countryside around her and in Amherst from the time she was eighteen years old and refused to stand up . . . and say she wanted to be saved. I'm sure that the metaphor was one that she quite ironically and with consciousness could draw on to talk about a very different kind of confirmation, self-confirmation.

—Adrienne Rich in a *Voices & Visions* interview

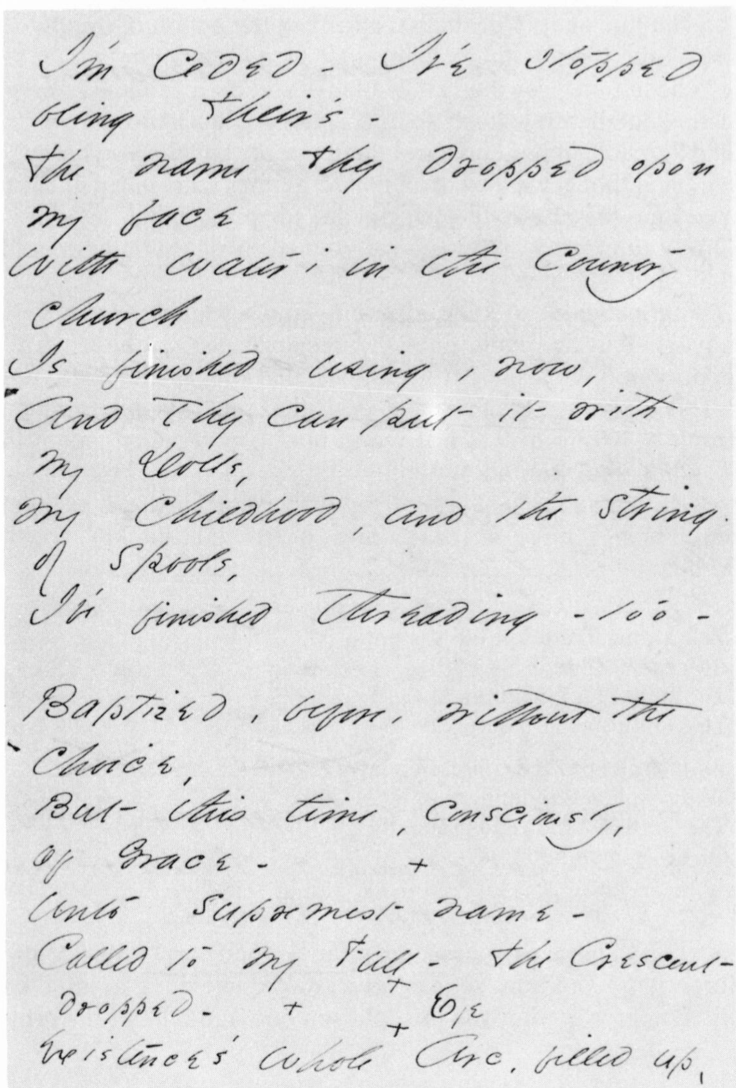

I'm ceded - I've stopped
being Their's -
The name They dropped upon
my face
With water, in the Country
church
Is finished using, now,
And They can put it with
my Dolls,
My Childhood, and the string
of spools,
I've finished threading - too -

Baptized, before, without the
choice,
But this time, consciously,
of Grace - +
Unto supremest name -
Called to my Full - The Crescent
dropped - + + Eye
Existence's whole Arc, filled up,

ciple is the same. Just as she refused to be explicit about the Truth that must be told slant (is it the truth of Life, Death, Immortality?), she withholds clues, in poem after poem, to the specifics that may have been in her mind. To put it as the philosophers would, Dickinson is concerned with essence, not accident. In "The Soul selects," she presents with stunning power the essence of an experience—"what it feels like" to make a final, ultimate commitment to a way of life that involves perhaps painful renunciation of many of the fine things of this world, including the pleasant society of friends. The last line is like the clank of a heavy door shutting. We are left to ponder the nature of such commitments *in general* and to fill in the specifics from our own experience.

In another poet-poem of the period, she declared herself in a way that, had the poem been read from an Amherst pulpit, the congregation would have been shocked and dismayed. (Even then, it was passed over in four editorial winnowings and did not see the light of day until 1929.) In the poem, she allies herself with the poetic "over-reachers," from the Renaissance on down, those who preferred to create the world anew in their own imaginations rather than accept the traditional views handed down by the generations. The poem is not atheistic—it is not God but God's Heaven that she rejects in favor of her own. But that would hardly lessen the shock of putting "Poets—All—":

I reckon—when I count at all—
First—Poets—Then the Sun—
Then Summer—Then the Heaven of God—
And then—the List is done—

But, looking back—the First so seems
To Comprehend the Whole—
The Others look a needless Show—
So I write—Poets—All—

Their Summer—lasts a Solid Year—
They can afford a Sun
The East—would deem extravagant—
And if the Further Heaven—

Be Beautiful as they prepare
For Those who trust in Them—
It is too difficult a Grace—
To justify the Dream—

No. 569, c. 1862

Although it might have been difficult to persuade a shocked congregation of this, the poem is not so much a rejection of an old theology as it is a song of praise of the good things of this world—the sun, the summer—so good, indeed, that she chooses them over the promises of the preacher. A word she used frequently is "ecstasy," and in the nearly thirty poems in which it occurs, the reference is mostly to things in nature—summer, sun, birds, flowers. A late poem begins, "Take all away from me, but leave me Ecstasy" (No. 1640), and Higginson records a remark of hers when he visited her in 1870: "I find ecstasy in living—the mere sense of living is joy enough" (*L,* 342a). In the poem, she chooses the present joy over the promise of future bliss because, as a poet, she can create her own.

Emily Dickinson was never discursive on the subject of poetry. She never wrote essays or gave lectures or carried on literary correspondences with fellow poets as, say, the English Lake Poets did a generation earlier. In a day when it was fashionable to keep a journal, she never, as far as we know, kept one. (Her sister Vinnie did for a few months, and Austin did, only to have most of it destroyed by fire in 1888.) Dickinson's journal was her poetry. Apparently, writing it (or her letters, into which she poured much of the same creative effort) was an almost daily exercise. For a few years in the early 1860s, it is estimated (mostly on the basis of handwriting, since she never dated a poem) that she averaged nearly a poem a day. As to letters, she seems to have been indefatigable. The thousand-odd letters in the current complete edition represent only a tenth of what we know she wrote; the others are lost or were destroyed upon the deaths of the recipients. And yet, although she never expanded (again, as far as we know) on what poets, from Sir Philip Sidney on down, have loved to write about in their off-hours—the nature and purpose of their art—she knew what she was doing. It is clear from the poet-poems and from certain revealing remarks in the letters that she thought theoretically about poetry. The materials are random; but we can put together, I think, a fairly reliable statement, a homemade poetics, by which she explained herself as poet.

In one of her phases, she thought of herself as a kind of Orpheus, commissioned—and here we go back to that reckless valentine—to wake people up, to be the "crowing cock and the singing lark" to a sleeping world. Higginson recorded her as saying in the 1870 conversation: "How do most people live without any thoughts? There are many people in the world (you must have noticed them in the street). How do they live? How do they get strength to put on their clothes in the morning?" (*L,* 342a) Her next few sentences as recorded by Higginson have to do with books ("so few *real* books"); with truth (". . . such a rare thing it is delightful to tell it"); and with the "ecstasy in living" as "joy enough." By 1870, she had been writing steadily for more than a dozen years, with well over a thousand poems to her credit and an untold number of letters. She may well have been summing up for Higginson, in her own slant way, her poetic credo. The bookish part of the conversation had begun with her own test for poetry—a way of saying, perhaps, that if poetry is to convey thought, or truth, or the joy of living, it must work through the senses, physiologically: "If I read a book and it makes my whole body so cold no fire ever can warm me I know *that* is poetry. If I feel physically as if the top of my head were taken off, I know *that* is poetry. These are the only way I know it. Is there any other way?" Higginson, the true formalist, could have suggested many. If he made an answer he did not record it. In her first full-length letter to him (April 1862), she had asked him, "Could you tell me how to grow—or is it unconveyed—like Melody—or Witchcraft?" Higginson's only answer then was to tell her to be less "spasmodic," less "wayward," less "uncontrolled"—the answer, that is, of the formalist. Although she never lacked form (Higginson seems to have been blind to it), the source of poetry, and its essence, was to her inspirational, partaking (as we shall see) of the divine, the God-given.

Here is one of her best "Orphic" poems, in which (presumably) she takes it upon herself to do no more than alert people to the sound of the wind in the trees. She sent the poem to Higginson (April 1862) and in a letter, shortly after, stated her Orphic purpose explicitly: "Then there's a noiseless noise in the Orchard—that I let persons hear" (*L,* 271).

Of all the Sounds despatched abroad,
There's not a Charge to me
Like that old measure in the Boughs—
That phraseless Melody—
The Wind does—working like a Hand,
Whose fingers Comb the Sky—
Then quiver down—with tufts of Tune—
Permitted Gods, and me—

Inheritance, it is, to us—
Beyond the Art to Earn—
Beyond the trait to take away
By Robber, since the Gain
Is gotten not of fingers—
And inner than the Bone—
Hid golden, for the whole of Days,
And even in the Urn,
I cannot vouch the merry Dust
Do not arise and play
In some odd fashion of it's own,

Some quainter Holiday,
When Winds go round and round in Bands—
And thrum upon the door,
And Birds take places, overhead,
To bear them Orchestra.

I crave Him grace of Summer Boughs,
If such an Outcast be—
Who never heard that fleshless Chant—
Rise—solemn—on the Tree,
As if some Caravan of Sound
Off Deserts, in the Sky,
Had parted Rank,
Then knit, and swept—
In Seamless Company—

No. 321, c. 1862

In another version of the poem (there are three, all written about the same time, a fact that may indicate the importance she attached to it), line eight reads "Permitted Men—and Me—" (that is, "all of us"). As with that other poem she sent Higginson, "I cannot dance upon my toes," one wonders if he understood all she was saying about her poetry—and, perhaps, about him. In another poem of the same year, she used the phrase "bolts of melody" as a metaphor for poems (No. 505); here (in line seven), she may be asking Higginson (and the rest of us) to listen more sharply to her "tufts of Tune," her poems. The second section of the poem expands upon the idea that poetry, like melody and witchcraft, *cannot* be taught or "earned." It has been well suggested (again by David Porter) that in the final section she is trying to explain the nature of this new song of hers (recall Arlo Bates's "new species of art") so unfamiliar to Higginson—this "Caravan of Sound" as it blends sound and sense in "seamless" prosody. At any rate, she never wrote a finer example of it. Curiously, even after the success of her poems in the 1890s, Higginson still criticized her lack of form, her "waywardness." One wonders (again) if he noticed the firm metrical control throughout this poem: eight four-line stanzas in the Common Meter of the hymns ("8's and 6's"), with the second and fourth lines in each stanza rhyming either perfectly or approximately. Something of a stylist himself, especially eloquent on the things of nature, he would have been an "outcast" indeed had he not responded at least in some measure to the lovely interplay of thought and sound and tempo throughout.

Although the Orphic voice, so clear in her great contemporaries Emerson and Thoreau, was not to be her permanent mode, it never entirely left her. Once, in an early letter to Susan Gilbert, she described a miserable day at home. Everybody was busy sweeping and dusting and washing clothes (she preferred pestilence to housekeeping [*L,* 318]), and the weather outside was cold and gray. In the midst of her doleful account, she made this little aside, actually a remark close to the center of her poetics: "Do I paint it *natural*—Susie, so you think how it looks?" (*L,* 85) (Italics hers.) All her life it was her aim to "paint it *natural,"* to get it true, whether it was a sunset or a bluejay or the experience of parting or the essence of pain. This she did for her own sake, surely, "to set in order the outward and inward" of her existence. But it seems clear that she always had an audience in mind, if only that ultimate audience when at last she would "take her place in summer." She wanted to enable people to "think how it looks," to help them hear the wind in the trees, to open their feelings to the major experiences of life, like pain, parting, death. She once boasted of being able to "arrest" the "light that never was, on sea or land" which Wordsworth in "Elegiac Stanzas" declared unarrestable. "But," she concluded, "we'll not chagrin him" (*L,* 315). A brash boast, perhaps, were it not that in countless poems and in many of her matchless letters she proved her competence.

Here is an instance of a light "arrested." It is the light of a late afternoon in winter, very New England, when the sun is setting and the shadows are lengthening. As often in Dickinson, the scene induces a meditation. If in the poem, "Of all the Sounds . . . ," the wind in the trees started her thinking about the "golden gain," the ecstasy (she might have said) of an experience many are deaf to, here the winter landscape leads to thoughts of mortality and despair. Both poems could be called Orphic in that they are directed to all of us: the meditations lead to perceptions in which Dickinson wants all to share.

There's a certain Slant of light,
Winter Afternoons—
That oppresses, like the Heft
Of Cathedral Tunes—

Heavenly Hurt, it gives us—
We can find no scar,
But internal difference,
Where the Meanings, are—

None may teach it—Any—
'Tis the Seal Despair—
An imperial affliction
Sent us of the Air—

When it comes, the Landscape listens—
Shadows—hold their breath—
When it goes, 'tis like the Distance
On the look of Death—

No. 258, c. 1861

Volcanoes be in Sicily
And South America
I judge from my Geography—
Volcanoes nearer here
A Lava step at any time
Am I inclined to climb—
A crater I may contemplate
Vesuvius at Home.

It was Higginson and Mrs. Todd who changed "Heft" to "weight" in the 1890 *Poems* and included the poem in the section entitled "Nature," even though it would have been more at home in their very next category, "Time and Eternity." Actually, the poem straddles both categories. The New England scene is sharp and clear, while the long, long thoughts it induces control our response to it. But what is that response? Are we left in a bleak, hurtful, hopeless world? When the light goes, are we in utter darkness? (The poem has been much discussed; see Suggestions for Further Reading: Anderson, Kher, Weisbuch, Porter.) I am reminded of the psychologist Carl Jung's phrase as he opposes the powerful, dangerous factors in our lives to the "grand, beautiful, and meaningful": he refers to this opposition as "the terrible ambiguities of immediate experience" (*Psychology and Religion,* 55). Here, the poem seems to say, "If, in the midst of life we die, it is also true that in the midst of death, we live." The oppressive tunes are "Cathedral," the hurt is "Heavenly," the despair is "imperial," of the "Air." And in this awareness we live more intensely, closer to the divine in our nature. It takes the shock of such awareness—"the look of Death"—to wake us up. A short, undatable, probably late poem is explicit:

By a departing light
We see acuter, quite,
Than by a wick that stays.
There's something in the flight
That clarifies the sight
And decks the rays.

No. 1714

Even as, in Kher's fine phrase, she was pursuing "the never-ending odyssey of her mind" and trying to explain herself and her poetry to Higginson—but O so slant—she was going through a major crisis in her life that has been the subject of much biographical speculation and controversy. Here the evidence is mainly in the poems—deeply troubled, anguished—while the letters remain, for the most part, noncommittal, often lighthearted, with only a hint here and there of trouble within. For long, the cause of her increasingly strange ways was thought to have been a frustrated love affair (the search for the lover still goes on.) Other theories posit a domineering father, an inadequate mother, a brother of whom she was inordinately fond, a woman with whom she was in love. Psychiatric theories range from the mildly neurotic to the psychotic and hinge on frustrations of various sorts—the hopeless position of women in her day, her failure to win public recognition as a poet, and of course sexual frustration. She has been seen as on the verge, during this critical period, of a complete nervous breakdown. She has been put under the medical microscope: it was the symptoms of Bright's Disease (the official cause of her death) that drove her into seclusion. Other observers stress the anxieties of her religious pilgrimage and see her as adopting, when all else failed, the role of the Bride of Christ. Facets of the truth, perhaps, but I find none of these theories ultimately convincing. What is incontrovertible is that, during her late twenties and early thirties, there *was* a crisis of some sort in her life that brought her suffering and sorrow. But these facts also remain: she never stopped writing (some of her finest poems come from this period) and, whatever caused the crisis, she weathered it —and went on to write some thousand more poems before she died in 1886.

And went on (to get back to her homemade poetics) to make some of her most revealing statements about her poetry, its nature and purpose. Her later mood is more serene, more assured, as if, having got her bearings (personal as well as aesthetic), she now is in a position to do some summing-up, to make some final pronouncements. Sometimes she turned prophetic, as when in a late letter to a friend she wrote, "I think if I should see you again, I sh'd begin every sentence with 'I say unto you—' " (*L,* 950). Again, since she was never discursive about such matters, we must assemble random remarks, and poems explicitly about poetry, to arrive at even an approximately coherent theory.

A simple poem of about 1864 shows the Orphic in her—the impulse to alert people to sights, sounds, feelings—blended with a liberal amount of Puritan didacticism and outreach, too much, perhaps, for our sensibilities, but an operative and unabashed phase of her own notion of what poetry should do:

If I can stop one Heart from breaking
I shall not live in vain
If I can ease one Life the Aching
Or cool one Pain

Or help one fainting Robin
Unto his Nest again
I shall not live in Vain.

No. 919

She was true to her native New England, "the teacher of America," in her impulse, not only to heal and comfort, but to teach. Fully half her canon could be called "wisdom pieces" (most of them following the crisis period), thoughts on life and living, sometimes exhortations, sometimes warnings, sometimes pure clinical analyses, as in her anatomizings of pain, hope, love—the definition poems I have earlier remarked upon. She seemed bent on making moral or psychological distinctions for the benefit of those whose vision was not so clear as hers.

Another phase of her poetics concerns her intense concentration on the word. One of the first full-length studies (by Henry Wells in 1947) of Emily Dickinson's poetry has this as its opening sentence: "In the beginning was the Word." He might have added, ". . . and at the last." Only a few months before she died, and in failing health, she wrote a friend: "I hesitate which word to take, as I can take but few and each must be the chiefest" (*L,* 873). All her life, once she had emerged from the reckless valentine stage, she was at pains to take the "chiefest." A letter to Joseph Lyman in the mid-1860s contains her mature view:

> We used to think, Joseph, when I was an unsifted girl and you so scholarly that words were cheap and weak. Now I dont know of anything so mighty. There are those to which I lift my hat when I see them sitting princelike among their peers on the page. Sometimes I write one [she had already written thousands], and look at his outline till he glows as no sapphire. (L, 78)

Remark after remark shows her sensitivity to the sound, the feel, the ring of the single word. Thanking Mrs. Holland for her "full sweetness, to which, as to a Reservoir the smaller Waters go," she paused to write, "What a beautiful Word 'Waters' is!" (*L,* 833). Commenting on "Antony's remark to a friend, 'Since Cleopatra died . . .' " she wrote: "That engulfing *'Since'*—" (*L,* 791). To her bereaved cousins: "You need the balsam word" (*L,* 281). Again: "A Word is inundation, when it comes from the Sea" (*L,* 965). Once she turned away a caller with the note: "I . . . have no grace to talk, . . . my own Words so chill and burn me" (*L,* 798). Several poems warn against the power of words to harm: a word "dropped careless on a Page" (No. 1261, c. 1873) may have devastating effect long after its author has died. In the poem "She dealt her pretty words like Blades" (No. 479, c. 1862), words can wound like steel. A quatrain written about 1877 sharpens the focus still further:

> Could mortal lip divine
> The undeveloped Freight
> Of a delivered syllable
> 'Twould crumble with the weight.
>
> No. 1409

Another poem, this one written in the late 1860s, goes beyond the power of the single word to heal or hurt or teach. It confronts the problem of the very source of the word itself—how the poet comes by it. Is it by conscious thought-process? By inspiration? (Once in a letter she asked Higginson what "inspiration" was.) The poem depicts a little drama of the poetic process. The scene is the poet's study. The characters are the poet and the words lined up as candidates for selection. The poet ponders the choice rationally, analytically, exploring the Lexicon for (as Dickinson would say) the "chiefest." Then, in the last six lines, something happens beyond reason.

A scene from the Voices & Visions *film* Emily Dickinson *depicting the "fascicles" into which she bound many of her poems. Of the close to 1800 poems she kept, only 10 were published during her lifetime.*

No one of her poems, let's put it this way, should be regarded as a signed and sealed position paper. It's the poetry, as Emerson put it, of portfolio. When she died, they found these poems in her room, in a bureau drawer, I think—it's not quite clear. . . . She'd never gone through the discipline of publication. They're the portfolio poetry of a poet who had written for herself, to herself, thinking out her life, investigating what was happening, especially inside, and coming out with an extraordinary, true, certainly realistic sense of the human psyche. She has been called the greatest realist of the interior that America has produced.

—Richard B. Sewall in the *Voices & Visions* film *Emily Dickinson*

Shall I take thee, the Poet said
To the propounded word?
Be stationed with the Candidates
Till I have finer tried—

The Poet searched Philology
And when about to ring
For the suspended Candidate
There came unsummoned in—

That portion of the Vision
The Word applied to fill
Not unto nomination
The Cherubim reveal—

No. 1126, c. 1868

Note that "word" in line two is not capitalized but in line ten it is. Dickinson was perplexingly liberal with capitals and often eccentric with them. But here she may have meant it—and we are at the threshold of what I take to be her mature conception of poetry, where it comes from and what it is on this earth to do. It is more than Orphic, beyond (say) Shelley's vitalism, beyond the didactic and therapeutic. There is something here of the Greek Muse (although I don't recall her ever using the word seriously); but if there is, it is transmuted by Scriptural theology into something quite her own. In the last five lines of the poem, the poet had a vision. The Word (now a term encompassing the entire poem) had come "unsummoned in," a divine gift.

In one of her Prose Fragments (those bits and pieces found among her things after she died), she jotted down a comment on a verse from the opening passage of St. John's Gospel which obviously fascinated her:

The import of that Paragraph "The Word Made Flesh"
Had he the faintest intimation Who broached it Yesterday!
"Made Flesh and dwelt among us."

(PF No. 4)

The fragment is undatable—and so is the poem in which she enlarged upon some of the "intimations" the passage had for her. But both the fragment and the poem seem late. The poem I take to be climactic and perhaps definitive:

A Word made Flesh is seldom
And tremblingly partook
Nor then perhaps reported
But have I not mistook
Each one of us has tasted
With ecstasies of stealth
The very food debated
To our specific strength—

A Word that breathes distinctly
Has not the power to die
Cohesive as the Spirit
It may expire if He—
"Made Flesh and dwelt among us"
Could condescension be
Like this consent of Language
This loved Philology

No. 1651

Let me look back a bit to explain my high claim for this poem. The late-Puritan atmosphere in which Emily Dickinson grew up was suspicious of "polite literature." In his inaugural address (1845) on assuming the presidency of Amherst College, Edward Hitchcock warned against its influence as "very disastrous to religion":

> For much of it has been prepared by men who were intemperate, or licentious, and secretly or openly hostile to Christianity. . . . And their writings have been deeply imbued with immorality, or infidelity, or atheism. Yet the poison has been so interwoven with those fascinations of style, or thought, characteristic of genius, as to be unnoticed by the youthful mind, delighted with smartness and brilliancy. (*Life,* 353)

Emily, a precocious fourteen, was even then acquiring a reputation among her schoolmates for smartness and brilliancy. She might very well have attended the inauguration, or she could have read the speech when, later, it was on sale at the town bookstore. It is not surprising, in view of such attitudes (and Hitchcock's could be called "official"), that, like her near-contemporary Hawthorne, she later approached her vocation with a sense of guilt. There is something clandestine in that curious, metaphoric announcement to Jane Humphrey centering on the "one gold thread . . . a long, big shining fibre," the meaning of which she never explains. "I have dared to do strange things," she wrote Jane, "bold things . . . I have heeded beautiful tempters, yet do not think I am wrong"—a boast that does not conceal the lingering guilt. When she sent her first group of poems to Higginson in April 1862, she did not sign the accompanying letter; she wrote her name on a card and enclosed it in its own envelope, asking (in the letter) that he not "betray" her (*L,* 260).

But by then, as we have seen, she had achieved independence—"I'm ceded—I've stopped being Their's"—and had selected her own society. She knew she was a poet and of the company of poets whose "Summer—lasts a Solid Year." It may be that she found her final self-justification (if, indeed, she needed any) in her notion of "The Word made Flesh." Here was the answer to Hitchcock and all his tribe. For "the Word was with God and the Word was God." This "consent of Language" which had been granted her, this "loved Philology" to the use of which she had devoted her life, were divinely sprung, types of the Incarnation.

That she came (probably late) to the idea of poetry as Incarnation, or Revelation, does not mean that she (perhaps ever) wrote in the security of Divine Sanction. Hers was a troubled spirit, as witness her difficulty with doctrines of the church. Throughout her life, she pondered the great questions. At twenty-seven she wrote a cousin, "I wonder how long we shall wonder; how early we shall *know*" (*L,* 190). Three years before she died, she asked a friend, "Are you certain there is another life? When overwhelmed to know, I feel that few are sure" (*L,* 827). A late poem (No. 1144) speaks of "the balm of that religion / That doubts as fervently as it believes." She "grappled," as she put it in poem No. 1221, with "a Theme stubborn as Sublime"—and the theme was "Immortality . . . the Flood Subject" (*L,* 319), Eternity that "sweeps around me like a sea" (*L,* 785). "On subjects of which we know nothing . . . we both believe, and disbelieve a hundred times an Hour, which keeps Believing nimble"—a remark in a letter of 1882 (*L,* 750) to her friend Judge Otis Lord, jocular in context but, generalized, helps explain the erratic spiritual course discernible in the poems: buoyant affirmations (Nos. 4, 827, 1052), and cries of despair (Nos. 280, 502) sometimes side by side. Her persistent questioning (every death in her family or circle of friends brought up anew for her the old agonizing doubts) led Charles Anderson to call her a *religious* poet, "using," he wrote, "that word in its 'dimension of depth' "—that is, in Tillich's terms, "asking passionately the question of the meaning of our existence . . . and of *being* universally." It is in this sense that I described her as the most religious in her family.

I like to think of her as an explorer, or experimenter, of the spirit, trying out on her own pulses, in that curiously isolated life of hers, mood after mood, passion after passion, "ideas-as-lived," felt on the pulse and in the bloodstream. She does not tell us how to live (although there is much wisdom if one has the patience to find it) so much as what it feels like to be alive. In this canon of nearly two thousand poems and in the thousand-odd indispensable letters (even that adjective is too weak), we meet with almost everything that touches our humanity. She was no Shakespeare; she never wrote a play or a novel ("When I try to organize," she wrote Higginson, "my little Force explodes" [*L,* 271]; hers is not the panoramic vision, say, of Whitman. But she made up in depth what she lacked in breadth. There *is* an external world in her poems and letters, much broader and more sharply realized than is generally supposed; but few poets have led us deeper into what she called "the Being's Centre" (No. 553) or have made us more keenly aware of the "internal difference / Where the Meanings, are." (Alfred Kazin recently called her, in this regard, "the greatest realist in our literature.") She spoke in many voices, often with the dramatist's capacity for projecting character (whether her own or a persona's is the crux of much critical controversy). She could be witty, wise, impudent, truculent, tough-minded. Her philosophical standing has recently been asserted (Benfey), and her significance as a religious and meditative poet is the subject of much recent study. But through it all she kept an eye on all that made for what she called "the ecstasy of mere living"—the sights, the sounds, the life of nature, the love of friends. She gloried in this earth: "I often wonder how the love of Christ, is done—when that—below—holds—so—" (*L,* 262). And through it all (again) was the constant discipline of the artist, the demands of the poet's craft to "paint it *natural,*" to get it true, to

The footpath between the Dickinson Homestead, where Emily lived, and the Evergreens, Austin and Susan's home.

achieve the blend of sound and sense and rhythm that satisfied her. In the short hymn forms she chose for herself, she worked hard for perfection and often achieved it.

I have called her an experimenter of the spirit. Let me repeat Kher's phrase, "the never-ending odyssey of her mind." A gnomic quatrain, found among her things in a penciled rough draft, probably written in 1870 and intended to go with a letter to Higginson, puts it in her own way. It probably would have shocked the pious folk of Amherst as still another declaration of independence.

Experiment escorts us last—
His pungent company
Will not allow an Axiom
An Opportunity

No. 1770

No Axioms, indeed! But had they read closely they might have seen that this impious bit is written in the precise meter of Isaac Watts's great hymn, "God, our help in ages past," a hymn she could have sung (and probably did) in complete reverence.

I want to write down here two or three cardinal principles that I wish you would think over and turn over now and again till we can protract talk.

I give you a new definition of a sentence:

A sentence is a sound in itself on which other sounds called words may be strung.

You may string words together without a sentence-sound to string them on just as you may tie clothes together by the sleeves and stretch them without a clothes line between two trees, but — it is bad for the clothes.

The number of words you may string on one sentence-sound is not fixed but there is always danger of over loading.

The sentence-sounds are very definite entities. (This is no literary mysticism I am preaching.) They are as definite as words. It is not impossible that they could be collected in a ~~book~~ dictionary though I dont at present see on what system they would be catalogued.

They are apprehended by the ear. They are gathered by the ear from the vernacular and brought into books. Many of them are already familiar to us in books. I think no writer invents them. The most original writer only only catches them fresh from talk, where

ROBERT FROST

RICHARD POIRIER

For nearly half a century, until his death in 1963 at age eighty-nine, Robert Frost was the unofficial poet laureate of America, recipient of so many honorary degrees that he allowed the various academic hoods to be sewn into a large blanket. This was before he received two especially coveted ones, from Oxford and Cambridge, in the same year, 1957, a distinction previously given only to two other American poets, Longfellow in 1868 and James Russell Lowell in 1873. Writing to his official biographer, Lawrence Thompson, about his trip to England to attend the ceremonies, he remarked, "I have had about everything I can have in my own country. Now for the mother country" (*Letters,* 565).

He had good reason to call England the mother country. It was, for one thing, the place where, except for Emerson's, the poetry in English that mattered most to him had been written. Time and again in talks and letters he expresses his special devotion to *The Golden Treasury,* Francis Palgrave's famous anthology of English songs and lyrics from their earliest to the nineteenth century. This was the book, first published in 1861 and with a second, expanded edition in 1896, which he often carried with him as a convenient way to read, reread, memorize, and study the English poets whose traces are to be found in his own work. These included Milton, from whom he derived that strong sense of the mythological dimensions of conjugal love that reverberate in one of the best of his sonnets, "Never Again Would Bird's Song Be the Same," and in the marital tensions of his long narrative-dramatic poems, like "Home Burial." In Spenser and Keats he found tropes for such beautiful songlike poems of mutability as "Spring Pools." Echoes of Pope's early pastorals can be heard in "A Prayer in Spring," of Marvell's mower poems in the great sonnet "Mowing," of Dante Gabriel Rossetti's "The Woodspurge" in "The Vantage Point." His tastes were wide-ranging and eclectic. At twenty, he wrote to Susan Hayes Ward, who had agreed to publish his first poem, "My Butterfly," that his favorite poems "are and have been these: Keats's 'Hyperion,' Shelley's 'Prometheus,' Tennyson's 'Morte D'Arthur,' and

Elinor Miriam White, 1895.

Robert Lee Frost, 1895.

They met at high school, and it just so happened that they were both valedictorians at the graduation ceremony. The title of the Frost piece was "Monumental Afterthoughts Unveiled." What's more important is the title of her valedictory talk, which was "Conversation as the Force of Life." Between those two you have the definition . . . of Frost's poetry, at least of that period, dating up to *North of Boston.*

—Joseph Brodsky in the *Voices & Visions* film *Robert Frost*

Browning's 'Saul'—all of them about the giants. Besides these I am fond of the whole collection of Palgrave's" (*Letters,* 20). Wordsworth helped him to bring into poetry "the language really spoken by men" ("Preface to Lyrical Ballads," 1800, in Stillinger, 452) and offered prefigurations of such sad, mutilated, and half crazy or stoical characters as populate the long dramatic narratives, notably "A Servant to Servants," "The Hill Wife," "The Witch of Coös," "The Wood-Pile."

England was the mother country, too, in another sense. It was there, and not in America, that Frost's career as a poet had its real beginnings. At thirty-eight, with a wife and four children, he moved to England late in 1912 for a stay of nearly two and a half years. Before that, only a scattering of his poems had appeared, and in quite inconspicuous American magazines and newspapers, though these included some important works like "The Trial By Existence," and "The Tuft of Flowers." He had supported his family by a combination of farming, schoolteaching, odd jobs, and with the help of a small annuity from a paternal grandfather. It was by the sale of a farm left him in the grandfather's will that he was able to afford the trip to England. Soon after his arrival he managed to meet Ezra Pound, Yeats, and a number of poets who wrote for an anthology called *Georgian Poetry* (a title referring to George V, who came to the throne in 1910). These included Wilfred Gibson, Lascelles Abercrombie, and W. H. Davies. He got acquainted with the recently appointed poet laureate Robert Bridges, who remained a lifelong admirer of Frost's poetry, and, above all, with the man who, until he was killed in action near the end of World War I, was probably the most beloved friend of his life, Edward Thomas, "the only brother I ever had," he wrote to Edward Garnet (*Letters,* 217).

These were all influential literary persons, far more so than any comparable group he could have found anywhere in America, and they proved to be enormously helpful to him. When he arrived in England he had with him enough poems in manuscript to make up his first book, a collection of lyrics entitled *A Boy's Will,* published in England in 1913, and a second, the collection of dramatic narrative poems called *North of Boston,* published there in 1914. He had nearly enough for a third book, *Mountain Interval,* which came out in 1916 after his return to America. "My dream," Frost wrote to a friend at home in December 1913, "would be to get the thing started in London, and then do the rest from a farm in New England," and that is very much what he succeeded in doing. Both of the first two books were very favorably reviewed by such new friends as Pound, the poet F. S. Flint, Gibson, Abercrombie and, most perceptively of all, by Edward Thomas, who reviewed *North of Boston* no fewer than three times. Frost was careful to mail the reviews to people at home who would assure them some degree of local publicity, and he also wrote a number of remarkable letters to American friends in which, partly to assist them in their writings about him, he elaborated his theories of poetry. Thus, to John Bartlett in July 1913, he writes that "I alone of English writers have consciously set myself to make music out of what I may call the sound of sense. . . . If one is to be a poet he must learn to get cadences by skillfully breaking the sound of sense with all their irregularity of accent across the regular beat of the metre" (*Letters,* 80–81). In his letters of this period Frost was no less anxious than was T. S. Eliot, in his essays a decade later, to encourage critics and reviewers to see the historical importance and originality of his poetic practices.

Throughout his life Frost was fiercely devoted to the making of a poetic career; he was determined that he should be not only the most popular but the greatest of American poets. So that while he shrewdly set about from London to create and enlarge an appreciative audience at home, he also displayed a masterful dedication to the formal and technical possibilities of English and classical verse. His sonnets are among the best ever written in the language, and include variations using thirteen lines, as in "The Line Gang," and fifteen, as in "Hyla Brook." He wrote two masques, *A Masque of Reason* and *A Masque of Mercy;* he composed occasional epigrams, one of which, entitled "From Iron," is characteristically tough-minded: "Nature within her inmost self divides / To trouble men with having to take sides." The satirical discourses of Horace inform his long poem "New Hampshire," while the hendecasyllabics of "For Once, Then, Something" are a nod to Catullus, for whom the eleven-syllable line was a favorite measure. In his great dramatic-narrative poems, of which the monologue "Mending Wall" is a famous example, he claimed that he had "dropped to an everyday level of diction that even Wordsworth kept above" (*Letters,* 83–84).

This evident devotion to the craft, the traditions, the forms of poetry makes it all the more peculiar that many readers even now tend to think of him as in some ways less sophisticated, less allusive or learned or worldly than are comparable figures like Yeats, Eliot, Pound, and Stevens. Eliot was aware of this curious misperception and aware, too, of how much it might mean to Frost if Eliot himself set out to correct it, which is what he tried to do in a toast that brought Frost nearly to tears during a dinner given in his honor in London in 1957:

> Mr. Frost is one of the good poets, and I might say, perhaps *the* most eminent, the most distinguished, I must call it, Anglo-American poet now living. I have a special weakness, perhaps—no, I shouldn't call it a weakness—I have a special understanding of a great deal of his work. Of course, I also have the New England background. But I think that there are two kinds of local feeling in poetry. There is one kind which makes that poetry only accessible to people who had the same background, to whom it means a great deal. And there is

> another kind that can go with universality: the relation of Dante to Florence, of Shakespeare to Warwickshire, of Goethe to the Rhineland, the relation of Robert Frost to New England. He has that universality. And I think that the beginning of his career, and the fact that his first publication and reputation was made in this country, and that he is now hailed in this country universally as the most distinguished American poet, points to that fact. (Thompson and Winnick, 243)

This is a most elevating and affecting tribute from one great poet to another, and all the more because, until this nearly closing moment in their lives, Eliot and Frost did not have a relationship that was either very amiable or very admiring. Their edginess illustrates, I think, a central and mostly unexplored episode in the history of twentieth century literary culture, an episode in which modernism, in Eliot's dazzling version of it, blinded nearly everyone to alternative ways of thinking about literature and culture, especially one that links Frost to William James and to Emerson. In the account I would like now to offer of these complex matters, it is nowhere suggested that Eliot is anything less than a poet of extraordinary magnitude. I am, however, not primarily concerned with his poetry but rather with modernist mythologies contrived to advance a certain reading of that poetry and which, at the same time, had a deleterious effect on the cultural-critical assumptions brought to a poetry like Frost's, or, for that matter, to the quite different but still Emersonian poetry of Stevens.

Allowing for the many differences among them, Emerson, William James, Frost, and Stevens all encourage a kind of skepticism about modernist assumptions, a scepticism so strong as to anticipate later theorizing about the deconstructive tendencies of language, even while advancing beyond it, to allow for an engendering human presence. In assessing the relation of Frost to Emerson and to William James, it will also be important to remember that all three aspired to be "popular" writers, and that they so far succeeded as to be treated by most modernist interpreters, at least until recently, as somehow insufficiently complicated. Frost has been especially ill served, for example, by modernist presuppositions about "difficulty" and its virtues which were brought to poetry largely at Eliot's behest.

Frost's admirers have had trouble making properly large claims for his work mostly because these seemed already preempted by a modernist aesthetic wherein Frost could not hospitably be located, and they have never energetically enough discovered a way to read him within the enlarging, alternative traditions of the Emersonian dispensation. Loved by some for his folksy toughness in the representation of the joys

William James.

James asks in "Humanism and Truth": "must not something end by supporting itself?" And he answers, in figures Frost would admire, that

> humanism is willing to let finite experience be self-supporting. Somewhere being must immediately breast nonentity. Why may not the advancing front of experience, carrying its immanent satisfactions and dissatisfactions, cut against the black inane as the luminous orb of the moon cuts the caerulean abyss? Why should anywhere the world be absolutely fixed and finished? And if reality genuinely grows, why may it not grow in these very determinations which here and now are made?

and pains of country life, he is by others considered local or insular. If, to meet that disparagement, he is shown to be ironic about his own apparent sincerities, he is as immediately perceived to be rather tiresomely arch. And if, in all these cases, it is at least allowed that he is a poet who instills confidence in the human ability to cope, he is then rescued from that presumed banality—in what is, is it not, the worst of centuries?—by the insistence, from Randall Jarrell, Lionel Trilling, and others since, that he is really at heart a "terrifying" poet, a sort of modernist manqué.

Each of these readings flounders into the embrace of the others, and one reason is that Frost himself offers no consistent signal that he leans toward any one of them. "You get more credit for thinking," he wrote Louis Untermeyer on January 1, 1917, "if you restate formulae or cite cases that fall in easily under formulae, but all the fun is outside saying things that suggest formulae that won't formulate—that almost but don't quite formulate. I should like to be so subtle at this game as to seem to the casual person altogether obvious" (*Letters to Untermeyer,* 47). Frost's importance consists largely in his subversions of accredited ideas of what it *means* to be serious, to "get credit for thinking." He does not do this, let me insist, by any consistent repudiation of traditional formulae or the big words that go with them. To do so would in itself be too systematic for him. He does not, any more than does William James, ever dismiss, for example, the idea of God or Truth. He merely mixes such terms with more ordinary or lesser ones, and then, by turns of voice and of metaphor, tests their endurance. The moment-by-moment effort of his writing is to disclose alternative ways of determining what only *might* be significant or important. The idea of a God in the heavens might "work" for some, as William James would say, but for others the idea of apple-picking or cutting wood might "work" just as well. When Frost, in this letter to Untermeyer, admits that he would not mind being thought "obvious," he would, as a scholar of Latin as well as Greek, have known that a root meaning of "obvious" is "in the way." He wants to show how obvious things are "in the way" of larger meanings because they are also *on* the way to them, as when, in "After Apple Picking," "My long two-pointed ladder's sticking through a tree / Toward heaven still."

So that when he talks, as he frequently does, about being "obvious," it is best to listen as carefully as one must to Wordsworth when he talks about bringing into poetry "the language really used by men." Being a poet for the People did not mean for Wordsworth, or for Frost, being a poet for the Public. Frost wrote to John Bartlett in November 1913 that "there is a kind of

A scene from the Voices & Visions *film* Robert Frost.

My long two-pointed ladder's sticking through a tree
Toward heaven still,
And there's a barrel that I didn't fill
Beside it, and there may be two or three
Apples I didn't pick upon some bough.
But I am done with apple-picking now. . . .
My instep arch not only keeps the ache,
It keeps the pressure of a ladder-round.
I feel the ladder sway as the boughs bend.
And I keep hearing from the cellar bin
The rumbling sound
Of load on load of apples coming in. . . .
One can see what will trouble
This sleep of mine, whatever sleep it is.
Were he not gone,
The woodchuck could say whether it's like his
Long sleep, as I describe its coming on,
Or just some human sleep.

—From "After Apple Picking"

success called 'esteem' and it butters no parsnips. I mean a success with the critical few who are supposed to know. But really to arrive where I can stand on my legs as a poet and nothing else I must get outside that circle to the general reader who buys books in their thousands. I may not be able to do that. I believe in doing it—don't you doubt me there. I want to be a poet for all sorts and kinds. I could never make a merit of being caviare to the crowd the way my quasi-friend Pound does" (*Letters,* 98). To reach an audience that "buys books in their thousands" sounds disreputable only on the assumption that in this century such an audience for great poetry ought to be forsworn. In fact, of course, neither Eliot nor Pound was in that sense abstemious; they merely made a virtue of being hard to get. As Frost adroitly notices, a poetry like Pound's, under the guise of its own exclusivity, is all the while aspiring to popular acclaim. It makes "a merit of being caviare to the crowd."

Frost's first meeting with Edward Thomas had taken place a month earlier, after Thomas's anonymous review of *A Boy's Will.* Though he began writing poetry at Frost's encouragement, Thomas was already a remarkably astute critic, notably of Pound's early work, as David Bromwich has argued in his essay "Edward Thomas and Modernism" (*Raritan Quarterly,* Summer 1983). Thomas paid sufficient credit to Pound's *Personae* in 1909 when he remarked that it was a "battlefield" in which, as Donald Davie puts it in *Ezra Pound,* he had challenged an enormous range of linguistic resources of which the English language was only one (17). This is a somewhat generous characterization, since the cultural burden it attributes to Pound would seem to include a weighty knowledge of foreign languages. He had, in fact, only some superficial acquaintance with any of them. Perhaps he was already an American Europeanist, but it was of the spirit rather than the tongue. Thomas came closer to the truth in a second review of *Personae,* when he asks us to "straightaway acknowledge the faults, the signs of conflict; the old and foreign words and old spellings that stand doubtless for much that the ordinary reader is not privileged to detect, the tricky use of inverted commas; the rhythms at one time so free as not to be distinguished at first from prose, at another time so stiff that 'evanescent' becomes 'evan'scent'; the gobbets of Browningesque." Some months later, in a review of *Exultations,* he complained that Pound is "so pestered with possible ways of saying a thing," that "if he is not careful he will take to meaning what he says instead of saying what he means" (Bromwich, 111).

Thomas's essential complaint about Pound, as Bromwich points out, is that instead of showing, as Frost was to do, how it might be possible to speak in poetry without being "poetic" in already tired ways, he was inventing yet another kind of aloofness for the language of poetry. He was making it still more remote from common usage. That did not mean, again, that such poetry necessarily cut itself off from the common reader. Such a reader would soon enough be persuaded that it was culturally incumbent upon him to pay respects to what he was not meant to understand. Explicate! Explicate! Nor does it mean that the alternative to Pound's kind of thing, insofar as it is represented by the poetry of Frost, was supposed to be "simple." Frost involves us in the most subtle kinds of voiced inflection against regularity of meter, and an equally subtle allusiveness, where echoes of earlier poetry are casually allowed to pass into sounds of ordinary speech.

The possibility that a poetry written for "all sorts and kinds" could have its own sort of difficulty was suggested much earlier, again by Wordsworth, in "Essay, Supplementary to the Preface" (1815) where we are asked to "remember . . . that the medium through which, in poetry, the heart is affected is language; a thing subject to endless fluctuations and arbitrary associations." Instead of passively accepting these "associations," "the genius of the poet melts these down for his purpose" (Stillinger, 479). No good poetry is ever obvious in the sense of being transparent, and it requires of us a strenuous effort if we are to divest ourselves of those "arbitrary associations" which language, under most other circumstances, excites. Wordsworth speaks of "the exertion of a co-operating *power* in the mind of the Reader" (Stillinger, 478). The movements in a poem can in that sense create and sustain a community of effort in which writer and reader might find ideal versions of themselves which, in life, are only intermittently audible.

In his criticisms of Pound, and in his admiring reviews of Frost, Thomas was saying no less than Wordsworth had said, and his views coincide with what Frost meant in the letter to Bartlett when, speaking of his determination to "get outside that circle [of the critical few] to the general reader," he insists that "I believe in doing it—don't you doubt me there." He believes in "doing this" not for the fame and fortune it might bring him, but because he believes in the power of poetry to create possibilities for communal life that a modernist kind of poetic "difficulty" has given up for lost. He believes that what he calls "sentence sounds" in poetry might make the experience of life seem less alienating, sentence sounds being at once familiar to the reader from life but better understood in their elevating mystery when they are put into a tense proximity to meter. Bromwich refers us to a passage in which Thomas remarks—

this was before he knew Frost and before he reviewed *North of Boston,* where the workings of sentence sounds are especially conspicuous—that "men understand now the impossibility of speaking aloud all that is within them, and if they do not speak it, they cannot write as they speak. The most they can do is to write as they would speak in a less solitary world" (Bromwich, 114).

Poetry, on these instructions, is to use language in such a way as to discover in it those possibilities for community of feeling with which we otherwise have only the most sporadic contact. The poet is to seek out or, indeed, bring into being a common or "general reader" and need not, in the interest of some larger cultural or spiritual quest, dissociate himself from such readers or despair of their existence. Over a hundred years before Thomas's reviews, in "Appendix to the Preface" (1802), Wordsworth had criticized poets who are "proud of modes of expression which they themselves had invented and which were uttered only by themselves," while allowing, as does Frost, that these can in fact offer a kind of specious pleasure. The pleasure consists in "impressing a notion of the peculiarity and exaltation of the Poet's character, and in flattering the Reader's self-love by bringing him nearer in sympathy with that character; an effect which is accomplished by unsettling ordinary habits of thinking" (Stillinger, 466).

The poet thus exalted is radically different from any imagined by Thomas or Wordsworth, by Emerson or Frost. He is instead more like the modernist poet described by Eliot in his essay of 1921, "The Metaphysical Poets." Eliot turns on its head Wordsworth's stricture about a poetry of "hieroglyphics and enigmas" (Stillinger, 466), and in the process gives to his own version of "complexity" and "difficulty" an aura of cultural heroism. "We can only say," he writes, "that it appears likely that poets in our civilization, as it exists at present, must be *difficult.* Our civilization comprehends great variety and complexity, and this variety and complexity, playing upon a refined sensibility, must produce various and complex results. The poet must become more and more comprehensive, more allusive, more indirect, in order to force, to dislocate, if necessary, language into his meaning" (*Sel. Essays,* 248). Despite efforts to sound as if considerable caution and scruple are at work—"we can only say that it appears likely"—the passage is anxious to press quite untenable positions. Has any poet in "our civilization" (which here is only what Eliot wants to imagine it to be) been "more comprehensive" than Spenser? "more allusive" than Tennyson? "more indirect" than Marvell? more anxious to "dislocate" language than is Shakespeare in *Troilus and Cres-*

sida? Nothing unique to our century compels anyone to write in these ways. Eliot is determined to assert a historical necessity for poetic practices that might also be explained by the personal stress and depressions that in the early 1920s brought him to a nervous collapse.

Eliot's cultural-historical arguments in his essays issue from a desire, no less strong than Frost's in his letters, that his poetry shall be enhanced, but they have their source even more in what William James calls "a strong temperamental vision." James uses the phrase in *Pragmatism* while proposing, as indeed did Santayana, that "the history of philosophy is to a great extent that of a certain clash of human temperaments, even though the philosopher tries when philosophizing"—or the critic-poet when theorizing—"to sink the fact of his temperament" under "impersonal reasons" (11). Like many writers of great ambition, Eliot chooses to believe that his differences from writers of the past are a matter not simply of "temperament" but of history. Another example of this is Henry James's curious little study *Hawthorne,* where he wants to claim that because of the Civil War "the good American, in days to come, will be a more critical person than his complacent and confident grandfather" (quoted, with discussion, in Poirier, *A World Elsewhere,* 100). Since Eliot was readying *The Waste Land* for publication the next year, it was a particularly opportune time to propose that "difficulty," "allusiveness," "complexity," and "dislocation" are a more or less direct literary result of some unprecedented cultural-historical crisis.

Two years later, and after the publication of his poem, Eliot was to add "the mythical method" to the list of a contemporary writer's necessary devices. In the *Dial* (November 1923) he courageously champions *Ulysses* which, with very few exceptions, had been treated in England with remarkable and often simple-minded resistance. He argues that "the novel is dead" and that what he calls Joyce's "mythical method" has the importance of "a scientific discovery." The method is, he says, "a step toward making the modern world possible for art," though in fact "the modern world" had proved quite wonderfully possible not only for Frost and Stevens but, among others, for D. H. Lawrence, E. M. Forster, and Virginia Woolf. What Eliot is saying is not especially appropriate even to *Ulysses,* where the so-called method is scarcely as necessary to an understanding of the book as he wants to make it out to be. He is, again, talking about his own poetry, and it is therefore not surprising that forty years later, in 1964, when he had no further need for these arguments, he characterizes them, in a note he appended to the essay, as "intemperate," "silly," "pompous," and "absurd." And

. . . the word "parochial" is one that I would apply to Frost positively within the redefinition of the word "parochial" offered by Eire's poet Patrick Kavanaugh. Kavanaugh made a distinction between what he called the parochial imagination and the provincial imagination. The parochial imagination, he says, is never in any doubt about the artistic validity of its parish as the subject for art; whereas the provincial imagination is always looking over its shoulder to the metropolis to see if it's getting approval.

—Seamus Heaney in a *Voices & Visions* interview

yet when the essay was written, the "method" was said to be indispensable for no less a reason than that the modern world made it so: it was "simply a way of controlling, of ordering, of giving a shape and a significance to the immense panorama of futility and anarchy which is contemporary history." Writers who fail of the example set by Joyce (and Eliot) may continue to write, he allows, but they will be unaware of their own "obsolescence."

The essay on *Ulysses,* like the essay on "The Metaphysical Poets," was to have profound consequences for critical practice and opinion, especially in the American academy, and thus for promoting an idea of modernism which helped make Frost an example of obsolescence. As Pound had said, he was "simple" or, as even so brilliant a critic as R. P. Blackmur had the misfortune to phrase it, in a review in 1936, he was "an easy going versifier of all that comes to hand" (Thompson, II, 454). Having, as we have seen, announced in a letter dated Fourth of July 1913 that "to be perfectly frank with you I am one of the most notable craftsmen of my time," and that "I alone of English writers have consciously set myself to make music out of what I may call the sound of sense" (*Letters,* 79), Frost became increasingly aware in the 1930s that most of "the critical few" had been persuaded to equate what was "new" in poetry not with poets who have "their ear on the speaking voice" but with the kind of poet who writes so as "to force, to dislocate, if necessary, language into his meaning."

Frost was far too intelligent about literary politics to set himself up as a public alternative to Eliot or to Eliot's modernism, especially in an American literary situation where he might then find himself in the company of Vachel Lindsay, Edgar Lee Masters, and Carl Sandburg. But before Eliot and Frost were to join, in London in 1957, in such wonderfully affectionate praise of each other, two grand old survivors of American poetry, Frost managed to suggest some essential distinctions between them just short of making a gap which would have left him irrevocably on a side where he could not have tolerated the company. In an interview of 1923, Frost was annoyed to find himself credited with saying, "I like to read Eliot because it is fun seeing the way he does things, but I am always glad it is his way and not mine" (Thompson, *Robert Frost,* Vol. 2, 220). A similarly tart, but not abrasive remark is reported by Untermeyer: "Eliot likes to play Eucharist, I like to play euchre" (*Letters to Untermeyer,* 321). After Eliot had honored him in London, however, he implied that a line in "Take Something Like a Star," written in 1943 —"Some mystery becomes the proud"—referred to Eliot. "You don't know how much that line cost me in the way of living," he said in some talk one evening in 1962 at the Breadloaf Summer School at Middlebury, as recorded by Reginald Cook in *The Living Voice.* "It took me a long time to accept obscurity in poetry, but I decided it was a lofty spirit made them obscure"*

*Cook says this is a remark about Pound, but earlier in his book (p. 136), he says, correctly, that a similar statement is about Eliot.

(p. 191). (He had claimed earlier, in a lecture given in 1962 called "On Extravagance," that "Take Something Like a Star" refers to "the Arabian Nights or Catullus or something in the Bible" (Lathem and Thompson, 459). Perhaps the most considered way of putting his difference from Eliot occurred to him in 1958 when, in a conversation recalled by Louis Mertins, he said, "He's a pessimistic Christian; I'm an optimistic pagan" (353). He had come a long way from what he had said in the privacy of a letter to his daughter Lesley in 1942: that Eliot is a "worlds-end-whimperer" (Thompson and Winnick, *Robert Frost,* Vol. 3, 89).

As against this testimony, the kinds of opposition to Eliot that critics of Frost wanted in the thirties to attribute to him, usually with the intent to place Frost in a relatively minor position, are much too sharp. Rolfe Humphries, professing in a review of *A Further Range* in 1936 to defend Eliot from a charge of "charlatanism," which Frost is not on record as ever having made, goes on to assert that as soon as Frost tries to extend his "range" he shows himself "incapable of getting up and going places. The man who, seated on his kallipyge, looks like Olympian Zeus, turns out, when he stands, to be of much less impressive stature, and when he strides the hustings, to be ridiculous and unimportant of gait. . . . *A Further Range?* A further shrinking" (Thompson, *Robert Frost,* Vol. 2, 455). The inference to be drawn from such nastiness is that Frost is at his infrequent best when he is most "local." This is an opinion that extends from Pound's early reviews, through Blackmur and on to the present with John Kemp's *Robert Frost and New England* in 1979 and to some views of the poetry even in William Pritchard's brilliant and invaluable revisionary biography* of 1984, *Robert Frost: A Literary Life Reconsidered.*

It was in fact not Frost but William Carlos Williams who chose to enunciate an "American" difference from Eliot on the basis of "local conditions," and who illustrates how unrewarding the distinction is. Williams in his *Autobiography* in 1951 makes a rather turgid complaint about the effect upon "us" of the appearance thirty years before of *The Waste Land.* "There was heat in us, a core and a drive that was gathering headway upon the theme of a rediscovery of a primary impetus, the elementary principle of all art, in the local conditions. Our work staggered to a halt for a moment under the blast of Eliot's genius which gave the poem back to the academics. We did not know

*The official biography in three volumes by Lawrence Thompson, assisted in Volume 3 by R. H. Wennick, is often misleadingly antagonistic toward its subject, as shown vividly in Stanley Burnshaw, *Robert Frost Himself* (New York: Braziller, 1986).

Edward Thomas, the British poet who befriended Frost and wrote perceptive reviews of his early books.

I meant, you meant, that nothing should remain
Unsaid between us, brother, and this remained—
And one thing more that was not then to say:
The Victory for what it lost and gained.

You went to meet the shell's embrace of fire
On Vimy Ridge; and when you fell that day
The war seemed over more for you than me,
But now for me than you—the other way.

How over, though, for even me who knew
The foe thrust back unsafe beyond the Rhine,
If I was not to speak of it to you
And see you pleased once more with words of mine?

—From "To E.T."

how to answer him" (146). Unfortunately, the "we" here, insofar as it refers to poets, includes such figures as Alfred Kreymborg, Maxwell Bodenheim, and Walter Arensberg, not Stevens, with whom Williams was friendly but not especially close, or Frost, who scarcely recognized Williams's existence, or Hart Crane, whom Williams upbraided for picking up Eliot's mannerisms.

The "answer" to Eliot, though he had not asked for one, was already implicit in an Emersonian tradition with which Frost and Stevens were more inwardly and powerfully engaged than Williams, by disposition, was able to be. It is a tradition in which no absolutes, no spiritual (or poetic) quests, no object or word is necessarily more significant than any other. "We ought," says James in *Principles of Psychology,* to say a feeling of *and,* a feeling of *if,* a feeling of *but,* and a feeling of *by,* quite as readily as we say a feeling of *blue* or a feeling of *cold"* (*Psychology,* 238). It is a tradition in which literalness, or the alleged thing in itself, is treated as a great trope of the mind equal to any figurations made about the "thing." In the essay "Art," Emerson claims:

> It is the right and property of all natural objects, of all genuine talents, of all native properties whatsoever, to be for their moment the top of the world. A squirrel leaping from bough to bough, and making the wood one wide tree for his pleasure, fills the eye not less than a lion,—is beautiful, self-sufficing, and stands then and there for nature. A good ballad draws my ear and heart whilst I listen, as much as an epic has done before. A dog, drawn by a master, or a litter of pigs, satisfies, and is a reality not less than the frescoes of Angelo. From this succession of excellent objects, we learn at last the immensity of the world, the opulence of human nature, which can run out to infinitude in any direction. But I learn that what astonished and fascinated me in the first work astonished me in the second also. (433)

This is an argument for pragmatism long before that term was introduced by Charles Pierce and reinterpreted by William James. It strikes at the heart of efforts to claim that some subjects are perforce more important than others or that some achievements of form are more satisfying because historically revered. Emerson focuses on the act of making, the "opulence" —the combination of power and wealth—by which human nature can take *any* direction it wants into "infinitude." As against the regulative mastery of concept over trope in most philosophical writing, Emerson asserts the superiority of trope over concept, and the power of the individual "workman" or agent over both. "The Figure a Poem Makes," the title Frost gave in 1939 to the preface for his *Collected Poems,* affirms these Emersonian principles as against any idea of a static poetic meaning ultimately arrived at. "The figure," he says, "is the same as for love," and from his language it is made wittily obvious that he refers not to the sentiment but to the act of lovemaking:

> No one can really hold that the ecstasy should be static and stand still in one place. It begins in delight, it inclines to the impulse, it assumes direction with the first line laid down, it runs a course of lucky events, and ends in a clarification of life—not necessarily a great clarification, such as sects and cults are founded on, but in a momentary stay against confusion. (Lathem and Thompson, 394)

Contrast with this Eliot's lines from "East Coker": "Love is most nearly itself / When here and now cease to matter," when "We must be still and still moving / Into another intensity / For further union, a deeper communion / Through the dark cold and the empty desolation." These lines, beautiful as they are, are also some measure of the differences between the "temperaments" of the two poets. Frost knew enough about old men and dark cold to write one of his best poems, "An Old Man's Winter Night." But even that old man tries to scare the outer night by "beating on a box," like Stevens's "The Man on the Dump" who "sits and beats an old tin can, lard pail. / One beats and beats for that which one believes. / That's what one wants to get near. Could it after all / Be merely oneself. . . ." One must do *something* "here and now," because this is the time that "matters," if any time does. So, too, with the speaker in "Desert Places," whose brusque assertion, "They cannot scare me with their empty spaces," both tropes and traduces the "vacant interstellar spaces," again of "East Coker." But the tone is itself a little scared, in an almost boyish way, and it nowhere claims exoneration from terror or despair. It only insists on locating these within the self. "I have it in me so much nearer home / To scare myself with my own desert places." "Home" is one of Frost's most recurrent figures, and he would have known what James said of it. "All 'homes' are in finite experience," he tells us in his essay "Pragmatism and Humanism," and "finite experiences as such are homeless" (*Prag.,* 125). Sometimes, for Frost's peripatetic figures, like the man in "The Wood-Pile," there seem to be no "homes" at all, only pathetic hints of their absence, as in the little cord of maple he happened upon "far from a useful fireplace."

Frost's differences from the modernism made fashionable by Eliot are a matter finally of cultural and historical perception, or, to put it in a way closer to their activity as poets, it gets down to whose metaphors are to govern your perception of what it is like to make a life for yourself in the twentieth century. In a

Robert Frost at home in Franconia, c. 1915.

letter to Untermeyer, dated November 25, 1936, Frost wrote that "Marx had the strength not to be overawed by the metaphor in vogue," meaning "the Darwinian metaphor." "We are all toadies to the fashionable metaphor of the hour. Great is he who imposes the metaphor" (*Letters to Untermeyer,* 225). For Frost "all thinking, except mathematical thinking, is metaphorical,"—as he says in "Education By Poetry" (Lathem and Thompson, 332), and the usefulness of poetry is that it can teach us how metaphors are made and managed, and also that each has its limit. We may enthusiastically commit ourselves to a metaphor, as when the speaker of "For Once, Then, Something" sees a white object at the bottom of a well. But what, then, do we call it, and in which of the many tones of voice invited by the last line? "What was that whiteness? / Truth? A pebble of quartz? For once, then, something."

That conclusion *refuses* to conclude and is as wry and skeptical as is Frost's observation in the letter to Untermeyer that in history the shift from one governing metaphor to another is usually made rather abruptly, "There are no logical steps from one to the other. There are no logical connections." What must be learned is a proper wariness of all metaphors, which is what his famous "mischievousness" in the management of his own poems is most significantly about. One must learn to be "at home in the metaphor," as he says, again in "Education by Poetry," because only then can you know "the metaphor in its strength and its weakness." Otherwise "you don't know how far you may expect to ride it and when it may break down with you. You are not safe in science; you are not safe in history" (Lathem and Thompson, 334). To know where you are, to be at "home," is, peculiarly then, to know danger without even having to look for it.

Suspicious of the metaphor of "the waste land," Frost was equally suspicious of the metaphor of "the New Deal." With the election of Roosevelt to a second term in 1936, just before the letter to Untermeyer (and close to another, still more important letter of the same year which we will see in a moment), Frost came to understand that the two metaphors had become fashionable because they had much in common. The one, of apocalyptic despair, conspired with the other, of bureaucratic "planning," to deny the individual the power to make his own fate, to turn, as William James expresses it in "What Pragmatism Means," away from his own "insufficiency" toward "concreteness and adequacy, toward facts, towards action, and towards power" (*Prag.,* 31).

For Frost, literary culture is necessarily political because it is either shaped by "the metaphor in vogue" or by resistance to it. So naturally was this the case for him, that his politics is seldom abstracted from his style. Style, for Frost, gives evidence of how a person manages not to surrender himself to any mere idea, including his own, how he manages not to be "overawed" even by his own metaphors. A man's "ideas are his ideas," he remarks in another letter to Untermeyer (March 10, 1924). "His style is the way he carries himself toward his ideas. Mind you, if he is down spirited it will be all he can do to have the ideas without the carriage. The style is out of his superfluity. It is the mind skating circles round itself as it moves forward. Emerson had one of the noblest, least egotistical of styles. By comparison with it Thoreau's is conceited" (*Letters,* 243). Style in itself constitutes a defense against the ideas on which it advances, and with this in mind we can better understand one of the most important of his letters. It was written in April 1936 to the student newspaper at Amherst College, where he taught off and on for most of his life. The letter was meant to thank the students for congratulating him on his sixtieth—it was actually his sixty-first—birthday.

This is another of those instances where Frost uses a letter to write what is essentially an essay; his letter to Sidney Cox and to John Bartlett in 1914 on the distinction between "ear" reading and "eye" reading are other examples. A standard collection of his prose pieces exclusive of letters, talks, or interviews edited by Hyde Cox and Edward Connery Lathem runs only to 15 pieces, a little over 118 small pages. In that respect, the letter to *The Amherst Student* is one of the most pondered and ponderable "essays" he ever wrote, a sort of position paper from someone who does not like to be held too closely to positions, which is perhaps why he chose to address the letter to a newspaper with no circulation outside a small collegial group in which he felt at home.

It is very, very kind of the *Student* to be showing sympathy with me for my age. But sixty is only a pretty good age. It is not advanced enough. The great thing is to be advanced. Now ninety would be really well along and something to be given credit for.

But speaking of ages, you will often hear it said that the age of the world we live in is particularly bad. I am impatient of such talk. We have no way of knowing that this age is one of the worst in the world's history. Arnold claimed the honor for the age before this. Wordsworth claimed it for the last but one. And so on back through literature. I say they claimed the honor for their ages. They claimed it rather for themselves. It is immodest of a man to think of himself as going down before the worst forces ever mobilized by God.

All ages of the world are bad—a great deal worse anyway than Heaven. If they weren't[,] the world might just as well be Heaven at once and have it over with. One can safely say after from six to thirty thousand years of experience that the evident design is a situation here in which it will always be about equally hard to save your soul. Whatever progress may be taken to mean, it can't mean making the world any easier a place in which to save your soul—or if you dislike hearing your soul mentioned in open meeting, say your decency, your integrity.

Ages may vary a little. One may be a little worse than another. But it is not possible to get outside the age you are in to judge it exactly. Indeed it is as dangerous to try to get outside of anything as large as an age as it would be to try to engorge a donkey. Witness the many who in the attempt have suffered a dilation from which the tissues and the muscles of the mind have never been able to recover natural shape. They can't pick up anything delicate or small any more. They can't use a pen. They have to use a typewriter. And they gape in agony. They can write huge shapeless novels, huge gobs of raw sincerity bellowing with pain and that's all they can write.

You take the lake. I look at it.
I see it's a fair, pretty sheet of water.
I stand and make myself repeat out loud
The advantages it has, so long and narrow,
Like a deep piece of some old running river
Cut short off at both ends. It lies five miles
Straight away through the mountain notch
From the sink window where I wash the plates,
And all our storms come up toward the house,
Drawing the slow waves whiter and whiter and whiter.
It took my mind off doughnuts and soda biscuit
To step outdoors and take the water dazzle
A sunny morning, or take the rising wind
About my face and body and through my wrapper,
When a storm threatened from the Dragon's Den,
And a cold chill shivered across the lake.

—From "A Servant to Servants"

> Fortunately we don't need to know how bad the age is. There is something we can always be doing without reference to how good or how bad the age is. There is at least so much good in the world that it admits of form and the making of form. And not only admits of it, but calls for it. We people are thrust forward out of the suggestions of form in the rolling clouds of nature. In us nature reaches its height of form and through us exceeds itself. When in doubt there is always form for us to go on with. Anyone who has achieved the least form to be sure of it, is lost to the larger excruciations. I think it must stroke faith the right way. The artist, the poet, might be expected to be the most aware of such assurance. But it is really everybody's sanity to feel it and live by it. Fortunately, too, no forms are more engrossing, gratifying, comforting, staying than those lesser ones we throw off, like vortex rings of smoke, all our individual enterprise and needing nobody's co-operation; a basket, a letter, a garden, a room, an idea, a picture, a poem. For these we haven't to get a team together before we can play.
>
> The background in hugeness and confusion shading away from where we stand into black and utter chaos; and against the background any small man-made figure of order and concentration. What pleasanter than that this should be so? Unless we are novelists or economists we don't worry about this confusion; we look out on [it] with an instrument or tackle it to reduce it. It is partly because we are afraid it might prove too much for us and our blend of democratic-republican-socialist-communist-anarchist party. But it is more because we like it, we were born to it, born used to it and have practical reasons for wanting it to be there. To me any little form I assert upon it is velvet, as the saying is, and to be considered for how much more it is than nothing. If I were a Platonist, I should have to consider it, I suppose, for how much less it is than everything (*Letters,* 417—19).

Some occasionally tiresome aspects of Frost are in evidence here. The punning at the outset on his "advanced age" ("The great thing is to be advanced") and then on his "age" and "the age" and the cheap shot about typewriters are typical of his mannerisms when he is imitating Thoreau at his most "conceited." There are, additionally, problems of a more substantial kind, as when he says, in effect, that since complaints about "the age" have recurred throughout history, that only proves that although one age may be a bit worse or better than another, they are all pretty much identical.

Marx did not live for nothing, and unless Frost is licensed to ignore social, economic, and religious-historical interests altogether, he is open to a question which he never asks of himself, any more than does Emerson or James. He never asks if perhaps Eliot and before him Arnold and before that Wordsworth and

Swift and Pope and Shakespeare—if each and all were not justified in finding something bad about "the age" because they were all alluding to essentially the same age, the economic-ecclesiastical systems peculiar to Western civilization since the beginnings of capitalism. In his customary blindness to the institutional sources and directions of power, Frost shares the deficiencies, as much as the strengths, of the Emersonian-pragmatist tradition. He liked to say, as he does, again in the mid-thirties in his introduction to Edward Arlington Robinson's *King Jasper,* that he preferred "grief" to "grievances" (Lathem and Thompson, 348), and for the reason that, like the Emerson of "New England Reformers," he finds "grievances" too partial. And yet, even if "griefs" are an irremediable consequence of human life, they can be immeasurably compounded—as when hunger in our own decade is turned into unnecessary famine or inevitable death into terrorism or mass murder—as a result of specific political systems and institutions of belief. The twentieth century may indeed not be worse than any other, but it can be *called* worse because now no one can claim anymore to be ignorant about the political and economic arrangements that have increased some of the necessary terrors of life for countless numbers of people.

But in response to those who say that this is the worst of centuries Frost is actually not quite so easily dismissive as he first sounds. One of the many peculiarities of his tone here is that while seeming to deny that his own is the worst of times, he does not quite do so. Rather, he is "impatient with such talk." The distinction is an important one, because what makes him "impatient" is a matter of "style," of carriage. He is bothered by the "immodesty" of the mongers of apocalypse. By contrast he strives for at least the effect of "modesty" in himself. He does this in part by movements of language that are characteristic also of his poetry and, in part, by refusing to elevate his own writing over other activities.

Like Emerson or Stevens, Frost is among the least paraphrasable or translatable of writers. The refutation of one idea by another idea becomes, as it issues from him, not so much an argument as a warning about the personal consequences of *holding* to a particular idea. The consequences are audible, he suggests, in the way a person sounds. He is concerned with what William James, in a phrase wrongly assumed to indicate his easy accommodation to the capitalistic ethos, frequently calls "the cash value" of an idea, a conception, or a word. Not is this idea true or false, but what will it eventually do to me if I think it is true rather than false. This is what mostly concerns him. What is lost or what is gained by thinking one way about "the age" rather than another? It is, Frost says, "dangerous to try to get outside of anything as large as an age," because then you "can't pick up anything delicate or small any more." The easygoing apparently extemporized way he proceeds in his arguments, or his poems, his intimate, homy familiarity with other writers like Wordsworth and Plato—this is meant, regardless of how artfully contrived, to exemplify his own capacity to deal grandly with small things and delicately with large ones, his refusal to be "overawed."

He wants his way of speaking to be by inference ours too, so that we should not think that by "form" he means only or even primarily the forms created by poetry. Emerson, who had promised in his *Journals* (July 7, 1839) that to be a "poet" you need simply and fully to "do your thing," would endorse Frost's assurance that "the least form" can be "engrossing, gratifying, comforting, staying . . . a basket, a letter, a garden, a room," all of which he casually mixes with "an idea, a picture" (possibly Emerson's "frescoes of Angelo"?), "a poem." He is talking about any form within which you might hope to make sense and outside of which you probably should not expect to make much.

The kind of human community or conversation shaped by Frost's letter is consistent with the very accent and tilt of it, which has a close resemblance stylistically to the letters and lectures of William James. So that while the sentence near the opening—"It is immodest of a man to think of himself as going down before the worst forces ever mobilized by God"—may constitute, as Frank Lentricchia argues in *After the New Criticism,* "a wickedly ironic remark about self-congratulatory modern pessimists," it is also quite confident and good-humored, a convivial sort of reprimand. Frost intends that the letter itself shall be a "form" that will contain rather than ostracize "modern pessimists." So that I would dissent from Lentricchia's further claim that Frost "slips back," as if he had ever been there, "into the solemn posture of *The Birth of Tragedy* when he speaks of 'the larger excruciations,' "—which sounds elegantly witty to me—the " 'background in hugeness and confusion,' the 'black and utter chaos.' " If an analogy is wanted, it is nearer home in the writings, again, of William James, whose works Frost taught and admired and who, like his father, Henry James, Sr., was a survivor of psychological exposure to "black and utter chaos." To expand a passage already alluded to in James's "Pragmatism and Humanism," "Truth grows up inside all finite experiences. They lean on each other, but the whole of them, if such a whole there be, leans on nothing. All 'homes' are in finite experience; finite experiences as such are homeless. Nothing outside the flux secures the issue of it. It can hope for salvation only from its own intrinsic promises and potencies" (*Prag.,* 125).

In all likelihood James is himself remembering here, without mentioning it, a passage in "Circles," where Emerson says, "There is no outside, no inclosing wall, no circumference to us. The man finishes his story,—how good! how final! how it puts a new face on all things! How he fills the sky. Lo! on the other side rises also a man, and draws a circle around the circle we had just pronounced the outline of the sphere. Then already is our first speaker no man, but only a first speaker. . . . Every man is not so much a workman in the world, as he is a suggestion of that he should be" (405). Here, as in the passage quoted from "Art," something gets to matter because someone for a moment *makes* it matter: "The figure a poem makes," is also "a momentary stay." It is in no sense a yearning for one of Eliot's "still points."

In the Emersonian tradition wherein Frost chose to locate himself, there is at last nothing to rely on except what may be discovered in and during the course of an individual action—like writing a poem or reading a poem, like working in a bean field in order, with Thoreau in *Walden,* "to know beans"; by the act of lovemaking or the fashioning of an ax-helve or in "the prayer of the rower kneeling with the stroke of the oar," to quote Emerson's "Self-Reliance" (276). As Emerson gets round to acknowledging in that essay, to talk even of the "self," as if it had an existence prior to an act, is "a poor external way of speaking. Speak rather," he says, "of that which relies because it works and is" (272). You discover what it is you may rely on only in the doing of it. In language less transcendental than Emerson's, James asks in "Humanism and Truth": "must not something end by supporting itself?" And he answers, in figures Frost would admire, that

> humanism is willing to let finite experience be self-supporting. Somewhere being must immediately breast nonentity. Why may not the advancing front of experience, carrying its immanent satisfactions and dissatisfactions, cut against the black inane as the luminous orb of the moon cuts the caerulean abyss? Why should anywhere the world be absolutely fixed and finished? And if reality genuinely grows, why may it not grow in these very determinations which here and now are made? (*The Meaning of Truth,* 55)

Such "determinations" include the "work" represented in—and also by—such poems as "Mowing," "The Tuft of Flowers," "After Apple Picking," "Putting in the Seed," "The Ax-Helve," "Two Tramps in Mud Time," even the digging of the child's grave in "Home Burial." "Mowing"—the first of what Frost called his "talk songs," written as early as 1905 and a poem he felt he might never surpass—may stand for his poems of work and the work going on in his poems:

There was never a sound beside the wood but one,
And that was my long scythe whispering to the ground.
What was it it whispered? I knew not well myself;
Perhaps it was something about the heat of the sun,
Something, perhaps, about the lack of sound—
And that was why it whispered and did not speak.
It was no dream of the gift of idle hours,
Or easy gold at the hand of fay or elf:
Anything more than the truth would have seemed too weak
To the earnest love that laid the swale in rows,
Not without feeble-pointed spikes of flowers
(Pale orchises), and scared a bright green snake.
The fact is the sweetest dream that labor knows.
My long scythe whispered and left the hay to make.

The line that is likely to matter most to us is not the last but the penultimate one, set off like an aphorism from the rest of the poem. The line is not "whispered" by the scythe, which is afterward still trying to say *something,* nor is the word "labor" a reference to the cutting of hay, since at the end the speaker has "left the hay to make." It aspires to become "one of the proverbs of nations." This is what, in the "Language" section of *Nature,* Emerson called "make hay while the sun shines," citing it as an example of how proverbs "consist usually of a natural fact" (24).

The Frost family at Franconia.

The people along the sand
All turn and look one way.
They turn their back on the land.
They look at the sea all day.

As long as it takes to pass
A ship keeps raising its hull;
The wetter ground like glass
Reflects a standing gull.

The land may vary more;
But wherever the truth may be—
The water comes ashore,
And the people look at the sea.

They cannot look out far.
They cannot look in deep.
But when was that ever a bar
To any watch they keep?

—Robert Frost, *Neither Out Far Nor In Deep*

So that the "fact" which is said to be "the sweetest dream that labor knows" is most likely the poem itself; the more so because the language of the poem is so clearly anxious to exorcise "poetic" falsifications. The "dream" is explicitly not of "easy gold," as it would be if borrowed effortlessly from Palgrave's *Golden Treasury;* and Marvell's "The Mower against Gardens" would not be expected to "scare a bright green snake." In 1916, in an interview reprinted in Edward Lathem's *Interviews with Robert Frost,* Frost remarks that "anything you do to facts falsifies them, but anything the facts do to you—yes, even against your will; yes, resist them with all your strength—transforms them into poetry" (18–21). Quite audibly, Frost plays on the idea of not "doing" anything to the "facts," as note the half-comic interrogation about the sound of the scythe, the admission that he did not know what, if anything, it was saying, his joke about its not wanting to raise its voice, or especially his disinclination to get agitated about its meaning: "perhaps something . . . something perhaps." "Earnest" is not meant to suggest that the poem or the mowing is to be taken solemnly, but rather that the "love" that laid the "swale in rows" (or that "laid" the lines of poem, as Frost liked to say) is a pledge, an assurance of something to follow.

What is apt to be most affecting about the poem is that it insists on reducing its promises to a minimum. It exploits the trope of "the thing in itself" which is also eloquently doing its job in the last line of "Hyla Brook" ("We love the things we love for what they are") or in the last lines of "The Oven Bird" ("The question that it asks in all but words / Is what to make of a diminished thing"). The only promise made in "Mowing" is in that gnomic next-to-last line, a line which only promises to *be* promising. We might be reminded here of how often the poems leave us in this way, suspended between hope and nothing at all. Thus, even as the apple picker falls more deeply than he has fallen all day into sleep and dreams, his "long two-pointed ladder" is "still" there, in the first line and in the deserted field, "sticking through a tree / Toward heaven still." We know from "Education by Poetry" that such a ladder is an image for Frost of how metaphor, two things in tandem that can never become one thing, projects us beyond either, or both together, into the unknown. "We still ask boys in college to think, as in the nineties, but we seldom tell them what thinking means; we seldom tell them it is just putting this and that together; it is just saying one thing in terms of another. To tell them to set their feet on the first rung of a ladder the top of which sticks through the sky" (Lathem and Thompson, 336).

The engendering power of "work" in Frost and in his Emersonian lineage attends upon a vision of the world that is often frighteningly blank, the "rock" of Emerson's essay "Experience" (490) or of Stevens's great poem "The Rock" or "the boulder-broken beach" from which the man of Frost's "The Most of It" would, of a morning, "cry out on life." Instead of finding himself at what James, in "Pragmatism and Religion," calls "our turning-places, where we seem to ourselves to make ourselves and

I never dared be radical when young
For fear it would make me conservative when old.

grow" (*Prag.,* 138), the poet in Frost can, by the same individualistic virtue, find himself in "Desert Places" where he is "too absent spirited to count," a line which, I suspect, is an intended echo of one from Stevens who, in an equivalent situation of psychic and imaginative barrenness, confesses that "I am too dumbly in my spirit pent" ("The Man Whose Pharynx Was Bad"). "The universal cataract of death / That spends to nothingness," in "West-Running Brook" is said to be "unresisted, / Save by some strange resistance in itself," and in Frost, as in Emerson, "resistance" to the consciousness of death or of imaginative impoverishment and impotence, is precariously expressed in efforts to be "at home in the metaphor," even while admitting, with James, that "finite experience as such is homeless," that outside the making of form there is, to recall Frost's Amherst letter, only "black and utter chaos." At the level of

There was a Boy: ye knew him well, ye cliffs
And islands of Winander!—many a time
At evening, when the earliest stars began
To move along the edges of the hills,
Rising or setting, would he stand alone
Beneath the trees or by the glimmering lake,
And there, with fingers interwoven, both hands
Pressed closely palm to palm, and to his mouth
Uplifted, he, as through an instrument,
Blew mimic hootings to the silent owls,
That they might answer him; and they would shout
Across the watery vale, and shout again,
Responsive to his call, with quivering peals,
And long halloos and screams, and echoes loud,
Redoubled and redoubled, concourse wild
Of jocund din; and, when a lengthened pause
Of silence came and baffled his best skill,
Then sometimes, in that silence while he hung
Listening, a gentle shock of mild surprise
Has carried far into his heart the voice
Of mountain torrents; or the visible scene
Would enter unawares into his mind,
With all its solemn imagery, its rocks,
Its woods, and that uncertain heaven, received
Into the bosom of the steady lake.

—William Wordsworth, from "The Prelude," Book VI

He thought he kept the universe alone;
For all the voice in answer he could wake
Was but the mocking echo of his own
From some tree-hidden cliff across the lake.
Some morning from the boulder-broken beach
He would cry out on life, that what it wants
Is not its own love back in copy speech,
But counter-love, original response.
And nothing ever came of what he cried
Unless it was the embodiment that crashed
In the cliff's talus on the other side,
And then in the far distant water splashed.
But after a time allowed for it to swim,
Instead of proving human when it neared
And someone else additional to him,
As a great buck it powerfully appeared,
Pushing the crumpled water up ahead,
And landed pouring like a waterfall,
And stumbled through the rocks with horny tread,
And forced the underbrush—and that was all.

—Robert Frost, "The Most of It"

"The Most of It" . . . is almost a dialogue with Wordsworth. In Wordsworth's "Prelude" there is a section in which the young boy awakens echoes . . .

—Seamus Heaney in a *Voices & Visions* interview

words—which in life, and not just in poetry, is where things begin and end—you therefore forgo any expectations of "some illuminating or power-bringing word or name," the "solving names" to which James alludes in "What Pragmatism Means." You inescapably use those names and words, like God or Reality or Energy, and they occur frequently enough in Emerson and in James himself, in Frost and Stevens. But, James continues with his sturdy audacity, "you cannot look on any such word as closing your quest." You can only "set it at work within the stream of your experience. It appears less as a solution then, than as a program for more work" (*Prag.,* 31–32).

SUBMITTED FOR BLINDMAN PRIZE.

FROM THE JOURNAL OF CRISPIN

I.

THE WORLD WITHOUT IMAGINATION

Nota: Man is the intelligence of his soil,
The sovereign ghost. As such, the Socrates
Of snails, musician of pears, principium
And lex. Sed quaeritur: Is this same wig
Of things, this nincompated pedagogue,
The sceptre of the unregenerate sea?
Crispin at sea creates a touch of doubt.
An eye most apt in gelatines and jupes,
Berries of villages, a barber's eye,
This eye of land, of simple salad-beds,
Of honest quilts, the eye of Crispin, hangs
On porpoises, that hung on apricots,
And on silentious porpoises, whose snouts
Dibble in waves that are mustachios,
Inscrutable hair in an inscrutable world.

One eats one paté, even of salt, quotha.
It is not so much that one's mythology
Is blotched by the sea. It was a boresome book,
From which one trilled orations of the west,
Based on the prints of Jupiter. Rostrum.

WALLACE STEVENS

HELEN VENDLER

> **To see the gods dispelled in mid-air and dissolve like clouds is one of the great human experiences.**
>
> —*Opus Posthumous,* 206

Wallace Stevens distinguished his twentieth-century version of the twilight of the Gods from Norse and Greek versions:

> It is not as if they had gone over the horizon to disappear for a time; nor as if they had been overcome by other gods of greater power and profounder knowledge. It is simply that they came to nothing.

The extinction of religious belief represented for Stevens a crisis of the imagination, which had possessed, in the past, various therapeutic, solacing, and inspiriting notions (those of God, heaven and hell, eternity, omnipotence, transcendence, Incarnation, and so on) which it had now to do without. "It was their annihilation," Stevens writes of the gods, "not ours, and yet it left us feeling dispossessed and alone in a solitude, like children without parents, in a house that seemed deserted." For many writers, the sense of religious loss provoked a religious nostalgia. Stevens thought this a false position. The gods are remembered, of course, because they are represented in our art and literature: "they had been a part of the glory of the earth. At the same time, no man ever muttered a petition in his heart for the restoration of those unreal shapes" (*OP,* 206–07).[1]

The essay "Two or Three Ideas," from which I have been quoting, was published in 1951, when Stevens was seventy-two. It rephrases Stevens's most famous early poem, "Sunday Morning," composed in 1915, when Stevens was thirty-six. The poem describes and quotes from a woman who deliberately does not go to church, because she knows Jesus was not divine; she knows that the Resurrection of Jesus, on which the worship of Jesus as God is based, never happened:

> The tomb in Palestine
> Is not the porch of spirits lingering.
> It is the grave of Jesus, where he lay.
>
> (*CP,* 70)

Wallace Stevens at Harvard, 1900.

Stevens never wavered in his conviction that the momentous change in human consciousness caused by disbelief in the supernatural implied a new conception of man and of art alike:

> There was always in every man the increasingly human self, which instead of remaining the observer, the non-participant, the delinquent, became constantly more and more all there was or so it seemed; and whether it was so or seemed so still left it for him to resolve life and the world on his own terms. (*OP,* 207)

To resolve life and the world, the private and the public, on his own terms is, as Stevens said, the work of everyone who has ceased to believe in commandments and conceptions prescribing God's terms for approved resolutions of life and the world. "Most people stand by the aid of philosophy, religion and one thing or another, but a strong spirit . . . stands by its own strength," Stevens wrote in 1940 (*L,* 348). The task of standing by one's own strength is for Stevens not a cognitive or religious act, but an imaginative one, the work of the arts. As painters turned from representing Annunciations and Nativities to landscapes, still lifes, and genre scenes; as composers turned from Masses and Sunday cantatas to symphonies and opera; so the poets, Stevens believed, had to turn from the poetry of heaven to the poetry of earth:

Poetry

Exceeding music must take the place
Of empty heaven and its hymns.

(*CP,* 167)

In dismissing the religious attitudes of the past, while still admiring the imaginative efforts they had elicited and the imaginative works they had produced, Stevens was also implicitly dismissing the European past and inscribing himself among the ranks of Emersonian Americans, striking out for a new beginning on new terrain:

The heaven of Europe is empty, like a Schloss
Abandoned because of taxes. . . .
It ceased to exist, became
A Schloss, and empty Schlossbibliothek, the books
For sale in Vienna and Zurich to people in Maine, Ontario,
Canton.

(*OP,* 53)

The abandoned castle and empty aristocratic library suggest the bankruptcy of European culture after the debacle of World War I. Like Eliot, Stevens felt keenly the end of the cultural ascendancy of Europe; but he accepted it with more buoyancy and more ironic humor than Eliot could manage. Stevens never once in his long life visited Europe (though he bought European books and, sight unseen through a dealer, French paintings). None of our modern poets, except for Eliot, is more European in cultural possession than Stevens (he had none of Pound's need to assume an aggressively American public manner); but in spite of his ease with European thought and taste, Stevens is resolutely American in his poetics. As he grew older, his investigations of both modern consciousness and American poetics deepened and broadened, embodying themselves in memorable poems of what it is to live in a world without gods, and what it is to be a poet writing in America.

I want to quote two of his late poems before going back to Stevens's beginnings. The first of these, "The Planet on the Table," is Stevens's farewell to his own life and work. This poem assumes that art resembles life, and that in the poet's little world we can see the great world reproduced and immortalized point for point, though in a compact and stylized form. Stevens's image for that form is the teacher's terrestrial globe, "the planet on the table" from which one learns elementary geography. "Here is Africa; here is the North Pole," says the teacher, and we agree, though we know that Africa is not a tiny pink triangle and that the North Pole is in fact invisible. So too the poet describes what he has remembered and loved, and we assent though we know he has stylized in reduced poetic tropes and lines his memories and his affections. The creations of nature, Stevens reminds us, die and rot; but the creations of the poet keep the world he lived in alive and visible, if in a miniaturized form:

THE PLANET ON THE TABLE

Ariel was glad he had written his poems.
They were of a remembered time
Or of something seen that he liked.

Other makings of the sun
Were waste and welter
And the ripe shrub writhed.

His self and the sun were one
And his poems, although makings of his self,
Were no less makings of the sun.

It was not important that they survive.
What mattered was that they should bear
Some lineament or character,

Some affluence, if only half-perceived,
In the poverty of their words,
Of the planet of which they were part.

(*CP*, 532–33)

The point of departure for this poem was probably the work Stevens did in choosing the pieces to be included in his *Selected Poems* (Faber and Faber, 1953). For the first time, Stevens reviewed all he had done, and envisaged what his American publisher had suggested in 1952, a *Collected Poems*—his life's work

. . . Swiftly in the nights,
In the porches of Key West,
Behind the bougainvilleas,
After the guitar is asleep,
Lasciviously as the wind,
You come tormenting,
Insatiable,

When you might sit,
A scholar of darkness,
Sequestered over the sea,
Wearing a clear tiara
Of red and blue and red,
Sparkling, solitary, still,
In the high sea-shadow.

Donna, donna, dark,
Stooping in indigo gown
And cloudy constellations,
Conceal yourself or disclose
Fewest things to the lover—
A hand that bears a thick-leaved fruit,
A pungent bloom against your shade.

—From "O Florida, Venereal Soil"

lying on the table in one book. (In 1954, Stevens finally agreed to a collected volume; when it appeared in 1955, it won both the National Book Award and the Pulitzer Prize.) In "The Planet on the Table," Stevens calls himself by the name of Shakespeare's airy singing nature-spirit, Ariel. And although he sees clearly that the planet on the table cannot equal (given the poverty of its means) the greater planet in the cosmos, he hopes for an accurate analogy between them, so that in the lesser planet his reader can recognize the greater one.

It is characteristic of Stevens's late simplicity that this poem should be naively constructed around families of letters. "S" stands for nature (self, sun, something seen); "W" stands for rot (waste, welter, writhed); and "P"—for poem—is the letter of art (perceived, poverty, planet, poems, part). It is also characteristic of Stevens, always, to be allusive—remembering here not only Shakespeare's *Tempest* but also, in a corrective way, Wordsworth's "Tintern Abbey." In that poem, Wordsworth refers to the "mighty world / Of eye and ear—both what they half create, and what perceive"—a famous formulation. Stevens suggests that we only half perceive (and therefore can only half create) the affluence of that world.

The great claim of this poem is one that is modestly made, and modestly hidden in the middle of the verse: "His self and the sun were one." There is, in short, no nature independent of man's perception of nature; though the noumenon may exist, only phenomena can be represented. It is for that reason that each artist's record of perceived phenomena is precious:

> The people in the world, and the objects in it, and the world as a whole, are not absolute things, but, on the contrary, are the phenomena of perception. . . . If we were all alike; if we were millions of people saying do, re, mi in unison, one poet would be enough. . . . But we are not all alike, and everything needs expounding all the time because, as people live and die, each one perceiving life and death for himself, and mostly by and in himself, there develops a curiosity about the perceptions of others. This is what makes it possible to go on saying new things about old things. (*OP,* 266–67)

The "old things" about which Stevens said new things include the disappointments of erotic love, the attachment to a particular region, the apprehensions of old age, and, above all, the change of seasons—both "the human seasons" (Keats's phrase) and the climatic ones. The second late poem I want to quote is one about Stevens's Connecticut, the state where he lived for almost forty years. The name "Connecticut" means "land of the great river," and here Stevens writes of the Farmington River, one of the tributaries of the Connecticut, near which he had lived for most of his adult life. The river is an old symbol for the current of life; Stevens opposes his "river of rivers in Connecticut" to the mythological river Styx, over which Charon ferries souls to Hades or, as Stevens calls it here, Stygia. The poem is the hymn of thanksgiving of a man returned to life after a glimpse of the shores of death:

THE RIVER OF RIVERS IN CONNECTICUT

There is a great river this side of Stygia,
Before one comes to the first black cataracts
And trees that lack the intelligence of trees.

In that river, far this side of Stygia,
The mere flowing of the water is a gayety,
Flashing and flashing in the sun. On its banks,

No shadow walks. The river is fateful,
Like the last one. But there is no ferryman.
He could not bend against its propelling force.

It is not to be seen beneath the appearances
That tell of it. The steeple at Farmington
Stands glistening and Haddam shines and sways.

It is the third commonness with light and air,
A curriculum, a vigor, a local abstraction . . .
Call it, once more, a river, an unnamed flowing,

Space-filled, reflecting the seasons, the folk-lore
Of each of the senses; call it, again and again,
The river that flows nowhere, like a sea.

(*CP,* 533)

Stevens has here re-presented the ancient cosmic struggle of light against darkness, consciousness against blankness, breath against death. Gradually, in the poem, the black shades of Stygia recede, and the vigor of the river of life flashes brilliantly again. Yet at the end, the mythological dark and the physical light alike flow into the nowhere of nonexistence.

"To me," Stevens wrote, "poetry is not a literary activity: it is a vital activity. . . . The good writers are the good thinkers. They are not able and skillful ink-slingers but people who put all they have into what they say in writing" (*L,* 815). In "putting all he had" into praising the American river, Stevens was doing for his landscape what Wordsworth had done in "Tintern Abbey" in praising the English river Wye:

How oft—
In darkness and amid the many shapes
Of joyless daylight; when the fretful stir
Unprofitable, and the fever of the world,
Have hung upon the beatings of my heart—
How oft, in spirit, have I turned to thee,
O sylvan Wye! thou wanderer through the woods,
How often has my spirit turned to thee!

Stevens, c. 1916.

For Stevens, it was important that the American landscape should have its poetry, just as the English landscape had. Otherwise, without its cloud of cultural representation (poems, paintings, music), the soil of the world would be encountered by each new generation as an uninhabited and dead terrain. Without the artist, says Stevens in "Somnambulisma,"

The ocean, falling and falling on the hollow shore,

Would be a geography of the dead: not of that land
To which they may have gone, but of the place in which
They lived, in which they lacked a pervasive being.

(*CP,* 304)

We have only to imagine what it would be to be born in a world with no past—no architecture, no music, no tradition, no literature at all—to know why Stevens considers the act of art a vital one. Only by inheriting, interpreting, and refashioning culture can we possess a deepened human identity.

In borrowing Charon, the Styx, and the blackness of Hades from Greek mythology, Stevens connects his poem to the Western past; in making it a hymn to American natural force and beauty, he confers on the Farmington River the dignity that European poets have given the Tiber or the Thames. Stevens continues here Longfellow's poetic program for bestowing literary interest on the American landscape. Just as Longfellow wrote "Hiawatha" to give Indian narrative the folk significance of the *Kalevala,* "The Wreck of the Schooner Hesperus" to memorialize native events and give ghosts to the New England shore, and "The Jewish Cemetery at Newport" (in Thomas Gray's quatrains) to create an American "Elegy in a Country Churchyard," so Stevens attempts to fill in the blanks on the American map, writing here about Connecticut, elsewhere about his Pennsylvania Dutch ancestors and his summers at Ephrata in Pennsylvania, placing poems in Mississippi and Tennessee and Florida and New England, commemorating other rivers like the Swatara and the Perkiomen. The poet is to "Call it, once more . . . / call it, again and again," by name, the physical landscape in which he finds himself:

One of the limits of reality
Presents itself in Oley when the hay,
Baked through long days, is piled in mows. It is
A land too ripe for enigmas, too serene.

(*CP,* 374)

These late poems, in which Stevens glances at his physical world, show his deepest American self. But when he came of age at the turn of the century his first models were the British poets taught in school—Shakespeare, Wordsworth, Keats, Shelley, and Browning. On the English influences were grafted, when Stevens went to college, the French symbolists, visible in the last and most accomplished poems he published in Harvard literary journals. (At Harvard, Stevens became the president of the *Advocate,* the literary magazine, and of the Signet, the literary society.) In college, Stevens came under the influence of the skeptical Spanish-born poet and philosopher George Santayana (1863–1952), who was teaching philosophy at Harvard while Stevens was in residence (1897–1900). The courtly civilized verses of Longfellow—the first American poet commemorated in the Poets' Corner of Westminster Abbey—still represented the notion of poetry acceptable to the genteel tradition in American letters: Robert Frost, after all, borrowed from Longfellow the title of his first book, *A Boy's Will,* as well as a good deal of his early technique.

Stevens spent only three years at Harvard. He had enrolled, by his father's wish, as a special student rather than as a degree candidate, since it was then possible to enter law school without a college degree, and the elder Stevens, himself a lawyer without a college education, sent his three sons into his own profession. Stevens hoped at first, when he left Harvard, for a career as a writer or journalist, but after one discouraging year, he realized that to earn a living he had to find a profession, and he entered New York Law School. He passed the bar in 1904 and met, on a trip home to Pennsylvania, the young woman six years his junior, wholly uneducated, whom he married in 1909. He had failed in a law partnership and in working for various law firms, but in 1908 he had found more secure employment with the legal staff of the American Bonding Company, an insurance firm. He remained in the insurance world for the rest of his life, moving in 1916 to the Hartford Accident and Indemnity Company, where, at the time of his death at seventy-five, he was a vice-president.

Stevens's mature style, in his long poems especially, may show the effect of his legal training and legal writing. The deliberate, ceremonious, and Latinate phrases of legal briefs and judicial decisions—with their qualifications and exceptions, their parentheses and backward glances—seem to have been congenial to Stevens, enough so that he could write, for instance, a passage like these lines from "A Primitive Like an Orb":

The central poem is the poem of the whole,
The poem of the composition of the whole,
The composition of blue sea and of green,
Of blue light and of green, as lesser poems,
And the miraculous multiplex of lesser poems,
Not merely into a whole, but a poem of
The whole, the essential compact of the parts,
The roundness that pulls tight the final ring

And that which in an altitude would soar
A vis, a principle, or, it may be,
The meditation of a principle,
Or else an inherent order active to be
Itself.

(*CP,* 442)

Some readers have found Stevens's deliberateness in this vein maddening and ponderous; this is only one of his many styles, but it is the one that may have been encouraged by the law.

Stevens waited a long time—until 1923, when he was forty-four—to publish his first book, *Harmonium.* It is a book as famous now, in the history of modern American poetry, as Eliot's *Prufrock* (1917) or Moore's *Observations* (1924). And Stevens was to say later that he liked some things in *Harmonium* as much as anything he had done later. The most ambitious poem in this first volume was a long Browningesque autobiographical narrative called "The Comedian as the Letter C." Stevens's skeptical and ironic humor acts as an astringent force throughout this narrative of its hero's life-voyage. Crispin, the hero, originally from France, leaves Europe behind and journeys to the New World, first to Yucatan and then, leaving the tropics behind, to North America, marrying and settling down like Voltaire's Candide to cultivate his garden and rear his four daughters. The poem proposes Stevens's lifelong belief that the poet's lot is the common lot ("Beginning with green brag, / Concluding fadedly"), but its chief energy is spent on rejecting European aestheticism and asserting that all poetry must be native to its region:

The man in Georgia waking among pines
Should be pine-spokesman. The responsive man,
Planting his pristine cores in Florida
Should prick thereof, not on the psaltery,
But on the banjo's categorical gut

(*CP,* 38)

True to his own prescription, Stevens called a later *ars poetica* "The Man with the Blue Guitar"—an instrument he connected with folk music. American music could be played on the unpretentious little harmonium, or the guitar or banjo, but not on the psaltery or lyre of Europe. If the American poet sat down to a European instrument like the clavier, he would play it, as the title of one of Stevens's early poems implies, like Shakespeare's Peter Quince, one of the "rude mechanicals" in *A Midsummer Night's Dream.*

Like other American poets influenced by the *chinoiserie* of Imagism, Stevens turned for a time from Western models to Eastern ones, and wrote his set of serial "views" after the manner of Chinese and Japanese painters, calling his set "Thirteen Ways of Looking at a Blackbird." In writing this poem, Stevens discovered his affinity for the aspectual poem—a series of variations on a theme. It was only later that he formulated his theoretical base for that form—his conviction that there is no such thing as unitary verity—"the" truth, or "a" truth, but only endless aspects of reality:

> It was when I said,
> "There is no such thing as the truth,"
> That the grapes seemed fatter.
> The fox ran out of his hole.
>
> You . . . You said,
> "There are many truths,
> But they are not parts of a truth."
>
> . . .
>
> You said,
> "The idols have seen lots of poverty,
> Snakes and gold and lice,
> But not the truth";
>
> It was at that time, that the silence was largest
> And longest, the night was roundest,
> The fragrance of the autumn warmest,
> Closest and strongest.

(*CP,* 203–04)

This is Stevens's baldest statement about the inadequacy of all religions, each of which claims either to be "the" truth or part of "a" truth. Truths, for Stevens, are many; and they are not hierarchical parts of "a" truth, but rather coordinate fellow-equals. The formal equivalent to this aspectual view of cognition is the sequence or the assembly of variations, the form Stevens always adapted (after his one experiment in narrative in "The Comedian") for his long poems:

Stevens in Elizabeth Park, 1922.

I said,
"Words are not forms of a single word.
In the sum of the parts, there are only the parts.
The world must be measured by eye"

(*CP,* 204)

Each of the "parts" of "Thirteen Ways of Looking at a Blackbird" is equally valid. Visual experience, measuring the world by eye, thus becomes the equable model (since we do not privilege one glance over another) for modern perception and cognition alike. Implication, innuendo, eccentricity of perspective, and summary aphorism become the condensed vehicles for Stevens's multiple "ways of looking":

I was of three minds,
Like a tree
In which there are three blackbirds.

(*CP,* 92)

As Stevens perceives a new naked sharp angularity in his aspectual aesthetic, he comes to identify that nakedness, angularity, and eccentricity of view with America itself. Many of the poems in *Harmonium* and later volumes attempt to define the predicament of the American poet. How is the poet to write of our American eroticism, which cannot draw from the elaborate Petrarchan erotic heritage of Europe? Botticelli's Venus arose from the sea borne on a shell, wearing drapery of royal purple on her arms—but our goddess is new and raw, a "paltry nude," as she begins her spring voyage:

> But not on a shell, she starts,
> Archaic, for the sea.
> But on the first-found weed
> She scuds the glitters,
> Noiselessly, like one more wave.
>
> She too is discontent
> And would have purple stuff upon her arms
>
> (*CP,* 5)

In another poem, Stevens represents America as an oafish male giant, needing to be civilized by Muses or Graces who will "whisper / Heavenly labials in a world of gutturals. / It will undo him" (*CP,* 7).

But Stevens could not remain in a world of heavenly labials, not in the American wilderness. He tries, in another famous poem, to "place a jar in Tennessee," exalting art over nature; but he discovers that the jar is ill at ease in its wild setting: "It did not give of bird or bush / Like nothing else in Tennessee" (*CP,* 76). Flights back to European aesthetics are of no help; in another comic version of the tropical American poet's predicament, Stevens asks what "floral decorations" would suit as accompaniments for that native American fruit, "bananas hacked and hunched":

> These insolent, linear peels
> And sullen, hurricane shapes
> Won't do with your eglantine. . . .
>
> Pile the bananas on planks . . .
>
> And deck the bananas in leaves
> Plucked from the Carib trees,
> Fibrous and dangling down,
> Oozing cantankerous gum
> Out of their purple maws.
>
> (*CP,* 53–54)

Many of the poems in *Harmonium* were what we would now call "conceptual poetry"—a kind of poetry in which the aim is not so much to produce a "beautiful poem" as to question what a "beautiful poem," these days, could possibly be. In the comic

"Anecdote of the Jar," for instance, Stevens deliberately makes each of his quatrains and rhymes formally inept and farcical, as though the American poet, vainly trying to integrate his stoneware "urn" with his wilderness, could only do prosodic pratfalls, scrawls defacing the classic British quatrain form:

ANECDOTE OF THE JAR

I placed a jar in Tennessee,
And round it was, upon a hill.
It made the slovenly wilderness
Surround that hill.

The wilderness rose up to it,
And sprawled around, no longer wild.
The jar was round upon the ground
And tall and of a port in air.

It took dominion everywhere.
The jar was gray and bare.
It did not give of bird or bush,
Like nothing else in Tennessee.

(*CP,* 76)

Such a poem repudiates the elegance of Stevens's borrowed British pentameters in "Sunday Morning" and "Le Monocle de Mon Oncle," and initiates his lifelong search for a flexible American meter, roughly iambic but no longer visibly reminiscent of Shakespeare, Keats, and Wordsworth. Stevens eventually found his new measure, both in long lines and short. We hear it in its long "pentameter" form in late poems like "The Rock," a poem he wrote about turning seventy, when he looked far back disbelievingly to sixty years earlier, when he was a child, and forty years earlier, when he married: both the dawn of life and the noon of life (the sexual embrace) seem chimerical now, in the "permanent cold" of age: even the poet's guitar seems an illusion:

SEVENTY YEARS LATER

It is an illusion that we were ever alive,
Lived in the houses of mothers, arranged ourselves
By our own motions in a freedom of air.

Regard the freedom of seventy years ago.
It is no longer air. The houses still stand,
Though they are rigid in rigid emptiness.

Even our shadows, their shadows, no longer remain.
The lives these lived in the mind are at an end.
They never were . . . The sounds of the guitar

Were not and are not. Absurd. The words spoken
Were not and are not. It is not to be believed.
The meeting at noon at the edge of the field seems like

An invention, an embrace between one desperate clod
And another in a fantastic consciousness,
In a queer assertion of humanity:

A theorem proposed between the two—
Two figures in a nature of the sun,
In the sun's design of its own happiness

(*CP,* 525)

We hear the music of the English pentameter as a ghost behind Stevens's free tercets; but he has found his own large-limbed American rhythms by which to move, and his own loose adaptation of Shelleyan *terza rima* in his tercets. "Nothing," said Stevens, "could be more inappropriate to American literature than its English source since the Americans are not British in sensibility" (*OP,* 176). We see him in poems like "Anecdote of the Jar" and "The Rock"—one from early in his career, one from his last decade—coping always, in different ways, with the difficulty of making the American sensibility and the American language present in a genuinely non-British way.

The poems published in *Harmonium* (1923) had been written between 1915 and 1922, but they do not show any impact from World War I, because Stevens did not include in his book some early poems (later published with other juvenilia in *Opus Posthumous*) that had the war as their subject. World War I was not fought by Stevens's generation but by younger men; and Stevens, living in America, was not exposed to the physical aftermath of the war in the way that Eliot and Pound, living in London, were. It was not until the thirties, in the Depression, that Stevens found himself thinking a great deal about the social function, and the social value, of poetry. At first, in "Mozart, 1935," he urged the poet, rather lamely, to be "the voice of angry fear / The voice of this besieging pain":

Poet, be seated at the piano.
Play the present, its hoo-hoo-hoo,
Its shoo-shoo-shoo, its ric-a-nic,
Its envious cachinnation.

(*CP,* 131–32)

Here, as always in Stevens, nonsense syllables stand for a ground of being—pure sound—as yet unarticulated into intelligible language. In this passage, the nonsense syllables, as Stevens's draft shows, are derived from the French words for

"Village Carnival" by Paul Klee.

. . . Suppose these houses are composed of ourselves,
So that they become an impalpable town, full of
Impalpable bells, transparencies of sound,

Sounding in transparent dwellings of the self,
Impalpable habitations that seem to move
In the movement of the colors of the mind, . . .

Confused illuminations and sonorities,
So much ourselves, we cannot tell apart
The idea and the bearer-being of the idea. . . .

—From "An Ordinary Evening in New Haven"

"howling," "whispering," and "sneering": "ses hurlements / ses chuchotements, ses ricanements." (I have corrected Stevens's French as transcribed by Peter Brazeau, in *Parts of a World,* 104). Sometimes the ground of being is the ocean, which "howls hoo and rises and howls hoo and falls": sometimes it is the wind, roaring, seeking for articulation in speech:

What syllable are you seeking,
Vocalissimus,
In the distances of sleep?
Speak it.

(*CP,* 113)

This address "To the Roaring Wind" was the poem that closed *Harmonium.* Now, in "Mozart, 1935," the massed social noises join the unarticulated noises of nature, and the poet's burden of expression grows heavier. In his long poem on the social meaning of art, "Owl's Clover," which he thought (*L,* 311) of calling "Aphorisms on Society," Stevens takes as his example of a socially successful art the noble European sculptural theme of winged marble horses, figures like Pegasus, rearing upward. He places next to this aspiring statue the Depression figure of an old woman, destitute, near death, a "bitter mind in a flapping cloak," full of blackness and fear. She stands for suffering and mortality, torture and need. She disturbs the universe. The statue collapses in her presence. Nature itself cannot but acknowledge her rebuke:

Without her, evening like a budding yew
Would still be brilliant, as it was, before
The harridan self and ever-maladive fate
Went crying their desolate syllables, before
Their voice and the voice of the tortured wind were one.

(*OP,* 45)

Stevens's poetry had been criticized for remoteness from the social scene by Stanley Burnshaw, reviewing Stevens's *Parts of a World* in the socialist journal *New Masses* (October 1, 1935). The review had stung Stevens sufficiently so that he retorted in "Owl's Clover," satirizing the Marxist concept of a populist art of social realism. Will we see, in place of the statue, Stevens asks, "bare and blunt" stones, carved, "The Mass Appoints These Marbles Of Itself To Be Itself"? Will we listen to "the latest Soviet reclame," "Concerto for Airplane and Pianoforte"? (*OP,* 48, 62). Poets are never, in this sense, "of the world in which they live": topicality and collectivity alone cannot form powerful art. And against the Marxist Utopian millennial view that the state will wither away and the dictatorship of the proletariat will be established, Stevens sets his bleaker view, a vision of the perpetual fall of all cultures. Stevens knows that all forms of art eventually die, including the European high art of the "white-maned horses' heads":

> A solemn voice, not Mr. Burnshaw's says:
> At some gigantic, solitary urn,
> A trash can at the end of the world, the dead
> Give up dead things and the living turn away. . . .
> There lies the head of the sculptor in which the thought
> Of lizards, in its eye, is more acute
> Than the thought that once was native to the skull;
> And there are the white-maned horses' heads, beyond
> The help of any wind or any sky:
> Parts of the immense detritus of a world
> That is completely waste, that moves from waste
> To waste, out of the hopeless waste of the past
> Into a hopeful waste to come.
>
> (*OP,* 49)

Stevens carried his social speculations further; of what relevance could the European marbles be to Africa, "the black sublime," "the greenest continent?" Pegasus is as impossible to imagine in Africa as Christianity is; and as Stevens faces the ruin or irrelevance of all culture, including his own, he sings a death chant to the Greek god of Fate: "Fatal Ananke is the common god."

Stevens eventually suppressed "Owl's Clover" from his *Collected Poems:* he had judged (*L,* 289) that it contained too many "stock figures (what is now called *Victorian ideology*)." Though the poem was too discursive to please Stevens as art, it formulated for him a press of social questions (the relation of the artist to society; the value of the art of the past; the obligation of art to be contemporary without being solely topical; the necessarily culture-bound nature of art) which he could never again ignore. These questions recur, stimulated by the giant crisis of World War II, in his later verse, and in the essays collected in *The Necessary Angel* (1951) and *Opus Posthumous* (1957). It is impossible to reduce Stevens's subtle and self-questioning prose to bare propositions, since the import of his essays lies as much in their manner—eddying, speculative, ironic—as in their matter. But some of his conclusions can be suggested.

Stevens concluded that we are all—whether we are poets or not—creatures who constantly construct a world, each of us perceiving a slightly (or enormously) different world from our fellows. Cultures differ from each other in the same way, as they construe the world differently, determining by their imagination how they dress, cook, draw, what they believe:

> The soul, he said, is composed
> Of the external world. . . .
>
> The dress of a woman of Lhassa,
> In its place,
> Is an invisible element of that place
> Made visible.
>
> (*CP,* 51–52)

The work of culture, abetted by tradition and change, goes on incessantly in a buzzing and blooming of consciousness. "Reality" is therefore, as the title of a late poem (*OP,* 110) puts it, "an activity of the most august imagination." There are not two poles, one called "Reality," the other "Imagination." There is only one. "Things seen are things as seen," as Stevens wrote in one of his *Adagia,* a series of aphorisms published in *Opus Posthumous* (*OP,* 162).

The thing seen changes at every moment, as poesis never ceases to occur, being the activity of consciousness itself. Culture changes over time and over space, and we are delighted as we see the variety of human cultural possibility. Art is only one version of culture; the dress of a woman of Lhasa is another

Officers of the Hartford Accident and Indemnity Company, 1938. Wallace Stevens is third from right, front row.

version. Both exhibit what Stevens would call "the poetry of the idea"; in addition, writing exhibits "the poetry of the words." Art is the version of culture that makes use of a specialized medium, and is consequently produced only by the few who can master the medium, and give to experience a symbolic form, incarnating it in an embodied shape. Because our cultural symbol for incarnation is the angel's annunciation to Mary, Stevens imagines the annunciation of form as the passage of an angel, too. His "necessary angel" speaks, emphasizing his human, nontranscendental being:

I am the angel of reality,
Seen for a moment standing at the door.

I have neither ashen wing nor wear of ore
And live without a tepid aureole,

Or stars that follow me, not to attend,
But, of my being and its knowing, part.

I am one of you and being one of you
Is being and knowing what I am and know.

Yet I am the necessary angel of earth,
Since, in my sight, you see the earth again,

Cleared of its stiff and stubborn, man-locked set,
And, in my hearing, you hear its tragic drone

Rise liquidly in liquid lingerings,
Like watery words awash; like meanings said

By repetitions of half-meanings. Am I not,
Myself, only half of a figure of a sort,

A figure half seen, or seen for a moment, a man
Of the mind, an apparition apparelled in

Apparels of such lightest look that a turn
Of my shoulder and quickly, too quickly, I am gone?

(*CP*, 496–97)

"There was a time," said Wordsworth in his Intimations Ode,

When meadow, grove, and stream,
The earth, and every common sight,
To me did seem
Apparelled in celestial light,
The glory and the freshness of a dream.
It is not now as it hath been of yore,
Turn whereso'er I may,
By night or day,
Those things which I have seen I now can see no more.

Wordsworth's lament for the lost apparel of celestial light is the classic locus of religious nostalgia in English poetry. Stevens announces, by his "apparition apparelled in / Apparels of such lightest look," that form itself, refreshing our vision and changing the drone of life to music, is the true glory of consciousness.

Stevens's poem on the angel was in fact suggested by a still life painted by the modern Breton artist Pierre Tal Coat. "The angel is the Venetian glass bowl on the left with the little spray of leaves in it. The peasants are the terrines, bottles and the glasses that surround it," Stevens wrote, describing the painting (*L,* 650). Stevens's conviction that poesis "leads to a fresh conception of the world" (*L,* 590) made him especially interested in the fresh conceptions of modern painting. His friend Walter Arensberg was a collector of modern art; the journal *The Dial*, edited by the poet Marianne Moore, regularly included photographs of new painting and sculpture; the Armory Show of 1913 had brought the inventions of modern art to the attention of everyone in the arts in New York. Stevens borrowed his figure of "The Man with the Blue Guitar" from Picasso; and his letters frequently express admiration for Klee, Brancusi, Duchamp, Cézanne, Modigliani, and others. Though he distrusted idle experimentation, Stevens was persuaded, as Williams and Crane and Moore were also, that modernist painters and sculptors were the medium of a new revelation of reality. "To a large extent," he wrote, "the problems of poets are the problems of painters, and poets must often turn to the literature of painting for a discussion of their own problems" (OP, 160).

In formulating his long *ars poetica,* "Notes Toward a Supreme Fiction," a didactic poem full of allegorical figuration, whimsical naming, and epigram, Stevens decided that any viable aesthetic invention—whether a cultural form like religious belief, or a form employing a medium, like poetry—must fulfill three conditions: "It Must Be Abstract," "It Must Change," and "It Must Give Pleasure." These are the three subheadings of his poem. By "It Must Be Abstract," Stevens means, as we would now say, "It Must be Stylized"—that is, it must have symbolic form, be in some way condensed, shaped, or focused by comparison with raw experience. By "It Must Change," he means "It Must Be of Its Moment"—that is, culture and art must derive constantly from contemporary history, and cannot be a stale repetition of past conceptions and past forms. And by "It Must Give Pleasure," Stevens signified his agreement with Coleridge, who had said in *Biographia Literaria* that poetry (and by extension all imaginative action) proposes as its immediate object pleasure, not truth.

If a cultural conception was accurately of its moment, had found realized form, and gave pleasure, it would satisfy the human mind, and would endure as long as its culture remained stable. Being of its moment, it would represent the human dimension of its age. It would be a production of the human, but of the human in its form of "Major Man," as Stevens called it —not man in a transcendent aspect, an aureoled angel, but rather man at his most acute and philosophic, and his most socially responsive, speaking for his whole culture and all his fellows:

> The major abstraction is the idea of man
> And major man is its exponent, abler
> In the abstract than in his singular,
>
> More fecund as principle than particle. . . .
>
> The major abstraction is the commonal,
> The inanimate, difficult visage. Who is it?
>
> (*CP,* 388)

The commonal is the unredeemed Chaplinesque common man, unable to articulate for himself a new culture, needing the philosophers, the statesmen, the scholars, and the artists to tell him who he is, to formulate his century for him:

> What rabbi, grown furious with human wish,
> What chieftain, walking by himself, crying
> Most miserable, most victorious,
>
> Does not see these separate figures one by one,
> And yet see only one, in his old coat,
> His slouching pantaloons, beyond the town,
>
> Looking for what was, where it used to be?
>
> (*CP,* 389)

This pantalooned *homme moyen,* helplessly caught in a nostalgia for the past, is a version of Crispin the clown, no longer elegant, only one of the ordinary masses. As Stevens continues, he speaks to the apprentice poet (called by his Greek name, the "ephebe") and explains to him his calling as an artist:

> Cloudless the morning. It is he. The man
> In that old coat, those sagging pantaloons,
>
> It is of him, ephebe, to make, to confect
> The final elegance, not to console
> Nor sanctify, but plainly to propound.
>
> (*CP,* 389)

Religion had wished to console the common man for his delinquency, to sanctify him into virtue. Stevens wishes instead to

"Still Life" *by Pierre Tal Coat. It was this painting by the Breton artist that inspired Stevens's poem. The "angel" is the Venetian glass bowl, the plainer vessels are the "paysans."*

. . . I have neither ashen wing nor wear of ore
And live without a tepid aureole,

Or stars that follow me, not to attend,
But, of my being and its knowing, part.

I am one of you and being one of you
Is being and knowing what I am and know.

Yet I am the necessary angel of earth,
Since, in my sight, you see the earth again,

Cleared of its stiff and stubborn, man-locked set, . . .

—From "Angel Surrounded by Paysans"

confect from the hapless ordinary the final elegance of major man—that man who has created the culture of Greece, the poetry of China, the order of Rome. To restore to man his human dignity, the poet needs to be at once beautiful and ordinary, learned and accessible.

> He tries by a peculiar speech to speak
>
> The peculiar potency of the general,
> To compound the imagination's Latin with
> The lingua franca et jocundissima.
>
> (*CP*, 397)

It is typical of Stevens's constitutive irony that he will name the speech of the populace by a Latin name (the "lingua franca et jocundissima") while referring to "the imagination's Latin" in English. The poet's Latin is English, his English is foreign; the medium has stylized the language.

Stevens's certainty that his only route toward communal authenticity was to render his own sense of the world as accurately as possible enabled him to write the imagination's Latin (especially in his complex long poems) without anxiety about the accessibility of his poetry to the ordinary reader. He did not live long enough to see his poetry generally understood; his fame came much later than the fame of Frost, Eliot, and Pound, even later than the fame of Williams. But he was confident that as long as his subject—how man reconceives culture—was one applying to everyone, he was writing of "common experience." If his language was uncommon—"Language [is] the material of poetry, not its mere medium or instrument" (*OP*, 171)—his subject was the broadest possible one.

Stevens's chief emotional crisis following his loss of faith ("Loss of faith is growth," *OP*, 172) was his disillusion in his marriage. Because he had fallen deeply—almost religiously—in love with the beauty of Elsie Moll, he persuaded himself that she must be a kindred spirit. But during the apparently incompatible marriage, she became withdrawn and reclusive. Though after fourteen years of marriage they had a daughter (named by Stevens "Holly Bright" because she was born near Christmas), Stevens and his wife seem to have become more estranged as the years of their marriage passed. There are some bitter poems in *Opus Posthumous* ("Red Loves Kit," "Good Man, Bad Woman," "The Woman Who Blamed Life on a Spaniard") about failed love:

> Your yes her no, your no her yes. The words
> Make little difference, for being wrong
> And wronging her, if only as she thinks,
> You never can be right. . . .
>
> That you are innocent
> And love her still, still leaves you in the wrong. . . .
> Her words accuse you of adulteries
> That sack the sun, though metaphysical.

True, you may love
And she have beauty of a kind, but such
Unhappy love reveals vast blemishes.

(*OP,* 30, 31)

When May came last
And [you] saw the blossoms, snow-bred pink and white,
Making your heart of brass to intercept
The childish onslaughts of such innocence,
Why was it that you cast the brass away
And bared yourself, and bared yourself in vain?
She can corrode your world, if never you.

(*OP,* 33)

Stevens's romantic idealization of his wife, so visible in all his early letters and poems to her during their courtship, led him, by its collapse, to realize that no faith is impregnable to ruin, no esteem impervious to contempt, no love insulated from change. "The mind," he wrote in "Man and Bottle," "Destroys romantic tenements / Of rose and ice" (*CP,* 238). The lover leaves the tropics of natural sensation and returns, bitter with self-laceration, to the homeless artifice of a hotel:

Home from Guatemala, back at the Waldorf.
This arrival in the wild country of the soul,
All approaches gone, being completely there,

Where the wild poem is a substitute
For the woman one loves or ought to love,
One wild rhapsody a fake for another.

(*CP,* 240)

Many of Stevens's poems concern "Desire and the Object"—as one late title puts it (*OP,* 85). Stevens's female characters run the gamut from the "innocent mother" (*CP,* 419) to the devouring death-mother "Madame La Fleurie" (*CP,* 507), from the bridally mimetic "prismy blonde" of Crispin to the evanescent "Woman in Sunshine," a pure creation of desire. There are many meditations on Venus and her doves, and a final terrible vision of a man who knows "desire without an object of desire / All mind and violence and nothing felt" (*CP,* 358). Stevens's personal retreat into a fairly unbroken inner solitude, reticence, and compositional intensity may be ascribed in part to his deep disappointment in desire. He never ceased meditating on the capacity of the mind for illusion—which is creation—and on the compulsions of desire. Increasingly, he wrote of the poverty of the world which we decorate and transform by desire, of "reality grimly seen," of "the total leaflessness" (*OP,* 475, 477). And yet, "the point of vision and desire are the same":

It is desire, set deep in the eye,
Behind all actual seeing, in the actual scene,
In the street, in a room, on a carpet or a wall,

Always in emptiness that would be filled.

(*CP,* 467)

"Inescapable romance, inescapable choice / Of dreams, disillusion as the last illusion" (*CP,* 468)—Stevens was far too reticent to address this theme in the first person. Writing in the third person, using a persona or simply saying "he," was the chief formal strategy, along with his joking titles, that he invented in order to sound different from his lyric predecessors, who had usually written of their desire and disillusion in the first person and with serious titles. To read Stevens, one has to substitute, at least provisionally, the pronoun "I" for "Professor Eucalyptus" or "the scholar" or "the planter" or "Ariel" or "the man with the blue guitar." These personae are inventions of Stevens's imaginative buoyancy, staving off the tragic implications of his cultural pessimism and skepticism. Stevens's long poems are full of fictional characters, while the shorter poems are more likely to employ a fictional "he." Once one has done the substitution of the first person, and has seen Stevens's personal predicament, one has to restore the persona to the poem, regrant the poem its fictional energy, and read it as an imaginative construct with its anecdotal freshness unimpaired. Stevens's extravagances of language are experiments in the refurbishing of diction, breaking the boilerplate of cliché. His experiments in diction respond to his sense of the swarming variety of the physical world:

One might have thought of sight, but who could think
Of what it sees, for all the ill it sees? . . .
And out of what one sees and hears and out
Of what one feels, who could have thought to make
So many selves, so many sensuous worlds,
As if the air, the mid-day air, was swarming
With the metaphysical changes that occur
Merely in living as and where we live.

(*CP,* 326)

The appetite of the imagination for change, in Stevens's view, exceeds even its appetite for the fulfillment of desire. Stevens's turbulent hymn to creation and destruction, "The Auroras of Autumn," marks his point of greatest resonance and imaginative amplitude: the auroras, invoked earlier by Emerson (in "The Poet") and Dickinson ("Of bronze and blaze"), stream across the heavens, their power destroying Crispin's cabin and all dreams of domestic permanence:

George Santayana.

. . . It is a kind of total grandeur at the end,
With every visible thing enlarged and yet
No more than a bed, a chair and moving nuns,
The immensest theatre, the pillared porch,
The book and candle in your ambered room,

Total grandeur of a total edifice,
Chosen by an inquisitor of structures
For himself. He stops upon this threshold,
As if the design of all his words takes form
And frame from thinking and is realized.

—From "To an Old Philosopher in Rome"

The man who is walking turns blankly on the sand.
He observes how the north is always enlarging the change,

With its frigid brilliances, its blue-red sweeps
And gusts of great enkindlings, its polar green,
The color of ice and fire and solitude.

(*CP,* 412–13)

The "Snow Man" in *Harmonium* had had "a mind of winter," and "had been cold a long time"; but the frigid whiteness of numb stoic endurance attempted in that great poem is imaginatively less powerful than Stevens's terrified rapture before the auroras:

He opens the door of his house

On flames. The scholar of one candle sees
An Arctic effulgence flaring on the frame
Of everything he is. And he feels afraid.

(*CP,* 416–17)

Whereas in *The Waste Land* Eliot had lamented the fall of cultures ("Falling towers / Jerusalem Athens Alexandria / Vienna London / Unreal"), Stevens hails the perpetual destruction that enables perpetual creation. His favorite seasonal moment is the cusp between one season and the next, when one reality is vanishing and another is being born, the Shakespearean moment where tragedy turns to comedy. In his old age, Stevens becomes a sublime poet of dawn and inception, as in the poem with which he closed his book, "Not Ideas About the Thing But the Thing Itself." In this poem, a man who has been afraid that he will never see another spring wakes up thinking that he has heard the cry of the first returning bird, the harbinger of the turning season. At first he denies his own perception, thinking that he has simply, out of desire, dreamed the bird-cry. Then he looks out the window, at the light, and realizes that already, at six o'clock, the sun has risen—a spring dawn-time, not a winter one. The poem breathes the deep gratitude of one who finds an incredible hope becoming credible day:

That scrawny cry—it was
A chorister whose c preceded the choir.
It was part of the colossal sun,

Surrounded by its choral rings,
Still far away. It was like
A new knowledge of reality.

(*CP,* 534)

Seventy Years Later

It is an illusion that we were ever alive,
Lived in the houses of mothers, arranged ourselves
By our own motions in a freedom of air.

Regard the freedom of seventy years ago.
It is no longer air. The houses still stand,
Though they are rigid in rigid emptiness.

Even our shadows, their shadows, no longer remain.
The lives these lived in the mind are at an end.
They never were. . . . The sounds of the guitar

Were not and are not. Absurd. The words spoken
Were not and are not. It is not to be believed.
The meeting at noon at the edge of the field seems like

An invention, an embrace between one desperate clod
And another in a fantastic consciousness,
In a queer assertion of humanity:

A theorem proposed between the two—
Two figures in a nature of the sun,
In the sun's design of its own happiness,

As if nothingness contained a métier,
A vital assumption, an impermanence
In its permanent cold, an illusion so desired

That the green leaves came and covered the high rock,
That the lilacs came and bloomed, like a blindness cleaned,
Exclaiming bright sight, as it was satisfied,

In a birth of sight. The blooming and the musk
Were being alive, an incessant being alive,
A particular of being, that gross universe.

—From "The Rock"

Stevens had written to Delmore Schwartz in 1948 that "Poetic form in its proper sense is a question of what appears within the poem itself . . . the things created and existing there" (*L,* 590). Form is the way the world unfolds as we read the poem. In "Not Ideas About the Thing But the Thing Itself" there are only five formal units of construction:

1. the bird cry
2. the rising sun
3. the man's fear that he has dreamt the cry
4. inside
5. outside

Stevens in his yard in Hartford, 1951.

As the poem unfolds, we see the intertwining choreography of these simple units, inscribed here in boldface:

At the earliest ending of winter,
In March, **a scrawny cry** from **outside**
Seemed like a sound **in his mind**.

He **knew** that he heard **it**,
A bird's cry, at **daylight** or before,
In the early March wind.

The **sun** was rising at six,
No longer a **battered panache** above snow . . .
It would have been outside.

> **It** was not from **the vast ventriloquism**
> **Of sleep's faded papier-mâché . . .**
> The **sun** was coming from **outside.**
>
> That **scrawny cry—it** was
> A **chorister** whose c preceded the choir.
> **It** was part of the colossal **sun,**
>
> Surrounded by its **choral rings,**
> Still far away. **It** was **like**
> **A new knowledge** of reality.
>
> (*CP,* 534)

This dance of signifiers, of doubt and confidence, uses simple counters of the sort Stevens liked best—a note of song, the wind, the sun, the season, the dawn, sleep, dreams. And it twists them around a single set of syntactic formulae—"It was this; it was not that." The poem reveals the joy of seeing the old formulations—the battered winter sun, the illusions of dream—vanish in favor of the radiant new formulations—the coming season of a colossal sun, surrounded by its choirs of birds—promised in the single pitch-pipe of the sun's first acolyte.

More and more, as he aged, Stevens simplified his counters. The world for him, finally, was a bare rock covered with leaves (of grass, almost), nature elaborated on by culture. His rhythms of the rock—dignified, sober, plain—could rise to quirkiness to exhibit the fronds and fruit of forms, the featheriness, as he said, of argentines. The names he gave the river of life ("Call it, again and again, the river") became talismans of affection for his American "local objects" like the ducks in Elizabeth Park in Hartford:

> Little existed for him but the few things
> For which a fresh name always occurred, as if
> He wanted to make them, keep them from perishing.
>
> (*OP,* 112)

Stevens felt things profoundly, but ironically and humorously and astringently, too; these qualities, and his reticence, preserve him from sentimentality. "The final poem will be the poem of fact in the language of fact. But it will be the poem of fact not realized before" (OP, 164). A poem was for Stevens never a matter simply of feeling; it always proposed an enigma to the mind: "The mind always proposes a solution" (OP, 168). Poetry "must resist the intelligence almost successfully" (OP 171), or it will not carry the pleasurable shock that we associate with insight. Stevens aimed constantly at a stylization of his subject (as the snowman is his stylization of stoic knowledge, or the auroras his stylization of imaginative freedom in the midst of tragic fatality). He aimed as well at an aesthetic distance proper to reflective meditation, and at what he called the gaiety of language, a diction freed from the prosaic obligation to be transparent, liberated into the holiday of expressive form. He undertook the great metaphysical subjects of the constructed nature of phenomenal reality and the necessary historical exhaustion of all cultural and erotic forms. He proposed, and exhibited, the symbolic, rhetorical, and prosodic independence of American poetry from British models; and he left a memorable record of a single inner life in this century, one extending from youth to old age, full of clarity and sobriety of vision, equally full of expression at once extravagant, buoyant, and austere.

Between walls

the back
wings
of the

hospital
where
nothing

will grow -
cinders
in which

shine
pieces of
a green

bottle

WILLIAM CARLOS WILLIAMS

MARJORIE PERLOFF

I

In 1917, the London *Egoist* published what was to be one of the most famous poems of the century, T. S. Eliot's "Love Song of J. Alfred Prufrock." A few months earlier, on the other side of the Atlantic, Alfred Kreymborg's little magazine *Others* published a short poem also called "Love Song," this one by William Carlos Williams, a resident of Rutherford, New Jersey, where he practiced general medicine and pediatrics. Here is Williams's "Love Song":

I lie here thinking of you:—

the stain of love
is upon the world!
Yellow, yellow, yellow
it eats into the leaves,
smears with saffron
the horned branches that lean
heavily
against a smooth purple sky!
There is no light
only a honey-thick stain
that drips from leaf to leaf
and limb to limb
spoiling the colors
of the whole world—

you far off there under
the wine-red selvage of the west![1]

What could English and American readers of 1917 make of this very odd "love song"? "Prufrock," after all, could be assimilated to the nineteenth-century Symbolist tradition: Williams himself dismissed it, not without a stab of jealousy, as the work of a "subtle conformist" who had "betrayed America," a "repetition in another way of Verlaine, Baudelaire, Maeterlinck" (*KH,* 24). "I knew," Williams was to recall some forty years later, "[Eliot] would influence all subsequent American poets and take them out of my sphere. I had envisaged a new

William Carlos Williams.

form of poetic composition, a form for the future. It was a shock to me that he was so tremendously successful" (*IWWP,* 30).

But what did this promised "new form of poetic composition" look like? "Love Song" is, to begin with, written in free verse, but not the "free verse" *(vers libre)* Eliot was writing, a verse in which, according to Eliot's own account, "the ghost of some simple metre should lurk behind the arras . . . to advance menacingly as we doze, and withdraw as we rouse." In the case of "Prufrock," the "ghost" is that of iambic pentameter, and it "advances," before we have gotten more than six lines into the seemingly irregular rhythms of the poem, in the couplet, "Of réstless níghts in óne-nîght chéap hotéls / And sáwdûst réstauránts with óyster shélls."

No such ghost lurks behind the arras in Williams's "Love Song." The lines range from three syllables ("heavily") to eight ("the wine-red selvage of the west"), from one stress to four. The rhythm seems to be intentionally prosaic. "I lie here thinking of you" or "you far off there under"—these heavily monosyllabic lines have the ring of actual speech. Again, Williams cuts his lines in quirky places—"the stain of love / is upon the world!" —and he tends to isolate words rather than to arrange them, as Whitman does, in repetitive rhythmic phrases. The aim is to provide a graph of the poet's actual experience, to chart the mental process itself. Accordingly, the poet begins with the simple fact, "I lie here thinking of you." As Williams puts it in *Spring and All,* "What I put down of value will have this value: an escape from crude symbolism, the annihilation of strained associations, complicated ritualistic forms designed to separate the work from 'reality.' . . . The word must be put down for itself, not as a symbol of nature but a part, cognizant of the whole" (*SAA,* 102).

"The word must be put down for itself"—again and again, Williams insists that the poet must "lift to the imagination those things which lie under the direct scrutiny of the senses, close to the nose" (*KH,* 14). But such declarations, like the later aphorism in *Paterson,* "No ideas but in things!" must be taken with a grain of salt. Williams—and I cannot stress this sufficiently—was never the happy Naturalist, patiently depicting the objects or persons in the world around him. On the contrary, his verbal constructs are characterized by a restless energy; like the Cubist and Dada artworks with which they have so much in common, his poems exploit the principle of "cut," of what Williams called, with reference to Gertrude Stein, "unlinking [words] from their former relationships in the sentence" (*IMAG,* 349).

"The stain of love / is upon the world!" What can these seemingly simple words mean? "Yellow, yellow, yellow" is, of course, the color of semen, and the poet may well be describing the act of love. But what sort of lovemaking is it that spreads its "stain . . . upon the world," that eats, like acid, into the leaves, and "smears with saffron" (a bitter spice) "the horned branches"? So thick is this "honey-thick stain" that it blots out the light and finally "spoil[s] the colors / of the whole world." Moreover, the "you" whom Williams's "Love Song" ostensibly celebrates is not with him, sharing a moment of joyful consummation. She is, on the contrary, "far off there under / the wine-red selvage of the west!"

In the first version of "Love Song" (1915, see *CEP,* 173), Williams is more explicit. The poem begins:

What have I to say to you
When we shall meet?
Yet—
I lie here thinking of you.

And after the account of "the stain of love" (lines 2–14 of the second version), three short stanzas follow:

I am alone.
The weight of love
Has buoyed me up
Till my head
Knocks against the sky.

See me!
My hair is dripping with nectar—
Starlings carry it
On their black wings.
See at last
My arms and my hands
Are lying idle.

How can I tell
If I shall ever love you again
As I do now?

In the 1916 version, these three stanzas are deleted and replaced by the abrupt couplet, "you far off there under / the wine-red selvage of the west!" Williams evidently decided that the direct statement of his feelings ("What have I to say to you / When we shall meet?") lacked subtlety, that the poem should render the complex of emotions as vividly and economically as possible. Indeed, the revised "Love Song" leaves open the question of whether the poet is alone, whether, that is to say, the "stain of love" is the projection of desire rather than the product of actual union. "You far off there," has been taken to refer to the sense of separation that follows orgasm. But read in the context of the first version, this separation is taken to be one of fact rather than feeling.

Williams is still all too often regarded as the poet of "easy" Imagist lyrics, pleasant little poems that lack the "depth" of, say, the poetry of Stevens or Eliot or Dickinson. Later in his career, of course, there is the "epic," *Paterson,* but this too, so many critics have argued, is a fairly slapdash performance, a patchwork quilt of memory and desire. "Oh, Carlos Williams," a British professor remarked dismissively, "nice enough, if you want Imagist bits about cats or housewives or flowerpots." And, indeed, as the poet Charles Tomlinson reminded us not long ago, in England much of Williams's work continues to be unavailable or out of print.

Imagist, I would argue, is precisely what Williams's poetry is not. Pound's call for "direct treatment of the thing" is here (as, for that matter, in Pound's own later poetry) met by the stubborn

refusal to let the words compose a coherent "picture." We can say, for instance, that "Love Song" is an erotically charged poem, but erotic in what sense? Does the poet want love to "eat" into his world or does he fear the power of its "stain"? In Williams's quasi-surrealist vision, the poet's semen becomes a mysterious flood, a kind of Yellow Peril silhouetted against the "smooth purple sky." Not only is the "you" finally "far off," but the word "selvage" (an edge of cloth so woven that it does not unravel) implies a certain desire to keep the self intact, free from actual contact. As Williams puts it in a related poem, "Danse Russe," "I was born to be lonely, / I am best so!" (*CEP,* 148), and again, in the slightly later "Waiting," "When I am alone I am happy" (*CEP,* 213).

Happy but also restless, as Williams's lineation everywhere testifies. "I lie here thinking of you:—." The colon, dash, and visual jump to the next stanza force us to move quickly on to "the stain of love." But "the stain of love" now becomes the subject of "is" in line three, so that again our attention is pushed ahead. This forward propulsion continues until the poem brings us down on the word "heavily," placed by itself, precisely at the midpoint of the fourteen-line stanza:

> the horned branches that lean
> heavily
> against a smooth purple sky!

The isolation of "heavily," surrounded only by white space, gives a sense of phallic power pressing against the "smooth purple sky." But the image of the "horned branches" also suggests the collapse of the phallus, all passion spent, reduced to a mere drip. We "see," finally, not a lover contemplating his mistress in a lovely pastoral setting, but limbs, horned branches, a yellow sticky substance, the hard edge of the sunset. Not love but the stain of love.

In his later years, especially in his *Autobiography* (1951), Williams was fond of presenting himself as a "natural" genius, an artist innocent of the ways of the world:

> I was an innocent sort of child and have remained so to this day. Only yesterday, reading Chapman's *The Iliad of Homer,* did I realize for the first time that the derivation of the adjective venereal is from Venus! And I a physician practicing medicine for the past forty years. I was stunned! (*Auto,* 3)

The reader should not be taken in by this "gee whiz!" manner. Williams's "innocence" was a carefully constructed pose, a

Williams's mother, Elena Hoheb Williams.

Yes, I said that [Williams] was the quintessential American poet in that his father was English, of old English stock, the mother was born in Puerto Rico, part Basque, part Jewish, mixed Mediterranean French stock. So, when his parents came to the U.S. and settled in Rutherford they wanted to be the perfect immigrants. . . . She dropped her Catholicism, he dropped his Anglicanism and they became charter members of the Unitarian Church, which meant being teetotalers, and meant doing all the right things and living in the right kind of house. His father worked very hard and the idea was to better yourself—the perfect immigrant experience. . . . I think that Williams adopted the American idiom aggressively because he was self-conscious about being an American. He was constantly talking about writing in the American idiom, writing the American poem . . . having American speech rhythms rather than British speech rhythms, which is something that a poet like T. S. Eliot—who was a fourth-generation American, as was Stevens, as was Pound—would never have dreamt of doing.

—From a *Voices & Visions* interview with Marjorie Perloff

mode of being that allowed him to be "the happy genius of [his] household" even as he devoted himself with the firmest discipline to his craft. It was also a brilliant way of dealing with the problem of his origins.

II

William Carlos Williams was born on September 17, 1883, the child of an English father and a mother, half-Basque, half-Jewish, who was born in Puerto Rico. The poet's middle name was taken from his maternal uncle who practiced medicine in Panama City. When Mr. and Mrs. Williams settled in the then small country town of Rutherford, New Jersey, where their son would marry a local girl named Florence ("Floss") Herman and practice medicine for the rest of his life, they renounced their respective Anglican and Catholic faiths and, wanting to assimilate into the local community, joined the Unitarian Church, then a bastion of temperance and respectability. William George Williams evidently led the most orderly of lives: he commuted daily to New York City, where he worked for a company that manufactured cologne. Raquel Helène Rose Hoheb Williams was, by contrast, what her poet son later called "a defeated romantic" (*YMW,* 33). As a young girl she had studied painting in Paris; she was artistic, temperamental, exotic—and thoroughly out of place in small-town Rutherford.

As the product of this union, William Carlos Williams was in many ways the quintessential first-generation American of his time. He admired his father's steadiness of purpose and respectability even as his own affinities were with his artistic and "difficult" mother. Further, to compensate for their foreignness, he himself became aggressively *American,* insisting that the poet must celebrate his own region, that he must write in none other than "the American idiom" and invent exclusively American rhythms. He deplored the defection to Europe of Eliot and, especially, of Ezra Pound, whom he had befriended at the University of Pennsylvania, even as Pound, himself from old American stock, twitted Williams about his patriotism:

> And America? What the h——l do you a blooming foreigner know about the place. Your *père* only penetrated the edge, and you've never been west of Upper Darby, or the Maunchunk switchback.
>
> Would H., [H.D.] with the swirl of the prairie wind in her underwear, or the Virile Sandburg recognize you, an effete easterner as a REAL American? INCONCEIVABLE!!!!! . . .
>
> You thank your bloomin gawd you've got enough Spanish blood to muddy up your mind, and prevent the current American ideation from going through it like a blighted colander.
>
> The thing that saves your work is opacity, and don't forget it.

> Opacity is NOT an American quality. Fizz, swish, gabble, and verbiage, these are *echt americanisch.* (*KH,* 11)

Playful as Pound was in this letter from London, he perceived something very important about Williams's poetry. "Enough Spanish blood" meant, in practice, an avoidance of the Carl Sandburg–Edgar Lee Masters realist model on the one hand, and a rejection of Genteel School idiom on the other. "Opacity," Williams style, was to be a matter not of Poetic Diction and verbal elegance, but, as we have seen in the case of "Love Song," a question of prosodic, syntactic, and semantic defamiliarization, the injection of a Dada or quasi-Surrealist strain into the down-to-earth world of what Pound called "American ideation."

But it did not happen overnight. Williams's first book, *Poems* (1909), of which only a hundred copies were printed, is written in the dominant "genteel" style of the period. As Williams himself put it some fifty years later, "The poems should be classified as sonnets, not the Shakespearean sonnet, but the sonnets of Keats and other romantic poems" (*IWWP,* 10). The results looked like this:

> Sweet Lady, sure it seems a thousand years
> Since last you honored me with gentle speech.
> Yet, when, forsaking fantasy, I reach
> With memory's index o'er the stretching tiers
>
> Of minutes wasted, counting, (as who fears
> Strict-chiding reason, lest it should impeach
> All utterance, must) a mighty, gaping breach
> 'Twixt truth and seeming verity appears.
>
> (*Poems* 1909, 14)

Inversion, contorted syntax (especially in the awkward parenthesis in the second quatrain), sing-song meter, predictable rhyme, and stock phraseology ("gentle speech," "memory's index," "Strict-chiding reason")—Williams in his early poetic discourse is closer to William Vaughan Moody than he is to Keats, let alone Shakespeare. And even four years later, in *The Tempers,* a book actively promoted by Pound, who had arranged its publication, Williams seemed not yet to have found his direction. Pound himself was, at best, a problematic model; on the one hand, he provided Williams with important negative prescriptions—"Go in fear of abstractions," "Compose in the sequence of the musical phrase, not in sequence of the metronome," "[avoid] false ornament," and so on—but the elegant and exotic renderings of Provençal, Greek, and Roman scenes that Pound prescribed were essentially alien to the sensibility of the poet-physician who had recently set up practice in Rutherford, having trained in the charity hospitals of New York's Hell's Kitchen. Dutifully, Williams wrote Poundian lines like "Mother of flames / You have kept the fire burning!" Or "O crimson salamander / Because of love's whim / sacred!" (*CEP,* 22–23). But it is only in rare instances like "The Revelation" (*CEP,* 39) that his own much quieter voice and his abrupt rhythms come through:

> I awoke happy, the house
> Was strange, voices
> Were across a gap
> Through which a girl
> Came and paused,
> Reaching out to me—
>
> (*CEP,* 39)

Here crimson salamanders and mothers of flame give way to ordinary incident, in this case, the act of trying to remember a particular moment of love. The line breaks enact the difficulty of remembering: the separation of the subject noun "house" from its predicate ("Was strange") creates a moment of suspension as the reader tries to decide whether "house" looks ahead to line two or back to the alliterating word "happy."

But such effects are still rare in *The Tempers,* and it was not until the publication of *Al Que Quiere* (1917) that Williams became recognizably himself. Indeed, the shift from a poem like "The Ordeal" ("O crimson salamander . . . !") to "Love Song" is so profound that one wonders what could have happened in four years to account for it. Where does it come from, the Williams mode, a mode that remains essentially intact despite the poet's progression from the short lyric to longer forms, from Imagism to Objectivism to the late manner of *Pictures from Breughel*?

Whitman is often cited as a source. James Breslin tells us that in March 1913, Williams received a copy of *Leaves of Grass* from his wife, a copy, now in the library of the University of Pennsylvania, that falls open to the beginning of "Song of Myself." Whitman could provide Williams with an American alternative to the "European" Pound; he was the poet of democracy who celebrated his native country, the innovator who defied European norms of verse form and diction and invented an American idiom. It is Whitman's voice we hear in such early Williams poems as "The Wanderer" (1914), especially in the lines from "The Strike" that celebrate "the electric":

"Ugly, venomous, gigantic!"
Tossing me as a great father his helpless
Infant till it shriek with ecstasy
And its eyes roll and its tongue hangs out!—

(*CEP,* 7)

We hear Whitman too in the concluding passage of the poem where "the filthy Passaic" becomes the poet's friend:

Then the river began to enter my heart,
Eddying back cool and limpid
Into the crystal beginning of its days.

(*CEP,* 11)

But Williams's most clearly Whitmanesque poem of this period is "January Morning," with its loving apostrophe to "Exquisite brown waves—long / circlets of silver moving over you! / enough with crumbling ice crusts among you!" its echo of "Crossing Brooklyn Ferry" in "The young doctor is dancing with happiness / in the sparkling wind, alone / at the prow of the ferry!" its celebration of "the curdy barnacles and broken ice crusts / left at the slip's base by the low tide" and the "green shell-crusted ledges among / the emerald eel-grass!"

The nature images, the oracular voice—these are Whitman's but the principle of structure is distinctly different. Consider the Whitmanesque part XI of "January Morning":

Who knows the Palisades as I do
knows the river breaks east from them
above the city—but they continue south
—under the sky—to bear a crest of
little peering houses that brighten
with dawn behind the moody
water-loving giants of Manhattan.

(*CEP,* 164)

Whitman's characteristic mode is one of repetition, parallelism, accumulation, parataxis:

Others will enter the gates of the ferry and cross from shore to
shore,
Others will watch the run of the flood-tide,
Others will see the shipping of Manhattan north and west, and
the heights of Brooklyn to the south and east,
Others will see the islands large and small. . . .

("Crossing Brooklyn Ferry")

Williams's lines have no such flow, no intensifying repetition and heightening. "I didn't go in for long lines," he told Edith Heal, "because of my nervous nature. I couldn't. The rhythmic pace was the pace of speech, an excited pace" (*IWWP,* 15). Which is to say, a curious disjunction. The seven-line stanza not only avoids Whitman's parallelism, it presents the poet's perceptions as being almost afterthoughts ("Who knows the Palisades as I do / knows . . ."), as qualifications ("but they continue south"), as parentheses ("under the sky"). The line breaks, moreover, undercut assertion—"to bear a crest of / little peering houses that brighten / with dawn"—all resolution being delayed until the eye and ear come down on the word "Manhattan." The stanza is characterized by what Hans Hoffman was to call "push and pull": it becomes a system of oppositions: above the city—under the sky; east—south; Palisades—Manhattan; brighten—moody. It is, to use Williams's own adjective, "nervous."

Where, then, if not in Pound or Whitman, did Williams find a "form for the future" that suited his own temperament? How did the poet of "O crimson salamander" come to write, just four years later, lines like:

> In brilliant gas light
> I turn the kitchen spigot
> and watch the water plash
> into the clean white sink.
>
> (CEP, 145)

Kitchen spigots: one looks in vain for such mundane images in the poetry of Williams's contemporaries. But even as *Poetry* and *The Little Review* were publishing delicate little lyrics by Rabindranath Tagore, Eunice Tietjens, Sara Teasdale, and George Soule, Alfred Stieglitz's journal *Camera Work,* and later his *291,* was beginning to expose New York to the avant-garde art of Paris. It is in the pages of these journals, as well as at Stieglitz's 291 (for 291 Fifth Avenue) Gallery, that Williams began to find possible alternatives for the structuring of poetic discourse. "Why," remarked Marius de Zayas in an essay on Picasso for *Camera Work* 36 (1911), "should a person in the foreground [of a painting] be larger than in the background?" The point was made more emphatically by Francis Picabia, newly arrived in New York from Paris, in the Preface to the Catalogue of his first exhibition of paintings at 291:

> The objective representation of nature through which the painter used to express the mysterious feelings of his ego in front of his

But even as *Poetry* and *The Little Review* were publishing delicate little lyrics by Tagore, Eunice Tietjens, Sara Teasdale, and George Soule, Alfred Stieglitz's journals *Camera Work* and later *291* were beginning to expose New York to the avant-garde art of Paris. It is in the pages

VOYAGE

A Mlle Paula Valmont

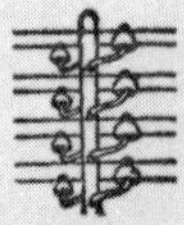

ADIEU AMOUR NUAGE QUI
FUIS REFAIS LE VOYAGE DE DANTE
ET N'A PAS CHU PLUIE FÉCON

TÉLÉGRAPHE
OISEAU QUI LAISSE SES AILES PARTOUT
TOMBER

OU VA DONC CE TRAIN QUI MEURT AU LOIN
DANS LES VALS ET LES BEAUX BOIS FRAIS DU

TENDRE ÉTÉ SI PALE ?

LA DOUCE NUIT LUNAIRE ET
ÉTOILÉE
C'EST TON VISAGE QUE
LA PEINE
NE
JE
VOIS
PLUS

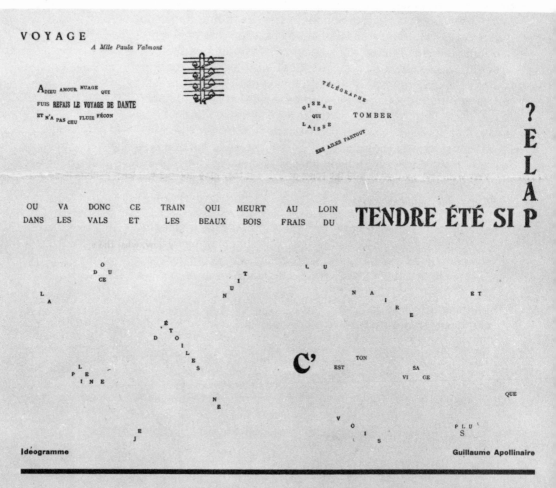

Idéogramme — Guillaume Apollinaire

ONE HOUR'S SLEEP——

THREE DREAMS

I.

I was to be buried. The whole family stood about. Also hundreds of friends. My wish was carried out. Not a word was uttered. There was not a single tear. All was silence and all seemed blackness. A door opened and a woman came in. As the woman came in I stood up; my eyes opened. But I was dead. All screamed and rushed away. There was a general panic. Some jumped out of the windows. Only the Woman remained. Her gaze was fixed upon me. Eye to Eye. She said: "Friend are you really dead?" The voice was firm and clear. No answer. The Woman asked three times. No answer. As she asked the third time I returned to my original position and was ready to be buried. —— I heard one great sob. I awoke.

II.

I was very ill and everyone asked me to take a rest. No one succeeded to induce me. Finally a Woman said: "I will go with you. Will you go?" We went. We tramped together day and night. In the mountains. Over snow. In the moonlight. In the glaring sun. We had no food. Not a word was said. The Woman grew paler and paler as the days and nights passed by. She could hardly walk. I helped her. And still not a word was uttered. Finally the Woman collapsed and she said, in a voice hardly audible: "Food—Food—I must have food." And I answered: "Food—Food—, Child, we are in a world where there is no Food—just Spirit—Will."—And the Woman looked piteously at me and said, half dead: "Food—Food" —— and I kissed the Woman, and as I did that there stood before the Woman all sorts of wonderful food—on a simple wooden table, and it was Springtime. And as the Woman began to eat ravenously—conscious of nothing but Nature's Cry for Food, I slipped away. And I continued walking Onward. —— I heard a distant cry. I awoke.

III.

The Woman and I were alone in a room. She told me a Love Story. I knew it was her own. I understood why she could not love me. And as the Woman told me the story—she suddenly became mad—she kissed me in her ravings—she tore her clothes and mine—she tore her hair. Her eyes were wild—and nearly blank. I saw them looking into mine. She kissed me passionately and cried: "Why are you not HE?" "Why not?" And I tried to calm her. But did not succeed. And finally she cried: "What makes me kiss you—it is He I want, not you. And yet I kissed you. Kissed you as if it were He."—I didn't dare to move. It was not fear that made me stand still. It was all much too terrible for Fear. I stood there spell-bound. Suddenly the woman moved away—it was ghastly. Her look. Her eyes. —— The Woman stood immovable, her eyes glued on mine; when suddenly she screeched: "Tell me you are He—tell me—you are He. And if you are not He I will kill you. For I kissed you." I stood there and calmly said, what I really did not want to say, for I knew the Woman was irresponsible and mad. I said, "I am not He." And as I said that the Woman took a knife from the folds of her dress and rushed at me. She struck the heart. The blood spurted straight ahead, as if it had been waiting for an outlet. And as the Woman saw the blood and saw me drop dead she became perfectly sane. She stood motionless. With no expression. She turned around. Upon the immaculate white wall she saw written in Blood Red letters: "He killed himself. He understood the kisses."——There was a scream. I awoke.

ALFRED STIEGLITZ

of these journals, as well as at Stieglitz's 291 (for 291 Fifth Avenue) Gallery, that Williams began to find possible alternatives for the structuring of poetic discourse. . . . The first issue of *291* (1915) reproduced Apollinaire's *calligramme* (here called "idéogramme") "Voyage."

When I arrived at 291 the Spirit of 291 was manifesting itself at its best; 291 himself was at the height of an animated discussion with the Professor.

291 is a trinity; a place, a person and a symbol, so be not surprised if I refer without transition to its separate entities.

Professor What I wonder at, is why *you* did not tell the world what *291* is.

291 I wanted the other people to tell me.

Prof. Have they done so?

291 Each one of the sixty odd contributors has said what *291* was to him; the sum total of what it is to each individual makes up the spirit of *291*.

Prof. Very well, they have given you the spirit of *291* but they have not told you what definite thing *291* represents.

291 It represents nothing definite; it is ever growing, constantly changing and developing.

Prof. And how is it going to develop?

291 That, I do not know; nobody knows.

Prof. But somebody should know; somebody should at least know what it should accomplish. If *291* is nothing definite but only a spirit, how can it do its work? We know now, what the spirit of *291* is, as nearly as a spirit can be known. What we should know for the future is *291* the machine which will provide the channels through which this wonderful spirit can accomplish useful work.

291 That will come of itself, in the course of events.

Prof. Precisely; but there is a logical sequence in the course of events. The past history of *291* shows it. . . You started with a fight for photography; you wanted your problem answered: "What is photography?"; you got the photographers together, you held exhibitions, you published reproductions of meritorious work; writers came who wrote about photography and out of all these efforts came an answer. We all know now what photography is, what it can accomplish; we have standards by which we can judge new work. What was *291* while all this was going on?

291 Nothing but a laboratory, a place for experiments.

Prof. And is it not still a laboratory, only with new problems to solve?

291 That is what it is.

Prof. And what is the object of a laboratory?

291 To experiment.

Prof. And what do experiments lead to?

291 To finding out.

Prof. Now, at last, we have a definition of what *291* is; a laboratory where experiments are conducted in order to find out something. Now, the inevitable sequence which man follows in experimental science is:

1st. *To establish facts or phenomena by observation and experimentation.*

2d. *To arrive through induction from these facts or phenomena to their general relationship or laws.*

3d. *To start from these laws to arrive by logical deductive reasoning to the discovery of other facts which may in turn be included in the general law.*

Now, I have noticed of late that you, *291*, have been, so to speak, marking time. You are waiting for the "*WHAT NEXT?*" For me, who have been watching you closely for many years the "*WHAT NEXT?*" is clear. You are at the end of your first period; you have gathered your data, you have made your observations. You are about to enter your second period in which you will arrive at the laws which govern the phenomena you have observed. This may be a long period, for new data will constantly be coming up which may cause you to modify or abandon the theories you will evolve before you strike the answer that will satisfy you. That must be your next step if all your experimenting is not to remain sterile, and when that is done, then we will talk about the last period.

291 But laws are the very things I have been fighting against all my life.

Prof. Let us not quarrel about words. You have been fighting against *FIXED* laws which impede progress and development. The laws I mean are but our conception of the relationship of phenomena which we use as guides in making new discoveries. That, I believe is what you have always sought to discover. If *291* sees clearly the path which is traced for it, great things may be expected from it for its preliminary work has been well done.

PAUL B. HAVILAND

subject "motive" no longer suffices for the fullness of his new consciousness of nature. . . .

For example: when we look at a tree we are conscious not only of its outside appearance but also of some of its properties, its qualities, and its evolution. Our feelings before this tree are the result of this knowledge acquired by experience through analysis. . . . Therefore, in my paintings the public is not to look for a "photographic" recollection of a visual impression or a sensation, but to look at them as but an attempt to express the purest part of the abstract reality of form and color in itself. (*Camera Work* 42 [1912–13]: 19–20)

And, as if to prove that the aesthetic of nonrepresentation could be transferred from the visual to the literary sphere, the special 1913 issue of *Camera Work* published Gertrude Stein's "abstract" "Portrait of Mabel Dodge at the Villa Curonia." Williams was later to remark: "Stein has gone systematically to work smashing every connotation that words ever had, in order to get them clean" (*SE,* 163).

Nineteen thirteen was also the year of the Armory Show. As Williams recalls in his *Autobiography:*

I went to [the Armory Show] and gaped at a "picture" in which an electric bulb kept going on and off; at Duchamp's sculpture (by "Mott and Co."), a magnificent cast-iron urinal, glistening of its white enamel. The story then current of this extraordinary and popular young man was that he walked daily into whatever store struck his fancy and purchased whatever pleased him—something new—something American. Whatever it might be, that was his "construction" for the day. The silly committee threw out the urinal, asses that they were. The "Nude Descending a Staircase" is too hackneyed for me to remember anything clearly about it now. But I do remember how I laughed out loud when first I saw it, happily, with relief. (*Auto,* 134)

"Relief," because such "readymades" as Duchamp's "Fountain" (the urinal) implied that art need no longer deal with exalted subject matter. Pound's "The Coming of War: Actaeon," H.D.'s "Oread"—these could now be supplanted by poems prompted by the turning on of the kitchen spigot. If a urinal could be presented as a sculpture, surely it must be possible to make poems that have neither meter nor rhyme, that begin lines with lowercase letters and omit punctuation.

The first issue of *291* (1915) reproduced Guillaume Apollinaire's *calligramme* (here called *"idéogramme"*) "Voyage." A lament for lost love (evidently prompted by the marriage of Apollinaire's mistress, Marie Laurencin, to another man), "Voyage" relies on typography to create its tone of mordant regret.

Nude Descending a Staircase *(# 2) by Marcel Duchamp.*

I went to [the Armory Show] and gaped . . . at a "picture" in which an electric bulb kept going on and off; at Duchamp's sculpture (by "Mott and Co."), a magnificent cast-iron urinal, glistening of its white enamel. . . . The "Nude Descending a Staircase" is too hackneyed for me to remember anything clearly about it now. But I do remember how I laughed out loud when I saw it, happily, with relief.

—From Williams's *Autobiography*

The foregrounding of cloud and train shapes against the starry "sky" (the empty space in which appear tiny words) below, reinforces a sense of distance and remoteness. The words composing the cloud (in translation, "Farewell Love Cloud that flees make again Dante's Journey and hasn't fallen fertile rain") and telegraph ("telegraph bird that lets fall his wings everywhere") may be read in different sequences, even as the C in the "sky" [*Ciel*] beneath it is also the moon, and the heavy lettering at the end of the "train" represents the locomotive. Thus, the train which, according to the words, "dies far away," graphically comes closer and closer, evoking the "tender summer so pale."

Williams rarely made *calligrammes* of this sort, but Apollinaire's emphasis on the poem as visual text made a great impression on him. Equally important were Picabia's "machine drawings," five of which were printed in the July-August 1915 issue of *291.* In these comically erotic works, the visual is played off against the verbal. Thus, what looks like a realistic black and white drawing of a sharply outlined spark plug, bearing the brand name "FOR-EVER," is labeled, in modest small letters above it, *Portrait d'une jeune fille américaine dans l'état de nudité*. The most obvious irony of this portrait is, of course, that the young girl is reduced to mere mechanism, a technological object. But, in another sense, she is a *spark* plug that lasts, in the words of valentines, "forever." Her "head" sits on a "body" that, so to speak, screws into a socket. The shutters of this screwing machine are closed. But if we ignore the title, the spark plug obviously has the form of the male phallus. Is the "jeune fille américaine" excessively masculine? Or is Picabia presenting his spark plug to us as a new sort of androgyne? Williams's own portraits of young (or older) American girls are never quite so nonrepresentational as this. If his poetry bears the imprint of Apollinaire's typographic experimentation and Picabia's verbal/visual punning, it also pays homage to the defamiliarization of the mundane object in the urban landscape characteristic of Stieglitz's photographs, for example, *The Steerage*, which appeared in the September-October issue of *291.* Thus, a poem like "The Young Housewife" is, at one level, a "realistic" observation of a woman perceived as she goes about her daily routine, even as that observation is gradually charged with playfully erotic connotations:

At ten A.M. the young housewife
moves about in negligee behind
the wooden walls of her husband's house.
I pass solitary in my car.

Then again she comes to the curb
to call the ice-man, fish-man, and stands
shy, uncorseted, tucking in
stray ends of hair, and I compare her
to a fallen leaf.

The noiseless wheels of my car
rush with a crackling sound over
dried leaves as I bow and pass smiling.

(*CEP,* 136)

Here the colloquial, matter-of-fact detail—"ten A.M.," "Then again she comes to the curb / to call the ice-man, fish-man"—brings to mind the Stieglitz photograph: Williams, it would seem, is foregrounding particular sights and sounds so as to give the reader the "feel" of a certain environment. But the defamiliarizing of rhythm and syntax, a technique learned, no doubt, from artists like Apollinaire and Picabia, creates an erotic undertone, quite at odds with the seeming realism of the portrait.

We might note, to begin with, that the first neat-looking quatrain is a parody stanza, its lines related neither by rhyme nor by metric recurrence. The "young housewife" is not quite a spark plug like Picabia's "jeune fille américaine," but a certain mechanistic aura is implicit in Williams's designation of her by the same four-syllable rhythmic group we find in "At ten A.M.":

At tén Á.M̂.   the yoúng hoúsewîfe

The second line, with its odd construction "in negligee" on the model of "in furs" or "in silks," is cut after the word "behind," a word that may thus be construed as a noun (her "in negligee behind") rather than as a preposition. But this enticing "in negligee behind" is to be found not where the "solitary" physician-poet, driving by in his car, can contemplate it, but, at least hypothetically, "behind / the wooden walls of her husband's house." Like a courtly knight longing for the lady of the fortressed castle, the poet can only *imagine* her *deshabillé.*

The erotic fantasy now continues to transform what seem like ordinary details. From the vantage point of his moving car, the physician may really see the young woman come to the curb to call ice-man and fish-man, but the poem focuses not on what is seen but on what is imagined. The young housewife emerges from "behind / the wooden walls of her husband's house" only to call, not the poet, but other men. The line

shy, uncorseted, tucking in

is cut before we reach the direct object of the verb ("stray ends of hair"), suggesting that what is to be tucked in (and is deliciously not tucked in!) is that which belongs inside a corset. But of course the poet only surmises that she is "uncorseted," even as the reference to "stray ends of hair" acts as a synecdochic image of arousal.

Line eight, with its internal rhyme, now raises further expectations:

> stray ends of *hair,* and I com*pare* her

To what, we wonder?

> to a fallen leaf.

An absurd comparison, since surely the young housewife, who is busily moving around performing her daily duties is the very opposite of a fallen leaf. Or is she? The authoritative period after "leaf" is an intentional false lead: the tercet brings the poet's fantasy out into the open:

> The noiseless wheels of my car
> rush with a crackling sound over
> dried leaves as I bow and pass smiling.

In some corner of his mind, the poet wants to turn this shy, uncorseted young housewife into a "fallen leaf," so that "the noiseless wheels of his car" can "rush with a crackling sound over / [her] dried leaves." But it is, after all, only a daydream. Normal life must continue, and the reality principle returns with the words, "I bow and pass smiling." The tercet has lines respectively of seven, eight, and nine syllables (three, four, and five stresses); the diagonal created by its line endings thus presents an image of step-by-step progression, as if to say that, fantasize all we like, we must get on with life. "I bow and pass smiling" brings the poem round full circle to the normality of 10 A.M. Time, probably, for the doctor to make his rounds.

In its playful treatment of the subject, "The Young Housewife" recalls the Picabia of the machine-drawings. Tonal balance is very important here. "The Young Housewife" is not a sexist dismissal any more than it is mere still life. Rather, its focus is on the subliminal, the erotic longing kept in check by the discipline of "normal," socially acceptable behavior, a longing that betrays, so to speak, the "Spanish," or maternal, element in Williams's otherwise "English" demeanor. And so subtly does the poem structure this tension that the reader, like the poet, is finally left "smiling."

III

"The Young Housewife" was one of twenty-two poems by Williams to appear in Alfred Kreymborg's little magazine *Others* during 1916. The July issue, edited by Williams himself, included Wallace Stevens's "The Worms at Heaven's Gate," Marianne Moore's "Critics and Connoisseurs," and Ezra Pound's "To-Em-Mei's 'The Unmoving Cloud,' " as well as poems by Amy Lowell, Carl Sandburg, John Gould Fletcher, Iris Barry, Conrad Aiken, Maxwell Bodenheim, Mina Loy, Skipwith Cannell, Alfred Kreymborg, Padraic Colum, and Witter Bynner. I list these names only to point up a curious difference: Williams stands apart from this avant-garde company (a company he has, after all, chosen for himself) in his introduction of graphic images of lower-class life and of urban blight. Thus Amy Lowell's "garden / With peonies, and tinkling pagodas" ("Chinoiseries") and Conrad Aiken's "stealth of white petals in the sun" ("Illusions") give way to "the yards cluttered / with old chicken wire" and "the fences and outhouses / built of barrel-staves / and parts of boxes" of Williams's ironically titled "Pastoral." A second "Pastoral" presents us with the image of an "old man who goes about / gathering dog-lime / [who] walks in the gutter / without looking up" (*CEP,* 124).

Such images of "the anarchy of poverty" reflect the larger anarchy Williams finds in nature. The chicory and daisies that dot the faceless New Jersey fields must struggle to lift their "bitter stems . . . out of the scorched ground" (*CEP,* 122); a "Crooked, black tree" is seen "straining / against the bitter horizontals of / a north wind" (*CEP,* 142) while, in the "silver mist [that] lies upon the back yards / among the outhouses," another tree, this time a big and sturdy one, "smiles and glances / upward," even as "Tense with suppressed excitement / the fences watch where the ground / has humped an aching shoulder for the ecstasy" (*CEP,* 141).

"Ecstasy," because in the "interpenetration, both ways" (*P,* 3) which is Williams's verbal universe, the snowy mound of "bleached grass" in the back yard is also the "aching shoulder" of the poet. There is no real separation between self and other. "When I spoke of flowers," Williams tells Edith Heal, "I *was* a flower, with all the prerogatives of flowers, especially the right to come alive in the Spring" (*IWWP,* 21).

This Romantic urge to enter into the life of the object or person contemplated recalls such poets as Whitman and Lawrence, but Williams's Laurentian animism is held in check by a curious, almost clinical detachment, by a quality Robert Lowell defined as his "hard, nervous, secular knowingness." Given his

Remorse is a virtue in that it is a stirrer up of the emotions but it is a folly to accept it as a criticism of conduct. So to accept it is to attempt to fit the emotions of a certain state to a preceding state to which they are in no way related. Imagination though it cannot wipe out the sting of remorse can instruct the mind in its proper uses.

—From *Kora in Hell,* V.

Beautiful white corpse of night actually! So the northwest winds of death are mountain sweet after all! All the troubled stars are put to bed now: three bullets from wife's hand none kindlier: in the crown, in the nape and one lower: three starlike holes among a million pocky pores and the moon of your mouth; Venus, Jupiter, Mars, and all stars melted forthwith into this one good white light over the inquest table—the traditional moth beating its wings against it—except there are two here. But sweetest are the caresses of the county physician, a little clumsy perhaps—*mais—!* and the Prosecuting Attorney, Peter Valuzzi and the others, waving green arms of maples to the tinkling of the earliest ragpicker's bells. Otherwise—: kindly, stupid hands, kindly coarse voices, infinitely soothing, infinitely detached, infinitely beside the question, restfully babbling of how, where, why and night is done and the green edge of yesterday has said all it could.

---

particular sensibility, Williams was, as we have already seen, drawn to Cubist and Dadaist, rather than to Expressionist models, and it is these models that played a decisive role in what we may call his "French decade," the period from 1917, when he began his book of prose improvisations, *Kora in Hell,* to 1927, when, on board the S.S. *Pennland* on his return from Europe to America (his two sons having remained behind with their mother for a year of schooling in Geneva), he composed the sequence of fragments called "The Descent of Winter." Within this great decade of experimentation, Williams published *Kora* (1920), *Sour Grapes* (1921), which contains some of his most famous lyrics, the prose-verse collage book *Spring and All* (1923), the antinovel *The Great American Novel* (1923), and his highly personal reinvention of American history called *In The American Grain* (1925).

According to Williams, *Kora* was composed backwards: first the Improvisations, then their appended notes, the title and cover design, the Stuart Davis frontispiece, and finally the Prologue. The cover design, Williams told Edith Heal, "represents the ovum in the act of being impregnated, surrounded by spermatozoa, all trying to get in but only one successful. . . . The cell accepts one sperm—that is the beginning of life." As for the frontispiece, the Stuart Davis drawing was chosen because "it was, graphically, exactly what I was trying to do in words, put the Improvisations down as a unit on the page. You must remember I had a strong inclination all my life to be a painter" (*IWWP,* 28–29).

The Improvisations themselves were written more or less as diary entries. "For a year I used to come home and no matter how late it was before I went to bed I would write *something.* And I kept writing, writing, even if it were only a few words, and at the end of the year there were 365 entries. Even if I had nothing in my mind at all I put something down" (*IWWP,* 27). No doubt, Williams had in mind the Dada writings of Picabia and Tristan Tzara, André Breton's *Champs magnétiques,* and, behind these, Rimbaud's *Illuminations.* But his choice of title runs counter to the anarchic, anti-art spirit of Dada: "I am indebted to Pound for the title. We had talked about Kora, the Greek parallel of Persephone, the legend of Springtime captured and taken to Hades. I thought of myself as Springtime and I felt I was on my way to Hell (but I didn't go very far). This was what the Improvisations were trying to say" (*IWWP,* 29).

The desire to ground his improvisatory discourse in some kind of symbolic structure, in this case, the Persephone myth, reflects what I take to be the Puritan streak in Williams, his uneasy sense that the center must somehow hold, that order must finally prevail. But of course the demand for a unifying theme runs counter to the very meaning of Improvisation, which is, in Gerald Bruns's words, "a species of unforeseen discourse . . . discourse that makes no provision for its future, not in the reader's mind and certainly not in the writer's; its teleology is entirely in the present." And futher, "Improvisation is the performance of a composition in the moment of its composition. One preserves such a moment by refusing to revise its results" (*Inventions,* 1984).

But Williams frequently does "revise its results," as in the following example:

> This that I have struggled against is the very thing I should have chosen—but all's right now. They said I could not put the flower back into the stem nor win roses upon dead briars and I like a fool believed them. But all's right now. Weave away, dead fingers, the darkies are dancing in Mayaguez—all but one with the sore heel and

Dr. Williams outside his home at 9 Ridge Road in Rutherford.

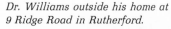

sugar cane will soon be high enough to romp through. Haia! leading over the ditches, with your skirts flying and the devil in the wind back of you—no one else. Weave away and the bitter tongue of an old woman is eating, eating, eating venomous words with thirty years' mould on them and all shall be eaten back to honeymoon's end. Weave and pangs of agony and pangs of loneliness are beaten backward into the love kiss, weave and kiss recedes into kiss and kisses into looks and looks into the heart's dark—and over again and over again and time's pushed ahead in spite of all that. The petals that fell bearing me under are lifted one by one. That which kissed my flesh for priest's lace so that I could not touch it—weave and you have lifted it and I am glimpsing light chinks among the notes! Backward, and my hair is crisp with purple sap and the last crust's broken. (XVII, 2 in *KH,* 62–63)

This Improvisation originates in the poet's momentary realization that "This that I have struggled against"—the fire inside—is his true self, a self he has been suppressing in submission to

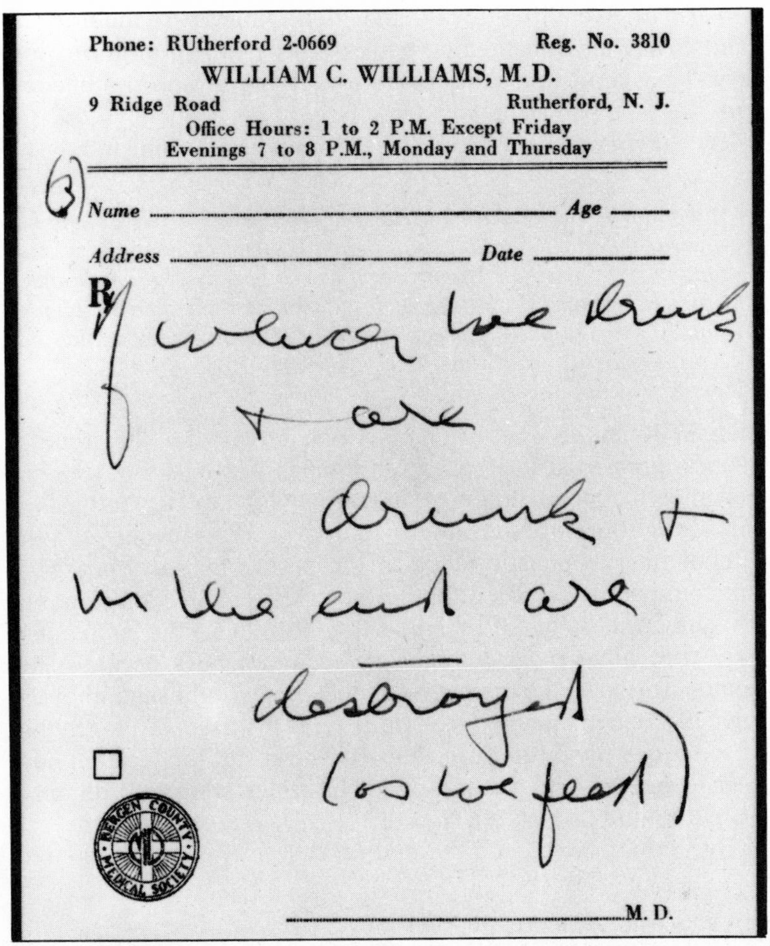
Phone: RUtherford 2-0669 **Reg. No. 3810**

WILLIAM C. WILLIAMS, M. D.

9 Ridge Road **Rutherford, N. J.**

Office Hours: 1 to 2 P.M. Except Friday
Evenings 7 to 8 P.M., Monday and Thursday

(6)

Name ______ *Age* ____

Address ______ *Date* ____

℞

which we drink
& are
drunk &
in the end are
destroyed
(as we fear)

BERGEN COUNTY MEDICAL SOCIETY

______ M. D.

One of the prescription pads on which Williams jotted lines and made notes between patients at the office and on his rounds.

the faceless "They" (family, community, the world outside) who "said I could not put the flower back into the stem." The incantation, "Weave away, dead fingers," generates a process whereby the poet's own consciousness merges with that of his mother: step by step, he becomes the young girl in Mayaguez she once was, romping through the sugarcane and "leading over the ditches, with your skirts flying and the devil in the wind back of you." But the incantatory repetition of "Weave" (the imperative verb occurs five times) cannot quite erase that other image which haunts the poet, the image of "the bitter tongue of an old woman . . . eating, eating, eating venomous words with thirty years' mould on them." The process of the prose poem is to subordinate this image to the "love kiss" and the "heart's dark" that once was. The ritual of exorcism finally brings the poet back to his Edenic origins: "The petals that fell bearing me under are lifted one by one." And so "my hair is crisp with purple sap and the last crust's broken."

Williams's prose effectively moves forward by allowing each sentence to generate the next. The reader cannot know, at the opening of the poem, in what sense "all's right now." But in the process of "weav[ing] away" the "dead fingers" of the present, the "flower" is once again "back into the stem," and the "last crust's broken." In a sudden epiphany, mother and son become one.

But now consider the italicized commentary that follows:

> *A woman on the verge of growing old kindles in the mind of her son a certain curiosity which spinning upon itself catches the woman herself in its wheel, stripping from her the accumulations of many harsh years and shows her at last full of an old time suppleness hardly to have been guessed by the stiffened exterior which had held her fast till that time.* (*KH,* 63)

Here Williams gives us a summary account of what the previous section presented in fragmented images. He tells what he has just shown. One might argue, of course, that the very flatness of this straightforward account is ironic when juxtaposed with the exclamatory, imagistic mode of the preceding section. Again, the commentary shifts attention from the old woman's "pangs of agony and pangs of loneliness" to her "old time suppleness hardly to have been guessed at," a suppleness perhaps just demonstrated in the Improvisation. Still, it would seem that the logic of the commentary is at odds with the associative rhythm of the prose poem that precedes it. The result is a certain coyness or self-consciousness—what H.D. referred to as Williams's "hey-ding-ding touch" (*KH,* 13).

By the time we reach the end of XVII, however, the balance

has been righted. In Part 3, the moon of the first section reappears in the "glassy twilight" where the poet sits alone. The moment of ecstasy when the petals are "lifted one by one" has passed, and we read:

> Feel your way up to the bed. Drop your clothes on the floor and creep in. Flesh becomes so accustomed to the touch she will not even waken. And so hours pass and not a move. The room too falls asleep and the street outside falls mumbling into a heap of black rags morning's at seven.

So much for the "light chinks among the notes" and the "purple sap." Time is once again perceived as linear, and the poet perceives that his mother can no more become the young girl she once was than he can escape his daily routine. Next to the body of his sleeping wife, he witnesses the passing of the night hours. And the final commentary is ambivalent:

> *Seeing a light in an upper window the poet by means of the power he has enters the room and of what he sees there brews himself a sleeping potion.*

Does the doctor literally take a sleeping potion? Maybe, so as to wipe out his own "pangs of loneliness." Or is the "sleeping potion" his poetic brew, the dream-image of Mayaguez conjured up so as to create "light chinks among the notes"? We can read the commentary either way (and other readings would be possible); the poem ends, in any case, on a note of irresolution. The reader is propelled forward: XVIII opens with the sentence, "How deftly we keep love from each other." And now another kind of love, adultery, is explored.

In his next serial work, *Spring and All,* Williams came closer to achieving the "simultaneity" he admired in the artworks of Picabia, Picasso, and Juan Gris. The intermittent coyness of *Kora* (e.g., "To you! whoever you are, wherever you are! [But I know who you are!], *KH,* 56) now gives way to what Williams would later call "a field of action," a "machine made of words" in which lyric passages (there are twenty-seven poems in all) modulate quite naturally into their prose analogues. Thus poem VIII ends with the lines:

> Impossible
>
> to say, impossible
> to underestimate—
> wind, earthquakes in
>
> Manchuria, a
> partridge
> from dry leaves

Wind, earthquakes in Manchuria, a partridge from dried leaves —what can unite such disparate items? The prose passage that follows answers the question by focusing on a Juan Gris still life:

> Things with which he is familiar, simple things—at the same time to detach them from ordinary experience to the imagination. . . .
>
> Here is a shutter, a bunch of grapes, a sheet of music, a picture of sea and mountains (particularly fine) which the onlooker is not for a moment permitted to witness as an "illusion." One thing laps over on the other, the cloud laps over on the shutter, the bunch of grapes is part of the handle of the guitar, the mountain and sea are obviously not "the mountain and sea," but a picture of the mountain and the sea. (*SAA,* 110, 111)

Not the mountain and sea but a *picture* of mountain and sea. In the Cubist poems dispersed among passages of prose that make up *Spring and All,* we witness what Williams calls, again referring to Gris, the "power TO ESCAPE ILLUSION," to avoid "likeness to nature." This does not mean that the poems renounce referentiality: "I do not believe," Williams insists, "that writing is music" (*SAA,* 150). It does mean that, as in the case of the visual images in Cubist painting, the verbal clues here contradict each other, thus preventing the formation of a coherent image of reality.

Consider Juan Gris's "Still Life Before an Open Window: Place Ravignan," (1915), a painting belonging to Williams's friend, the great collector Walter Arensberg. Here we can identify the objects on the table—carafe, bowl of fruit, goblet, newspaper—and the window view—shuttered windows across the street, trees, balcony rails—quite easily. We can also make out the wine label "MEDOC" and the block letters of "LE JOURNAL." But these "real" objects are seen as if through a distorting lens; they are rigidly subordinated to the geometric grid of the painting: a complex set of interlocking triangles and rectangular planes whose spatial positions are ambiguous. Thus the balcony rail on the right seems to intersect the house across the street, or again the table top becomes a reflecting mirror, endowing the letters of "LE JOURNAL" with different sizes and shapes. The canvas thus records the oscillation of representative reference and compositional game: the "still life" seems to be in constant motion.

The *Spring and All* lyrics, all too often taken out of their context and printed separately, provide verbal analogues of such Cubist fragmentation and superposition of ambiguously located planes. Take poem IX, which follows Williams's discussion of Juan Gris. It begins:

Region of Brooklyn Bridge Fantasy
by John Marin.

What about all this writing?

O "Kiki"
O Miss Margaret Jarvis
The backhandspring
I: clean
clean
clean: . . New York

Wrigley's, appendicitis, John Marin:
skyscraper soup—. . .

—From "Young Love"

What about all this writing?

O "Kiki"
O Miss Margaret Jarvis
The backhandspring

I: clean
  clean
  clean: yes . . . New-York

Wrigley's, appendicitis, John Marin:
skyscraper soup—

Either that or a bullet!

Once
anything might have happened
You lay relaxed on my knees—
the starry night
spread out warm and blind
above the hospital—

(*SAA,* 113)

The scene (evidently a memory of Williams's internship) is a New York hospital, the view from the window providing a kind of John Marin cityscape, with its "skyscraper soup" punctuated by advertising posters for Wrigley's chewing gum. But who is Miss Margaret Jarvis, also known, perhaps in tribute to the great French cabaret dancer of the twenties, as "Kiki"? She is obviously someone to whom the poet has been close, a nurse perhaps, judging from the last lines of the poem:

fifteen years ago and you still
go about the city, they say
patching up sick school children

But the heroine of this fragmented narrative may also be a patient:

You sobbed, you beat your pillow
you tore your hair
you dug your nails into your sides

Or, for that matter, the poet may be recalling a number of women with whom he was involved during his internship in New York. Williams does not, in any case, want us to reconstruct the narrative. Rather, the poem juxtaposes images of eroticism—"The backhandspring," "Once anything might have happened / You lay relaxed on my knees— / the starry night / spread out warm and blind / above the hospital"—with a nagging fear of involvement and that which is "unclean":

In my life the furniture eats me

the chairs, the floor
the walls

which heard your sobs
drank up my emotion—

And again:

It is not onion soup
Your sobs soaked through the walls
breaking the hospital to pieces

A breakage that recurs eleven lines later:

All I said was:
there, you see, it is broken

stockings, shoes, hairpins
your bed, I wrapped myself round you—

It is interesting to compare Williams's "Kiki" poem with *The Waste Land* published just a year earlier and greeted by Williams, still almost entirely unknown to a larger public, as "the great catastrophe to our letters" (*Auto,* 146). Like "The Fire Sermon," Williams's poem records a series of what might be considered sordid affairs, but here the lover and his mistress (or mistresses) are not, like Eliot's typist and clerk or Thames daughters, treated as representative of the sterility of the modern world. Rather, the poet-physician in the poem is torn between responsibility toward his mistress and the drive to be "clean / clean / clean" and to get on with "all this writing," all the while being absorbed in the mechanical routine of hospital duties:

beds, beds, beds
elevators, fruit, night-tables
breasts to see, white and blue—
to hold in the hand, to nozzle

To present this conflict in all its immediacy, as if it were taking place *now,* Williams juxtaposes fragmented images—the voiced threat of suicide ("Either that or a bullet!"), the sobs "soak[ing] through the walls," the windows and chairs "spinning— / white, blue, orange / —hot with our passion," a pair of legs, "turning slowly / end over end in the air!" In this context, the poet's recollection that "All I said was: / there, you see, it is broken," may refer to the mattress spring, the bed, the woman's hymen—or, for that matter, to their love affair. What is interesting, in any case, is that the role he assumes is that of voyeur:

> I watched
>
> You sobbed, you beat your pillow
> you tore your hair
> you dug your nails into your sides
>
> I was your nightgown
>   I watched!

This sense of withdrawal, of wanting to stand outside experience, is one we shall meet frequently in the later Williams, especially in the short stories collected in *Life Along the Passaic River.* Empathy ("I wrapped myself round you," "I was your nightgown") gives way to the cool clinical detachment of "but I merely / caress you curiously." For the poet, survival finally depends upon separation:

> Clean is he alone
> after whom stream
> the broken pieces of the city—
> flying apart at his approaches.

By the end of the poem, the affair has become just another of "the broken pieces of the city— / flying apart at his approaches."

It is these "broken pieces" that constitute Williams's poetic collage. Further, the poem itself is juxtaposed to the prose passage that follows, which contains the cryptic remark, "When we name it, life exists. To repeat physical experiences has no—" (*SAA,* 115). The sentence breaks off even as the poem implies that "to repeat physical experiences" is much less interesting than to name them. And the naming takes place, not in the order the events occurred, nor, for that matter, in any sort of causal or logical sequence. The poem's images do not carry symbolic weight; they point to no external sphere of reality outside themselves. Rather, items are related along the axis of contiguity: the "backhandspring" prepares us for the "bullet," which in turn leads to "not straight to the mark," and then to the images of breakage that culminate in "the broken pieces of the city." Or again, "skyscraper soup" makes way for "onion soup" and, by inversion, for the furniture that "eats me" and the "chairs, the floor / the walls" that "drank up my emotion."

In a larger sense, the whole book constitutes just such a field of contiguities. Williams's recurrent images—wind, flower, star, white, dark—are perfectly ordinary, but it is their *relationships*

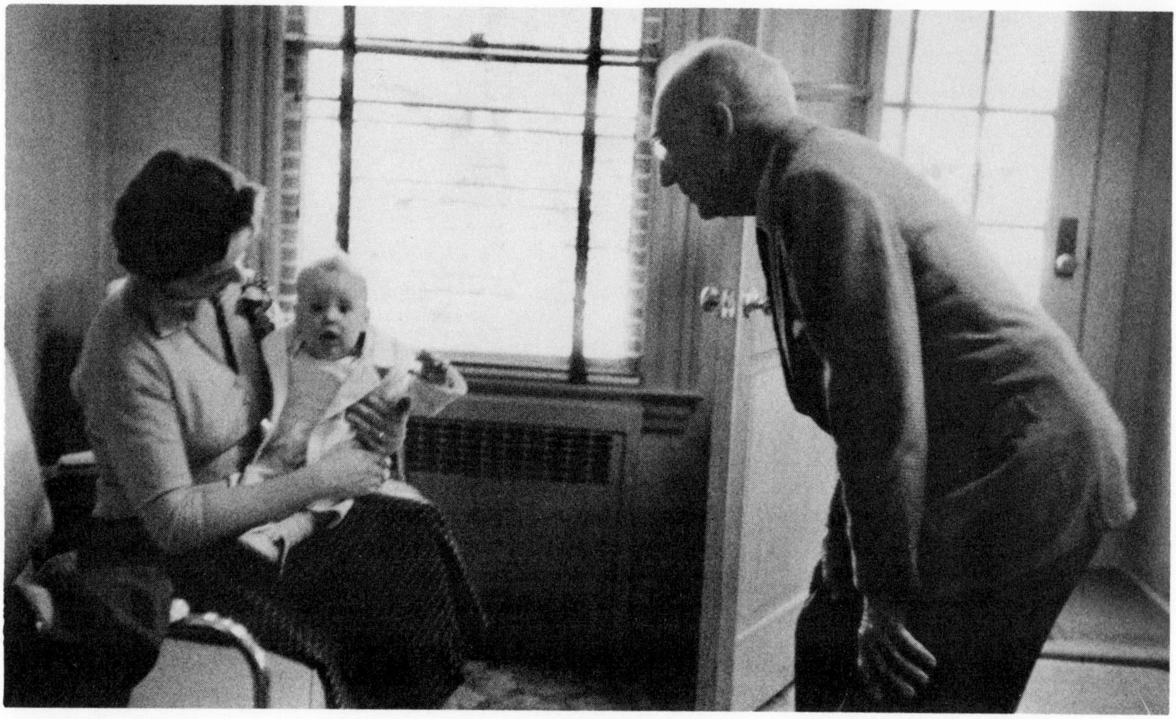

Dr. Williams greeting a patient.

And my "medicine" was the thing that gained me entrance to these secret gardens of the self. It lay there, another world, in the self. I was permitted by my medical badge to follow the poor, defeated body into those gulfs and grottos. . . . In illness, in the permission I as a physician have had to be present at deaths and births, at the tormented battles between daughter and diabolic mother, shattered by a gone brain—just there—for a split second—from one side or the other, it has fluttered before me for a moment, a phrase which I quickly write down on anything at hand, any piece of paper I can grab.

—From Williams's *Autobiography*

that matter. The final poem in *Spring and All,* which acts as a coda, provides what is perhaps the best clue to the structural dynamics of the serial poem:

Black eyed susan
rich orange
round the purple core

the white daisy
is not
enough

Crowds are white
as farmers
who live poorly

But you
are rich
in savagery—

Arab
Indian
dark woman

(*SAA*, 151)

Read independently, this is no more than an attractive little flower poem in which the black-eyed susan is treated animistically as a savagely sensual woman. To compare flowers to women—what could be more hackneyed? Yet a reader who comes across this poem in an anthology and hence does not know its context must surely wonder about the third tercet: what do white crowds and poor farmers have to do with the "savagery" of the "Arab / Indian / dark woman"?

Within the confines of the poem, there is no particular connection. But in terms of the larger structure of *Spring and All,* the words "white," "crowds," and "farmers" are charged with meaning because of their nagging recurrence (e.g., "beside the white chickens," "the whitish moonlight," "Pink confused with white / flowers"; or again, "Nightly the crowds," "The crowds at the ballgame," "the crowd is laughing"; "The farmer in deep thought," "the quality of the farmer's / shoulders"). Again, the images "black," "eyes," "orange," "purple," "core," and "white" recur in any number of different contexts. Against this backdrop, comes the astonishing final tercet:

Arab
Indian
dark woman

We have been introduced to the notion of "Indian" "savagery" in the reference to the "dash of Indian blood" that characterizes the poor slatternly Elsie of XVIII. "Arab" harks back to the smiling gipsy of XXI and the "Gipsy lips pressed / to my own" of XXIV. "Dark" has, of course, occurred frequently, from the "dark" but "wholly gay" flowerpot of II, with its "darkened" petals, to the light which becomes "darkness and darkness light" of XIV. But although the word "woman" has been used once or twice in the sequence, it is only at the very end of the poem that she is endowed with the attributes *Arab, Indian, dark.* Furthermore, the conclusion of the lyric points back to the opening line, which contains the only mention of the word "susan" in the whole sequence.

By relating these items, Williams thus suddenly opens up the text: the "Arab / Indian / dark woman" who is also a "susan" is verbally a *discovery* even if she has been present all along as a subliminal image. Only as we read the last words of the coda poem, do we suddenly see that this image of "rich . . . savagery" has been at the core of *Spring and All* from the beginning. Indeed, the poet's sexual desire for just such a "dark woman" has been a latent theme all along, from the reference to "Thither I would carry her / among the lights" of poem IV, to the image of Elsie, the "voluptuous water" of XVIII, to "The sea that encloses her young body" of XX. Indeed, the thrust of *Spring and All* is to bring the "dark woman" to life out of the surrounding death. The "broad, muddy fields / brown with dried weeds" and "patches of standing water" of the opening poem finally give birth to the "Black eyed susan / rich orange / round the purple core." Out of the "messy" and unwieldy prose, out of the disorder of language, out of the "broken pieces of the city" where the poet works, the "dazed spring" of poem I "approaches."

IV

By 1934, when Louis Zukofsky's Objectivist Press published Williams's *Collected Poems 1921–1931,* the poet was fifty-one. The new direction his work would take in the thirties is prefigured in a poem originally published in *Spring and All* and later reprinted under the title "The Red Wheelbarrow":

so much depends
upon

a red wheel
barrow

glazed with rain
water

beside the white
chickens

(*CEP,* 277)

This famous, and frequently lampooned, minimal poem belongs less to the erotically charged landscape of *Spring and All* than to the more severe, hard-edged Objectivist space of Williams's Depression America. Williams had met Louis Zukofsky in 1928, and in an article on "Objectivism" for the *Princeton Encyclopedia of Poetry and Poetics,* he wrote:

OBJECTIVISM. A term used to describe a mode of writing, particularly the writing of verse. It recognizes the poem, apart from its meaning, to be an object to be dealt with as such. O[bjectivism] looks at the poem with a special eye to its structural aspect, how it has been constructed. The term originated in 1931 with a small group of poets calling themselves "The Objectivists," who used it to signalize their work: George Oppen, Louis Zukofsky, Charles Reznikoff, Lorine Niedecker and W. C. Williams. Individually they published several books and together, in 1932, *An "Objectivist" Anthology.* The movement, never widely accepted, was early abandoned. It arose as an aftermath of imagism, which the Objectivists felt was not specific enough. . . . O[bectivism] concerned itself with an image more particularized yet broadened in its significance. The mind rather than the unsupported eye entered the picture.

Zukofsky was later to demur that there never was any such thing as "Objectivism," but, as Hugh Kenner points out in *Homemade World,* what the term meant in practice was that the poet "look[s] at the interaction of the lines, not at their rapport with their subject." Such "interaction" had always mattered to Williams, but the Objectivist phase brought a new concern for objectivity, construction, and, as Williams notes, "the mind rather than the unsupported eye." In keeping with the radicalism of the thirties (a radicalism from which Williams stood somewhat apart), Objectivism emphasized the materiality of the object.

"The Red Wheelbarrow" is a good example of a poem in which "so much depends" precisely on "the interaction of lines" apart from its "subject." "Try to imagine," says Kenner, "an occasion for this sentence to be said:

> So much depends upon a red wheelbarrow glazed with rainwater beside the white chickens.

Try it over, in any voice you like: it is impossible. . . . Not only is what the sentence says banal, if you heard someone say it, you'd wince. But hammered on the typewriter into a *thing made,* and this without displacing a single word except typographically, the sixteen words exist in a different zone altogether."

The zone is that of four identical two-line stanzas, identical, at least, to the eye. "Wheel" is separated from "barrow," "rain" from "water," using cuts that makes us rethink the meaning of these compound nouns. Further, the morphemes "bárrow," "wáter," and "chíckens" each constitute a trochee, the "weight" of the red wheelbarrow being what "so much (the food supply? the farmer's survival?, the pastoral order?) depends upon." Like a hard-edge painting, "The Red Wheelbarrow" is a composition in simple, primary colors—red and white—a red offset just slightly by the "glaze" of rainwater. The white chickens beside the red wheelbarrow: a synecdoche for an image of "the farm." And the picture is "framed" neatly by its stanzaic structure: the syllable count is 4/2, 3/2, 3/2, 4/2.

The attention to lineation is, of course, nothing new for Williams. What is new is the "stanzaic" uniformity, the compactness of structure, the reduction of the connotative power of the image. I once had a student who insisted that "The Red Wheelbarrow" could yield a hidden meaning. He argued that the "red wheelbarrow" of Communism would soon have the "white chickens" of Capitalism decapitated and inside it. But he didn't know what to do with "glazed," rather than, say, "flooded" with rainwater. By the same token, "The Red Wheelbarrow" cannot be read as a poem about the red of passion and the white of being "chicken"—that is, virgin. The poem is what it is, a "mobile-like arrangement," as Wallace Stevens said critically, a system of tensions, a structure of checks and balances.

The thirties yielded dozens of such poems from Williams, among them such famous lyrics as "Young Sycamore," "Poem: As the cat," "On Gay Wallpaper," "Nantucket," "This Is Just to Say," "Young Woman at a Window," "A Chinese Toy," and "The Term." To take just one example of the "Objectivist" Williams, here is "Between Walls." Characteristically, the title is part of the poem:

BETWEEN WALLS

the back wings
of the

hospital where
nothing

will grow lie
cinders

in which shine
the broken

pieces of a green
bottle

(*CEP*, 343)

If we insert two small function words, "the" in the title and "of" at the beginning of the first line, and place a comma after "grow," we have a perfectly "normal" sentence:

> Between the walls of the back wings of the hospital where nothing will grow, lie cinders in which shine the broken pieces of a green bottle.

An independent clause, its subject and verb inverted, lies embedded in multiple prepositional modifiers. Williams drapes this sentence across ten lines so that each and every word is taken out of its proper syntactic slot and hence defamiliarized:

> of the . . .
> will grow lie . . .
> in which shine . . .

and so on. But there is something more. The visual pattern—five symmetrical couplets in which a long line is regularly followed by a short one, contradicts the aural one. Compare, for example, the first and third couplets:

the back wings of the	will grow lie cinders

On the page, these are matching couplets, each having a syllable count of 3/2, each of the first lines, moreover, containing three monosyllables. But when the poem is spoken, "of the" receives no stress at all, whereas line five gets three ("wíll grów / / líe").

What looks symmetrical is, in other words, characterized by difference. This is precisely what Williams's scrupulously bare, minimal, "Objectivist" poem tells us. The poem fixes its objects in an anonymous space; there is no observer here to tell us what "depends upon" the image. Just as the pieces of the green bottle are broken, so the words of the poem are separated from their grammatical neighbors, creating jagged patterns like "will grow lie" and "of the." The poem means, so Williams tells Babette Deutsch, "that in a waste of cinders loveliness, in the form of color, stands up alive" (*SL,* 265). Stated thus flatly, this is pure sentimentality; indeed, the poem, as it stands, "means" something a little different.

The word "wings" in line one naturally brings to mind images of birds in flight, but here there are only the "back wings / of the / hospital." The hospital is a repository of disease, not of growth, and we all know how dingy and unappetizing the waste spaces "between [its] walls" can be. "Nothing" appropriately gets a line to itself as does "cinders." What flower can root itself in such soil? The meaning is suspended: first we perceive that something (as opposed to "nothing") does "shine" here; then we realize that it is "broken," and only with the presentation of the last word in the poem, do we comprehend that the "green" that shines here is not grass or leaf but only the broken pieces of a bottle.

It is not, then, so much a matter of "loveliness, in the form of color" standing up "alive" in the cinders. For there is nothing at all lovely about broken green glass in a parking lot or alley. The normal way to perceive such "broken pieces" is as part of the trash. But what Williams's poem really "says" is that, "hammered on the typewriter," the poet's words become nodes of energy in the verbal field, particles in a process of discovery. Having read "Between Walls," one perceives the bleak scene at "the back wings" with new eyes. The words, anchored in their odd linear configurations, imply that, if we pay attention, a hidden radiance may be ours.

V

Quite possibly, Williams never surpassed the accomplishment of these small Objectivist poems. Imitated by countless later poets, they are only now beginning to be understood as works that are, in fact, extremely difficult to construct. But the poem that was to make him famous, that was to pave the way for the enthusiastic reception of such late, and to my mind, lesser works as *The Desert Music* (written in 1951 after Williams had suffered a severe stroke) was, of course, the "epic" *Paterson,* the first book of which was published in 1946. The fourth (and supposedly final) book appeared in 1951; a fifth book was added in 1958. By this time, just five years before his death, Williams had finally become famous: when *Pictures from Breughel* appeared in 1962, any response other than total enthusiasm seemed out of order.

If less space than usual is devoted here to *Paterson* and the late works, it is for two reasons. First, more has been written about *Paterson* than about all Williams's earlier poems and prose works put together: I refer the reader to Paul Mariani's authoritative biography (1981) and to the studies of Joel Conarroe, Benjamin Sankey, Walter Peterson, Bernard Duffey, Stephen Tapscott, and others. Secondly, *Paterson* and the fifties poems have been, I think, rather overrated, or at least admired for the wrong reasons. Let me explain.

Williams's correspondence of the late thirties and early forties reveals that he conceived of *Paterson* essentially as a response to Pound's *Cantos.* Pound had been writing, since 1917, a major epic, whereas he, Williams, seemed unable to articulate a coherent long poem. In 1936, he wrote Pound: "And then there's that magnum opus I've always wanted to do: the poem PATERSON. Jeez how I'd like to get at that. I've been sounding myself out in these years working toward a form of some sort" (*SL,* 163). But what sort? By 1943, Williams was still unsure. " 'Paterson,' " he wrote his new publisher James Laughlin, "I know, is crying to be written; the time demands it; it has to do

To Elsie

The pure products of America
go crazy—
mountain folk from Kentucky

or the ribbed north end of
Jersey
with its isolate lakes and

valleys, its deaf-mutes, thieves
old names
and promiscuity between

devil-may-care men who have taken
to railroading
out of sheer lust of adventure—

and young slatterns, bathed
in filth
from Monday to Saturday

to be tricked out that night
with gauds
from imaginations which have no

peasant traditions to give them
character
but flutter and flaunt

sheer rags—succumbing without
emotion
save numbed terror

under some hedge of choke-cherry
or viburnum—
which they cannot express—

Unless it be that marriage
perhaps
with a dash of Indian blood

will throw up a girl so desolate
so hemmed round
with disease or murder

that she'll be rescued by an
agent—
reared by the state and

sent out at fifteen to work in
some hard-pressed
house in the suburbs—

some doctor's family, some Elsie—
voluptuous water
expressing with broken

brain the truth about us—
her great
ungainly hips and flopping breasts

addressed to cheap
jewelry
and rich young men with fine eyes

as if the earth under our feet
were
an excrement of some sky

and we degraded prisoners
destined
to hunger until we eat filth

while the imagination strains
after deer
going by fields of goldenrod in

the stifling heat of September
Somehow
it seems to destroy us

It is only in isolate flecks that
something
is given off

No one
to witness
and adjust, no one to drive the car

just with all the peace movements, the plans for international infiltration into the dry mass of those principles of knowledge and culture which the universities and their cripples have cloistered and made a cult" (*SL*, 214). And a few months later to his friend Robert McAlmon:

"Lackawanna Station, February, 1968" by George Tice.

I'm in process of writing a book, the book I have contemplated doing for many years—prose and verse mixed: "Paterson"—an account, a psychologic-social panorama of a city treated as if it were a man, the man Paterson. I want to work at it but I shy off whenever I sit down to work. It's maddening but I have the hardest time to make myself stick to it. (*SL,* 216).

How do we account for these nagging doubts? Pound's *Cantos* had proved that it was, after all, possible, in the twentieth century, to write a long encyclopedic poem. Williams was dazzled by the example even as he seems to have felt the obligation to write a kind of anti-*Cantos,* a poem of "local pride" written in the American idiom and celebrating the daily circumstances of his own locality. Given this context, the Author's Note to Book One is revealing:

> This is the first part of a long poem in four parts—that a man is himself a city, beginning, seeking, achieving and concluding his life in ways which the various aspects of a city may embody—if imaginatively conceived—any city, all the details of which may be made to voice his most intimate convictions. Part One introduces the elemental character of the place. (*IWWP,* 71)

As for the choice of city, Williams explains:

> The problem of the poetics I knew depended upon finding a specific city, one that I knew, so I searched for a city. New York? It couldn't be New York, nor anything as big as a metropolis. Rutherford wasn't a city. Passaic wouldn't do. I'd known about Paterson, even written about it as I've mentioned. Suddenly it dawned on me I had a find. I began my investigations. Paterson had a history, an important colonial history. It had, besides, a river—the Passaic, and the Falls. I may have been influenced by James Joyce who had made Dublin the hero of his book. I had been reading *Ulysses.* But I forgot about Joyce and fell in love with my city. The Falls were spectacular; the river was a symbol handed to me. (*IWWP,* 72)

"A man is himself a city": here is the central identification that was to give Williams trouble, even as the Passaic River and its Falls were to become problematic symbolic properties. For what was Paterson, New Jersey, really to stand for? As Michael A. Bernstein points out in his important study of modern verse epic, Williams wholly idealized the real historical significance of the New Jersey town. Except for a short period during the American Revolution, Paterson played no important role in the colonial history of the United States. Its commercial importance during the nineteenth century was fleeting, and by 1946, the date of Book One, it would have carried few, if any, associations for American readers. Accordingly, it could only stand, in a general way, for the despoliation of the once-pastoral landscape by modern industrialization and economic greed. Hence the Romantic commonplaces of the opening:

A man like a city and a woman like a flower
—who are in love. Two women. Three women.
Innumerable women, each like a flower.

But

only one man—like a city.

(*P*, 7)

**Jostled as the waters approaching
the brink, his thoughts
interlace, repel and cut under,
rise rock-thwarted and turn aside
but forever strain forward—or strike
an eddy and whirl, marked by a
leaf or curdy spume, seeming to forget
Retake later the advance and
are replaced by succeeding hordes
pushing forward—they coalesce now
glass-smooth with their swiftness,
quiet or seem to quiet as at the close
they leap to the conclusion and
fall, fall in air! as if
floating, relieved of their weight,
split apart, ribbons; dazed, drunk
with the catastrophe of the descent
floating unsupported
to hit the rocks: to a thunder,
as if lightning had struck**

—From *Paterson*

The Passaic Falls

The identification is asserted rather than realized in the poem; indeed, in the course of *Paterson,* the existence of Paterson as a *city* is all but forgotten. Instead of examining the political, historical, and economic reality of Paterson, the text provides a somewhat static and repetitive opposition between natural beauty (the unspoiled landscape, the poet's desire for the "Beautiful Thing!") on the one hand and the "divorce" that results from economic and sexual exploitation on the other.

As such, the poetic of *Paterson* is curiously at odds with that of the earlier poems. In *Spring and All,* the tension between "cleanliness" and "savagery," between what we may call the poet's "English" self-discipline and his "Spanish" passion, is at the core ("Kore") of his own self; he cannot, indeed does not want to, separate the two. Or again, in "Between Walls," discovery can come only by attentiveness to the tiniest of local manifestations—the broken pieces, for instance, of a green bottle. But in *Paterson,* Williams erects an elaborate typological structure that, as Michael Bernstein says, "violates just that specificity of surface detail which had given Williams's earlier writing its energy and sharpness of focus." Thus the thunder of the Falls symbolizes the inarticulate language of Paterson's citizens, out of which the poet must "comb" his meaning. The Falls are further identified with the destructive fire and "Beautiful Thing" of Book Three, and with the experiments of Madame Curie in Book Four. Unlike Joyce, for whom every insignificant detail of Dublin could prove to be epiphanic, Williams did not quite know how "To make a start, / out of [the] particulars" of his locale. And unlike Pound, for whom Malatesta and Adams were *alive,* living in the very verbal space which the poet occupied, Williams had to force the historical documents inserted into the text to yield up "relevant" meaning.

Why, then, given the neglect of the earlier work, was *Paterson* so immediately popular? No doubt, because Williams had finally written a poem that could be explicated, a poem with a universal theme: namely, the search for a natural language, an idiom that could recover the lost innocence of genuine communication between landscape and mind, between the artist and his world. Again, *Paterson* was America's answer to the mythic mode of Eliot and Pound, a genuinely American epic in the tradition of Whitman. It seemed to answer the demand for an "open" process-poem, an action model, whose perspective is repeatedly dissolved so as to allow for new beginnings. Yet the very texture of the verse, I would argue, is a measure of the poem's closure. Consider the opening of Book One, ii:

There is no direction. Whither? I
cannot say. I cannot say
more than how. The how (howl) only
is at my disposal (proposal) : watching—
colder than stone

                    a bud forever green,
tight-curled, upon the pavement, perfect
in juice and substance but divorced, divorced
from its fellows, fallen low—

                              Divorce is
the sign of knowledge in our time,
divorce! divorce!

                    with the roar of the river
forever in our ear (arrears)
inducing sleep and silence, the roar
of eternal sleep . .   challenging
our waking—

—unfledged desire, irresponsible, green,
colder to the hand than stone,
unready—challenging our waking.

(*P,* 18)

The usual way to talk about this passage is to note how despair and lassitude ("There is no direction") gradually gives way, thanks to the inspiriting "roar of the river," to newly awaked "desire, irresponsible, green." In the stanzas that follow, this desire finds a fantasy object in "Two halfgrown girls hailing hallowed Easter." We may also note such devices as the ironic echo, mimetic of the Falls, of "how (the howl)" and "disposal (proposal)," the separation of letters from punctuation marks, and the spread of words across the page.

But if "Between Walls" functions as a mobile or suspension system, the lines here seem merely to droop. "A bud forever green": the line break predictably comes at the end of the noun phrase, before the appositive, "tight-curled, upon the pavement." Again, "unfledged desire, irresponsible, green" (a standard free-verse line) is, not surprisingly, "colder to the hand than stone" (an echo of line five), but also, predictably, "unready—challenging our waking." In a poem like "The Young Housewife," every word counts; in the "divorce" passage in question, substitution for words like "substance," "unfledged," or "unready" would be entirely possible. The ambiguity of assertions like "The stain of love / is upon the world" gives way to the flatness of "Divorce is / the sign of knowledge in our time."

Yet, if the dialectic of *Paterson* often seems too neatly Hegelian, as Robert Lowell termed it, the poem is saved by its brilliant use of prose. The idea of inserting documentation, personal letters, diary entries, and other "found objects" into the lyric fabric may well have come from Pound, but nothing in the *Cantos* can equal the sense of presence and immediacy that characterizes, say, the neurotic letters from the woman who signs herself only as "C," the histories furnished by patients like that of the retarded "T," who tells the doctor about her lobotomized sister "Billy" (*P,* 26–27), or the report, in the third person, of Dr. Paterson's attempt to remove the label from a mayonnaise jar in which some patient had brought a specimen—an action that synecdochically defines his subconscious refusal to participate in the lives of others, even as he "talk[s] pleasantly the while and with great skill to the anxious parent" (*P,* 33).

The juxtaposition of such prose passages with their lyric analogues or opposites creates interesting collage patterns. In "The Library" (Book Three), for example, we find a letter from a certain D.J.B. that begins:

> Hi Kid
>
> I know you just about to shot me. But honest Hon. I have really been to busy to write. Here, there, and everywhere.
>
> Bab I haven't wrote since October so I will go back to Oct. 31, (Oh by the way are friend Madam B. Harris had a party the 31, but only high browns and *yellow* so I wasn't invited) (*P,* 123)

The letter continues on in this dialect vein, recording how the speaker got into a drunken driving accident, the persons who went to jail, and how many mutual friends are pregnant. Both poignant and funny, the broken prose of the unknown girl's letter now "cuts" into the poet's lyrical address:

> Later
> Beautiful thing
> I saw you:
> Yes, said
> the Lady of the House to my questioning.
> Downstairs
> (by the laundry tubs)
>
> (*P,* 124)

There is, in other words, more than one way of looking at the poor black girl in question: her inside view may not match his external one but both are essential to the poet's exploration.

Such shifts in perspective, the modulation of the text from high lyricism, to historical record, to the black dialect letter of D.J.B., make *Paterson* a remarkable poetic text, a paradigm later poets could adapt. Interesting as the experiment is, however, *Paterson* cannot quite match the achievement of such serial poems as *Spring and All,* poems in which form is genuinely an act of discovery. By the mid-fifties, when Williams, having suffered a series of strokes, wrote the famous triad poems "The Sparrow" and "Of Asphodel, That Greeny Flower," the act of discovery, the "nervous" toughness that makes the earlier work so arresting, had given way to sculpturesque stasis:

> Approaching death,
>   as we think, the death of love,
>   no distinction
> any more suffices to differentiate
>   the particulars
>   of place and condition
> with which we have been long
>   familiar.
>   All appears
> as if seen
>   wavering through water.
>   We start awake with a cry
> of recognition
>   but soon the outlines
>   become again vague.
> If we are to understand our time,
>   we must find the key to it. . . .
>
> (*PB,* 162)

Robert Lowell has recorded a moving account of Williams reading this poem:

> It was at Wellesley. I think about three thousand students attended. It couldn't have been more crowded in the wide-galleried hall and I had to sit in the aisle. The poet appeared, one whole side partly paralyzed, his voice just audible, and here and there a word misread. No one stirred. In the silence he read his great poem, "Of Asphodel, That Greeny Flower," a triumph of simple confession. . . .

Given the circumstances, it would have been churlish to question the structure of that "simple confession." But today, some thirty years later, we cannot help wondering what has happened to the principle that "a poem is a small (or large) machine made of words," that "it isn't what [the poet] *says* that counts as a work of art, it's what he makes" (*SE,* 256–57). For despite its network of unifying symbols, "Asphodel" is a poem of *saying.* In the passage from Book Two cited above, Williams's characteristic strategy of "cut" and juxtaposition so as to create a field of action, a suspension-system of opposed forces, gives way to a new reliance on direct abstract statement and smooth transition. The three-step grid is an attractive frame but it remains largely external to the articulation of meanings within it.

But there is something else. Reading Williams's lines

("no distinction / any more suffices to differentiate / the particulars / of place and condition / with which we have been long familiar" or "We start awake with a cry / of recognition / but soon the outlines / become again vague"), the voice we hear has a familiar ring. And for good reason. In old age, it seems, Williams quite unwittingly submits to the voice of his supposed arch-enemy, T. S. Eliot, to the inescapable rhythms and inflections of the *Four Quartets:*

There is, it seems to us,
At best, only a limited value
In the knowledge derived from experience.
The knowledge imposes a pattern, and falsifies,
For the pattern is new in every moment
And every moment is a new and shocking
Valuation of all we have been. We are only undeceived
Of that which, deceiving, could no longer harm.
("East Coker," II)

Or again:

It seems as one becomes older,
That the past has another pattern, and ceases to be a mere
  sequence—
Or even development: the latter a partial fallacy
Which becomes, in the popular mind, a means of disowning the
  past.

("The Dry Salvages," II)

If we realign these lines in triads—

It seems
          as one becomes older,
                    that the past has another pattern—

we might indeed "start awake with a cry / of recognition." No wonder the Wellesley audience of 1955, a year when Eliot's fame was at its height, loved "Asphodel."

Surely, the more challenging Williams, the Williams who sounds like no other poet and whom no other poet has quite managed to imitate, is not the author of "Asphodel," but the poet of that other "greeny flower," "Queen Anne's Lace," a flower which is never once described in the poem by that title (1920), even as it becomes the impetus for a remarkable meditation on the moment of love as it comes to climax:

Her body is not so white as
anemone petals nor so smooth—nor
so remote a thing. It is a field
of the wild carrot taking
the field by force; the grass
does not raise above it.
Here is no question of whiteness,
white as can be, with a purple mole
at the center of each flower.
Each flower is a hand's span
of her whiteness. Wherever
his hand has lain there is
a tiny purple blemish. Each part
is a blossom under his touch
to which the fibres of her being
stem one by one, each to its end,
until the whole field is a
white desire, empty, a single stem,
a cluster, flower by flower
a pious wish to whiteness gone over—
or nothing.

(*CEP,* 210)

Here is the "field" of language, taking each "cluster" of morphemes "by force" so as to create, finally, the satisfaction of that "white desire."

5

Made courage or made order or made grace
 Pull down thy vanity , pull down ,

Learn of the green world what can be thy place
In scaled invention or true artistry
Pull down thy vanity
                    Pacquin pull down !
  The green casque has outdone your elegance,

" Master thyself, then others shall the beare "
  Pull down thy vanity
Thou art a beaten dog beneath the HHHH hail
  A swolen magpie in a fitful sun
Half black half white
Nor knowst'ou wing from tail
Pull down thy vanity
                    How mean thy hates
Fostered in falsity
                    Pull down thy vanity
      Rathe to destroy , niggard in charity/
Pull down thy vanity
                    I say pull down .

But to have done instead of not doing
          this is not vanity
To have ,with decency , knocked
That a Blunt should open ;
      To have gathered from the air a live tradition
 or from a fine old eye the unconquered flame
This is not vanity.
   Here error is all in the not dHHHH done,
 all in the diffidence that faltered,

earlier ref To lizzard & katydid small green etc

(CANTO)

When with his hunting dog I see a cloud

" Guten Morgen , Mein Herr " yells the black boy from the jo-cart
 (Jeffers , Lovell and Harley
    also Mr Walls who has lent me a razor
   Persha , Nadasky and Harbell)

Swinburne my only miss
                    and I didn't know
he he'd been to see Landor
                    and they told me this that an8 tother
and when old Mathews
 went, he saw the three teacups
   two for Watts Dunton who liked to let his tea cool,
So old Elkin had only one glory :
   He did carry Algernon's suit case once
 when he , Elkin // first came to London.
 But given what I know now I'd have broken the door in
 or got thru it somehos ... Direce's shade
                    or a blackjack .

whence french
 ench fisher;men hauled him ...

EZRA POUND

HUGH KENNER

I

Homer L. Pound was deputy assayer at the mint in Philadelphia; his wife Isabel believed in high decorum. Their house in Wyncote, Pennsylvania, had a stained glass window. Growing up surrounded by studied gentility, their son Ezra (born in 1885) experienced day by day a comfortable culture of fervid blankness. Its rationale is well described by Peter Makin:

> At a certain point the *raison d'être* for the whole economic structure was the Sunday-afternoon tea and chat, this being the ideal end of the consumer chain: for this heavy industry fed light industry, that ultimately some might sit among the latter's products and chat, and that others might aspire to.[1]

Spelled out, some unthinking assumptions sound parodic. Thus the purpose of two light industries, painting pictures and framing them, was to decorate the spaces where tea was taken. Thus Michelangelo had existed that in rooms so ornamented women might come and go and chat of him. Thus the University, yet another light industry, was valued for equipping the sons of the more favored with qualifications easy chat could allude to. T. S. Eliot's first subject would be the suffocation induced by such a world, and the first bond between him and Pound, when they met in London in 1914, would be the way they had both put distance between it and themselves.

And the poet? The role of the poet could only be to fill awkward spaces in *The Atlantic* and other magazines with rhythmic accolades to the refinement of the browser's soul. Pound would remember a time when he had supposed that appearing in *The Atlantic* was an honor to aspire to. He went to a good school where he was taught Latin so well he would read Latin verse at sight for the rest of his life, and at fifteen he was duly enrolled in the University of Pennsylvania, to study what we now call comparative literature, though the phrase was yet to be coined. In those years the four percent of college-age youths who went to college might be understood to be fulfilling their families' aspirations. A boy learning Provençal was a boy to be proud of!

Ezra Pound as a youth.

It was college that freed Pound from those aspirations, though he was never estranged from the mother and father who held them; one thing we can hear behind his lifelong didacticism is the effort to bring them along, to explain himself to them.[2] Talent and fortune had brought him a vocation. In classrooms at Penn and Hamilton, and through the languages he picked up there, he glimpsed what he aspired to join—the world community of poets, the sons of Homer.

II

Homer drew on unrecorded bards. Vergil read and emulated Homer. Dante, twelve centuries later, shut off from Greek, read Vergil, to visit the dead as Aeneas had and as before him had

Odysseus. A poet using English centuries later had better be familiar with all three. So much would have come as no surprise to Tennyson, who praised Vergil, and envied Dante the Italian vowels, and even Englished a few vignettes of Homer's.

But the generation of Pound and Eliot had access to a new way of thinking about languages and their masters, rooted in studies that had come to fruition long after the great Victorians' minds were formed. It was possible to ignore the national literatures, to conceive poetry as international and interlingual, and to imagine poetry in English as intertwined with poetry in Greek, Latin, Italian, French, in much the way those languages were themselves intertwined. By 1900, the affiliations of languages stood documented and comprehended. The literature of Europe, like its speech, could be conceived as one rich organism, and the study of poetry be seen as inextricable from the study of philology.

In the classrooms where Pound developed this sense of tradition, the nineteenth century's chief intellectual adventure still quickened. That was the vast cooperative effort that had ordered the lore of the Indo-European languages, a subject unsuspected before 1788, when Sir William Jones announced his great discovery that Sanskrit held the key to the kinship of the tongues of Europe. (So, in *The Waste Land* [1922], T. S. Eliot's quester after lost origins would hear an Indo-European root, *DA,* uttered by thunder near the Ganges.)

By the mid-nineteenth century it had grown clear that dictionaries wanted organizing on historical principles, not starting from current usage but ending with it. So old texts needed faithful old-spelling editing for dictionaries to cite, and decade after decade lexicography and textual scholarship went hand in hand. Manuscripts were transcribed, collated, arranged by families; principles of emendation were arrived at; scholars devised fine-print apparatus to record intricate webs with economy. Something like Ugo Canello's edition of Arnaut Daniel (only twenty years old when Ezra Pound used it in W. P. Shepard's seminar) was in effect a new kind of book, neatly compressing into notes and appendices the cross talk of dozens of scholars. Much detail was understood to be not yet settled, and all this information was meant to assist further thought. One lesson for Pound was the way light came incrementally as minds grappled with minutiae; that foreshadows the role into which he would maneuver the reader of his *Cantos.* He himself shirked no detail. For help with one word on which Canello was unpersuasive, he was to seek out the lexicographer Emil Levy in Freiburg; the story is told in Canto xx. And Sweet's *Anglo-Saxon Reader,* which he'd used in college, went with him to

London. It's arresting, that glimpse of old textbooks claiming space in a poet's luggage.

Whoever retraces Pound's dealings with a source will be struck by the extent of his engagement with its notes and appendices. It was always to the apparatus that he turned, in a scholarly book. Fred Robinson[3] has beautifully documented his engagement with Sweet's notes as he worked on the Anglo-Saxon "Seafarer," making textual decisions as he went. (They have passed for guesses and misreadings, and are often, to say the least, debatable; but they were demonstrably *pondered.*) That was in 1911. By a decade later he was incorporating fragments of academic fact into the very page he showed his reader. Thus in Canto XXV we confront the committee minutes that enabled the slow creation of the Ducal Palace in Venice:

1335. 3 lire 15 groats to stone for making a lion.
1340. Council of the lords noble, Marc Erizio
Nic. Speranzo, Tomasso Gradonico:
                                                  that the hall
be new built over the room of the night watch
and over the columns toward the canal where the walk is . . .

because of the stink of the dungeons. 1344.
1409 . . . since the most serene Doge can scarce
stand upright in his bedroom . . .
                                        vadit pars, two gross lire
stone stair, 1415, for pulchritude of the palace

                                        254 da parte
                                          de non 23
                                          4 non sincere
Which is to say: they built out over the arches
and the palace hangs there in the dawn, the mist,
in that dimness,
or as one rows in from past the murazzi
the barge slow after moon-rise
and the voice sounding under the sail.

(*C,* 117[4])

The first part of this is the poetry of the footnote, disclosing the minute particulars of research. "Which is to say" introduces a translation, into the poetry of sonorous evocation. Pound's mastery of sonorous evocation has never been doubted, but the poetry of the footnote was his major discovery, a flashing of "gists and piths."

(And though the five sonorous lines make a formal sentence, the gists and piths that precede it—fourteen lines—consist of discrete phrases and clauses, implying structures of surround-

Ezra Pound, 1913.

From "Cino"

Bah! I have sung women in three cities,
But it is all the same;
And I will sing of the sun.

ing syntax but never spelling them out. Increasingly, the economy of such a procedure would enter Pound's system of poetic and discursive habits, until there were times when he resembled a lecturer who disdains to comment on the slides he is showing. We'll return to this theme.)

He came to define the epic as "a poem including history" and thought that there was no other worthy subject. History, ideas of history, dominated the century that discovered evolution and made it a regnant metaphor. The very word "Renaissance" was a nineteenth-century coinage. And the very idea of an interlingual community of poets cohered with the great idea that languages were siblings, that a creating urgency flowed across their (miscalled) boundaries. "Provençal, Italian, Spanish, French, Portuguese, Catalan, Roumanian and Romaisch," so Pound told the readers of his first prose book, were at first simply "ways of speaking Latin somewhat more corruptly than the Roman merchants and legionaries spoke it."[5] A commonplace by 1985, that truth in 1910 had the power to excite imagination. Latin was not a dead language. There are no dead languages, nor dead poets save the nonpoets who were always dead.

We may pause to notice the two conceptions of history involved here. If like a nineteenth-century scholar you attended to the process by which Latin got "corrupted" into several Romance tongues, then you were thinking of something irreversible, related to the theme of entropy that was occupying scientific imaginations. After some centuries, Latin is simply *gone*. French, Italian, Spanish, Portuguese have replaced it, no doubt to be supplanted in their turn by future derivations (though the printing press to be sure has slowed the rate of change). Even Renaissance Latin is a specialist's tongue, newly emerged and, despite all efforts at elegance, never to be confused with the Latin they spoke without effort in a culture long since vanished from the earth. So runs an evolutionary reading of history, dominated by the sense of the past's irretrievability that underlies much of the ache of Romanticism.

The Romantic nostalgia set at a hopeless distance whole ages, customs, cultures; and that was a new way to think of the past. True, a Horace may seem a poet of nostalgia: "Eheu, fugaces . . ." he writes; "labuntur anni . . ." Alas, the years slip by, unbiddable. But what Horace laments is personal aging. That we cannot expect a second Regulus, a second Hercules even, was a different theme that did not enter his head. For Horace the better times gone were, yes, reclaimable; "et veteris revocavit artes," he wrote of Caesar Augustus: he has brought back our former way of life, the old way that made us glorious.

We need not think that Horace, or any pre-Romantic, had a

special sense of history, different from ours, any more than painters who lived before perspective was invented had a special sense of space. Pictorial space was an invention of the Renaissance, ineluctable history an invention of the Romantics. But with their invention came the option of denying them, electing with Picasso a special sense of space, or with Ezra Pound a special sense of time.

For if, in the twentieth century, you perceived with a poet's x-ray eye the Latin language, for instance, still durable under shifting guises—if you could say, as Pound said in 1940, "Rome is where they speak LATIN"—then you were extolling the durability of tough patterns beneath recorded mutability. To that sense of history the past is always reclaimable, and whatever was possible once remains possible now. Circumstance continues to present similar dilemmas, similar options. So we study history to learn from recorded experience which courses of action are favorable, which foolhardy. Though "labuntur anni" remains a human constant, though all men age and die ("Thy work in set space of years, not over an hundred" [*C,* 210]), yet the quality of human experience alters little, and the relevance of what we can learn from the past.

It was toward this latter sense of history that Pound tended, and in turning to it he allied himself with a disused tradition that ran from Plutarch's time clear to Pope's. Plutarch's parallel *Lives* offer patterns of good and bad judgment in situations we are to regard as comparable, both with one another and with what we ourselves may expect to confront. A Venetian painter of the sixteenth century could depict the troops before Troy in sixteenth-century Italian costume, so little, to minds of his era, had anything really changed. And for English Augustans the moral decline of Rome was a cautionary tale, modern men having left semibarbarism behind much as the Romans had and having climbed to a comparable plateau only to hear the same voices that tempted Rome with luxury, idleness, avarice, rootless novelty.

That way of perceiving the past survived in odd places. As late as 1896, his mind on the fiscal crises of his own decade, Brooks Adams in the first chapter of *The Law of Civilization and Decay* was examining anew and in new detail the lesson of Rome's misfortune, inextricable from Roman mismanagement of monetized wealth. "The stronger type exterminated the weaker; the money-lender killed out the husbandman; the race of soldiers vanished, and the farms, whereon they had flourished, were left desolate."[6] Pound was past fifty when he heard about Adams's book, but he instantly found it congenial. It read the past, in his own way, into the present.

III

"You have an obligation," Pound would say late in life, "to visit the great men of your own time." By 1909 he had settled in London, partly because Yeats was in London, Yeats whom he considered the greatest poet alive. By 1911 he had achieved his first unqualified success, the recreation of the Anglo-Saxon "Seafarer," moving it bodily, nearly word for word, into a diction through which we can hear the sounds of our early tongue:

> bitre breostceare gebiden haebbe,
> gecunnad in ceole cearselda fela . . .
>
> Bitter breast-cares have I abided,
> Known on my keel many a care's hold . . .
>
> (*P*, 64[7])

It is a poem of exile, and Pound felt exiled; he was not only transposing a poem many centuries old, but achieving personal expression simultaneously, the dead bard coming alive to voice the live man's feelings. That extends a device of Browning's. But Browning had made up his monologues; Pound's way was to work through textual recreation. No language could have suited his purposes better than English. It still contains enough Anglo-Saxon words to make "The Seafarer" strike fire; later he would exploit its Latin derivatives to lend Propertius a voice.

You'd not guess from "The Seafarer" that its author had been seeing Yeats almost weekly for two years; rather, it's the verse he wrote before they met that is stamped with Yeatsian "Celtic" mannerisms. But the Yeats of 1909–10 was passing through a sobering phase, turning to public themes and to blunt speech in despair over modern Dublin's rejection of imaginative opportunity. Dubliners preferred to

> fumble in the greasy till
> And add the halfpence to the pence
> And prayer to shivering prayer. . . .[8]

The Yeats of the *Green Helmet* poems (1910) and of *Responsibilities* (1914) set Pound his first modern example of forceful plain speech in verse, to be set beside many instances in Dante. In 1914 too the prose of Wyndham Lewis was posing a like challenge. But though he'd emulate the manner many times, as though out of moral obligation, it never came naturally. His imagination flourished best in the past.

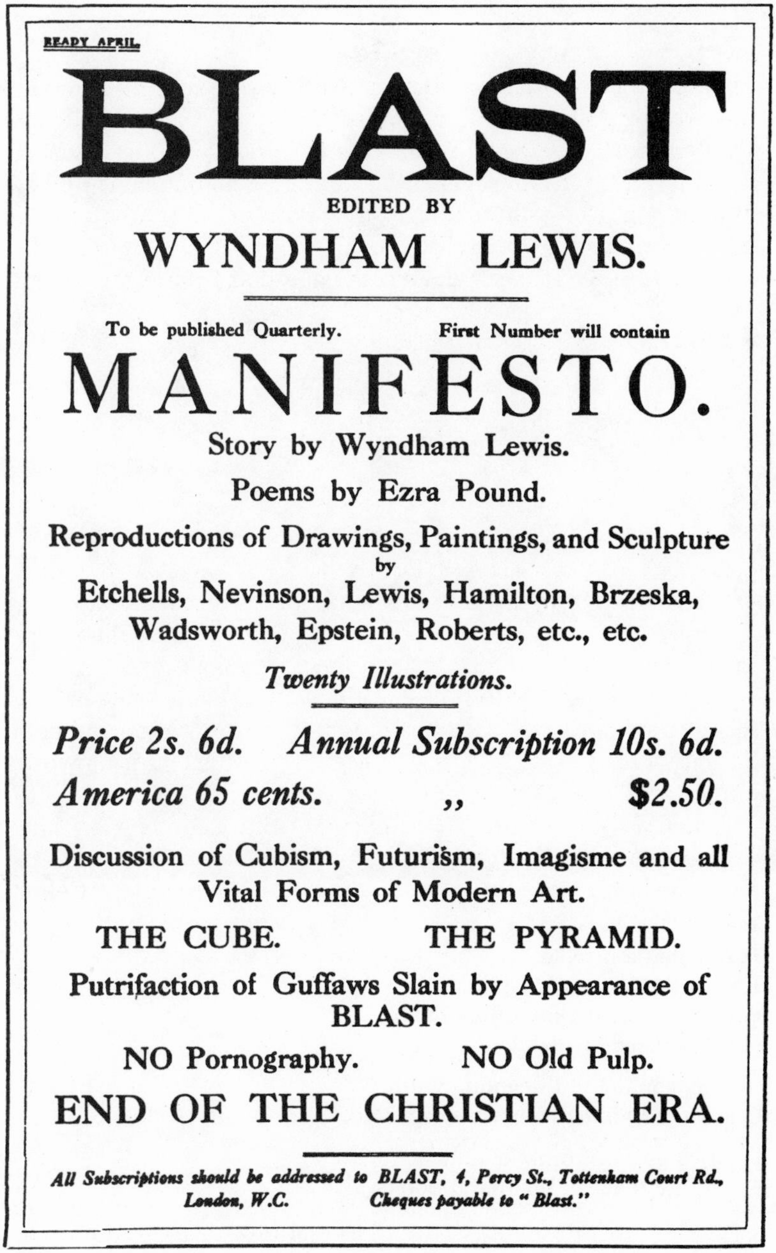
READY APRIL.

BLAST

EDITED BY

WYNDHAM LEWIS.

To be published Quarterly. First Number will contain

MANIFESTO.

Story by Wyndham Lewis.

Poems by Ezra Pound.

Reproductions of Drawings, Paintings, and Sculpture by

Etchells, Nevinson, Lewis, Hamilton, Brzeska, Wadsworth, Epstein, Roberts, etc., etc.

Twenty Illustrations.

Price 2s. 6d. Annual Subscription 10s. 6d.

America 65 cents. ,, $2.50.

Discussion of Cubism, Futurism, Imagisme and all Vital Forms of Modern Art.

THE CUBE. THE PYRAMID.

Putrifaction of Guffaws Slain by Appearance of BLAST.

NO Pornography. NO Old Pulp.

END OF THE CHRISTIAN ERA.

All Subscriptions should be addressed to BLAST, 4, Percy St., Tottenham Court Rd., London, W.C. Cheques payable to "Blast."

The announcement for Pound and Wyndham Lewis's magazine, Blast.

Henri Gaudier-Brzeska was killed in action at Neuville St. Vaast on June 5, 1915.

There died a myriad,
And of the best, among them,
For an old bitch gone in the teeth,
For a botched civilization,

Charm, smiling at the good mouth,
Quick eyes gone under the earth's lid,

For two gross of broken statues,
For a few thousand battered books.

—From *Hugh Selwyn Mauberley*

More deeply congenial was the sculptor Henri Gaudier-Brzeska (1891–1915), for whom successive spatial idioms—the sphere, the parallelogram—moved from culture to culture and metamorphosed in gathering up local energies. By extricating structure from mannerism, so Gaudier implied, a sculptor could re-create Egypt, re-create China, and make his "modern" forms speak with implacable authority. And had Pound in "The Seafarer" not done something similar? And was it not, for all its archaisms of surface, indisputably a modern poem? For it is surely inconceivable in any other age of English poetry.

So in *Cathay* (1915) he extended its method. The title page tells us that the poems are adapted from the ancient Chinese, via the notes of Ernest Fenollosa. This time the philological approach had to be oblique. Nothing in English corresponds to Chinese save the custom of building compounds out of simples. By writing "at morning there are flowers to cut the heart," Pound kept the necessary texture of linguistic strangeness; yet he was transcribing almost literally a philological note of Fenollosa's. On reflecting how nearly his line reproduces the etymology of "poignant," a word he might have used but didn't, we may wonder if we've glimpsed some universal principle of thought.

The little book, in khaki-colored paper covers, aimed at another order of universality. Three of the poems, at the beginning, middle, and end of the book, tell us that men of war keep weary watch on remote frontiers, and the other poems remember good times long gone, and reenact separations, and voice loneliness. For the hidden subject of *Cathay* is the first winter of World War I, a winter of departures and homesickness and waiting, in a war that had not yet become an epic of slaughter.

> Flying snow bewilders the barbarian heaven.
> Lice swarm like ants over our accoutrements,
> Mind and spirit drive on the feathery banners,
> Hard fight gets no reward. . . .
>
> (*P*, 139[9])

Gaudier, in the weeks before a bullet killed him, read those and similar lines to his fellows in the trenches. "The poems depict our situation in a wonderful way."

All this says that some orders of human experience are changeless, so that one can see a European war by reflection in a remote Chinese mirror. In 1917 a suite of twelve poems called "Homage to Sextus Propertius" mirrored Imperial London in Augustan Rome:

Oh august Pierides! Now for a large-mouthed product.
Thus:
"The Euphrates denies its protection to the Parthian and
apologizes for Crassus."
And "It is, I think, India which now gives necks to your
triumph,"
And so forth, Augustus. "Virgin Arabia shakes in her
inmost dwelling."
If any land sink into a distant seacoast,
it is a mere postponement of your domination.
And I shall follow the camp, I shall be duly celebrated
for singing the affairs of your cavalry.
May the fates watch over my day.

(*P,* 216)

Once more, albeit with much creative distortion, this comes word by word from an alien source, the *Elegies* of the Roman poet Sextus Propertius (c. 50–16 B.C.) "It presents certain emotions as vital to me in 1917, faced with the infinite and ineffable imbecility of the British Empire, as they were to Propertius some centuries earlier, when faced with the infinite and ineffable imbecility of the Roman empire," he wrote fourteen years later. "These emotions are defined largely, but not entirely, in Propertius' own terms. . . ."[10] In those years, when one-quarter of the world map was colored red, the British empire habitually reassured itself by comparisons with the imperial enterprise of Rome. Pound's *Homage* takes the comparison at its word. He adduces, though, not Vergil, who in lines much quoted had hymned the Roman mission, but Propertius, who was bored by public vacuities (and tended to be excluded from school curricula).

That emotions endure, that loss and pain and hardship are alike in 1914 and in ancient China, in a way that transcends all difference between China and England, then and now: for the sake of the poetry most readers will comply without a qualm. But that in 1917 history's finger had re-created certain Roman imbecilities of the first century B.C.: that proposition goes much further. It can imply not an intuition of human constancy but something as formal as a theory of history. And we may recognize here the Augustan note we've already detected in Pound's historicism. The present reenacts the past; and behold, uninstructed men fall afoul of precedent snares. May it be that poets, whose sense of linguistic formality entails a deep valuing of recurrence—the meter of a line, the repeated shape of the stanza, the perennial usefulness of a convention—are especially apt to discern repetition in historic time itself? Yeats even conjured up a two-thousand-year law, bringing something anew to

Bethlehem to be born. In the *Propertius,* written only three years after *Cathay,* Pound was making a long step toward *The Cantos,* the "poem including history" for which he was already drafting trial openings.

He was also expanding his circle of allusion. The poem's ironies of elaborate circumlocution, with every now and then a colloquial American word, were studied from Henry James, the international novelist par excellence. James had died the previous year, and Pound had read through his work entire to write an essay of homage. He may have been the first to perform that feat conscientiously since James himself did it to prepare the New York edition. He was certainly the first to perceive, in James's mannerisms of language, resources for a poet.

One more major poem preceded *The Cantos,* on which he would spend the second half of his life. That was *Hugh Selwyn Mauberley* (1919–20). At different times he called it "a farewell to London," "an attempt to condense the James Novel," and a popularization of his own *Propertius.*

IV

The kind of James novel he had in mind is the novel of missed sexual opportunity, most saliently *The Ambassadors.* In the U.S. edition of *The Ambassadors* two chapters were accidentally transposed and the error went unnoticed for decades. This mishap illustrates James's way of composing by "scenes" rather than by advancing the story; the completed work resembles an array of pictures, meant to be viewed in a certain order, but with little harm done if their sequence is slightly disrupted. Pound's *Mauberley* likewise is a sequence of numbered vignettes, thematically interrelated. The principle deserves a little attention.[11]

In the *Iliad,* the *Aeneid,* the *Divine Comedy, Paradise Lost,* long poems cohere thanks to narrative. That is the "epic" tradition, into which taxonomists have sometimes uneasily fitted Dante. But by the eighteenth century the epic was ailing, and Pope, although he assiduously modeled his career on Vergil's, achieved its climax not with a new epic but with *The Dunciad,* a mockery of the genre's pretensions. It was succeeded in the nineteenth century by a new genre that still goes unnamed, the Romantic Long Poem, at the center of which we discern not the story but the poet. Stories get slighter or triter, and less central. Vignettes and timeless moments grow in salience. The autobiographical "story" of *The Prelude* is commonplace; it serves Wordsworth simply as an ongoing context for the numinous moments. Similarly, the "story" of Yeats's first published work, *The Wanderings of Oisin* (1889), is unimportant save in

A scene from the Voices & Visions *film* Ezra Pound/American Odyssey *showing the castle Altaforte.*

framing his dilations on three psychic states, "Vain gaiety, vain battle, vain repose."

Then in 1919 Yeats published *The Wild Swans at Coole,* essentially a long poem about mortality and immortality that he had made by cunningly arranging short ones. The book can be read as though it were an ordinary collection of verse, much as Pound's *Propertius* can be read as though it were no more than an unreliable translation, but to read it so is to miss its arc, from swans anybody can see to the "Double Vision" only Michael Robartes can see; also to ignore such structural effects as the meditations on the death of Robert Gregory (named) and the death of Mabel Beardsley (left anonymous): two heroic deaths even though one seemed senseless and the other was slow and bedridden.

Pound had already made sequences out of *Cathay* and *Propertius,* which can be dipped into like collections but ought to be read in order. Yeats would make two major poems on Irish

Sestina: Altaforte

LOQUITUR: En Bertrans de Born.
Dante Alighieri put this man in hell for that he was a stirrer up of strife.
Eccovi!
Judge ye!
Have I dug him up again?
The scene is at his castle, Altaforte. "Papiols" is his jongleur. "The Leopard," the device *of Richard Cœur de Lion.*

I

Damn it all! all this our South stinks peace.
You whoreson dog, Papiols, come! Let's to music!
I have no life save when the swords clash.
But ah! when I see the standards gold, vair, purple, opposing
And the broad fields beneath them turn crimson,
Then howl I my heart nigh mad with rejoicing.

II

In hot summer have I great rejoicing
When the tempests kill the earth's foul peace,
And the lightnings from black heav'n flash crimson,
And the fierce thunders roar me their music
And the winds shriek through the clouds mad, opposing,
And through all the riven skies God's swords clash.

III

Hell grant soon we hear again the swords clash!
And the shrill neighs of destriers in battle rejoicing,
Spiked breast to spiked breast opposing!
Better one hour's stour than a year's peace
With fat boards, bawds, wine and frail music!
Bah! there's no wine like the blood's crimson!

IV

And I love to see the sun rise blood-crimson.
And I watch his spears through the dark clash
And it fills all my heart with rejoicing
And pries wide my mouth with fast music
When I see him so scorn and defy peace,
His lone might 'gainst all darkness opposing.

V

The man who fears war and squats opposing
My words for stour hath no blood of crimson
But is fit only to rot in womanish peace
Far from where worth's won and the swords clash
For the death of such sluts I go rejoicing;
Yea, I fill all the air with my music.

VI

Papiols, Papiols, to the music!
There's no sound like to swords swords opposing,
No cry like the battle's rejoicing
When our elbows and swords drip the crimson
And our charges 'gainst "The Leopard's" rush clash.
May God damn for ever all who cry "Peace!"

VII

And let the music of the swords make them crimson!
Hell grant soon we hear again the swords clash!
Hell blot black for always the thought "Peace!"

Hand scroll by Ch'u Ting, "Summer Mountains."

public events, *Nineteen Hundred and Nineteen* and *Meditations in Time of Civil War,* into explicit sequences with numbered parts. In 1922 Eliot would publish *The Waste Land* and Pound would be well embarked on *The Cantos.* In the second decade of the twentieth century, in short, it grew clear to several intelligences, in touch with one another, that the key to a possible long modern poem—by "long" meaning anything more than a page or two—lay in sequential contrasts of themes and tonalities and pitches of feeling. In this respect *Mauberley* was Pound's most ambitious work to date.

It commences with an epitaph, as it were in the *Times,* fussy with classical tags and with qualified homage.

The River-Merchant's Wife: A Letter

While my hair was still cut straight across my forehead
I played about the front gate, pulling flowers.
You came by on bamboo stilts, playing horse,
You walked about my seat, playing with blue plums.
And we went on living in the village of Chōkan:
Two small people, without dislike or suspicion.
At fourteen I married My Lord you.
I never laughed, being bashful.
Lowering my head, I looked at the wall
Called to, a thousand times, I never looked back.

At fifteen I stopped scowling,
I desired my dust to be mingled with yours
Forever and forever and forever.
Why should I climb the look out?

At sixteen you departed,
You went into far Ku-tō-en, by the river of swirling eddies,
And you have been gone five months.
The monkeys make sorrowful noise overhead.

You dragged your feet when you went out.
By the gate now, the moss is grown, the different mosses,
Too deep to clear them away!
The leaves fall early this autumn, in wind.
The paired butterflies are already yellow with August
Over the grass in the West garden;
They hurt me. I grow older.
If you are coming down through the narrows of the river Kiang,
Please let me know beforehand,
And I will come out to meet you
As far as Chō-fū-Sa.

—Rihaku (Li T'ai Po)

For three years, out of key with his time,
He strove to resuscitate the dead art
Of poetry; to maintain "the sublime"
In the old sense. Wrong from the start—

No, hardly, but seeing he had been born
In a half-savage country, out of date; . . .

(*P,* 187)

This is a British commemoration of an "E.P." so touchingly provincial as to think poetry still possible; one whose unwillingness to be affected "by the 'march of events' " has caused him to drop out of men's memory "en l'an trentiesme de son eage." (His thirtieth year: that was the year Pound published *Cathay.* The following year he was unable to get a collection called *Lustra* printed intact.) Many pages later, near the end of the sequence, we find a second epitaph, scrawled on an oar set up on a tropical island:

> "I was
> And I no more exist;
> Here drifted
> An hedonist."
>
> (*P,* 203)

That epitaph commemorates "Hugh Selwyn Mauberley," whose array of precious names bespeaks "sensibility." No "half-savage country" was responsible for him; he has been an assiduous frequenter of the British Museum, a connoisseur of porcelains and glazes and of such exotica as Arthur Evans was excavating in Crete—

> A Minoan undulation,
> Seen, we admit, amid ambrosial circumstances
> Strengthened him against
> The discouraging doctrine of chances,
>
> And his desire for survival,
> Faint in the most strenuous moods,
> Became an Olympian *apathein*
> In the presence of selected perceptions.
>
> (*P,* 202)

Even the lady who (by Jamesian convention) might have changed his life met his eye simply as one more exquisite object:

> Thus, if her colour
> Came against his gaze,
> Tempered as if
> It were through a perfect glaze. . . .
>
> (*P,* 201)

Not caricatured but rotated before us with tactful compassion, this man is the fine flower of a culture that has lost its will and direction and prefers "appreciation" to creativity. The London that once drew active minds in from the provinces and from overseas now resembles a wealthier, more articulate Wyncote. Hence the pointlessness of the war recently ended:

> Charm, smiling at the good mouth,
> Quick eyes gone under earth's lid,

For two gross of broken statues,
For a few thousand battered books.

(*P,* 191)

So much for the "civilization" that has been "saved" at such frightful cost. Three deft portraits array the inheritors. "Brennbaum," incarnate culture, is all costume and demeanor. "Mr. Nixon," a knowing hack modeled on Arnold Bennett, is generous with advice on how to get on ("give up verse, my boy, there's nothing in it"), and he owns a steam yacht. "The stylist" (anonymous, but drawn from Ford Madox Ford) makes do in a cottage with a leaky roof.

The "Envoi," one of Pound's ineradicable lyrics, quietly protests that a live tradition does exist in England, reaching forward from Chaucer's time and from the time of Edmund Waller and Henry Lawes. "Go, dumb-born book," it commences; instructed ears may hear Chaucer's "Go, litel bok" and Waller's "Go, lovely rose." (And Waller need not have read Chaucer; that is one meaning of "tradition.")

Go, dumb-born book,
Tell her that sang me once that song of Lawes:
Hadst thou but song
As thou hast subjects known,
Then were there cause in thee that should condone
Even my faults that heavy upon me lie,
And build her glories their longevity. . . .

(*P,* 197)

Lawes had set Waller's song, and someone has been singing their joined words and notes in the twentieth century, accompanied not by a lute but by a grand piano, the boom of whose bass is audible in the sound of "dumb-born."*

"Hadst thou" . . . the verbs and pronouns are archaic. Does the "book"—the first part of *Mauberley*—understand no other mode of address? No, the language of the first part of *Mauberley* is elaborately "modern," so it may be in that respect that it is

*Not a fanciful idea once you're familiar with Pound's studied reechoing of his own effects. After twenty-five years he recalled the "Envoi" in a set of variations:

Has he tempered the viol's wood
To enforce both the grave and the acute?
Has he curved us the bowl of the lute?
Lawes and Jenkyns guard thy rest
Dolmetsch ever be thy guest . . . (*C,* 520)

and there we don't find the easy rumble of "Go, dumb-born book" but a succession of crisp initial and terminal sounds for which the tongue must adroitly, rapidly reposition itself.

"dumb-born," partaking of the prose of an age that has lost all song save the old songs. But there are two more stanzas, and in these the archaisms disappear. Toward the end, modern words have gained the confidence of song:

Tell her that goes
With song upon her lips
But sings not out the song, nor knows
The maker of it, some other mouth,
May be as fair as hers,
Might, in new ages, gain her worshippers,
When our two dusts with Waller's shall be laid, . . .

(*P,* 197)

So, obscured by obtuseness, by pedantry, by avarice, a tradition lies await to be gathered from the air. Meanwhile public London has little to offer save

usury age-old and age-thick
and liars in public places.

(*P,* 190)

For the capital that once drew Conrad and Henry James (and Pound and Eliot) now (in Eliot's phrase of a few years later) "merely shrivels, like a little bookkeeper grown old."[12] "Bookkeeper" is exact. The City's preoccupations are fussily fiscal. If there's hope, it's in the fact that the "E.P." of the first epitaph is not dead. He is just overlooked. He obligingly left for the Continent.

V

Mauberley was not only Pound's farewell to London, it was his farewell to the first half of his career. Thenceforward he would be engaged with the long poem he had already been trying to plan for several years. At the threshold of *The Cantos,* it's worth surveying the resources he had developed on their behalf.

1. He had a repertoire of voices. Unlike, say, Wallace Stevens, who always sounds like himself, Pound in sounding like himself could sound like people as disparate as the "Seafarer" bard, the Roman ironist, and the Chinese connoisseur of light rain falling on the light dust. The adoption of a range of voices —he called them "personae," masks—was from the very first intrinsic to his method.

2. Out of his passion for condensed fact of the kind that gets tucked into footnotes, and his impatience with such long words

George Antheil and Olga Rudge in Paris, 1920.

as end in "—ation," he'd developed an eloquence of the isolate phrase—

> A wet leaf that clings to the threshold
>
> (*P*, 108)

—that names something and with rhythmic assistance surrounds the thing it names with auras of emotion. At one stage (1912—13) this got theorized as "Imagism." Later, talking of "the ideogrammic method," he would draw on an imperfect analogy with the components of the Chinese written character to indicate what happens when several such concretions are placed in each other's company. It is like what happens when five sharp words come together:

> Air hath no petals now
>
> (*C*, 630)

—with which compare,

Poikilothron' athanat' Aphrodita

—every word of Sappho's a surprise, or

IN A STATION OF THE METRO

The apparition of these faces in the crowd;
Petals on a wet, black bough.

(*P*, 109)

—the second image not only unforeseeable, but a new way to view the first one.

Such writing puts a premium on concreteness, definition, concision. There is little metaphor in Pound's language; he came to shun metaphor as a *mis*calling, and to value the short definite words at the core of the language:

Hay new cut on hill slope,
And the water there in the cut
Between the two lower meadows; sound,
The sound, as I have said, a nightingale
Too far off to be heard.

(*C*, 90)

Such concreteness moves the poem easily to its "visionary" episodes:

  or Anchises that laid hold of her flanks of air
drawing her to him
                  Cythera potens, Kuthera deina
no cloud, but the crystal body
        the tangent formed in the hand's cup
      as live wind in the beech grove
          as strong air amid cypress.

(C, 456–57)

It also conduced to what could be an unfortunate mannerism, when the withdrawal of syntactic support leaves us at a loss what to make of floating elements whose context is not the visionary imagination but some book we haven't read or some historic nexus we haven't grasped. Here one reader's trenchant condensation is another's hopeless obscurity; that was a risk *The Cantos* always ran. Pound's belief that poetry inheres in condensation, that nothing damps it more than unnecessary words, especially words that do niggling syntactic chores, shaped alike the poem's most and least successful passages.

3. An incomparable melodic sense, innate and his lifelong resource. "Ere the season died a-cold" (*C,* 519) runs as if effortlessly up the scale of the vowels A, E, I, O. And such a detail as

Behind the monk's bell
borne on the wind.
Sail passed here in April; may return in October
Boat fades in silver; slowly;
Sun blaze alone on the river

(*C,* 244)

draws its authority from its pauses and stops, its alliterations, its intertwining of vowels and liquids. That all sounds pedantic till you let yourself experience it. Experiencing the sound of words is for most modern readers the awful daring of a moment's surrender. We've been taught to abstract, abstract, to sniff after "meaning." For Ezra Pound speech was always physical, bodied. And the words were *these* very words, not lexical substitutes: hence his tags of French, Latin, Greek, at moments when the very phonemes mattered.

4. The sense of the past's steady relevance we've already glanced at; now combined with

5. a new set of convictions, and these need particularizing. During the war years he frequented the *New Age* circle, and there one day he met Major Charles H. Douglas, who had noticed something about how currency flows. It was Douglas's conclusion that the books never balance, no factory ever distributing enough wages for its workers to buy back its product. That is because of "finance charges," and there is consequently a perpetual shortage of purchasing power, coped with in the short term either by starting wars to gain markets or by issuing new currency as interest-bearing debt (the so-called deficit). So War and Want inhere in a bookkeeping system, and for Pound this had the importance of a scientific discovery. His villains became the international bankers, the present system's sole beneficiaries. His hero would be whoever should put the insights of Douglas into practice. History suggested that scientific discoveries were normally in practice within a generation or so. (Clerk Maxwell's equations, 1873; Marconi's radio, 1896.) The hero he elected was Mussolini, in whom people as diverse as Winston Churchill and Secretary Mellon at one time also discerned a positive force.[13]

6. Finally, there was the accumulation of his own published prose, in effect a growing body of commentary. During the war years especially, he had kept himself fed and clothed in London by ceaseless intellectual journalism; for 1917 alone his bibliog-

Roman wall painting of a lady playing the cithara.

Me happy, night, night full of brightness;
Oh couch made happy by my long delectations;
How many words talked out with abundant candles;
Struggles when the lights were taken away;
Now with bared breasts she wrestled against me,
Tunic spread in delay;
And she then opening my eyelids fallen in sleep,
Her lips upon them; and it was her mouth saying:
Sluggard!

—From "Homage to Sextus Propertius"

rapher lists 117 items. The best of these (which turned out to be the ones for which he'd been paid the least, or not paid at all) were gathered into books. So a reader of Canto I, wanting help with the name "Andreas Divus" and finding none in the *Encyclopaedia Britannica*, might turn to Pound's 1920 *Instigations,* which reprinted his *Little Review* articles on Renaissance translators of Greek, and exhibited as a sample of Divus's Latin *Odyssey* (1538) the identical pages the first Canto draws on. Later collections extracted the gists of the early ones; in the thirties "Translators of Greek" reappeared in *Make It New,* and since 1960 it has been in print in *Literary Essays.*

As over the years *The Cantos* grew to unforeseen length (802 pages in the complete edition), the ancillary prose grew too. By now there is scarcely a sentence Pound wrote anywhere that has no bearing at all on the poem. Even collections of his private letters abound in rewards for the student. This reflects in part the way the poem came to express his whole mind; in part, too, his loss of touch, over forty years, with any definable body of readers. In Rapallo (1926–40) he fell insensibly into the assumption that his own energies were creating and educating the poem's audience. And in Washington (1946–58) the friends and correspondents who sustained his alertness were the readers he could assume would follow its thought.

VI

A Draft of XVI Cantos for the Beginning of a Poem of Some Length appeared in 1925 in a sumptuous limited edition. That volume has one evident unity. It begins in prehistory and ends in the twentieth century, and as *Cathay* was built around three war poems, so this section of *The Cantos* is built around three wars. It starts with Odysseus sailing home from the war at Troy, it ends amid the confusions of the 1914–18 war, and at its center we find a fifteenth-century Italian free-lance. Human history, then, has moved from war to war, its most recent war its most horrible and anticlimactic. And the pretexts for warfare have altered. Greeks fought Trojans over the beauty of Helen. Sigismundo Malatesta's various employers had less noble but intelligible incentives (and his purpose in taking their money was to build his Tempio). But what so many died for in our time will remain obscure until Canto XLV waxes explicit about Usury, and Canto XLVI about banks.

But more important than wars at this stage of the poem is the complex laying down of themes; Canto I is an especially rich instance. The poem begins not only *in medias res* but as it were in midsentence, with the word "And":

The "cages" where Pound was detained by the occupying American army toward the end of World War II.

The Detention Training Center, Mediterranean Theater of Operations, United States Army, lay north of Pisa on the coastal plain, near the village of Metato, by the via Aurelia which for 17 centuries has run along the sea from the Palatine Gate through Pisa, Viareggio, Carrara, Rapallo, Genoa, all the way to Arles. White oxen now shared the Aurelian Way with jeeps, and down a side road past the camp moved more traffic than the road builders had envisaged, raising slow clouds of dry dust. A half-mile square of barbed wire enclosed the place; birds settled on the strands, the prisoner (Pound) was to observe, like notes of silent music. North and East stretched mountains, one cone-shaped above delicate trees (he named it Taishan, for China's sacred peak), two to the left of it low and hemispherical (he named them the Breasts of Helen). Pisa lay south; peering through the dangling laundry on clear days one could see the Tower. Sun and moon rose over the mountains, set over the invisible sea. Lizards basked in the heat; grass clung to friable earth; one could watch a wasp building her nest, or ants marching or crickets singing, or men at the Obstacle Fence working out the 14-hour days and looking uncommonly like figures at the grape arbor in the Schifanoia frescoes in Ferrara.

—From *The Pound Era* by Hugh Kenner

A fresco from the Schifanoia Palace in Ferrara.

And then went down to the ship,
Set keel to breakers, forth on the godly sea, and
We set up mast and sail on that swart ship,
Bore sheep aboard her, and our bodies also
Heavy with weeping, and winds from sternward
Bore us out onward with bellying canvas,
Circe's this craft, the trim-coifed goddess.
Then sat we amidships, wind jamming the tiller,
Thus with stretched sail, we went over sea till day's end.

(*C,* 3)

We have entered the *Odyssey* at Book XI. If we look back before "and" we see the preceding books, then beyond them in time the matter of the *Iliad,* and beyond that, unrecorded darkness. But if Homer's predecessors are lost they are not quite obliterated. In the Mediterranean way, he built with old stones, and Pound thought the narrative of Book XI, the *Nekuia,* the journey down to the realm of the dead, was manifestly *"older* than the rest

. . . hinter-time."[14] Thus the oldest verse we have in a Western language is celebrating the oldest of human concerns: rites to keep us in touch with our dead.

And what this Canto does is open communications with dead masters; Homer for one, and for another the "Seafarer" poet whose strong alliterative line,

> We set up mast and sail on that swart ship

is audible throughout, the oldest Greek sounding through the oldest English. The Canto has other archaic qualities. Its rush of narrative is presyntactic; the first verb has no subject, the first adverb ("forth") works like a verb, and no Flaubertian subordinations conceal the simplest narrative connective, "and." Contrast the Loeb translator's more formal sentence:

> But when we had come down to the ship and to the sea, first of all we drew the ship down to the bright sea, and set the mast and sail in the black ship, and took the sheep and put them aboard, and ourselves embarked, sorrowing and shedding big tears.

Though "correct," this makes both tidy and naive the utterance of a bard whose strong units were phrasal and metrical.

In the underworld they fill a pit with sheep's blood. And the shades gather, frantic for blood such as once made them feel alive.

> Souls out of Erebus, cadaverous dead, of brides
> Of youths and of the old who had borne much;
> Souls stained with recent tears, girls tender,
> Men many, mauled with bronze lance heads,
> Battle spoil, bearing yet dreory arms,
> These many crowded about me; with shouting,
> Pallor upon me, cried to my men for more beasts;
> Slaughtered the herds, sheep slain of bronze;
> Poured ointment, cried to the gods,
> To Pluto the strong, and praised Proserpine;
> Unsheathed the narrow sword,
> I sat to keep off the impetuous impotent dead,
> Till I should hear Tiresias.

Impetuous, impotent . . . these are all the people who have ever lived. One man confronts the whole past of the world: that is one meaning of this episode in *The Cantos.* And his confrontation will one day, in another land, inspire the sixth book of the *Aeneid,* the author of which will in turn guide Dante on a like journey through three realms of the Christian underworld.

When this Canto that began with "And" makes its end with an open-ended "So that:" the *Divina Commedia* is one term we can append to the colon.

When Tiresias speaks, it is with the aid of the blood Odysseus brought.

> "Stand from the fosse, leave me my bloody bever
> "For soothsay."
>   And I stepped back,
> And he, strong with the blood, said then: "Odysseus
> "Shalt return through spiteful Neptune, over dark seas,
> "Lose all companions."

In reducing to twelve words the thirty-eight lines Homer gave Tiresias, Pound makes us attend to the transaction with the blood. For the dead speak only thanks to blood we bring them; Odysseus and Homer and the Seafarer-poet are speaking now, enabled by the blood of a live man, Ezra Pound. The drunk blood is a communion, the act of translating by implication a sacrament. We should recall that Chaucer was esteemed as *le grand translateur* before "originality" came into esteem. We may also ponder a story Robert Fitzgerald tells.

Fitzgerald before translating the *Odyssey* made a ritual visit to Pound, as it were to Tiresias, for benediction. He said he intended to do only the high spots, and was told: "Oh no, don't do that. Let him say everything he wanted to say."[15] A successful translation, this means, is less a feather for its maker's cap than a new opportunity offered to the dead. Two things at least we owe them: voices, and a hearing. Before this long poem is over the dead will have spoken in hundreds.

And among the ghosts in the Canto there's an un-Homeric ghost, whom a voice new to the poem suddenly addresses:

> Lie quiet, Divus.

And as if aware that we're disoriented, this modern voice supplies information, embedding the poem's first footnote in the text itself:

>   I mean, that is Andreas Divus,
> In officina Wecheli, 1538, out of Homer.

For, Pound's Latin being superior to his Greek, he's been working from a sixteenth-century Latin version he'd found about 1909 at a Paris bookstall. (That, by the way, is why the sea is "godly"; for Homer's *dian,* bright, Divus had *divum*, divine.) It's indicative of the poem's increasingly austere criteria for relevance, that the incident of the Paris bookstall was present in early published drafts, to hint at a parallel with Browning's *The Ring and the Book,* but later got pruned and now must be retrieved from Pound's *Literary Essays.* That happened when he decided to attenuate the Browning theme, to state it openly only in four lines of Canto II and diminish it to a single quoted phrase in Canto III. It's arguable that the poem gains in distracting us less with early indications of its author's successorship to Browning. It's equally true that such artistic decisions have had the side effect of erasing seamarks we might wish were in the text.

What Divus had made was no ornate "rendering" of Greek but a serviceable pocket-size crib, meant to match, page for page and line for line, the Aldine octavo *Odyssey.* Before Aldus there'd been folio Homers, but folios are for venerating; a pocketable octavo is meant for *use,* and by a busy man away from home.

So here, superimposed on Homer (the beginning of Greek) and on The Seafarer (the beginning of English), is yet another beginning: the unquenchable romance of the Renaissance, when western Europe rediscovered Greek and discovered printing almost simultaneously. In Canto I we may perceive in triumphant embodiment the young Pound's classroom vision of European poetry, a rich multilingual organism which develops in time but keeps all times simultaneous, and is preserved for us in strings of printed letters.

The presence of the Renaissance, here and throughout the first thirty Cantos, should detain us a little, since men's historical interests are guided by their deep concerns. In the eighteenth or "Augustan" century the most applicable part of the past was the story of Rome and what happened to it; Gibbon's work could be read as a cautionary tale. Early in the nineteenth century, the invention of the word "Renaissance" marks a need for an updated paradigm. Things were beginning anew; three revolutions, American, French, and Industrial, helped prompt new scrutiny of Europe's last time of new beginnings. Soon the Renaissance was a happy hunting ground for enthusiasts. Browning's imagination returned to it repeatedly, and so did Pound's. It was Jacob Burckhardt's *Die Kultur der Renaissance in Italien* (1860; English translation, 1878) that supplied, in a chapter title, "The State as a Work of Art," the romantic metaphor by which Pound would fatefully misjudge Mussolini. He was always prepared for yet one more new beginning—to resolve the world's fiscal mess there *had* to be one—and how the first Renaissance had succeeded and failed was to engage him much of his life.

But that is a later story; we are still in Canto I. It ends with an evocation of Aphrodite, who shimmers through a mosaic of Latin phrases Pound took from the *Hymni Deorum* appended to Divus's book. Gold and copper (later to be coin-stuff) ornament her. And one recurrent ritual of *The Cantos* is established: after a fabulous journey, a vision of a goddess.

"So that:" concludes it. From "And . . . and . . . and" to "So That:" from succession to causality: come to think of it, the progression of Greek thought.

VII

Such is a partial engagement with any Canto; an encounter, first, with the authority of its local rhetoric; consideration, next, of any prior documents it refracts;[16] and always, attention to minutiae. Gradually, we collect a sense of the poem's rituals. Its first cats attend an apparition of Dionysios; any cat thereafter will always precede a theophany. Its first drink is blood, its first eating (in Canto IV) a human heart; eating and drinking will thenceforward be sacramental acts: sometimes profaned, as when the Emperor Tçin Ou "ended his days as a gourmet" (*C,* 282). And the way China makes its first appearance in Canto XIII, right after the first Canto to be situated in America, prepares us for the way the two countries will invariably be juxtaposed (as they were in the fortunes of Columbus, who encountered the one while seeking the other). The successive volumes in which the work appeared constitute structural units, most often units of eleven; from the moment of its launching with Book XI of *The Odyssey,* eleven was to be the poem's magic number. Names recur, lines recur, verbal motifs recur, while different Muses preside over different parts.

In 1940, the year of Cantos LI–LXXI (ten China Cantos, ten John Adams Cantos), the poem was still proceeding more or less according to plan, much though chance might have altered the plan's details. But the *Pisan Cantos* (published in 1948) reflected an unforeseen emergency. Writing in an American army stockade near Pisa in the summer and autumn of 1945, a poet who confronted the wreckage of all his hopes was thrown back on monologue and reminiscence. And the remaining sections—a third of the poem's pages—came from a Washington hospital to which friends brought the needed books: mostly books of which the man who wrote the first two-thirds had not suspected the existence. Their convention is marginalium, commentary, cross-light, excerpt: the Poetry of the Footnote, indeed.

Getting familiar with it all can take years, a consideration that has inspired charges of charlatanry. But until quite late in history, when the Easy Book was devised, it was normal to

Pound typing during his detention at Pisa.

assume that major works of literature lent themselves to lifelong study. Milton did not expect to be skimmed. If his "story" yields itself quickly, little else does. (His first readers even had trouble with the story, which is why the second edition of *Paradise Lost* was equipped with prose summaries.) Our "desire to make the poem add up to something quickly"[17] comes from reading habits formed on texts of contrived simplicity, and we need to acknowledge that Pound set out systematically to frustrate any such appetite. One intention of *The Cantos,* Margaret Dickie has argued, is to restore the old art of "slow reading": creative reading: such a reading as (Fred Robinson has shown) Pound gave the Anglo-Saxon "Seafarer," when he scrutinized the credentials of each word. The poem demands, and also offers to

The enormous tragedy of the dream in the peasant's bent shoulders
Manes! Manes was tanned and stuffed,
Thus Ben and la Clara *a Milano*
by the heels at Milano
That maggots shd/ eat the dead bullock
DIGONOS, διγενες, but the twice crucified
where in history will you find it?
yet say this to the Possum: a bang, not a whimper,
with a bang not with a whimper,
To build the city of Dioce whose terraces are the color of stars.
The suave eyes, quiet, not scornful,
rain also is of the process.
What you depart from is not the way
and olive tree blown white in the wind
washed in the Kiang and Han
what whiteness will you add to this whiteness,
what candor?

---

and there was a smell of mint under the tent flaps
especially after the rain
and a white ox on the road toward Pisa
as if facing the tower,
dark sheep in the drill field and on wet days were clouds
in the mountain as if under the guard roosts.

Tempus tacendi, tempus loquendi.
Never inside the country to raise the standard of living
but always abroad to increase the profits of usurers. . . .

I don't know how humanity stands it
with a painted paradise at the end of it
without a painted paradise at the end of it
the dwarf morning-glory twines round the grass blade
magna NUX animae with Barabbas and 2 thieves beside me. . . .

—From "Canto LXXIV" (written at Pisa)

train, "the attention usually reserved for partially destroyed Renaissance documents." "If reading were simply a copying of the palimpsest, or if reading were only an affirmation of the figure in the carpet, it would be a task easily assignable to clerks or to particularly sensitive geometricians. But reading is something beyond this passive copying and active affirming, as Pound himself had discovered in a lifetime."[18]

Lest we fear, with the frontier warrior in *Cathay,* that "hard fight gets no reward," jewels lie scattered for the picking up. They include historical curiosities like the Jefferson letter—

"Could you," wrote Mr. Jefferson,
"Find me a gardener
Who can play the french horn?"

(*C,* 97)

(as he did: in June 1778); also the lyric interludes and the matchless evocations of landscape:

From Val Cabrere, were two miles of roofs to San Bertrand
so that a cat need not set foot in the road,
where now is an inn, and bare rafters,
where they scratch six feet deep to reach pavement
where now is wheat field, and a milestone,
an altar to Terminus, with arms crossed
back of the stone
Where sun cuts light against evening,
where light shaves grass into emerald . . .

(*C,* 243)

A former generation of readers tended to deem these the successful parts of the poem, from which the rest fell away into incoherence. But the poem is a continuum, and everywhere it is anchored in factuality. We note that it cites the Jefferson letter by date, and tells us where to find the altar to Terminus. The library contains the one, southwest France the other. One learns to trust the surface indications. No poet since Wordsworth (an analogy that would have surprised him) has been so tenacious in fidelity to fact. "Mount Taishan at Pisa" designates the one mountain on the skyline in question that looks indisputably oriental, as you'll see if you go there. Much obscurity dissipates as one begins to take the literal sense on trust.

And the place of entry which every passage affords is its most accessible one: its verbal surface, its locally contrived "style." There is no more dramatic event in the early Cantos than the turn of the page that discloses prose documents frankly offered as prose: the contents of Sigismundo Malatesta's mailbag (*C,* 37–40). Browning, Pound's predecessor in the use of Renaissance documents, had transformed everything in *The Ring and the Book* into blank verse, postulating that there is a poem, and also a domain of language outside the poem, and that to merit inclusion in the former the latter needs transforming into "poetry." But Pound's Poetry of the Footnote acknowledges no sharp boundary between verse and prose, or between fact and imagination; only an ineluctable boundary between live writing and dead:

> Perspicax qui excolit se ipsum,
> Their writings wither because they have no curiosity,
> This "leader," gouged pumpkin
>   that they hoist on a pole.
>
> (*C,* 545)

VIII

The Cantos were never finished. About 1959, aged seventy-four, Pound simply felt unable to write any more. Nine years later he published the *Drafts and Fragments* into which the end of the poem had dissipated. Some are of unparalleled limpidity:

> A blown husk that is finished
>   but the light sings eternal
> a pale flare over marshes
>   where the salt hay whispers to tide's change.
>
> (*C,* 794)

Nothing to paraphrase there, nothing to footnote. Something autumnal to see, caught in a few common words, with embed-

ded in their solemn rhythm that trope of the singing light. He might have wished that more of the poem could have been made of details so simply turned, but learning the way of them had taken long, and "There is no substitute for a lifetime" (*C,* 691).

He died in Venice on November 1, 1972, two days after his eighty-seventh birthday.

I have said nothing about the political controversies that stormed round the last third of Pound's life: the rant of the wartime broadcasts, the indictment, the imprisonment near Pisa and in a Washington madhouse. The emphasis belongs where I keep it, on the continuities of the life of the mind and on the pleasures of his craggy texts. "These are the Alps," wrote his friend Basil Bunting in a poem called "On the Flyleaf of Pound's Cantos." It ends,

> Fools! Sit down and wait for them to crumble.

Pound in Venice near the end of his life.
He is buried there on Isola San Michele.

Marianne Moore,
14 St. Luke's Place,
New York City

AN OCTAPUS

of ice. Deceptively reserved and flat,
it lies "in grandeur and in mass"
beneath a sea of shifting snow dunes;
dots of cyclamen red and maroon on its clearly defined pseudopodia
made of glass that will bend--a much needed invention--
comprising twenty-eight ice fields from fifty to five hundred feet thick,
of unimagined delicacy.
"Picking periwinkles from the cracks"
or killing prey with the concentric crushing rigor of the python,
it hovers forward "spider fashion
on its arms" misleadingly like lace;
its "ghostly pallor changing
to the green metallic tinge of an anemone starred pool."
The firtrees in "the magnitude of their root systems,"
rise aloof from these manoevers "creepy to behold"--
austere specimens of our American royal families,
"each like the shadow of the one beside it.
The rock seems frail compared with their dark energy of life,"
its vermilion and onyx and manganese blue interior expensiveness
left at the mercy of the weather;
"stained transversely by iron where the water drips down,"
recognized by its plants and its animals.
Completing a circle,
you have been deceived into thinking that you have progressed,
under the polite needles of the larches
"hung to filter not to intercept the sunlight"--
met by tightly wattled spruce twigs
"conformed to an edge like clipped cypress
as if no branch could penetrate the cold beyond its company;"
and dumps of gold and silver ore enclosing The Goat's Mirror--
that lady-fingerlike depression in the shape of the left human foot,
which prejudices you in favor of itself
before you have had time to see the others;
its indigo, black, green, blue-green, and turquoise,
from a hundred to two hundred feet deep,
"merging in irregular patches in the middle lake
where like gusts of a storm,
obliterating the shadows of the firtrees, the wind makes lanes of ripples."
What spot could have merits of equal importance
for bears, elk, deer, wolves, goats, and ducks?
Preempted by their ancestors,
this is the property of the exacting porcupine,
and of the rat "slipping along to its burrow in the swamp
or pausing on high ground to smell the heather;"
of "thoughtful beavers
making drains which seem the work of careful men with shovels,"
and of the bears inspecting unexpectedly
ant hills and berry bushes.
Composed of calcium gems and alabaster pillars,
topaz, tourmaline crystals and amethyst quartz,
their den is somewhere else, concealed in the confusion
of "blue stone forests thrown together with marble and jasper and agate
as if whole quarries had been dynamited."

MARIANNE MOORE

JOHN M. SLATIN

In March 1914, a weekly magazine called the *Literary Digest* published a scathing review of *Des Imagistes,* a new anthology of verse edited by the American poet Ezra Pound:

> "Imagisme" is the latest poetic fashion—its devotees would give it a more dignified name. The writers of this school (many of whom, like Ezra Pound, are Americans living in London) share with the Futurists a dislike for rime and the other established conventions of poetry. They are concerned chiefly, it seems, with the presentation of beautiful images, and, for some reason not readily understood, they believe in only the homeopathic use of capital letters. (*Digest,* 48 [1914]: 450).

This is commonplace stuff, expressing commonplace critical opinions; attacks on imagism (with or without the final "e"), futurism, cubism, fauvism, and other literary and artistic movements were easy to come by in those days.

The only thing that makes this one special is that it found its way into the hands of twenty-six-year-old Marianne Moore, an aspiring poet who lived at 343 North Hanover Street in Carlisle, Pennsylvania, where news of avant-garde literary movements was a precious commodity. She clipped the review of *Des Imagistes* from the magazine, pasted it into a scrapbook (now part of the Moore Archive at the Rosenbach Museum and Library in Philadelphia) and thought about it.

The very terms of its attack on Pound and the poems in his anthology indicated that *Des Imagistes* was not simply a book of poems that the reviewer happened not to like. In its flagrant disregard for "rime and the other established conventions of poetry"—such as the use of capital letters at the beginning of every line—*Des Imagistes* raised questions which the reviewer thought of as having been settled long ago.

These were questions about the nature of poetry itself; the very fact of their having been raised was a clear indication that the definition of poetry could no longer be taken for granted. Anyone who wanted to be a poet would be expected to take sides in what was clearly a heated debate. (And even if she

Marianne Moore, 1924.

refused to align herself with either party, she would probably be treated as if she had done so. Neutrality is also a provocative posture.) Before she could do that, moreover, she would have to try to work out for herself what poetry was.

Moore's response to this typically modern problem of definition is breathtakingly direct: She takes the problem itself as one of her major subjects. Perhaps only Wallace Stevens, among her contemporaries, uses poetry as a medium for speculation about poetry (and art in general) as much as Moore does. It is in the writing of the poems themselves that Moore works out her ideas about poetry, so that each poem is part of a continuing effort to think through what poetry is. This is why so many of Moore's poems, especially those written before 1940, are so explicitly concerned with questions pertaining either to art in general or to poetry in particular (though these concerns are never very far from the surface, even in poems that seem to be about other things entirely).

Asking how poetry should be written involves looking at what other poets have done in the past and are doing now; it involves looking at prose as well as poetry; and it involves looking at painting, sculpture, and the decorative arts. These are the things Moore examines in her poems; even when she observes natural objects (animals or the sea or a glacier), she does so through eyes which have been trained on and by *art.*

When she sees them in relation to herself and her work, moreover, as she inevitably and rightly does, the objects of her attention take on an added dimension. What Moore finds to admire in the things she looks at are often abstract qualities like precision and compression; humility and restraint; self-sufficiency and endurance; clarity and simplicity; and these are also qualities she aspires to in herself. Conversely, the tensions between these admirable qualities and the opposing tendencies—to expansiveness and pride; dependency and a fondness for ephemeral things; complexity and opacity—point to tensions and contradictions within Moore's own character. Thus the general question of how poetry should be written is made personal: How am *I* to write poetry? And it is at this point, when the objects of attention in the poems become metaphors not only for poetry but for the self, that the search for a way to write poetry becomes a search for identity as well.

I

In an early poem that is probably a response to the *Literary Digest*'s critique of *Des Imagistes,* Moore turns to the Bible for assurance and discovers the prophet Habakkuk as a possible model for herself. This may seem an arrogant thing for a young poet to do—especially one as devout as Moore was throughout her life. (Until 1894, when she was seven, Moore lived in Kirkwood, Missouri, in the home of her maternal grandfather, the Reverend John Riddle Warner; her brother, John Warner Moore, was ordained a minister in 1914.) But in fact the choice of a Hebrew prophet is an expression of devotion and of an anxious desire for immortality. According to one of Moore's favorite biblical commentators, Habakkuk remains a shadowy figure of whom little is known beyond his name, so Moore may legitimately claim to resemble him in her anonymity; but of course she has no way of telling whether her words will last as his have done.

This poem has been called "The Past Is the Present" (*CP,* 88) since 1924. But it was originally published in December 1915 under a much longer and clumsier title, which reads as follows: "So far as the future is concerned, Shall not one say with the Russian philosopher, 'How is one to know what one doesn't know?' So far as the present is concerned . . ." (*Others,* 1 [1915]: 105). This is based on a passage from Ivan Turgenev's novella *The Diary of a Superfluous Man,* in which a young man dying of tuberculosis laments the futility of trying to predict the future. Like the reference to Habakkuk, then, the original title betrays the young poet's uncertainty about her place in history. In much the same way, the poem itself expresses uncertainty about the current state of poetry.

The question it asks is what to do "If external action is effete/ And rhyme is outmoded. . . ." The answer is to do what Habakkuk did—that is (according to the commentary on which Moore relied), to define a vantage point, "however narrow," and hold it against all comers. Moore succeeded well enough to attract the attention of William Carlos Williams's friend Alfred Kreymborg of Grantwood, New Jersey, the editor of a magazine called *Others* (it was Kreymborg who published Pound's anthology *Des Imagistes*). "So far as the future is concerned" was published, along with four other poems by Moore, in the December 1915 issue.

In "So far as the future is concerned," Moore dispenses with the "external action" of narrative and proposes a definition of at least one kind of poetry. According to a man named XY, whose "identical words" the poem repeats, "Hebrew poetry is/Prose with a sort of heightened consciousness." This sounds surprisingly like a modernist notion; it is reminiscent of Ezra Pound's repeated insistence that poetry should be at least as well written as prose. XY is even "speaking of unrhymed verse" —but Moore's poem rhymes *(abxbx/acxcx),* though perhaps not in quite the way the conservative *Literary Digest* would approve. In avoiding external action, Moore also ignores another of Pound's commandments: to "go in fear of abstraction" (*Literary Essays,* 5). Moore would tell an interviewer many years later that she "wondered why" anyone would call himself an imagist (*Reader,* 260); here, she uses the form of her poem to steer between the conservative and radical positions.

Now she will have to hold the middle ground she has staked out for herself. This is the plot of another early poem, "Critics and Connoisseurs," in which William Carlos Williams saw Moore's mature poetic method showing itself for the first time (*Selected Essays,* 130). And in fact everything here works so well that "Critics and Connoisseurs" makes "So far as the future is concerned" seem like a preliminary sketch. Evidently, Moore has decided that narrative is not effete after all: The poem revolves around an anecdote in which the poet tries to feed a reluctant swan.

"Critics and Connoisseurs," which appeared in *Others* in July 1916, displays all the confidence that is lacking in "So far as the future is concerned": There no longer seems to be any question about where to find poetry. "There is a great amount of poetry," Moore begins, "in unconscious/Fastidiousness." Ming vases and other fine objects are "well enough in their way," she continues, but she prefers the image of a child trying to get "an imperfectly ballasted animal" to "stand up," or forcing "a pup/[To] eat his meat from the plate." These are instances of unconscious and, therefore, poetic fastidiousness; they are succeeded by the recollection of "a black swan on the Cherwell in Oxford," where Moore had gone with her mother in the summer of 1911. (Another early poem, "Counseil to a Bacheler" [*sic*], published in *Poetry* in May 1915, came out of the trip to Oxford, and in Elkin Matthews's London bookshop Moore picked up two books by Ezra Pound. Perhaps the most important result of the trip, though, was a conversation several years later in which Moore's mother, speaking of how her daughter learned to read, said that as a child the poet had taken "no more interest" in the alphabet than she had taken in *Baedeker's Guide* to England—"in fact had a perfect contempt for it" [*Rosenbach,* 1250/24: 35]—and thus provided a way of describing how to read poetry: "Reading it, however, with a perfect contempt for it, one discovers that there is in/it after all, a place for the genuine.")

The world had changed since that summer, however. An unpublished poem entitled "Our Imported Grasshopper, 'North of Boston' " (the reference is to Robert Frost's second book, *North of Boston*) indicates how the war in Europe had imposed itself on Moore's consciousness: "As I unfolded [the grasshopper's] wings," Moore writes, "in examining it for the first time,/I forgot the war . . ." (*Unfinished Poems,* 57). She couldn't forget the war for long, though—especially since her brother received his navy commission in 1916: She writes in "Critics and Connoisseurs" of how the swan "reconnoitered like a battleship" and would not take the "bits/Of food" she tossed it: "Disbelief and conscious fastidiousness were the staple/Ingredients in its/Disinclination to move."

A test of wills ensues: The poet keeps tempting the swan,

tossing it food until finally the bird's "conscious fastidiousness" breaks down.

> Finally its hardihood was not proof
> against its
> Inclination to detain and appraise
> such bits
> Of food as the stream
> Bore counter to it; it made away with what I gave
> it
> To eat. . . .
>
> (*Others,* 3 [1916]: 4)*

We are just into the poem's middle stanza when the point of the story begins to be made clear. Suddenly, the mood changes, and lazy reminiscence gives way to anger: "I have seen this swan," says the poet, "and/I have seen you; I have seen ambition without/Understanding in a variety of forms." In its initial refusal to accept the poet's offer of food, the consciously fastidious black swan is a critic, not a connoisseur. The connoisseur, like the child trying to make a puppy eat from a plate, has an instinctive sense of the way things ought to be (even if, as in the case of the child and the puppy, that sometimes means forcing things into unnatural postures); the critic, however, simply rejects things out of hand.

Moore is not especially fond of critics during these early years, and she pokes fun at them in poem after poem. There is something unnatural about critics, she seems to imply: The swan, for instance, deliberately restrains its native "inclination" to examine what comes its way on the "stream." The "immovable critic" of Moore's famous poem "Poetry" twitches when he reads "like a horse that feels a flea"; like him—like "all of us"—the swan does "not admire what/[it] cannot understand," and wants nothing to do with what the poet has to offer. But as I shall explain, that resistance is what gives poetry its chance.

It isn't enough, however, to say "There is a great amount of

*Here I should alert the reader to a potential problem. As of fall 1986, the only available text of Moore's poems is the revised "Definitive Edition" of the *Complete Poems* (originally published in 1967) issued in 1981. But the *Complete Poems* is not complete —it omits roughly half of the poems Moore published before 1925, for instance—and most of the early poems it does contain have been very substantially revised. (Compare the version of "Poetry" on p. 36 of the *Complete Poems* with the "Longer Version" reprinted in the Notes, on pp. 266–67.) Of course Moore had the right to revise her poems; but the fact that she revised so heavily means that *Complete Poems* cannot be used as a reliable guide to Moore's early development as a poet. This is why, in most cases, I have quoted from the earliest published text.

poetry in unconscious/Fastidiousness." One has to know how to *see* the poetry—otherwise one ends up like the critics in "My Apish Cousins" (1917; later renamed "The Monkeys"):

> ". . . trembling about
> In inarticulate frenzy, saying:
> It is not for all of us to under-
> stand art—finding it
> All so difficult, examining the thing
>
> As if it were something inconceivably arcanic
> [*sic*], as
> Symmetrically frigid as something carved out of
> chrysoprase
> Or marble—strict with tension, malignant
> In its power over us and deeper
> Than the sea when it proffers flat-
> tery in exchange for hemp,
> Rye, flax, horses, platinum, timber, and
> fur."
>
> (*Kreymborg,* 83–84)

There is a dynamic in these poems of which Moore may be only partially aware. Each poem needs its stubborn critic, just as "Critics and Connoisseurs" needs the recalcitrant swan. There is no poetry, though, until resistance breaks down—the swan has to accept the offer of food, the critic has to read the poem, or nothing happens. This is fine, so long as the critic/swan remains distinct from the poet. But the distinction breaks down.

The swan, like the critic, has a position to hold; but so does Moore—which makes her uncomfortably kin to the swan and "the immovable critic" the bird resembles so closely. Several years later, T. S. Eliot will write, and Moore will quote approvingly, that "it is to be expected that the critic and the creative artist should frequently be the same person" (Eliot, 16); but for the time being, the lurking presence of the critic in the poet is something to distrust and disavow—a problem, and not a solution. The kinship between poet and critic—their complementarity, as Eliot would say—is doubly dangerous, as we shall see, because the swan is not quite immovable, and neither is Moore. Thus "Critics and Connoisseurs" sets the stage for the interplay of temptation and resistance on which a good deal of Moore's subsequent poetry depends for its drama.

What is at stake not only here but throughout Moore's career is the distinctiveness she depends upon for her sense of identity, a distinctiveness that is nonetheless a source of anxiety because it imposes the very isolation Moore wants (and fears) so

The female argonaut (paper nautilus).

From "The Paper Nautilus"

For authorities whose hopes
are shaped by mercenaries?
Writers entrapped by
teatime fame and by
commuters' comforts? Not for these
the paper nautilus
constructs her thin glass shell.

badly to overcome. In order to achieve and sustain an identity for herself, Moore has to differentiate herself and her poems from other poets and *their* poems; the "attitude of self-defense" that she seems to be questioning in "Critics and Connoisseurs" is actually essential to her. And if she is to succeed in distinguishing herself, her poems will have to exemplify that attitude in form as well as content. Thus, despite what some readers have perceived as the apparent arbitrariness of Moore's poetic forms, there is no meaningful distinction between form and content in her poems, especially "in view of the fact that spirit creates form" (as Moore writes in "Roses Only" [1917]); form becomes "the outward equivalent of a determining inner conviction" (Benet and Pearson, 1339).

The threat comes from other poets, other poems—or, more precisely, from Moore's response to them. Like her swan, Moore has a natural inclination to "detain and appraise" things as a connoisseur should, to reach out and take what she admires and hold it in her "predatory hand" (that last phrase is from "Roses Only"). But, she feels, that inclination has to be restrained. In resisting that inclination she becomes immovable, a critic, thinking that in doing so she saves herself from melting into a nondescript similarity to other poets.

This is why Moore's poems are so "strict with tension," why they so often appear to be "as/Symmetrically frigid as something carved out of chrysoprase/Or marble." The forbidding, almost mechanically precise look of Moore's poems on the page has led many readers to believe that the poems lack feeling and passion; but if they lacked feeling there would be no need for such strictness of form. As Moore says in "Silence" (1924), "the deepest feeling always shows itself in silence;/not in silence, but restraint" (*Dial,* 77 [1924]: 290)—restraint in the present context being supplied by form.

It is not only feeling that needs to be restrained, however. Moore never really explained why she wrote in rhyming syllabic verse (in which the freedom of proselike diction and syntax is restrained by the rules of rhyme and syllable counting). But she gives us a few clues in her essay "The Accented Syllable," published in the *Egoist* in October 1916. This was her first piece of published criticism and, partly because it was heavily cut by the *Egoist,* it is rather cryptic; but it is still possible to see that it amounts to an indirect defense of the kind of syllabic verse Moore herself was writing.

"The Accented Syllable" addresses the question of how to write in such a way that not only one's meaning but also one's tone of voice will be unmistakable. "[If] an author's tone of voice is distinctive," Moore says, "a reader's speaking tone of voice will not obliterate it" (*Prose,* 32). This is fine in theory; in practice, however, it often happens that "written tones of voice may resemble one another, and that a distinctive tone of voice employed by one author may resemble that same tone of voice as employed by another author" (33). It is difficult to maintain true distinctiveness in prose (Moore finds that certain passages of critical prose by Poe resemble passages from the notebooks of Samuel Butler, for instance)—and in "rhymed verse" it is even harder. For "In the case of rhymed verse, a distinctive tone of voice is dependent on naturalistic effects, and naturalistic effects are so rare in rhyme as almost not to exist" (34). That would seem to make free verse the best alternative; but Moore rejects free verse as well, writing that "so far as free verse is concerned, it is the easiest thing in the world to create one intonation in the image of another . . ." (34). In other words, free verse encourages conscious imitation of another writer's voice (a notion whose significance we will come to later). But imitation, conscious or unconscious, is just what Moore wants to avoid.

Ralph Waldo Emerson—the guiding spirit behind such important early poems as "Roses Only" and "My Apish Cousins" as well as later poems like "Silence" and "The Student"—says flatly in "Self-Reliance" that "imitation is suicide" (Emerson, 2: 46). That assertion underlies all of Moore's early poems. No wonder, then, that Moore should have developed a form whose main function is to "repel influences" (as Emerson says the transcendentalist does [Emerson, 1: 323]), first of all by suppressing her tendency to quote from other people's work and, at the same time, by inhibiting the inclination to echo or otherwise imitate other poets. Moore had experimented with quotation as early as 1915; but she scrupulously and conspicuously resists the temptation to quote in a series of crucial poems published between 1916 and 1918—including "Critics and Connoisseurs," "Roses Only," "Black Earth" (later called "Melancthon"), and "The Fish." All of the poems I have just named are concerned with the problem of responding to an "experience of beauty," which Moore finds herself compelled to resist because, as she puts it in "Marriage" (1923), "it tears one to pieces." "Black Earth" and "The Fish," in particular, are dominated by the effort to resist the "light," to withstand the "electricity" Moore increasingly sees as a power generated by the work of other writers.

As "Roses Only" suggests, Moore shares with Emerson's transcendentalist a fondness "for everything/self-dependent." Like Ben Franklin practicing Humility, however, she "cannot boast of much Success in acquiring the *Reality*" of absolute self-sufficiency—though, like Franklin, she certainly "had a good deal with regard to the *Appearance* of it" (Franklin, 462). On the whole, too, Moore's readers have been content to take the appearance for the reality. Introducing Moore's *Selected Poems* in 1935, T. S. Eliot wrote that so far as he knew "Miss Moore [had] no immediate poetic derivations," no traceable genealogy (viii–ix); and until very recently most students of Moore have treated her work as if it had no connection either with the practice of her contemporaries or with anything that had ever been done before.

II

But Moore does have "poetic derivations," both immediate and distant, and her work is closely connected with that of her contemporaries—especially with the work of Eliot himself. Emerson had been the most important source of ideas for Moore during the period of her comparative isolation from 1915 to 1918, when she lived first in Carlisle, Pennsylvania, and then, from the autumn of 1916 to the winter of 1918, in Chatham, New Jersey, where her brother had been appointed pastor of the Ogden Memorial Presbyterian Church. Eliot became an increasingly dominant figure, however, in the late teens and early twenties, after Moore and her mother moved to a basement apartment at 14 St. Luke's Place, a quiet, fashionable street in Greenwich Village.

Moore's shift from Emersonian self-reliance to Eliot's brand of twentieth-century neoclassicism does not occur the moment she arrives in the city, and it cannot be explained simply as the result of a move from a small town to the great metropolis. But there is a connection, although it takes some two years to develop.

Moore and her mother moved to the Village in December 1918, a month after the signing of the armistice. It was a move Moore had been eager to make ever since her first visit to the city in 1915; the precipitating cause, however, was her brother Warner's decision to reenlist in the navy after the war. His mother and sister could not continue living in the Chatham parsonage, and the need to move gave Moore the opportunity she had been waiting for.

In the words of the critic and novelist Malcolm Bradbury, "Modernism is a particularly urban art" (97), and moving to New York gave Moore the chance to immerse herself in the "modernizing" experience of the city. The city, Bradbury writes, "is itself the spirit of a modern technological society. [It] has appropriated most of the functions and communications of society, most of its population, and the furthest extremities of its technological, commercial, industrial and intellectual experience." As Moore put it in the phrase she borrowed from Henry James for the closing line of her poem "New York" in 1921, what she found most exciting (and most threatening) about the city was that it offered "accessibility to experience."

But in moving from the provincial "wilderness" to the metropolis, in modernizing herself as Pound said Eliot had done several years earlier, Moore would have to give up the Emersonian dream of self-dependency that she had nurtured in Chatham. The idea that she could go on writing indefinitely without incur-

Ashmolean Museum, Oxford

Study of Gneiss Rock at Glenfinlas
by John Ruskin.

In her notebooks Moore recorded this passage from John Ruskin's *Modern Painters:* "The greatest thing a human soul ever does in this world is to see something, and tell what it saw in a plain way. Hundreds of people can talk for one who can think, but thousands can think for one who can see. . . ."

II

But Moore does have "poetic derivations," both immediate and distant, and her work is closely connected with that of her contemporaries—especially with the work of Eliot himself. Emerson had been the most important source of ideas for Moore during the period of her comparative isolation from 1915 to 1918, when she lived first in Carlisle, Pennsylvania, and then, from the autumn of 1916 to the winter of 1918, in Chatham, New Jersey, where her brother had been appointed pastor of the Ogden Memorial Presbyterian Church. Eliot became an increasingly dominant figure, however, in the late teens and early twenties, after Moore and her mother moved to a basement apartment at 14 St. Luke's Place, a quiet, fashionable street in Greenwich Village.

Moore's shift from Emersonian self-reliance to Eliot's brand of twentieth-century neoclassicism does not occur the moment she arrives in the city, and it cannot be explained simply as the result of a move from a small town to the great metropolis. But there is a connection, although it takes some two years to develop.

Moore and her mother moved to the Village in December 1918, a month after the signing of the armistice. It was a move Moore had been eager to make ever since her first visit to the city in 1915; the precipitating cause, however, was her brother Warner's decision to reenlist in the navy after the war. His mother and sister could not continue living in the Chatham parsonage, and the need to move gave Moore the opportunity she had been waiting for.

In the words of the critic and novelist Malcolm Bradbury, "Modernism is a particularly urban art" (97), and moving to New York gave Moore the chance to immerse herself in the "modernizing" experience of the city. The city, Bradbury writes, "is itself the spirit of a modern technological society. [It] has appropriated most of the functions and communications of society, most of its population, and the furthest extremities of its technological, commercial, industrial and intellectual experience." As Moore put it in the phrase she borrowed from Henry James for the closing line of her poem "New York" in 1921, what she found most exciting (and most threatening) about the city was that it offered "accessibility to experience."

But in moving from the provincial "wilderness" to the metropolis, in modernizing herself as Pound said Eliot had done several years earlier, Moore would have to give up the Emersonian dream of self-dependency that she had nurtured in Chatham. The idea that she could go on writing indefinitely without incur-

Ashmolean Museum, Oxford

Study of Gneiss Rock at Glenfinlas
by John Ruskin.

In her notebooks Moore recorded this passage from John Ruskin's *Modern Painters:* "The greatest thing a human soul ever does in this world is to see something, and tell what it saw in a plain way. Hundreds of people can talk for one who can think, but thousands can think for one who can see. . . ."

ring (or seeming to incur) any obligation to other writers came to seem increasingly absurd in a city dominated by commercial transactions. That idea—delusion might be a better word—is what the opening line of "New York" calls "the savage's romance"; like a forest or a coral reef, it has "accreted where we need the space for commerce," and will have to be cleared away before progress can occur.

The masts of the ships plying New York's harbor were clearly visible from St. Luke's Place, and Moore took pleasure in the sight of all the commerce going on in the space along the riverfront, a short walk from her apartment. There was a great deal of it: New York handled more than a third of America's exports and about two thirds of the nation's imports (Still, 263). In "Dock Rats," first published in Alfred Kreymborg's *Others for 1919,* Moore celebrates shipping as "the most interesting thing in the world." But the celebration is somewhat muted. As in the earlier poem "Black Earth" (1918), in "Dock Rats" Moore speaks in the guise of an animal; but whereas in the earlier poem she had adopted the persona of a self-aggrandizing elephant, here she represents herself as a wharf rat, belittling herself as if to indicate that the city makes her feel small:

There are human beings who seem to regard the
place as craftily
as we do—who seem to feel that it is a good
place to come
home to. On what a river; wide—twinkling
like a chopped sea under some
of the finest shipping in the

world: the square-rigged four-rigged four-master,
the liner, the battleship like the
two-
thirds submerged section of an iceberg; the
tug
dipping and pushing, the bell striking as it
comes; the steam yacht, lying
like a new made arrow on the

stream; the ferry-boat . . .

From this catalog of ships, Moore goes on to list the cargoes they bring in:

. . . When the wind is from the east,
the smell is of apples, of hay; the aroma
increased and decreased
as the wind changes;

of rope, of mountain leaves for florists; as from
the west,
it is aromatic of salt. Occasionally a par-
rakeet
from Brazil arrives clasping and clawing; or
a monkey—tail and feet
in readiness for an over-

ture; all arms and tail; how delightful! There is
the sea, moving the bulk-
head with its horse strength; and the
multiplicity of rudders
and propellers; the signals, shrill,
questioning, peremptory, diverse;
the wharf cats and the barge dogs. . . .
(*Observations,* 53–54)

Just when the poem is most strongly reminiscent of Whitman —when we hear those "signals, shrill,/questioning, peremptory, diverse"—Moore suddenly backs off, and the voice of the critic asserts itself: "it/is easy to overestimate the value of such things," she says as she moves into the final stanza, and though she goes on to the concluding phrase I have already quoted— "shipping is the most interesting thing in the world"—the spell is broken.

Despite her own resistance, however, Moore's conception of poetry is beginning to change as a result of her exposure to commerce. It is in this context that we should read such passages as the famous one in "Poetry" (first published in the last issue of *Others* in 1919 and roughly contemporary with "Dock Rats") in which Moore asserts that it is not "valid/to discriminate against 'business documents and/school-books.' " The exotic animals and other "phenomena" she is coming to regard as being potentially so "important" to poetry—"The bat,/holding on upside down or in quest of something to/eat, elephants pushing, a wild horse taking a roll, a tireless wolf under/a tree"— these are the kinds of things which have conventionally been relegated to prose, and they are closely akin to the cargoes she sees coming in to the docks of New York every day.

Moore implies in "Poetry" that everything—even "the immovable critic twinkling his skin like a horse that feels a flea," even "business documents and/school-books"—is at least potential material for poetry; her position is very close to the one Eliot had taken in an essay called "The Borderline of Prose" in 1917. She comes even closer to Eliot in "Picking and Choosing," a poem about critics and criticism written at about the same time as "Dock Rats" and "Poetry" and first published in the *Dial.* (As Moore tells the story, Scofield Thayer and his partner,

James Sibley Watson, Jr., at first rejected the poems she sent them; but then Thayer heard her read one of those poems, "England." "Would you send that to us at the *Dial?*" he asked. "I did send it," Moore said, to which he replied, "Well, send it again" [*Reader,* 265]. She did, and "England" and "Picking and Choosing" were printed as companion pieces in April 1920.)

"Picking and Choosing" shows Eliot's influence most clearly in the way it redefines the critic's relationship to the poem. The first thing to go in "Picking and Choosing" is the idea of the critic as mere blocking agent like the swan of "Critics and Connoisseurs," a naysayer who performs the Emersonian function of resisting possible influences so that the poet can develop her own distinctive tone of voice. This conception is replaced in the closing lines by a metaphor which defines the critic as an enabling (though still more than slightly ridiculous) figure, who puts the poet "on the scent" in the manner of a hunting dog leading the hunter to the prey:

> Small dog, going over the lawn, nipping the linen
> and saying
>
> that you have a badger, remember Xenophon;
> only the most rudimentary sort of behavior is
> necessary
> to put us on the scent; a "right good
> salvo of barks," a few "strong wrinkles"
> puckering the
> skin between the ears, are all we ask.
>
> (*Dial,* 68 [1920]: 422)

As Moore indicates in the notes to *Observations,** the hunting metaphor derives from Eliot's essay "In Memory," a tribute to Henry James (d. 1916), which had been published in the *Little Review* in August 1918. Eliot writes that James's best criticism is "in the highest sense creative," so that it "preys not upon

*Moore was probably emulating Eliot, who added notes to *The Waste Land* when it was published in book form in 1922, when she provided notes to the poems in *Observations* (1924), indicating the sources of her quotations and other odd bits of information. Many readers have found these notes (and the ones to later books) charming, as indeed they are; but they serve a more important function, too, as guides to the relationships between Moore's poems and other phases of life or literature.

Moore has suggested that readers who find her notes worrisome might simply "disregard" them (*CP,* 262). But this is exasperation, not modesty, and, like everything else in *Complete Poems,* her annoyance has been toned down considerably. Here is the way she ended the first version of this "Note on the Notes" in 1941: "Perhaps those who are annoyed by provisos, detainments, and postscripts could be persuaded to take probity on faith, the will for the deed, the poem as a self-sufficiency, and disregard the notes" (*What Are Years,* 46). The very existence of the notes argues that the poem is anything but "a self-sufficiency," and in that case we had better not disregard the notes.

ideas, but upon living beings" (45). Crucially, this highly creative criticism is to be found not in what Eliot perversely calls James's "feeble" critical essays, but rather in the fiction itself. Thus criticism is seen as complementary to the creative process, not antagonistic to it; the critic is necessary to the artist.

This conception of the critic's role goes a long way toward resolving the problem of "influence," which had concerned Moore so deeply. Being influenced by another writer is no longer a matter of being forced out of one's own orbit, as Emerson had implied; instead, as Eliot says, "To be influenced by a writer is to have a chance inspiration from him; or to take what one wants" (44). The writer who is being influenced is no longer passive; on the contrary, she is actively engaged in a process of informed selection, picking and choosing material that (as Moore writes in an early draft, now in the Rosenbach Archive) she "can use" in her poems.

Moore's new understanding of the complementary relationship between criticism and creation was confirmed and deepened by her reading of Eliot's first collection of critical essays, *The Sacred Wood* (1920), which she reviewed for the *Dial* in March 1921:

> . . . [I]n what [*The Sacred Wood*] reveals as a definition of criticism it is especially rich. The connection between criticism and creation is close; criticism naturally deals with creation but it is equally true that criticism inspires creation. A genuine achievement in criticism is an achievement in creation; as Mr Eliot says, "It is to be expected that the critic and the creative artist should frequently be the same person." Much light is thrown on the problems of art in Mr Eliot's citing of Aristotle as an example of the perfect critic—perfect by reason of his having the scientific mind. Too much cannot be said for the necessity in the artist, of exact science.
>
> (*Dial,* 70 [1921]: 336)

The constant repetition of the terms *criticism* and *creation* in this passage is deliberate: It blurs the distinction between the two activities, so that by the end of the paragraph Moore is able to prove their complementarity by moving from Eliot's discussion of Aristotle's "scientific" criticism to the question of "exact science" for the artist.

The best known essay in *The Sacred Wood* is called "Tradition and the Individual Talent"; as its title implies, Eliot is concerned throughout *The Sacred Wood* not only with the relationships between individual writers and their contemporaries, but, on a much broader and more general scale, with the relationship between the work of any given writer and, as he puts it, "the whole of the literature of Europe from Homer"—that is,

BIRD, BEAST OR FISH? The rare Plumet Basilisk lizard from Costa Rica, newest arrival in the London Zoo. It is brilliant green, with a plume, or fin, down its back in contrasting color.

Underwood

N.Y. Herald Tribune 26 Jan. 1930

Marianne Moore's clipping of the London Zoo's "rare Plumet Basilisk from Costa Rica."

As by a Chinese brush, eight green
bands are painted on
  the tail—as piano keys are barred
by five black stripes across the white. This octave of faulty decorum
  hides the extraordinary lizard
till night-fall, which is for man the basilisk whose look will kill;
                                                                                    but is

for lizards men can
  kill, the welcome dark—

—From "The Plumet Basilisk"

with the whole of the past. It did not matter to Eliot's conception of tradition that individual works—say, the *Odyssey* or *The Inferno* or *Paradise Lost*—might have been written hundreds or even thousands of years apart; what mattered was that all those works existed simultaneously in the mind of the person sitting down *now* to write a poem.

Eliot's way of thinking about literature infuriated Moore's friend William Carlos Williams, who was convinced that under Eliot's influence poetry would become little more than a collection of museum pieces. Museums would eventually provide the material for some of Moore's most interesting poems, and indeed she praises Eliot in her review of *The Sacred Wood* for "opening a door upon the past and indicating what is there" (*Dial,* 70 [1921]: 339); but she seems to have found the air a bit chilly the first time she went through that door.

"Museums," she writes in an unfinished poem of that name written sometime between 1918 and 1925,

> are good things, never wholly barren, superficial,
> ignorant. "Where was it
> made and by whom was it worn?" The collection of
> armor, at
> first sight no more than so much hardware, becomes
>
> upon examination, cause for burning speculation . . .

This is hardly an expression of unbridled enthusiasm; it is as if the order of things in the museum, so carefully laid out in accordance with someone's conception of the "ideal order" formed by the "existing monuments" of the past (Eliot, 50), were too rigid to permit the free movement of the mind. The closing lines confirm this: What one looks for in a museum, Moore writes, is not the excitement generated by "the new (the really new) work of art," but something quieter:

> One
> takes a horse from the stable for the purpose of
> visiting
> a customary scene; one follows a stream,
>
> every turning of which is a foregone conclusion.
> It is similarly
> that one goes to a museum to refresh one's mind
> with the
> appearance of what one has always valued.
> (Quoted *MMN,* 1 [spring 1977]: 8)

Reading "Museums" feels a bit like going through a museum: There is a good deal to look at, but all of it is under glass, and one has seen it before. The past remains enclosed, neatly arranged for display; the present is carefully excluded. (The desire to retreat into a carefully preserved but inaccessible past will come increasingly to dominate Moore's later poetry, and finally deaden it.)

A good deal more energy is generated in the slightly later poem "When I Buy Pictures," published in the *Dial* in July 1921. Here Moore begins to "regard [herself] as the imaginary possessor" of a series of art objects that resemble the ones she sees in "Museums"—except that they are available for purchase. And yet Moore is not really out to "buy pictures." Instead, like Thoreau pretending in the second chapter of *Walden* to buy each of his neighbors' farms, she is only *pretending* to buy pictures: She doesn't want to get her "fingers burned by actual possession" (Thoreau, 129). Moore's understanding of how commerce works seems a bit odd (she writes in "Novices" [1923], for instance, that the artist is "the only seller who both buys, and holds onto the money"); nonetheless, it is when Moore begins to imagine herself as engaged directly in a kind of commerce that she makes major changes in the very structure of her poems.

Eliot wrote in 1923, in a belated review of Moore's *Poems* (1921; Eliot's review was delayed, presumably, by his breakdown and recuperation during the period of *The Waste Land*), that if Moore were to make another discovery as important as the "new rhythm" he believed she had invented, she would first have to *"shatter"* the "formation" she had perfected and then "painfully reconstruct" her art (Tomlinson, 49). But Moore had already anticipated him: She had begun the process of breaking down her own resistance and reconstructing her verse.

First she gave up the elaborately patterned syllabic stanzas that had become her poetic signature and transformed them into free verse. Beginning with "When I Buy Pictures" and "A Graveyard" (later called "A Grave"), both of which exist in earlier syllabic drafts, Moore embarked on a three-and-a-half-year experiment in free verse, the characteristic modern form. She used it in everything she published between July 1921 and January 1925, except for a few poems that were printed for the first time in *Observations* in 1924—"Peter" and "An Egyptian Pulled Glass Bottle in the Shape of a Fish," for instance, both of which were written several years earlier. At the same time, Moore began relying more and more heavily on quotation as a structural device—so much so, in fact, that her longest poems, "Marriage" (1923) and "An Octopus" (1924), seem to be tissues composed almost entirely of quotation.

Again it was Eliot who made the difference. Eliot had written in "Tradition and the Individual Talent" that the "ideal order" formed by "the existing monuments" of literature "is modified by the introduction of the new (the really new) work of art among them" (50). This sounds modest enough. But not so, as *The Waste Land* clearly reveals. Eliot's poem yokes together a multitude of "fragments" out of the literary past in a desperate effort to impose at least a provisional "order" upon the "ruins" of the speaker's life and his civilization. As if she had suddenly *seen* exactly what Eliot meant, Moore adapted his methods in her next poem, "Novices," which appeared in the *Dial* in February 1923, just four months after the first American publication of *The Waste Land* (also in the *Dial*) in November 1922.

Thirteen lines from the end of "Novices," a sarcastic but otherwise seemingly unexceptional critique of the hacks "who write the sort of thing that would in their judgement interest a lady" is shattered by the emergence of a completely different way of writing and seeing. The poem is

> "split like a glass against a wall"
> in this "precipitate of dazzling impressions,
> the spontaneous unforced passion of the Hebrew
> language—
> an abyss of verbs full of reverberation and
> tempestuous energy,"
> in which action perpetuates action and angle is
> at variance with angle
> till submerged by the general action;
> obscured by fathomless suggestions of colour,
> by incessantly panting lines of green, white with
> concussion,
> in this drama of water against rocks—this "ocean
> of hurrying consonants"
> with its "great livid stains like long slabs of
> green marble,"
> its "flashing lances of perpendicular lightning"
> and "molten fires swallowed up,"
> "with foam on its barriers,"
> "crashing itself out in one long hiss of spray."
>
> (*Dial,* 74 [1923]: 184)

In this passage, what had appeared moments before as the "detailless perspective of the sea" is "split" into a myriad of individual "impressions," each consisting of a single quotation.

Here we have thirst
and patience, from the first,
and art, as in a wave held up for us to see
in its essential perpendicularity;

not brittle but
intense—the spectrum, that
spectacular and nimble animal the fish,
whose scales turn aside the sun's sword by their polish.

—From "An Egyptian Pulled Glass Bottle in the Shape of a Fish"

(There are eight marked quotations and two unmarked ones in this passage; like virtually all of Moore's quotations, they all come from prose sources.) Taken together, these quotations or impressions form a composite and highly detailed image of the sea in motion—a phenomenon far too large in scope and far too complex to be seen in its entirety by a single individual.

What Moore has created here is not just an image of the sea; the method she uses in composing that image makes it a model, also, of the literary community she had been looking for ever since she began writing. This community is international in scope, like Eliot's version of modernism; and, like modernism, it reaches across historical and linguistic as well as geographical boundaries to join writers working in different countries (England, Italy, France, the United States); different languages

(Italian, French, English, Hebrew); and different points in time (from the Italian Renaissance to the present) in a common search for a universal and enduring truth. Moore's conception of truth is ultimately religious: The idea of using quotations in this way was suggested by *The Waste Land,* but the specific arrangement was suggested to Moore by a technical commentary on the Book of Isaiah.

Moore cannot hope to do more than approximate Isaiah's effects, as she would try to approximate the rhythms of the French when translating La Fontaine's *Fables* twenty years later; after all, she is writing secular verse in a different language—"not in Spanish, not in Greek, not in Latin, not in shorthand/but in plain American which cats and dogs can read!" (as she said in "England," 1920). But approximation is the best anyone can do in a fallen world; anything more requires "such power as Adam had and we are still devoid of," as Moore would write in "An Octopus" in 1924. One can only hope that successive approximations will bring one "closer to the truth."

III

During the 1930s and '40s, Moore approached the question of her place in the American community with the same seriousness with which we have seen her tackle the problem of her relation to the literary community. She was named acting editor of the *Dial* in 1925 and appointed editor the following year; she held the position until the magazine ceased publication in 1929. She wrote no new poems during this time, and even after she and her mother had left Greenwich Village for Brooklyn once the *Dial* closed its doors, she remained silent for another three years. She did not publish poetry again until June 1932, when the appearance in *Poetry* of "The Steeple-Jack," "The Student," and "The Hero" (under the collective title "Part of a Novel, Part of a Poem, Part of a Play") launched her examination of the ambiguous place of art in the American community.

In these new poems, Moore returns to the syllabic stanzas that had characterized her work during the teens, as if to say that in leaving Manhattan she was also resuming her old identity. I don't mean to suggest that she is merely reverting to a prior stage in her own career; on the contrary, the stanzaic patterns of the new poems show traces of Moore's three-and-a-half-year experiment with the openness of free verse. The new poems tend to be longer and a good deal more complex than the earlier ones—as Eliot said of "The Jerboa," they all have "a very wide spread of association" (*SP,* xi)—and their stanzaic patterns are correspondingly larger and more elaborate; their rhythms are more complex and various than in the past.

Marianne Moore with her mother, 1938.

The poems are often quite difficult; it is unfortunate, in a way, that they are the first ones a new reader of Moore is likely to come across. These are the poems that stand at the beginning of Moore's *Complete Poems* (1967, 1981); they owe their position to an editorial decision made by T. S. Eliot more than thirty years earlier. As editor of Moore's *Selected Poems,* Eliot decided to place her newest poems first—precisely because they *were* very difficult, and he wanted to get rid of conventionally minded readers right away. (His strategy worked, unfortunately: *Selected Poems* had been remaindered by 1940, and it has been out of print ever since.)

The poems are not impossible, however. As I have already suggested, they are all concerned with the relationship between the artist and the community in which she lives, and, like the poems we looked at earlier, many of them have to do with the troubling relationship between art and commerce. Thus we can look at the poems to see what kinds of oppositions they establish. For there has been a change in Moore's attitude. There is very little sense now that commerce is *good* for art.

"The Steeple-Jack" may be the most difficult of all the poems Moore wrote in the thirties. It transposes Moore's ironic representation of America as Paradise from the remote, glacial landscape of her previous major poem, "An Octopus" (*Dial,* 77 [1924]: 475–81), to a deceptively tropical—and deceptively simple—villagelike setting much closer to home. "An Octopus," set on Washington State's Mt. Rainier (which Moore visited in 1922), celebrates America's multiplicity and stylistic variety by incorporating more than fifty separate quotations, each providing a sightly different perspective on the scene as it unfolds. As in "Novices," the "relentless accuracy" of Moore's vision requires that all the quotations be taken together. There are so many shifts of perspective, however, and they occur so rapidly that it is very nearly impossible to hold them all in mind. And it is precisely in bringing the reader to acknowledge that such comprehensiveness of vision is impossible that Moore enforces her own understanding of what it means to be fallen: To be fallen is to be in Paradise and not know it.

"The Steeple-Jack" takes the opposite tack, tempting us to think we're in Paradise when we are really someplace else. The apparent simplicity of "The Steeple-Jack," like the complexity of "An Octopus," is also produced by Moore's careful manipulation of perspective; but the poet's hand is more carefully concealed here, and the shifts in point of view are more difficult to detect.

The steeplejack stands atop the whitewashed church at the center of the poem and of the community; he is "gilding the solid-/pointed star, which on a steeple/stands for hope," and he seems to be repairing the damage caused earlier in the poem by "the whirlwind fifeanddrum" of a storm that "bends the salt/marsh grass, disturbs stars in the sky and the/star on the steeple." But this is a storm that breeds "much confusion"; one of its effects is to make us think we are in some kind of tropical paradise; another is to make us think the steeplejack is working to restore the order that was disrupted by the storm.

In fact the steeplejack has *caused* the storm, and the consequent damage to the church: Moore's representation of the steeplejack was inspired, in part, by a sixteenth-century account of how, on a summer day in 1533, while the priest was celebrating mass, the devil climbed the steeple of the church in Shrewsbury, England, causing a great tempest and destroying both the town clock and the church bell (*Reading Diary,* 35–36). The steeplejack is wearing scarlet because that is the color the devil conventionally wears; the rope he lets down like a spider's fine-spun thread is meant to snare those sinners who are too foolish to heed the danger signs he has planted.

None of this is immediately apparent. But the idyllic appearance of this little village is a function of the perspective established by the carefully framed opening stanza. That stanza tells us that the German artist Albrecht Dürer, known among other things for his skillful and often deceptive manipulation of what was in his day the novel technique of perspectival drawing, "would have seen a reason for living/in a town like this, with eight stranded whales/to look at . . ." The reader is hooked, and it is easy to miss the moment later when the poem defines an alternative point of view.

The new perspective is established by the presence of a "college student/named Ambrose," who sits a little apart from the scene, which "he knows by heart." It is from his vantage point "on the hill-side" that we see that "the pitch of the church/spire" is "not true," and it is from that hillside that we watch while "a man in scarlet lets/down a rope as a spider spins a thread . . ." Ambrose's connoisseurship, his sense for what is true, reveals how dangerous it really is "to be living/in a town like this."

The difficulty of Moore's position is that she is committed to the perspectives of both Ambrose and the steeplejack, as well as to a third perspective—call it Dürer's—which includes them. Moore's goal is to persuade her community that the fearful danger she sees at its center is real; her strategy requires that she begin by representing the community as the community sees itself, and then delicately suggest the falseness of the representation. This is a dangerous course to pursue, since it deliberately courts misreading and risks the possibility that she will make matters worse by perpetuating the Edenic delusion of innocence she is trying to expose.

The stakes are especially high because Moore is not describing an imaginary village. "The Steeple-Jack" is an impassioned defense of Brooklyn, where for the first time in her career she feels really "at home," against the encroachments of the urban conditions she had lived under in Manhattan. Moore was prompted to write "The Steeple-Jack" when construction of the

"Adam and Eve"
by Lucas Cranach.

**This institution,
perhaps one should say enterprise
out of respect for which
one says one need not change one's mind
about a thing one has believed in,
requiring public promises
of one's intention
to fulfil a private obligation:
I wonder what Adam and Eve
think of it by this time,
this fire-gilt steel
alive with goldenness;
how bright it shows—
"Of circular traditions and impostures,
committing many spoils,"
requiring all one's criminal ingenuity
to avoid!
Psychology which explains everything
explains nothing,
and we are still in doubt.
Eve: beautiful woman—
I have seen her
when she was so handsome
she gave me a start,
able to write simultaneously
in three languages—
English, German and French—
and talk in the meantime;
equally positive in demanding a commotion
and in stipulating quiet . . .
And he has beauty also;
it's distressing—the O thou
to whom from whom,
without whom nothing—Adam;
"something feline,
something colubrine"—how true!**

—From "Marriage"

new IND Eighth Avenue subway line from Manhattan into Brooklyn undermined the foundation of the Lafayette Avenue Presbyterian Church, which she and her mother attended, forcing the removal of its steeple; a steeplejack named C. J. Poole —his name appears in the poem—was employed on the job. An entry in Moore's daily diary for Friday, November 6, 1931, tells the story in two words: "Subway construction" (*Daily Diary*, 1931).

But the poem is not only about Brooklyn. Just as the closing lines of "Novices" form a composite image of the sea, so the village in "The Steeple-Jack" is a composite made up of details from a number of villages and towns along the Eastern seaboard, including, most important, Brooklyn itself (*MMN,* 1 [Fall 1977]: 7). Brooklyn's historical associations with the American War of Independence (which is explicitly evoked in the companion poem "The Hero") make it clear that the village of "The Steeple-Jack" is also an image of what Moore sees as the quintessential American community. Not just Brooklyn, then, but the whole American community, governed as it is by "presidents who have repaid/sin-driven/senators by not thinking about them," is spiritually at risk.

With more than two and a half million inhabitants, Brooklyn was by far the most populous borough of Greater New York when Moore moved there in 1929; but the Clinton Hill district where she and her mother lived was still fashionable, in part because the neighborhood was small enough (like St. Luke's Place in the Village) and sufficiently self-contained to have kept the trappings of an earlier and more decorous era; it made Brooklyn seem much smaller than it actually was.

The Depression was about to begin, but New York had been in the throes of a construction boom for some time, a boom that saw the city's current skyline beginning to form in sharp contrast to that of Brooklyn. (Park Avenue, for instance, became a fashionable thoroughfare during the twenties; the 77-story Chrysler Building was completed in 1929, and construction was started on the 102-story, 1250-foot Empire State Building, which opened in 1931.)

Thus the separately titled sections of "The Jerboa," "Too Much" and "Abundance," respectively, draw a metaphorical contrast between the massive opulence of Manhattan's urban art forms and the far more modest scale of Brooklyn life. And just as "The Steeple-Jack" sets Ambrose against the more outrageously brilliant figure of the steeplejack, so "The Jerboa" pits its small desert rat, a "simplified creature," against the heavy, complicated mass created long ago, when "A Roman hired an/artist, a freedman,/to make a cone—pine cone/or fir cone—with holes for a fountain." This strange object was then "Placed" as emblematically as the steeplejack on the steeple, "on/the Prison of St. Angelo," where it "passed/for art" (*Hound and Horn,* 6 [1932]: 108).

The conical fountain bears a strong resemblance to another emblematic object that Moore describes in "The Plumet Basilisk" (1933):

. . . In
Copenhagen the principal door
of the bourse is roofed by two pairs of dragons
standing on
their heads—twirled by the architect—so
that the four
green tails conspiring upright, symbolize fourfold
security.

(*Hound and Horn,* 7 [1933]: 31)

The dragon figures, "conspiring" over the door of the Danish stock exchange, have had to be turned upside down in order to make them mean what those who paid for them want them to mean.

The opposition between the natural symbols of true art and the perversions engendered by commerce is most clearly stated in the poem's superb closing stanzas. Moore writes that the basilisk is America's "Tower-of-London/jewel that the Spaniards failed to see" because they were blinded by visions of wealth:

Thinking himself hid among the yet unfound jade
axeheads,
silver jaguars and bats, and amethysts and
polished iron, gold in a ten-ton chain, and pearls
the size of pigeon-eggs,

he is alive there
in his basilisk cocoon beneath
the one of lizard green; his quicksilver ferocity
quenched in the rustle of his fall into the sheath
which is the shattering sudden splash that marks
his temporary loss.

Moore is writing herself into an increasingly difficult corner in these poems. She makes it clear in "Virginia Britannia" (published in December 1935, but not grouped with the poems I have just been discussing because it was finished too late for inclusion in *Selected Poems*) that the folly she ascribes to the Spaniards in "The Plumet Basilisk" was not confined to one locality:

. . . pale fiercely
unpretentious North American, and Dutch
trader, and noble
Roman, in taking what they
pleased—colonizing as we say—
were not all intel-
lect and delicacy.

(*Life and Letters Today,* 13 [December 1935]: 69)

Whatever the Spaniards may have failed to see, they are no different from the Dutch and the Englishmen who colonized North America, or for that matter from the ancient Romans who colonized Britain: They all made their way by "taking what they/pleased" from those who were already there.

Moore cannot claim to be exempt from the charge of taking what she pleased, either. As the long catalogs of exotica that fill these poems testify, she too is possessed by the American in-

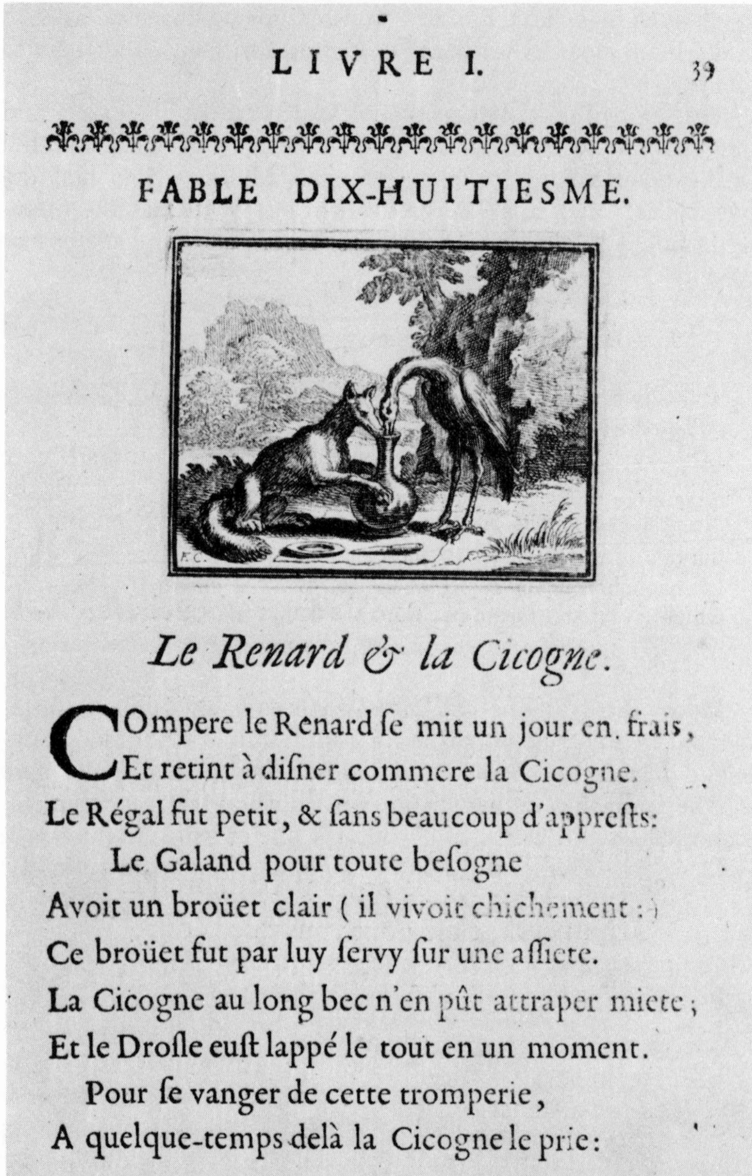

LIVRE I. 39

FABLE DIX-HUITIESME.

Le Renard & la Cicogne.

COmpere le Renard ſe mit un jour en frais,
Et retint à diſner commere la Cicogne.
Le Régal fut petit, & ſans beaucoup d'appreſts:
Le Galand pour toute beſogne
Avoit un broüet clair (il vivoit chichement :)
Ce broüet fut par luy ſervy ſur une aſſiete.
La Cicogne au long bec n'en pût attraper miete;
Et le Droſle euſt lappé le tout en un moment.
Pour ſe vanger de cette tromperie,
A quelque-temps delà la Cicogne le prie:

Moore's translations of the Fables *of La Fontaine appeared in 1954. The page reproduced is from* La Fontaine's *first edition, printed in 1668.*

stinct "to amass and reiterate" which she noted in Henry James in 1934 (*Prose,* 316), and for her as for James and all the other colonists, that instinct is closely allied with "the rapture of observation" (321).

It is instructive, in this context, to consider what these colonizing figures do with what they take; in "Virginia Britannia," at least, what they do is to create a facsimile of the English landscape they had left behind:

> . . . The Old Dominion has
> all-green grass-hoppers
> in all-green, box-sculptured grounds;
> an almost English green surrounds
> them. Care has formed, a-
> mong unEnglish insect sounds,
> the white wall-rose.

The colonists' careful work produces something that looks "almost English," just as the rhythm of Moore's lines is *almost* iambic pentameter—but the illusion holds only so long as you can ignore those "unEnglish insect sounds" and fail to see the grotesquely thickened stem of the wall rose, "As/thick as Daniel Boone's grape-/vine" and covered with "os-/trich-skin warts that were thorns."

Moore is a colonizer, too. There is no such thing in a Moore poem as "just looking." Though again and again she adopts the posture of the neutral observer, observation is always compromised by the desire for possession. There is a vivid illustration of this in "Bird Witted" (1936: another poem in the "Old Dominion" sequence which includes "Virginia Britannia"). Three young mockingbirds are waiting to be fed by their mother: The crisis comes when a "piebald cat" which has been "observing them" decides to join them on their branch; the whole scene is frozen (by typography among other things) as the mother bird dives down to attack "the intellectual, cautious-/ly c r e e p i n g cat" (*New Republic,* 85 [1936]: 311). This repeats the moment in "Virginia Britannia" when the command to "Observe" turns a mockingbird into a piece of statuary, "still standing there alone/ on the round stone-/topped table with lead cupids grouped to/ form the pedestal."

Colonists place no special value on originality—on the contrary, they prize imitations and memorials, monuments to the past and to what they still think of as home. Thus they transform the landscape into a museum dedicated to the preservation of obsolete forms—that is, to nostalgia, which means a longing for home; and, after 1940, Moore's poetry increasingly becomes what she called it in the foreword to *A Marianne Moore Reader*

Marianne Moore's desk, by Robert Andrew Parker.

in 1961—"if not a cabinet of fossils, a kind of collection of flies in amber" (xv).

She was speaking about her quotations, but the comment is an apt general description of her later poems. In May 1940, in a lecture she prepared for delivery at Sarah Lawrence College but never actually gave, Moore wrote that what she had learned from "Virginia Britannia" was that "one must overcome one's reluctance to be unoriginal" (Rosenbach Archive). This is a far cry indeed from her early, romantic determination to repel influences even at the cost of what her friend Williams called "incomprehensibility" (*Spring and All,* 101); we should note, in this connection, that Moore's definition of "colonizing"—"taking what they/pleased"—is very close to the definition of literary influence in Eliot's essay on Henry James ("To be influenced by a writer is to . . . take what one wants").

In their deliberate "unoriginality," Moore's later poems, those written after 1940, reveal a steadily deepening nostalgia, an intensifying desire to return to an earlier and more elegant but somehow simpler world. References to the eighteenth century, for example, recur with increasing frequency in her poems, and even in her costume—in the famous three-cornered hat and the black cape which made her easily recognizable. (The desire to simplify is evident in the abandon with which Moore slashed whole passages of complex detail while preparing the text of her *Collected Poems* in 1951; the poems of the 1930s sustained by far the heaviest damage. One might have expected readers to complain at this wholesale mutilation; but there were only a few complaints, and they were drowned out by general applause. *Collected Poems* won the Pulitzer Prize, the Bollingen Prize, and the National Book Award.)

In "A Carriage from Sweden" (1944), Moore regards the eighteenth century much as the eighteenth century had regarded the Augustan Age: as a model to emulate and a yardstick by which to measure how far the community had fallen. Here Moore discovers an emblem of "resined straightness" in the image of a "country cart/that inner happiness made art" sometime in the eighteenth century, in "Sweden's once-opposed-to-/compromise archipelago/of rocks."

The Holocaust casts a faint pall over the poem as Moore observes that, unlike Denmark with its "sanctuaried Jews," Sweden is no longer so firmly opposed to compromise; nor is Brooklyn, "this city of freckled/integrity." And so Moore asks forgiveness of two heroic eighteenth-century figures, one American and one Swedish: "Washington and Gustavus/Adolphus," she pleads, "forgive our decay."

Despite the general moral decay, however, Moore writes in the opening stanza that she has found something in Brooklyn that "makes [her] feel at home." That something is the carriage; but this is an instance of pure nostalgia. Moore had seen the carriage in the Brooklyn Museum in 1931 (*MMN,* 4 [Fall 1980]: 10–12); but, like the "Old Amusement Park" she would wistfully recall twenty years later (*CP,* 210), the carriage was no longer there when she wrote the poem. The amusement park was torn down to make way for commerce on a massive scale: LaGuardia Airport stands where it stood. So, too, the Swedish cart had fallen victim to commerce well before Moore's poem was written. A "put-away/museum piece," the carriage was sold in 1937 to a New York art dealer, and has subsequently disappeared.

WORDS FOR AN OLD MAN.

~~to Stephane Mallarmé.~~

The tiger in the tiger-pit

Is not more irritable than I.

The whipping tail is not more still

Than when I smell the enemy

Writhing in the essential blood

Or dangling from the friendly tree.

When I lay bare the tooth of wit

The hissing over the ~~flattened~~ archèd tongue

Is more affectionate than hate,

More bitter than the love of youth,

And inaccessible ~~to~~ by the young.

~~Garlic and sapphires in the mud~~

~~Clot the bedded axle-tree.~~

Reflected in my golden eye

The dullard knows that he is mad

Tell me if I am not glad!

T. S. ELIOT

FRANK KERMODE

Thomas Stearns Eliot became a British citizen in 1927, so for half of his lifetime he was not, technically, an American. In the same year he was baptized and received into the Church of England, a state church. He had already been editing *The Criterion* for five years, and *The Criterion* was a journal founded with the purpose of strengthening European cultural unity. He continued the journal until 1939; as war threatened and his editorial labors came to seem futile he expressed discontent with the condition of England. But he did not leave it; he suffered as everybody did during those dismal and dangerous years. His last important poem, *Little Gidding,* written in 1942, is both a war poem and a patriotic poem. It is difficult to imagine a career such as Eliot's occurring outside Europe, or even outside London. In the post-war years he was treated as a European sage, but his life was a London life. He was not only a poet and dramatist of world-wide reputation but an eminent English publisher. He wore the Order of Merit, an honor allowed to only twenty-six people at any one time. He was the patron of English poets but also a spokesman for English conservatism and Anglo-Catholicism. He was a member of several London clubs. Most of his friends were English, and both his wives. After fifty years abroad he had lost the Southern accent of his boyhood and the New England accent of his youth, if indeed he ever acquired one. In view of all this, it might be thought reasonable to ask whether he should be treated as in any important sense an American poet.

Perhaps the answer is in some lines from *Little Gidding*[1]:

> See, now they vanish
> The faces and places, with the self which, as it could, loved
> them,
> To become renewed, transfigured, in another pattern.
>
> (*CPP,* 195)

Eliot, who meditated so intensely on time, on moments of the past that are lost, or apparently lost, could not think of himself as indifferent to the lost America of his youth. If the river of *The*

Eliot during his first year at Harvard.

Waste Land is the Thames, the river of *The Dry Salvages* is the Mississippi as he remembered it at his birthplace, St. Louis. When he writes of that river he remembers Whitman and Mark Twain; when he writes of the ocean his thoughts are never far from his boyhood, when he sailed off Cape Ann, and with the fishermen of Gloucester and the "true owner" (*CPP,* 142) of that territory, "the tough one, the sea-gull" ("Landscapes" V: "Cape Ann"). He particularly admired Henry James, who although naturalized British and honored in Westminster Abbey where his monument is a near neighbor of Eliot's, never lost his sense of himself as American. James's ghost story, "The Jolly Corner" —in which an American returning late in life to the scene of his youth encounters a ghostly self that had remained behind— meant a good deal to Eliot. Speaking at his old school, Milton Academy, in 1933, he said he was addressing not the boys of today but his own ghost, aged about seventeen. We may also remember that he kept in touch with his teacher Irving Babbitt of Harvard—not a thinker to attract much European notice— and quoted Poe with more respect than is usual among English (though not among French) writers. Though his poetic career began in London, his early counselor was American, and he entrusted the delivery of his first great poem, *The Waste Land,* to the man-midwife Pound. Asked whether he was an American or an English poet, he replied jocosely that he was whatever W. H. Auden wasn't, Auden having taken U.S. citizenship in his thirties. The truth is rather that, like Auden, he was both, the old allegiance renewed, transfigured, in another pattern.

Eliot's mother, a woman greatly interested in sanctity, was an adherent also of Emerson; and her son inherited both traits, though he seems to have brooded on the first more than the second. Yet we may find something of Emerson in his lifelong insistence on making everything new. He never repeated himself; the lines at the beginning of the last section of *East Coker* say that

every attempt
Is a wholly new start, and a different
kind of failure . . .

(*CPP,* 182)

Another deep conviction was of the heroic role of the poet, separate and yet charged to speak for the rest of us. But his notion of the poet is also European; his views on suffering as a means to art owe more to Baudelaire than to the American tradition. And instead of a bold rejection of the past, he preferred to rebuild it in terms of the traditions of Latin civilization as he understood it, so that Virgil and Dante were canonical, and newness had only incidentally any connection with the passage of time. These opinions and attitudes, together with his high regard for Catholic and royalist views of history and politics, distanced him from the Unitarianism of his own distinguished family tradition, from American democratic assumptions, and from some of his American poet contemporaries, whose Emersonianism was less diluted. Wallace Stevens avoided reading much of Eliot, taking the side of his friend William Carlos Williams, who said outright that Eliot was a disaster for American poetry; for he "has turned his back on the possibility of reviving my world. And being an accomplished craftsman, better skilled in some ways than I could ever hope to be, I had to watch him carry my world off with him, the fool, to the enemy."[2]

Although Eliot was certainly, to use Philip Rahv's distinction, Paleface to Williams's Redskin, and undoubtedly preferred the English class system to the American, the ideals he took to Europe were surely American, though paleface American. His powerful sense of election surely derives something from his New England Puritan ancestry; and so does his sense of obligation to the community.

The relation of "major man" to man in general preoccupied Wallace Stevens, who thought that the poets who had once created the gods must after their death create new fictions to enable men to lead their lives on earth. Eliot's version of this vocation is different because it has from the beginning a religious tone, and that tone deepens as his career progresses. There is something in him of that Catholic belief in victimage, suffering borne on behalf of others, or "offered up." The poet may be such a victim, saint or sinner or both, and in any case is extraordinary. To be a saint or a great sinner is to be different, apart; for most people are neither, and Eliot tends to represent most people as barely alive at all, or as deficient in consciousness and certainly in spirituality. This is a theme in much of his poetry, even in the verse plays. He saw the theater as the most promising place for a poet to make contact with his community and labored to achieve a verse manner that approximated ordinary speech; but always there was an ulterior purpose and a message for the elect. *The Cocktail Party,* his greatest popular success, sorts out human beings thus; and he often thought of common humanity as barely existing, a spiritless herd.

He held aloof from practical or political plans to change this state of affairs, believing with Socrates that the intelligent man is concerned only with the politics of that republic which is laid up as a pattern in heaven; and he joined the Church of England not because he thought it a perfect church on earth but because of its relation to the Church Triumphant, laid up in heaven. Of an American aristocracy himself, he was most interested in the English upper classes. He did not forget his birthplace, though he would have found himself uneasy in modern America, where elites form, dissolve, and reform with such undesirable rapidity. His ashes are in the beautiful old church at East Coker in Somerset, the village from which his ancestors fled to America; thus,

Eliot's mother, Charlotte Champe Eliot.

without ceasing to be English, he arranged for his end to be his beginning in a cycle that will not allow us to decide that he belonged in some simple fashion to one tradition or the other.

Newly graduated from Harvard, Eliot first went to Europe in 1910. Honoring an American tradition, he went to Paris, but visited Munich and London. There was a moment when he considered settling in Paris and writing in French, but he returned to graduate school at Harvard to study philosophy. He was a serious student, distinguishing himself in the seminar of Josiah Royce, a philosopher of Christian community, and attracting the attention of Bertrand Russell, then a visiting professor. Russell was to remain for some time an influence in Eliot's life in other than philosophical ways; indeed his kind of philosophy was not congenial to Eliot, who decided to write his thesis on the English idealist philosopher F. H. Bradley. In 1914 he perforce cut short a visit to Germany and went to Merton College, Oxford, Bradley's own college, to continue his studies. This turned out to be the decisive move, not because it launched a philosophical career but because Eliot thenceforth lived in England; and because he was soon to meet Ezra Pound.

However, his philosophical training was important; and we have become more and more aware of the fact that Bradley had a considerable effect on Eliot as a poet as well as a thinker. He was already a poet, of course, but it was part of his singularity as a poet that he could assimilate very disparate material and turn it to his own use. His reading of Arthur Symons's *The Symbolist Movement in Literature* (1899), which he came across at Harvard in 1908, is a case in point: Symons not only introduced him to Jules Laforgue, with immediate effect on his poetic style, but gave him a knowledge of French Symbolism that he would improve, purge, and combine with his study of the English Elizabethan and Jacobean drama, in which Symons was also expert. Yet this combination of interests became very much Eliot's own and not at all derivative from the Ninetyish Symons. In a rather similar way he drew heavily on Ezra Pound without ever sounding like an imitator. And he steeped himself in the philosophy of Bradley without changing the color of his own mind.

His essay on Bradley (1926) is chiefly concerned with the philosopher's prose style and polemical resources, though it expresses admiration also for his intelligence, saying he was much too good a thinker to be popular. Eliot's thesis *Knowledge and Experience in the Philosophy of F. H. Bradley,* published in 1964, is a difficult book even for philosophers, and Eliot himself later professed not to understand it. Learned disputes about the exact character of Bradley's lasting influence on the poet turn on the quotation in the note to l.411 of *The Waste Land:* "My external sensations are no less private to myself than are my thoughts or my feelings. In either case my experience falls within my own circle, a circle closed on the outside; and, with all its elements alike, every sphere is opaque to the others which surround it . . . In brief, regarded as an existence which appears in a soul, the whole world for each is peculiar and private to that soul" (*CPP,* 80). In the context of the poem this means that we are each of us locked into the prison of the self. And in his thesis Eliot went beyond Bradley in the direction of solipsism, for Bradley insisted on the community of self and world, and held that individual minds were aspects of a single consciousness, the isolation of consciousness being a matter of appearance rather than of reality.

The philosopher Richard Wollheim, a great authority on

Bradley, argues that the *Waste Land* note quotes the philosopher out of context and so offers an interpretation which Eliot ten years earlier would have rejected. He was *using* Bradley for poetry. Wollheim thinks that Eliot came to fear philosophy. Certainly he abandoned it. His early work contains a good many philosophical essays and reviews, but later he said he had "little capacity for sustained, exact, and closely argued reasoning."[3] His failure to return to Harvard to defend his thesis is perhaps, among other things, an indication of his choice of poetry. There may be an incompatibility between the two careers; Eliot seems to have thought so, and remembered the sad example of Coleridge.

The idea of my consciousness as an entirely private and finite relation to the world, opaque to all others, is an alarming one, but it suited the late romantic concept of the artist as outcast, cut off, accursed, which Eliot was to hold in a very refined form. Hence his use of Bradley; it has a certain characteristic ruthlessness. There are also some touches of Bradley in early critical essays, where Eliot, writing about other poets or proposing a view of tradition congenial to his own program of work, was sketching his new poetic. All his reading could be forced to contribute, in very unexpected ways, to the splendidly self-regarding propositions of the poet. There is here a touch of that arrogance often seen in artists; it is what Eliot admired in Dante's Brunetto Latini, who, though in hell, "seemed like him who wins, and not like him who loses."

So Bradley made his contribution. But Eliot's decision to study in England had another important consequence: he met Ezra Pound. Three years senior to Eliot, Pound was much better known. He had been secretary and mentor to W. B. Yeats, the current "king of the cats." He threw himself energetically into propaganda for the New. He had arrived in England in 1908, and by 1914, when Eliot turned up, was on terms of easy familiarity with most of the writers for whom he saw any hope at all. He encouraged Eliot to stay in London and join the campaign; for, as he told Harriet Monroe, his new protégé had "trained himself *and* modernized himself *on his own.*"[4] Monroe bowed to Pound's demands and published "The Love Song of J. Alfred Prufrock" in June 1915. It was Eliot's first publication. In the same month he married. He had settled in London, by vocation an avant-garde poet, but with a wife to support. Neither the vocation nor the wife was pleasing to his American family; far away across the dangerous Atlantic they mourned Eliot's imprudence while he set about establishing himself in these new roles.

It is easy to agree that an avant-garde was needed. One can

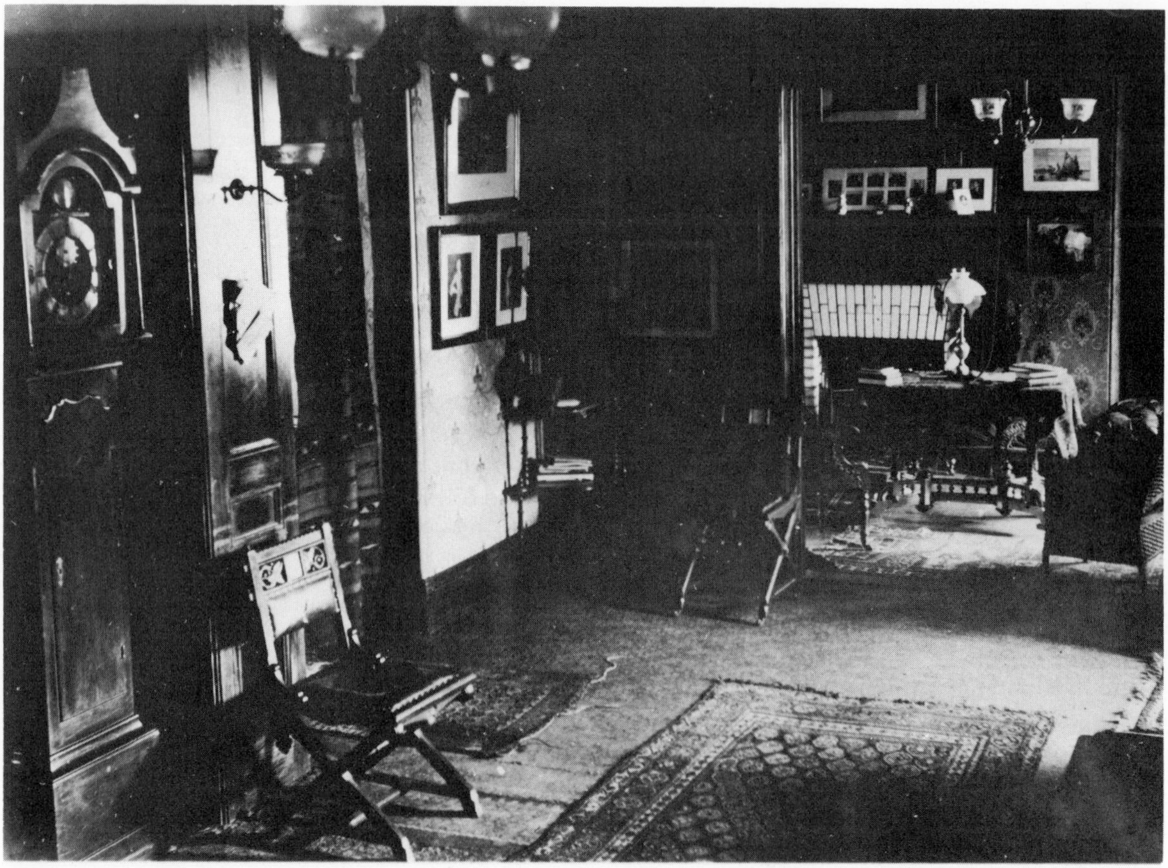

The Eliots' St. Louis parlor.

point to Yeats, Lawrence, and Hardy, all working at this time; but at first Eliot showed little interest in them, for they were not, so to speak, pointed in the direction in which he wanted to go. In 1933 he was to class them all—and Pound, too—as "heretics," deviants from the orthodoxy he had worked out for himself. He would have even less time for Shaw and Wells and Bennett, though he later came to value Bennett's advice on his first theatrical venture, *Sweeney Agonistes.* These were all English—or Anglo-Irish—writers of importance, but they were irrelevant to the avant-garde; Pound and Eliot embraced Joyce instead, and, to a lesser extent, Conrad; and it is one measure of their extraordinary success that we tend to think of the others as off the main modern track or as of the second rank. In short, we think of the Pound group as a historical necessity, and of Pound and Eliot in particular as the founders of modernist poetry in English.

And yet we do well to remember how unpromising their program must have seemed at the time. Two young Americans making their way in a foreign country—a country involved in a vast exhausting war while their own remained neutral—undertook to change the direction not only of poetry but of the other arts also, and not only of the arts but of culture in general. The principal English members of the group were T. E. Hulme and Wyndham Lewis. Hulme was killed in France in 1917, and Eliot never met him. The main part of Hulme's work was published only in 1924 *(Speculations),* but before and after that date he influenced Eliot greatly. At first it was Hulme's handful of brief poems, highly valued by Pound and the "Imagists," that affected him most, but Hulme's philosophy was also congenial. This was anti-Romantic (he called Romanticism "spilt religion") and authoritarian. He believed in original sin and regarded the replacement of that doctrine by a humanism that dated from the Renaissance as the source of all error. His notion of the good society was repressive and hieratic; his notion of good writing was similar, for he detested sentiment and inexactness, demanding that the poet find "the exact curve of the thing." Poetry should be dry and precise, society hierarchical, religion Catholic. In the visual arts he favored geometrical abstraction; he was a disciple of the German art historian Wilhelm Worringer, who associated good art with rigid societies like those of Egypt and Byzantium, and bad art with democratic societies obsessed with human individuality; the first had an art of "abstraction," the second an art of "empathy." The fight for abstraction against empathy was carried on in the work of the two principal artists of the group, the French sculptor Henri Gaudier-Brzeska, who was also killed in France at the age of twenty-four, and the cosmopolitan (Percy) Wyndham Lewis, who survived the trenches and achieved fame as painter, novelist, essayist, and pamphleteer.

Lewis was always important to Eliot, who championed his prose (especially the novel *Tarr* [1918]) and shared many of his opinions, though Lewis had nothing to do with religion. Of the "men of 1914," as this group is sometimes called, Lewis was the most versatile and pugnacious. Vorticism, as defined by Pound and Lewis, was one of the few moments in the history of English art that was characterized by the European practice of issuing manifestos and defiant periodicals. In painting it implied abstraction, independence of the fortuitous and the human; in literature a severance from the soft conventions of the recent past; in politics contempt for the masses, the *Massenmenschen,* to use the word chosen by Eliot when congratulating Lewis. In painting the movement owed much to Cubism and something to the Italian Futurism of Marinetti. In its devastation of earlier literature it used some of the techniques of the French, and especially of Guillaume Apollinaire, ardent proponent of a new poetry and a new art. Lewis edited the journal *Blast,* a visually striking, verbally violent affair, blasting this and blessing that; only one number appeared before the war began, and one more after that. The war indeed was the end of the Vortex. Its adherents would, in any case, have gone their own way; and Eliot, though junior to the others and not as loud a voice, was from the outset his own man. His association with Lewis and Pound remained important to him, but his work, to their irritation, diverged inexorably from their programs. For a while the influence of Pound continued to mark his work in obvious ways—his use, for instance, of the French critic Rémy de Gourmont derives from Pound, though as usual it is Gourmont ruthlessly adapted to the private aims of Eliot, which were just as radical as Pound's or Lewis's but radically independent of theirs.

So we find Eliot in 1915 prepared for a literary career. "Prufrock" was a work of even greater originality than it now seems: a drastic modernization of the old Browning-style dramatic monologue, lacking steady narrative or steady persona, mixing elaborate and protracted metaphysical conceits with the ironies and surprises of Laforgue, the poet who at this time was his chief model (though the need to be surprising, which Eliot always believed in, derives also from Edgar Allan Poe). However, he needed another career and one more likely to support himself and a wife. His marriage was a desperate affair, and lately a great deal, I think a great deal too much, has been written about it. A man beset by sexual difficulties of various kinds (including a fear of women that gets into his poetry, especially his unpublished verse) married a woman deeply neurotic and exhibiting symptoms that were in a disastrous sense complementary with his; and for both of them this meant years of misery, though the evidence of a close and sometimes fruitful bond between them is also not lacking.

It is important to remember that illness and anguish were, in Eliot's view, aspects of one mode of poetic election. He inherited, though he scrupulously worked to modernize the inheritance, the tradition of the *poète maudit,* condemned to malady and debauch; hence his admiration for Charles-Louis Philippe's novel *Bubu of Montparnasse,* and, above all, for the poetry and the life of Charles Baudelaire.

The essay on Baudelaire included in his *Selected Essays* was written later, in 1930, when he had found a solution to some of his problems, religious and poetic; but it still tells us something about the Eliot of the earlier years. Eliot needed a Baudelaire

Gloucester, Massaschusetts, at the turn of the century, when Eliot summered there.

stripped of the "Romantic detritus"[5] and of his historical association with the likes of Swinburne, who first introduced him into England. Like all great poets, Baudelaire is timeless, though incapable of avoiding the trappings of his period, its satanism and other "decadent" properties. Having got rid of these one sees that Baudelaire, though his poetry has imperfections, was a great man: not a good man, but a man who has a knowledge of good and evil.

This brings us close to a central idea, that great poetry is a poetry of orthodoxy. Good and evil are theological expressions and not at all synonymous with Right and Wrong. And to have knowledge of them may be the achievement of a saint, but it can be had also by the great sinner—not by trifling *Massenmenschen,* who are barely alive and know nothing of all this, not men enough to be damned. Saints rarely bother to be poets, so *pecca fortiter* (a Lutheran formula Eliot naturally does not use) is more likely to be the way of the great poet. Baudelaire's morbidity is as valuable as Goethe's health. He was a blasphemer, but blasphemy is a way of affirming belief; earlier Eliot had admired the blasphemy of Marlowe for the same reason. Baudelaire chose to suffer, but this kind of suffering implies a possibility of beatitude. Baudelaire's *ennui* is best understood theologically, as *acedia,* a condition arising from the unsuccessful struggle towards the spiritual life. We may admire him for showing how urban imagery—a new feature of poetry—can be raised to the first intensity (we may also imitate him in that, as Eliot did) but the important point is that Baudelaire understood what really matters—the pattern of Sin and Redemption. ". . . The possibility of damnation is so immense a relief in a world of electoral reform, plebiscites, sex reform and dress reform, that damnation itself is an immediate form of salvation —of salvation from the ennui of modern life, because it at last gives some significance to living."[6] So, we learn, Baudelaire "walked secure in this high vocation, that he was capable of a damnation denied to the politicians and the newspaper editors of Paris." He had discovered, for instance, that the unique pleasure of sexual love lay in the certainty of doing evil. It is better to do evil than to do nothing. This may mean that one treats woman as a symbol (*viz.,* of evil).

The whole extraordinary essay turns on its concluding quotation from Baudelaire himself: "true civilization lies not in gas or steam or spiritualist séances, but in the diminution of the traces of original sin." Eliot ends with a long passage from T. E. Hulme on that topic and its implications for social order; it hardly helps the essay, but it does show how, for Eliot, highly personal preoccupations were reflected in his thinking about other subjects. From the necessary sins and maladies of the orthodox poet one moves to the requirement of repressive institutions for those incapable of damnation.

The Baudelaire essay is a beautiful example of the audacity with which Eliot refined his view of another poet for his own ends. Here is the *poète maudit* in his stripped twentieth-century version, ready to pay the same price for the same access to high poetry as his bedizened ancestor. An early image of Eliot's was that of Saint Sebastian, his flesh in love with the arrows; another was Narcissus, identified in an early poem with the dancer Nijinsky, whose art cost him not less than madness. These figures made their contribution to the last great section of *The Waste Land.* The related conviction, that after the saint comes the great sinner, so utterly distinguishable from the crowd, is expressed by Eliot's admiration not only for the damned Brunetto Latini but for the troubadour Arnaut Daniel as he appears in Dante's *Purgatorio;* Dante gives him Provençal to speak, and the lines haunted Eliot, who quotes them repeatedly:

Baudelaire was man enough for damnation: whether he *is* damned is, of course, another question, and we are not prevented from praying for his repose. In all his humiliating traffic with other beings, he walked secure in this high vocation, that he was capable of a damnation denied to the politicians and the newspaper editors of Paris.

—From "Baudelaire" by T. S. Eliot

Ara vos prec, per aquella valor
que vos guida al som de l'escalina,
sovegna vos a temps de ma dolor.
Poi s'ascose nel foco che gli affina.

And so I pray you, by that Virtue which
leads you to the topmost of the stair—
be mindful in due time of my pain.
Then dived he back into that fire which refines them.

Arnaut was a strong sinner and a sexual sinner. Eliot called his first book *Ara Vos Prec,* and was still remembering Arnaut in *Four Quartets.* The poet, isolated from those incapable of damnation, might also hope for purgation in the refining fire by the very nature of his difference, his recognition of sexual evil and the strength of his sinning.

When he thus appropriated Baudelaire to his own purposes, Eliot was continuing a practice established in his first literary criticism. Though he worked for a time as a schoolmaster, and then for many years in a bank, he had also established himself, before 1920, as an important and respected reviewer. The relative brevity of reviews—typically the *Times Literary Supplement* lead or "middle," running to perhaps three thousand words, like the famous essay on *Hamlet*—suited his purposes well, since he could be provocative, test his notions, and display an unusual range of learned reference with urbanity rather than exhaustiveness. These early writings are remarkable for their tone of authority, for their polish (though they were often written by a weary and overworked man), and for their egotism; the word is not exactly right, but what he was doing was to stake out the claims of his own poetic while writing about other matters, which involved a just and necessary measure of self-regard.

One of the most celebrated of these pieces is the essay "Tradition and the Individual Talent," first published in 1919 and then in Eliot's first critical collection *The Sacred Wood* (1920). The proposition that tradition is essential to poetry is not astonishing until one sees what Eliot understands by tradition. It isn't, as might have been supposed, something handed down; "it cannot be inherited, and if you want it you must obtain it by great labour."[7] Once obtained, it confers a sense of the past not only as past but also as present; and a poet should write "with a feeling that the whole of literature from Homer . . . has a simultaneous existence and composes a simultaneous order." That order is outside time, and new works may join it; as they do so they modify the existing elements of the order, so that one has an interdependent canon of classic works, its internal relations free of chronology. But the work that joins the canon will be from the hand of one who has made something *new,* yet deferred to the tradition so defined. This requirement doesn't make him a scholar; if he is a true poet, he will find what he needs without turning into a dryasdust. Having found it, however, he must submit to its authority and sacrifice to it his own personality.

This is how the doctrine of tradition entails the doctrine of impersonality. Nowadays we have less trouble with the tradition than with the impersonality, for no one really supposes that there is a fixed past, unaffected by present interests and prejudices. But impersonality is another matter, since it has been shown that much of the poetry of Eliot is in an obvious way personal; he himself used the word "personal" of *The Waste Land,* which certainly uses language and incidents deriving from his private life. But these difficulties arise partly from the brevity of the essay and partly from the writer's need to make his points with emphasis. We have seen that as a philosopher Eliot had considered the problem of individual consciousness; he was well aware that our perception of the world is subjective, tinged with feelings proper to ourselves. But it was just that awareness that made him wish to be part of the community of great literature. The only way to achieve that was through a work which should join the canonical consort and which, being out of time, was independent of the suffering person who produced it. There must be a voluntary surrender of personality. The poet must act only as a catalyst, a medium by which disparate thoughts and feelings enter into new combinations. That is what makes him a poet and a servant of the tradition. His own experience will be disjoined from the poem; though the poem may be thought in some sense correlative with the experience or the emotion, it must also possess objectivity. (This is the point at which the idea of impersonality meets that of the "objective correlative," as it is stated in the essay on *Hamlet,* written in the same year.)

We know that throughout his career Eliot allowed poems to accrete in their own time rather than writing them to some plan; he remarked on this himself in his *Paris Review* interview. That is what he had in mind when he spoke of catalysis. He did not mean that the suffering of the poet was dispensable, and he makes that clear in the Baudelaire essay. He had many "dry" periods, but poetry was silently collecting; he said at one very difficult period of his life that he had written nothing for six months but lived through enough material for several long poems. The poetry is not in the pain, but the pain is essential to its production. Sometimes the poem will almost write itself, like the last section of *The Waste Land.* Mrs. Valerie Eliot tells us that when he wrote in his essay on Pascal (1931) that nonmystics have experiences that are mystical, and that poor health may conduce to such experiences, he was thinking of himself, and especially of those concluding lines, which give the poet "the sensation of being a vehicle rather than a maker."[8] This is an "escape from personality." "But of course, only those who have personality and emotions know what it means to escape from these things."[9] Here again is that rather contemptuous declaration of apartness from the "poor loveless ever-anxious crowd," as Coleridge called them; from the commuters shuffling across London Bridge at nine in the morning; from those who are the subject of sour jokes in *The Family Reunion* and receive therapy in *The Cocktail Party* and cannot hope even for salvation by damnation. It is a doctrine of election that makes of the poet a remote spiritual figure; one catches a glimpse of him in the Thomas of *Murder in the Cathedral.* The kind of poetry such a man would write is the kind upon which Eliot embarked at the time when he was writing "Tradition and the Individual Talent."

The essay has been much criticized for looseness of expression and terminology; yet it is very revealing. The notion of surrender to, or possession by, some poem belonging to the tradition is central to Eliot's success as poet and critic. An instance of this is his response to some lines in *The Revenger's Tragedy,* a play by Middleton or Tourneur published in 1607. They include this passage, now famous though it was not so when Eliot pointed it out:

> Does the silkworm expend her yellow labours
> For thee? For thee does she undo herself?
> Are lordships sold to maintain ladyships
> For the poor benefit of a bewildering minute?

This is valued not merely as a beautiful account of sex as at once fascinating and repellent but because it offers a sexual figure for the process of surrendering to poetry. In May 1935 Eliot wrote to Stephen Spender: "You don't really criticize any author to whom you have never surrendered yourself. . . . Even just the bewildering minute counts; you have to give yourself up, then recover yourself, and the third moment is having something to say, before you have wholly forgotten both surrender and recovery. Of course the self recovered is never the same as the self before it was given."[10] So the critic is the same kind of agent as the poet—a maker of the new transformed by contact with the old. The vivid "minutes" stud Eliot's poetry as well as his criticism, fragments of that transcendent canon. Many lines of Dante are now familiar to us only because Eliot chose them, or was chosen by them. The second-rate artist is concerned to emphasize his difference from others; the great one forgets himself. So should it be with critics; their concern is not with their own quirks and oddities but with "the common pursuit of true judgment";[11] and that pursuit has nothing to do with the Inner Voice that asserts individuality, but with attention to Tradition. The difference is the same as the difference between the vanity of nonconformity and the acceptance of a Catholic authority ("The Function of Criticism," 1923).

The notion of some order behind or beneath the drab appearances of modern life was very important to Eliot, and it accounts not only for his timeless Tradition but for his interest in ritual and myth. Hence his interest in Sir James Frazer and in Jessie Weston; hence his famous review of *Ulysses,* describing the Homeric parallels as "a way of controlling, of ordering, of giving a shape and a significance to the immense panorama of futility and anarchy which is contemporary history."[12] Eliot imagined a time in the past when this kind of effort was unnecessary, a time when poets, by a "direct sensuous apprehension of thought and feeling,"[13] conveyed a truer relation to the world. He thought he found this in the lyric poetry of the seventeenth century but not in Milton; he attributed the disaster to the Civil War; he thought poetry must strive again for the unified sensibility that was then dissociated. The real agent of disaster was science and attendant irreligion. In Eliot an interest in dance as a sort of liturgy, in myth, in the English seventeenth century, and in the English Catholic church are all part of the same pattern, a pattern to be made visible in the desolate modern world only by very great effort.

The chief exemplar of the classical and catholic tradition was Dante, to whom Eliot dedicated what is probably his finest long essay. Professional Dante scholars seem to think little of it. Eliot had no particular command of the language or of the scholarship; he treated Dante as the model of orthodoxy and the source of many bewildering minutes. Indeed he gives us another version of the letter to Spender: "The experience of a poem is the experience both of a moment and of a lifetime. It is very much like our intenser experiences of other human beings. There is a first, or an early moment which is unique, of shock and surprise, even of terror . . . ; a moment which can never be forgotten, but which is never repeated integrally; and yet which would become destitute of significance if it did not survive in a larger whole of experience; which survives inside a deeper and calmer feeling."[14] Some such experience explains his fascination with

T. S. Eliot at his desk at Faber and Faber.

the lines on Arnaut and those who suffer in the fire that refines because they wish to suffer. That moment survives in a larger whole: the conviction that the pain of the poet suggests the hope of beatitude. Arnaut, the sexual offender, remembers folly but can expect joy. Perhaps nobody can grasp much of the poetry of Eliot without understanding the Dante essay, and above all this passage on Arnaut.

Conrad Aiken tells us that in 1921–22, when he was seeing a lot of Eliot, the poet always carried in his pocket the little Temple Press edition of Dante, with the English prose translation facing the Italian text. This was the period of the long strange composition of *The Waste Land;* it was a time of overwork, illness, and mental anguish, but Dante was there also. The earliest poems Eliot published, the "Preludes" and the "Rhapsody," for instance, seem to owe most to Laforgue and Baudelaire and, in the satirical "Mr. Apollinax," to Pound; but the poems which open and close the volume are Italian: the epigraph to "Prufrock" and "La Figlia che Piange." The epigraph is untranslated; Eliot often played that trick, but it is related to his conviction that "genuine poetry can communicate before it is understood," and he wanted his modern poem to partake of the illustrious vernacular of Dante as well as to give the clue that the interlocutor of Prufrock is taken to be a suitable recipient for a confession the speaker finds it necessary to keep secret from the world; it helps to seal off the poem from those who would, by trying to puzzle out an ordinary narrative, destroy its secrecy, flatten out the surprise in the collocation of sordid streets, fog, and the head of John the Baptist. Dante is necessary, along with Laforgue, and in the context of a remarkable metrical experiment: the old essential to the new.

"Gerontion," however, was the poem that cleared the way for *The Waste Land,* with its incantations and its muted apocalypse; it is (as its Shakespearian epigraph suggests) a dream, dreamed as it were, in the Last Days, in spiritual drought. It is made up of broken images signifying the confusions of history and an imminent end. Jesus was so angered by the request for a sign that he declared "there shall be no sign given unto this generation" (Mark 8:12); Eliot, characteristically, locates this remark in a sermon by Lancelot Andrewes, from whom he also takes "The word within a word, unable to speak a word"[15]—altering Andrewes's *"Verbum infans,* the Word without a word." Here is a useful instance of the manner in which such "bewildering minutes" stayed in the poet's mind: in his essay on Andrewes (1926) he quotes the same passage, but in the errant form he had imposed upon it ("The word within a word, unable to speak a word"). In *Ash Wednesday,* a little later, he restores Andrewes but does not forget what he had made of him, writing "The Word without a word, the Word within / The world"—a sort of emendation, expansion or consolidation of the original and the deviant form of it. Thus these talismanic phrases echo round Eliot's poetry as round the consciousness of Gerontion, mixed with all the others, the echoes of Chapman and Henry Adams and also the names occurring here and here only, Madame de Tornquist, Hakagawa, Mr. Silvero, by contrast sinister because without reference, like the secret rite, the mysterious bowing, shifting, pausing. We are not to look for a story in this dramatic monologue, but for juxtapositions more unmotivated by story than any devised by Conrad or Ford Madox Ford in the novel, or any cinema director. We need to be bewildered, surrender, withdraw changed. Those are the terms on which the poetry of Eliot is offered.

At the end of 1920, sick and distressed, disappointed by the reception of *The Sacred Wood,* Eliot thought himself to be at a standstill, though some time before he had spoken of a projected long poem. He was involved in preliminary negotiations concerning the journal he was to begin editing in 1922; and he was also contemplating a play about Sweeney, a character he had used in some quatrain poems published in 1920. But he also began to put together a number of drafts and poems under the title *He Do the Police in Different Voices.* Then he had a breakdown, was given three months' leave by his bank, and went first to Margate, a seaside resort near London, and then to Lausanne for treatment. His illness was thought to be aboulia, an inability to experience emotion. He benefited by the treatment and it was in Lausanne that the final section of *The Waste Land* emerged in the manner described in the Pascal essay. Eliot had stopped in Paris on the way to Lausanne to show the batch of manuscripts to Pound, who had moved there; on his way home he saw Pound again, and gave him "What the Thunder Said."

Since the publication of Mrs. Eliot's edition of the manuscript (1971), a great deal of attention has been paid to the changes and cuts made by Pound and Eliot himself, and the whole subject is certainly of interest. But these alterations, although they well justify the dedication to Pound, are not the primary business of the reader. The poem as revised was considered complete, and Eliot published it in the first issue of *The Criterion* in 1922. Even the notes added later he did not consider essential. By November 1922, a month after its first publication, he could call the poem "a thing of the past";[16] and the changes it underwent he remembered only because they testified to Pound's skill. The reader is confronted with five poems that are one poem, but not because they have a continuous narrative. They are to be thought of as a unique constellation of images rather than as a sequence of simple succession. Of course this doesn't mean there are no "stories" in the poem—the seduction of the typist is obviously one such, and there are others less rounded off; mere episodes without outcome, like the encounter with Mr. Eugenides or the scene in the pub. But these are treated as elements in a much more complex whole which is not narrative. That is what Eliot had in mind when he suggested that Tiresias and what he sees (remember that he was blind) are the bond of the poem. It is not a story about Tiresias, however many roles he may be given. It is a once-for-all complex of figurations brought together in a poet's consciousness and expelled thence, to be assimilated and structured by other consciousnesses equally private, insofar as they can do it. Its logic, to use an expression of Eliot's, is a logic of the imagination and not a logic

"A cold coming we had of it,
Just the worst time of the year
For a journey, and such a long journey:
The ways deep and the weather sharp,
The very dead of winter."

—From "Journey of the Magi"

It was no summer progress. A cold coming they had of it at this time of the year, just the worst time of the year to take a journey, and specially a long journey in. The ways deep, the weather sharp, the days short, the sun furthest off, *in solstitio brumali,* "the very dead of winter."

—From "Nativity Sermon" XV
by Lancelot Andrewes

One of the surest tests is the way in which a poet borrows. Immature poets imitate; mature poets steal; bad poets deface what they take; and good poets make it into something better, or at least something different.

—From *Essays on Elizabethan Drama* ("Philip Massinger")
by T. S. Eliot

of concepts. "People who do not appreciate poetry always find it difficult to distinguish between order and chaos in the arrangement of images . . ."[17] Some good readers of poetry, however, still find some difficulty in believing that the order of this poem is inherent in it, and not something we have been persuaded to find in it by potent suggestion; indeed, since the academy long since endorsed its presence, by authority and inertia. We are so familiar with it, so accustomed to respond to its juxtapositions and allusions, that we feel certain, when we look at the manuscript versions, that all the changes, whether by Pound or Eliot, were for the better; and in the same way we can only with great difficulty imagine the poem as having any other shape than the one it now has.

Despite the allusions to the Fisher King and the Chapel Perilous, and the clue in the Notes about Jessie Weston, it may be questioned whether the background of myth is as persistent as these hints suggest. Jessie Weston provided the title—the Waste Land is a phase of the romance cycle about the Grail, the land laid waste by the impotence of its king. She was also devoted to Wagner. Much in the poem derives from Wagner's operas. Most obviously, there are the Thames Daughters, based on the Rhine Daughters of *Das Rheingold* and *Götterdämmerung.* There are two quotations from *Tristan und Isolde,* one from the opening moments, which touches on the parting of lovers, the other from the third act when Tristan, mortally hurt, awaits the arrival of Isolde, which will be followed by his death. In between come the lines about love and silence, a mystical love-recognition, utterly disastrous for the lovers in Wagner's opera; when they have drunk the love potion they gaze silently at each other. All this presumably has to do with the certainty of doing evil in sex. Finally there is *Parsifal,* here remembered at one remove in Verlaine's allusion to it (l.202) and ironically juxtaposed with another scene of feet-washing, Mrs. Porter and her daughter. Wagner was an important influence on the Symbolists, and for a moment at any rate he seems to have joined Dante as an influence on Eliot.

"What the Thunder Said" opens with an impression of the moment between crucifixion and resurrection, and the drought and the desert are associated with that moment. The longing for water, the failure to recognize the third person (as on the road to Emmaus) preludes an apocalypse, the destruction of cities; all this is again the ending world of Gerontion, with the emblems of isolation—Coriolanus, *Le prince d'Aquitaine*—menaced, as it were, by hints of hope: the bold sin in the past that entitles us to the salvation of damnation, the transient experience of sympathy or love: "The sea was calm, your heart would have responded . . ." (*CPP,* 74). It seems clear enough that the theme is religion or its desperate lack. Eliot was not a Christian at the time; he told Spender he almost became a Buddhist. He had studied Buddhism and other Eastern religions at Harvard, and was interested in the universality of mystical experience. But he was intellectually convinced that his poetry must belong to the Western tradition, the tradition of Virgil and Dante as qualified by the language and custom of his own province of their empire. That is why, five years after *The Waste Land,* he joined the Church of England. He had already been studying the works of the Fathers of that church. Religion is the great lack in *The Waste Land,* its absence is the drought. The world might go on with its "experiment of attempting to form a civilized but non-Christian mentality. The experiment will fail; but we must be very patient in awaiting its collapse; meanwhile redeeming the time: so that the Faith may be preserved alive through the dark ages before us; to renew and rebuild civilization, and save the World from suicide."[18] So Eliot wrote at the end of his critique of the Church of England in *Thoughts After Lambeth* (1931). Meanwhile he had brought his own roots rain.

Perhaps only an American poet could have ventured upon the extraordinary formal experiment of *The Waste Land.* Yet as Eliot presented himself in 1922—London editor, rejector of his native Unitarianism and of American humanism—he looked thoroughly cut off from his sources, and emphasized his new allegiances in all sorts of ways, even in his dress and his speech. Yet his next project seemed to reaffirm a fidelity to his origins.

He believed that the best way for poets to act upon, and with, the community at large was the theater. When he turned his thoughts to the theater it was, as always, with the intention of making something new; but now the novelty would come from the transformation of popular forms, of the English music hall certainly (his essay on Marie Lloyd [1923] treats her as the genius of the English people) but also of jazz; and jazz is not the only American component of *Sweeney Agonistes,* for there is Sweeney himself.

Eliot never finished the play; it was perhaps too daring and novel. Even Stravinsky, in *Le Sacre du printemps,* an audacious work greatly admired by Eliot at this time, and perhaps in his thoughts as he planned his drama, wrote within the conventions of the short ballet and the existing orchestra. Eliot had no such guidelines or constraints, and though he consulted men of theatrical experience he could not bring it off. He wrote a good deal more than he printed, and someday the details will be published; but there is not enough for anybody to be confident in surmising the shape of the whole. He thought the work the most original of his compositions, requiring a new style of verse, to be spoken to drumbeats by masked actors. There is behind the ritual and behind the vacuous repetitions and vulgarities of the dialogue a sordid sex crime, of the kind that makes the gutter press happy, yet is in essence not different from the killing of Agamemnon in his bath. Though entitled "an Aristophanic Melodrama," the play has epigraphs from Aeschylus and St. John of the Cross; they concern retribution and the achievement of freedom from practical desire.

Sweeney Agonistes, in fact, probably engages in one work more of Eliot's preoccupations than any other of his attempts before *Four Quartets.* It allowed him to show his gifts as tragedian and also farceur; there is probably no scene in any of his plays that has the concentrated power of the "Fragment of an *Agon.*"

About the same time he was, in his more usual way, accumulating the poems that turned into the sequence called *The Hollow Men* (1925). In these dreamlike limbo poems incantatory passages, often reminiscent of Dante, are interspersed with passages in which near synonyms are seemingly distinguished by shape and form, shade and color, force and motion; or natural sequences are interrupted, as in

Between the idea
And the reality
Between the motion
And the act
Falls the Shadow . . .

(*CPP,* 85)

Here the conception owes much to *Julius Caesar* ("Between the acting of a dreadful thing / And its first motion all the interim is / Like a phantasma or a hideous dream"). But the qualities between which the shadow falls grow stronger: between desire and spasm, between potency and existence, between essence and descent. The first of these is clearly sexual; the second, though it begins by sounding sexual with "potency," turns into straightforward Aristotelian doctrine; "existence" suggests "essence" in the same context of thought, but it is perverted by its partner, "descent," into a version of "ascent." The Shadow, Eliot agreed, probably came from Ernest Dowson's poem *Non sum qualis eram bono sub regno Cynarae.* These associations are in themselves like those of dream, so it seems we have dream within dream, framed once more by the muttered choric interventions of the final section. In general we feel again the poetry of impotent or frustrated desire: "Lips that would kiss / Form prayers to broken stone"[19] reminds us of some lines by James Thomson quoted by Eliot in his Harvard lectures in 1933: "Lips only sing when they cannot kiss."

Once again, at this time, Eliot thought himself finished as a poet. There was much else to occupy him: business, *The Criterion,* an enlarged circle of friends which by now included many members of the Bloomsbury Group, a milder avant-garde. There was also his still more painful marriage. Above all, there were religion and politics, the latter a topic on which he tried to maintain a high level of abstraction. For the sake of convenience I shall here give a drastically abbreviated account of the social and political sides of Eliot; they are not really separable from his religious side.

Eliot's conversion put some distance between him and the writers he most admired. There was still much in common between them on the surface, for they all hated liberalism, what Arnold called "machinery," and the half-educated masses. But Eliot now believed that only religion could save, and his kind of religion meant a hierarchical society and some severity in social institutions. Postwar Europe seemed to him evidence that our cultural, political, and physical decay could be ended only when our apostasy from the faith ended.

There had formerly existed the union of political and religious forces embodied in the Empire and the Church. England and its church were a provincial remnant of that arrangement; as for America, there was a belief that both Empire and Church had fled there in the seventeenth century, but the dream had faded long before with freedom of religion and a thousand sects. In England at least the inseparability of bishop and king had been historically demonstrated. "The problem of Toryism,"

T. S. Eliot with the actors in a 1951 revival of Murder in the Cathedral.

Eliot said, "should be . . . to make the Church of Laud survive in an age of universal suffrage."[20] This would mean dealing with the dissidence of dissent, sometimes taking the form of cheery atheism, sometimes that of obedience to the "inner voice" which, as a critic, Eliot had identified with Romanticism, expressiveness, and personality. Politics becomes on this scheme a branch of theology, economics of ethics. In practice he denounced all egalitarian ideas, schemes of reform, and extended public education.

An important influence was Charles Maurras, founder of the French royalist-Catholic movement Action Française. This movement had its origin as a response to Émile Zola's defense of Dreyfus and was thus from the outset anti-Semitic as well as given to violence. Its thugs roamed Paris with loaded canes and bludgeons. In 1926 Action Française was condemned by the Vatican, somewhat to Eliot's dismay; not because he approved of its violence but because he shared some of its religious and political ideals, and its dread of "modernism" and democracy.

Eliot knew Maurras, and almost always spoke well of him. This has added plausibility to accusations of anti-Semitism. The work in which Eliot came closest to giving them substance was *After Strange Gods,* assembled from lectures given at the University of Virginia in 1933 and never reprinted after the first edition. Early in the book he remarked that the kind of society he liked would, for "reasons of race and religion," regard "any large number of freethinking Jews undesirable."[21] He is reported to have rebutted the charge of anti-Semitism by stating that as a Christian he was forbidden to hold such views. They were much more common at the time; nobody goes out of his way to call Galsworthy or Bertrand Russell anti-Semitic; and as Orwell remarked, before 1934 anti-Semitic talk was a familiar social reflex. The Jews disturbed Eliot's social and religious paradigms.

He was not attracted to fascism in the way Pound was, though at first he was, like many others, excited by Mussolini's march on Rome. Perhaps his *Coriolan* may be taken as an ambiguous meditation on this kind of greatness. In reality he feared absolutism as much as he did socialism, certain kinds of Order as much as disorder. Fascism and communism made claims to be religions, which they were not; on the other hand, if England were to give up its native ideology, which was Christian, it might find itself worse off than either Germany or Russia. Perhaps he despised the dictators less than he did the run-of-the-mill English Conservatives, riding the bandwagon of the democratic vote, and totally neglecting the true Tory tradition as expressed in the "moral imagination" of Edmund Burke.

He found himself unable to denounce the Fascists in popular terms, refusing, for instance, to write for or against Franco in Spain. As the Second World War approached he grew more and more isolated; his *Criterion* commentaries paid little direct attention to the series of disasters that ravaged Europe. On one occasion he complained about the damage done in England by "irresponsible anti-fascists." In such times his program for organizing the *clercs* or intellectuals into a force that would in time leaven the lump of English society seemed hopelessly quietist. In *The Idea of a Christian Society* he attacked liberalism and democracy without religion, saying we could not claim to be defending the Christian against the pagan, since our mechanized and polluted society was thoroughly pagan anyway. What should be done? The answer is the same: sit still; redeem the time, wait for the doomed experiment to end, as the Royalists had done in 1649.

Eliot thought education the most important of social problems. He opposed the Education Act of 1944, which raised the English school-leaving age from fourteen to fifteen. He thought education should be unequal, based not on merit or achievement but on the chance of birth or income; the very smart might climb a few ladders and get themselves educated provided they did not thereby change their class. In *Notes towards the Definition of Culture* (1948) he denies that this system entails a waste of much first-class ability. People should keep the station to which they are called in the first place. It is not a doctrine one would expect to have much appeal to Americans.

Lifelong admirers of Eliot, among whom I count myself, will sometimes feel themselves uneasy at the unreality of all this. The degree of intellectual detachment it required of so intelligent a man, in such a time, seems almost outrageous until one remembers that it can be good for poetry if not for politics. A theocratic poetry disconcerts us less, since, as Eliot himself knew well, in the reading of poetry "*acceptance* is more important than belief." The *Criterion* withered away during the thirties and died in 1939, no longer a force under its tired and disappointed editor. But Eliot the poet, with all the same beliefs, continued his career.

After a dry spell he was induced to write the Ariel poems, one-poem booklets published by Faber. He drew on Andrewes once more for "The Journey of the Magi" and in "A Song for Simeon" developed a text in Luke; both poems bring together the times of birth and death; "Animula," almost the simplest of Eliot's poems, meditates on a passage in Dante; a brief meditation on the human lot, the warping of the simple soul, the coincidence of life and death ("Living first in the silence after the viaticum" [*CPP,* 107]). Of these poems the finest is "Marina," a meditation on the great recognition scene at the end of Shakespeare's *Pericles* set against another, on the tragic recognition in Seneca's *Hercules Furens;* the opposites again coinciding, though the prevailing tone is of the awed reverence of Pericles.

Ash Wednesday, a sequence of poems accumulated, then arranged, between 1927 and 1929, was Eliot's longest devotional work to date. Characteristically it returns to Dante's *Vita Nuova,* and characteristically it distinguishes itself from the poetry of the Pre-Raphaelites who did the same. It is an important work. The first section is developed from a line of Cavalcanti, a poet of the "sweet new style" that preceded the advent of Dante; only Eliot would have continued the meditation with a line from Shakespeare's Sonnet 29, and in the same context again remember a sermon of Andrewes. The poem is like a prayer or a spell; sometimes it is like an allegory, as strange as

A 1960 party at Faber and Faber. (From left to right) Stephen Spender, W. H. Auden, Ted Hughes, Eliot, and Louis MacNeice.

Dante's in the *Vita Nuova* and indeed more so, since it has no referent for its three white leopards and jeweled unicorns. But the stair on the third poem is a Dantesque stair Eliot has made his own; and so is the view from the window at the first turning of the third stair, for it recurs in *Murder in the Cathedral,* when Thomas rejects the old temptation of sensuous pleasure. *Ash Wednesday* is a poem of "the higher dream"—a visionary poem of great beauty and a hint that so far as he himself was concerned Eliot was right to understand the poetic trance as analogous with the spiritual meditation.

Again there followed a lull, broken this time by accident or luck in the form of an invitation to write verses for a large-scale church pageant. This was not exactly theater, but it came close, and the invitation had the effect of loosening the poet, who may have felt stiff after his year lecturing in the United States. It also made him a friend, the director E. Martin Browne, who was to advise him on the composition of later plays. *The Rock* as a whole is not important, though some themes are heard in its verse that will become important later. Its significance is that it started Eliot out on a new road.

> What life have you if you have not life together?
> There is no life that is not in community,
> And no community not lived in praise of God.
>
> (*CPP*, 152)

So the second chorus of *The Rock.* For the poet the place of community was the theater; and when he was asked to write a play for performance in Canterbury Cathedral the poet had all he needed, a commission to write drama for a Christian community, in the cathedral church of the Primate of All England. At forty-seven the Unitarian from St. Louis was fulfilling a strange destiny. Thomas will be martyred in the cathedral; but first he must be tempted, for the victory over sin precedes the victory over death. The last temptation is the temptation of doing the right deed for the wrong reason. We are to think that Thomas overcomes it.

Murder in the Cathedral is a work of high originality, very theatrical, even, in the speeches of the murdering knights, farcical; but it contains some highly wrought verse, both in the speeches of Thomas and the Tempters, and in the choruses spoken by the women of Canterbury. It enjoyed great success; I saw it on its provincial tour, where the audiences made it plain that Eliot was now in touch with a community. To write a poem, a play, about a great saint, a high spiritual aristocrat, so to speak, must have been very satisfying; to represent so fully the more proletarian agonies of the women of Canterbury as a background to Beckett's agon, and in so doing to move just those audiences ("decent godless people: / Their only monument the asphalt road / And a thousand lost golf balls" [*CPP*, 155]) was a remarkable achievement in a new manner.

The success of this play encouraged Eliot to continue with drama, and outside the church. But it also, as if by accident, started him on another course, the result of which was to be *Four Quartets;* for *Burnt Norton* originated in part with material cut from *Murder in the Cathedral.* His second play, *The Family Reunion,* opened six months before the war began, which removed the possibility of an immediate successor. Instead Eliot wrote another Quartet, *East Coker,* which appeared in

1940. The third play was *The Cocktail Party,* which did not appear until 1949; the third and fourth Quartets appeared during the war, *The Dry Salvages* in 1941 and *Little Gidding* in 1942. There is a good deal of intertwining between the poems and the plays, but for convenience I shall separate them, saying little about the plays.

It is quite typical of Eliot that none of its successors bears much resemblance to *Murder in the Cathedral. The Family Reunion* is based on the *Oresteia,* with a reminiscence of *Sweeney Agonistes,* since its hero (though as unlike Sweeney as can be imagined) supposes that he has done a girl in; pushed his wife overboard in the mid-Atlantic. Guilt, in this poet, is rarely unrelated to sex. The attempt to bring down to modern theatrical size the ritual grandeur of Aeschylus only partly succeeds, and Eliot himself disparaged the play in later comment. Later, though he still liked to have as armature for his drama some ancient play, he dispensed with the formally hieratic, reducing it to the merely gnomic in *The Cocktail Party,* in which a mysterious healer intervenes in the lives of some upper-middle-class persons to sort out the sheep from the goats, the saints from those incapable of damnation. *The Cocktail Party* is a lively piece, and it attracted large audiences in a long run; they may have been surprised to learn from the author that the play was based on the *Alcestis* of Euripides. Of *The Confidential Clerk* (1953), one can say that it is based on the *Ion* of Euripides; and that it has realized in a higher degree than ever Eliot's ambition of writing theatrical verse so near to prose as to be for the most part indistinguishable from it. The last play, *The Elder Statesman* (1958), came in time to celebrate Eliot's seventieth birthday. Although its theme is a guilty secret buried in a distant past, it is a sort of celebration of a release from the suffering thus caused; a release due not to old age, in the silence after the viaticum, but to human love. The play is a tribute to his second wife, and in that sense the most personal of his works; of the plays, it is probably the least regarded, yet it has its shadows and its surprises, and is the work of a man who had spent a great many years exploring the theater as a mode of communication with other consciousnesses.

But claims for Eliot as the central poet of his time (the king of the cats) rest not on these dramas but on the poems, of which the last and most ambitious is *Four Quartets.* The genesis of this extremely original long poem (it is indeed hardly necessary to specify the originality of any of this poet's works) is admirably described in Helen Gardner's *The Composition of Four Quartets* (1978). *Burnt Norton,* without the poet's conscious design, set

The Anglican church at Little Gidding is the point of departure for Eliot's meditations in the last of his Four Quartets. *The church served the small religious community founded by Nicholas Ferrar in the early seventeenth century. In 1646, Cromwell's parliamentary troops sacked the church and scattered the community.*

the pattern. Eliot, at the request of Martin Browne, had written into *Murder in the Cathedral* a brief passage for the Second Priest to speak after the exit of the Second Tempter; the speech was not used, and became, with little change, the opening fourteen lines of *Burnt Norton,* which appeared in Eliot's *Collected Poems* (1936). It was thought of as complete in itself. The opening meditation on time gives one of the principal themes of the whole set of poems; it is not an easy passage, but sounds familiar notes about the redemption of time past. A distinctive feature is the anchoring of such meditations to a particular place, Burnt Norton, a country house in the English Cotswolds, with a beautiful garden, which Eliot visited around 1934. It was not a place that had any personal associations, except that he saw it at a time of relative happiness; the garden poetry that remembers "our first world" (*CPP,* 171) was prompted by a particular experience there, but draws not only on the empty ponds of the garden itself but on stored clusters of images, personal and literary, in Eliot's usual way. The second section or movement begins with a difficult lyric that quotes from Mallarmé, followed by a meditative passage on moments out of time, which opens with a quotation from his own *Coriolan.* The third movement is also discursive, an infernal meditation on London and its underground railways that distinguishes their subterranean dark from another darkness that might be not unhealthy but purifying. The fourth movement is a brief lyric; the fifth a discourse, with a lyrical coda.

This pattern Eliot followed more or less closely in the other quartets. He admired the last five quartets of Beethoven and had resolved to do something like them in poetry; he had in mind, I think, the unpredictable but self-justifying transitions and alternations of mood in those works, as well as "the use of recurrent themes" which "is as natural to poetry as to music,"[22] as he put it in a lecture of 1942. He spoke also of possibilities of transition and contrapuntal arrangement; and the complex self-references of the four poems, especially prominent in the last, *Little Gidding,* testify to the value of the analogy.

The village of East Coker, which gave its name to the second Quartet, is in Somerset. It is a place of extraordinary calm and beauty, which Eliot visited only once. From that place the Eliots went to New England, and T. S. Eliot wished to be buried there, bringing together an end and a beginning, as in the motto of Mary Queen of Scots which opens the poem. It was published on Good Friday, 1940, in the *New English Weekly;* I remember going to the newsstand to buy my copy, lost, alas, during the war. There is a progressive simplification of language as the *Quartets* progress, which may have something to do with their enormous sales when they appeared in pamphlet form; also war somehow gave people an appetite for poetry. Eliot once remarked in an interview that writing plays had enabled him to simplify his language, but that maturity also had something to do with it. "By the time of the *Four Quartets,* I couldn't have written in the style of *The Waste Land.* In *The Waste Land,* I wasn't even bothering whether I understood what I was saying."[23] His final judgment was that the *Quartets* got better as they went on, the last being the best.

It was probably during the writing of *East Coker* that he formed the idea of a four-part work, though at the time of *The Dry Salvages* his friends could still speak of his "trilogy." Had this third been the last of the *Quartets,* Eliot's farewell to poetry (for the *Quartets* amount to that) would have had a strong American flavor. Here the title refers to the dangerous rocks off Cape Ann; the ocean of the poem is off the Massachusetts coast, where a boy might inspect the rockpools and the shattered lobsterpots, and hear the wail of the foghorn. The river is the Mississippi, and the opening lines not only remember the St. Louis of the poet's childhood but the words he himself had written in an introduction to *Huckleberry Finn* (a book he surprisingly did not read as a boy). But this ocean grows abstract, a figure for time, considered as the medium of right action; and the figures of Krishna and Arjuna arrive from the east onto the American scene.

The last of the *Quartets* chooses as its place the home of the Anglican community established by Nicholas Ferrar, where the fugitive Charles I once took refuge. Eliot visited Little Gidding in 1936, 290 years after the king. In this poem, if anywhere, one hears all Eliot's voices together, on the ground of his choosing: that unexplored area he spoke of as lying between poetry and devotional verse, "the experience of man in search of God, and trying to explain to himself his intenser human feelings in terms of the divine goal. . . ."[24] Its greatest moment is the long imitation of Dante in Section II, a scene that combines the ruined streets after an air raid with a powerful impression of purgatory; it is confessional, not as Yeats, the most potent element in its "familiar compound ghost" (*CPP,* 193), was confessional, but in a new mode—new, though derived from Dante and the fruit of many years of submission to that poet.

Apart from all this, *Little Gidding,* for all its complexity, is, as I remarked earlier, a patriotic poem and a war poem. The dove is ambiguously the Holy Spirit and a German night bomber; the fire (which is the element of this poem as earth, air and water had been of its predecessors) is the fire of London after the raids as well as that of Purgatory, the fire of Arnaut.

The western campanile of St. Paul's Cathedral seen through a Victorian shop front after a bombing raid.

The dove descending breaks the air
With flame of incandescent terror . . .

—From *Little Gidding*

Contemplating so vast an achievement it would be absurd to carry on an inquisition into the final nationality of the poet.

> So, while the light fails
> On a winter's afternoon, in a secluded chapel,
> History is now and England—
>
> (*CPP,* 197)

but history is a pattern of timeless moments. In accordance with that truth, Eliot can present the pattern, with its poems of many ages in consort, its memories real and imagined, Italian, French, American, English, as independent of time and "folded into a single party" (*CPP,* 196). Moreover, to be simple and sensible about the question, why can't the English and the Americans share a poet as they share a language? Eliot has probably made certain that they must.

He lived twenty-two years more after finishing *Four Quartets,* the last of them made happy by a second marriage. Honors crowded upon him and he was probably the most famous poet in the world. Pound, after years of incarceration, died silent and oppressed. Wyndham Lewis struggled on, defiant in blindness, until his death in 1957. It was the poet of drought, spiritual agony, physical malady, who survived to be universally acclaimed. The last lyric he published was the dedication of *The Elder Statesman* to his wife, a celebration of his love for a woman. To write such a poem was, for this poet, an act of originality, another surprise, something new. And since the desire to do those things in verse is, as we all think, American, we can end by saying that after all, and in spite of all, he was an American poet.

Frondage of dark islands, breathing
the crocus lustres of the stars--
repeated ease, repeated awe
enclose me with the night that trails

enclose me, aching with the night
that trails its rites from isle to isle.

VOYAGES - II

Frondage of dark islands, breathing
the crocus lustres of the stars-- minstrel mansions,
repeated ease, repeated awe
enclose me, aching with the night aching
that trails its rites from isle to isle.

out like sliding
Silhouettes of sceptres roving swimming
flash ~~mark the white~~ shoulders, O sadly
soothing as a vanished lily grove;
and you whose arms dip now in mine,
in turn, you too, immeasurably —
~~will smile and~~ dive with phantom ease!
to see you smiling

Bells ringing off San Salvador
~~on~~ scrolls of silver , ivory sentences
brimming confession, O prodigal,
in which your tongue slips mine,--
~~the perfect diapason danced~~
~~In minstrel mansions~~
the perfect diapason dancing lifting;
~~Its~~ ~~To~~ ~~the~~ where in minstrel mansions sling

~~I know~~

~~The~~ Fervent crosses of the tide,
Obey ~~the light that you have seen to~~
Repeated joy, repeated awe —

HART CRANE

ALAN WILLIAMSON

Of the American poets who emerged during, or shortly before, the 1920s, Hart Crane remains the most controversial, dazzling, and hard to evaluate. The efforts, a generation back, to take Eliot's reputation down a peg—and the tendency of some of Eliot's admirers to overlook Frost, or Williams, or Stevens—have faded into literary history, as we realize just how great, and how various, a Renaissance we actually had. Crane alone continues to divide sensitive readers squarely down the middle, some considering him a great poet, others a magnificent, or an exasperating, failure. Perhaps that is because he is our great Romantic, our great overreacher. His poetry takes place on a heightened, often ecstatic plane, as if unable to tolerate the limitations of ordinary life. And—in spite of Crane's known zest for restaurants, vulgar jokes, good cigars—critics have been quick to find the evidence for such an inability in his biography. It is, indeed, the biography of a Byron, a Shelley, or a Rimbaud: intense, turbulent, and brief, ending at the age of thirty-two with an impulsive suicidal leap into the Caribbean, which had been, in many of his poems, the symbol for overreaching, for union with the Absolute.[1]

To make matters still more complicated, Crane is also one of our most difficult poets, as difficult, in his way, as the classical poets of learned allusion, Eliot and Pound. The very intensity of his feelings made him find ordinary speech inadequate, and he ransacked the literature of the past and the technological vocabularies of the future for a denser, lovelier, more sensuous idiom. He tends to overdetermine, to load each word with as much connotation and suggestiveness as it will bear, so that his sentences are sometimes almost unintelligible without these undermeanings. Only a few of his lines could be spoken in conversation, though they read aloud magnificently, with something of the surge and grandeur of Elizabethan drama.

All of this tends to make Crane a poet for an elite audience. And yet—another irony—he was ideologically one of the few true democrats among the poets of his age. He enrolled himself in Whitman's tradition of faith in America, which was not jin-

Hart Crane in 1916.

Hart Crane in 1931.

goism, still less a blind faith in capitalistic progress, but a faith that a new, undoctrinal, post-Christian religion would be formulated here: as he put it in his essay "General Aims and Theories," "certain as yet unknown spiritual quantities, perhaps a new hierarchy of faith not to be developed so completely elsewhere." He saw a new vocabulary of spiritual heights and depths in the sensations of the machine age: the towers and bridges, the new sense of speed and space that had come with the airplane, the great violence of the factories and turbines, the beat of jazz. In his own time, these predilections made it difficult for Crane to find a wholly sympathetic audience, since the very readers who were most capable of appreciating his experimentalism as a poet were the least likely to be sanguine about the twentieth century. And as succeeding decades have given us more and more reason to be afraid of the technological powers we have unleashed, Crane's transcendental interpretation of them has remained as problematic as his transcendental claim on life generally.

To understand who Crane was, it is important to understand where he was from. He was one of the first poets of unquestionable stature to come from the Midwest, a region that has seemed to many the most American part of America. But it is also a strangely indeterminate place. Its half dozen provincial metropolises (Crane's were Akron and Cleveland) are strung out along the mysterious central pulse of the railroad, linking them in one direction to the tingling life of the Eastern cities and, beyond, of Europe; in the other direction to the ever vaster, quieter spaces where America had never really belonged to the white man. F. Scott Fitzgerald has described the strange charm of that doubleness, especially for a well-to-do young Midwesterner before the First World War, in one of the most memorable paragraphs of *The Great Gatsby:*

> When we pulled out into the winter night and the real snow, our snow, began to stretch out beside us and twinkle against the windows, and the dim lights of small Wisconsin stations moved by, a sharp wild brace came suddenly into the air. We drew deep breaths of it as we walked back from dinner through the cold vestibules, unutterably aware of our identity with this country for one strange hour, before we melted indistinguishably into it again.
>
> That's my Middle West—not the wheat or the prairies or the lost Swede towns, but the thrilling returning trains of my youth . . .

Crane uses the same image in "The River": the train emerging from a garble of information, advertising, and Shakespeare ("WALLSTREET AND VIRGINBIRTH WITHOUT STONES OR / WIRES OR EVEN RUNning brooks"), but reaching to the distances where

> The last bear, shot drinking in the Dakotas
> Loped under wires that span the mountain stream

and where the Indian body of the land waits, corn-maiden and Pocahontas,

> Time like a serpent down her shoulder, dark,
> And space, an eaglet's wing, laid on her hair.
>
> (62–66)

What Crane was geographically, he was in some way as a writer. It was not in him to feel that American literature should be the opposite of European; to become an anti-intellectual populist or Naturalist, like the slightly older writers who first put the Midwest on the literary map—Dreiser, Anderson, Sandburg, Lindsay. But neither was it in him to identify totally either with

Eliot's tradition or with Mencken's smartness, and then to harangue the Midwest as a soulless place, puritanical and mercenary, where a cultured person cannot survive for five minutes. (He says all those things about the Midwest, now and again; but he always says, or feels, more.) In a letter written when he was barely twenty, Crane contrasts himself with Sherwood Anderson and with Matthew Josephson, one of the most Europeanized writers of the twenties, now best known for his memoir *Life Among the Surrealists:*

> He (Anderson) and Josephson are opposite poles. J. classic, hard and glossy,—Anderson crowd-bound, with a smell of the sod about him, uncouth. Somewhere between them is Hart Crane with a kind of wistful indetermination, still much puzzled.
>
> (*Letters,* 27)

It is characteristic of Crane's modesty that he portrays his middle position as a weakness. Certainly many of his contemporaries considered it one: Allen Tate and Yvor Winters excoriated him for his allegiance to Whitman and Whitman's hopes for America; William Carlos Williams, on the other hand, regarded him with suspicion because he wrote of American things in meter, and in a style influenced by the French Symbolists. To us, Crane's refusal to be forced to a choice may seem a largeness in him. Keats, after all, said that the supreme quality of a poet was to be "capable of being in uncertainties, mysteries, doubts, without any irritable reaching after fact and reason." Crane did not want to relinquish anything that seemed valuable to him simply in order to be consistent or partisan. He wanted all the tools international Modernism offered for a fresher rendering of atmospheres, perceptions, states of soul; but he wanted to bring them home to the experiences, the familiar sights and sounds, the stubborn loyalties, of a Midwestern American at the beginning of the great age of technology. The result was one of the strangest, but also one of the most sensuously vivid, poetries the love of America has yet inspired. Most of it is concentrated in Crane's long poem, *The Bridge,* to which we will return later—an extraordinary work, not only in its ambition but in the range of American experiences it incorporates, from New York harbor at dawn—

> Insistently through sleep—a tide of voices—
> They meet you listening midway in your dream,
> The long, tired sounds, fog-insulated noises:
> Gongs in white surplices, beshrouded wails,
> Far strum of fog horns . . . signals dispersed in veils
>
> (54)

—to the "cobalt desert closures" and their primordial attendant spirits:

> The swift red flesh, a winter king—
> Who squired the glacier woman down the sky?
> She ran the neighing canyons all the spring;
> She spouted arms; she rose with maize—to die.
>
> (70)

But all this is not to say that Crane's relation to America was harmonious or uncomplicated. His family alone would have prevented that. His father was a moderately successful businessman, a candy manufacturer, with the prejudices, and the overbearing aggressive drive, of his type. His mother was a great beauty, a good amateur musician, and a Christian Scientist. The portrait of her in *The Bridge* makes us feel Crane's devotion to her, her ingrown religiosity, and her essential inability to respond to the claims of others:

> the Sabbatical, unconscious smile
> My mother almost brought me once from church
> And once only, as I recall—?
>
> It flickered through the snow screen, blindly
> It forsook her at the doorway, it was gone
> Before I had left the window. It
> Did not return with the kiss in the hall.
>
> (60–61)

When Crane was in his teens, his parents went through an extremely turbulent divorce—so turbulent that in the throes of it they simply forgot to send him to college. In this crisis, his mother won him over to her side, with endless and inappropriate confidences; he later wrote her that his adolescence had been a "bloody battleground for yours and father's sex life and troubles." Yet he chose his middle name, his mother's maiden name, for his first name as a writer; and he often punned it into "heart." Later, his friends were quick to find in this intense intimacy with a "peculiarly selfish and stupid" mother (Allen Tate's phrase) an explanation for Crane's homosexuality.

Crane's sexual character was, in fact, a complex one. His last love affair was with a woman; and his poems are full of images of an idealized goddess, interfused with sky, sea, and land—violent, victimized, yet transcending both roles—as the ultimate object of love; whereas the male lover is rarely distinguishable from the idealized self. Crane's friends, in their memoirs, repeatedly insist on the "masculinity" of his personality; and one has

The Crane home on East 115th Street in Cleveland. Crane marked his tower bedroom on this picture postcard in 1925 when the house was sold.

only to look at his letters, with their mixture of rude gusto and a helpless American downrightness about serious matters, to see what his friends meant.

But if Crane was sexually ambivalent, he was anything but ashamed of his homosexuality. He flaunted it—his affairs with sailors, even the beatings he suffered—just as, in those Prohibition years, he flaunted his illegal drinking. His homosexuality seems to have crystallized him in a paradoxical relation to his background, a relation at once defiant and sacrificial. It was as if he chose to live out one of the great roles of the Romantic artist: an artist who neither accepts his society nor escapes it, but who, by playing his part of outsider and martyr, reminds his society of the larger life it refuses to live. Crane saw an unforgettable instance of such a performance in 1922, when the great dancer Isadora Duncan appeared in Cleveland:

MY GRANDMOTHER'S LOVE LETTERS

There are no stars to-night
But those of memory.
Yet how much room for memory there is
In the loose girdle of soft rain.

There is even room enough
For the letters of my mother's mother,
Elizabeth,
That have been pressed so long
Into a corner of the roof
That they are brown and soft,
And liable to melt as snow.

Over the greatness of such space
Steps must be gentle.
It is all hung by an invisible white hair.
It trembles as birch limbs webbing the air.

And I ask myself:

"Are your fingers long enough to play
Old keys that are but echoes:
Is the silence strong enough
To carry back the music to its source
And back to you again
As though to her?"

Yet I would lead my grandmother by the hand
Through much of what she would not understand;
And so I stumble. And the rain continues on the roof
With such a sound of gently pitying laughter.

It was like a wave of life, a flaming gale that passed over the heads of the nine thousand in the audience without evoking response other than silence and some maddening cat-calls. After the first movement of the *Pathetique* she came to the fore of the stage, her hands extended. Silence,—the most awful silence! I started clapping furiously until she disappeared behind the draperies. . . . When it was all over she came to the fore-stage again in the little red dress that had so shocked Boston, as she stated, and among other things told the people to go home and take from the bookshelf the works of Walt Whitman, and turn to the section called "Calamus." Ninety-nine percent of them had never heard of Whitman, of course, but that was part of the beauty of her gesture. Glorious to see her there with her right breast and nipple quite exposed, telling the audience that the truth was not pretty, that it was really indecent, and telling them (boobs!) about Beethoven, Tchaikovsky, and Scriabin. She is now on her way back to Moscow, so I understand, where someone will give her some roses for her pains.

(*Letters,* 109)

This image of the artist (the woman artist, the *anima,* the "heart") exposing herself, body and soul, to the anger of the Midwesterners in order to bring them sexual liberty, culture, "truth," and Whitmanian democracy in one zany but electrifying package, spoke to the very core of Crane's own incipient enterprise. Here the "masculine" and the "feminine" were joined: courage lay in being more vulnerable, more open to sexuality, to affection, to artistic surprise, than his fellow citizens chose to be. Thus, in one early poem, he makes another great teacher and victim, Charlie Chaplin, say to his tormentors,

> We can evade you, and all else but the heart:
> What blame to us if the heart live on.
>
> (11)

All these strands of feeling come together in the great poem "Lachrymae Christi." I turn to it at the risk of subjecting the reader to a rude total immersion in Crane's obscurity; but it will at least give us an opportunity to consider the nature of that obscurity, and how it may best be unraveled. The poem begins:

> Whitely, while benzine
> Rinsings from the moon
> Dissolve all but the windows of the mills
> (Inside the sure machinery
> Is still
> And curdled only where a sill
> Sluices its one unyielding smile)
>
> Immaculate venom binds
> The fox's teeth, and swart
> Thorns freshen on the year's
> First blood. From flanks unfended,
> Twanged red perfidies of spring
> Are trillion on the hill.
>
> (19)

The scene is at night, on the outskirts of an industrial city (the speaker is looking at factories, but also at the "flanks" of the hills, covered with spring flowers). The time is probably near Easter: "Lachrymae Christi" means "the tears of Christ." But it is also the name of a wine Crane could get from Italian bootleggers around Cleveland—which suggests something about what "Immaculate venom" might mean and what the poet has come to such a lonely place, on an early spring night, to do.

Crane begins with a grammatically unattached adverb, "Whitely," setting the poem under a sign, or within a process, of purification. The moonlight dissolves almost the entire industrial landscape, except for a bit of machinery caught—"curdled" —where a shaft of light "sluices" onto it past the windowsill. The light seems almost aggressively undiscouraged by what it illumines ("unyielding smile"). Yet it is not wholly the opposite of the factory; it is "benzine," a cleansing agent which is also a poison, hence "Immaculate venom."[2]

What emerges is a sense of one force or attitude precariously "binding" another of almost equal power. The purifying force is moonlight, wine, imagination, the cleansing poison, the "unyielding smile" of acceptance and Christ-like sacrifice. (For the word "immaculate" begins a dense series of references to the life and particularly the Passion of Christ—the crown of thorns, the blood springing from the undefended, "unfended," side.) Against this force stand "the fox's teeth." If Crane means the rending teeth of the machinery (held "still," "curdled" by moonlight in the first stanza), he is suggesting that the rapacious side of technological progress can somehow be "bound" by the visionary side. But Crane also uses the ferocity of the world of machines, here and elsewhere, as a wider metaphor for experiences of cruelty or unbearable intensity. Perhaps some specific betrayal in his erotic life has prompted the solitary drinking spree. "Perjuries / Had galvanized the eyes," he says later in the poem. The technological metaphor is both vigorous and apt. To "galvanize" is to plate one metal with another by the application of an electric current; just so, the searing experience of betrayal has sealed the poet's eyes under a layer of disillusionment, indifference. But by responding to this experience with "not penitence, but song"—and wine—he recovers his Christ-like, flammable powers of vision: "Thy Nazarene and tinder eyes." It is the central plot of this poem, and of many of Crane's poems: by refusing to protect himself from suffering or to give up his imaginative openness—"unyielding" and "unfended"—the poet discovers possibilities, whether in industry or in love, that are invisible without this attitude.

I said at the beginning that Crane's difficulty arises from his tendency to overdetermine, to pack as much connotation as possible into a line or a word. We can see a beautiful instance of this in the last three lines of the second stanza:

> From flanks unfended
> Twanged red perfidies of spring
> Are trillion on the hill.

The whole passage is in a way a condensation: it describes two things at once, the individual drops of blood springing from Christ's side—as they might be shown in an early Renaissance

(From left to right) Hart Crane, Allen Tate, and William Slater Brown, February 1925 in New York.

The poetry of Hart Crane is ambitious. It is the only poetry I am acquainted with which is at once contemporary and in the grand manner. It is an American Poetry. Crane's themes are abstractly, metaphysically conceived, but they are definitely confined to an experience of the American scene. In such poems as "The Wine Menagerie," "For the Marriage of Faustus and Helen," "Recitative," he is the poet of the complex urban civilization of his age: precision, abstraction, power.

—From the "Introduction" by Allen Tate to Hart Crane's first book, *White Buildings* painting, perhaps caught by an angel with a cup—and the individual flowers emerging from the "flanks" of the Ohio hills. But why are the flowers "trillion," rather than the more usual thousand or million? There are, I think, three reasons. "Trillion" puns on "trillium," a common spring flower. Unlike "thousand" or "million," it is too large a number to have been part of common speech before modern physics and astronomy; so that it belongs to the same new energy and terror that gives us "benzine" for moonlight, "galvanize" for excruciating love. Finally, in conjunction with "twanged" in the preceding line, "trillion" puns on a musical "trill" (indeed, the passage from "tw-" to "tr-" is itself a kind of trill, a playful alternation of contiguous sounds). By this pun, Crane introduces a metaphor that will grow increasingly important through the rest of the poem, the old metaphor of music as universal harmony, to which the world is "recalled" by sacrifice and by art.

Instances like this could be multiplied if we read the poem through to the end; but I think it's clear how Crane's overdeterminations work, interweaving the many strands of feeling and subject-matter in a poem, but at the same time making it hard to seize on any single surface meaning. Readers have wondered, from the beginning, just how and why Crane arrived at such a difficult way of writing. Let us start with the why, and then return to the how, the question of literary growth and influences.

Crane was hardly a professional critic, but he did undertake to explain his own intentions at least twice, in the essay "General Aims and Theories" and in a famous letter to Harriet Monroe, the editor of *Poetry,* who had refused to publish a particularly dense poem called "At Melville's Tomb." In the essay, Crane contrasts what he calls "impressionist" and "absolute" poetry. "Impressionist" poetry would include for him most of what is easily admired in the literary magazines, in his time and in ours: crisp, vivid description, that can be reread for nuance, but does not need to be reread for understanding. Such poetry offers a "retinal registration" of the world, "along with a certain psychological stimulation"; what it cannot convey, Crane believes, are the "emotional derivations" and the "utmost spiritual consequences" of the poet's way of seeing the world. "Absolute poetry," by contrast, aims at conveying a "state of consciousness" or an "apprehension of life." It uses "our 'real' world somewhat as a springboard" to leap into its own independent "orbit"; it aims at the unity, and the uniqueness, of "a single, new *word"* (220–21). But Crane should not be thought of as anticipating current doctrines of the self-referentiality of the text; his "word" is a gift from the poet to the reader, and it is a word concerned with life, a "morality essentialized from experience" rather than deduced from "precepts." While Crane is careful to make clear that "absolute poetry" need not be about "absolute," or mystical, experience, he strongly suggests that if *"causes* (metaphysical)" are to be found in poetry at all, they will be found in such poems.

The technical problem, of course, is how poetry can achieve the unity of the "single, new word," the pervasive, atmospheric diffusion of the "state of consciousness," when the inherent tendency of discourse is to select, analyze, divide. Crane's answer, essentially, is to break the logical backbone of discourse by allowing connotation ("associational meaning") to predominate over denotation whenever a choice has to be made. I say "break the backbone" deliberately, because Crane often seems at war with the logical progression, though not the rhetorical sweep, of the sentence. He allows almost any word to modify almost any other ("circuit calm," "wine talons"), creating sentences that sound nonsensical when reduced to a subject-verb-object skeleton ("dice . . . bequeath an embassy," "star . . . bleeds infinity"). Crane intends the poem to take place not on the level of discourse, but on the level of the mind's interior and overdetermined connections, of a "logic of metaphor" which, Crane believed, was the fundamental process of the mind, the matrix out of which not only "pure logic" but "all speech, hence consciousness and thought-extension," arose.

Crane makes all this a little clearer by giving examples, from himself, Eliot, and Blake, of passages in which the emotional nexus of associations is foregrounded at the expense of logic or clear description. Here are two of his self-explications:

> When, in "Voyages" [II], I speak of "adagios of islands," the reference is to the motion of a boat through islands clustered thickly, the rhythm of the motion, etc. And it seems a much more direct and creative statement than any more logical employment of words such as "coasting slowly through the islands," besides ushering in a whole world of music. Similarly in "Faustus and Helen" [III], the speed and tense altitude of an aeroplane are much better suggested by the idea of "nimble blue plateaus"—*implying* the aeroplane and its speed against a contrast of stationary elevated earth.
>
> (221–22)

One might say that Crane allows us to glimpse the objective world only through a screen of subjective associations or emotional responses that have already transformed it. In a sense, he is aiming at an impossible, and a religious, transcendence of human isolation: he wishes the reader to have the *same* consciousness as the poet, for the duration of the poem. Though it leads to obscurity, it is also a democratic ideal: a new brother-

Charlie Chaplin and Jackie Coogan in The Kid, *the Chaplin film that inspired Crane's poem.*

And yet these fine collapses are not lies
More than the pirouettes of any pliant cane;
Our obsequies are, in a way, no enterprise.
We can evade you, and all else but the heart:
What blame to us if the heart live on.

—From "Chaplinesque"

hood will arise from the transmission of the "single, new word," the "morality essentialized from experience" which is itself, usually, the "unfended" democratic openness expounded in "Lachrymae Christi." Crane speaks of this ideal whenever he talks about poetry within his poems: "This competence—to travel in a tear / Sparkling alone, within another's will"; or

In alternating bells have you not heard
All hours clapped dense into a single stride?
Forgive me for an echo of these things,
And let us walk through time with equal pride.

(26)

As Allen Grossman has observed, this ideal would of itself incline Crane to suppress the prosaic, discursive voice found intermingled in most poems; such a voice accepts the separation between people, by explaining them, one to another.

One might well ask how such an almost Mallarméan aesthetic occurred to a young man growing up in Ohio, with no formal education beyond high school. The answer involves a good deal of the history of taste in the first quarter of this century. Of course—as is often pointed out—the earlier American Romantics Emerson and Whitman stand behind many of Crane's ideas: the vaguely pantheistic religious optimism; the acceptance of technology; even the sense of interidentity between the poet and his audience, which is as prominent, and as complex, in "Crossing Brooklyn Ferry" as in Crane's poems. But Emerson and Whitman had almost no influence on Crane as a stylist. And the magazine verse he encountered as he was growing up—Maxwell Bodenheim; William Vaughn Moody; pale imitations of Oscar Wilde and the Nineties—could not have been farther from "absolute poetry." Then, like many another young man in the 1920s, Crane discovered T. S. Eliot.

For Crane, Eliot was to be in some ways the great menace, the great rival. His "negations" (Crane's word) challenged Crane's desire to praise; his theory of the modern "dissociation of sensibility" had the potential to undermine Crane's whole sense of new spiritual possibility in the machine age. Yet Crane never managed to hate Eliot, unlike the more threatened William Carlos Williams, who said *The Waste Land* "wiped out our world as if an atom bomb had been dropped upon it." Crane found in Eliot not only brilliant, comic, defiant incorporations of the modern landscape into poetry ("When the evening is spread out against the sky / Like a patient etherised upon a table"), but also, in lines such as "Every street lamp that I pass / Beats like a fatalistic drum," a precedent for an "emotional dynamics" short-circuiting ordinary logic. He wrote to Allen Tate in 1922:

> In his own realm Eliot presents us with an absolute *impasse,* yet oddly enough, he can be utilized to lead us to, intelligently point to, other positions and "pastures new." Having absorbed him enough we can trust ourselves as never before, in the air or on the sea.
>
> (*Letters,* 90)

From Eliot, Crane quickly proceeded to the tastes Eliot was recommending in the literature of other times and countries—in particular, to the French Symbolists. Of the Symbolists, his immediate favorite was Rimbaud, and it is not hard to see why. Like Crane, Rimbaud was a rebel, a strikingly masculine homosexual poet who explored mystical borderlands of sensation and died an early death. The poet, he said, should "make himself a seer" by "the systematic disorientation of all the senses" —a doctrine which surely influenced Crane's view of alcoholic and sexual excess as religious Ways. Rimbaud was also avidly interested in the new sensations of the nineteenth-century city. But most important of all, he spoke of an "alchemy of the word," a "poetic word accessible . . . to all the senses," by which he "wrote down silences and nights, noted the inexpressible," and "pinned down vertigos." This is the same impossible equivalence between writing and consciousness that Crane called "absolute poetry"; and Rimbaud's chief method for achieving it —a synaesthetic blending of the different senses, derived from Baudelaire—seems a narrower version of Crane's stress on polyvalent mental connections, the "logic of metaphor." To see how deep an influence Rimbaud's way of representing the disintegrations and ecstatic fusions of the self had on Crane, one has only to juxtapose this passage from Louise Varèse's translation of "The Drunken Boat"—

> I've dreamed green nights of dazzling snows,
> Slow kisses on the eyelids of the sea,
> The terrible flow of unforgettable saps,
> And singing phosphors waking yellow and blue.

—with this from "The Dance":

> Spears and assemblies: black drums thrusting on—
> O yelling battlements,—I, too, was liege
> To rainbows currying each pulsant bone:
> Surpassed the circumstance, danced out the siege!
>
> (73)

The other great influence that came to Crane by way of T. S. Eliot was the Elizabethan and Jacobean dramatists, in particular Marlowe and Webster. This influence turned Crane, around 1922, from a predominantly free-verse poet to a predominantly metrical one. For some readers, Crane's meter, and his Elizabethan "O"s and "Thou"s, form a troubling contrast with his interest in spanking-new American things; they make him an old-fashioned, as well as a difficult, poet. Crane, of course, had

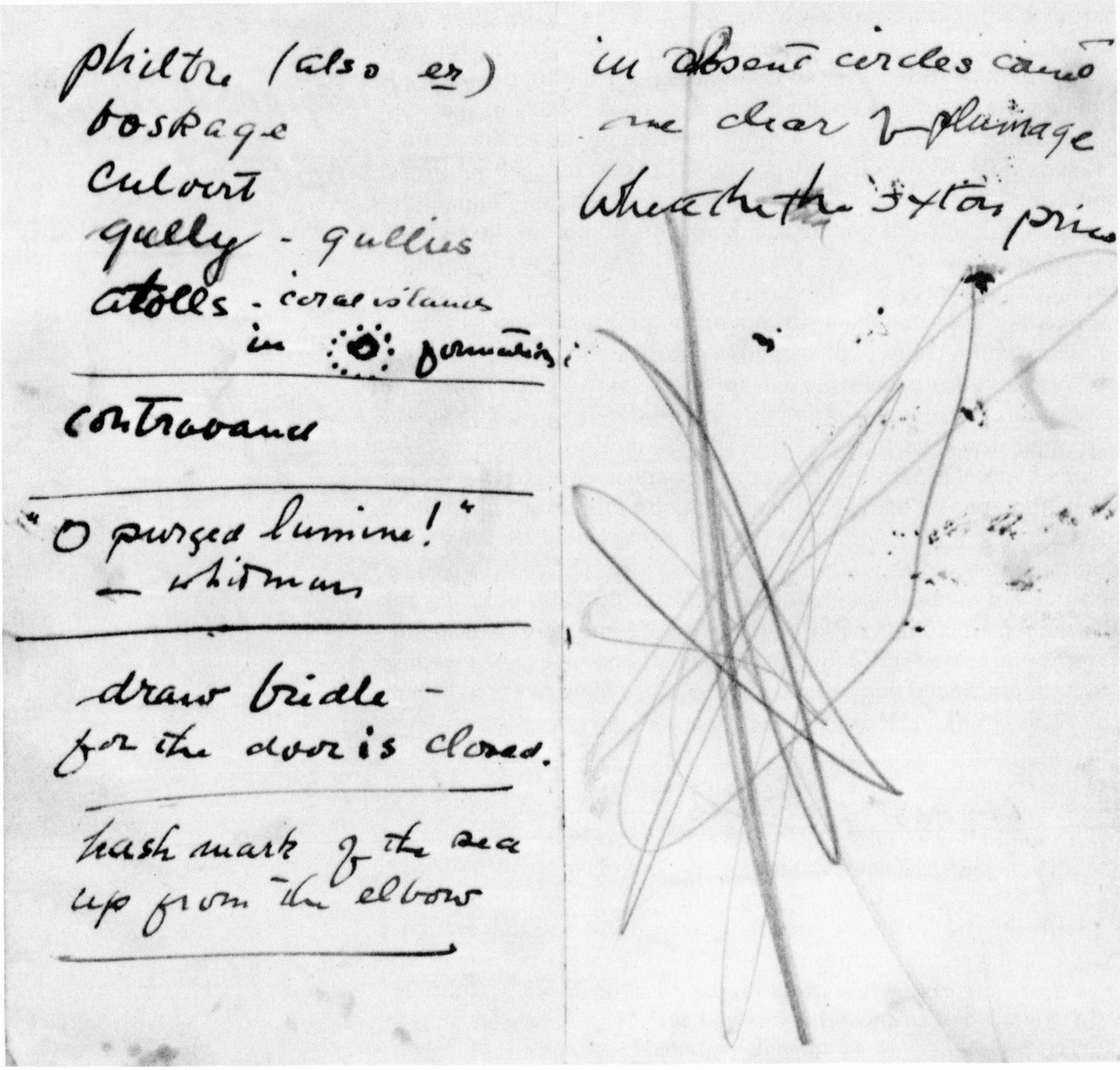

Crane's Vocabulary Notebook.

little interest in a conversational norm for poetry. He needed a style that could manage enormous intellectual quickness and complexity, and at the same time convey the ecstatic lift of feeling which, for him, was the precondition of poetry. Such styles are rare in any language, and the Elizabethan style is the great instance in ours. With so daring a Modernist as Eliot pointing back to it as one of the last examples of unified sensibility in English poetry, Crane would hardly have thought of it as a regressive model. For us, I suppose, it becomes part of Crane's Romantic claim to be at once of his time and timeless, or "absolute"; and we are likely to accept, or reject, the two together.

Finally, Crane received a much vaguer, but equally crucial, kind of encouragement from the generally heady atmosphere of all the arts in the 1920s. Charlie Chaplin was important to him; and cinematic techniques for suggesting more than is actually shown are invoked in "To Brooklyn Bridge." In the quick shifts of melody and timbre in modern composers (D'Indy, Stravinsky, Strauss), he found a precedent for his own mixture of Elizabethan, contemporary, and scientific vocabularies. "Striated with nuances, nervosities"—his line from "For the Marriage of Faustus and Helen"—seemed a motto for the art of the age (*Letters,* 129). Speed is, again, the theme in Crane's unfinished essay on Alfred Stieglitz's photography:

> The eerie speed of the shutter is more adequate than the human eye to remember, catching even the transition of the mist-mote into the cloud, the thought that is jetted from the eye to leave it instantly forever. Speed is at the bottom of it all—the hundredth of a second caught so precisely that the motion is continued from the picture infinitely: the moment made eternal.
>
> (*Letters,* 132)

As Crane praises the unique modern rapidity that captures the very act of "thought-extension" ("the thought that is jetted from the eye") and at the same time makes it seem to open out onto the "eternal," it is clear that he could be describing his own intentions as a poet. His style, like Stieglitz's camera, is a machine designed to capture an "invisible dimension."

Thus Crane took what he needed, and what would encourage him, from an immense variety of sources. By 1922, his essential style was formed: grand and metrical; difficult and rapid; audacious in its combinations of the anachronistic and the ultracontemporary. Between then and 1927, Crane wrote most of the poems that give him a claim to greatness. He published two books in his lifetime, *White Buildings* in 1926 and his long poem, *The Bridge,* in 1930. The lyrics in *White Buildings* are—with one important exception—only obliquely concerned with the affirmation of America or the machine age. They are concerned with the search for the ideal and the testing of the ideal by (often self-imposed) suffering; with the communication, or communion, between the artist and his audience; and with love. The great poems of quest and purgatorial suffering are "Lachrymae Christi," "Possessions," and "Repose of Rivers"—perhaps also

"Passage" and "The Wine Menagerie." The image of the artist who offers his society truths like the truth of quixotically persistent idealism—and who is forever laughed at, or feared, for doing so—is developed comically in "Chaplinesque," tragically in "Praise for an Urn" and "Recitative." But the section of *White Buildings* that has won Crane the affection of more readers, probably, than anything else he ever wrote, is the sequence of love poems called "Voyages."

The sequence was written after Crane moved, more or less permanently, from Ohio to New York City in 1923. Crane had fallen in love with a young man, Emil Opffer, who was both an intellectual and a sailor, and who periodically left Crane to ship out for South America. The anxiety of these absences, on the one hand; on the other, the glamour of his friend's image superimposed on the languid, dangerous, unbounded, maternal body of the sea, generated in Crane one of the richest metaphors ever conceived for the risks and gains of love. The opening poem—written long before the others, and a good instance of Crane's clearer early style—warns children at the beach against the dangers of the sea and, implicitly, of sexual awakening:

> O brilliant kids, frisk with your dog,
> Fondle your shells and sticks, bleached
> By time and the elements; but there is a line
> You must not cross nor ever trust beyond it
> Spry cordage of your bodies to caresses
> Too lichen-faithful from too wide a breast.

(35)

Yet the succeeding three poems are a celebration of an oceanic loss of identity, in which the speaker's body becomes indistinguishable from the lover's, and both from a kind of primordial Being:

> Infinite consanguinity it bears—
> This tendered theme of you that light
> Retrieves from sea plains where the sky
> Resigns a breast that every wave enthrones. . . .

(37)

And yet, the themes of drowning, death, and fate persist underneath. Perhaps individual personalities will not bear this kind of archetypal expansion for very long. In the one poem in which the lover actually speaks, and thereby manifests his separate will ("Voyages V"), the poet begins to feel a "tidal wedge" driven between them. The last poem records their separation, mingling images of shipwreck and "the death of kings" with the

Emil Opffer, for whom Crane wrote his great sequence "Voyages."

Whose counted smile of hours and days, suppose
I know as spectrum of the sea and pledge
Vastly now parting gulf on gulf of wings
Whose circles bridge, I know, (from palms to the severe
Chilled albatross's white immutability)
No stream of greater love advancing now
Than, singing, this mortality alone
Through clay aflow immortally to you.

—From "Voyages IV"

hope that art will capture, more satisfactorily, the image of that goddess, whose "unbetrayable reply" haunts so many of Crane's poems:

> Creation's blithe and petalled word
> To the lounged goddess when she rose
> Conceding dialogue with eyes
> That smile unsearchable repose. . . .
>
> (40)

Like Rilke's *Duino Elegies,* it is a poem that reveals an utter incapacity for the sustained relationships most of us consider normal; and thereby speaks all the more powerfully to a radical dream in us, of love as a cosmic fusion, a permanent departure from the opacities and limitations of our single bodies and minds.

The epic side of Crane's work, if one wants to call it that, begins with the other sequence in *White Buildings,* "For the Marriage of Faustus and Helen." The sequence is, in part, a high-spirited attempt to capture modern sensations for poetry. At first, they are the grimy urban sensations that Eliot had described, but seen from a different, transcendent angle—instead of "the damp souls of housemaids," Helen of Troy herself with "hands . . . that count the nights / Stippled with pink and green advertisements." Then Crane turns to sensations that were, as yet, in no one's poetry: the rhythm and weird humor of jazz—

> And you may fall downstairs with me
> With perfect grace and equanimity.
> Or, plaintively scud past shores
> Where, by strange harmonic laws
> All relatives, serene and cool,
> Sit rocked in patent armchairs
>
> (30)

—or the airplane and the terror of warfare in the air:

> We know, eternal gunman, our flesh remembers
> The tensile boughs, the nimble blue plateaus,
> The mounted, yielding cities of the air!
>
> That saddled sky that shook down vertical
> Repeated play of fire—no hypogeum
> Of wave or rock was good against one hour.
>
> (32)

The whole thing is held together by the kind of "mythic parallel" Joyce and Eliot had made popular—the myth in this case being

Marlowe's story of how Faustus receives, as his most tangible reward for selling his soul to the devil, a night with Helen of Troy. (But in Marlowe, the two cannot be married, marriage being a sacrament, and so beyond the devil's power.) The very choice of such a myth suggests that Crane only half disagrees with Eliot's view of the modern age as plunging toward damnation. Indeed, the war passages echo Faustus' last speech before the devil comes to carry him off. Crane is simply insisting that modern man, before his plunge, has consummated once again an eternal marriage with an "absolute conception of beauty," in the very terms of jazz solos, airplanes, new poetic forms.

When Crane moved to New York in 1923, he had already conceived of a long poem about Brooklyn Bridge, to be written in the same spirit of praise for "our constructive future" and the "mystical synthesis of America" that partly animates "Faustus and Helen." The conjunction of the move and the new project was a momentous one. For the America one remembers from Crane's poetry is New York, even more than it is the Midwest: the "Crap-shooting gangs in Bleecker"; the "penguin flexions" of people entering the subway; the new Art Deco towers whose "ribs palisade / Wrenched gold of Nineveh"; "The Harbor Dawn" where "steam / Spills into steam, and wanders, washed away / —Flurried by keen fifings."

But it was three years before *The Bridge* got well under way —a delay that made the poem darker, more in conflict with itself, but incomparably greater than it could have been in 1923, because of Crane's intervening struggle with what he found most alien in the intellectual premises of his time.

Crane's own age, as he saw it, was obsessively concerned with judging itself as an age, and predicting its future, triumphant or catastrophic. And Crane particularly disliked the sense in Eliot, Tate, and others that individual spiritual experiences were a helpless reflection of the spirit of the age, rather than, as he believed them to be, timeless and ahistorical:

> I think that this unmitigated concern with the Future is one of the most discouraging symptoms of the chaos of our age, however worthy the ethical concerns may be. It seems as though the imagination had ceased all attempts at any creative activity—and had become simply a great bulging eye ogling the foetus of the next century . . . I find nothing in Blake that seems outdated, and for him the present was always eternity.
>
> (*Letters,* 322)

Crane's satiric view of his own time is echoed elsewhere. Even the insensitive Tom Buchanan, in *The Great Gatsby,* reads and worries over long books predicting the downfall of the "white

Hart Crane on the roof of 110 Columbia Heights in Brooklyn.

From "To Brooklyn Bridge"

How many dawns, chill from his rippling rest
The seagull's wings shall dip and pivot him,
Shedding white rings of tumult, building high
Over the chained bay waters Liberty—

Then, with inviolate curve, forsake our eyes
As apparitional as sails that cross
Some page of figures to be filed away;
—Till elevators drop us from our day . . .

I think of cinemas, panoramic sleights
With multitudes bent toward some flashing scene
Never disclosed, but hastened to again,
Foretold to other eyes on the same screen;

And Thee, across the harbor, silver-paced
As though the sun took step of thee, yet left
Some motion ever unspent in thy stride,—
Implicitly thy freedom staying thee!

race" which has invented "science and art and all that." Crane worried over such a book—Spengler's *The Decline of the West*—to the point of paralysis in the early summer of 1926, when he was trying to progress beyond the first completed part of *The Bridge,* the Columbus section. He spoke in letters of "my delusion that there exist any real links between that past and a future worthy of it"; the Bridge, far from being a transcendent symbol, was perhaps only "an economical approach to shorter hours, quicker lunches, behaviorism and toothpicks." Then came a strange and drastic countermovement of spirit. Crane wrote to his friend Waldo Frank:

> Isn't it true—hasn't it been true in your experience, that beyond the acceptance of fate as a tragic action—immediately every circumstance and incident in one's life flocks toward a positive center of action, control and beauty? I need not ask this, since there is the metaphor of the "rotted seed of personal will," or some such phrase, in your *Spain.*
>
> (*Letters,* 274)

L. S. Dembo, in one of the most important studies of Crane yet written, *Hart Crane's Sanskrit Charge,* suggests that the liberating influence—here and elsewhere—was Nietzsche's *The Birth of Tragedy.* From Nietzsche, Crane learned that "the acceptance of fate as a tragic action" could be a very desirable step indeed, because it alone reconciled the Apollonian and Dionysian principles.

Apollo, for Nietzsche, represents the principle of individuation, the "personal will," the strengths and the limitations of selfhood. Dionysus represents the loss of self in the oneness of the cosmos, the ecstasy in which "indiscreet extravagance revealed itself as truth, and contradiction, a delight born of pain, spoke out of the bosom of nature." In Greek tragedy, Nietzsche believes, the two perspectives come together. The fate of the tragic hero enacts the pain of individuation—the sense that all finite human purposes are illusions. But it is also, like the dismemberment of the god Dionysus, a religious rite leading to a resurrection, to a new, more than Apollonian, sense of the beauty of particular life as a manifestation of the One. So, Nietzsche writes,

> For a brief moment we become, ourselves, the primal Being, and we experience its insatiable hunger for existence. Now we see the struggle, the pain, the destruction of appearances, as necessary, because of the constant proliferation of forms pushing into life, because of the extravagant fecundity of the world will.

Whether Crane received these ideas precisely, from *The Birth of Tragedy* itself, or loosely, from popularizations of Nietzsche, has never been proven. But proof is hardly necessary: the sense of "personal will" as a limitation, and of a kind of triumph and "fecundity," in which "we become . . . the primal Being," arriving with the "acceptance of fate as a tragic action," is too clear in poems like "Lachrymae Christi" and "Voyages." The next step was the application of the pattern to history. As we have seen, "Faustus and Helen" allows the possibility that modern man is racing toward destruction. Near the end of that poem, there are two historical images—

> Anchises' navel, dripping of the sea,—
> The hands Erasmus dipped in gleaming tides
>
> (33)

—that remain opaque, until one realizes that both refer to the deaths of civilizations, turned, by a "sea-change," into a fertilizing force for the future. Anchises, carried out of burning Troy on the back of Aeneas, died during the voyages that ended with the founding of Rome. When Rome in turn fell, Erasmus reached back across the Dark Ages to recover its literary energies ("Gathered the voltage of blown blood and wine") for the Renaissance. The important questions are not Spengler's, or even Eliot's, because creative energy does not die with the institutions that originally accommodated it. When Crane returned to *The Bridge,* with renewed confidence, that summer of 1926, I think he saw America, or the machine age, as the tragic hero manifesting both the beauty and the pain of individuation. The "new religious quantities" would come not only from America's accomplishments, but from the Dionysiac experience of accepting and, in the imagination, surviving the possible "decline of the West."

All of Crane's conflict is in a way summed up in the opening poem, "To Brooklyn Bridge," a work of subtle moral discrimination as well as great splendor. It has a triptych-like arrangement: the Bridge is placed between the open sea, on the one hand, and the jammed-in, cavernous streets of the Financial District and the Lower East Side on the other. In a letter, Crane compares his "space and detail division" in this poem to El Greco's in "Christ on the Mount of Olives," where the central figure of Christ is flanked, on one side, by an angel, on the other, by the distant figures of Judas and the soldiers. The angel, in the poem, is a seagull asleep out on the water:

Stick your patent name on a signboard
brother—all over—going west—young man
Tintex—Japalac—Certain-teed Overalls ads
and lands sakes! under the new playbill ripped
in the guaranteed corner—see Bert Williams what?
Minstrels when you steal a chicken just
save me the wing for if it isn't
Erie it ain't for miles around a
Mazda—and the telegraphic night coming on Thomas

a Ediford—and whistling down the tracks
a headlight rushing with the sound—can you
imagine—while an EXPRESS makes time like
SCIENCE—COMMERCE and the HOLYGHOST
RADIO ROARS IN EVERY HOME WE HAVE THE NORTHPOLE
WALLSTREET AND VIRGINBIRTH WITHOUT STONES OR
WIRES OR EVEN RUNning brooks connecting ears
and no more sermons windows flashing roar
breathtaking—as you like it . . . eh?

So the 20th Century . . .

—From "The River"

Rolling Power *by Charles Sheeler.*

How many dawns, chill from his rippling rest,
The seagull's wings shall dip and pivot him,
Shedding white rings of tumult, building high
Over the chained bay waters Liberty. . . .

(45)

The gull's awakening flight anticipates many of the principles of motion Crane will discover in the architecture of the Bridge: the "dip and pivot" of the main cable, "shedding" the subsidiary cables from it in "white rings," like arcs of endless concentric circles. But in "building," out of the gull's flight, an image of "Liberty," Crane draws an implicit contrast with the image which is there for all to see—the statue across New York harbor. By the contrast, the statue is made to seem heavy, metallic, fixed, part of the world of "chained bay waters" that reminds one of Blake's "charter'd Thames." Even before the gull escapes "with inviolate curve" in the next stanza, Crane has posed the question which the Bridge must attempt to mediate: whether there can be any social, institutional incarnation of a principle as absolute as "Liberty."

Flanking the Bridge on the other side is the world of Wall Street, where the poet drudges through his nine-to-five job, and "Liberty" seems as remote as the Melvillean past of clipper ships, "As apparitional as sails that cross / Some page of figures to be filed away." This world is, in its own way, full of energy, but an energy confined and potentially violent: the sunlight "leaks" into its depths, at noon, like the "rip-tooth" of an "acetylene" torch. Only the "cloud-flown derricks" remind one of the world as it looks from out on the Bridge, where energy and peace are one: "Thy cables breathe the North Atlantic still."

For the Bridge has, from the beginning, a mediating function in the poem. It is, in a way, the symbol of a symbol: what a religious icon would have to be, to speak to modern America and yet avoid the rigidity of the abstraction "Liberty." It belongs to industry, and to nature ("the North Atlantic"), and to art. It is a fixed artifact, yet when one walks across it it seems in endlessly renewing motion. Sometimes it even seems like a Mayan chronometric temple, a vast order bringing the skies down to earth:

And Thee, across the harbor, silver-paced,
As though the sun took step of thee, yet left
Some motion ever unspent in thy stride,—
Implicitly thy freedom staying thee!

But its position in the city is problematic. It changes nothing there; and to the victims of the city's very real and ruthless energies, those who must live crammed into "some . . . cell or loft," so intangible an image of perfection can be a source of despair as easily as of hope. The first human being to enter the poem, other than the shadowy image of Crane himself as office-worker, is a suicide:

A bedlamite speeds to thy parapets,
Tilting there momently, shrill shirt ballooning,
A jest falls from the speechless caravan.

And so the poem turns to a lofty, but rather anguished, meditation on what the Bridge—one of the "new religious quantities" —has to offer America. Tangible reward is not the point, any more than the afterlife is the point in Judaism ("And obscure as that heaven of the Jews, / Thy guerdon"). The Bridge's "accolade" is a transcendent "anonymity": neither its builder, Roebling, nor its "prophet," Whitman, nor Columbus himself—the "pariah" whose "prayer" will be heard in the next section—had the recognition he deserved in his own lifetime. "Reprieve and pardon" must spring from the "vibrant" image itself, as the "altar" of the flat-topped cable tower seems to grow out of the "harp" of "choiring strings." For Crane, as for Whitman, as for the great English Romantics, art becomes the type of the religious act as an act of pure consciousness, in the absence of tangible promises or dogmatic certainties.

As we read, the poem moves us unobtrusively through a single day in New York, from dawn to full morning to "street noon" to "all afternoon." Now it is suddenly evening, and the Bridge becomes a tender, merciful Mary:

Again the traffic lights that skim thy swift
Unfractioned idiom, immaculate sigh of stars,
Beading thy path—condense eternity:
And we have seen night lifted in thine arms.

(46)

For once, the Bridge seems to reach down to help the city, tenderly including the "traffic lights" in its cosmic space, translating them into "stars." And watching the strange, sad "sigh" of their passage across the river, we feel we are attending at the births and deaths of galaxies—the Bridge becoming an absolutely primordial creative force. Creative, but also entombing: for the suggestion of the Pietà in the fourth line leads into the grimmest stanza of the poem—

Under thy shadow by the piers I waited;
Only in darkness is thy shadow clear.
The City's fiery parcels all undone,
Already snow submerges an iron year. . . .

The Brooklyn Bridge: Variation on an Old Theme *by Joseph Stella.*

O harp and altar, of the fury fused,
(How could mere toil align thy choiring strings!)
Terrific threshold of the prophet's pledge,
Prayer of pariah, and the lover's cry,—

Again the traffic lights that skim thy swift
Unfractioned idiom, immaculate sigh of stars,
Beading thy path—condense eternity:
And we have seen night lifted in thine arms. . . .

O Sleepless as the river under thee,
Vaulting the sea, the prairies' dreaming sod,
Unto us lowliest sometime sweep, descend
And of the curveship lend a myth to God.

—From "To Brooklyn Bridge"

This is a Dark Night of the Soul, in which the ideal is clarified only by its "shadow," the terror of its absence. As in John of the Cross, one aspect of this night is an erotic "waiting": the sailors' bars where Crane sought casual pickups, and was often beaten, were "under thy shadow by the piers." But there is a public aspect as well: the third line fuses, in Crane's characteristic manner, an image of discarded Christmas wrappings with the random patterns of light in the night skyscrapers. To paraphrase crudely, the Christian festival has faded into the capitalist one, and both into a bitter aftermath. The city is "submerged"—a first hint of Crane's great symbol for the tragic possibilities of America's future, the drowned Atlantis. Out of this desperation, Crane prays to the Bridge to connect, in its "sweep," the "lowliest" with the highest experience; and to generate a new, post-Christian religion—"lend a myth" to the wholly unknowable "God"—out of its "unfractioned" aesthetic unity, its "curveship."

The poem that follows from this introduction bewildered its first readers by its seeming phantasmagoria of times, places, and characters. The narrative voice is by turns Crane himself, Columbus, a pioneer youth, a pioneer woman. The action strays over four hundred years, and as far away from New York as the Caribbean and the Southwest. And it all, somehow, has something to do with the Brooklyn Bridge.

Crane's first readers, we must remember, had read only one poem at all like this—the poem Crane thought he was answering, *The Waste Land.* We, who have also had the chance to read the complete (or incomplete) *Cantos, Four Quartets, Paterson, The Maximus Poems, The Dream Songs,* know that Crane's form is not an aberration, but the dominant form of the modern long poem, all but excluding the epic or extended narrative. What we have come to know about depth psychology and the archetypal, and what we have ceased to know—or to judge confidently—about the public world, both incline us to write epics that "include" history, in Pound's phrase, but take place in a kind of mental space, where all experiences are interpenetrable. And literal place is treated strangely in these poems: at once overburdened with importance—as if Paterson, East Coker, the Brooklyn Bridge were the navel of the universe—and yet somehow made dreamlike, internalized.

Crane could at least claim a certain historical justification for using the Brooklyn Bridge in this way. The Bridge's designer, John Roebling, had been a student of Hegel, and actually believed that he was creating a new kind of religious object for the machine age. And the opening of the Bridge followed shortly after the completion of the transcontinental railroad, and was seen, in public rhetoric, as part of the same phenomenon: the technological linking together of the entire world which, Whitman hoped, would become a mystical linking, the "Passage to India" discovered at last.

So it is not inappropriate that a poem about the Bridge should concern itself obsessively with journeys and have a composite hero who might be called the quester. In the long central section "Powhatan's Daughter," an indigenous American goddess (dreamed of at dawn in a room in Brooklyn Heights) leads the poet westward and backward in time: to childhood memories of trains and the hoboes who jumped them; then to a grand set-piece on the Mississippi River; then to a nineteenth-century alter ego, a pioneer youth who leaves his village and witnesses the death-dance, or initiatory vision, of another quester, the Indian chief Maquokeeta. In the structure of the poem as a whole, one can discern an alternating rhythm of westward and eastward movement. Westward journeys tend to be solitary, toward a visionary encounter with the Absolute: Columbus' discovery of what he thought was "Cathay"; Maquokeeta's transfiguration. Eastward journeys are equally crucial and more dangerous: they represent the incorporation of the vision into the fabric of society and its institutions; and the question is always, as in the opening poem, whether that incorporation can be anything but a betrayal. We meet Columbus on his return voyage, afraid of what King Ferdinand's desire for gold and Queen Isabella's desire to convert the heathen will make of his discovery. The Indian vision is brought back to white society—so Crane wants us to feel—by a pioneer woman who has a moment of wordless communion with an Indian squaw; but the woman's son feels confined on the farm in "Indiana," and must set out again, this time to sea. Disappointed questers tend to turn into beautiful losers, like the hoboes in "The River," "born pioneers in time's despite." Crane seems to agree with the historian Frederick Jackson Turner that the frontier was a necessary safety valve for American restlessness and Romanticism, our need to believe that ideal "Liberty" exists somewhere, our inability to tolerate the compromises of settled life. The bottling-up of this restlessness can be dangerous. In the second half of the poem, when the frontier is definitely closed, that energy either goes into commerce or literally up into the air, in airplanes and the technology of modern war. These sections of the poem are the most problematic, Crane's wish to find the energy itself "religious" clashing head on with his barely suppressed loathing of some of the forms it takes.

The other dominant, recurring theme in the poem, I would say, is the distortion and redemption of sexuality. Like Whitman, Crane hopes that the American wilderness itself will inspire us to an acceptance of the "natural" in ourselves, an Edenic sexual simplicity and splendor. Like almost every other American writer, he finds by experience that the ravages of Puritanism have been worse in America than elsewhere. On the "mythical and smoky soil" of the Indian, he imagines titanic figures of violent, apocalyptic sexuality, Maquokeeta and Pocahontas, whose self-immolations lead to a reawakening as simple as—and identical with—nature's own:

> High unto Labrador the sun strikes free
> Her speechless dream of snow, and stirred again,
> She is the torrent and the singing tree;
> And she is virgin to the last of men . . .
>
> (74)

But these figures are grimly contrasted with Crane's own parents, the father whose violence is merely violence ("the whip stripped from the lilac tree / One day in spring my father took to me"), the mother who finds her ecstasy in the "dream of snow," the "Sabbatical, unconscious smile," and not the reawakening. What he finds in his parents he finds everywhere in America: degradation and idealization, but never the calm acceptance of sexuality as a part of complete human identity. There are the traveling salesmen's reminiscences, "like a pigeon's muddy dream"; the burlesque show; the ragtime singer's

Hart Crane sent this postcard to Solomon Grunberg sometime around 1931.

The bell-rope that gathers God at dawn
Dispatches me as though I dropped down the knell
Of a spent day—to wander the cathedral lawn
From pit to crucifix, feet chill on steps from hell. . . .

The bells, I say, the bells break down their tower;
And swing I know not where. Their tongues engrave
Membrane through marrow, my long-scattered score
Of broken intervals . . . And I, their sexton slave! . . .

And so it was I entered the broken world
To trace the visionary company of love, its voice
An instant in the wind (I know not whither hurled)
But not for long to hold each desperate choice. . . .

—From "The Broken Tower"

frail idealization of his "Saturday Mary," "smiling the boss away." And, courageously, Crane includes himself, the mixture of indistinct hope ("The Harbor Dawn") and sheer nightmare (the "simian Venus" and corrosive "phosphor" of "Southern Cross") that he encounters when he ventures onto the suppressed heterosexual terrain of his own personality.

Since Crane's time, a series of venturesome critics, from D. H. Lawrence to Leslie Fiedler, have taught us to see the under-

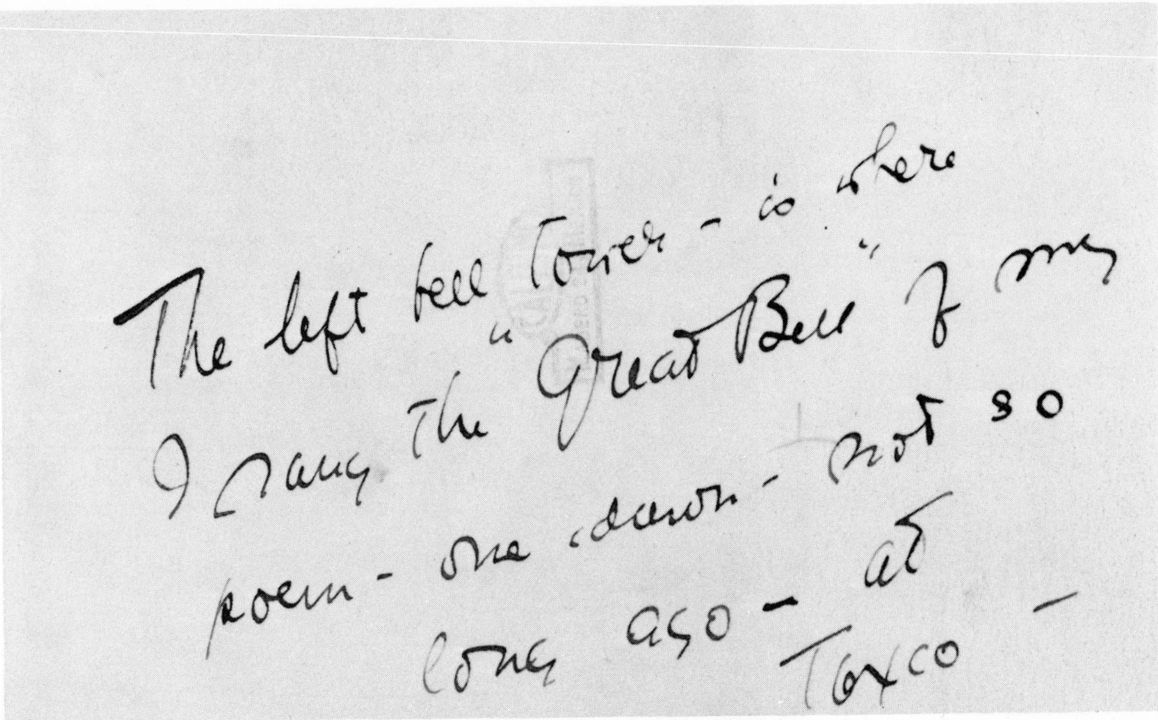
The left bell tower — is where
I rang the "Great Bell" of my
poem — one dawn — not so
long ago — at
Taxco —

themes of *The Bridge* as the great themes of classic American literature. With this perspective, we read *The Bridge* differently from its first readers, finding its "myth of America" both darker and truer. If the myth appears, on the surface, to be a new connection to "God" and "Love," just under the surface the myth is restlessness and the beauty of failure, and a sexual longing that remains provisional in its long battle with Puritanism and the fear of the settled life. *The Bridge* is a great poem, finally, because it sees so much that is wrong with America and sees at the same time how that wrongness has contributed to our peculiar national sense of beauty, and even of the sacred. It is able to do this partly because of the affirmative sense of tragedy that Crane picked up from Nietzsche, and that crowds the last stanzas of *The Bridge*—like the last stanzas of "Faustus and Helen"—with references to glorious fallen civilizations, Atlantis, Troy, and Tyre.

Discussion of *The Bridge* has been given a peculiar focus, from the start, by the insistence of some of its first critics that it was a "failure." By this, they meant three things: that it tries, and fails, to maintain an optimistic view of modern America; that it is structurally arbitrary and incoherent; and that some of

[Poets] to whom I speak . . . when we sit and talk about writers we admire, usually have some odd apprehension of Crane . . . he's the joker in the pack. For each poet he represents something that they don't have. . . . I almost always hear [in these conversations] a note of a special kind of intimacy and gratitude.

—Richard Howard in a *Voices & Visions* interview

its sections are disastrously weaker than others. The first two objections have lost much of their force simply through the passage of time, and a deeper reading both of *The Bridge* and of other modern long poems. The third objection remains true. The best sections of *The Bridge,* by a general consensus, are "To Brooklyn Bridge," "Powhatan's Daughter"—especially the subsections "The Harbor Dawn," "Van Winkle," "The River," and "The Dance"—"Cutty Sark," "Three Songs," and "The Tunnel." The worst sections are "Cape Hatteras," "Quaker Hill," and "Indiana," and there is some very bad writing indeed in the first of these. These poorer sections are the ones Crane rushed through, in a state of alcoholic and emotional collapse, in order to finish the poem in 1929. But perhaps there is a deeper explanation. "Cape Hatteras" and "Quaker Hill," in particular, are sections in which Crane tries to argue out, and balance, his admiration and his dislike of modern America. This cooler act of the mind was outside Crane's natural sense of what poetry could and should do. He could embody terror, disgust, the "negative" (and does so, in "Three Songs" and "The Tunnel") as powerfully as he could embody ecstasy. What he could not do, or at any rate could not do discursively (for he does it, in symbolic terms, in the structure of "To Brooklyn Bridge"), was to stand aside and weigh the claims of both on his imagination. If *Paterson* and *Four Quartets* are in any sense more satisfying long poems than *The Bridge,* it is because both Williams and Eliot had that capacity.

It is clear that the completion of *The Bridge* left Crane feeling rudderless and desperate, as a poet and as a man. Perhaps the tendentious, ideological reception the poem got from his former friends Tate and Winters had something to do with this; perhaps it was more a matter of personal difficulties. Mainly, I suspect, intermittent Romantic ecstasy—particularly with the masochistic tinge it had for Crane—no longer seemed to him an adequate basis for life; it rarely does, at the age of thirty. Shelley died at that age; Rimbaud had long since stopped writing; Byron turned to the all-encompassing, nihilistic worldly irony of *Don Juan.* The little work Crane did—aside from completing *The Bridge*—after 1927 is more jaunty and conversational, more open to the crude humor of his letters; but there is an underlying despair. The absolute—in the shape of the heat, the vastness, the hurricanes of the Caribbean landscape—is often invoked, but now it seems to dwarf the "personal will" without offering very much in return. Opinions differ about these poems. I know a distinguished contemporary poet who does not like any of Crane's denser earlier poems quite so well as "Eternity," with its low-key description of the aftermath of a hurricane:

The President sent down a battleship that baked
Something like two thousand loaves on the way.
Doctors shot ahead from the deck in planes.
The fever was checked. I stood a long time in Mack's talking
New York with the gobs, Guantanamo, Norfolk,—
Drinking Bacardi and talking U. S. A.

(183)

But this remains a minority opinion.

There is more unanimity about the merits of Crane's last poem, "The Broken Tower." It was written in Mexico, a few months before his suicide, to celebrate his last, and only heterosexual, love affair. But it takes its symbolism from an earlier experience helping the bellringers at dawn in the cathedral at Tepoxtlan, during a half-Aztec, half-Christian religious festival. The symbolism is complex. On one level, the tower is phallic, and stands for the new sexual confidence Crane felt in his relation with Peggy Cowley: "What I hold healed, original now, and pure. . . ." But the tower also recalls the old ascensions of religious consciousness, and the efforts of the Romantic poets to equal them by private intensity, or intensity of utterance (the phrase "The Broken Tower" itself comes from a French Romantic, Gérard de Nerval). But this straining upward seems always to create a counterbalancing abyss at its feet:

The bell-rope that gathers God at dawn
Dispatches me as though I dropped down the knell
Of a spent day—to wander the cathedral lawn
From pit to crucifix, feet chill on steps from hell.

(193)

Finally, these efforts and ascensions are judged in the light of the bodily symbolism. The "tower that is not stone"—the phallic tower that must lose its rigidity in the act of fulfilling itself—becomes the model of what is really possible to human experience. The writing, too, seems to embody a new acceptance of limit. The best stanzas of the poem combine high style and clear style as little in Crane's earlier work does. One such stanza has almost passed into the language, providing the title for Harold Bloom's famous study of the English Romantics, and the epigraph for Tennessee Williams's *A Streetcar Named Desire:*

And so it was I entered the broken world
To trace the visionary company of love, its voice
An instant in the wind (I know not whither hurled)
But not for long to hold each desperate choice.

The poem makes a good self-epitaph, as it were, and is often read in that spirit. But it is equally possible to read it as a gesture toward self-integration, the beginning of a new poetry that was never written.

Whether one considers Crane a great poet depends, in part, on the value one sets on that very straining against limits which he seems to renounce at the end. As Allen Grossman has pointed out, Crane's poetics implicitly denies the separateness of individual minds, by attempting to conjure up the most inward, incommunicable overtones of the poet's feelings in the reader. At the same time, he sacrifices many of those more oblique ways of gaining a reader's sympathy that come with the imitation of a speaking voice. He regards language less as speech than as a fascinating object, full of hidden depths and inner perspectives; and he does more with that side of language than any poet in English since Hopkins. He uses high style, not because he is old-fashioned, or narrow in his sense of the poetic, but because it seems the only adequate way to test the power of his feeling against the world's resistance. He is never a smooth or a facile artist; the intense, downright provincial boy of the letters can be felt even in his most spectacular moments of poetic achievement. And yet, the world is there in his poems —not only in a thousand right details, but in the seethe of responsive excitement, the "springboard" that sends him off into exultant "orbit." Robert Lowell wrote of him, "He somehow got New York City; he was at the center of things in the way that no other poet was. All the chaos of his life missed getting sidetracked the way other poets' did, and he was less limited than any other poet of his generation." And one of the best poet-critics of my generation, Robert Hass, has compared the combination of resources in Crane's poetry with what Miłosz brought to Polish poetry, and regretted that it did not lead to more in America: "Hart Crane's *The Bridge,* with its social concerns, its appropriation of the baroque, its surreal and visionary imagery, and its futurist fascination with machines, appeared to be a sort of splendid entryway to a building that was never built."

Hass is essentially right. Crane founded no school; and as the pendulum of taste has moved more toward Williams, toward free verse, simplicity, and the "American language," he seems more of a loner even than before. When I teach him, I often make one or two immediate converts; but for the majority of students he requires patience, study, and suspension of prejudices, as few other modern poets do. And yet, parts of his enterprise have persisted, as an active force, in the poetry of the last forty years. The enormous tension of his grand style against the world reappears, thanks to the intervening influence of Allen

Herman Melville in 1868.

At Melville's Tomb

Often beneath the wave, wide from this ledge
The dice of drowned men's bones he saw bequeath
An embassy. Their numbers as he watched,
Beat on the dusty shore and were obscured.

And wrecks passed without sound of bells,
The calyx of death's bounty giving back
A scattered chapter, livid hieroglyph,
The portent wound in corridors of shells.

Then in the circuit calm of one vast coil,
Its lashings charmed and malice reconciled,
Frosted eyes there were that lifted altars;
And silent answers crept across the stars.

Compass, quadrant and sextant contrive
No farther tides. . . . High in the azure steeps
Monody shall not wake the mariner.
This fabulous shadow only the sea keeps.

Tate, in Robert Lowell's *Lord Weary's Castle.* A later poem, "Words for Hart Crane," makes much the same point I have made about the social significance of Crane's self-imposed martyrdom. And there is an oblique tribute to Crane in the final stanzas of the grandest and, to my mind, the best of Lowell's later poems about America, the *Near the Ocean* sequence. (Crane is mentioned by name in the early drafts of the poem in the Houghton Library at Harvard.) Crane is also an important influence on Karl Shapiro's early, and still remarkably fresh, scenes of urban America. Crane's extremely active, energized sense of how a poet moves from one word to the next makes him one of the few predecessors, other than Pound and Williams, who really exist for the Black Mountain poets; Charles Olson, Robert Creeley, and Clayton Eshleman have all written movingly of him. His chosen role, the loyal but unacceptable homosexual son of the Republic—the gadfly who takes democratic brotherhood literally—he handed down to Allen Ginsberg, as he received it from Whitman. I even detect a trace of his verbal alchemy, his condensation, in two poets who nowhere speak of him as an influence, John Ashbery and Sylvia Plath. So he seems a kind of great dismembered Osiris of our poetry; bits and pieces of him turn up wherever it is most experimental and intense. Or perhaps, to alter the metaphor, an Orpheus: for to some of us he seems, as Marina Tsvetaeva wrote of Rilke, not a poet, but poetry. This feeling can even accompany uncertainty about his purely artistic success; thus, Allen Grossman writes of a "proximity to the sources of art inconsistent with the life of art itself." I think he means that Crane embodies an oceanic dream of what art might (but never quite does) do. It is the idea of an Edenic language, impossibly deep and substantial, impossibly attuned to the essence, the early morning freshness, of things—a language accessible to all minds equally, so that within it we stand, in the words of a late poem, "struck free and holy in one Name always."

The Weary Blues

Drowning a drowsy syncopated tune,
Rocking back and forth to a mellow croon,
I heard a Negro play.
Down on Lenox Avenue the other night
By the pale dull palor of an old gas light
He did a lazy sway....
He did a lazy sway....
To the tune o' those Weary Blues.
With his ebony hands on each ivory key
He made that poor piano moan with melody.
O Blues!
Swaying to and fro on his rickety stool
He played that sad raggy tune like a musical fool.
Sweet Blues!
Coming from a black man's soul.
O Blues!
In a deep song voice with a melancholy tone
I heard that Negro sing, that old piano moan—
"Ain't got nobody in all this world,
Ain't got nobody but ma self.
I's gwine to quit ma frownin'
And put ma troubles on the shelf."
Thump, thump, thump, went his foot on the floor.
He played a few chords then sang some more—
"I got the Weary Blues
And I can't be satisfied.
Got the Weary Blues
And can't be satisfied—
I ain't happy no mo'
And I wish that I had died."
And far into the night he crooned that tune.
The stars went out and so did the moon.
The singer stopped playing and went to bed
While the Weary Blues echoed through his head.
He slept like a rock or a man that's dead.

Langston Hughes

LANGSTON HUGHES

ARNOLD RAMPERSAD

On the countless occasions over more than forty years when Langston Hughes, smiling his boyish, disarming smile, mounted a podium as "Poet Laureate of the Negro Race" (a term he may have invented for himself) to read his verse before audiences, most of them mainly black, in a variety of church and school halls, he often told the same droll story about how he came to be a poet. "It happened like this," he would write about his fellow students in the seventh grade between 1915 and 1916 in Lincoln, Illinois, where he lived for a year. "They had elected all the class officers, but there was no one in our class who looked like a poet, or had ever written a poem. There were two Negro children in the class, myself and a girl. In America most white people think, of course, that *all* Negroes can sing and dance, and have a sense of rhythm. So my classmates, knowing that a poem had to have rhythm, elected me unanimously—thinking, no doubt, that I had some, being a Negro."[1] Helped by his mother and a teacher, Hughes penned some verses that lavished praise on his fellow students and the faculty. At graduation, when he read his poem to a packed hall, the applause seemed so sweet that he resolved there and then to be a poet.

If this tale contains an element of truth to go with its self-deprecating yet double-edged charm, there were other factors in Langston Hughes's decision early in life to attempt what no other black American had succeeded in doing: to live exclusively by writing, and to write primarily as a poet. In fact, as with the best writers, his decision was really an endorsement of the inevitable. The major elements of Hughes's life compelled him to a career of expressive language. In addition to the seventh-grade melodrama of election, Hughes might have told his listeners about a lonely, passed-around childhood spent in various places but mainly in Lawrence, Kansas, that left him vulnerable and sensitive about his identity and basic worth; a mother with ambitions for the stage who flitted theatrically into and out of his life with heartbreaking irregularity; a father who, scorning life as a black in the United States, had expatriated himself to Mexico and left his baffled son behind; an aged grandmother

Langston Hughes, 1920.

who indoctrinated a dreamy little brown boy with stories of men and women fighting to end slavery, but who had failed to pass on also a sense that he was wanted and needed and loved. *"Nobody loves a genius child,"* Hughes would write in a poem of uncharacteristic self-reference, not to say vanity. *"Kill him—* and let his soul run wild!"[2]

Hughes grew up poor. Nevertheless, he was also taught to be proud of certain persons whose heroism in the name of freedom he would be expected to try to match in his lifetime. One such person had been his maternal grandmother's first husband, Sheridan Leary, who was killed at Harpers Ferry in John Brown's band ("Perhaps / You will remember / John Brown,"

Hughes would write. "Harpers Ferry / Is alive with ghosts today, / Immortal raiders / Come again to town—" ["October 16," *SP,* 10]). On cool nights in Lawrence, Mary Leary Langston, who had served with her husband at the fanatical Oberlin station of the underground railroad, would draw his bullet-riddled shawl over her grandson as he went to sleep. Her second husband, Charles Langston, also an ardent Abolitionist, had fought for freedom mainly with words, but also with deeds; he had been arrested and tried after leading the rescue of a fugitive slave during one of the most celebrated of such actions before the Civil War. Charles's younger brother, John Mercer Langston, a graduate of Oberlin College, had been elected to Congress from Virginia and represented the United States in Haiti. Although his autobiography, *From the Virginia Plantation to the National Capitol,* was in many ways a tedious book, its details of honors and accomplishments, privileges and property, formed a challenge to the impoverished young Langston Hughes that he could hardly ignore. He would want to write his own book.

By his own account, from some point in the second grade, while he was living with his aging and increasingly remote grandmother, books rescued Hughes from excruciating loneliness: "Then it was that books began to happen to me, and I began to believe in nothing but books and the wonderful world in books—where if people suffered, they suffered in beautiful language, not in monosyllables, as we did in Kansas" (*BS,* 16). His earliest memories of books, he would recall, were of the Bible and W.E.B. Du Bois's historic collection of essays on Afro-American life, *The Souls of Black Folk* (1903). The great poems of his childhood undoubtedly were those of Longfellow, Whittier, and other New England poets—and of the masterful black poet from Ohio, Paul Laurence Dunbar, who wrote in dialect of a comic and pathetic black world, of little brown babies "wif spa'klin' eyes," and in lacquered English of a sorrow that many of his black readers recognized at once ("I know what the caged bird feels, alas! / When the sun is bright on the upland slopes").[3] Young Hughes read widely and well. If later he seemed to turn his back on books, and opened his autobiography *The Big Sea* with a dumping of texts overboard at the start of a voyage to Africa, it was definitely not out of ignorance of what they might contain.

Books alone could not save Hughes from loneliness, let alone give him the strength to be a writer. At least one other factor was essential in priming him for creative obsession. In the place in his heart, or his psychology, vacated by his parents entered the black masses. No Afro-American writer has seemed to love

Sheridan Leary.

[Hughes's] maternal grandmother's first husband, Sheridan Leary, [had been] killed at Harpers Ferry in John Brown's band. . . . On cool nights in Lawrence, Mary Leary Langston . . . would draw his bullet-riddled shawl over her grandson as he went to sleep.

his people more. The truth is that no black writer has *needed* to be loved by the race more; no black writer has so craved the affection of the masses. The great celebrant of blackness approached Afro-America from a distance, which his art would bridge; Hughes once confessed privately that he was more than twenty-five years old before he began to feel truly at home among his people. His race entered Hughes's consciousness, in a sense, both objectively and subjectively. Objectively it came in the neo-Abolitionist challenge to duty explicit in the words of persons such as W.E.B. Du Bois and Mary Leary Langston. In a far more powerful way, however, independent and yet reinforcing the neo-Abolitionist challenge, blacks came unmediated and unsponsored to capture the mind of the young boy. They worked their power essentially in three main areas: through the music, drama, and emotional commitment of the black church (by far the greatest single institution in black culture); through specific, loving examples that touched Hughes personally; and, especially as he grew more adult, through black secular music, notably the blues, which would orchestrate his private melancholy and give it form.

Since few visitors were invited to his home, Hughes met the folk mainly in the churches of his youth: above all, the St. Luke's A.M.E. Church, where he was the star of the Sunday School, and the Ninth Street Baptist Church, both in Lawrence. There he first experienced the powerful music and drama, the *commotion* of black faith.

> Glory! Hallelujah!
> The dawn's a-comin'!
> Glory! Hallelujah!
> The dawn's a-comin'!
> A black old woman croons
> In the amen-corner of the
> Ebecaneezer Baptist Church.
> A black old woman croons—
> The dawn's a-comin'!
>
> ("Prayer Meeting," *SP,* 27)

A skeptic almost by nature, Hughes was deeply moved in church not by religion but by the power of blacks to feel it. They worshipped Jesus; Hughes worshipped them. He marveled at their apparently boundless capacity for faith and hope:

> At the feet o' Jesus
> Sorrow like a sea.
> Lordy, let yo' mercy
> Come driftin' down on me.
>
> At the feet o' Jesus
> At yo' feet I stand.
> O, ma little Jesus,
> Please reach out yo' hand.
>
> ("Feet o' Jesus," *SP,* 17)

Shepherding the boy to church usually was not his grandmother (who, barred by racism from the church of her own religion, stayed at home altogether), but Mrs. Mary J. Reed, the supervisor of the St. Luke's Sunday School. From time to time, when their poverty demanded it, Hughes and his grandmother lived with Mrs. Reed and her husband, James Reed, who dug ditches for the city, raised chickens and milk cows on the side, and avoided church completely on Sunday. The Reeds grounded in Langston Hughes what would become his craving for the affection and regard of blacks. Of Mrs. Reed and her husband, Hughes would write words he never approached in reference to his own family, but that might apply perfectly to his view of the black race: "For me, there have never been any better people in the world. I loved them very much" (*BS,* 18).

The churches were not all ecstatic groans and cries. Both St. Luke's and the Ninth Street Baptist offered more high-toned debates and musicales that drew students from the nearby University of Kansas on Sunday afternoons, and helped to instill in young Hughes a balanced respect for the ability of blacks. But on the Lawrence streets, and in downtown Kansas City, not far from Lawrence, at a barbershop run by an uncle, Hughes also encountered a tradition that would be of far greater importance to his poetry. He never forgot the first time he heard the blues:

> I got de weary blues
> And I can't be satisfied.
> Got de weary blues
> And can't be satisfied.
> I ain't happy no mo'
> And I wish that I had died . . .
>
> (*SP,* 33)

The blues, Hughes would come to realize, embodied the classical black response to African experience in modern America. Here the masses articulated their philosophy of life in song—"gay songs, because you had to be gay or die; sad songs, because you couldn't help being sad sometimes. But gay or sad, you kept on living and you kept on going." Perhaps no twentieth-century American poet listened more attentively than Hughes did to music. To him, black music at its best was not mere entertainment but the metronome of Afro-American racial grace: "Like the waves of the sea coming one after another, always one after another, like the earth moving around the sun, night, day—night, day—night, day—forever, so is the undertow of black music with its rhythm that never betrays you, its strength like the beat of the human heart, its humor and its rooted power" (*BS,* 209).

A full understanding of all this significance would come to

Hughes only much later in his life. In Cleveland, where he would spend his four years of high school (1916–20), and where he began to publish verse as a sophomore, he found a home at the prestigious Central High School, the oldest secondary school west of the Alleghenies, and the most prominent in Cleveland (its best known alumnus was John D. Rockefeller). Cosmopolitan in its mixture of "native" whites, a small stream of blacks (many fresh from the South), and the children of European immigrants, both Christian and Jewish, Central High School provided Hughes with an excellent education. Studious and yet athletic, reserved but sweet-tempered, he performed very well in his courses, lettered in track and field, served as an officer in a number of clubs, and in his senior year won election as editor of the yearbook and Class Poet. This time he could not ascribe his election to benevolent racism; from his sophomore year Hughes had published poems regularly in the expertly produced Central High School *Monthly.*

While his earliest published poems suggest no particular talent, they are noteworthy in certain ways. Their form is traditional. The poems have almost nothing to do with race, although one was in Dunbar-like dialect ("I loves to see de big white moon / A shinin' in de sky").[4] Curious for the work of an athletic boy, they are dominated by the image of the poet as a little child, anxious for a loving mother ("Come with me to Little-Boy Land / Where the houses are castles big and grand").[5] Hughes had not yet properly apprenticed himself. He had also not yet found his subject, which is to say that the vacancy left by his absconding parents remained unfilled. Then, in January 1919, just before his seventeenth birthday, an unusually long, rambling, sometimes prosaic but affecting ode, "A Song of the Soul of Central," appeared in the *Monthly* above his name.

> . . . Children of all peoples and all creeds
> Come to you and you make them welcome.
> Oh Central, you know no race.
>
> . . . .
>
> You take beneath your roof
> Those with the blood of far away China,
> Those with the blood of the Congo,
> Those with the blood of Abraham and Jacob
> Flowing through their veins.
> You are mother to the rich and poor . . .[6]

Clearly Hughes had fallen under the spell of Walt Whitman, who had died not thirty years before ("Old Walt Whitman / Went finding and seeking," he would write; "Finding less than sought / Seeking more than found" ["Old Walt," *SP*, 100]). With Whitman's influence came a break with the genteel tyranny of rhyme and the pieties of the Fireside poets and the majority of black versifiers, including Dunbar. Hughes was on the brink of becoming a modern. Attuned as he already was to black life, however, he could not accept, much less internalize, a vision of the modern defined largely by the fate of Europe after the War. Sharing little or nothing of J. Alfred Prufrock's sense of an incurably diseased world, Hughes looked with indifference on the ruined splendors of the Waste Land. In practice, Modernism for him would mean not Ezra Pound (whose poetry he would claim to like, but not remember well, in an exchange of letters initiated by Pound in 1931), T. S. Eliot, or Wallace Stevens, but Whitman, Vachel Lindsay, and, above all, Carl Sandburg. The last became "my guiding star" (*BS*, 29).

A Midwesterner from Abe Lincoln country in Illinois, and a hyphenated-American like Hughes, Sandburg sang of democracy and the worker, humble immigrants and even humbler blacks, jazz and folk songs, the peaceful countryside and the harsh face of industry, injustice and the coming dawn. His poetic talk was too fiercely plain for fancy rhythms, too dirt-honest for rhyme. If Pound wanted to carve fancy images on Whitman's felled tree trunk, Sandburg would take a saw to the wood to carry on the great populist work. Hughes, who had spent a hot, excruciating summer in "vast, ugly, brutal, monotonous" Chicago in 1918, read Sandburg's *Chicago and Other Poems* and saw verse in a new light.[7]

> Carl Sandburg's poems
> Fall on the white pages of his books
> Like blood-clots of song
> From the wounds of humanity.
> I know a lover of life sings
> When Carl Sandburg sings.
> I know a lover of all the living
> Sings then.
>
> (*BS*, 29)

But Hughes did not remain star-struck for long; within a year or so he had emancipated himself from direct influence. In one instance, where the well-meaning Sandburg had written: "I am the nigger. / Singer of Songs, / Dancer,"[8] Hughes had responded with the more dignified (though not superior) "The Negro": "I am the Negro: / Black as the night is black, / Black like the depths of my Africa" (*SP*, 8).

The key to his release as a poet was his discovery of the significance of race, as well as his final, full admission of his

Carl Sandburg.

A Mid-Westerner from Abe Lincoln country in Illinois, and a hyphenated-American like Hughes, Sandburg sang of democracy and the worker, humble immigrants and even humbler blacks, jazz and folk songs, the peaceful countryside and the harsh face of industry, injustice and the coming dawn. . . . Hughes, who had spent a hot, excruciating summer in "vast, ugly, brutal, monotonous" Chicago in 1918, read Sandburg's *Chicago and Other Poems* and saw verse in a new light.

aloneness in the world. The discoveries came virtually together during an ill-fated summer in Mexico in 1919, where he lived with his father for the first time (apart from a few months when Langston was five or so) and discovered that he hated the man. Aggressive and acquisitive, his prosperous father openly despised the poor; he seemed particularly to despise his fellow blacks for being black and poor. He also despised poets—or at least he hated the thought that his only child might become one. At the end of the summer of 1919, Langston Hughes returned to Cleveland a changed person. In the coming year, he would achieve his fetal identity as a poet. He would do so by consciously accepting the challenge of Whitman and Sandburg but also by assigning as his own special task, within the exploration of modern democratic vistas in the United States, the search for a genuinely Afro-American poetic form.

At the center of his poetic consciousness now stood the black masses, rejected like himself but

> Dream-singers all,
> Story-tellers,
> Dancers,
> Loud laughers in the hands of Fate—
> My people.[9]

Or, as he soon more calmly, and yet more passionately, would express his admiration and love:

> The night is beautiful,
> So the faces of my people.
>
> The stars are beautiful,
> So the eyes of my people.
>
> Beautiful, also, is the sun.
> Beautiful, also, are the souls of my people.

("My People," *SP,* 13)

Within a year, before he was nineteen, Hughes had written at least three of the poems on which his revered position among black readers would rest. The most important, and the one most illustrative of his poetic process, was composed on a train in July 1920, when, after graduating from high school, he traveled to Mexico to attempt a reconciliation with his father. According to the poet, the place was a train crossing the Mississippi River near St. Louis, the time was near sunset, and his mood something like despair after a long dwelling on his unhappiness with his father and his father's contempt for blacks. A phrase came to Hughes, then the whole poem, "The Negro Speaks of Rivers":

I've known rivers:
I've known rivers ancient as the world and older
than the flow of human blood in human veins.

My soul has grown deep like the rivers.

I bathed in the Euphrates when dawns were young.
I built my hut near the Congo and it lulled me
to sleep.
I looked upon the Nile and raised the pyramids
above it.
I heard the singing of the Mississippi when Abe Lincoln
went down to New Orleans, and I've seen its muddy
bosom turn all golden in the sunset.

I've known rivers:
Ancient dusky rivers.

My soul has grown deep like the rivers.

(*SP,* 4)

If the details of its inspiration are true (and they appear to be), then "The Negro Speaks of Rivers" reflects the classic motion of Hughes's creativity as a poet. The poem begins in a sense of hurt mingled with indignation, but the affliction and the rage are transcended. In this case, the image of his father, the primal source of anxiety, even of a death-wish, dissolves into the superior power with which it would contend, the beauty and historicity of the black race, which nourishes the poet as a mother nourishes her child. Quietly, without anger, much less invective, the father (the hurt) is liquidated in the inexorable flow of the river, whose despised "muddy bosom," irradiated by the poet's filial vision, turns now "all golden" in the sunset of the poem. Buried deep within the work, deep in the river, is an act of violence—parricide—which nevertheless brings peace both to the brown river-race and to the poet who honors it.

Published in Du Bois's *Crisis* magazine in June 1921, when Hughes was nineteen, "The Negro Speaks of Rivers" would remain in some ways the centerpiece of his verse to the end of his life.

Another poem written that year, "When Sue Wears Red," drew on the ecstatic cries of the black church to express a tribute to the historic beauty of black women unprecedented in the literature of the race. Again, hurt is transcended so perfectly that virtually no trace of it is left for the casual reader. Only black readers, painfully aware of their despised color and features and the denial of their history by the Anglo-Saxon world, would feel in the poem both the impact of a wound and the balm of poetic healing.

When Susanna Jones wears red
Her face is like an ancient cameo
Turned brown by the ages.

Come with a blast of trumpets,
    Jesus!

When Susanna Jones wears red
A queen from some time-dead Egyptian night
Walks once again.

Blow trumpets, Jesus!

And the beauty of Susanna Jones in red
Burns in my heart a love-fire sharp like pain.

Sweet silver trumpets,
    Jesus!

(*SP,* 68)

The third major poem of this first phase of Hughes's adult creativity was "Mother to Son," a quiet dramatic monologue, sentimental to be sure, but a revelation to members of a race haunted by self-doubt. Black dialect, so often derided as a vehicle only for low-verse comedy ("A jingle in a broken tongue," Dunbar once dejectedly called his own similar lines[10]), empowers an epic challenge in "Mother to Son":

Well, son, I'll tell you:
Life for me ain't been no crystal stair.
It's had tacks in it,
And splinters,
And boards torn up,
And places with no carpet on the floor—
Bare.
But all the time
I'se been a-climbin' on,
And reachin' landin's,
And turnin' corners,
And sometimes goin' in the dark
Where there ain't been no light.
So boy, don't you turn back.
Don't you set down on the steps
'Cause you finds it's kinder hard.
Don't you fall now—
For I'se still goin', honey,
I'se still climbin',
And life for me ain't been no crystal stair.

(*SP,* 187)

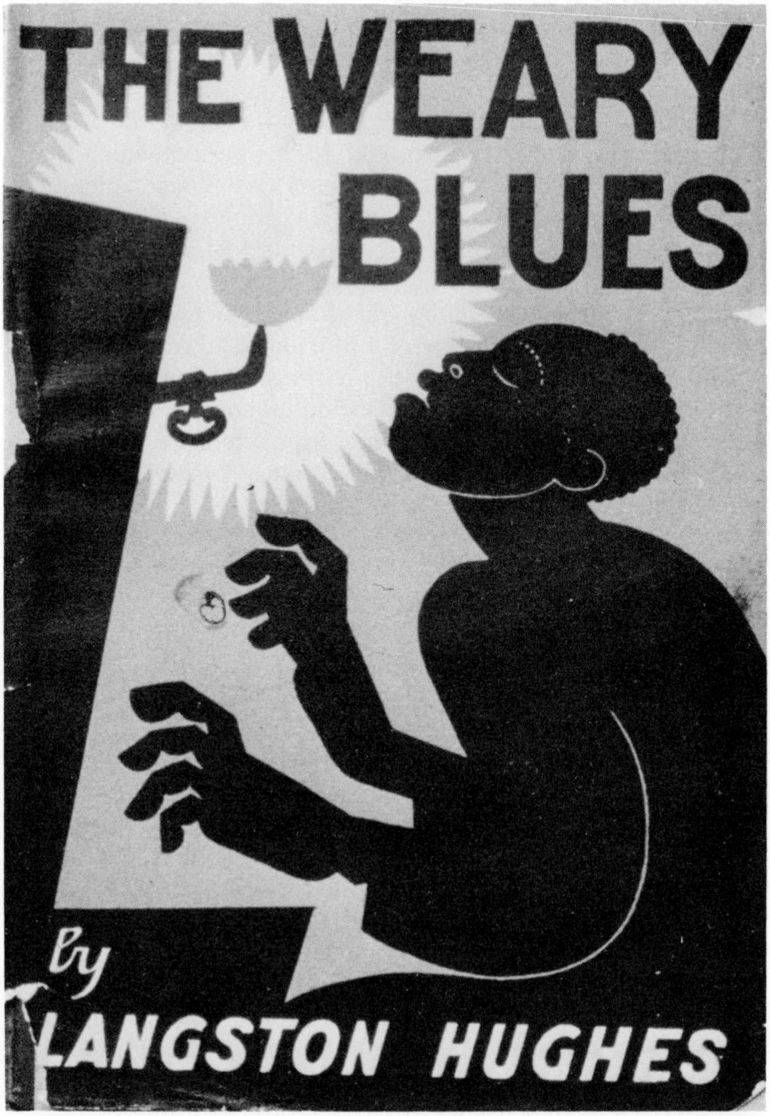

Miguel Covarrubbias did the jacket art for Hughes's first book, The Weary Blues.

In coming to terms with his race, Hughes had clearly taken upon himself, along with his other duties, something of the charge assumed by the Fireside poets in the previous century. He would also have to accept the main liability of this assumption —the contempt of critics for the poetry of social service.

After a year in Mexico with his father, Hughes attended Columbia University in New York for one year before withdrawing from school to begin four unsteady years of odd jobs and apparent drifting that took him as far from home as the west coast of Africa, France, and Italy. The nonchalance of this period was contrived; Hughes understood the need to saturate himself in experience, as Whitman and Sandburg had done, in order to write the populist poetry he prized. In this period, which found him now voyaging up the Congo River, now beachcombing in Genoa, stranded without a passport, he cannily managed nevertheless not only to write but also to publish steadily. At first his work appeared mainly in black magazines such as *Crisis* (of the N.A.A.C.P.) and *Opportunity* (of the Urban League); then it began to creep into a variety of white journals from *The World Tomorrow* to the fashionable *Vanity Fair.* These years of wandering would end in 1926 with his simultaneous entry into black Lincoln University in Pennsylvania, from which he would graduate, and the publication of his first volume of verse, *The Weary Blues* (Knopf). Moderately well received, this collection was followed in 1927 by another, *Fine Clothes to the Jew.*

Between 1921 and 1927, by far the most fertile period of his life as a poet, Hughes established his authentic range. That range was not narrow. An examination of his work suggests, in fact, that Hughes worked essentially in three major modes as a poet. These modes may usefully be seen, I believe, to reflect the three major stages in his basic creative process, with the third or last mode representing his art at its most mature. In turn, these three poetic stages reflect the three main stages of his psychology in grappling with circumstances that demanded a profoundly serious, or a poetic, response. In "The Negro Speaks of Rivers" we have already seen the three stages: melancholic passivity, concealed outrage, and transcendence. Poetic transcendence comes usually with some quiet assertion of black beauty and historicity, which the sensitive reader immediately understands to be in response to a negation, even if the hurt is not directly expressed. Melancholic passivity and outrage were not always as veiled in Hughes's verse as they had been in "Rivers." Each, indeed, led to a strain of poetry that is accomplished in itself—even if one concludes that the accomplishment is minor compared with that of Hughes's poetry of transcendence.

Closest perhaps to the source of language in Hughes was his sense of loneliness, abandonment, and despair. Neither romantic rehearsing nor existential modishness, but an intravenous gloom led him to write as often as he did about nihilism and death, about suicide and "my mother, / Death," and, more philosophically, of

Dear lovely Death
That taketh all things under wing
Never to kill—
Only to change
Into some other thing
This suffering flesh . . .[11]

To Hughes, the difference between living and dying is that "between tears and crying"; the distance between "here and there" is "nowhere."

There are
No clocks on the wall,
And no time,
No shadows that move
From dawn to dusk
Across the floor.

There is neither light
Nor dark
Outside the door.

There is no door!

("End," *SP*, 86)

"Anybody," he would write, is "better than nobody."

In the barren dusk
Even the snake
That spirals
Terror on the sand—

Better than nobody
In this lonely
Land.

("Desert," *SP*, 93)

Sometimes, as in "Afro-American Fragment," he links nihilism to cultural loss, to passages of historically induced sorrow when, with the drums of Africa now all "subdued and time-lost,"

There comes this song I do not understand,
This song of atavistic land,
Of bitter yearnings lost
Without a place—
So long,
So far away
Is Africa's
Dark face.

(*SP*, 3)

Josephine Baker is the music hall queen depicted in this 1925 poster for the Revue Nègre.

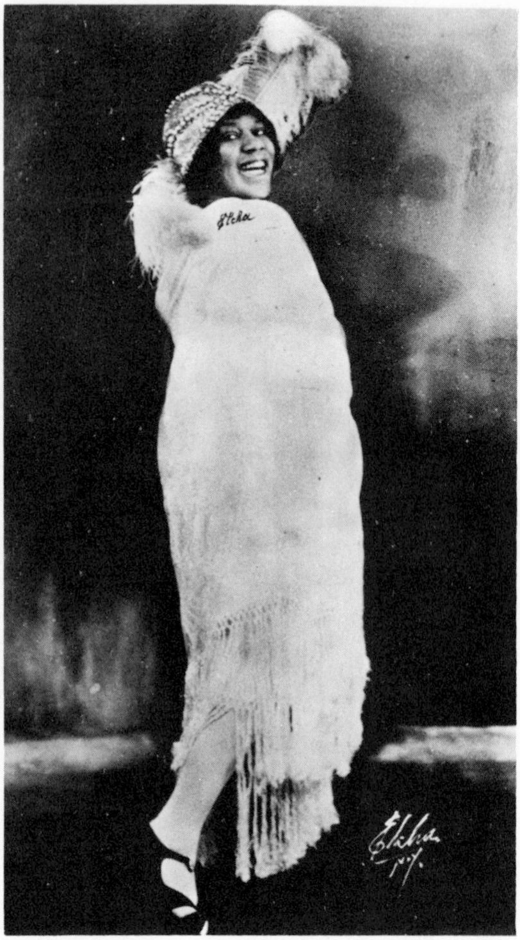

Bessie Smith.

Far more often, because its source is not perceived by Hughes as political or cultural, his poetry of nihilism, loss, and despair proposes no racial reference. Ironically, in their famished spirit —and their absence of racial reference—such poems would normally be perceived as perhaps Hughes's most "universal" and "modern" work. They are also, aside from the doggerel he later took an almost perverse pleasure in writing (apparently in order to leave no member of the masses unsolicited, not even the near-illiterate), perhaps his least satisfying work. Such poems are seen as being so contrary to Hughes's typically engaged style that their very existence is barely acknowledged. And yet they form, in a sense, the magma on which his more clearly wrought work, stabilized by race, rests. The judgment that these

Fats Waller.

poems are more "universal," or more poetic, is unfortunate. Hughes's distinction as a writer derives precisely from his concern with race and culture, which made him a better poet.

This was one mode of Hughes's writing. Another was the poetry of open protest in which, in a sense, he honored the spirit of John Brown and fulfilled his ancestral obligation to Sheridan Leary. Such poetry is itself varied, beginning with a plaintive call for admission to the American family and stretching far toward revolution. Perhaps the best known of his milder poems of protest, composed while Hughes was stranded in Genoa and saw ship after ship flying the American flag refuse to take him home because of his race, is "I, Too." Here, he modifies one of Whitman's greatest chants to assert that "I, too, sing America":

I am the darker brother.
They send me to eat in the kitchen
When company comes,
But I laugh,
And eat well,
And grow strong. . . .

Tomorrow they will see "how beautiful I am / And be ashamed— / I, too, am America" (*SP*, 275). Other poems were less petitionary, less equivocal. What Hughes had seen of British, French, and Belgian colonialism in Africa had led him to more caustic lines. "I do not hate you, / For your faces are beautiful, too," he wrote. "Yet why do you torture me, / Oh, white strong ones, / Why do you torture me?"[12] Of "the Johannesburg mines," where there were "240,000 / Native Africans working," Hughes demanded to know "What kind of poem / Would you / Make out of that?"[13]

Virtually from the start, Hughes knew and generally sympathized with radical socialism, even if he did not always seek to endorse its extreme viewpoint, and even if he eventually would repudiate it as a solution for blacks or, indeed, the world.

I am so tired of waiting,
Aren't you,
For the world to become good
And beautiful and kind?
Let us take a knife
And cut the world in two—
And see what worms are eating
At the rind.[14]

Initially, his sympathy came from three main sources. One was the universal communalism of Whitman and Sandburg. Another was the example of his Jewish schoolmates in Cleveland, who "lent me *The Gadfly* and *Jean-Christophe* to read, and copies of the *Liberator* and the *Socialist Call.* They were almost all interested in more than basketball and the glee club. They took me to hear Eugene Debs. And when the Russian Revolution broke out, our school almost held a celebration" (*BS,* 31).

The *Liberator* was crucial. "I learned from it the revolutionary attitude toward Negroes," he remembered. "Was there not a Negro on the staff?" The Negro on Max Eastman's magazine (the successor to *Masses,* edited by Eastman, Floyd Dell, and John Reed) was the Jamaican lyric poet and intellectual Claude McKay. "It was Claude McKay's example that started me on this track," Hughes would recall, and he sent his own radical poems—without success—to Dell.[15] Years later, in the Depression, during a year in the Soviet Union, where he had gone to work on a film on race relations in the United States, Hughes began a phase in his career in which he virtually adopted a radical socialist aesthetic, and discovered that he had a talent for sloganeering. In this period came much verse that Hughes would later try to hide, partly because of right-wing intimidation and partly out of shame—poems such as "Good Morning Revolution" (after Carl Sandburg's "Good Morning America"?), "Ballads of Lenin," "A New Song" ("I speak in the name of the black millions / Awakening to action"), "Put One More 'S' in the U.S.A." (to make it Soviet), and one poem that would haunt him the rest of his life, and which he tried to expunge, "Goodbye Christ" ("Make way for a new guy with no religion at all— / A real guy named / Marx Communist Lenin Peasant Stalin Worker ME").[16]

With radical socialism, as with race, Hughes had no goals that were incompatible with what he considered the aboriginal American ideals. Perhaps his finest poem of the thirties combined his will to revolution with his Whitman-like nostalgia for a vanishing America. In "Let America Be America Again," Hughes wrote a sometimes awkward and wooden but still noble anthem for a nation in Depression:

Let America be America again.
Let it be the dream it used to be.
Let it be the pioneer on the plain
Seeking a home where he himself is free.

(America never was America to me.)

Let America be the dream the dreamers dreamed—
Let it be that great strong land of love
Where never kings connive nor tyrants scheme
That any man be crushed by one above . . .

. . . .

Say who are you that mumbles in the dark?
And who are you that draws your veil across the stars?

I am the poor white, fooled and pushed apart,
I am the Negro bearing slavery's scars . . .[17]

Although his radical verse is sometimes effective, Hughes's best writing, as we have seen, comes when the poet retains his racial or other social concern but transcends overt rage and a sense of hurt by explorations of human nobility and beauty. Such explorations fare better, in general, the greater their distance from didacticism—although "The Negro Speaks of Rivers" is both a moving and a teaching poem. Hughes's greatest single insight, however, led him to understand that no tribute in "high" art to the black race would be greater than one in which the race spoke for itself, as it spoke for itself in its folk songs and folklore. Within a few weeks of his twenty-first birthday, Hughes discovered the form appropriate to this most radical step in his art, and the courage within himself to try to take it.

By the winter of 1923, having already written several important poems, he had not yet written a poem (nor had any other black poet even come close to doing so) that had emerged integrally out of the most significant artistic expression of black America—blues and jazz. What is the blues? Although W. C. Handy was the first musician to popularize it, notably with "St. Louis Blues," the form is so deeply based in the chants of Afro-American slave labor, field hollers, and sorrow songs as to be ancient, and comprises perhaps the finest art of Africans in North America. Oral and improvisational by definition, the blues nevertheless has a classical regimen. Its most consistent form finds a three-line stanza, in which the second line restates the first, and the third provides a contrasting response to both. The blues most often sings of misfortune, but, as Hughes himself wrote of the songs, "when they are sung people laugh."[18] "The blues speak to us simultaneously of the tragic and the comic aspects of the human condition," Ralph Ellison would write in *Shadow and Act* almost forty years after Hughes's pioneering literary work; they must be seen "first as poetry and as ritual," and thus as "a transcendence of those conditions created within the Negro community by the denial of social justice."[19] "It was a language," Samuel Charters asserts in his *Legacy of the Blues;* "a rich, vital, expressive language that stripped away the misconception that the black society in the United States was simply a poor, discouraged version of the white. It was impossible not to hear the differences. No one could listen to the blues without realizing that there were two Americas."[20]

A long brooding on the psychology of his people, and a Whitmanesque predisposition to make the native languages of America guide his art, led Hughes early in 1923 to begin his greatest single literary endeavor: his attempt to resuscitate the dead art of Afro-American, and American, poetry and culture by invoking the blues (exactly as George Gershwin, the following year, would try to elevate American music in his "Rhapsody in Blue"). Inspiration came one night in March after a visit to a little Harlem cabaret, when Hughes set, within an otherwise conventional poem, the first blues he had heard as a child in Kansas. In doing so, he honored at one and the same time the poetic traditions of Europe and Afro-America. Nevertheless, the poem is a dialogue between poetical, cultural, and psychological forms: between, on the one hand, the white or the "cultivated"

Harlem belles, 1920's.

When Susanna Jones wears red
Her face is like an ancient cameo
Turned brown by the ages.

Come with a blast of trumpets, Jesus!

When Susanna Jones wears red
A queen from some time-dead Egyptian night
Walks once again.

—From "When Sue Wears Red"

Negro persona, who is overwhelmed by but does not fully understand what he hears, and, on the other, the black bluesman, Afro-America, who plays and plays before sleeping like an innocent. The technical virtuosity of the opening lines of the poem is seen only when they are measured against the cadences of urban black speech, derived from the South, with its glissandos, arpeggios, and sudden stops. The poem was "The Weary Blues":

Droning a drowsy syncopated tune,
Rocking back and forth to a mellow croon,
    I heard a Negro play.
Down on Lenox Avenue the other night
By the pale dull pallor of an old gas light
    He did a lazy sway. . . .
    He did a lazy sway. . . .
To the tune o' those Weary Blues.
With his ebony hands on each ivory key
He made that poor piano moan with melody.
    O Blues!
Swaying to and fro on his rickety stool
He played that sad raggy tune like a musical fool.
    Sweet Blues!
Coming from a black man's soul.
    Blues!
In a deep song voice with a melancholy tone
I heard that Negro sing, that old piano moan—
    "Aint got nobody in all this world,
    Ain't got nobody but ma self.
    I's gwine to quit ma frownin'
    And put ma troubles on the shelf."
Thump, thump, thump, went his foot on the floor.
He played a few chords then he sang some more—
    "I got the Weary Blues
    And I can't be satisfied.
    Got the Weary Blues
    And can't be satisfied—
    I ain't happy no mo'
    And I wish that I had died."
And far into the night he crooned that tune.
The stars went out and so did the moon.
The singer stopped playing and went to bed
While the Weary Blues echoed through his head.
He slept like a rock or man that's dead.

(*SP,* 33)

Just as the classically trained Scott Joplin had labored to notate ragtime in order to enshrine its beauty as art, so Hughes worked to lift the lowly blues—which would not have been allowed into many decent black homes—in order that its fineness might be recognized by the world. Uncharacteristically but shrewdly, he kept the poem unpublished for two years until, when it was finally released, it led directly to the acceptance of his first book.

Hughes did not stop, however, with this concessionary introduction of the blues. Over the next four years he moved to the ultimate position, which dominated *Fine Clothes to the Jew* in 1927 and helped it to become both the finest and the most condemned and financially unsuccessful of his more than forty books. By that time Hughes was offering the blues as a form unto itself, without need of mediation by European verse forms, or framing by a conventional, "refined" poetic sensibility. Both the peculiar stanzaic form and the psychology of the blues (the psychology of the black masses, as Hughes saw it) were enough to certify a poem.

The bluesman, after all, knows how to etch a rare image:

De railroad bridge's
A sad song in de air.
De railroad bridge's
A sad song in de air.
Ever time de trains pass
I wants to go somewhere . . .

("Homesick Blues," *FC,* 24)

But most blues singers are not so abstract. Love and loss of love, violence and despair, saturate the blues and, therefore, Hughes's blues poems. The happier poems swell with an exuberant sexuality, the sadder deflate with a mixture of sex and pathology. One man beats his wife and "ma side gal too": "Don't know why I do it but / It keeps me from feelin' blue" ("Bad Man," *FC,* 21). Another met "a gal I thought was kind. / She made me lose ma money / An' almost lose ma mind" ("Po' Boy Blues," *FC,* 23). The blues, however, are sung most brilliantly by women. One warns young girls to "Listen here to me: / Gin an' whiskey / Kin make you lose yo' 'ginity" ("Listen Here Blues," *FC,* 85). Another sees in love only inevitable sorrow:

I hope ma chile'll
Never love a man.
I say I hope ma chile'll
Never love a man.
Cause love can hurt you
Mo'n anything else can.

("Lament Over Love," *FC,* 81)

Most often, the sorrow is not in the future, but in the present or the still aching past. Loss is mixed with despair and pathetic self-abnegation, as in "Gal's Cry for a Dying Lover":

. . . Hound dawg's barkin'
Means he's gonna leave this world.
Hound dawg's barkin'
Means he's gonna leave this world.
O, Lawd have mercy
On a po' black girl.

Black an' ugly
But he sho do treat me kind.
I'm black an' ugly
But he sho do treat me kind.
High-in-heaben Jesus
Please don't take this man o' mine.

(*FC,* 82)

Fine Clothes to the Jew horrified most of its black reviewers: Hughes had exposed the secret shame of their race to the white world. The New York *Amsterdam News* denounced him as a "SEWER DWELLER," and the book as "about 100 pages of trash [reeking] of the gutter and the sewer." The Pittsburgh *Courier* found it "piffling trash" that left its critic "positively sick." The Chicago *Whip* denounced "the lecherous, lust-reeking characters that Hughes finds time to poeticize about. . . . These poems are unsanitary, insipid and repulsing."[21]

Other reviewers understood what Hughes had done. More than one compared his effort to rewrite the language of black poetry, and American poetry, to the attempt by Wordsworth and Coleridge in *Lyrical Ballads.* Perhaps the most perceptive review came from the cultural historian Howard Mumford Jones. Although Hughes sometimes lapsed, like Wordsworth, into "vapid simplicity," he had succeeded dramatically in scraping the blues form down to the bone, and in the process had raised a folk form to the level of literary art. "In a sense," Jones concluded, Hughes "has contributed a really new verse form to the English language."[22]

Hughes's initiative was firmly resisted by the other major young black poet of what would be called the Harlem Renaissance, Countee Cullen, who himself had already published *Color* (1925) when *The Weary Blues* appeared in 1926. Captivated by the romantic lyricism of Keats and A. E. Housman in particular, Cullen saw the jazz and blues verse in *The Weary Blues* as exemplifying "the gaping pit that lies before all Negro writers, in the confines of which they become racial artists in-

stead of artists pure and simple. There is too much emphasis here on strictly Negro themes; and this is probably an added reason for my coldness toward the jazz poems—they seem to set a too definite limit upon an already limited field."[23] To this argument Hughes replied vigorously in the *Nation* in the greatest essay of his life, "The Negro Artist and the Racial Mountain," which would serve as a manifesto for most of the younger black writers of the age. The mountain was "this urge within the race toward whiteness, the desire to pour racial individuality into the mold of American standardization, and be as little

"Summer Magic" by Ellis Wilson.

Negro and as much American as possible." Jazz is "one of the inherent expressions of Negro life in America; the eternal tom-tom beating in the Negro soul—the tom-tom of revolt against weariness in a white world."

> Let the blare of Negro jazz bands and the bellowing voice of Bessie Smith singing Blues penetrate the closed ears of the colored near-intellectuals until they listen and perhaps understand. . . . We younger Negro artists who create now intend to express our individual dark-skinned selves without fear or shame. If white people are pleased we are glad. If they are not, it doesn't matter. We know we

Dream Variations

To fling my arms wide
In some place of the sun,
To whirl and to dance
Till the white day is done.
Then rest at cool evening
Beneath a tall tree
While night comes on gently,
  Dark like me—
That is my dream!

To fling my arms wide
In the face of the sun,
Dance! Whirl! Whirl!
Till the quick day is done.
Rest at pale evening . . .
A tall, slim tree . . .
Night coming tenderly
  Black like me.

are beautiful. And ugly too. The tom-tom cries and the tom-tom laughs. If colored people are pleased we are glad. If they are not, their displeasure doesn't matter either. We build our temples for tomorrow, strong as we know how, and we stand on top of the mountain, free within ourselves.

(*Nation* 122 [June 23, 1926]: 692–94)

With this essay and his books of verse, Hughes became the most influential of black poets, a position reinforced by his extreme generosity to other writers. The spirit of the blues infused the best book of verse by a black in the thirties, Sterling Brown's *Southern Road* (1932). Hughes also encouraged Melvin Tolson, author of the posthumously published *A Gallery of Harlem Portraits* (1979) and also the acclaimed *Rendezvous with America* (1944) and *Libretto for the Republic of Liberia* (1953). Margaret Walker, who won the Yale Younger Poets prize with *For My People* (1942), repeatedly acknowledged the importance of Hughes's help as well as his artistic example. Although he looked quizzically on the complex high modernism of Gwendolyn Brooks and the later stages of Melvin Tolson's career, Hughes remained a reliable supporter of both poets. To the end of his life he took pride in being a friend to young writers; in two landmark anthologies, *The Poetry of the Negro* (1949) with Arna Bontemps, and *New Negro Poets* (1964), he brought several to public recognition for the first time. Throughout the explosive

1960s, even as his reputation faded among most academic or otherwise privileged critics, white or black, Hughes was unquestionably the single most important older poet for the younger writers, particularly admiring and befriending the most militant and gifted of these, LeRoi Jones (Amiri Baraka)—although Hughes was frequently shocked by Jones's excesses. Moreover, if the full extent of the older writer's achievement had begun to be forgotten generally, his pioneering work in Afro-American forms was now the foundation of black verse. The blues, if frequently in modified ways, had come to be accepted as the quintessential black poetic form—often without credit to Hughes. Although few white poets would work in the form (Elizabeth Bishop was one exception), several books of verse in recent years by accomplished poets such as Michael Harper, Sherley Anne Williams, and Raymond Patterson attest to the validity of Hughes's insights in the 1920s.

After 1927 and *Fine Clothes to the Jew,* however, in part because of the powerful reaction in the black press, in part because of changed circumstances in his life, Hughes did not

Song for Billie Holiday

What can purge my heart
Of the song
And the sadness?
What can purge my heart
But the song
Of the sadness?
What can purge my heart
Of the sadness
Of the song?

Do not speak of the sorrow
With dust in her hair,
Or bits of dust in eyes
A chance wind blows there.
The sorrow that I speak of
Is dusted with despair.

Voices of muted trumpet,
Cold brass in warm air.
Bitter television blurred
By sound that shimmers—
Where?

build immediately on his achievement in verse. Often in desperate need of money as he continued to try to live by his writing, he turned his attention in the next decade mainly to fiction, with a novel and a collection of stories, and to drama, including a half dozen plays written and produced either on Broadway or semiprofessionally at the Karamu Playhouse in Cleveland. His publication of verse dwindled. *The Dream Keeper* (Knopf, 1934) comprised a selection of already published poems intended mainly for youths; the pamphlet *A New Song* (International Workers Order, 1938) brought together a number of his most radical pieces.

In spite of his radical writing, antithetical to the blues, Hughes continued to believe in the centrality of the latter, although not many black poets, even among his many admirers, followed his lead closely (he and Richard Wright, however, collaborated on one blues). With the onset of the war, the heyday of Hughes's radicalism passed. In the forties, M. Margaret Anderson's centrist journal, *Common Ground,* published more of his poems than did any other single magazine. When Knopf brought out his *Shakespeare in Harlem* in 1942, the book was saturated with the blues, in which Hughes had grown expert. Whether he had grown in other ways as a poet was less clear,

Mother to Son

Well, son, I'll tell you:
Life for me ain't been no crystal stair.
It's had tacks in it,
And splinters,
And boards torn up,
And places with no carpet on the floor—
Bare.
But all the time
I'se been climbin' on,
And reachin' landin's,
And turnin' corners,
And sometimes goin' in the dark
Where they ain't been no light.
So boy, don't you turn back.
Don't you set down on the steps
'Cause you finds it's kinder hard.
Don't you fall now—
For I'se still goin', honey,
I'se still climbin',
And life for me ain't been no crystal stair.

as his main creative effort became the development of his highly successful Jesse B. Semple, or "Simple," prose stories in his weekly column in the black Chicago *Defender.* The question seemed fair again with the appearance of *Fields of Wonder* (Knopf, 1947), a collection mainly of "pure" lyrics that added little to Hughes's reputation. He took up the blues influence again in *One Way-Ticket* (Knopf, 1949), where he offered one of his more inspired recent personae, Alberta K. Johnson, in the "Madam to You" suite of a dozen satirical pieces.

His major poetic achievement since the 1920s, however, came with *Montage of a Dream Deferred* (Henry Holt, 1951). *Montage* is consciously a portrait of Harlem. Hughes also hoped that it would be seen as one long, fragmented poem representing the variety of circumstance and humanity that make up black America. The collection had surged from him in response to a commitment he made early in the mid-forties to Harlem (which he had first seen in 1921), to live there for the rest of his life as its *griot.* (By the early 1960s Hughes would claim proudly that he alone of all prominent black writers still lived squarely in the middle of a typical black community, the others having fled for their lives.) In this volume, as in *Fine Clothes to the Jew,* Hughes took his cultural and poetic cues from the music of black America, which he continued to see as the infallible guide to the race. In this case, the music was the recent evolution of blues and jazz

The wife of an evicted sharecropper.

into the entropic tendencies of "be-bop" and the early manifestations of "progressive" jazz. To Hughes, the new music both reflected and prophesied the realities of a community often said to be "in transition" (in the euphemistic jargon of sociology) but in reality headed, in some respects, toward Armageddon.

"This poem on contemporary Harlem," he wrote in a prefatory note to the book, "like be-bop, is marked by conflicting changes, sudden nuances, sharp and impudent interjections, broken rhythms, and passages sometimes in the manner of the jam session, sometimes the popular song, punctuated by the riffs, runs, breaks, and disc-tortions of the music of a community in transition."

Good morning, daddy!
Ain't you heard
The boogie-woogie rumble
Of a dream deferred?

Listen closely:
You'll hear their feet
Beating out and beating out a—

You think
It's a happy beat?

Listen to it closely:
Ain't you heard
something underneath
like a—

What did I say?

Sure,
I'm happy!
Take it away!

Hey, pop!
Re-bop!
Mop!

Y-e-a-h!

("Dream Boogie," *SP,* 221)

From his townhouse at 20 East 127th Street, not far from the steamy intersection of Lenox Avenue and 125th Street, Hughes listened to the rising rhetoric of integration emanating from afar, looked out on the detritus of cracked promises and broken dreams, and warned of a coming disintegration.

What happens to a dream deferred?

Does it dry up
like a raisin in the sun?
Or fester like a sore—
And then run?
Does it stink like rotten meat?
Or crust and sugar over—
Like a syrupy sweet?

Maybe it just sags
Like a heavy load.

Or does it explode?

("Harlem," *SP,* 268)

About a decade after the appearance of *Montage of a Dream Deferred,* years in which Hughes enjoyed more material suc-

At a revival meeting.

Fire,
Fire, Lord!
Fire gonna burn ma soul!

I ain't been good,
I ain't been clean—
I been stinkin', low-down mean.

Fire,
Fire, Lord!
Fire gonna burn ma soul!

—From "Fire"

cess as a writer than at any previous time in his life, came his last major poem, the book-length *Ask Your Mama* (Knopf, 1961). If integration had finally come to the United States, there seemed a fatal quality to the black world's lurch into its prescribed, whitened future. The two cultures seemed destined to integrate by collision. A note before *Ask Your Mama* (the title is taken from a key phrase in the Afro-American tradition of ritualized, therapeutic insult called the "dozens") announced

You've taken my blues and gone—
You sing 'em on Broadway
And you sing 'em in the Hollywood Bowl,
And you mixed 'em up with symphonies
And you fixed 'em
So they don't sound like me. . . .

But someday somebody'll
Stand up and talk about me,
And write about me—
Black and beautiful—
And sing about me,
And put on plays about me!
I reckon it'll be
Me myself!

Yes, it'll be me.

—From "Note on Commercial Theatre"

that the "Hesitation Blues" is "the leit motif for this poem. In and around it, along with the other recognizable melodies employed, there is room for spontaneous jazz improvisation, particularly between verses, where the voice pauses." Throughout the twelve-part poem are instructions for accompanying music, from lieder on the piano to "very modern jazz burning in the air eerie like a neon swamp-fire cooled by dry ice until suddenly there is a single ear-piercing flute call." At the end of the work, as if in genially insulting parody of T. S. Eliot's impedimenta in *The Waste Land,* come "LINER NOTES: *For the Poetically Unhep."* The prevailing drive of the poem is varied—that of the old blues and the be-bop of the forties, as well as the still greater complication of "progressive" jazz; the mood is both retrospective of dreams deferred and a token of chaos come:

IN THE
IN THE QUARTER
IN THE QUARTER OF THE NEGROES
WHERE THE DOORS ARE DOORS OF PAPER
DUST OF DINGY ATOMS
BLOWS A SCRATCHY SOUND.
AMORPHOUS JACK-O'-LANTERNS CAPER
AND THE WIND WON'T WAIT FOR MIDNIGHT
FOR FUN TO BLOW DOORS DOWN.

BY THE RIVER AND THE RAILROAD
WITH FLUID FAR-OFF GOING
BOUNDARIES BIND UNBINDING
A WHIRL OF WHISTLES BLOWING
NO TRAINS OR STEAMBOATS GOING—
YET LEONTYNE'S UNPACKING.

IN THE QUARTER OF THE NEGROES
WHERE THE DOORKNOB LETS IN LIEDER
MORE THAN GERMAN EVER BORE,
HER YESTERDAY PAST GRANDPA—
NOT OF HER OWN DOING—
IN A POT OF COLLARD GREENS
IS GENTLY STEWING . . .

(3–4)

Ask Your Mama went largely unnoticed. For the major critical journals, Langston Hughes was passé as a poet. On the front page of the *New York Times Book Review,* the black essayist and fiction writer James Baldwin had delivered a crushing assessment of Hughes's career in poetry. "Every time I read Langston Hughes," Baldwin began, "I am amazed all over again by his genuine gifts—and depressed that he has done so little with them" (March 29, 1959). The occasion was the appearance of

Hughes's *Selected Poems* in 1959. (Curiously, in this act Baldwin had behaved not unlike William Carlos Williams, the modernist master whose work most closely resembles that of Carl Sandburg. In 1951, writing in *Poetry* magazine, Williams had savaged Sandburg's *Collected Poems* on its appearance.)

By the end of his career, even as election to the National Institute of Arts and Letters (the waiting room outside the American Academy) and the awarding of the annual Spingarn Medal of the N.A.A.C.P. brought Hughes his greatest public honors, he was calling himself, self-deprecatingly and on cue from one of his critics, a "documentary" poet. Certainly he had seemed for several years a sometime poet, with the great volume of his creativity expressed in other genres—in plays, gospel and more conventional musicals, children's books, an institutional history, libretti for operas and cantatas, and other literary schemes—appearing to confirm his evolution within his lifetime from a brave new poet into a mere man of letters. "Chesterton in burnt cork," an English newspaper sneered.[24]

Whatever the critics had written, however, by this time Hughes had achieved his greatest goal; without a doubt, no poet was held in higher esteem by black Americans. Even the cultural nationalists of the 1960s, inquisitional in their zeal, found texts for the militant times in many of his poems. But Hughes's achievement almost certainly went further. To judge him accurately one must measure him both in a purely American context, as a voice echoing in the dank hold of the national slaveship, and against the background of international cultural change in the twentieth century. By the age of twenty-one, driven by his private gift and by the exigencies of race in North America, he was already toward the front of an international advance guard of writers, largely from the yet unspoken world outside Europe and North America, that would include Pablo Neruda, of Chile; the young Jorge Luis Borges, of Argentina; Federico García Lorca, of Spain; Léopold Sédar Senghor, of Senegal; Jacques Roumain, of Haiti; Aimé Césaire, of Martinique; Léon Damas, of French Guiana; and Nicolás Guillén, of Cuba. Collectively, their aim was to develop, even as they composed in the languages of Europe and faced the challenge of Modernism, an aesthetic tied to a sense of myth, geography, history, and culture that was truly indigenous to their countries, rather than merely reflective of European trends, whether conservative or avant-garde.

While virtually all these other writers, although often nationalistic, were still grappling uncertainly with the legacy of racism and exploitation in their countries, Hughes had begun to merge his Whitman-like love of American ideals with a search for a racial song, a merging that would reflect the actuality of North

American culture rather than its archaic prejudices. Hughes must be judged with reference to painters such as Diego Rivera, David Siquieros, and José Orozco, who would found a revolution in the art of Mexico by venerating its long-despised Indian past, and to a poet like García Lorca (who had written at least one poem about Harlem), with his revolutionary emphasis on gypsy art and culture. Appearing in *Contemporáneos* magazine (1928–31), the most controversial journal of culture in Mexico, various translations of his poetry exemplified the nationalist and folk expression that many Mexicans considered vital to the future of their art. In his *Nostalgia of Death,* the relatively conservative Xavier Villaurrutia dedicated his "North Carolina Blues" to Hughes; Carlos Pellicer, among the most honored of nationalist Mexican writers, would remember the Afro-American writer as a personal friend and an inspiration. In 1931, Borges translated and published "The Negro Speaks of Rivers"; the same year, Roumain of Haiti wrote a poem in homage to Hughes, and Guillén of Cuba published testimony that his major breakthrough as a poet had come because of Hughes and the blues. Strongly internationalist, Hughes (who spoke French and Spanish) himself translated and published, or attempted to publish, works by Mexican, Cuban, Chilean, Haitian, and Spanish writers, and he translated and published books by Guillén, Roumain, García Lorca, and Gabriela Mistral of Chile.

More than any other poetry, his poems of racial pride in the 1920s had inspired black writers in Cuba, Haiti, Martinique, Guadeloupe, and the rest of the Caribbean. A visit to Cuba in 1930 had led to a revolution in the art of Cuba's future national poet, Nicolás Guillén. Heeding Hughes's direct advice that he should employ in his poetry the most popular Afro-Cuban song and dance form, the *son,* within six weeks Guillén had published in the Havana newspaper *El Diario de la Marina* the eight landmark poems of *Motivos de Son,* to be followed by *Sóngoro Cosongo* and other volumes that would make him the most radical and probably the finest poet in the Caribbean. The racial spirit of the Harlem Renaissance, of which Hughes's poetry was quintessential, had suffused the journal *La Revue du Monde Noir,* founded by blacks in Paris in 1931; his poems appeared in several numbers. In a successor and more radical journal, *Légitime Défense,* Hughes and Claude McKay were hailed as "les deux poètes noirs révolutionnaires" who most inspired black pride.[25] In 1935, young Senghor, Césaire, and Damas, who would become the leading French-speaking black poets, endorsed this view of Hughes in founding their newspaper *L'Étudiant Noir.* They would not hesitate to credit him as the supreme influence, among poets, in the formation of the

"Red Jackson—Harlem Gang Leader" by Gordon Parks.

Harlem

What happens to a dream deferred?

Does it dry up
like a raisin in the sun?
Or fester like a sore—
And then run?
Does it stink like rotten meat?
Or crust and sugar over—
like a syrupy sweet?

Maybe it just sags
like a heavy load.

Or does it explode?

concept of *négritude,* by which these and other black writers attempted to develop an aesthetic suffused by an African sensibility. In 1966 in Dakar, Senegal, at the First World Festival of Negro Arts, Senghor (then president of the republic) would pay tribute to Hughes as the greatest single figure in the history of black poetry. And young African writers "followed him about the city and haunted his hotel," according to a New York *Times* reporter, "the way American youngsters dog favorite baseball players" (April 24, 1966).

To the end of his life, Hughes saw no irreconcilable conflict between his love of country and his devotion to his race, or between racial themes and the universal goals of the writer. In his main address at Dakar, one of the last of his life, composed against the backdrop of racial turmoil in the United States, he quietly lamented the fact that "the most talented of the young Negro writers have become America's prophets of doom, black ravens cawing over carrion." The racial and the universal were both authentic, and were linked. *Négritude* and Afro-American "soul" were inescapably related. The latter, Hughes argued, was "a synthesis of the essence of Negro folk art redistilled—particularly the old music and its flavor, the ancient beat out of Africa, the folk rhymes and Ashanti stories. . . . *Soul* is contemporary Harlem's *negritude,* revealing to the Negro people and the world the beauty within themselves." As for the universal principles behind art: the prime function of all creative writing is "to affirm life, to yeah-say the excitement of living in relation to the vast rhythms of the universe of which we are a part, to

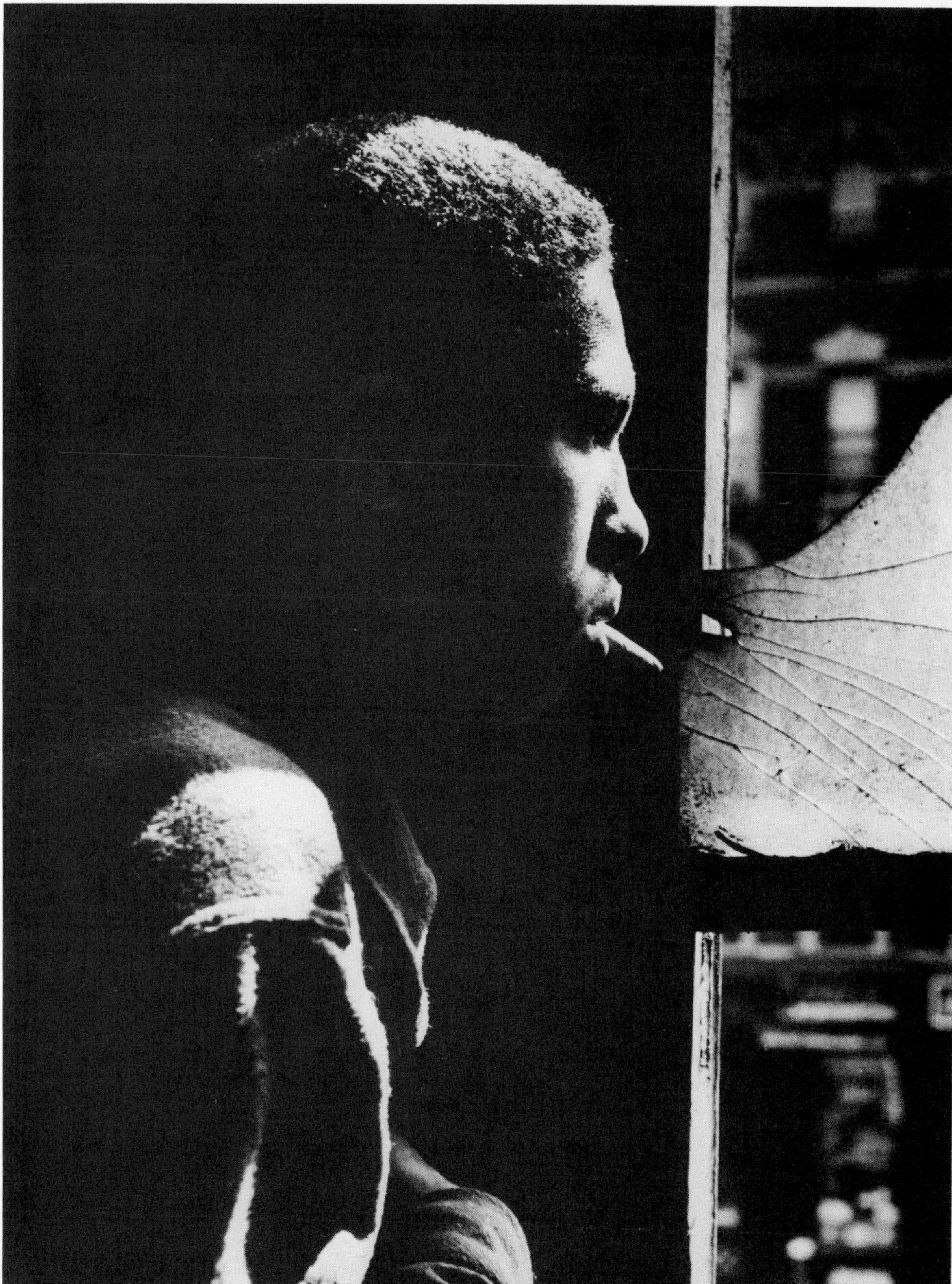

Langston Hughes providing autographs for young admirers.

untie the riddles of the gutter in order to closer tie the knot between man and God."[26]

To respect what Hughes has accomplished as a poet one must first do what has been difficult for many blacks, as well as for whites: one must respect his love of his people, if one cannot actually respect and love the people themselves. Second, one must accept the aesthetic that emerged from his desire to say little that his people, treated so shabbily by history and the master culture, could not understand and, understanding, accept. Fearing abstruseness and confabulation, because they were barriers between himself and his primary audience, he fashioned an aesthetic of simplicity born out of the speech, music, and actual social condition of his people.

On March 1, 1927, in the midst of enduring some of the most violent reviews ever visited on an American poet for *Fine*

Consider me,
A colored boy,
Once sixteen,
Once five, once three,
Once nobody,
Now me.
Before me
Papa, mama,
Grandpa, grandma,
So on back
To original
Pa.

(A capital letter there,
He
Being Mystery.)

Consider me,
Colored boy,
Downtown at eight,
Sometimes working late,
Overtime pay
To sport away,
Or save,
Or give my Sugar
For the things
She needs. . . .

Consider me,
Descended also
From the
Mystery.

—From "Consider Me"

Clothes to the Jew, Hughes had stated the central doctrine of his art. "I believe," he told a little gathering, "that poetry should be direct, comprehensible and the epitome of simplicity."[27] Hughes understood that simplicity, no less than the baroque or the rococo or the Modern, has its discipline and its standards, just as the black race, no less than the white, has its humanity and its great art. He knew and drew strength from the fact that he and his blacks were not less but perhaps *more* American than their enemies. Fittingly, he made his little speech in the house of his poetical grandfather—on a lecture at the invitation of the Walt Whitman Foundation at the poet's old home on Mickle Street in Camden, New Jersey. From which place Hughes, in the middle of his troubles, sent to a close friend a postcard bearing a brief but flashing line from Whitman's "Song of the Open Road": "All seems beautiful to me."[28]

[Draft 3]

ARRIVAL AT SANTOS

Here is a coast; here is a harbor;
here, after a meagre diet of horizons, is some scenery:
impractically-shaped, and, who knows? self-pitying, mountains
sad and harsh beneath their ~~[illegible]~~ frivolous greenery,

with a little church on top of one. And some warehouses,
some of them painted a ~~[illegible]~~ feeble pink, or blue,
and some tall, ~~[illegible]~~ uncertain palms. Oh tourist,
is this ~~[illegible]~~ how this country is going to answer you

and your ~~[illegible]~~ immodest demands for a different world,
and a better life, and complete comprehension
of both at last, and immediately,
after eighteen days of suspension?

Finish your ~~[illegible]~~ breakfast. The tender is coming,
a strange and ancient craft, flying a strange and brilliant rag
So that's the flag. I never saw it before.
I somehow never thought of there being a flag,

but of course there was, all along. And coins, I presume,
and paper money; they remain to be seen.
And ~~[illegible]~~ gingerly now we climb down the ladder backwards,
myself and a fellow-passenger named Miss Breen,

ELIZABETH BISHOP

HELEN MCNEIL

For Elizabeth Bishop, poetry began in observation. Writing about another great observer, Charles Darwin, Bishop found that

> Dreams, works of art, (some) glimpses of the always-more-successful surrealism of everyday life, unexpected moments of empathy (is it?), catch a peripheral vision of whatever it is one can never really see full-face but that seems enormously important. . . . What one seems to want in art, in experiencing it, is the same thing that is necessary for its creation, a self-forgetful, perfectly useless concentration.[1]

Art, then, gives over the artist's discoveries intact to the reader, who can subsequently have the same essential but curiously "self-forgetful" experience. This is at once a very modest and a very ambitious definition of the work of the poem; art doesn't transform, but it yields some immensely important knowledge that is not available through will. For Bishop, the most important prerequisite for all discovery is self-forgetfulness, a giving-over of oneself to whatever is glimpsed or half-seen. Poetry requires this essential self-forgetfulness. Scientific observation and the surreal insights of dream and the uncanny also need a setting-aside of self. Bishop marks the similarity of process and grants these different modes of seeing equal weight.

By age and by stylistic affinity, Bishop was part of the generation of American poets who succeeded Eliot, Pound, Moore, Williams, and Stevens. She began to publish in 1935, shortly after her graduation from Vassar College, and her first collection, *North & South* (1946), was well received by the same journals that were reviewing Robert Lowell's *Lord Weary's Castle* (1944, 1946) and Randall Jarrell's *Little Friend, Little Friend* (1945). Yet Bishop's poetry of observation has always eluded precise placement within that modernist project to which it now seems so central.

Bishop exhibits many resemblances, none of them definitive, to her modernist contemporaries. Her discoveries, as the Darwin letter makes clear, recall both surrealism and its ostensible

Elizabeth Bishop,
age twelve.

Wrote poetry from the age of eight. Literary career started at the age of twelve with a prize, a $5.00 gold piece, awarded by the American Legion for an essay on AMERICANISM. This has vanished, but the first sentence, something about "From the icy regions of the frozen north to the waving palm trees of the burning south . . ." seems to have been prophetic, indicating directions taken later by both life and work.

—From an unpublished autobiographical sketch

opposite, the attentive, "scientific," objectivist gaze of Williams. Bishop's poetic voice usually does not distinguish itself from the voice of the woman Elizabeth Bishop. Yet, although we may, as readers, well discover our own selves represented through the experiences her poems depict, Bishop is not a poet of self and self-representation like Theodore Roethke, Sylvia Plath or the later Lowell; the autobiographical in Bishop tends to be submerged or displaced until late in her career. Like Marianne Moore, her mentor and friend, Bishop can use formal beauty as part of an argument for order; and like Moore, she opened her poems to the disordered and the banal. However, Moore's disorder tends to be geological or allusive, her banality a deliberate use of modern commercial or conventional language. Bishop's disorder is emotional, her banality that of a deliberately adopted inconsequentiality. Bishop's lifelong attention to the phenomenology of perception is comparable to that of Stevens, whose work she admired, but the role of perception in her work is different. Her attitude is curiously antimodernist, perhaps more like that of Frost in its consistently ethical implications.

Bishop's gaze was appreciated from the start; indeed, it may have been overappreciated, since her poetry was praised into a pigeonhole as a typically female art of the miniature.[2] The ethical goals and the kinds of knowledge shown by Bishop's poetry are, however, only now becoming clear. By consistently endowing the gaze at ordinariness with value, and by letting the object of her gaze act out its unexpectedness in her poetry, Bishop has in fact provided a way for the image-dominated poetic of this century to regain the moral and epistemological authority usually associated with an earlier age. To look was for Bishop to act, and acts for her carried moral weight. Bishop's modernist "look" leads to much older kinds of knowledge, to lessons concerning the integrity of all life and the wisdom to be gained by looking steadily at it. To read her poetry is to experience that skilled wisdom.

As a good modernist, however, Bishop lets the reader arrive at his or her own conclusions by experiencing the act of the poem. Didactic address isn't an important element in Bishop's rhetorical armory, nor does she seduce the reader into agreement by the intimate second-person address of so much American poetry of the 1970s. Bishop's "self" seems most powerfully present in her poems as the formal intelligence shaping them, and her lyric "I" works as our guide or as the instance of the questioner. Thus in "The Fish" (1946) a first-person speaker, who is not distinguished from Bishop herself, gazes for a long time at a "tremendous" old fish she has happened to catch:

He hung a grunting weight,
battered and venerable
and homely. Here and there
his brown skin hung in strips
like ancient wallpaper.[3]

This is the classic fish story of the big one that got away, only with the macho moral reversed: Bishop lets it get away. Her generous "victory" has been to give this old man of the sea that victory which is survival. The fish is weird, uncanny, almost an object, the irises of his eyes seeming "backed and packed / with tarnished tinfoil." By turning his yellow eyes away when Bishop looks into them, the fish places himself beyond any Romantic identification. Nonetheless he is alive and he deserves life. Just when the impact of the fish's primordial right to survive strikes the reader, the poem explodes with its own epiphanic recognition of ordinary natural splendor:

. . . everything
was rainbow, rainbow, rainbow!
And I let the fish go.

Bishop's poetry always assumes this self-forgetful, revelatory gaze. Upon this base it develops three major areas of investigation to which Bishop addressed her poetry throughout her career: lyric meditation, the uncanny, and homelessness. I shall discuss her manner of meditation in the early poem "The Map," and proceed through "At the Fishhouses" to the late "Poem" (1976). Then I shall return to trace the uncanny in Bishop, as her gaze rests on the part-objects of her early poetry, and turns to the banal uncanny in her late work. Finally I shall treat homelessness, a condition of Bishop's orphaned childhood and later life which she transformed into a mode of knowledge. In this last context we shall return to the question of "placing" Bishop.

The meditative line of English lyric which runs from George Herbert to Wordsworth and across to the Americans Emerson and Dickinson is continued and deepened by Elizabeth Bishop's poetry. Bishop's half-forgetful moments of observation are her equivalent to Wordsworth's half-remembered moments of charity by which the soul is made whole in "The Old Cumberland Beggar" and "Tintern Abbey." Bishop is a poet of profound, intent investigation, a prime bearer of that characteristically "Northern," Protestant, highly detailed sensibility whose female line has also produced Emily Dickinson and Marianne Moore.

From "In the Village"

A scream, the echo of a scream, hangs over that Nova Scotian village. No one hears it; it hangs there forever, a slight stain in those pure blue skies, skies that travelers compare to those of Switzerland, too dark, too blue, so that they seem to keep on darkening a little more around the horizon—or is it around the rims of the eyes?—the color of the cloud of bloom on the elm trees, the violet on the fields of oats; something darkening over the woods and waters as well as the sky. The scream hangs like that, unheard, in memory—in the past, in the present, and those years between. It was not even loud to begin with, perhaps. It just came there to live, forever—not loud, just alive forever. Its pitch would be the pitch of my village. Flick the lightning rod on top of the church steeple with your fingernail and you will hear it.

When Bishop blurs the margins of self at moments like the conclusion of "The Fish," she is not so much engaging in a Whitmanesque absorption of world into ego as giving permission for the object of her gaze to become itself a subject. Hence, perhaps, the sense of leisure in Bishop's poetry. Her respect for the object gives it the space to display its uncanny otherness, different yet always recognizable. Nature, art, dreams, and other people are all teachers for Bishop, but never a priori. Wisdom is gained as a consequence of act, not as a faculty to be absorbed from the object being contemplated. Because of this post-Wordsworthian, characteristically American, stress on process, Bishop's poetry isn't quite part of the emblem tradition, despite her stress on the tutelary image.

Bishop's earliest poetic affinity was with the metaphysical poet George Herbert, whose meditative lyrics she discovered at fourteen. Herbert remained a source for Bishop all her life, his dream-poem "Love-unknown" probably providing the closest model for Bishop's celebratory investigations.[4] Herbert's poetry, like that of John Donne and Richard Crashaw (whose bizarre conceits resemble some of Bishop's metaphors), formed part of the new, antiromantic, modernist canon of English poetry that T. S. Eliot set forth in *The Sacred Wood, For Launcelot Andrewes,* and other critical essays which soon became academic orthodoxy. Bishop did not, however, depend upon Eliot to alert her to the metaphysicals. Instead, her own natural connection of sensuous imagery and metaphysical questioning make her work a kind of missing modernist link with meditative tradition. In this role Bishop resembles Gerard Manley Hopkins, another of her early, long-term favorites, who became a kind of influence-in-retrospect in the critical reconstruction of modernist origins.[5]

In her earlier poems Bishop often directs gaze by inventing its object, generally something unusual, which may be variously a borderline object (mannequin, artwork, anthropomorphized machine, etc.), an emblem, a dream-image, a symbolic figure ("The Man-Moth" or the Stevensian tramp in "Anaphora"), or a surreal *objet trouvé.* As Bishop grew older, however, she took greater risks; she makes us feel it is absolutely essential to probe the unsettling ordinariness of an ill-tended gas station, or to consider what happens when a moose crosses a road.

"The Map," the opening poem of *North & South,* was written when Bishop was in her early twenties, but it sets out many of the issues that have dominated her poetry from beginning to end. Bishop's technique is to present her investigation as if it were the idle gaze of a flaneur, wandering felicitously across a map. A map is, however, an overdetermined object, since it is a system of both representation and interpretation:

Land lies in water; it is shadowed green.
Shadows, or are they shallows, at its edges
showing the line of long sea-weeded ledges
where weeds hang to the simple blue from green.

Solid land, then, is seen set upon the surrounding water; what it displays—green shadows—and what those shadows represent converge pleasantly, like the punning words that denote them. Is one seeing deep shadows? or their connotative opposite, mere shallows? Borderlines between an object and what it signifies are blurred, and the blurring permits a shift of perspective by which we are taken underwater, where weeds hang from sea ledges. The closed a-b-b-a rhyme of the quatrain and the numerous susurrating half-rhymes and repetitions combine with an underlying pentameter which notably slows near the line-ends to produce a wave of lyric whose soothing rhythm continues unsettlingly, even when its sense is broken in the next line: "Or does the land lean down to lift the sea from under . . ." It is just as likely that this appearance signifies the opposite of what we have been told: land, not sea, is the basis, raising the sea from beneath. Yet our pleasure is, if anything, heightened by semiological inversion: "We can stroke these lovely bays."

In its stress upon image and its fascination with borderline states, "The Map," like many poems in *North & South,* looks back to the Imagism of H.D. and across to the transformations of Stevens's *Ideas of Order.* It is almost too well resolved a poem, yet the soothing aesthetic of its conclusion heralds one of Bishop's sternest meditations: "More delicate than the historian's are the mapmaker's colors." Time, and fear of its passing, are deep themes of pure lyric, since mutability destroys the eternal present of song. The extent to which time is seen as enemy may even mark the boundary between the lyric and the philosophical or meditative poem. If, as Bishop concludes, the representation of space is more pleasurable than the representation of time, then we may safely look to Bishop's pleasure-imagery of space and place as a way of addressing their opposite, fear of time's works. To the extent to which Bishop accepts time as a source of knowledge as well as of pain, she writes meditatively. However, with the exception of the early, Herbertian "The Weed," these meditations are not about her own death, but about "look" and its consequence, knowledge.

In "At the Fishhouses," from Bishop's second collection *Poems: North & South—A Cold Spring* (1955), Bishop notices how "an old man sits netting" by the sea. The net is "almost invisible," while a completely invisible but overwhelming

Elizabeth Bishop (front row, center) as editor in chief of the 1934 Vassarion.

codfish stench pervades the scene. Silvery, scale-covered benches turn transparent as Bishop looks, while the sea, at first "opaque," begins to invert itself under the pressure of her meditative gaze:

> All is silver: the heavy surface of the sea,
> swelling slowly as if considering spilling over,
> is opaque, but the silver of the benches,
> the lobster pots, and masts, scattered
> among the wild jagged rocks,
> is of an apparent translucence. . . .

In the Bishop poem, the image is less "an intellectual and emotional complex in an instant of time," as Pound put it in "Some Don'ts by an Imagiste," and more an encounter with an actuality. That actuality displays itself by the reversal of assumptions. Bishop's images are complex and unexpected because to her the world's detailed resistance to idealization provides a model (Bishop often writes "equivalent") for the mind's equally complex realization that knowledge involves accepting a lack of control; we cannot control the flow of thought and thought does not—must not—control the objects of its attention or desire.

Then, in the poem, Bishop looks again, this time into the chill water. Northern water, "bitter / then briny," is the element which is "like what we imagine knowledge to be." Now the water is no longer opaque but "Cold dark deep and absolutely clear." Such water is an "element bearable to no mortal," yet the seals and the fish sport in it. Intensely cold, it feels paradoxically "burning" to the touch and "bitter, yet briny" to the taste; it is of the world and above it at once. The list of attributes accelerates: "Dark, salt, clear, moving, utterly free," watery knowledge wells out from our cold mother, the earth,

> . . . derived from the rocky breasts
> forever, flowing and drawn, and since
> our knowledge is historical, flowing, and flown.

Bishop uses water to represent temporal knowledge to show that knowledge-in-time is not merely a track (indeed it is trackless); that you can believe in the value of baptizing yourself into it by total immersion; that it is transparent; and that it is the bitter, necessary milk of our earthly nurturance: "Our knowledge is historical."

"At the Fishhouses" is, typically for Bishop, set in a present tense punctuated by necessary memory. Yet even the stillest Bishop landscapes or place-pictures are overlaid by layers of time. "The Bight," a descriptive picture of a harbor's flotsam and jetsam, is, as Bishop notes in her half-title, a birthday poem. Poems from Bishop's third, most topographical collection, *Questions of Travel* (1965), depict the effects of time past, as in "Cape Breton," time present, as in "Arrival at Santos," or a prophetic time to come, as in "Brazil, January 1, 1502."

In "Poem," one of the fullest meditative statements of her aesthetic, Bishop draws wisdom from a great-uncle's amateur landscape painting. Uncherished but (terms that are central to Bishop) "useless and free," the oil painting is "About the size of an old-style dollar bill," although it expresses another register of value. The uncle's painting is a kind of miniature window into the past. Carefully looking in, Bishop sees

> Up closer, a wild iris, white and yellow,
> fresh-squiggled from the tube.
> The air is fresh and cold; early spring
> clear as gray glass; a half inch of blue sky
> below the steel-gray storm-clouds.
> (They were the artist's specialty.)

Petropolis was the favorite place of Pedro II, the last emperor, & Therezopolis, about 20 miles away, the favorite place of his wife, Teresa. —Maybe they didn't get along. I don't know.

—From a postcard Bishop sent to Dr. Anny Baumann

Self-referentially entitled "Poem," since it is about making, this poem shows Bishop focusing on the point where the art object starts to generate reality by its act of depiction, while still calling attention to itself as object; by virtue of their lack of mimetic skill, amateur works of art inevitably present that self-referentiality that modernist and post-modernist aesthetics must achieve through conscious foregrounding of the art process.

The close-focus Northern landscape of "Poem" looks like the objectivism of William Carlos Williams's "Spring and All" or "The Red Wheelbarrow," but it is actually a rebuff to unmediated presentation of the object. For Bishop, an organizing vision—her own or someone else's—must intervene explicitly to generate the life the poem investigates. Acts of representation —literally, re-presentation—are what the poem depends upon for its knowledge.

The autobiographical speaker in "Poem" suddenly realizes, with a colloquial shock, that the painting is depicting the Nova Scotia landscape of her long-ago childhood:

> Heavens, I recognize the place, I know it!
> It's behind—I can almost remember the farmer's name.
> His barn backed on that meadow. There it is,
> Titanium white, one dab.

The painted "copy" becomes a precious vision (or, as Bishop half-deprecatingly corrects herself, a "look") into "life and the memory of it"; the mimetic mirror is also a door. She sees through the poem, not into an eternal world of art, but into the past. She reexperiences the source of her own memory, at first indirectly, and then, through this stimulus, directly. This kind of temporally doubled postsurreal perception also characterizes the opening chapters of Luis Buñuel's autobiography *My Last Breath*:[6] a major basis of the bizarre vividness of the present is memory, so that what is most deeply seen is being seen twice, uncannily *déjà-vu.*

Bishop's vision is meant to be shared; the reader experiences the speaker's pleasurable jolt in "Poem" when she recognizes that someone else had seen, and been moved by, what she herself once saw and almost forgot forever. Nor is vision transcendent for Bishop; rather, it concentrates and intensifies what might otherwise have been lost. Inside the great-uncle's picture is another picture of love. "The little that we get for free" is "live" and "touching in detail," as in Dutch landscape painting. The free gift will suffice, even if Bishop concludes that it is

> Not much.
> About the size of our abidance
> along with theirs: the munching cows,
> the iris, crisp and shivering, the water
> still standing from spring freshets,
> the yet-to-be-dismantled elms, the geese.

All gifts and all conclusions are provisional, "to-be-dismantled."

Beginning in the 1930s, Bishop worked out her own, "Northern," skeptical version of surrealism.[7] If her poetry now and then looks like that American poetry of the 1970s which has taken on Latin-American surrealism, that is because Bishop was there first time round in the 1930s and then, living in Brazil, came to know Latin-American poetry at first hand.[8] Bishop certainly felt close to surrealist art and poetry. She translated four poems by Max Jacob. She liked Joseph Cornell's surreal boxes so much that she made at least one herself, and she translated "Objects and Apparitions," Octavio Paz's poem about Cornell.[9] In her poem "Cirque d'Hiver" she saw a horse whose "mane and tail are straight from Chirico." Bishop's many surreal dream-poems such as "Some Dreams They Forgot," "Love Lies Sleeping," "Sleeping on the Ceiling," "A Summer's Dream," "Sunday 4 A.M.," and "Sleeping Standing Up" welcome the hypnogogic state and what "Sleeping Standing Up" calls "the armored cars of dreams." For Bishop, dream facilitates and reveals, but its recognitions are incomplete. In "Sleeping Standing Up," the dream machine has "tracked" its desires, crushing some in the process, but it has never quite "found out where the cottage was."

In the dialogue-poem "The Monument," her most sustained meditation on surrealism, Bishop enlarged Max Ernst's series of *frottages* from *Histoires Naturelles* (1926) to make a Frankenstein's monster of signification in which the shoddy decorations of a "temple of crates" reveal it to be a signifying object:

> The monument's an object, yet those decorations,
> carelessly nailed, looking like nothing at all,
> give it away as having life, and wishing;
> wanting to be a monument, to cherish something.
> The crudest scroll-work says "commemorate."

In *frottage,* images are created by pressing an inked object against paper. Thus an image of "earth" or "eye" bears the imprint of the wood grain in the block of wood that made it. While signifying, say, earth, it also recalls the technique and materials of its own creation. Bishop brings Romantic theory of origin to bear upon her monument, as she uses pathetic fallacy to attribute desire to a wooden structure; her own desire may thus be expressed in displaced form. Perhaps a signifying structure also has an inside and an outside, like the body. Certainly "it can shelter," like a house. Whatever meanings it contains or doesn't contain, the monument still remains "all of wood," its powers of signification eerily expanding. "Watch this closely," Bishop warns about this object which, like her own poem, travels across barriers between object and signification.

Yet Bishop is not a true surrealist, disrupting bourgeois rationalism with the subversive irrational of dream and fantasy.

The equanimity with which she treats dream material points rather to an integration of subjective and objective observation. Also, Bishop's poems have a distinct closure, even if their thematics are often those of incompletion. The Bishop poem may disguise its internal route by leisurely examination or by effects of diction such as colloquial exclamations, but the route is there. By contrast, as Mary Ann Caws has noted,[10] the surreal poem is an act of passage, ideally without origin or end. The intelligence of the surrealist poem is an intelligence always in transit.

A Bishopesque attention to the object may, however, be a quality more surreal than histories such as André Breton's *Le Surréalisme et la peinture* (1926–27) might lead one to conclude. In Breton's own poem "Fata Morgana," for example,

> La petite place qui fuit entourée d'arbres qui diffèrent
> imperceptiblement de tous les autres
> Existe pour que nous la traversons sous tel angle dans la vraie
> vie
> Le ruisseau en cette boucle même comme en nulle autre de tous
> les ruisseaux
> Est maître d'un secret qu'il ne peut faire nôtre à la volée
>
> (The little square fleeing, surrounded by trees imperceptibly
> different from all others
> Exists for us to cross it at a certain angle in real life
> The stream in this very curve as in no other among the streams
> Has hold of a secret which it can't reveal to us at will)

For the Anglophone reader, Breton's insistence upon the particular object seen from a distinct perspective at a moment in "real life" inevitably recalls Williams and—were the object more elaborated—Marianne Moore. The similarity is close enough to permit speculation that Bishop may have derived her intent gaze equally from French and Anglophone sources. Yet Bishop, like Moore and Williams, concentrates on one object or scene, while Breton sees the scene as a privileged moment, a crossing of a consciousness which will then fly onwards and alight wherever its "internal model" directs it.[11]

Paradoxically, Bishop's poetry readily assimilates the unknown while seeing the domestic or banal as curiously strange.[12] Her poetry is filled with signifying objects, borderline cases between signifier and signified, whose ambiguity she never quite resolves. These surreal effects arise from a cast of mind in Bishop which is also found in surrealist art and poetry, but never defined by the surrealists as a distinct quality. This cast of mind is the Freudian uncanny, which is Bishop's central technique of recognition.

Among Bishop's voyages was a trip up the Amazon River in 1961. This slide of a river port in the interior was taken during that trip.

That golden evening I really wanted to go no farther;
more than anything else I wanted to stay awhile
in that conflux of two great rivers, Tapajós, Amazon,
grandly, silently flowing, flowing east.
Suddenly there'd been houses, people, and lots of mongrel
riverboats skittering back and forth
under a sky of gorgeous, under-lit clouds,
with everything gilded, burnished along one side,
and everything bright, cheerful, casual—or so it looked.
I liked the place; I liked the idea of the place.
Two rivers. Hadn't two rivers sprung
from the Garden of Eden? No, that was four
and they'd diverged. Here only two
and coming together. Even if one were tempted
to literary interpretations
such as: life/death, right/wrong, male/female
—such notions would have resolved, dissolved, straight off
in that watery, dazzling dialectic. . . .

Two rivers full of crazy shipping—people
all apparently changing their minds, embarking,
disembarking, rowing clumsy dories.
(After the Civil War some Southern families
came here; here they could still own slaves.
They left occasional blue eyes, English names,
and *oars.* No other place, no one
on all the Amazon's four thousand miles
does anything but paddle.) . . .

Side-wheelers, countless wobbling dugouts . . .
A cow stood up in one, quite calm,
chewing her cud while being ferried,
tipping, wobbling, somewhere, to be married. . . .

In the blue pharmacy the pharmacist
had hung an empty wasps' nest from a shelf:
small, exquisite, clean matte white,
and hard as stucco. I admired it
so much he gave it to me. . . .

Then—my ship's whistle blew. I couldn't stay.
Back on board, a fellow-passenger, Mr. Swan,
Dutch, the retiring head of Philips Electric,
really a very nice old man,
who wanted to see the Amazon before he died,
asked, "What's that ugly thing?"

—From "Santarém"

As Freud noted in his 1919 essay "The Uncanny,"[13] many of our most frightening and sinister sensations do not arise from the hitherto unknown. Bishop, for example, welcomes the surprising, golden foreign plenitude of "Santarém." The alien, frankly baroque landscape of "too many waterfalls" and "crowded streams" in Bishop's famous poem "Questions of Travel," isn't the place she flees from, as Yeats does in "Sailing to Byzantium," but the goal of her desire. What is most deeply unsettling, for Bishop as for most of us, is something awry in an apparently known place.

In German, "heimlich," meaning homelike, domestic or cozy, also carries the opposite meaning of secret, frightening, sinister, indeed uncanny, which it shares with its negative, "unheimlich." Especially powerful uncanny effects arise, according to Freud, from borderline cases, such as objects that look mechanical but may be alive or vice versa. In his admittedly speculative essay Freud offers only the instance of the automaton in E.T.A. Hoffmann's story "The Sandman," but Bishop's practice suggests wider parameters for the uncanny. Bishop's uncanny takes in objects whose extreme ambiguity makes them both signifiers and things signified. Bishop's poetry is rife with such objects, many of them houses or houselike, from "The Monument" through numerous self-conscious, strategic uses of pathetic fallacy. To take an instance of apparent safety, the overexplicit, explanatory realism of familiar, cheap Bible illustrations in Bishop's poem "Over 2000 Illustrations and a Complete Concordance" comes uncannily to produce "what frightens most of all,"—the empty sepulchre of a meaningless death. In "Faustina, or Rock Roses," a poem about a courtesy visit to a sick old woman, the servant's

> . . . sinister kind face
> presents a cruel black
> coincident conundrum.

Bishop had not entirely succeeded in entering black consciousness in her four early "Songs for a Colored Singer," though her Brazilian poems show sustained empathy for the poor. Here she takes on Faustina's uncanny opacity as signifying either love or its opposite, "the unimaginable nightmare" of sadism. "There is no way of telling." This ending makes Bishop ponder origins, as she asks: "Whence come the petals?" of the rose she has brought.

Bishop was drawn to what might be called part-signifiers, inefficient vehicles of meaning. She wrote often about primitive and "bad" art, both in poems and in her essay "Gregorio

Valdes," and she addressed herself to landscapes of either improbable excess or chilling poverty. She clearly enjoyed the uncanny, the incomplete sensing of a possible origin or a possible meaning, two areas of knowledge inside the seen which she treats as if they were the same thing.

The myth of origin and the myth of meaning may indeed, from an uncanny perspective, be the same thing. For Freud, the apparently contradictory meanings of "heimlich" were resolved when he noted Schelling's dictionary definition of "heimlich" as what "ought to have been hidden but has come to light",[14] namely, the repressed. What is most "heimlich" of all, Freud suggests, is that secret place where we were once at home, the mother's body from which we have been expelled, never to return.

Freud does not seem fully aware of some potential consequences of his speculation. Since all things seen—the female body, houses, and automata in particular, but also material landscape—can generate the uncanny, when they do so they are being read according to their intimate provenance as parts of or equivalencies to the body of the mother. For our society, that body in turn hides the secret of origins. Far from being a minor psychological phenomenon, the uncanny can provide a nontranscendent way of accounting for our sense of the peculiar otherness of the everyday world.

When Freud speaks in general, he speaks of the experience of the male. But what is the case when a female child, who will grow up to have the same body as the mother and thus share in or reenact her secret, becomes a writer? Is there a female uncanny? Bishop offers an answer.

For Bishop, "home" can be obsessively repetitious and frighteningly uncanny in the direct Freudian sense. In her brilliant, eerie "Sestina," a child is trapped in the repetition-and-variation of sestina rhyme words: "house," "grandmother," "child," "Little Marvel Stove," "almanac," and "tears." Tears only seem to be the extraneous element, since as part of the material of the sestina's verse form, they are transformed in a kind of magic circle of obsession carried forward by the child's magical grandmother. Grandmother practices the transformative arts of cooking on the stove ("tears" become "tea") and she interprets the prophetic declarations of the almanac, the book of time:

> *It was to be*, says the Marvel Stove.
> *I know what I know*, says the almanac.
> With crayons the child draws a rigid house
> And a winding pathway. Then the child
> Puts in a man with buttons like tears
> And shows it proudly to the grandmother.

At the end of "Sestina" the child "draws another inscrutable house"—an uncanny house. Although its suffering has clearly been derived from Bishop's childhood, the sestina-child is significantly and painstakingly neuter: it offers the general case.

When Bishop writes in a female persona, the role of the uncanny shifts towards pleasure. For the woman, that houseful of secrets is where she too lives. Since she can hope to "know" or to reenact the secret, her experience of the uncanny need not necessarily be fearful. It may, of course, be unsettling nonetheless, particularly if the woman poet experiences some alienation from her body. Sylvia Plath's uncanny doubles and her many poems about hostility to her physical self do not yield a mode of knowledge like Bishop's. In Bishop the uncanny phenomenon is so well accepted that it can verge on the comic. The huge moose that looms uncannily in front of the bus in Bishop's late poem "The Moose" is female, "homely as a house, / (or, safe as houses)"—a perfect definition of the beneficent "heimlich."

This acceptance of at-homeness did not always come easily to the orphaned Bishop. Her poem "In the Waiting Room," inexorably placed in Worcester, Massachusetts, fifth of February, 1918, represents the girl child Elizabeth waiting for her aunt in the dentist's office. She looks "sidelong" around the banal, uncanny room, and realizes that "nothing stranger / had ever happened, that nothing / stranger could ever happen," than for her to be herself, in her own time. Leafing through the *National Geographic,* and finding herself forced to recognize her kinship with the bodies of strange native women, Elizabeth wonders how it can be that

> . . . those awful hanging breasts—
> held us all together
> or made us all just one?
> How—I didn't know any
> word for it—how "unlikely" . . .

The word the Bishop-child wants is "uncanny."

In "O Breath," the last of "Four Poems" from *A Cold Spring,* the body of the beloved is the house of secrets. "Beneath that loved and celebrated breast" of centuries of Petrarchan love poetry, "silent bored really," is the hidden self of the beloved. This absence-in-presence of the beloved is uncannily unsettling, "equivocal." Caesuras separating Bishop's words suggest distance even while the speaker hopes for the partial solution of some equivalency, a roof over her head, a dwelling made of the body of the beloved:

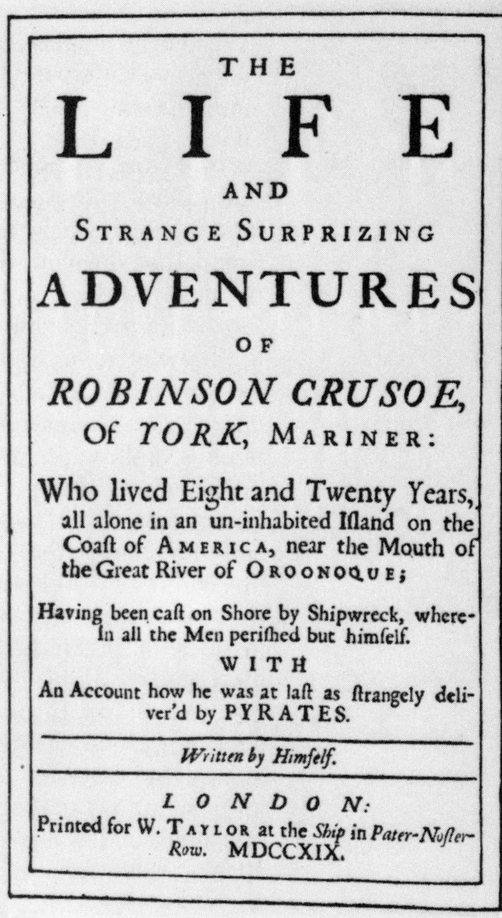

THE

LIFE

AND

STRANGE SURPRIZING

ADVENTURES

OF

ROBINSON CRUSOE,

Of *YORK,* MARINER:

Who lived Eight and Twenty Years, all alone in an un-inhabited Iſland on the Coaſt of AMERICA, near the Mouth of the Great River of OROONOQUE;

Having been caſt on Shore by Shipwreck, wherein all the Men periſhed but himſelf.

WITH

An Account how he was at laſt as ſtrangely deliver'd by PYRATES.

Written by Himſelf.

LONDON:

Printed for W. TAYLOR at the *Ship* in *Pater-Noſter-Row.* MDCCXIX.

Robinson Crusoe: *frontispiece of the first edition, published in London in 1719.*

Now I live here, another island,
that doesn't seem like one, but who decides?
My blood was full of them; my brain
bred islands. But that archipelago
has petered out. I'm old.
I'm bored, too, drinking my real tea,
surrounded by uninteresting lumber.
The knife there on the shelf—
it reeked of meaning, like a crucifix.
It lived. How many years did I
beg it, implore it, not to break?
I knew each nick and scratch by heart,
the bluish blade, the broken tip,
the lines of wood-grain on the handle . . .
Now it won't look at me at all.
The living soul has dribbled away.
My eyes rest on it and pass on.

—From "Crusoe in England"

something that maybe I could bargain with
and make a separate peace beneath
within if never with.

As one would expect, Bishop's happiness uses the house-image too. Literally these images were those of Bishop's cherished homes, particularly the houses in Persepolis and Ouro Preto, Brazil, that she shared with Lota de Macedo Soares; figuratively the house is the female body accepting its inhabitant. In "Song for the Rainy Season," the water (once again Bishop's emblem for knowledge) flows sensuously around "the house we live in" where "the waterfalls cling, / familiar, unbidden." This "house, open house" does not have to hide secrets from an equally female "milk-white sunrise."

Yet since Bishop is also the poet who knows (in "At the Fishhouses") that "our knowledge is historical," she forces herself to recognize that this joyous repetition will end and "a later era will differ." When that later era of loss did come she traced its trajectory of human need in the powerful and moving poem "Crusoe in England." Leading, perhaps, into the poem from her own reading about the new (northern) volcanic island of Surtsey, off Iceland, Bishop inverts the situation, taking on the persona of a male castaway on a southern island "with fifty-two volcanoes" (one for each week), with turtles that hissed like kettles, and waterspouts like "sacerdotal beings of glass." Even startling similes are "not much company," however, and the speaker soon falls victim to the orphan's disease, masochism:

I often gave way to self-pity.
"Do I deserve this? I suppose I must.
I wouldn't be here otherwise. . . ."

Though the madness of longing is fiercely transformative, it is still madness. With no one to love him, the speaker transmutes the Christian lesson of *caritas* and sinks into a solipsistic self-pity:

. . . I told myself
"Pity should begin at home." So the more
pity I felt, the more I felt at home.

The sun set in the sea; the same odd sun
rose from the sea,
and there was one of it and one of me.

In such lines Bishop challenges the American rhetoric of self-reliance and oneness which runs from Emerson through Stevens's First Idea of the sun in "Notes Toward a Supreme Fiction." For her the goal is not to ignore or sublimate the pain of wanting love, but to accept that need. Then, "Just when I thought I couldn't stand it / another moment longer, Friday came." When Friday dies and Crusoe is returned to England (larger, but still an island), he finds himself marooned in a world without significance: The knife that had "reeked of meaning, like a crucifix" during the years of longing now "won't look at me at all." After the death of his beloved Friday, "the living soul has dribbled away."

Bishop could also face loss with sardonic directness; in "One Art," she chronicles her ever-increasing skill in losing all she loves: maternal time, home, lover:

> I lost my mother's watch. And look! my last, or
> next-to-last, of three loved houses went.
> The art of losing isn't hard to master.

Nevertheless, as the repetition-and-variation of the villanelle indicates, even the most awful loss can be structured into truth:

> —Even losing you (the joking voice, a gesture
> I love) I shan't have lied. It's evident
> the art of losing's not too hard to master
> though it may look like *(Write it!)* like disaster.

Elizabeth Bishop had particular cause to fear time's thefts, and her steady encounter with time as knowledge bears witness to her personal strength in living with tragedy. Bishop was in effect an orphan: her father, William Bishop, died eight months after her birth on February 8, 1911, and her mother, Gertrude Bulmer Bishop, suffered after her husband's death the first of many breakdowns that led to lifelong insanity. Initially Mrs. Bishop's in-laws had her treated at MacLean's Hospital in Boston, then she and the infant Elizabeth were returned to the home of grandmother Bulmer, in Great Village, Nova Scotia, the scene of many vividly remembered poems and stories. There Gertrude Bishop suffered a final breakdown and Elizabeth, then aged five, never saw her again, though Gertrude lived until 1934.

Bishop used the circumstances of her life as the occasion for her poems; her lyric "I" is usually autobiographical. Yet while it is possible to see moments in Bishop's life in her poems, it is not appropriate to attempt to derive an intimate biography from them. Bishop's interest was not in her self but in the human knowledge gained from that self's experience. If her losses do appear in her poetry, they appear by an inverse rhetoric of attachment. The intent care with which she constructs the part sensed, part sentient sign-objects of *North & South* and the intensity of her engagement with the semitransparent landscapes of her later poetry may hint, by their very "attack," at a wish to enact the process of making, feeling, and being within life, lest it slip away.

Bishop's poetry resists the assignment of psychological causality, but her prose does bear witness to an attempt to learn where she was once at home, and how homes, and lives, are lost. In Bishop's great short story "In the Village" (included with her essays and memoirs in *Collected Prose*),[15] the mad mother's terrifying scream is said to have come "there to live, forever—not loud, just alive, forever." The sound of the clear bell of honest labor at the blacksmith's shop is always tempered by the pitch of the scream, which, like the moon's orbit in Ptolemaic cosmology, marks the upward limits of human time:

> Its pitch would be the pitch of my village. Flick the lightning rod on top of the church steeple with your fingernail and you will hear it.

Elizabeth Bishop in 1954.

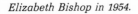

The village is "my village" to the little girl; her experience is addressed out to us, heightening our hearing up to the level of the scream.

There is a case, in such circumstances, for being less than human. The cow simply "looks up at me, drooling glass strings." But everyday life, in the village of the scream, takes on the pitch of distortion and fear. Uncle Neddy, the drunken, miserably married devil-like tinsmith whom the child visits, lives in an uncanny house, with "terrifying pictures" of the sinking Titanic. The all-remembering grandmother rules: "And she set the rocking chair rocking, as if it were, and it probably was, a memory machine."

The bucolic "North" of Bishop's Nova Scotia was broken by Bishop's abrupt removal at six back to Worcester, Massachusetts, and the home of her paternal grandparents, whose wealth failed to make up for their coldness; Elizabeth got eczema, asthma, and bronchitis—illnesses of the lost child. In the autobiographical story "The Country Mouse" her misery solicits pity; the child Elizabeth's nausea on the train is neatly paralleled later by the tale of Beppo, the bull terrier with a delicate stomach. When Beppo was "bad" he was punished by isolation:

> Once, when I was playing with him, he disappeared and would not answer my calls. Finally he was found, seated gloomily by himself in the closet, facing the wall. He was punishing *himself.* We later found a smallish puddle of vomit in the conservatory. No one had ever before punished him for his attacks of gastritis, naturally; it was all his own idea, his peculiar Bostonian sense of guilt.

The Calvinist North is also the place where even a dog internalizes punishment into guilt. It is a Kafkaesque formulation; those who are punished must be guilty.

With its character sketches and straightforwardly consecutive narrative, "The Country Mouse" has couched its plea in the most traditionally realistic fictional mode of Bishop's memoir pieces. Bishop never printed "The Country Mouse" and she came to dislike "The Farmer's Children," a fully fictional, rather melodramatic tale with a similar theme of suffering orphan and wicked step-parent. Bishop may have concluded that direct autobiographical pleading can make for an ultimate opacity in the literary work, as if what the speaker most wants the reader to know is precisely what can never be known.

Questions of knowledge are also at stake. The ironic omniscience of the realist narrator arises from a very different model of knowing from that adopted by Bishop's poems in their hard-won knowledge-by-look. Bishop has a narrative of discovery in

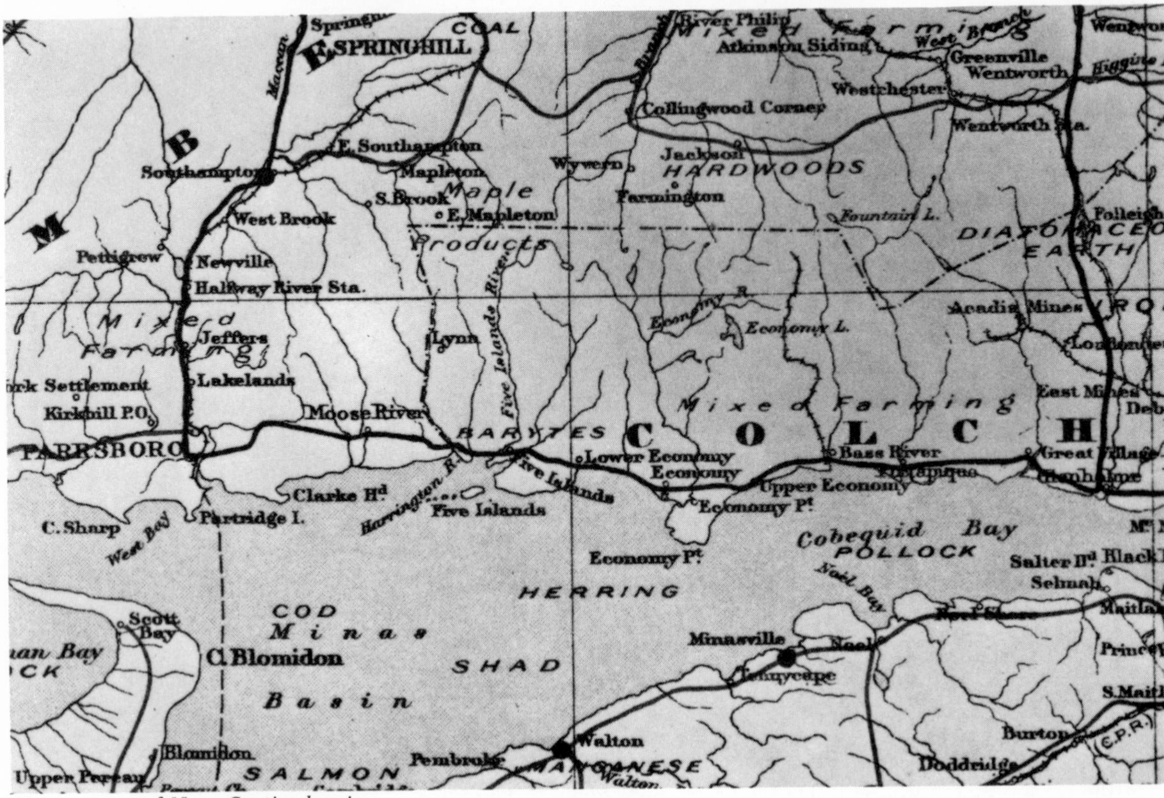

From a map of Nova Scotia showing the towns named in "The Moose."

all her poems, but narrative of action does seem to her to require a kind of initial confidence about the status of event. The substitution of image-clusters for narrative is, of course, one of the hallmarks of modernist poetry, but Bishop does not quite fit the image-based model. She has an unusual relation to narrativity in that while she is a brilliant storyteller, she chooses to put her linear narratives in the mouths of others or write them about other people. When she writes out of her own experience, Bishop restricts herself to moments of recognition or moral incident. Perhaps, having lost the native country of the family, Bishop saw the secure, straight line of episodic narrative to be a property of those who are at home.

The Brazilian fairy tale of Bishop's poem "The Riverman," the mishaps of "Manuelzinho," and the tour-de-force of her tragicomic ballad "The Burglar of Babylon" are all distanced.[16] These narrative poems are about people who are at home, integrated, with a high proportion of the "given" in their lives. Indeed, some of Bishop's first-person narrators, like the Giant

The bus starts. The light
grows richer; the fog,
shifting, salty, thin,
comes closing in. . . .

One stop at Bass River.
Then the Economies—
Lower, Middle, Upper;
Five Islands, Five Houses,
where a woman shakes a tablecloth
out after supper. . . .

The passengers lie back.
Snores. Some long sighs.
A dreamy divagation
begins in the night,
a gentle, auditory,
slow hallucination. . . .

In the creakings and noises,
an old conversation
—not concerning us,
but recognizable, somewhere,
back in the bus:
Grandparents' voices

uninterruptedly
talking, in Eternity:
names being mentioned,
things cleared up finally:
what he said, what she said,
who got pensioned. . . .

Talking the way they talked
in the old featherbed,
peacefully, on and on,
dim lamplight in the hall,
down in the kitchen, the dog
tucked in her shawl.

Now it's all right now
even to fall asleep
just as on all those nights.
—Suddenly the bus driver
stops with a jolt,
turns off his lights.

A moose has come out of
the impenetrable wood
and stands there, looms, rather,
in the middle of the road.
It approaches: it sniffs at
the bus's hot hood. . . .

—From "The Moose"

Toad or the Giant Snail (from the prose poems of *Rainy Season: Sub-tropics*) are excessively at home, knowing what they are and nothing else. Even worse are those who do not know who or where they are and obsessively, endlessly figure forth their dilemma, like the repetitious bird of "Sandpiper," the irredeemably sad seamstress in "House Guest," or the incarcerated Ezra Pound, "the man / that lies in the house of Bedlam."

The Diary of "Helena Morley," Bishop's translation of Alice Brandt's Brazilian classic *Minha Vida de Menina (My Life as a Young Girl)* is usually regarded as an exercise in exoticism, but it actually constitutes Bishop's most extreme homage to at-homeness. Comic, materialist, and delightfully fallible, "Helena" lives in a world whose God-given center is her enormous happy family, powerful grandmother and all, in Diamantina, Brazil, circa 1890:

> Everyone has the weakness of thinking anything that's foreign is better than what they have at home. . . . Even I used to think this way. But from now on I'm not going to.[17]

Everything in Helena's world is known or knowable; both time and meaning are measured by the Catholic church, a system of belief inhospitable to the uncanny. In Protestant tradition, God's presence may be revealed through some half-legible language of Nature. Nature may be read to discover the God beyond it. In Helena's Catholicism every object, act, or representation is an instantly understandable, specific act of God. Reading doesn't come into it; immanence is the usual state of things. In Helena, Bishop found the obverse of her own childhood.

Bishop's later childhood and adulthood were marked by further moves. From 1918 she lived in Massachusetts with her aunt, attending Walnut Hill Boarding School and then Vassar College, where she took her B.A. in 1934, a year after Mary McCarthy, her lifelong friend. After Vassar, Bishop worked at odd jobs, but mainly she began the pattern of deliberate wandering that characterized much of the rest of her life: New York, Europe, Key West, Brazil (1951 to early 1970s), Boston, and North Haven, Maine.[18]

During the late 1940s Bishop formed her long-term friendship with Robert Lowell, who had already praised *North & South* prophetically as the work of "one of the best craftsmen alive" with "a marvelous command of shifting speech-tones" and a "simple" structure of "description or descriptive narrative" growing into reflection.[19] When Lowell and his then girlfriend visited Bishop in Maine in 1947, Bishop became the object of one of Lowell's manic infatuations. Although Lowell asserted at various times that he was in love with "My Darling Elizabeth [Bishop]" as an unpublished poem puts it,[20] Bishop kept their relationship on the more productive terrain of close friendship and mutual respect. During the 1950s, when Bishop, Lowell, and Elizabeth Hardwick met frequently, and the early 1960s, when Lowell visited Bishop in Brazil during a disastrous lecture tour, Bishop and Lowell must be seen as holding a continuing creative conversation, with Bishop probably exercising the greater influence. Bishop dedicated "The Armadillo," with its conversational quatrains and its imagery of the failed transcendence of fire-balloons, to Lowell. In return, Lowell dedicated "Skunk Hour" (the concluding poem in *Life Studies*) to Bishop "because re-reading her suggested a way of breaking through the shell of my old manner . . . 'Skunk Hour' is modelled on Miss Bishop's 'The Armadillo,' a much better poem."[21]

Lowell felt Bishop occupied that essential prosodic middle ground "between [Allen] Tate's formalism and [William Carlos] Williams's informal art,"[22] that he himself was trying to reach after the occasionally turgid Miltonic pentameters of his earlier volumes. Bishop helped Lowell reach this ground. When Lowell was writing the prose autobiographical notes that led to the "91 Revere Street" section of *Life Studies,* he had available, at the very least, Bishop's "In the Village" and "Gwendolyn" (a story about children playing with a doll and learning about death), both of which had been published in the *New Yorker* in 1953. Bishop's practice offered Lowell a model of how to take intensely imaged shards of childhood memory and assemble them in both prose and poetry. Lowell's "91 Revere Street" and the "Life Studies" family poems address themselves to the paradox of Lowell's sense of alienation, even though his ancestry, class, and education had prepared him to be one of the American inheritors, one of those quintessentially "at home" in American culture. In a letter, Bishop the exile affectionately criticizes Lowell for exploiting his advantages while setting himself apart from them:

> And here I confess . . . that I am green with envy of your kind of assurance. I feel I could write in as much detail about my uncle Artie, say,—but what would be the significance? Nothing at all. He became a drunkard . . . whereas all you have to do is put down the names.[23]

Lowell's poetry of self is, however, more public, more self-critical, and infinitely more self-dramatizing than Bishop's meditations. When Lowell later alluded to the classic model for memories of poetic self-development by calling *Life Studies* a "small-scale Prelude,"[24] his stress on Wordsworth rather than

Untitled construction by Joseph Cornell (known as Medici Slot Machine).

Hexahedrons of wood and glass,
scarcely bigger than a shoebox,
with room in them for night and all its lights.

Monuments to every moment,
refuse of every moment, used:
cages for infinity.
. . .

Slot machine of visions,
condensation flask for conversations,
hotel of crickets and constellations.
. . .

A comb is a harp strummed by the glance
of a little girl
born dumb.
. . .

The apparitions are manifest,
their bodies weigh less than light,
lasting as long as this phrase lasts.

Joseph Cornell: inside your boxes
my words became visible for a moment.

—From Elizabeth Bishop's translation
of "Objects & Apparitions" by Octavio Paz

Bishop (or W. D. Snodgrass or Randall Jarrell) is entirely appropriate. Lowell's re-created youth, like Wordsworth's, is about preparation for the sacred role of prophetic poet; it is a life defined backwards from a present of a major poet's midcareer impasse. Bishop's child-speakers awake to the more general, but horrifying, recognition that they are, like other people, merely human.

Despite her decades as an expatriate, there is no hint in Bishop's poetry of felt distance from the English lyric tradition or of complexly blocked effort to enter it. She is that rare phenomenon, a natural modern, at ease in traditional and free-verse forms, her sensuous imagery always informed by an antiromantic, questioning intelligence. Indeed, Bishop's sex, ostensibly a barrier to feeling "at home" in literary tradition, may have proved an advantage.

The struggle of the second-generation moderns Schwartz, Roethke, Lowell, Berryman, and (more arguably) Jarrell concerned the taking up of the mantle, the consecrated role of great poet in the tradition. A youthful, ambitious seizing of role proved particularly difficult for Bishop's contemporaries, domi-

5

An untitled watercolor by Elizabeth Bishop.

nated as they were by Eliotic diction and taste, and by still-vigorous older poets like Pound, Williams, and Stevens, all of whom wrote some of their best work after World War II. As a woman, Bishop didn't have this goal fully available to her. Whatever her talent, the social reading of gender would have made it virtually impossible for her to dominate the development of American poetry. As a consequence, the tradition, while ready to hand, did not have to be perceived by her as a challenge. Bishop's necessary distance, not from tradition but from its traditionally male prophetic burden, may partly account for her famously unplaceable style. She was a second-generation modern, but her poetry looks both earlier and considerably later. Her diction was American (indeed educated Eastern seaboard), but it also had English and Latin-American resonances. She had a mode of address which is gender-free (in the sense that some of her poems, such as "The Unbeliever," may be read without reference to their female authorship), but that same mode of address is also, in its epistemology and imagery, womanly.

While Bishop's work doesn't show signs of a quest for an alternative female tradition, she did adopt a "mother" in Marianne Moore, to whom she was introduced by a helpful librarian when Bishop was still an undergraduate at Vassar College. After Bishop's youthful discipleship, with Moore introducing three of Bishop's poems in a 1935 anthology,[25] the two remained friends, and in "Efforts of Affection,"[26] Bishop's memoir of Moore, Bishop saw Moore as her tutor in prosody, in "reticence," in the need for meticulous revision, over a period of years if necessary. By her example, Moore may also have taught Bishop to accept her own uniqueness.

Bishop was an unbeliever from a Protestant background. The place where her poetry is spiritually at home is a real, sensuous, uncanny world which yields meaning to unwilled meditation. Bishop's rhetoric of investigation diverges from that of Herbert or Emerson in Bishop's lack of pressure toward a "beyond." Incident in Bishop is also not "immanent" after the fashion of 1960s American poetry, though its intensity may lead to superficial resemblances. When, as in her famous "The Man-Moth," Bishop is dealing with attempted transcendence, she substitutes an uncanny myth of literary birth. The man-moth

> . . . climbs fearfully, thinking that this time he will manage
> to push his small head through that round clean opening
> and be forced through, as from a tube, in black scrolls on the
> light. . . .

The romantic man-moth "fails, of course," in his Romantic quest because the only "beyond" is this world, only inverted.

Elizabeth Bishop's poetry exhibits the pleasure of deep gaze without a corresponding desire to control the object of the gaze. Her poetry has the generous ability to look at anything, however painful, trivial or apparently alien it may seem, to read that "thing," and to give over that act of knowing intact to the poem's audience. It is a body of work without pose or inflation. It is also, by the same token, without a final truth, if truth is a transcendent Emersonian "beyond." Bishop's truths are the repeatable acts of traveling inwards through the transparencies of water and air, through the dream, the image, the landscape, the house, and the body; her uncanny mysteries are resolved here. Bishop is as good a guide as this century is likely to find for reading experience and its metaphors. Bishop's route to this knowledge is by a universal, but also particularly womanly, epistemology. The habit is that of curiosity.

Skunk Hour

Nautilus Island's hermit
Heiress still lives through winter in her Spartan cottage;
Her sheep still graze above the sea.
Two sons are bishops. Her farmer
Is first selectman in our village;
She's in her dotage--

Thirsting for
The hierarchic privacy
Of Queen Victoria's century,
She~~'s tried to~~ buys up all
The ~~bad houses~~ facing her shore,
And lets them fall.

The season's ill--
We've lost our summer millionair,
Who seemed to leap from an L. L. Bean
Catalogue. His ten-knot yawl
Was ~~sold to Deer Isle~~ lobstermen.
A red fox stain covers Blue Hill.

And now our fairy
Decorator brightens his shop for fall;
His fishnet's filled with orange cork,
Orange, his cobbler's bench and awl;
There is no money in his work,
He'd rather marry.

One dark night,
My Tudor Ford climbed the hill's skull;
I watched for love-cars. Lights turned down,
They lay together, hull to hull,
Where the graveyard shelves on the town...
My mind's not right--

It was one thing to sing,
Love, loveless Love... ~~another to~~ hear
~~The~~ ill spirit sob in each blood cell,
As if my hand were at its throat...
I myself am hell;
Nobody's here;

~~And~~ the skunks search,
All ~~elbows~~ for a bite to eat.
~~They are roaming out on~~ Main Street:
White stripes, ~~in~~ moonlight, eyes' red fire
Under the chalk-dry and spar spire ~~spire~~
Of the Trinitarian Church.

I stand on top
Of our back steps and breathe the rich air--
A skunk swills ~~in our~~ garbage pail,
~~It~~ jabs ~~its~~ wedge-head in a cup
Of sour cream, drops ~~its~~ ostrich tail,
And will not scare.

ROBERT LOWELL

VEREEN BELL

If there was ever an American writer who had reason to be at home in the world, it should have been Robert Lowell. His mother and father by lineage—Winslow on the one side, Lowell on the other—flowed unreflectively in the mainstream of New England history. Their wealth, though modest by American standards, freed them and Lowell himself, eventually, from undue anxieties about money. In his apprentice years he was tutored and encouraged by the most important established writers of his time, Richard Eberhart, Allen Tate, Ford Madox Ford, John Crowe Ransom. His closest friends at Kenyon College had been Peter Taylor and Randall Jarrell. By the time he was thirty he had won a Pulitzer Prize (1947) and had established a secure position in all the standard American literature anthologies—at a time when there were no modern poetry courses and the youngest American poet being taught in any course was T. S. Eliot.

But something obviously went and stayed wrong. An alert reader would suspect this from the poems themselves. Nothing is more characteristic of Lowell's poems—even in his early highly formalist phase—than their refusal or inability to achieve a satisfying resolution. A conventional poetic structure may be said to resemble a narrative in that it sets out, experiences complications, and finally achieves closure. Lowell's poems are not like that: they are sent out into an alien environment and never find their way back. They either simply stop—abruptly arresting the movement toward resolution—or they achieve parodies of resolution, at home finally only in an ironic awareness of what is absent. Collectively they express disinheritance and unaccommodated anxiety and yet they are sick for home. After those of the first three volumes—two, in effect—the poems are not even at home in poetry itself, their idiom becoming increasingly ordinary and banal, out of place in their own conventional environment where discourse is still expected to be formal and at least polite. As a young man, Lowell struggled obsessively to be an important poet; as he matured he came to call poetry itself into question, relentlessly confronting and

Robert Lowell.

challenging by that means the whole tradition of aesthetic false consolation. The Puritans did not care for lying and intellectual self-deception either. American Puritanism had worked its way through him to a modernist standoff, all the more stark for being, ironically, without a god. Ralph Waldo Emerson's classic idealism—the opposing strain to Puritanism in American intellectual history, one carried forward by poets as disparate as Whitman, Wallace Stevens, and Hart Crane—had disappeared from this world without a trace. A strange but characteristically American logic had worked itself out.

It is true, as Stephen Gould Axelrod has argued, that Lowell in a sense had fulfilled a prophecy of Emerson's that the poet in America would come to value authentic seeing over "skill and command of language," would "[traverse] the whole scale of experience" and "tell us how it was with him," and that this was an affirmation in art of democratic individualism, each man's experience being all men's. But Emerson was perhaps more characteristic when advancing much stranger notions—

that, for example, Idealism was an attractive philosophy because "it presents the world in precisely that view which is most desirable to the mind." Characters like Jay Gatsby come into the world embodying that naive appraisal of human possibility; characters like Robert Lowell in Lowell's poems dream of such freedom, but when it goes bad and one has recourse to no metaphysical principle beyond mere experience—or cannot go on and believe, as Emerson tended to, in the benignity of Nature anyway—then what is most acceptable to the human mind will begin to seem ironically remote. Eliminate Emerson's unempirical optimism from his aesthetic of democratic individualism and you have a wholly different report on what is common in human experience. When that happens, the Poet might practice, as Lowell did, an art that rehearses the only experience he knows to be authentic—his own; such an art would enact the process by which we who are not poets work daily to achieve some transcendence of our own lives, seemingly always gaining and falling back, gaining and falling back. To represent that process faithfully, the art cannot be contrived so as to seem an alternative to real existence: that would be bad faith. The task instead would be to achieve an art that enacts the effort—the labor, Yeats would say—of transcending while remaining continuous with experience itself. Elizabeth Bishop was eloquent on this point when she wrote to Lowell of her satisfaction with *Life Studies.* "They all . . . have that sure feeling, as if you'd been in a stretch . . . when everything and anything suddenly seemed material for poetry—or not material, seemed to be poetry, and all the past was illuminated here and there, like a long-waited-for sunrise. If only one could see everything that way all of the time! It seems to me it's the whole purpose of art, to the artist (not to the audience)—life is all right, for the time being."[1]

Life Studies gave celebrity and respectability to a mode of writing in America that would soon become known, imprecisely, as "confessional." As a model and as a symbolic breakthrough this volume would become a landmark in the history of American poetry's evolution. It made new possibilities of meaning accessible to poetic understanding and had a strong influence upon two different generations of younger poets, particularly upon poets who had been Lowell's friends and students as well—Anne Sexton, Sylvia Plath, Adrienne Rich, Alan Williamson, Frank Bidart. The poems of *Life Studies* were mainly about Lowell's own family and their poignantly thwarted expectations. Both realistically detailed and thematically coherent, they showed how the poet's way of seeing caused human lives to become poetry as if by apotheosis. "After one has abandoned a belief in God," Wallace Stevens said,

John Lowell (1743–1802), known as the Old Judge. He was a member of the Continental Congress.

James Russell Lowell, poet, editor of The Atlantic Monthly.

And here I must confess . . . that I am green with envy of your kind of assurance. I feel I could write in as much detail about my uncle Artie, say,—but what would be the significance? Nothing at all. He became a drunkard, fought with his wife, and spent most of his time fishing . . . and was ignorant as sin. It is sad; slightly more interesting than having an uncle practising law in Schenectady maybe, but that's about all. Whereas all you have to do is put down the names!

—Elizabeth Bishop to Robert Lowell, December 14, 1957

"poetry is that which takes its place as life's redemption." The wary Puritan strain in Lowell ran too deep for him to be able to take such a new dispensation as seriously as Stevens did, especially the redemption part, but at some less sententious level such a belief motivated and sustained his creative impulse from this point forward. Allen Tate, Lowell's mentor, thought the poems in *Life Studies* "bad" because they lacked "the imagina-

Percival Lowell, who, by deduction, discovered and located the planet Pluto but died shortly before it was sighted.

tive thrust toward a symbolic order": he had managed simultaneously to see the point and to miss it.

Life Studies had given some indication of why the young poet who seemed to be American history's godson never really found a comfortable place in the world and, in part, therefore, why he spent so much of his life trying to make sense of his own displacement. His parents' relationship had exhibited about as much love as a fourteenth-century dynastic marriage. His mother was a distraught, overbearing woman, obsessed with her patrician status in the world and its associated privileges and obligations. She pampered her son—her only child—and also manipulated him in her conflict with her husband. It must have been hard for Lowell to know the difference between being loved and being used. For the rest of his life Lowell remained dependent upon strong women and upon the attention of women generally, and was given to assuming that what he wanted was more or less what he was supposed to want—a problem for his friends and wives. Charlotte Lowell told her son later in his life that when she was pregnant she used to pace the shore of Staten Island saying to the ocean, "I wish I were dead, I wish I were dead." Lowell records this episode in a very late poem called "Unwanted." He reports in the same poem that Merrill Moore—with dubious judgment for a psychiatrist and his mother's friend, perhaps lover—told him that he was an unwanted child. Characteristically Lowell takes refuge in the thought that we are all unwanted in "the medical sense— / lust our only father." That this humiliation resurfaces so late in his life shows how deeply hurting that thought had remained and how analytically skeptical he was of his mother's attention.

The main cause of friction in Bob and Charlotte Lowell's marriage was Charlotte's sense of being displaced from her rightful station in society by the obtuse complacency of her husband, a career naval officer until he retired from the navy to work, unsuccessfully, for Procter & Gamble. The only place in the world that was suitable for Charlotte Lowell's delicate temperament was Boston, and there they eventually lived, precariously, in the Hub, at the cost of her husband's naval career, such as it was, and her son's childhood. Boston was like an extension of Lowell's family—possessive, unintrospective, demanding. He went to correct schools and was taught breeding and manners, taken on coerced "strolls on the polite, landscaped walks of the Public Garden." (Even his father was persuaded to take carving lessons when they moved to Boston.) Seemingly intuiting the danger, the young Lowell became rebellious, and eventually a violent break with his family ensued that was never wholly repaired. Ironically, his mother and father closed ranks behind him. He was never free of Boston but, of course, was never at home there—or in Cambridge when he taught periodically at Harvard in his later years. Charlotte Lowell died in 1954 in Rapallo (four years after her husband). Lowell escorted her body back in a suitably Napoleonic coffin he had bought for her, though aboard ship because of the heat she was "wrapped like *panettone* in Italian tinfoil." Lowell would have recorded that odd detail not simply because of its pathos but because for him it would have called ironic attention to the impurity of Boston's real culture. When Lowell himself died, one of the Boston papers proclaimed, on the front page, "Hub Poet Dies." His mother would have liked that. Lowell himself, on the other hand, always exaggerated his relationship to exotic ancestors, one of whom, his great-great grandfather, Mordecai Meyers, was a Mediterranean Jew.

Of course one other consequence of his patrician background was that Lowell could never have become another Whitman or William Carlos Williams, though one can see how he might have wanted to. His manner, his upbringing, his education were too indelibly aristocratic for that. He became a famous poet in the first place by acting out an exalted version of that identity in the High Modernist style, pitting culture, classical learning, Christian typology, and Miltonic rhetoric against the crassness, slackness, and venality of the modern age. In the High Modernist style, as it was expounded by Allen Tate, Lowell's first mentor, the poet is not a person but a role, the poet in the opposite of the Emersonian sense. The poet is the custodian of a privileged language and of a privileged vision derived from its association with tradition, unembarrassed by pretension and unrestrained by ironic introspection.

Even after the high manner had disappeared, Lowell remained a Brahmin intellectually, a student of music and art, translator of Juvenal, Horace, and Dante, deeply immersed in human history, a reflective and compulsive reader. For a writer who was also influenced by the Metaphysical Poets and who worked mainly by association it was therefore not ostentation but second nature to see any circumstance as summoning an analogous one from some other context, as if real life were of indeterminate status and scope. The volume of his that was most obviously democratic by Emerson's standard, as indicated by its title, was *Notebook.* Both its plan and its style were notational, but it was hardly confined to the poet's own experience, except in that his experience was refracted through that of Flaubert, Harpo Marx, Charles I, Tacitus, Mao Tse-tung, Plutarch, John Calvin, King David, Robespierre, Saint-Just, Christopher Marlowe, Dante, Christoph Glück, Schubert, Potter and Albert Cuyp, Margaret Fuller, George Grösz, Velásquez, Che Guevara, Thoreau, and so on. Hardly a page exists only in the simple present, and yet the present is what *Notebook,* any notebook, is about. For Lowell, reporting how it was with him always entailed dense cross-reference. He had given a new complexity, encouraged by Ezra Pound's *Cantos,* to Emerson's

Jonathan Edwards (1703–58), philosopher, theologian, minister in Northampton, Massachusetts, brought the religious revival known as the Great Awakening to New England. Lowell quotes Edwards's sermon "Sinners in the Hands of an Angry God" in this poem in which he singles out Josiah Hawley, a member of Edwards's congregation who, convinced that he was one of the damned, cut his throat.

conviction that one man's experience is all men's. "I am large," Whitman had said, not meaning to be immodest. "I contain multitudes." Lowell's pluralism was not populist, but it was—eventually—inclusive; and he was never more American than when he seemed to see everything at once and could therefore never rest secure in any single place or with any one perception of things. It was as if the abundance and contradictions and the disorienting pace of American life had been condensed and introjected into the space of a single consciousness, overriding

Mr. Edwards and the Spider

I saw the spiders marching through the air,
Swimming from tree to tree that mildewed day
In latter August when the hay
Came creaking to the barn. But where
The wind is westerly,
Where gnarled November makes the spiders fly
Into the apparitions of the sky,
They purpose nothing but their ease and die
Urgently beating east to sunrise and the sea;

What are we in the hands of the great God?
It was in vain you set up thorn and briar
In battle array against the fire
And treason crackling in your blood;
For the wild thorns grow tame
And will do nothing to oppose the flame;
Your lacerations tell the losing game
You play against a sickness past your cure.
How will the hands be strong? How will the heart endure?

A very little thing, a little worm,
Or hourglass-blazoned spider, it is said,
Can kill a tiger. Will the dead
Hold up his mirror and affirm
To the four winds the smell
And flash of his authority? It's well
If God who holds you to the pit of hell,
Much as one holds a spider, will destroy,
Baffle and dissipate your soul. As a small boy

On Windsor Marsh, I saw the spider die
When thrown into the bowels of fierce fire:
There's no long struggle, no desire
To get up on its feet and fly—
It stretches out its feet
And dies. This is the sinner's last retreat;
Yes, and no strength exerted on the heat
Then sinews the abolished will, when sick
And full of burning, it will whistle on a brick.

But who can plumb the sinking of that soul?
Josiah Hawley, picture yourself cast
Into a brick-kiln where the blast
Fans your quick vitals to a coal—
If measured by a glass,
How long would it seem burning! Let there pass
A minute, ten, ten trillion; but the blaze
Is infinite, eternal: this is death,
To die and know it. This is the Black Widow, death.

Lowell's temperamental and hereditary disposition toward selectivity, form, stability, and established certainties.

It is the essence of the American vision historically that experience should not be subjugated to form, particularly to old forms or imposed forms; this was Emerson's point. But the cost of that freedom is an American version of existential anxiety. Commander and Charlotte Lowell were not happy in their life but they were secure in their sense of who they were and of what their proper station in society entailed. Their perspective on such things was European and conventional and not susceptible to examination or modification, since the psychological virtues of certainty and assurance are as compelling as the virtues of the superior station itself. When their son did not behave in the acceptable manner he was unwittingly challenging their station and its norms, and therefore their identity. This accounts for the ease with which they closed ranks in response. Whatever else they suffered they did not suffer doubt over how their identities and the nature of existence coincided.

Lowell's temporary move south—recommended by Merrill Moore as a therapeutic measure—turned out to have been a kind of transition for him into, so to speak, the unknown. There is something sad and emblematic about the image of this tense young scion of an old Boston family, an émigré from Harvard, where an illustrious ancestor had been president, suddenly showing up in Clarksville, Tennessee, and then (so the story goes) living in a Sears, Roebuck tent on the front lawn of Allen Tate and Caroline Gordon. (This may have been the only occasion in history when a Lowell was in a Sears, Roebuck store. At Newport, shortly after her wedding, Mrs. Lowell had been vexed to learn that naval wives had to order their own groceries.) Lowell was eager to learn, to be famous in his own right, and to be measured on his own terms, but he was also displaced. He had cast himself into the unfamiliar world like a novice pioneer. For the whole of his life, Lowell had a willful child's enthusiasm for disruption and adventure—domestic, intellectual, sexual, political. Though he was trapped in his mandarin's role—he was eventually instantly recognizable anywhere in educated society—this too was an American trait, the indiscriminate restlessness and inability to stay put. He could not even let his poems stay put, always treating published work, as he himself said, as if it were manuscript. Conceivably the ruthlessly disciplined style of his early manner, his absorption at Kenyon College in classical languages and literature, and his brief but ardent conversion to the Roman Catholic faith were all over-corrections for, or ways of organizing, a tendency to go off

Charlotte Winslow, 1915.

In 1924 people still lived in cities. Late that summer, we bought the 91 Revere Street house, looking out on an unbuttoned part of Beacon Hill bounded by the North End slums, though reassuringly only four blocks away from my Grandfather Winslow's brown pillared house at 18 Chestnut Street. . . . My mother felt a horrified giddiness about the adventure of our address. She once said, "We are barely perched on the outer rim of the hub of decency." We were less than fifty yards from Louisburg Square, the cynosure of Boston's plain-spoken, cold-roast elite—the Hub of the Hub of the Universe. Fifty yards!

—From "91 Revere Street"

Robert Traill Spence Lowell, Sr., and Jr., about 1920.

"I have always believed carving to be *the* gentlemanly talent," Mother used to proclaim. Father, faced with this opinion, pored over his book of instructions or read the section on table carving in the Encyclopædia Britannica. Eventually he discovered among the innumerable small, specialized Boston "colleges" an establishment known as a carving school. Each Sunday from then on he would sit silent and erudite before his roast. He blinked, grew white, looked winded, and wiped beads of perspiration from his eyebrows. His purpose was to reproduce stroke by stroke his last carving lesson, and he worked with all the formal rightness and particular error of some shaky experiment in remote control. He enjoyed quiet witticisms at the expense of his carving master—"a philosopher who gave himself all the airs of a Mahan!" He liked to pretend that the carving master had stated that "no two cuts are identical," *ergo:* "each offers original problems for the *executioner.*" Guests were appeased by Father's saying, "I am just a plebe at this guillotine. Have a hunk of my roast beef hash."

—From "91 Revere Street"

in many different directions at once. Under the tutelage of Ford Madox Ford, who taught him to revere "the sacredness of the poet's function in the world," and of Allen Tate, John Crowe Ransom, Cleanth Brooks, and Robert Penn Warren, and under the influence of Hart Crane, for all of whom High Modernism and New Criticism were symbiotic, Lowell launched himself onto the literary scene as a zealous artificer writing powerfully and ostentatiously from within the assurance of a closed system. When he won the Pulitzer Prize for *Lord Weary's Castle* in 1947 he was barely thirty years old. The manuscript had been completed two years before that. But he had already exhausted the possibilities of his vatic role. *The Mills of the Kavanaughs,* published four years later, was almost self-parody, a *Lord Weary's Castle* style presenting what would turn out to be *Life Studies* subjects.

Then for six years Lowell was stalled. Whether he was jolted out or whether he worked his way out cannot be said for certain. But these events, because of their proximity, seem important. His mother had died in March 1954. By June he had been recommitted to Payne Whitney psychiatric hospital after a particularly bizarre manic-depressive episode, by now a tragically regular occurrence. While recovering in Payne Whitney he was permitted to substitute poetry-writing for the ordinary occupational therapy. His manuscripts (in the Houghton Library) show that he had already been working on a prose memoir (eventually published as "91 Revere St") which included an account of his mother's death and the return home with her body. (This portion breaks off before he enters the hospital.) But when he tries to begin again with poetry, the "labor and cynicism and maturity of writing in meter became horrible. I began to write rapidly in prose and in the style of a child." What he then wrote was to become most of Part IV of *Life Studies,* some of it carefully pared back and revised, some of it simply rearranged into a verse pattern. Other circumstances impinged: the continuing encouragement of William Carlos Williams; his avid reading of Freud; the new models of Philip Larkin in England and of W. D. Snodgrass in America; the influence, oddly enough, of the Beat poets in California. But for whatever combination of forces, Lowell with *Life Studies* had radically Americanized his own poetry, as if in that irritable rejection of "the labor and cynicism and maturity of writing in meter" he had reenacted American history itself. The writing like a child hints at a sense of rebirth (after the death of both parents), though of course the poems are in the voice of a mature and shaping poet. Lowell had heard Williams say that the form of a poem *is* its meaning. Elizabeth Bishop had written to him that it was the "whole purpose of art" to be able to see life as if it *were* poetry, as "all right" for the time being. Emerson had said that the poet's representing what he himself truly sees is what counts. Lowell had written to Williams saying that there was "no ideal form for any two of us"; in saying so, he restated Emerson's point and affirmed the principle of organic, empirical form: each form is the effect of a special way of seeing. Poetry for him is no longer an answering to restraints ("cynicism *and* maturity," he oddly says). The poem does not subject the material to an obedience to a "higher" meaning; nor does it record the revelation of a meaning. It *is* the meaning while the meaning lasts, and the only meaning: "everything and anything suddenly seemed material for poetry—or not material, seemed to *be* poetry" and life itself "all right, for the time being." The "for the time being" in Elizabeth Bishop's definition is an important qualification: it puts emphasis upon the immediacy of the experience from the poet's point of view and therefore upon its transitoriness as well. To put this in another, redundant, way, poetry is the nature of experience seen in this way; the made poem itself is the record, not quite the same as the experience but close, and perhaps no more or less valuable. What is democratic about this is that it assumes, as Emerson would have us assume, that the value of each person's experience as he or she moves through it—at eye level, so to speak—is always being made and remade and that a poet is different only in having left the record behind and in having the skill with form and words to reconstitute the experience—or, rather, not the skill *with* form but the skill *of* form.

Of course Lowell had not invented this aesthetic. William Carlos Williams and even earlier imagists, Lowell's cousin Amy included, had covered some of this theoretical ground forty years before. But what the experience of imagism had shown unintentionally was that form *does* matter: that if a poem has only the virtues of good prose and yet presents itself as a poem on the page—that is, devoid of experienceable poetic form—then it imparts the aesthetic satisfaction of neither poetry nor prose. Form is more than just meter or structure or even the perceived and represented inner logic of the experience: it is also the texture and coherence of the language itself; and this sense of form is a gift that one either has or does not have. One of the remarkable aspects of the Payne Whitney sketches, prior to their being made into *Life Studies,* is that they are equally, if mysteriously, formal either as poetry or as prose. Abandoning or relegating meter and rhythm exacts a very great cost from a poem—sometimes a disastrous one, as the work of Lowell's imitators has tended to illustrate—because in terms of aesthetic gratification what one immediately loses is the resistance that it is our pleasure to see gracefully overcome. But subordinating the obvious formal effects of meter and rhyme has the merit of letting the other more elusive kind of form become apparent. Meter and rhyme are in fact so visible that they tend to bully other manifestations of form into retreat. It was a transaction in these terms that Lowell was trying to negotiate, and he was successful, though a majority of his readers did not at first see this—largely because his own sense of the authority of form was innate and most other people's is not.

When Lowell says that he began writing in "the style of a child" he was being disingenuous, of course, since the tone of the Payne Whitney sketches—though they are of his childhood memories—is very sophisticated. He certainly did not mean to romanticize childhood as Wordsworth or Dylan Thomas might have done. He appears to have meant only that he was being open to the experience of his past and receptive to his material without prior restraint, and that he was writing relatively spontaneously. He was also seeing things not as a generic or literary child would—whatever that might be—but as a very eccentric and particular one like the one he was. "I wasn't a child at all. / Unseen and all-seeing, I was Agrippina in the Golden House of Nero." There is a story about himself in disguise in these same unpublished papers called "The Boy with the Raspberry Sherbet Heart." Charles, as the boy is called, keeps telling his father that he is cold, that his heart is in the refrigerator. "Neither Charles's father nor mother had any idea of what he was saying, but being grown-ups they pretended as though they had. They said, 'Charles is a surrealist. He is improving on nature. Last night he said the stars are blossoming. . . .' They didn't try to understand him. They were already looking forward to telling their friends how their son was able to mingle all sorts of beautiful and unlikely things together in his mind. Charles said, 'Help me!' " The child that comes back to life in *Life Studies* remains an innocent witness in Lowell's poems to some very strange permutations of experience. He is innocent not in the sense of being either inexperienced or guiltless, but in the sense of being innocent of understanding and therefore always in a state of need and in a state of thwarted and disturbed wonder. Before *Life Studies,* the poems are always this way—"Always inside me is the child who died"—groping, baffled, and solipsistic—and inexhaustibly observant. The poet is also, as the story of Charles shows, terribly exposed: unloved and exposed to the unknown, a dangerous, un-Emersonian combination, but American for all of that. The only meaning he can have after this is that which, from one day to the next, he can make himself. Bob and Charlotte Lowell were definitively dead.

The Winslow family graveyard in Dunbarton, New Hampshire. The graves of Lowell's parents can be seen in the left foreground. The poet is buried there also.

A few years after *Life Studies* had been published Lowell was saying in an interview, "One side of me . . . is a conventional liberal, concerned with causes, agitated about peace and justice and equality, as so many people are. My other side is deeply conservative, wanting to get at the roots of things, wanting to slow down the whole modern process of mechanization and dehumanization, knowing that liberation can be a form of death too." This is a little naive and muddled, suggesting as it does an incompatibility between the two aims; but it shows Lowell thinking of himself as torn between an allegiance to change on the one hand and to stability on the other. A year later with Albert Alvarez he is puzzling over the oddly seductive quality of American life: "You can't touch a stone in London that doesn't point backwards into history; while even for an American city, New York seems to have no past. And yet it's the only city that provides an intellectual, human continuum to live in . . . [If] you removed it, you'd be cutting out the heart of American culture. Yet it is a heart with no past . . . [It] has a sheer

While the passengers were tanning
on the Mediterranean in deck-chairs,
our family cemetery in Dunbarton
lay under the White Mountains
in the sub-zero weather.
The graveyard's soil was changing to stone—
so many of its deaths had been midwinter.
Dour and dark against the blinding snowdrifts,
its black brook and fir trunks were as smooth as masts.
A fence of iron spear-hafts
black-bordered its mostly Colonial grave-slates.
The only "unhistoric" soul to come here
was Father, now buried beneath his recent
unweathered pink-veined slice of marble.
Even the Latin of his Lowell motto:
Occasionem cognosce,
seemed too businesslike and pushing here,
where the burning cold illuminated
the hewn inscriptions of Mother's relatives:
twenty or thirty Winslows and Starks.
Frost had given their names a diamond edge. . . .

In the grandiloquent lettering on Mother's coffin,
Lowell had been misspelled LOVEL.
The corpse
was wrapped like *panettone* in Italian tinfoil.

—From "Sailing Home from Rapallo"

feeling of utter freedom. And then when one thinks back a little bit, it seems all confused and naked." It is in this context that Lowell says that in America "the artist's existence becomes his art. He is reborn in it, and he hardly exists without it." One might say that America both requires this rebirth and also permits it, or requires it *by* permitting it, and for one who was repeatedly struggling back from madness during his middle years, the idea of rebirth was no vague metaphor. The self in the poems could achieve form, but not without the associated fear that the fluidness of the present that permits it—the "human continuum"—will also take it away.

Existing in one's art for Lowell meant being in control (even when writing about not being in control), reconstructing a world (out of a wilderness, so to speak), making a form where there was none and then for its duration—for we are not talking about Platonic form or anything akin to it—being contained by it and self-aware in relation to it; and for this purpose any form is suitable, even a grim one. In *Life Studies,* the form was that of a repeating process. It is a story about how things change and give way, about how what is in motion stops, about a sad stillness underlying the animation of human lives. In the central poem of the volume, "My Last Afternoon with Uncle Devereux Winslow," this theme is first focused on the gardener at Lowell's grandfather's farm who is making cement for the root-house cellar, mixing earth and lime. The boy Lowell sits watching, one hand warm on a pile of lime, the other cool on a pile of earth; he is metaphorically mixing earth and lime. At the end of the poem, which seems until the end to have no plot and not much point, we learn that Uncle Devereux, aged twenty-nine, military and hierarchical, and off this day with his wife for Europe, is dying of Hodgkin's disease. The child remembers his hands on piles of earth and lime, "a black pile and a white pile," and the point is then made explicit: "Come winter / Uncle Devereux would blend to the one color" (*LS,* 64). Uncle Devereux's story is the story of the poem and the story of the volume. One would want to call it elegiac except that the strange mixture of the child's and the adult's point of view keeps it from being that, keeps the form of seeing from becoming too conventional. This poem reminds us that a child is incapable of elegiac feelings. In so doing it causes us to recognize that elegy as a form oversimplifies the experience of death, is an adult's way of organizing the unthinkable. The child in *Life Studies* is frightened, and he is mystified because, being a child, he is all-seeing, and details speak intelligibly and unintelligibly from all directions.

The form in the texture is both the meaning and the nature of the meaning, shows how the meaning can be disclosed and hidden at once. Grandfather Winslow's "manly" and "overbearing" artifacts all seem like something frozen in time, or like metaphors that haven't been fully worked up: a little figurine of Huck Finn fishing in a hollowed-out millstone; "octagonal red tiles / sweating with a secret dank"; a chaise longue made of "shellacked saplings." Both the little Huck Finn and the saplings suggest something imperiling childhood. This implication is oddly reinstated by the grandfather's saying to his dying son Devereux and his daughter-in-law, "You are behaving like children." Uncle Devereux is dressed in the "war uniform of a volunteer Canadian officer"; young Robert is wearing a "sailor blouse"; he picks at its anchor. The farm has been a place of childhood happiness, and of adventure and shelter: "No one had died there in my lifetime"—except their puppy, Cinder, paralyzed from gobbling toads (which doesn't make sense from an adult's point of view but would be all too plausible to a child). Little Robert Lowell is five and a half, perfectly poised and perfectly dressed (like Uncle Devereux) and in his water basin he suddenly sees his own face distorted by drops of water into that of a "striped toucan with a bibulous, multicolored beak." Form erodes, motion stops. Youth and age, being alive and being dead, all too readily coincide.

In the very next poem of *Life Studies,* Uncle Devereux is dead and Lowell's father is gone at sea; Grandfather and the boy Lowell have become companions, the one as childish as the other; Grandfather, freed from Karl the chauffeur, letting his car "roller-coaster out of control down each hill," drinking root beer, making jokes about pumping ship as they urinate together at a tavern, the two of them happily headed to the family cemetery at Dunbarton to rake leaves from around the graves of "our dead forebears." This is one of those poems of Lowell's that just dramatically stops, as if switched off in mid-progress, these last three lines hanging above the void of an otherwise blank page.

> In the mornings I cuddled like a paramour
> in my grandfather's bed,
> while he scouted about the chattering greenwood
> stove.
>
> (*LS,* 67)

Aesthetically speaking this conclusion is not very satisfying; no catharsis or resolution is supplied. But of course the form of the poem is answering to the form of the vision, the way of seeing that brought it into being. Abrupt endings are never satisfying. That is the subtextual point. The point is complicated by the echo of the green wood chattering in the stove with the shellacked saplings in the earlier poem and with the dead leaves he and his grandfather strive to clear away. The young Lowell identifies with the newts he has caught in the stream, grounded and numb

> as scrolls of candied grapefruit peel.
>
> (*LS,* 66)

Lowell's father remains a child in these stories, beaming and ineffectual, playing with his car, loafing at the maritime museum —a kind of grown-up's playhouse in Salem. When he dies, his death is "abrupt and unprotesting. / His vision was still twenty-twenty" (*LS,* 74). The now-adult Lowell finds a book in his father's surprisingly dainty bedroom with "Robbie from Mother" written in the flyleaf, causing childhood and death to become once again identified.

Lowell's father's death is reported in the poem eerily titled "Terminal Days at Beverly Farms." Beverly Farms is the place near Salem where his parents had bought a house, so that Commander Lowell could relax and protect his health. Like his car, the house is a "plaything." It is the subject of a poem called "For Sale," short enough to show how form in Lowell's poems works from within.

> Poor sheepish plaything,
> organized with prodigal animosity,
> lived in just a year—
> my Father's cottage at Beverly Farms
> was on the market the month he died.
> Empty, open, intimate,
> its town-house furniture
> had an on tiptoe air
> of waiting for the mover
> on the heels of the undertaker.
> Ready, afraid
> of living alone till eighty,
> Mother mooned in a window,
> as if she had stayed on a train
> one stop past her destination.

(*LS,* 76)

The poem is slight by itself but it resonates with the other poems of *Life Studies* in ways that are intriguingly formal. The seer is still seeing the adults as children. The house itself seems helplessly vulnerable. A house ought to be stable; this one is tentative, ready itself to move, its furniture out of place from the start, an image of transience. The human life in it had given what value there was to the things. But for Mrs. Lowell now the house is only a place where she doesn't belong, like the furniture, like even the house itself. Odd rhymes and near-rhymes draw out the subject's strangeness—*sale, plaything, waiting, undertaker, afraid, eighty, stayed, train, destination*—as if some evil spirit was at work on a separate poem inside. Mrs. Lowell herself, in the next poem, is dead, brought home wrapped in her Italian tinfoil, and, ironic with rebirth, the "whole shoreline of the *Golfo di Genova* / was breaking into fiery flower" (*LS,* 77).

The poems of this part of *Life Studies* seem very simple on the surface—or "benign" and "detached," as Ian Hamilton has said—but that seeming normalcy is disrupted by the strangeness of connections beneath the surface, so that not only lives but the normalcy of the poems themselves is threatened and eroded. Mr. Lowell and Uncle Devereux Winslow are children in that they are *un*-seeing, and because they believe that life takes a form that cannot be infiltrated, except of course by disease and death. The all-seeing child who is the poet meanwhile registers disaccommodation and fear, attuned to how

Robert Lowell and Elizabeth Hardwick, 1949.

You were in your twenties, and I,
once hand on glass
and heart in mouth,
outdrank the Rahvs in the heat
of Greenwich Village, fainting at your feet—
too boiled and shy
and poker-faced to make a pass,
while the shrill verve
of your invective scorched the traditional South.

—From "Man and Wife"

human life remains mysterious despite our rational assaults upon it. At Beverly Farms, the Lowells

had no sea-view,
but sky-blue tracks of the commuters' railroad shone
like a double-barrelled shotgun
through the scarlet late August sumac,
multiplying like cancer
at their garden's border.

(*LS,* 73)

"I lean heavily to the rational," Lowell said in the "Afterthought" to the first *Notebook,* "but am devoted to surrealism."

Charles's parents in "The Boy with the Raspberry Sherbet Heart" thought being a surrealist was cute. Little did they know.

When in *Life Studies* Lowell's parents and grandparents are dead, he is suddenly a fully grown man, having fulfilled his surrealist bias by having *become* a kind of surrealism: in the hospital, tense and manic, among the other "thoroughbred mental cases," each by now an old-timer in his ironically normal state; or among pimps and pacifists in the West Street jail in New York. He is in jail as a conscientious objector because of the mass killings by the allies in Europe, but he is housed with Czar Lepke, a professional killer, who with his flags and Easter ribbons seems as American as apple pie. Lowell is least at home in his own home where his daughter is, wanting to play, where everyone on the street is a Republican of the "tranquilized Fifties," where his wife has led him back once more from "the kingdom of the mad."

From here on, Lowell's special way of seeing things will be an antiform within form. He will inhabit a world visible to him alone, nonetheless real for being surreal and nonetheless exhilarating for being threatening. He will be out of place anywhere else, in place only when there is no rest. In *For the Union Dead,* America itself begins to seem obliviously estranged from its own reality and the poet therefore from it. There is an odd, glancing allusion to this incompatibility in "The Old Flame," where the unorthodox and drunken exhilaration of his first marriage—he and his wife snowbound in their house, "quivering and fierce," "simmering like wasps in our tent of books"—is disrupted by the approach of the snowplow moving into this domestic bohemia with heraldic color,

> groaning uphill—
> a red light, then a blue,
> as it tossed off the snow
> to the side of the road.
>
> (*FUD,* 6)

That was in the past. The house, with new owners, is now itself a model of complacent Americana.

> Now a red ear of Indian maize
> was splashed on the door.
> Old Glory with thirteen stripes
> hung on a pole. The clapboard
> was old-red schoolhouse red.
>
> (*FUD,* 5)

Elsewhere, in his more famous poem about isolation, "On a thousand small New England greens, / The old white churches hold their air of sparse, sincere rebellion"; "The stone statue of the abstract Union Soldier / grows slimmer and younger each year . . ."; and a bas-relief image of Robert Shaw, stern and proud amidst his Negro cavalry, still stands across from the State House on the Boston Common. But an eerie counterforce is on the move: "yellow dinosaur steamshovels" grunt as they scoop up "tons of mush and grass / to gouge their underworld garage"; parking spaces "luxuriate like civic / sandpiles"; "giant finned cars nose forward like fish; / a savage servility slides by on grease" (*FUD,* 70–72). In New York at the mouth of the Hudson "chemical air / sweeps in from New Jersey / and smells of coffee. / Across the river, ledges of suburban factories tan / in the sulphur yellow sun"; the poet feels, absurdly, "like a birdwatcher" (*FUD,* 10). It is then fall 1961, and all of the talk is of nuclear holocaust, even the moon is "radiant with terror," while the state is out of reach, "a diver under a glass bell":

> A father's no shield
> for his child.
> we are like a lot of wild
> spiders crying together
> but without tears.
>
> ("Fall 1961," *FUD,* 11)

On the traffic circles in Washington, "green statues ride like South American / liberators above the breeding vegetation." "The elect, the elected" come here "bright as dimes, and die dishevelled and soft" ("July in Washington," *FUD,* 58). In *For the Union Dead,* Lowell's country is like his family, both smug and unconscious of a reality they cannot attend, drifting toward inertia, weirdly threatened, even more weirdly oblivious. (His father's voice, he had said in his Payne Whitney writing sketches, sounded to him like that of "a robot criticizing strawberry shortcake"). The effect, as before, except now more vivid for being an adult's experience, is one of estrangement, as if being cut off in a genre where different conventions apply. "I see / a dull and alien room, / my cell of learning"; "What has disturbed this household? / Only a foot away, / the familiar faces blur" ("Myopia: A Night," *FUD,* 70). He identifies movingly with Jonathan Edwards in his last years:

> I love you faded,
> old, exiled and afraid
> to leave your last flock, a dozen
> Houssatonic Indian children;

afraid to leave
all your writing, writing, writing,
denying the Freedom of the Will.
You were afraid to be president

of Princeton, and wrote:
"My defects are well known;
I have a constitution
peculiarly unhappy:

flaccid solids,
vapid, sizzy, scarse fluids,
causing a childish weakness,
a low tide of spirits.

I am contemptible,
stiff and dull.

Why should I leave behind
my delight and entertainment,
those studies
that have swallowed up my mind?"
("Jonathan Edwards in Western Massachusetts," *FUD,* 43–44)

There is no ease in this time and place from seeing things darkly. He says in "Eye and Tooth," "Nothing can dislodge" the images that threaten and isolate: "Young, my eyes begin to fail. / Nothing! No oil / for the eye, nothing to pour / on those waters or flames." He has always seen things like this, too much at once, surrealistic, like Charles.

Ian Hamilton calls *Life Studies* the most "American" of Lowell's volumes, but this is clearly not the case when *For the Union Dead* is read carefully and measured by the same standard. There is hardly any point in this fifth volume of Lowell's where the nature of American life itself is not somehow implicated in the discontinuity between the surreal way of seeing and the tunnel vision of the normal world. Around this theme in "Soft Wood," the volume's strongest and most accomplished poem, the personal and political are beautifully and characteristically brought together. Only momentarily at home in his cousin Harriet's house in Maine—where "things bend to the wind forever" and where the wind cleans and the salt heals—Lowell is unable not to think of what gradually erodes the sense of well-being. This is not surrealism at work now but a meditative inclusiveness of understanding, the mature child's inability not to see or to hold ordinary facts at bay. The wood of the house is clean because it is soft and wearing away. The house is not only not his but not really his cousin's before him; nor is the place, Castine, one where summer people rightfully belong. The town is a

Randall Jarrell, Robert Lowell, and Peter Taylor, 1948.

fishing village, the fine houses were formerly the old sea captains' houses whose "square-riggers used to whiten / the four corners of the globe." All that is gone, that power dispersed, except for the houses, which, truly known, are like shed skin and can "never fit another wearer." The surrealistic anxiety of *Life Studies* has taken on the authority of a rational form drawing the poem from a dreaming, Emersonian transcendence back into harsh fact. Mortality is real, not just a theme for poems. Harriet Winslow is far from her summer home, disabled by a stroke, "in Washington / breathing in the heat wave / and air-conditioning, knowing / each drug that numbs alerts another nerve to pain" (*FUD,* 63–64). Lowell has thought of her there; it seems logical now that he has been alerted again to suffering. In point of fact, Harriet Winslow *is* in Washington, but in this volume, with its suggestive title, it is inevitable that the otherwise unimaginable distance between quaint and remote Castine and urban and indisputably authentic Washington be measured, and that Washington be associated with pain.

It is a rule of thumb for poems of Lowell's like these, idiosyncratically modern and American, that the wider the field of vision—the more fact or matter one includes in a given meditative sequence—the less at home one is likely to feel anywhere. "Soft Wood" is explicitly a case in point. Even in *For the Union Dead* the poet cannot identify either with Colonel Shaw or with modern Boston; he is as "out of bounds" by disinheritance as single-mindedly heroic Shaw was; so he can yearn only for a vanished dream of oblivion: "I often sigh still / for the dark downward and vegetating kingdom / of the fish and reptile" (*FUD,* 70).

The house in Castine reappears in *Near the Ocean* in a different role. *Near the Ocean* is Lowell's Vietnam volume, and it shows him stranded in somewhat the same way he had seemed in *For the Union Dead.* His poems strive to sustain public utterance and to recover the old rhetorical formality. In both respects he is working from Andrew Marvell's example but achieves only wavering authority in a forced and awkwardly managed tetrameter line. But the public utterance does not suit any longer because Lowell is too radically displaced to be able to find the right idiom or the motivation to struggle for it. (Even the hoary old Tenth Satire of Juvenal is brought to bear in a new translation—seeming to be relevant but really quaintly extraneous to the contemporary situation.) There is no doubt that the war is a disastrous error. The problem is that the poet has lived long enough now to see America's military power once again blindly misused. History is now so hopelessly overdetermined that it seems pointless to resist.

> No weekends for the gods now. Wars
> flicker, earth licks its open sores,
> fresh breakage, fresh promotions, chance
> assassinations, no advance.
> Only man thinning out his kind
> sounds through the Sabbath noon, the blind
> swipe of the pruner and his knife
> busy about the tree of life . . .
>
> Pity the planet, all joy gone
> from this sweet volcanic cone;
> peace to our children when they fall
> in small war on the heels of small
> war—until the end of time
> to police the earth, a ghost
> orbiting forever lost
> in our monotonous sublime.

("Waking Early Sunday Morning," *NO,* 23–24)

Lowell is obsessed with minutiae, as if only unthreatened or unfatigued by things that do not even pretend to have a point. (In an earlier poem, he had imagined Hawthorne brooding, "eyes fixed on some chip, / some stone, some common plant, / the commonest thing, / as if it were the clue" and dissatisfied finally by his meditation "on the true and insignificant" (*FUD,* 39). He fantasizes about escape—from history altogether, certainly from being involuntarily responsible: "O to break loose"; "my body wakes / to feel the unpolluted joy / and criminal leisure of a boy"; "O that the spirit could remain / tinged but untarnished by its strain"; "O to break loose. All life's grandeur / is something with a girl in summer . . ." (*NO,* 16–23). The forced cynicism of the last remark—in the terrible historical context—shows how desperately alienated he has become. He is like an overeducated—and underactive—Frederick Henry (in *A Farewell to Arms*) trying to achieve, or just imagine, a separate peace—the American archetype casting himself back upon his own resources. This is how Harriet Winslow's house comes back into focus. There is an unconstraining charm to the patriotic pageantry in "Fourth of July in Maine," precisely because of its otherworldly normalcy and irrelevance, not much more or less in the grim mainstream of things than his daughter Harriet's pacific, munching guinea pigs. The house in this same way is like an appealing digression; a momentary access to a time of unambiguous creative zeal.

> This white Colonial frame house,
> willed downward, Dear, from you to us,
> still matters—the Americas'
> best artifact produced en masse.
> The founders' faith was in decay,
> and yet their building seems to say:
> "Everytime I take a breath,
> my God you are the air I breath."
>
> (*NO,* 29)

—as if there really were a moment of Byzantium back somewhere in America's past. It is as an artifact that the house appeals, *because* it is an artifact but having parity also with the guinea pigs and the Independence Day Parade: all representing states of intellectual innocence that the poet is drawn to but finally estranged from. He is back in his own genre at the poem's end, where the symbolic night wind is blowing the symbolic maps, and the sun cinders instead of warming and the whiskey burns instead of gratifying. It is the obsessed truth seer of the volume who imagines lovers in Central Park wishing "to leave this drying crust, / borne on the delicate wings of lust" (*NO,* 39).

Near the Ocean is a deeply demoralized volume, and the return to a stringent meter and couplet rhymes—like ghosts of form—cannot disguise that fact and barely tries to. Pondering this circumstance compels us to recall Lowell's statements about the writer's existence becoming his art and how he hardly exists without it. More than once in the poems Lowell will come upon a cold hollowness that inhibits, perhaps, any genuine freedom. *Notebook* (he says at one point in it) is like a honeycomb "that proves its maker is alive."

In the last decade of his life, Lowell's poems will be most concerned with the survival of the inner life, while at the same time testing the boundaries of experience and the reach of his understanding of it, putting himself in a kind of metaphysical jeopardy in the process. The testing is shown in the notational style that dominates his technique (until the last volume). This style is intended to serve the instant, to set down what has just passed, whether it conforms to what preceded or what will come or not, or whether it is flattering or not or impressive artistically. Everything in this method begins to compete for parity with everything else. Value, involving premeditated choice, requiring selection and emphasis, becomes distributed into a democratic welter of minutely registered detail; and because thoughts and feelings are layered and contradictory and, often enough, not even fully formed, identity itself begins to lose definition. Whatever else may be said of *Notebook,* the burden of the vatic role of *Near the Ocean* has been decisively cast off. The interesting and predictable new event is that in this newly won freedom nothing coheres. The poems are made to cohere more or less arbitrarily by their sonnet length and shape; and that threatened, because inorganic, control remains visible to us throughout a very long volume. Lowell's style has risked laying everything on the line by giving everything a chance to count.

Since *Notebook* is so startlingly radical, it is worth pausing to remember that the persona in Lowell's poems after *Life Studies* has always been threatened by seeing more at once than a good analyst would regard as healthy. He is alive, in the very midst of life, in the poem, not aesthetically cloned or even socialized; but the price that he has to pay for life in that sense is a constant edgy anxiety (anxiety indeed *is* the life) and a refusal of sanctuary. Such passion produces odd and existentially intriguing results. Since the survival of the life is a main issue in *Notebook,* a recurring subject is the poet's surprisingly active sexual life; many such episodes are frankly recounted. Ian Hamilton quotes one of Lowell's younger partners as saying that she understood of course that he came to her for "renewal." The theme of sexual renewal reminds us of Lowell's interest in being reborn in his poems, and whatever else one might say about the affairs and infatuations in real life—in any other man conventional signs of a midlife crisis—sexual affairs *can* be made to seem renewing once translated into poems and given the right treatment. There is nothing inherently offensive or absurd about Lowell's doing this, so long as it works poetically. But what rescues these poems about sexual euphoria from the banality that threatens them is Lowell's own insomniac apprehension and attention. The progression of "Soft Wood" could be thought of as a model here, too. One of the main points of sexual passion is to lose oneself to the passion—to override thought and irony —and to try to achieve a banal and momentary peace. In this respect, sexual gratification is a kind of blessed regression into biological normalcy—it is even in a real sense, dehumanizing. So the "renewal" Lowell was said to have sought could be a recovery of his youth and vigor (he was around fifty when the episodes took place) but also a renewal of his bearings in, so to speak, the real and generic world. But as if he were thinking again—"Dearest, I cannot loiter here / in lather like a polar bear"—each such normalizing occasion in *Notebook* is soon disrupted by a thought or an image that brings the mode of surrealism once again into play. Even this pattern seems bleakly American, as if sexual enchantment were a kind of clearing, a new and open space, which is eventually closed in on so as to require pulling up stakes and once again moving on.

> Our leeway came so seldom, fell so short,
> overwatched by some artist's skylight in the city,
> or some suburban frame-house basement window,
> angular, night-bluish, blear-eyed, spinsterish—
> still this is something, something we can both
> take hold of willingly, go smash on, if we will.
>
> (*NB,* 80)

The physical world in these poems is an urban world, close enough to touch at any given moment, crowding in to restrict space and freedom, to mock love and the voluptuous flesh.

> We open the window, and there is no view,
> No green meadow pointing to *the* green meadow,
> to dogs, to deer, Diana in her war-skirt,
> Heaven must be paved with terra-cotta tile . . .
>
> (*NB,* 63)

He is absorbed by signs of nature struggling—stranded, ragged last leaves, sumac growing through cracks in stone—not so much because of his age as because of his conviction that some incomprehensible force in life threatens human and natural things with subjugation and extinction. Repeatedly this anxiety breaks through in images that do not on the other hand assimilate (as metaphors are supposed to do) but are all the more compelling for their opaqueness:

> I've slept so late here, snow has stubbled my throat;
> students in their hundreds rise from the beehive,
> swarm-mates; they have clocks and instincts,
>   make classes. In the high sky, a parochial school,
>   the top floor looking like the Place des Vosges—
> a silk stocking, blown thin as smog, coils in a twig-fork,
> dangling a wire coathanger, rapier-bright,
> a long throw for a hard cold day . . . wind lifting
> the stocking like a lecherous lost leg.
>
> Each hour the stocking thins, the hanger dulls;
> cold makes the school's green copper cupola
> greener over the defoliated playground. . . .
>
> (*NB,* 79)

It would be hard to say why that eerie stocking deserves as much attention as it gets in this sequence of lines (crossing two poems in the suite called "Harvard"), but it clearly suggests a sinister displacement, a perversion of nature and the flesh. It associates with the way in which the copper cupola has taken to itself the green of the now defoliated playground; and the word "defoliated" in 1971 would have inescapably invoked American military strategy in Vietnam, which had brought the term into currency. The span of implication in these few lines is very great—oddly immeasurable—and yet read in conventional terms, they hardly seem to be *about* anything at all. There is a fierce pressure of meaning which does not release itself for us by becoming clear, as if the world were an allegorical code that cannot be broken. The threatening things seem to inhabit a kingdom of their own within ours but secret, taking what seems to be our achievements into their own. This world of Lowell's is one in which being able to feel at home is so unlikely that it becomes a progressively receding, wistful dream.

And yet when we hold *Notebook* in our hands—two hundred and forty-two pages of text, roughly two poems to a page—and then begin reading in it once more, we gradually realize that being at home or being happy and secure in time were at this point irrelevant to Lowell, and that the deep, almost mannered pessimism of this volume is offset by its sheer abundance and intellectual range. The variety and complexity of the world, the sensations of it, the quirks of it, calling for thought and meditation, the richness and density of the world's being tend to override any darker thoughts or feelings we may have about its purpose or future. This is a difficult paradox, perhaps impossible to state in any way other than the way Lowell has done. But a book like *Notebook* in itself—in its richness of interest and subject, of historical reference, of intimate disclosure, of mystified pleasure and pain, of exposure and striving—is the very reverse of the demoralized fatigue that characterizes so much of its tone otherwise. Thought and feeling do seem separated into one category, and mediated experience into another, as if thought and feeling rather than having a privileged status had instead the same status as what is filtered through them. The sexual adventures in this light seem metonymic, both a part of and standing for a rapacious psychic energy that is the true and undying eros.

The poet here is in thrall to thought only because of the range of experience it can comprehend. The comprehensiveness itself is beyond both good and evil and reason. The power to contain these multitudes supersedes and consumes the will toward negation and despair. Once everything is allowed to count, suddenly everything *does* count, and the painful longing for home, for a secure dwelling, is implicitly forsaken, undone by the raw will to encounter the real inexhaustibility of the world. Ezra Pound had written: "Art very possibly ought to be the supreme achievement, the 'Accomplished'; but there is the other satisfactory effect, that of man hurling himself at an indomitable chaos and yanking and hauling as much of it as possible into some sort of order (or beauty) aware of it both as chaos and as potential." Even in this context Elizabeth Bishop's words are again meaningful: "The whole purpose of art" is in showing "everything and anything" as "material for poetry," to make it "*be* poetry," so that "life *is* all right, for the time being." Lowell thinks of and writes about such things obliquely:

> And now, the big town river, once hard and dead as its
>   highways,
> rolls blackly into the country river, root-banks, live ice,
> a live muskrat muddying the moonlight.
>
> (*NB,* 66)

What he feared most had become temporarily what would save him.

Then in an odd way this reading is confirmed by his next wholly new book, *Dolphin. Dolphin* and his last book, *Day by Day,* both deal primarily with his affair with, marriage to, and finally separation from Caroline Blackwood, in the course of

For the Union Dead

"Relinquunt Omnia Servare Rem Publicam"

The old South Boston Aquarium stands
in a Sahara of snow now. Its broken windows are boarded.
The bronze weathervane cod has lost half its scales.
The airy tanks are dry.

Once my nose crawled like a snail on the glass;
my hand tingled
to burst the bubbles
drifting from the noses of the cowed, compliant fish.

My hand draws back. I often sigh still
for the dark downward and vegetating kingdom
of the fish and reptile. One morning last March,
I pressed against the new barbed and galvanized

fence on the Boston Common. Behind their cage,
yellow dinosaur steamshovels were grunting
as they cropped up tons of mush and grass
to gouge their underworld garage.

Parking spaces luxuriate like civic
sandpiles in the heart of Boston.
A girdle of orange, Puritan-pumpkin colored girders
braces the tingling Statehouse,

shaking over the excavations, as it faces Colonel Shaw
and his bell-cheeked Negro infantry
on St.-Gaudens' shaking Civil War relief,
propped by a plank splint against the garage's earthquake.

Saint-Gaudens's monument to Colonel Shaw and the Massachusetts 54th.

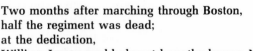

Two months after marching through Boston,
half the regiment was dead;
at the dedication,
William James could almost hear the bronze Negroes breathe.

Their monument sticks like a fishbone
in the city's throat.
Its Colonel is as lean
as a compass-needle.

He has an angry wrenlike vigilance,
a greyhound's gentle tautness;
he seems to wince at pleasure,
and suffocate for privacy.

He is out of bounds now. He rejoices in man's lovely,
peculiar power to choose life and die—
when he leads his black soldiers to death,
he cannot bend his back.

On a thousand small town New England greens,
the old white churches hold their air
of sparse, sincere rebellion; frayed flags
quilt the graveyards of the Grand Army of the Republic.

The stone statues of the abstract Union Soldier
grow slimmer and younger each year—
wasp-waisted, they doze over muskets
and muse through their sideburns . . .

Shaw's father wanted no monument
except the ditch,
where his son's body was thrown
and lost with his "niggers."

The ditch is nearer.
There are no statues for the last war here;
on Boylston Street, a commercial photograph
shows Hiroshima boiling

over a Mosler Safe, the "Rock of Ages"
that survived the blast. Space is nearer.
When I crouch to my television set,
the drained faces of Negro school-children rise like balloons.

Colonel Shaw
is riding on his bubble,
he waits
for the blessèd break.

The Aquarium is gone. Everywhere,
giant finned cars nose forward like fish;
a savage servility
slides by on grease.

which also a son is born. The theme of renewal is prominent in the first of the two volumes. The many women of *Notebook* have become one, and that one is idealized as the Dolphin to serve the theme: "I spout the smarting waters of joy in your face — / rough weather fish, who cuts your nets and chains" (*D,* 54). He has left his wife of twenty-one years and his daughter of fourteen to achieve this rescue in a new life. Gradually in a strange country, England, he begins to feel at home, more at one with his life and feelings—despite residual guilt—than he has ever expressed himself as being. It is not easy. He is, as he says, "overtrained for England"; and he is kept off-balance by the anxiety of his choices. Eventually, in the period reported in *Day by Day,* he will succumb to a voluptuous torpor. In *Dolphin* there is animation, ardor, intimacy, but the poet who contains multitudes is constrained now by the very conventionality of what he is doing. Even in this ruthless act of self-renewal Lowell cannot escape the ironic awareness that he has suddenly become a conventional character in a conventional plot, a plot which by definition closes out the outside world. This plot limits the range of his interests and freedom, the range of his mind and its access to experience. The irony is not allowed to be lost: "We follow our script as timorously as actors, / unalterably divorced from choice by choice" (*D,* 53). He, in fact, finds many ways to call attention to it: "Living with you is living a long book / *War and Peace,* from day to day to day, / unable to look off or answer my name" (*D,* 51)—unable, that is to respond to the outside world or to be sure who in fact he is. Caroline has a dream in which she is strolling happily with "Lizzie," talking of a simple plot about a woman and a man, versifying her tragedy in which "you"—Lowell—"did not exist" (*D,* 50). "The price of freedom is displacing facts," he says in another place. "Good narrative is cutting down description." But good narrative is inhibiting, too, especially if one is part of it is, as his is, a "common plot" (*D,* 45).

> Focus about me and a blur inside;
> on walks, things nearest to me go slow motion,
> obscene streetlife rushes on the wheelrim,
> steel shavings from the vacillating will.
>
> (*D,* 42)

In *Notebook* "obscene streetlife" is at the hub, not rushing by, an indistinguishable blur, on the rim. To enhance his existence Lowell has isolated and stylized his existence and thus created by his choice a paradoxical countereffect: the very act of choosing, of acting out choice, has subverted choice.

Correspondingly, the weakness of *Dolphin*—measured by *Notebook*'s standard—is that it is a better book. It has form—a subject, a plot, and a structure—though it also has a poet in it who cannot simply subdue himself to the pleasures of lust and love but must watch and think about and write about himself doing so. Conventionality is a bondage mainly when it is seen as such, as it is here, and admitted to be. One poem that Lowell starts out in the old *Notebook* vein, "Tired Iron," free-associating about the "great war of our youth" compared with the new war, Vietnam, of someone else's youth, suddenly simply stops, and everything—as in *Dolphin* is always the case—turns back inward:

> We promised to put back Liberty on her feet . . .
> I can't go on with this, the measure is gone:
> a waterfall, the water white on green,
> like the white letters on my olive keyboard. . . .
>
> (*D,* 55)

"I am in bondage here," he says in the next poem, "and cannot fly; / when marriage is surmounted, what is left?" Existential proving grounds are now behind him, as if when sprawling, not-to-be-contained existence no longer supersedes essence, essence itself becomes false. Form is a self, but it is not a Whitman-like self, not American in Whitman's and the other Lowell's scary way of being so. The theme of loss of identity in *Dolphin* is the surviving Whitman-Lowell's critique of what he otherwise affirms: "my eyes have seen what my hand did" (*D,* 78).

The warring of these two claims within Lowell goes on in *Day by Day* to the end, with an inevitable preoccupation with death taking precedence. Tranquillity and solitude and death are too much alike not to induce thoughts of each other. It becomes natural for Lowell to look for the winter skeletons in summer trees and to be barely conscious of what a blossom is ("Notice"). The scene of *Day by Day* is largely that of the short soporific period of withdrawal with Caroline into a version of country life at their home in Kent. The home-seeking impulse in Lowell draws him further inward but its opposite is wary and resistant:

> "These days of only poems and depression—
> what can I do with them?
> Will they help me to notice
> what I cannot bear to look at?"
>
> (*DD,* 118)

© 1967 JILL KREMENTZ

Robert Lowell on the march on the Pentagon, October 21, 1967.

In the middle of these speakers Robert Lowell was called up. He had been leaning against a wall in his habitual slumped-over position, deep in revery at the side of the steps—and . . . the call for him to say a few words caught him partly by surprise. He now held the portable hand microphone with a delicate lack of intimacy as if it were some valuable, huge, and rare tropical spider which he was obliged to examine but did not have to enjoy. "I was asked earlier today" he began in his fine stammering voice which gave the impression that life rushed at him like a series of hurdles and some he succeeded in jumping and some he did not, "I was asked earlier this afternoon by a reporter why I was not turning in my draft card," Lowell said with the beginnings of a pilgrim's passion, "and I did not tell him it was a stupid question, although I was tempted to. I thought he should have known that I am now too old to have a draft card, but that it makes no difference. When some of us pledge to counsel and aid and abet any young men who wish to turn in their cards, why then you may be certain we are aware of the possible consequences and do not try to hide behind the technicality of whether we literally have a draft card or not. . . ."

It was said softly, on a current of intense indignation and Lowell had never looked more dignified nor more admirable. Each word seemed to come on a separate journey from the poet's mind to his voice, along a winding route or through an exorbitant gate. Each word cost him much—Lowell's fine grace was in the value words had for him, he seemed to emit a horror at the possibility of squandering them or leaving them abused.

—From *The Armies of the Night* by Norman Mailer

What he cannot bear to look at is, in effect, the "obscene street-life" on the rim in *Dolphin.* At home he knows that he can walk blindfolded, so familiar is it, but he knows too the danger of that assurance: "But we must notice— / we are designed for the moment" (*DD,* 118). Being at home is not noticing; being at home is a drift toward inertia and peace. The opposite is a *"dream of hell"—"packing up a house / with demons eternally asking / thought-provoking questions"* (*DD,* 116). It is in this volume that Lowell records remembering his mother stalking the beaches of Long Island bearing him, her only child, wishing she were dead, and Merrill Moore reporting that he had been unwanted. In other poems in the volume his mother appears weirdly, almost deliberately, thwarting her child's need to take a home for granted.

> Your parlor was a reproach. . . .
> you used to brush mantelpiece and banister
> with the forefinger of a fresh white glove for dust.
>
> "Why do we keep expecting life to be easy,
> when we know it never can be?"
>
> ("To Mother," *DD,* 78)

. . . .

> Is the one unpardonable sin
> our fear of not being wanted?
> For this, will mother go on cleaning house
> for eternity, and making it unlivable?
>
> ("Unwanted," *DD,* 124)

Now approaching the age of his mother's and his father's deaths, Lowell can relish the common peace denied him as a child; but he is no longer a child and therefore no longer innocent of what true peace is or where it tends.

> I seek leave unimpassioned by my body,
> I am too weak to strain to remember, or give
> recollection the eye of a microscope.
>
> ("Shifting Colors," *DD,* 119)

His double in this particular poem is an ageless white horse—"slightly discolored by dirt"—who seems to graze a whole field without moving. And as the poet equivalent to that horse, what he writes about is "horse and meadow, duck and pond, / universal consolatory / description without significance, / transcribed verbatim by my eye" (*DD,* 120). This receptiveness is a passivity that is the volume's profoundest influence; yet only

An Artist in His Studio *by Jan Vermeer.*

Epilogue

Those blessèd structures, plot and rhyme—
why are they no help to me now
I want to make
something imagined, not recalled?
I hear the noise of my own voice:
The painter's vision is not a lens,
It trembles to caress the light.
But sometimes everything I write
with the threadbare art of my eye
seems a snapshot,
lurid, rapid, garish, grouped,
heightened from life,
yet paralysed by fact.
All's misalliance.
Yet why not say what happened?
Pray for the grace of accuracy
Vermeer gave to the sun's illumination
stealing like the tide across a map
to his girl solid with yearning.
We are poor passing facts,
warned by that to give
each figure in the photograph
his living name.

five poems later, in the last poem, "Epilogue," he is refusing inertia, wanting to make / "something imagined, not recalled." "I hear the noise of my own voice: / *The painter's vision is not a lens, / it trembles to caress the light"* (*DD,* 127). But this voice is one that comes from his past life, a different, more voracious state of being, the eros of *Notebook* rather than that of *Day by Day,* where idly observing the stability of nature is the norm, or watching "The stars' / extravagant, useless journey across the sky." That drift away from energy, from language itself—"age is nothing voiced"—is interrupted by unpredictable psychotic episodes and by the resurfacing of his most painful childhood memories. And in the end England, home, and peace do not prevail, for he abandons it all and returns to America.

Perhaps that peace that he yearned toward was not really there in the first place. Certainly his prized and high-strung Dolphin was no surrogate mother, let alone "Queen of Heaven" (who "never doubted / the divided, stricken soul / could call her Maria, / and rob the devil with a word" ["Home," *DD,* 115]).

But the old Brahmin-Whitman Lowell, otherwise Charles, the surrealist, with the raspberry sherbet heart, was most assuredly "overtrained for England." In the real-life chronology of *Day by Day* the poet has two new doubles: a demented male swan, escaped from "his safe, stagnant, matriarchal pond" gallanting "down the stout-enriched rapids to Dublin, / smirking drunkenly . . . / as if to show a king had a right to be too happy" ("Last Walk," *DD,* 14); and Ulysses, returning warily to his Penelope, escaping Circe, "risk" still "his metier" after all, circling Penelope's house like a shark, "flesh-proud, sore-eyed, scar-proud, / a vocational killer / in the machismo of senility" ("Ulysses and Circe," *DD,* 9). One who can think of himself in this way has not been unmanned by his dream of home, still yearns not just to perceive but "to caress the light," remains insatiable and unfulfilled like the Horace of "Intermissa, Venus, diu," pursuing his Ligurian girl only to see "her lost / in the Tiber he could not hold" ("Departure," *DD,* 17). He still fears death more than life, even where life is a mingling "of all sorts of beautiful and unlikely things" in the mind and where each voice that is true to its fear is saying, "Help me!"

We know from Ian Hamilton's biography that the period of Lowell's life spanned by *Day by Day* was a much greater turmoil than the book itself shows, though the book is certainly troubled and wary as it is. His manic seizures and Caroline Blackwood's nervous and anxious temperament had made for a disastrous combination. But he seems to have wanted the book to commemorate even this troubled peace that he had known, and he had arranged the poems achronologically to create this effect, as if in art trying to achieve a stability he could not have—for internal and external reasons—in life. By the time *Day by Day* was published in August 1977, Lowell was back again in America. Milgate, the country house in Kent, had been abruptly sold. Caroline was living with the children in an inhospitable castle outside Dublin. Lowell had rooms alone in Cambridge. Congestive heart failure had put him for a short period in Phillips House (where his grandfather Winslow, whom he had written about, had died of cancer). Then on September 12, after a last terrible trip to Dublin, Lowell himself died in New York in a taxicab returning to his and Elizabeth's old place on West 67th Street, in transit as usual. After an Episcopal high Mass in Boston, he was buried in the family graveyard in Dunbarton, itself having been moved only a few years before to make way for a Corps of Engineers dam project.

Ian Hamilton ends his biography by citing Christopher Ricks on Lowell's death, who had remembered William Empson on Lear:

> The scapegoat who has collected all this wisdom for us is viewed at the end with a sort of hushed envy, not I think really because he has become wise but because the general human desire for experience has been so glutted in him; he has been through everything.

Lowell had allowed his desire to keep him from peace until the very end without even very much wisdom to show for it. Empson's words remind us that he had therefore fulfilled, in an ironic way, Emerson's vision of the poet who would traverse "the whole scale of experience" and "tell us how it was with him." He had also extended the reach of another poignantly American idea expressed by Robert Frost. "There is at least so much good in the world that it admits of form and the making of form. And not only admits of it but calls for it." Against the background of "hugeness and confusion shading away from where we stand into black and utter chaos," Frost had said, "any little form I assert . . . is velvet, as the saying is, and to be considered for how much more it is than nothing. If I were a Platonist, I should have to consider it . . . for how much less it is than everything." As after Whitman and William Carlos Williams, American poetry could never be the same.

Ariel (3) October 27 1962

Stasis in darkness,
Then the substanceless blue
Pour of tor & distances.

God's lioness!
How one we grow!
Pivot of heels & knees! The furrow

Splits & passes
Sister to the brown arc
Of the neck I cannot catch,

Nigger-eye
Berries cast dark
Hooks, ~~but do not catch black~~

Black ~~black~~ sweet blood mouthfuls!
Shadows!
Something else

Hauls me through air-
Thighs, hair;
Flakes from my heels. → White Godiva, I unpeel—
Dead hands, dead stringencies!

And now I
Foam to wheat, a glitter of seas.
The child's cry

Melts in the wall.
O bright beast, I
Am the arrow, the dew that flies
Suicidal, at one with the drive
Into the red
Eye, the cauldron of morning.

SYLVIA PLATH

HELEN MCNEIL

Sylvia Plath was a brilliant and compelling lyric poet, particularly in the poems of *Ariel* (1965) which even now, more than twenty years after her suicide, seize the reader with their stunning, immediate power. At the same time, Plath herself, or a fictional figure bearing Plath's name, has become a modern totem, a symbolic figure of angry suffering whose precise import shifts according to the needs of her readers. It is not accident that intense interest has fastened upon Plath as protagonist of the psychological dramas which her poems and prose are thought to chronicle. Her autobiographical novel *The Bell Jar*, the poem "Daddy," and a score or so other poems from her last year depict a subjectivity instantly recognizable to the female—and feminist—consciousness which constitutes much contemporary sensibility; indeed, Plath (or the Plath-totem) is one of the creators of that sensibility.

All of Plath's writings have a double dynamic which arises—to put the case at its simplest—from the revealed and the repressed speaking at the same time. This essay will examine the development of that dynamic, bringing in Plath's life and its totemic representations where necessary. The dynamics of repression generate much of the power of Plath's voice, but the interplay of declaration and repression plays more than a purely formal role in Plath's work; when we follow the traces left by the energizing but hidden self we are also pursuing what I take to be Plath's commanding themes.

The simultaneous process of repression and the surfacing of the repressed is particularly visible in Plath's prose, as it is in Kafka and some of the works of Virginia Woolf.[1] Typically, in Plath, a biting satiric stance distances her unexamined speaker from the human dross that she surveys. Indeed, the absoluteness of this technique of satiric rejection makes it a particularly convenient secondary mode for a writer of great lyric imagination. For Plath, as occasionally for Blake, Shelley or indeed Woolf, destructive satire offers a release from the inexorable sincerity of the lyric "I."

Plath's short story "The Daughters of Blossom Street" (whose

Sylvia Plath, 1950.

material, like that of the story "Johnny Panic and the Bible of Dreams," was taken from Plath's brief 1958 secretarial employment typing records at the psychiatric clinic of Massachusetts General Hospital) shows the workings of Plath's satire of repression. The narrator, a young woman, describes a fellow secretary:

> Cora, in Psychiatric Social Service down the hall from Dotty and me, is nowhere the person Dotty is—pushing forty, you can tell it by the pleats around her eyes, even if she does keep her hair red, thanks to those coloured rinses. Cora lives with her mother, and to hear her talk you'd think she was a green teenager . . . Cora keeps taking these bus trips to Lake Louise and these cruises to Nassau in her vacations to meet Mr Right, but all she ever meets is girls from

Tumour Clinic or Amputee Clinic and every one of them on the self-same mission. (*Johnny Panic,* 81–82)

The tone is that of one of Eudora Welty's harpies, but unrelieved by Welty's humane, comic understanding. Dread of becoming middle-aged and failing to find any sexual partner reveals itself through the narrator's jaunty put-down. Yet "pushing forty" happens to us all, if we are lucky; by transferring aging to the pathetic Cora, Plath declares it "other," though she also severely limits her narrative authority by the same act. Not far from this text is the figure of Plath's celibate mother, Aurelia, who had never remarried after the death of her husband. The "Amputee Clinic" that is said to pursue Cora recalls the amputation of Plath's father's foot shortly before his death, a real and symbolic mutilation that pursued Plath all the way to her 1962 poem "Daddy."

Plath's most powerful mode was the lyric poem, in which a subjective speaker is already assumed. In Plath, however, one function of the subjective lyric voice is to mask the acts of a deeper self while simultaneously tracing their presence by an otherwise inexplicable vehemence. Plath's later poems, the basis for her lasting fame, show her characteristic doubled voice in its full complexity. Although these poems are syntactically straightforward, beautifully rhythmic, and vividly imaged, their full meaning can seem held back. Plath's voice structures her poems. Yet it often depicts a self whose subjectivity is displayed while the bases of that subjectivity are hidden.

In "Fever 103" (1962) the speaker declares:

I am too pure for you or anyone.
Your body
Hurts me as the world hurts God.

We never learn why the speaker is injured; it is simply, irrefutably the case; the stylistic authority of Plath's voice is what makes the statement believable. This wounded speaker may be an invented *persona,* but if so, her situation appears in poem after poem. "Fever 103" may be what it seems, namely, a depiction of impressions during illness, but it carries too much emphasis to be only that; some more profound alienation from the body's organs and their sensations has been condensed into the state of feverishness. The stronger Plath's subjectivity is, the more there seems to be hidden behind it. The more arbitrary the emotion, the stronger the passion pushing it out.

There is, however, a second dynamic to Plath's voice. While the hidden self comes and goes, Plath's mythological imagery is generating meaning directly. "Fever 103° continues:

I am a lantern—

My head a moon
Of Japanese paper, my gold beaten skin
Infinitely delicate and infinitely expensive.

Plath developed a characteristic image-vocabulary whose terms are recognizable and shared. In "Fever 103°" the image of the moon-balloon also evokes a Japanese paper lantern and the beaten gold death masks of Mycenae. As the speaker ascends, she is becoming a pale bodiless lamp, generating her own light and heat. Finally she transcends the masks and "old whore petticoats" of the world of sexual relationships and representations. It is as if the female body has been a weight imposed upon her by her lover's gaze and touch. Much postwar American poetry explicitly addresses problems of the self, but that self can usually be presumed to be arriving at speech directly through the imagery it uses; this is certainly the case with Theodore Roethke's mythic and psychological self-examinations. Plath's poetic voice, however, lures the reader back to a hidden self while at the same time addressing itself outwards through interpretable imagery. This unusual doubling is the source of much of Plath's peculiar power, stressful and exhilarating at once.

When Plath's hidden self achieved an absolute closure by suicide, it took on the shape of fiction. That shape, the Plath-totem, is not part of the poems, but it haunts our reading of them. The bereaved and betrayed child (Plath's father died when she was eight), the dutiful daughter, the young woman caught in a classic double bind between a fifties model of femininity and her conviction of artistic vocation, the seductive chronicler of breakdown and suicide, the mythologizer of womanly archetypes, the exalted wife in a marriage of true minds, the passionately loving mother, the tormented truth-teller, the cold death-voice: all these speaking images are screens. No single image or combination of images wholly identifies the voice of the Plath poem. Rather, these self-generated icons stand totemically behind the poems, hiding and figuring forth still deeper ghosts whose power they imply.

The availability of almost all of Sylvia Plath's writing, some admittedly in heavily edited form,[2] means that it is now possible to see her driving consciousness displayed across different genres. Plath was both a prolific and a multigeneric writer. Having had a poem published when she was eight years old and other work published while she was a high school student, Plath arrived at Smith College in 1950 already defined as a writer. From 1956, when she met and married the English poet Ted

Hughes (now poet laureate) while she was studying for the English Tripos on a Fulbright fellowship at Newnham College, Cambridge, to 1963, when she died, Plath wrote over two hundred poems and prepared almost all of them for publication. During Plath and Hughes's time in the United States, July 1957–December 1959, when Plath taught at Smith and then, having decided against an academic career, worked at odd jobs, she wrote the children's poems of *The Bed Book* and the short stories subsequently collected in *Johnny Panic and the Bible of Dreams. The Bell Jar*, based upon Plath's 1953 breakdown, suicide attempt, and partial recovery, was written in 1962, when Plath and Hughes were living in Devon, England, after the birth of their daughter Frieda (b. 1960). Frieda and Nicholas (b. 1962) were the subjects of a number of poems, including the lovely "You're" (1960) in which the newborn Frieda is "my little loaf," and "A clean slate, with your own face on." In her last nine months, while separating from Hughes and trying to set up home in London with her children, Plath wrote her greatest poems, some composed only days before she gassed herself in February 1963.

Of Plath's hundreds of letters, those to her mother have been collected and edited by Aurelia Plath in *Letters Home*. Most of the self-analytic, passionate, and occasionally savage *Journals,*[3] Plath's chronicle of her struggle to survive and create, have now been published. Yet despite Plath's energetic literary output, and her highly professional attitude towards magazine publication, only her first poetry collection, *The Colossus* (1960, 1962), and *The Bell Jar* (1963), published under the pseudonym Victoria Lucas, appeared in book form during her lifetime. Plath's fame is posthumous, based upon the relentless *Ariel* poems, published in 1965.

Plath's youth and her literary apprenticeship were determined by the strongly enforced cultural conventions of the 1950s. Because Plath died young, all her work offers the shared discoveries of youth: the positive joy in discovery itself; energy, idealism, and belief in the limitless capacities of language; and the negatives of disillusion, false stances and conflict over sex role. The same youthfulness meant that her work until her last year shows the marks of the quite explicit repression of emotion and sexuality that was expected of a young woman writer seeking entry into the literary establishment.

When Plath arrived at Smith College in 1950, it was the heyday of the New Criticism. T. S. Eliot's "impersonality" and his anti-Romantic English canon had been wholeheartedly adopted; unsurprisingly, Plath never was moved by the Romantics, except for Blake, whom she read later, with Hughes. The poetic models readily available to the youthful Plath were

Mlle's last word on college, '53
We're stargazers
this season, bewitched
by an atmosphere of
evening blue. Foremost in the
fashion constellation we spot MLLE's
own tartan, the astronomic versatility of sweaters,
and men, men, men—we've even taken the shirts off their backs!
Focusing our telescope on college news around the globe, we debate and deliberate.
Issues illuminated: academic freedom, the sorority controversy, our much labeled (and libeled)
generation. From our favorite fields, stars of the first magnitude shed a bright influence on
our plans for jobs and futures. Although horoscopes for our ultimate orbits aren't yet in, we
Guest Eds. are counting on a favorable forecast with this send-off from MLLE, the star of the campus.
—Sylvia Plath, Smith College, '54

Sylvia Plath won a Mademoiselle *guest editorship in 1953. She is number one in this group photograph.*

Yeats, Auden ("He is my conception of the perfect poet," *Letters,* 107), Eliot himself, and the metaphysicals. Plath was drawn to the more aesthetic modern American poets, such as "the lyric clarity and purity of Elinor Wylie" (*Journals,* 32), a poet who, though Plath doesn't comment on it, described female frustration and guilt in her famously cool rhymed quatrains and sonnets. She also enjoyed e. e. cummings, Archibald MacLeish, Conrad Aiken, Louis Untermeyer; with the possible exception of Wylie, it is a typical list for a young educated reader of the period. While at Smith, in Northampton, Massachusetts, Plath read and imitated Emily Dickinson, the poet of nearby Amherst,

First, are you our sort of person?
Do you wear
A glass eye, false teeth or a crutch,
A brace or a hook,
Rubber breasts or a rubber crotch,

Stitches to show something's missing? No, no? Then
How can we give you a thing?
Stop crying.
Open your hand.
Empty? Empty. Here is a hand

To fill it and willing
To bring teacups and roll away headaches
And do whatever you tell it.
Will you marry it? . . .

Now your head, excuse me, is empty.
I have the ticket for that.
Come here, sweetie, out of the closet.
Well, what do you think of *that?*
Naked as paper to start

But in twenty-five years she'll be silver,
In fifty, gold.
A living doll, everywhere you look.
It can sew, it can cook,
It can talk, talk, talk.

It works, there is nothing wrong with it.
You have a hole, it's a poultice.
You have an eye, it's an image.
My boy, it's your last resort.
Will you marry it, marry it, marry it.

—From "The Applicant"

Sylvia Plath's "jobiography" as a Mademoiselle *guest editor.*

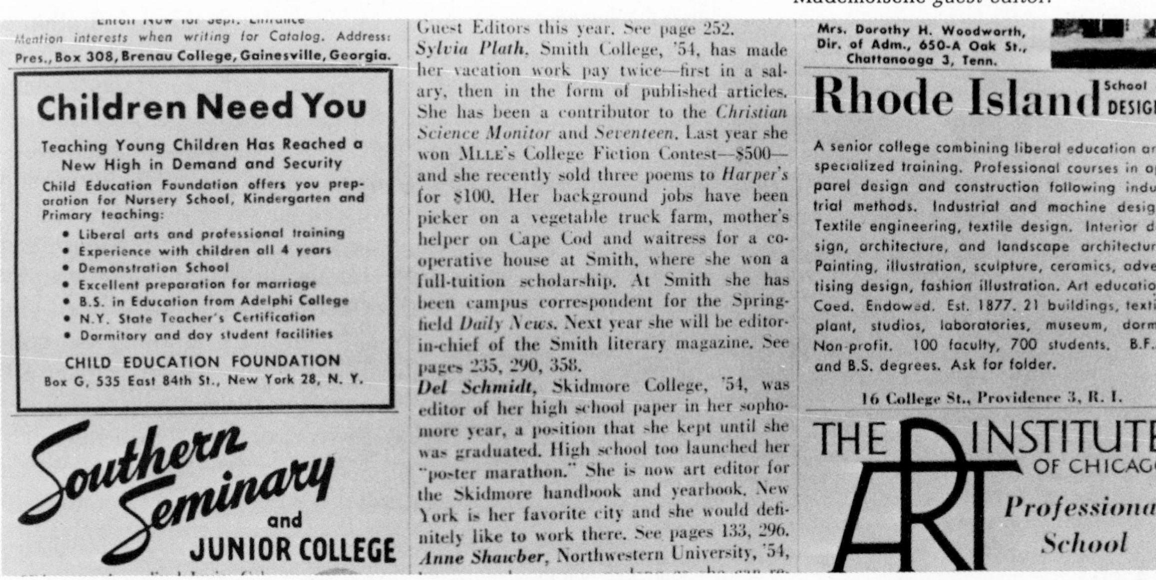

Mention interests when writing for Catalog. Address: Pres., Box 308, Brenau College, Gainesville, Georgia.

Children Need You

Teaching Young Children Has Reached a New High in Demand and Security

Child Education Foundation offers you preparation for Nursery School, Kindergarten and Primary teaching:

- Liberal arts and professional training
- Experience with children all 4 years
- Demonstration School
- Excellent preparation for marriage
- B.S. in Education from Adelphi College
- N.Y. State Teacher's Certification
- Dormitory and day student facilities

CHILD EDUCATION FOUNDATION
Box G, 535 East 84th St., New York 28, N. Y.

Southern Seminary and JUNIOR COLLEGE

Guest Editors this year. See page 252.

Sylvia Plath, Smith College, '54, has made her vacation work pay twice—first in a salary, then in the form of published articles. She has been a contributor to the *Christian Science Monitor* and *Seventeen*. Last year she won MLLE's College Fiction Contest—$500—and she recently sold three poems to *Harper's* for $100. Her background jobs have been picker on a vegetable truck farm, mother's helper on Cape Cod and waitress for a cooperative house at Smith, where she won a full-tuition scholarship. At Smith she has been campus correspondent for the Springfield *Daily News*. Next year she will be editor-in-chief of the Smith literary magazine. See pages 235, 290, 358.

Del Schmidt, Skidmore College, '54, was editor of her high school paper in her sophomore year, a position that she kept until she was graduated. High school too launched her "poster marathon." She is now art editor for the Skidmore handbook and yearbook. New York is her favorite city and she would definitely like to work there. See pages 133, 296.

Anne Shawber, Northwestern University, '54,

Mrs. Dorothy H. Woodworth, Dir. of Adm., 650-A Oak St., Chattanooga 3, Tenn.

Rhode Island School of DESIGN

A senior college combining liberal education and specialized training. Professional courses in apparel design and construction following industrial methods. Industrial and machine design. Textile engineering, textile design. Interior design, architecture, and landscape architecture. Painting, illustration, sculpture, ceramics, advertising design, fashion illustration. Art education. Coed. Endowed. Est. 1877. 21 buildings, textile plant, studios, laboratories, museum, dorms. Non-profit. 100 faculty, 700 students. B.F.A. and B.S. degrees. Ask for folder.

16 College St., Providence 3, R. I.

THE ART INSTITUTE OF CHICAGO
Professional School

but Plath is only truly Dickinsonian in the mode of address of her late poems. Plath didn't draw upon the New England tradition, except perhaps through her work ethic, even though she grew up in Winthrop, Wellesley, and Northampton, Massachusetts. Her tradition is the English lyric itself, supported by a lifelong habit of voracious, intense reading.

The young woman Sylvia Plath experienced the social conventions of the fifties as a murderously repressive force. Plath's early letters and journals, like the thoughts of *The Bell Jar*'s college girl heroine Esther Greenwood, reflect her fears about contradictions that seemed to her to be inherent in growing up female. Plath and Esther desire men but they fear getting trapped in marriage through having sex. For both the author and her character, intellect and creativity offer no escape from biological fate:

> I also remembered Buddy Willard saying in a sinister, knowing way that after I had children I would feel differently, I wouldn't want to write poems any more. So I began to think maybe it was true that when you were married and had children it was like being brainwashed, and afterwards you went about numb as a slave in some private, totalitarian state. (*The Bell Jar,* 89)

Plath has caught an issue whose explicitness shows it to have been at a cultural crisis point. Like the older Vassar women whom Betty Friedan was soon to interview for *The Feminine Mystique* (1963), Plath saw herself entering a society in which marriage and childbearing were irreconcilable with a career. Yet she wanted both. Like Friedan's subjects, but more startlingly, considering her talent, Plath seems to have assumed her fate from the clichés of popular magazine culture.

These clichés were familiar to Sylvia Plath through firsthand experience. When the highly competitive Plath won one of the 1953 *Mademoiselle* Guest Editorships, she had to face the cultural onslaught of meeting Marianne Moore, Elizabeth Bowen, Vance Bourjaily, and Paul Engle and writing about such well-regarded poets as Richard Wilbur and Anthony Hecht, among others. At the same time she was expected to comport herself as a young lady about town, impeccably turned out in matching dress, hat, gloves, and pumps for the inevitable photography session. Plath's reaction to this "test" seems to have been one of excitement followed by panic. After her crumbling self-confidence was further undermined by failure to get into Frank O'Connor's prestigious creative writing course at Harvard Summer School, Plath had a breakdown and tried to kill herself.

J. D. Salinger's *The Catcher in the Rye* (1951) showed that a sensitive and intelligent boy might well dread growing up to fit the stifling conventional male model of the fifties. Salinger suggested that his hero might well consider madness to be a fair riposte to a mad society. Plath's *The Bell Jar* is a deliberately female reply, using Esther Greenwood, a slightly older, even more death-drawn girl to match Salinger's slangy Holden Caulfield. Again like Salinger, whose work she admired, Plath used satire against society, but wrote the most moving passages about Esther's breakdown in a cool, detached voice, leaving space for our empathetic pity to enter between author and character.

Plath's sense of conflict between literary vocation and conventional sex role made womanliness a central issue for her poetry. In this Plath exemplifies a debate whose terms have since become more explicit. Adrienne Rich (b.1929), the woman poet whom Plath correctly assessed as her great rival in her private, self-generated competition for the title of best American woman poet,[4] has argued that since social discourse has been taken by men for their own use, women must invent their own "common language." Although Rich, like Plath, began her career with formal impersonal lyrics, she has subsequently loosened her poetic form while seeking to develop a recognizably female language. In *The Dream of a Common Language* (1978) and subsequent collections, Rich has developed a public womanly voice, uncommon in American poetry.

Plath, by contrast, took pride, for most of her life, in giving men the first place;[5] indeed, her contempt for sisterhood and her fearful loathing of female celibacy, childlessness, and aging form the material of a number of poems (e.g., from 1962–63, "Barren Woman," "Widow," "Lesbos," which is not about lesbianism but a nihilistically splenetic account of a visit to another, sentimentally sympathetic, mother, "Amnesiac," "The Tour," "Eavesdropper," "Childless Woman"). Some of Plath's most rewarding poems from the period of *The Colossus* meditate upon her ambivalent reactions to female identity, an identity that it was not easy for Plath to accept. In "All the Dead Dears" (1957) the female skeleton displayed in the Fitzwilliam Museum is "no kin / Of mine . . . yet kin she is." To be womanly can mean to be drawn into death, not life:

> Mother, grandmother, greatgrandmother
> Reach hag hands to haul me in. . . .

Yet Rich's argument for a female language finds a curious echo in Plath. When Plath followed Hughes's suggestion and read Robert Graves's *The White Goddess,* she found traditional female symbols of moon and blood which she took for her poetry;[6] bit by bit, using mythology and mysticism, she made her-

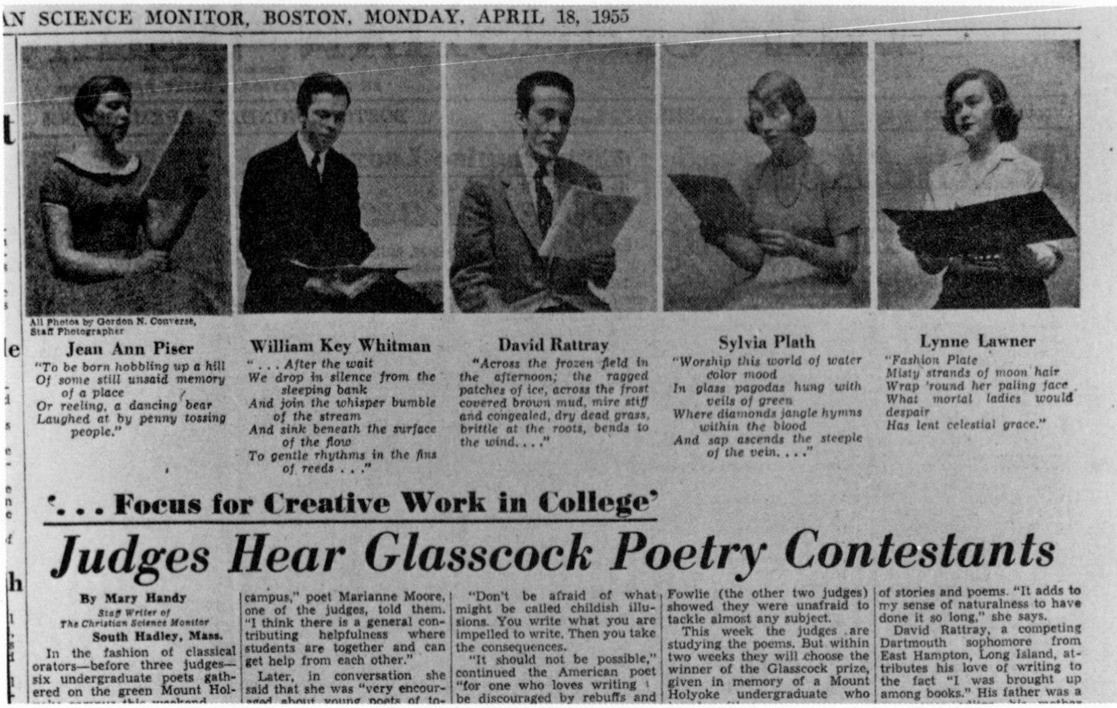

AN SCIENCE MONITOR, BOSTON, MONDAY, APRIL 18, 1955

All Photos by Gordon N. Converse, Staff Photographer

Jean Ann Piser

"To be born hobbling up a hill
Of some still unsaid memory
of a place
Or reeling, a dancing bear
Laughed at by penny tossing
people."

William Key Whitman

". . . After the wait
We drop in silence from the
sleeping bank
And join the whisper bumble
of the stream
And sink beneath the surface
of the flow
To gentle rhythms in the fins
of reeds . . ."

David Rattray

"Across the frozen field in the afternoon; the ragged patches of ice, across the frost covered brown mud, mire stiff and congealed, dry dead grass, brittle at the roots, bends to the wind. . . ."

Sylvia Plath

"Worship this world of water
color mood
In glass pagodas hung with
veils of green
Where diamonds jangle hymns
within the blood
And sap ascends the steeple
of the vein. . . ."

Lynne Lawner

"Fashion Plate
Misty strands of moon hair
Wrap 'round her paling face
What mortal ladies would
despair
Has lent celestial grace."

'. . . Focus for Creative Work in College'

Judges Hear Glasscock Poetry Contestants

By Mary Handy
Staff Writer of The Christian Science Monitor

South Hadley, Mass.

In the fashion of classical orators—before three judges—six undergraduate poets gathered on the green Mount Hol- [...] campus," poet Marianne Moore, one of the judges, told them. "I think there is a general contributing helpfulness where students are together and can get help from each other."

Later, in conversation she said that she was "very encour- [...]

"Don't be afraid of what might be called childish illusions. You write what you are impelled to write. Then you take the consequences.

"It should not be possible," continued the American poet "for one who loves writing to be discouraged by rebuffs and [...] Fowlie (the other two judges) showed they were unafraid to tackle almost any subject.

This week the judges are studying the poems. But within two weeks they will choose the winner of the Glasscock prize, given in memory of a Mount Holyoke undergraduate who [...] of stories and poems. "It adds to my sense of naturalness to have done it so long," she says.

David Rattray, a competing Dartmouth sophomore from East Hampton, Long Island, attributes his love of writing to the fact "I was brought up among books." His father was a [...]

A Christian Science Monitor *account of the competition for the Glascock Poetry Award in 1955.*

self into a woman poet. Plath's lunar imagery is, however, often about death or sterility; in "The Moon and the Yew Tree" (1961) the moon is "white as a knuckle and terribly upset." In "The Rival" (1961),

> If the moon smiled, she would resemble you.
> You leave the same impression
> Of something beautiful, but annihilating.
> Both of you are great light borrowers.
> Her O-mouth grieves at the world; yours is unaffected . . .

Lunar imagery refers to woman as fertile whole, waxing and waning in her monthly cycle; to the extent that Plath could not believe this of herself, her moon image also came to mean sterility, otherness. The white goddess can range from Artemis, the virgin huntress, to Hecate, the wrinkled lunar witch. Plath worked at the deathly end of the range. Her moon is not so much a mythic figuring-forth of a cyclical power so vast it effortlessly encompasses individuals as it is the deathly double of a modern alienated self.

Because it climaxed in a burst of pure lyric, Plath's career seems to follow the classic Keatsian model of poetic self-discovery through both formal and imaginative leaps. Yet Plath actually developed her own model by pressing harder on fewer materials. Keats reinvented the ode, wrote narrative poetry and romantic epics: "Endymion," "Hyperion," and "The Fall of Hyperion." Hart Crane, developing in the Keatsian mode, followed the lyrics and lyric sequence "Voyages" of *White Buildings* with the structurally innovative, if problematic, *The Bridge*. Plath wrote the seven-part "Poem for a Birthday" (1959), another seven-part poem, "Berck-Plage" (1962), the verse play for BBC Radio "Three Women" (1962), and a group of four poems about bees and beekeeping, but she wrote no long narratives, and she didn't develop the idea of the symbolic poem-sequence. The separate lyric was Plath's basic form.

Plath developed by changing the way her voice, the lyric "I," related to the poem's declarations. Once she could alter voice, then her poems changed the way they related to their perceived audience. Plath began by knowing all too well to whom her poetry spoke. She spent the first years of her career trying to please readers: initially, her mother, the editors of *Seventeen* and *Mademoiselle,* and her teachers at Smith, later the more inspiring and exigent single audience of Hughes. Gradually Plath worked her way forward to a stance of sheer utterance, thrust outwards without fixed audience; when Hughes and she separated in late 1962, that independence became a necessity.

With a few exceptions like "The Disquieting Muses" (1957), Plath's poems prior to 1958 are dense, syntactically complex, with regular metric and stanza form. The structure of the poem protects the voice, even though relatively few poems are written in an individualized first person. As a student Plath had trained herself in the tight form of the villanelle. She wrote a number of the *Colossus* poems in syllabics, teaching herself the differing length and weight of syllables, as in "The Hermit at Outermost House" (seven-syllable line), "Man in Black" (six-syllable line), and "Dark Wood, Dark Water" (five-syllable line). There are many run-on lines in *The Colossus,* and many qualifications in the manner of Stevens. Several poems resemble the highly rhetorical lyrics of John Crowe Ransom, others the formally controlled imagery of Howard Nemerov, who was publishing at the time in *The New Yorker.* In 1959 Plath wrote in her journal that she had "40 unattackable poems" (*Journal,* 300). There is no such thing as an unattackable poem; what Plath had written were forty armored poems.

Plath's later poems use ordinary events as the springboard for emotion. Practice gave Plath the confidence to be direct. During the *Ariel* period, virtually any action or reflection revealed itself as the occasion for a poem. Earlier, however, Plath had some trouble finding topics; Hughes and she occasionally used a ouija board to "find" themes. Striving to avoid the colloquial, Plath used a thesaurus to extend her vocabulary. In the poems of *The Colossus,* for example, there are 2360 words that appear just once, while in the *Winter Trees* group of poems contemporary with *Ariel*, the figure is only about half, 1254 unique words (the *Ariel* selection comes in between with 1741).[7]

The *Ariel* poems read smoothly; when run-on lines appear, they tend to be part of a colloquial sentence broken for emphasis. Thus "Balloon" (1963), a poem about small pleasures, addresses Frieda, Plath's daughter, saying

> Your small
>
> Brother is making
> His balloon squeak like a cat.

While *Ariel* is often deliberately colloquial, it has fewer contractions and possessives than *The Colossus,* though these are usually signs of a conversational style. In *Ariel* the individual word stands out displaying its own strength; it isn't busy doing extra syntactic work packing meaning into a line.

The Plath poem is always the work of a voice, but that voice is written in her earlier work, while it is spoken in *Ariel* and the *Winter Trees* poems.[8] If the earlier poems are parcels, the later ones are shouts. The later Plath poem continues for as long as it has voice; its length defines what's interesting about its subject. (In this habit Plath's closest parallel is—perhaps less oddly than it may seem—with Whitman.) Sometimes Plath's voice yields knowledge, as when "Crossing the Water" (1962) concludes of the "expressionless sirens" who mark the passage across Lethe that "This is the silence of astounded souls." Yet Plath wasn't an epistemological poet. The conclusion of "Crossing the Water" is itself a kind of image-examination, a bringing-forth of potentialities already present in the initial image, rather than a narratively or rhetorically gained "conclusion." While her poetry is rich in startling metaphor, Plath was not a poet of the conceit, the intellectually daring metaphoric linking of disparate images. The ever-clearer goal of her poetry is the display of that particular type of self-knowledge called authenticity, and authenticity is not necessarily rational, epistemologically firm, or rhetorically justified.

In *The Bell Jar* Esther had been about to embark upon a sterile-sounding thesis "on some obscure theme in the works of James Joyce" (35) without even having read much Joyce. In July 1953 Plath found herself in the same position. After her breakdown and recovery, Plath changed her topic to the theme of the

D. H. Lawrence.

Virginia Woolf.

. . . how does Woolf do it? How does Lawrence do it? I come down to learn of those two: Lawrence because of the rich physical passion —fields of forces—and the real presence of leaves and earth and beasts and weathers, sap-rich, and Woolf because of that almost sexless, neurotic *luminousness*—the catching of objects: chairs, tables and the figures on a street corner, and the infusion of radiance . . .

—From *The Journals of Sylvia Plath*

double, a myth she examined not through symbol-hunting but according to its psychic necessity. For her thesis Plath read Dostoievsky's *The Double*, Poe's "William Wilson," Stevenson's *Dr. Jekyll and Mr. Hyde,* Wilde's *The Picture of Dorian Gray,* Jung, Frazer, Freud's 1916 essay "The Uncanny" and the E.T.A. Hoffmann tale "The Sandman," which is Freud's main source.

The double was a resonant choice for Plath. Her use of it

indicates her early awareness that the experience of doubling gave an apt image for her own experience of self. Plath's poetry and *The Bell Jar* are filled with doubles and uncanny effects. Esther has a double in Joan Gilling, who is her rival for Buddy Willard's affections, her fellow inmate at McLean's, and the bearer of two areas of her dread: lesbianism and suicide.

> I looked at Joan. In spite of the creepy feeling, and in spite of my old, ingrained dislike, Joan fascinated me. It was like observing a Martian, or a particularly warty toad. Her thoughts were not my thoughts, nor her feelings my feelings, but we were close enough so that her thoughts and feelings seemed a wry, black image of my own.
>
> Sometimes I wondered if I had made Joan up. (231)

When Joan is found dead, Esther realizes she has been freed to live. Earlier Esther had sat in a doctor's office like the child in Elizabeth Bishop's poem "The Waiting Room" who reads the *National Geographic* and feels an uncanny alienation from the female bodies which are both different from her and uncannily like her. Since Esther has come to be fitted for a contraceptive, she feels particularly threatened by the waiting room bursting with her doubles: mysteriously happy-looking mothers with their babies and copies of *Baby Talk*—the future reading material for the fecund.

One of Plath's earliest "mature" poems, "Tale of a Tub" (1956), describes the classic uncanny sensation of looking in a mirror and seeing a stranger:

> . . . caught
> naked in the merely actual room,
> the stranger in the lavatory mirror
> puts on a public grin, repeats our name
> but scrupulously reflects the usual terror.

In the conclusion to the poem, only death "makes us real" because the corpse, by definition, is no longer part of the world of reflected images.

If one's own body can seem "other," then Nature, the traditional "other" to the poetic subject, is likely to seem consistently uncanny, the weird resemblances to oneself in Nature being a cause for terror. Plath never accepted an uncanny, maternal body of Nature in the way that Elizabeth Bishop did. Her uncanny is not about pleasure, as Bishop's can be. Nor did she follow Hughes's vision in *Hawk in the Rain* (1957) and *Lupercal* (1960) and see the brutality of Nature as part of an encounter with local place and inevitable instinct.[9]

When objects in nature address themselves to Plath's speaker, they signify death. "The Moon and the Yew Tree" (1961), a poem on a topic set for her by Hughes, and based upon an actual tree near their home in Devon, begins with an uncompromising internalization: "This is the light of the mind." Moonlight becomes a symbol, a deathly "mother." Nearby stands a church, but, the poem concludes,

> The moon sees nothing of this. She is bald and wild.
> And the message of the yew tree is blackness—
> blackness and silence.

To the extent that the self is being represented by these familiar but uncanny natural symbols, it is doomed. In "Elm" (1962), the tree says that its bottom "is what you fear." A face "in its strangle of branches" brings out "the isolate, slow faults / That kill, that kill, that kill." In "Little Fugue" (1962), "The yew's black fingers wag" until "Death opened, like a black tree, blackly." In "Tulips" (1961), "The tulips are too red in the first place, they hurt me." In "Poppies in July" (1962), the poppies are "little hell flames," their "clear red" like a bloodied mouth. Plath's symbolic colors—black, white, red, and occasionally gold, gray, and ivory—are the colors of ancient art, not of nature. They are absolute colors: death, erasure, blood, statues.

"I know how she feels; I've felt like that." This is the immediate instinctive response to Plath's voice, even when what we've actually felt is not our own feelings but the poem's voice as it refers back to a hidden self. It is important to remember that not all reading of poetry is directed towards aesthetic or formal understanding; indeed, with a poet like Plath, understanding may be the by-product of an encounter with text-as-personality. Such encounters center upon power and empathy. Plath draws empathy from her reader without offering it. "For the eyeing of my scars," she remarks sardonically in "Lady Lazarus" (1962), "there is a charge, a very large charge"—the reader's voyeuristic thrill has a high moral price tag. Plath's speaker is made to put on a "big strip tease" as she is unwrapped after each suicide attempt; the line also implies that the teasingly confessional poem constitutes another contract to perform for a greedy crowd; only death can break the contract. Lady Lazarus rises again, reborn as fire, to wreak revenge upon her audience. She has precisely the power that the poem's lyric assertion has claimed for her: "Beware . . . I eat men like air."

How much of herself does Plath expose in her poetry? The editor of Plath's Journals has written that ". . . it's important to understand that the autobiography does not work in Plath as it

Queen of *Bombus ternarius* sipping nectar. About natural size.

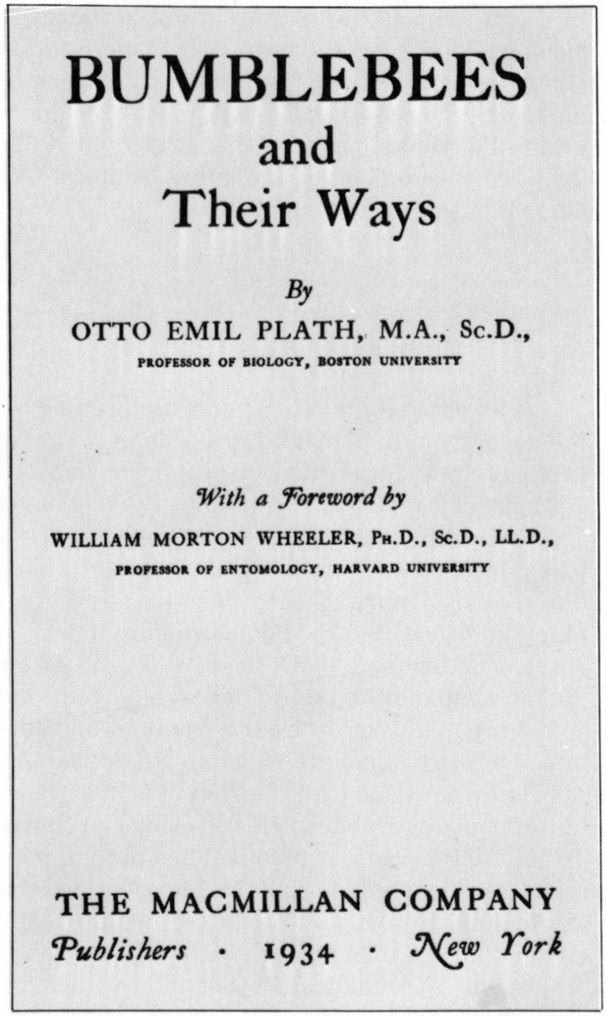

BUMBLEBEES
and
Their Ways

By
OTTO EMIL PLATH, M.A., Sc.D.,
PROFESSOR OF BIOLOGY, BOSTON UNIVERSITY

With a Foreword by
WILLIAM MORTON WHEELER, Ph.D., Sc.D., LL.D.,
PROFESSOR OF ENTOMOLOGY, HARVARD UNIVERSITY

THE MACMILLAN COMPANY
Publishers · 1934 · *New York*

Sylvia Plath's father was a distinguished entomologist whose work on bees is among the standard treatments of its subject.

does in the 'confessional' writers," but rather in a mythological sense . . ."[10] This statement needs clarification. When M. L. Rosenthal wrote *The New Poets: American and British Poetry Since World War II,*[11] he used the term "confessional" to describe the intimate and unmediatedly personal work of Robert Lowell, Sylvia Plath, Allen Ginsberg, Theodore Roethke, John Berryman, and Anne Sexton. Ignoring Eliot's version of literary history, Rosenthal saw confessional poetry as the "culmination" of what he considered a continuing "Romantic and modern tendency to place the literal self more and more at the center of the poem" (*New Poets,* 27). The confessional poem brought

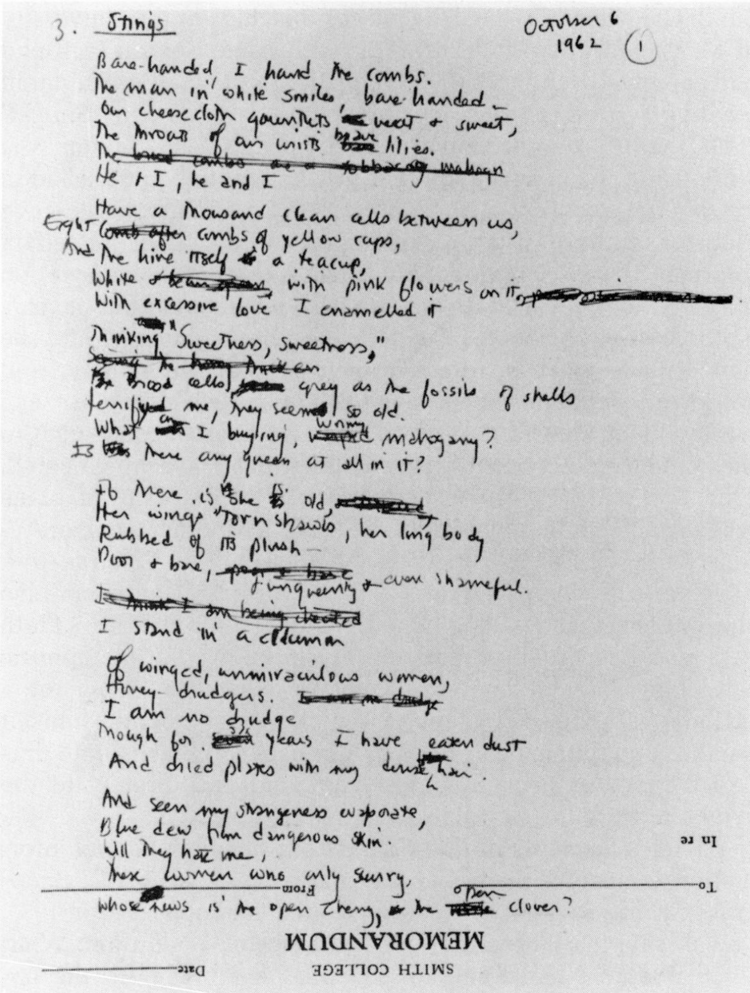

3. Stings
October 6
1962 (1)

Bare-handed I hand the combs.
The man in white smiles, bare-handed —
Our cheesecloth gauntlets neat & sweet,
The throats of our wrists brave lilies.
He & I, he and I
Have a thousand clean cells between us,
Eight combs of yellow cups,
And the hive itself a teacup,
White with pink flowers on it,
With excessive love I enamelled it
Thinking "Sweetness, sweetness,"
The brood cells grey as the fossils of shells
Terrify me, they seem so old.
What am I buying, wormy mahogany?
Is there any queen at all in it?
If there is, she is old,
Her wings torn shawls, her long body
Rubbed of its plush —
Poor & bare, unqueenly & even shameful.
I stand in a column
Of winged, unmiraculous women,
Honey-drudgers.
I am no drudge
Though for years I have eaten dust
And dried plates with my dense hair.
And seen my strangeness evaporate,
Blue dew from dangerous skin.
Will they hate me,
These women who only scurry,
Whose news is the open cherry, the open clover?

SMITH COLLEGE
MEMORANDUM
To / From / In re / Date

"private humiliations, sufferings, and psychological problems into the poems . . . usually developed in the first person and intended without question to point to the author himself" (*New Poets,* 26). Rosenthal's "confessional" was never more than a working hypothesis, but he recognized that a separation between speaker and author is a convention rather than a necessity in the lyric poem. The intimate speaker is simply another way by which the poet directs his or her relations with the reader. Its expressions can range from ironic realism to mythic iconography, or offer both at once.

During the spring of 1959, after she had finished teaching at

Smith College and while Hughes was teaching at the University of Massachusetts, Plath, together with Anne Sexton (a friend and perceived poetic rival), attended Robert Lowell's seminar in creative writing at Boston University. Lowell's *Life Studies* (1959) had just come out to mixed reviews, and Sexton was working on the poems about her breakdown to be published in *To Bedlam and Part-Way Back* (1960). Lowell's example gave Plath an authoritative precedent for writing about herself in informal first-person verse, but he didn't direct the conception of self in her poems. Plath had already begun to use her psychic history directly in poems like "The Disquieting Muses," and she had already been reading Graves, African mythology, and works on demonic possession. While in Lowell's class she wrote "Electra on Azalea Path," a poem based upon a visit to the actual cemetery path where Otto Plath's grave was located. This "actuality" soon becomes part of a play "on" a place whose name punningly cannibalizes Plath's mother's name, Aurelia Plath, while bluntly giving the classic title—Electra—to a daughter's sense of loss. In a darker wordplay, the poem also shows Electra/Sylvia "on" a path leading "into the dirt." Plath had also been reading and closely imitating the metaphoric reworkings of childhood in Theodore Roethke; "Poem for a Birthday" is a direct homage to Roethke. Since Roethke himself had been adapting the symbolism of Yeats and Blake, Plath thus had a renewed access both secondhand and directly to the symbolic tradition in English.

Lowell's accounts in *Life Studies* offer enough factual information to sustain themselves as narratives; like W. D. Snodgrass, whose sequence "Heart's Needle" had appeared in 1957, Lowell saw his illness and guilt as food for meditation. What Plath does, is, like Roethke, to admit the reader to the unresolved, unworked-through situation behind any narrative; the most useful term for such representation might be self-poetry. Plath's poems present the situation of the self as given, using a mixed, adaptable inheritance of mythic imagery to convince the reader of the authenticity of the self's situation. Plath's "myth" of self includes not only classical myth but also fairy tale, the magical repetitions of children's rhymes so tellingly used by Roethke. There are even revisions of Freud himself.

In "Daddy," perhaps Plath's most famous poem, we are not given the original motivating circumstance: Plath's father, Otto Plath, an eminent entomologist and professor of biology at Boston University, died in 1940 after having a leg amputated because of diabetes. In "Daddy," Otto Plath appears coded, first as the patriarchal statue, "Marble-heavy, a bag full of God / Ghastly statue with one grey toe." Then, shockingly, he becomes a Nazi, playing tormentor to Plath's Jew. Although Otto Plath came from Silesia, in what was then Germany, he was not a Nazi, nor was his daughter Jewish, nor is there evidence that he mistreated her. In a classic transference, "Daddy" transforms the abandoned child's unmediated irrational rage into qualities attributed to its object: if Daddy died and hurt me so, he must be a bastard; I hate him for his cruelty; everyone else hates him too: "the villagers never liked you." The invalid scientist Otto has disappeared, and "Daddy" is not about knowing him or understanding his loss. Lowell's "My Last Afternoon with Uncle Devereux Winslow" or "Commander Lowell," by contrast, try to accept loss by recapitulating its history. Plath knew that she hadn't ever completed the process of mourning for her father, and both she and "Daddy" recognize that in some way she had used Hughes as a double of her lost father.[12] However, "Daddy" does not console. For Plath her father's German speech is an "obscene engine,"

> An engine, an engine,
> Chuffing me off like a Jew.
> A Jew to Dachau, Auschwitz, Belsen.
> I began to talk like a Jew.
> I may well be a Jew.

The speaker's staggering effrontery in likening her emotional state to the Holocaust is a kind of psychic conceit, as if she is daring her reader to disbelieve what has been so passionately felt and powerfully expressed. "Daddy" operates by generating a duplicate of Plath's presumed psychic state in the reader, so that we reexperience her grief, rage, masochism, and revenge, whether or not these fit the "facts." Plath's own properly New-Critical interpretation of "Daddy," in notes prepared for a BBC reading, reduces "Daddy" to a bizarre case history by objectifying it as a story: "a poem spoken by a girl with an Electra complex . . . Her case is complicated by the fact that her Father was also a Nazi and her mother very possibly part Jewish" (*Collected Poems,* 293).

The impact of "Daddy" depends precisely upon that girl not being a "case" but recognizable, so that her despairing rage seems only a more brightly colored instance of our own. "Daddy" triumphantly lays bare the secret mechanism of all women's masochism:

> Every woman adores a Fascist,
> The boot in the face, the brute
> Brute heart of a brute like you.

This picture of Sylvia Plath and Ted Hughes accompanied a 1959 article in Mademoiselle *entitled "Four Young Poets."*

. . . I have written the seven best poems of my life which make the rest look like baby-talk. . . . Ted reads in his strong voice; is my best critic, as I am his. . . .

—From a letter of Sylvia Plath to her mother, April 29, 1956

Plath's radio account does not deal with the clear invitation to biographical reading that occurs when, after the near-perfect fit of the father's death, the speaker is, like Plath in autumn 1962, said to be "through" with a man who liked to dress in black and whom she had known for seven years. "Daddy" is self-poetry. The self is the subject whose sensations make up the poem. This may seem a small frame, but if that subject undergoes psychic torment, then for the subject herself that torment, being absolute, may indeed be worthy of the imagery of the most profound horror of our age. Better to be reminded this way of the absoluteness of Dachau and Hiroshima (used in "Fever 103") than not to be reminded at all.

"The Disquieting Muses," written in spring 1957, may in fact mark a more important discovery for Plath than what she learned later from Roethke and Lowell. It is Plath's earliest expression of deep ambivalence towards her maternal "inheritance." It marks her realization that her poetic "landscape" is not nature but the altered, worked-upon significant scenery of memory, dream or violent emotion. By using the Italian artist Giorgio de Chirico's "The Disquieting Muses," Plath found an enigmatic imagery which could express unresolved power.

Plath's and Chirico's image is that of a woman with a featureless head like a darning egg, a woman without origins or issue because she is organless and fabricated. Once this image enters Plath's poetry, it stays. In "The Disquieting Muses," the speaker asks,

> Mother, mother, what illbred aunt
> Or what disfigured and unsightly
> Cousin did you so unwisely keep
> Unasked to my christening, that she
> Sent these ladies in her stead
> With heads like darning-eggs to nod
> And nod and nod at foot and head
> And at the left side of my crib?

Her mother cannot or will not say

> Words to rid me of those three ladies
> Nodding by night around my bed,
> Mouthless, eyeless, with stiched bald head.

It is significant that "The Disquieting Muses," while mythic, is actually a *bricolage* or patchwork of mythic, artistic, and fairy-tale images picked up because they fit the case at hand, or can be changed to approximate it. This is a radically different operation from Anne Sexton's demythologizing poems like "Cinderella," which deconstruct one myth at a time.

Chirico's "The Disquieting Muses" shows three women: a maternal seated figure, a more phallic figure whose darning-egg head is set upon a pillar, and a draped statue in shadow. Plath stresses the threesome, because these uncannily disquieting Muses are her Fates. The speaker is also the princess in "Sleeping Beauty"; the revenge of the uninvited bad fairy is not, however, to have her pricked by a pin and die, but to abduct her, as in the Erlkönig tale, and make her one of them—enigmatic, nonhuman, signifying, stony, magical, and fatal. As the Muses close in on their chosen prey, the speaker's mother floats mysteriously away in an ever-tinier Blakean bubble of pastoral bliss.

Everything that happens in "The Disquieting Muses" is the mother's fault; the poem states the case without explanation. The mother has been too protective, or not protective enough:

> Day now, night now, at head, side, feet,
> They stand their vigil in gowns of stone,
> Faces blank as the day I was born,
> Their shadows long in the setting sun
> That never brightens or goes down.
> And this is the kingdom you bore me to,
> Mother, mother. But no frown of mine
> Will betray the company I keep.

The mother is to blame ultimately for having given birth to something that is in the process of recognizing itself as nonhuman.

Plath's favorite artists, Chirico, Klee, Gauguin, and Rousseau, all painted symbolic, deliberately "unconscious" images using flat, nonatmospheric, often fantastic light. There is no mimetic modeling of shadow and space, only parodic or evocative references to it.[13] Chirico displays distorted objects in an exaggerated perspective of shallow planes; Klee, Rousseau, and Gauguin (usually) use no perspective at all. The landscape is that of the mind. In her *Journal* (210), Plath noted several statements by Chirico, one of which—"What shall I love unless it be The Enigma?"—is actually the title of a Chirico self-portrait. The self is the source of the enigma, a mystery displayed not as "inward" or subjective, but spread out over the entire landscape; Chirico called this mode "metaphysical."

Chirico found a way, perhaps the only credible twentieth-century way, to use classical myth and mythic imagery in art. He depicts myth not directly but as the modern mind must perceive it, as a monumental relic. This relic bears the same relation to the imagination as the heroic statue bears to the living body. Such statues are not mimetic, they are representations not of the living person but of its desires turned to stone. Some of Chirico's figures are like dressmaker's dummies, their insides made up of interlocking parts, others are more seamless, resembling Plath's "The Munich Mannequins" (1962), "naked and bald in their furs," their sterile "perfection," making a calm, mindless, deathly alternative to the demanding "blood flood" of

Sylvia Plath with her children, Frieda and Nicholas.

Kindness glides about my house.
Dame Kindness, she is so nice!
The blue and red jewels of her rings smoke
In the windows, the mirrors
Are filling with smiles. . . .

And here you come, with a cup of tea
Wreathed in steam.
The blood jet is poetry,
There is no stopping it.
You hand me two children, two roses.

—From "Kindness"

love that involves other people. Other Chirico sculptures look like plaster casts over a hidden body, like the foot of the father in "Daddy" or Plath's numerous other uses of sculpture to depict the double, from "The Lady and the Earthenware Head" (1957) onwards. A metaphysical "nostalgia of the infinite" (as another Chirico title puts it) is still present in Chirico's works, but the nostalgia is present as precisely that, namely, desire for an imaginary object that cannot ever be possessed because the mind has invented it. And that desire, in Plath as in Chirico, has its source and object in the emblems of patriarchy: the tower, the pillar, the great edifice, the heroic statue, the man in black, the king.

Plath's imagery of the darning-egg woman appears with startling accuracy as the image of the schizoid body in *Anti-Oedipus* (1972, trans. 1983), an iconoclastic theoretical work by the French psychoanalysts Gilles Deleuze and Félix Guattari,[14] although they appear not to know Plath's poetry. In Deleuze and Guattari's usage, "schizophrenia" is not merely the clinical term but stands for a form of Nietzschean revolt against the narrowness of the Freudian Oedipal triangle. By removing the body from its production role in the familial economy, the schizoid, egglike "organless body" frees itself, though ultimately it frees itself unto death:

> The full body without organs is produced as antiproduction, that is to say it intervenes within the process as such for the sole process of rejecting any attempt to impose on it any sort of triangulation implying that it was produced by parents (15). . . . The body without organs is an egg . . . Nothing here is representative; rather, it is all life and lived experience . . . Nothing but bands of intensity, potentials, thresholds, and gradients. A harrowing, potentially overwhelming experience, which brings the schizo as close as possible to a burning, living centre of matter. (19)

In using Deleuze and Guattari's terminology I am not offering a psychoanalytic diagnosis of Plath or seeking to read her work as clinical evidence; her work reads as part of the English lyric tradition, and there is every reason to believe that Plath herself sought health. What Deleuze and Guattari do offer is an understanding of why we perceive Plath's work as radical, in the way that Roethke's "The Lost Son" is radical or Antonin Artaud's journals are radical, far more so than the work of Lowell, Sexton, or even the recent French autobiographical novel of a woman's breakdown, Marie Cardinal's *The Words to Say It*.

In "Face Lift" (1961),

> Now she's done for, the dewlapped lady
> I watched settle, line by line, in my mirror—
> Old sock-face, sagged on a darning egg.

The "old" egg is reborn as a new, motherless, asexual, and even more featureless one:

> Mother to myself, I wake swaddled in gauze,
> Pink and smooth as a baby.

In "Death & Co" (1962) "Somebody's done for" when death appears in one of his two guises as William Blake's egglike death mask, "one who never looks up, whose eyes are lidded and balled, like Blake's." The poems of Plath's last nine months seem to be becoming "a case without a body" as "The Detective" (1962) puts it, but they never become entirely so. The body in Plath's late poems is an egglike sac which nevertheless is still full of blood, and still writes, even when mouthless, with blood: "the blood jet is poetry" ("Kindness," 1963).

As the egg images increase in frequency in Plath's poetry, combining with imagery of balloons and the image of the sterile moon, mirror images, which are associated with others, with the world of representation and presentation of self, gradually decrease. For Plath in "Purdah" (1962) the "bridegroom" is "lord of the mirrors." In a variation, the second face of death in "Death & Co" is a disgusting lover, "masturbating a glitter," demanding a reaction; the only way to resist is to be still as death oneself.

In Plath's last poems (November 1962–February 1963) the mirror image disappears or is both literally and colloquially "cracked." In "Eavesdropper" (1962), a malice-poem, the speaker fantasizes that her neighbor's light can magically draw out her words and catch

> The zoo yowl, the mad soft
> Mirror talk you love to catch me at.

"Thalidomide" (1962) uses the thalidomide-deformed infants who had been born in England in 1960–61, near the time of Plath's own second pregnancy, to address Plath's maternal dread that she might give birth to the ultimate "other," a monster, but love it nonetheless. The speaker refuses to look:

> The glass cracks across,
> The image
>
> Flees and aborts like dropped mercury.

The reflecting mirror is not replaced this time by another double; "Contusion" (1963) ends, "The mirror is sheeted."

Sometimes the code of Plath's later poems is uncrackable, as in "The Secret" (1962), or it is enigmatically assembled, as in the repertory offered by the well-titled "Totem" (1962); in some

Axes
After whose stroke the wood rings
And the echoes!
Echoes traveling
Off from the center like horses. . . .

Words dry and riderless,
The indefatigable hoof-taps.
While
From the bottom of the pool, fixed stars
Govern a life.

—From "Words"

other poems Plath seems to look at other people the way the photographer Diane Arbus looked at them, as grotesque phenomena whose uncanny likeness to herself both fascinates and appalls.

Yet to the very end, language is always "with" Plath, always strong and flexible, always exempted from rage. In Plath's very last poems the saclike body of the subject is no longer distinguished from the object, the world; everything is wound. In "Contusion"

> Color floods to the spot, dull purple.
> The rest of the body is all washed out,
> The color of pearl.
>
> In a pit of rock
> The sea sucks obsessively,
> One hollow the whole sea's pivot.

These poems are free the way Emily Dickinson's poetry is free, removed from the market of any audience at all. They remain one with their author the way newborn infants remain one with their mother (Images of infants, of Plath's "two children, two roses" ["Kindness," 1963] provide rare flashes of light in these last works.) In "Edge" (1963), her last poem, Plath concludes coldly:

> The moon has nothing to be sad about,
> Staring from her hood of bone.
>
> She is used to this sort of thing.
> Her blacks crackle and drag.

These last poems are what Deleuze and Guattari call celibate machines. They are anti-production, production addressed nowhere. In Plath's case, they are also productions so deeply rooted in lyric that they finally address the wound in us all.

NOTES

WALT WHITMAN

1. In this essay I have quoted from the following: H. L. Mencken, *The American Language,* ed. Raven I. McDavid, Jr. (New York: Knopf, 1982), here abbreviated *AL;* Herbert Marcuse, *Eros and Civilization: A Philosophical Inquiry into Freud* (New York: Vintage Books, 1962), abbreviated *EC;* Ralph Waldo Emerson, *Emerson's Essays,* intro. Irwin Edman (New York: Apollo Editions, n.d.), abbreviated *EE;* Paul Ricoeur, *Freedom and Nature: The Voluntary and the Involuntary*, trans. Erazim V. Kohák (Evanston: Northwestern Univ. Press, 1966), abbreviated *FN; The Native Muse: Theories of American Literature,* vol. 1, ed. Richard Ruland (New York: E. P. Dutton, 1972), abbreviated *NM;* Georg Wilhelm Friedrich Hegel, *The Philosophy of History,* trans. J. Sibree (New York: Dover, 1956), abbreviated *PH; Walt Whitman: Complete Poetry and Complete Prose* (New York: The Library of America, 1982), abbreviated *W;* Czesław Miłosz, *Visions from San Francisco Bay,* trans. Richard Lourie (New York: Farrar, Straus & Giroux, 1983), abbreviated *V.*

EMILY DICKINSON

1. Unless otherwise indicated, quotations from Dickinson's poems and letters are from *The Poems of Emily Dickinson,* ed. Thomas H. Johnson, 3 vols. (Cambridge: The Belknap Press of Harvard University Press, 1955) and *The Letters of Emily Dickinson,* ed. Thomas H. Johnson and Theodora Ward, 3 vols. (Cambridge: The Belknap Press of Harvard University Press, 1958). I have followed the numbering of the poems and letters in these editions. In my essay, *P* and *L* refer to poems and letters respectively. Other sources are Millicent Todd Bingham, *Emily Dickinson's Home* (New York: Harper & Row, 1955), abbreviated *H;* Richard B. Sewall, *The Lyman Letters* (Amherst: University of Massachusetts Press, 1965), abbreviated *LL;* Richard B. Sewall, *The Life of Emily Dickinson,* 2 vols. (Farrar, Straus & Giroux, 1974), referred to as *Life.*

ROBERT FROST

Sources for works referred to or quoted in text are as follows:

David Bromwich, "Edward Thomas and Modernism," *Raritan Quarterly* 3 (Summer 1983): 101–23.

Reginald Cook, *Robert Frost: A Living Voice* (Amherst: University of Massachusetts Press, 1974), Part Two, pp. 29–195 (text of recorded talks given by Frost from 1953 to 1962).

Hyde Cox and Edward Connery Lathem, eds., *Selected Prose of Robert Frost* (New York: Collier Books, 1968).

James M. Cox, ed., *Robert Frost: A Collection of Critical Essays* (Englewood Cliffs, N.J.: Prentice-Hall, Inc., 1962); includes essays by Randall Jarrell and Lionel Trilling.

Donald Davie, *Ezra Pound* (New York: Viking Press, 1975).

T. S. Eliot, *Four Quartets* (New York: Harcourt Brace Jovanovich, 1943).

———, *Selected Essays 1917–1932* (New York: Harcourt Brace Jovanovich, 1932).

Robert Frost, *The Letters of Robert Frost to Louis Untermeyer* (New York: Holt, Rinehart and Winston, 1963).

William James, *The Meaning of Truth* (Cambridge: Harvard University Press, 1982).

———, *Pragmatism* (Cambridge: Harvard University Press, 1975).

———, *The Principles of Psychology* Cambridge: Harvard University Press, 1983).

Edward Connery Lathem, ed., *Interviews with Robert Frost* (New York: Holt, Rinehart and Winston, 1966).

———, *The Poetry of Robert Frost* (New York: Holt, Rinehart and Winston, 1969).

———, and Laurence Thompson, eds., *Robert Frost: Poetry and Prose* (New York: Holt, Rinehart and Winston, 1972).

Joel Porte, ed., *Emerson: Essays and Lectures* (New York: The Library of America, 1983).

Wallace Stevens, *The Collected Poems* (New York: Alfred A. Knopf, 1954).

Jack Stillinger, ed., *Selected Poems and Prefaces by William Wordsworth* (Boston: Houghton-Mifflin, 1965).

Laurance Thompson, *Robert Frost: The Early Years, 1874–1915* (New York: Holt, Rinehart and Winston, 1970).

———, *Robert Frost: The Years of Triumph, 1915–1938* (New York: Holt, Rinehart and Winston, 1970).

———, ed., *Selected Letters of Robert Frost* (New York: Holt, Rinehart and Winston, 1964).

——— and R. H. Winnick, *Robert Frost: The Later Years, 1938–1963* (New York: Holt, Rinehart and Winston, 1976).

William Carlos Williams, *The Autobiography of William Carlos Williams* (New York: Random House, 1951).

WALLACE STEVENS

Works by Stevens referred to in my essay are:

The Collected Poems (New York: Knopf, 1955), abbreviated *CP; Opus Posthumous,* ed. Samuel French Morse (New York: Knopf, 1957), abbreviated *OP; Letters,* ed. Holly Stevens (New York: Knopf, 1966), abbreviated *L; The Necessary Angel* (New York: Knopf, 1951).

WILLIAM CARLOS WILLIAMS

1. In this essay, Williams's books are cited using the following abbreviations:

AUTO *The Autobiography of William Carlos Williams* (1951; reprint, New York: New Directions, 1967).

CEP *The Collected Earlier Poems of William Carlos Williams* (New York: New Directions, 1951).

IMAG *Imaginations,* Schott (New York: New Directions, 1970).

IWWP *I Wanted to Write a Poem: The Autobiography of the Works of a Poet,* reported and edited by Edith Heal (Boston: Beacon Press, 1958).

KH *Kora in Hell* (1920), in *Imaginations,* ed. Webster Schott (New York: New Directions, 1970).

P *Paterson* (1958; New York: New Directions, 1963).

PB *Pictures from Breughel and Other Poems* (New York: New Directions, 1962).

SE *Selected Essays of William Carlos Williams* (1958; reprint, New York: New Directions, 1969).

SL *The Selected Letters of William Carlos Williams,* ed. John C. Thirlwall (New York: McDowell, Obolensky, 1957).

SAA *Spring and All* (1923), in *Imaginations,* ed. Webster Schott (New York: New Directions, 1970).

EZRA POUND

1. Peter Makin, *Pound's Cantos* (London: George Allen and Unwin, 1985), 1–2.
2. Thus his most general statement about *The Cantos* is a 1927 letter to Homer L. Pound: "Dear Dad: . . ." D. D. Paige, ed., *The Letters of Ezra Pound 1907–1941* (New York: New Directions, 1950 1st edition, 1971), 210.
3. Fred C. Robinson, "Pound's Anglo-Saxon Studies," *Yale Review* Vol. 71, No. 2 (Winter 1982): 199–224.
4. *C,* 117 refers to page 117 of *The Cantos of Ezra Pound* (New York: New Directions, 1970). All Canto references will appear in the text in this form.
5. Ezra Pound, *The Spirit of Romance: An Attempt to Define Somewhat the Charm of the Pre-Renaîssance Literature of Latin Europe* (London: J. M. Dent & Sons, Ltd., 1910), 12.
6. Brooks Adams, *The Law of Civilization and Decay,* (New York: Knopf, 1951), 89.
7. This means Ezra Pound, *Personae* of Ezra Pound (New York: New Directions, 1949), 64. All references to this collection of the short poems will be given in the text in this way.
8. "September 1913," *The Poems of W. B. Yeats*, ed. Richard Finneran (New York: Macmillan, 1983), 108.
9. This poem ("South Folk in Cold Country") ended the original *Cathay.* When the four that now follow it in *Personae* were added, the 1915 focus on war was dispersed.
10. Paige, *Letters,* 231.
11. For an extended treatment see M. L. Rosenthal and Sally M. Gall, *The Modern Poetic Sequence* (1982). They adduce Poe on the long poem as he knew it ("a contradiction in terms"). Sequencing permits omission of prosy bridges.
12. T. S. Eliot, "London Letter," *Dial,* May 1922, 510.
13. For an excellent brief exposition, see Makin, *Pound's Cantos*, 105–14.
14. In a 1935 letter to W.H.D. Rouse, Paige, *Letters,* 274.
15. "Interview with Robert Fitzgerald," *The Paris Review* 94 (Winter 1984): 51.
16. Locating these is greatly facilitated by Carroll F. Terrell's *Companion to the Cantos of Ezra Pound,* Vol. 1 (Orono: National Poetry Foundation, University of Maine at Orono; Berkeley: University of California Press, 1980–84) Vol. 2, in press.
17. From Margaret Dickie's fine essay, *"The Cantos:* Slow Reading," *ELH* 51–54 (Winter 1984): 819–35.
18. Ibid., 823, 833.

MARIANNE MOORE

The following are sources of material quoted or referred to in text (see also footnote p. 248):

William Rose Benet and Norman Holmes Pearson, eds., *The Oxford Anthology of American Literature* (New York: Oxford University Press, 1938).

Malcolm Bradbury, "The Cities of Modernism," in Malcolm Bradbury and James McFarlane, eds., *Modernism* (Harmondsworth, England: Penguin Books, 1976), pp. 96–104.

T. S. Eliot, "In Memory," *The Little Review* 5 (August 1918): 44–45.

Ralph Waldo Emerson, *The Complete Works of Ralph Waldo Emerson*, 9 vols. (Boston: Houghton, Mifflin, 1884).

Benjamin Franklin, *The Autobiography* in Baym, Nina, and Ronald Gottesman, et al., eds., *The Norton Anthology of American Literature* (New York: W. W. Norton and Co., 1985), 1: 390–528.

Alfred Kreymborg, ed., *Others: An Anthology of the New Verse(1917)* (New York: Alfred A. Knopf, 1917).

Marianne Moore, *A Marianne Moore Reader* (New York: Viking Press, 1961).

———, *Collected Poems* (New York: Macmillan, 1951).

———, *Complete Poems* (New York: Viking/Macmillan, 1981).

———, *Complete Prose* (New York: Viking, 1986).

———, *Daily Diary 1931*, Rosenbach Archive, Series VIII:01:31.
———, *Notebook*, Rosenbach Archive, 1250/24.
———, *Observations* (New York: The Dial Press, 1924).
———, *Predilections* (New York: Viking, 1955).
———, *Reading Diary 1930–1943*, R1250/6, Rosenbach Museum and Library.
———, *Selected Poems*, introduction by T. S. Eliot (London: Faber and Faber, 1935).
———, *Unfinished Poems* (Philadelphia, Pa.: Rosenbach Museum and Library, 1972).
———, *What Are Years* (New York: Macmillan, 1941).

Pound, Ezra, *Literary Essays* (New York: New Directions, 1954).

Bayrd Still, *Mirror for Gotham: New York as Seen by Contemporaries from Dutch Days to the Present* (New York: New York University Press, 1956).

Henry David Thoreau, *Walden; or, Life in the Woods* (Boston and New York: Houghton, Mifflin, 1897).

Charles Tomlinson, ed., *Marianne Moore: A Collection of Critical Essays* (Englewood Cliffs, N.J.: Prentice-Hall, 1968).

William Carlos Williams, *Kora in Hell*, rpt. in *Imaginations*, ed. Webster Schott (New York: New Directions, 1970).

———, *Selected Essays* (New York: New Directions, 1954).

———, *Spring and All*, rpt. in *Imaginations*, ed. Webster Schott (New York: New Directions, 1970).

T. S. ELIOT

1. T. S. Eliot, *Complete Poems and Plays* (New York: Harcourt Brace, 1969), hereafter abbreviated *CPP.*
2. William Carlos Williams, *Autobiography of William Carlos Williams* (1951; reprint, New York: New Directions, 1967), 174.
3. Richard Wollheim, in *T. S. Eliot,* ed. S. Spender (London: Fontana, 1975), 31–34; (New York: Viking Press, 1976), 25, 27–29.
4. Letter to H. Munroe, in *Letters to E. P., 1907–1941* ed. D. D. Paige (London: Faber and Faber, 1950), 40.
5. Charles Baudelaire, *Selected Essays* (1932), 339.
6. Ibid., 344.
7. T. S. Eliot, *Selected Essays, 1917–1930* (1932; reprint New York: Harcourt Brace, 1950), 4.
8. Valerie Eliot, ed., *The Waste Land,* a facsimile and transcript of the original drafts including the annotations of Ezra Pound (New York: Harcourt Brace Jovanovich, 1971), 71.
9. W. F. Trotter, trans., "The Pensées of Pascal," introduction to Blaise Pascal, *Pensées* (London: J. M. Dent, 1908, and Everyman Library, 1931). See also T. S. Eliot, *Selected Essays.*
10. Letter to Spender: "Remembering Eliot," in *T. S. Eliot: The Man and His Work,* ed. Allen Tate (New York: Delacorte Press, 1966), 55–56.
11. T. S. Eliot, "The Function of Criticism," in T. S. Eliot, *Selected Essays, 1917–1932* (London: Faber and Faber, 1932), 14.
12. T. S. Eliot, *"Ulysses,* Order and Myth," in *Selected Prose,* ed. Frank Kermode (New York: Harcourt Brace, 1975), 175–78.
13. T. S. Eliot, *Selected Essays,* 246.
14. Ibid., "Dante," 212.
15. Ibid., 297.
16. Valerie Eliot, *The Waste Land.*
17. T. S. Eliot, in Foreword to Saint-John Perse, *Anabasis,* in Saint-John Perse, *Collected Poems* (Princeton: Princeton Univ. Press, Bollingen Series, 87, 1971), 676.
18. T. S. Eliot, *Selected Essays,* 332.
19. T. S. Eliot, *The Use of Poetry and the Use of Criticism* (London: Faber and Faber, 1933, and New York: Farrar, Straus & Giroux, 1965).
20. T. S. Eliot, *After Strange Gods* (London: Faber and Faber, 1934), 20.

21. Ibid.
22. T. S. Eliot, *On Poetry and Poets* (New York: Farrar, Straus & Cudahy, 1957), 32.
23. Interview in *Writers at Work,* Second Series, the *Paris Review* Interviews (New York: Viking, 1963).

HART CRANE

1. All quotations from Crane's poems are taken from *The Complete Poems and Selected Letters and Prose of Hart Crane,* ed. Brom Weber (New York: Doubleday, 1966). All page numbers refer to that edition unless otherwise noted. Page numbers preceded by *Letters* refer to *The Letters of Hart Crane,* ed. Brom Weber (New York: Hermitage House, 1952).
2. In this discussion of "Lachrymae Christi," and in the discussion, farther on, of the journey motif in *The Bridge,* I owe a great deal to the late Laurence Holland, who introduced me to Crane's poetry at Haverford College in 1963. As far as I know, Professor Holland never put his remarkable insights about Crane down on paper.

LANGSTON HUGHES

1. Langston Hughes, *The Big Sea* (New York: Knopf, 1940), 24; hereafter abbreviated *BS.*
2. Langston Hughes, "Genius Child," in *Selected Poems* (New York: Knopf, 1959), 83. All citations from *Selected Poems* are hereafter abbreviated *SP.*
3. Paul Laurence Dunbar, "Little Brown Baby," in *The Poetry of the Negro: 1746–1970,* ed. Langston Hughes and Arna Bontemps (New York: Doubleday, 1970), 40. Dunbar, "Sympathy," in *Poetry of the Negro,* 34.
4. "My Loves," Central High School *Monthly* 19 (April 1918): 13.
5. "Play-Toy Land," *Monthly* 20 (Jan. 1919): 12.
6. "A Song of the Soul of Central," *Monthly* 20 (Jan. 1919): 9–10.
7. "The Fascination of Cities," *Crisis* 31 (Jan. 1926): 138.
8. Carl Sandburg, "Nigger," *Complete Poems* (New York: Harcourt, Brace, Jovanovich, 1970), 23.
9. "My People," *Crisis* 24 (June 1922): 72.
10. Paul Laurence Dunbar, "The Poet," in *Complete Poems* (New York: Dodd, Mead, 1913), 191.
11. "Dear Lovely Death," *Opportunity* 8 (June 1930): 182.
12. "The White Ones," *Opportunity* 1 (March 1924): 68.
13. "Johannesburg Mines," *Messenger* 7 (Feb. 1925): 93.
14. "Tired," *New Masses* 6 (Feb. 1931): 4.
15. Langston Hughes, "Claude McKay: The Best" (1933); Ms. 29, Langston Hughes Papers, James Weldon Johnson Memorial Collection, Beinecke Library, Yale University.
16. "A New Song," *Crisis* 40 (March 1933): 59. "Goodbye Christ," *The Negro Worker* 2 (Nov.–Dec. 1932): 32.
17. "Let America Be America Again," *A New Song* (New York: International Workers Order, 1938), 9.
18. Langston Hughes, *Fine Clothes to the Jew* (New York: Knopf, 1927), n.p.; hereafter abbreviated *FC.*
19. Ralph Ellison, *Shadow and Act* (New York: New American Library, 1966), 249–50.
20. Samuel Charters, *The Legacy of the Blues* (New York: Da Capo), 22.
21. *New York Amsterdam News,* Feb. 5, 1927; *Pittsburgh Courier,* Feb. 5, 1927; *Chicago Whip,* Feb. 26, 1927.
22. *Chicago Daily News,* June 29, 1927.
23. *Opportunity* 4 (Feb. 1926): 74.
24. *The Guardian* (Manchester), Dec. 5, 1966.
25. *Légitime Défense* 1 (June 1, 1932): 12.
26. Langston Hughes, "Black Writers in a Troubled World," March 26, 1966; Ms. 3390, Langston Hughes Papers, Beinecke Library.

27. *Camden Evening Courier,* March 3, 1927.
28. Hughes to Carl Van Vechten, March 1, 1927; Carl Van Vechten Papers, James Weldon Johnson Collection, Beinecke Library.

ELIZABETH BISHOP

1. Letter to Anne Stevenson, first printed in her *Elizabeth Bishop* (New York: Twayne, 1966), 66. David Kalstone also cites this letter in his excellent essay on Bishop, *Five Temperaments* (New York: Oxford Univ. Press, 1977), 12–40.
2. For example, in 1948 Oscar Williams praised Bishop's "exquisite detail" and "charming little stained-glass bits," quoted in *Elizabeth Bishop and Her Art,* ed. Lloyd Schwartz and Sybil P. Estess (Ann Arbor: Univ. of Michigan Press, 1983), xvii; hereafter referred to as Schwartz and Estess.
3. All poetry citations are from Elizabeth Bishop, *The Complete Poems* (New York: Farrar, Straus & Giroux, and London: Chatto & Windus, 1983).
4. In an interview with Ashley Brown, Bishop said that her poem "The Weed" is modeled on Herbert's "Love-unknown" (Schwartz and Estess, 295), and Richard Howard (in a short comment reprinted in Schwartz and Estess, 208–09) sees "Love-unknown" as the model for "In the Waiting Room."
5. Schwartz and Estess, 298.
6. Luis Buñuel, *My Last Breath* (London: Jonathan Cape, 1984), chapter 1.
7. Richard Mullen, "Elizabeth Bishop's Surrealist Inheritance," *American Literature* 54 (March 1982): 63–80, notes similarities between Bishop's work and a number of surrealist texts, and also her nonsurrealist interest in the external world. Although, as Mullen and others have pointed out, Bishop acknowledged a specific debt to Ernst, none of the *frottages* of *Histoires Naturelles* depicts a monument or monumental image. Some, however, have a huge eye that looks out ambiguously from a wooden, block-printed sky.
8. See Elizabeth Bishop and Emanuel Brasil, eds., *An Anthology of Twentieth-Century Brazilian Poetry* (Middletown, Conn.: Wesleyan Univ. Press, 1972).
9. This biographical detail comes, like some others, from "The Art of Poetry XXVII: Elizabeth Bishop," *Paris Review* 80 (1981): 56–83 (interview with Elizabeth Spires). Bishop's translations of Jacob appeared in *Poetry,* May 1950.
10. Mary Ann Caws, *A Metapoetics of the Passage* (Hanover and London: New England Univ. Press, 1981). The translation of Breton's "Fata Morgana" is quoted from Caws.
11. André Breton, *Le Surréalisme et la peinture,* cited in *The Autobiography of Surrealism,* ed. Marcel Jean (New York: Viking Press, 1980), 198.
12. The range of the domestic and the strange in Bishop has been mapped in Helen Vendler's extensive review of *Geography III,* "Domestication, Domesticity, and the Otherworldly," first published in *World Literature Today I* (Winter 1977), reprinted in Vendler's *Part of Nature, Part of Us* (Cambridge, Mass.: Harvard Univ. Press, 1980), 97–110.
13. Sigmund Freud, "The 'Uncanny' " [*Das Unheimliche*] *Standard Edition,* vol. XVII, 219–52.
14. *Standard Edition,* vol. XVII, 225.
15. Elizabeth Bishop, *The Collected Prose* (New York: Farrar, Straus & Giroux, and London: Chatto & Windus, 1984), 121–56. All citations of Bishop's prose, unless otherwise indicated, are from this volume.
16. Bishop would have also known *Macunaíma,* the modernist, picaresque reworking by Mario de Andrade of a Brazilian folk tale (New York: Random House, 1984), trans. E. A. Goodland.
17. Elizabeth Bishop, *The Diary of "Helena Morley"* (New York: Farrar, Straus & Cudahy, 1957, and London: Victor Gollancz, 1958), 107; entry for March 14, 1894.
18. After the critical success of *North & South* in 1946, Bishop led the life of a respected poet, receiving fellowships and awards, e.g., a Guggenheim Fellowship in 1947; in 1949–50 the post of poetry consultant for the Library of Congress in Washington, D.C.; in 1956 the Pulitzer Prize for *Poems: North & South—A Cold Spring* (1955). In 1969 Bishop won the National Book Award for the somewhat prematurely titled *The Complete Poems.* Only in 1966, when she began to

spend most of the year back in the United States, did Bishop teach in a sustained way (at Harvard), and she never gave many readings of her poetry. These dates are derived from Bishop's own chronology prepared for *World Literature Today* 51 (Winter 1977), an issue devoted to Bishop and including several critical articles and homages.

19. Robert Lowell, from "Thomas, Bishop and Williams," in Schwartz and Estess, 187; this review first appeared in *Sewanee Review* 55 (Summer 1947): 97–99.
20. Ian Hamilton, *Robert Lowell: A Biography* (New York: Random House, 1982, and London: Faber, 1983), 134, hereafter referred to as Hamilton. The draft poem, "The Two Weeks' Vacation," in the Houghton Library, Harvard University, is also quoted by Hamilton, 238.
21. Schwartz and Estess, 199; the comments first appeared in *The Contemporary Poet as Artist and Critic*, Anthony Ostroff, ed., (Boston: Little, Brown), 107–10. Lowell wrote Bishop another homage in "For Elizabeth Bishop 4" in *History* and Bishop wrote for Lowell the meditative elegy "North Haven" in 1978.
22. Hamilton, 235.
23. Letter to Lowell December 14, 1957 (Houghton Library), reprinted in Hamilton, 233.
24. Robert Lowell, "After Enjoying Six or Seven Essays on Me," *Salmagundi* 37 (Spring 1977): 112–15; cited in Hamilton, 233. Lowell also acknowledged influences from Randall Jarrell and the younger poet W. D. Snodgrass.
25. Ann Winslow, ed., *Trial Balances* (New York: The Macmillan Company, 1935); this was Bishop's first publication in book form.
26. *Collected Prose,* 121–56.

ROBERT LOWELL

1. Quoted in Ian Hamilton, *Robert Lowell: A Biography* (New York: Random House, 1982). I have cited from the following editions of Lowell's poems: *Lord Weary's Castle* and *The Mills of the Kavanaughs* (New York: Meridian Books, 1961), abbreviated *LWC* and *MK; Life Studies* and *For the Union Dead* (New York: Farrar, Straus & Giroux, 1967), abbreviated *LS* and *FUD; Near the Ocean* (New York: Farrar, Straus & Giroux, 1971), abbreviated *NO; Notebook* (New York: Farrar, Straus & Giroux, 1971), abbreviated *NB; History* (New York: Farrar, Straus & Giroux, 1973), abbreviated *H; The Dolphin* (New York: Farrar, Straus & Giroux, 1973), abbreviated *D;* and *Day by Day* (New York: Farrar, Straus & Giroux, 1976), abbreviated *DD.*

SYLVIA PLATH

1. At Smith College and again at Cambridge, Plath was reading Woolf in the deliberate way she read writers she wanted to be influenced by—with Woolf, Plath was influenced by her suicide and her ways of dealing with recurrent depression as well as by her writing. "Bless her. I feel linked to her, somehow." Feb. 25, 1956 (part of a long entry on Woolf), *Journals,* 152; the May 20, 1959, entry shows Plath rejecting Woolf as "gossamer," literally and symbolically sterile, *Journals,* 305.
2. *The Colossus* (London: Heinemann, 1960, and New York: Knopf, 1962); the British edition includes several poems not found in the American edition, most importantly "Two Sisters of Persephone" and the seven-part "Poem for a Birthday," of which the American edition prints two poems, "Flute Notes from a Reed Pond" and "The Stones." *Crossing the Water* (London: Faber and Faber, 1971, and New York: Harper & Row, 1971), with differing contents in the British and American editions, represents the period between *The Colossus* and *Ariel. Ariel* (London: Faber and Faber, 1965, and New York: Harper & Row, 1966), also with differing contents, is a selection made by Ted Hughes based mainly upon a collection Plath was assembling at the time of her death. *Winter Trees* (London: Faber and Faber, 1971, and New York: Harper & Row, 1972), again with differing contents, is a second culling of work from the *Ariel* period, together with the verse play "Three Women," broadcast by the BBC in 1962. Despite *Ariel*'s sense of a drive towards release, it is not an organic collection; the chronologi-

cal *Collected Poems* (London: Faber and Faber, 1981, and New York, Harper & Row, 1982), edited with an introduction and valuable notes by Ted Hughes, shows the precise sequence of Plath's development. *Johnny Panic and the Bible of Dreams* (London: Faber and Faber, 1977, and New York: Harper & Row, 1978), with an introduction by Ted Hughes, gathers short stories written and (except for "Snow Blitz") published in magazines from 1956 to 1963. *The Bed Book* (London: Faber and Faber, 1966, with illustrations by Quentin Blake, and New York: Harper & Row, 1976, with illustrations by Emily Arnold McCully), an effort to break into the children's poetry market, was written in 1959.

3. There is not yet a Plath *Collected Letters* and her *Letters Home: Correspondence 1950–1963* (New York: Harper & Row, 1975, and London: Faber and Faber, 1976), edited and with a commentary by Plath's mother, Aurelia Schober Plath, has many editorial omissions. Plath's *Journals* (New York: Dial Press, 1982), edited by Ted Hughes and Frances McCullough, includes about a third of the surviving journals. (Two journal volumes covering the period from 1962 to a few days before Plath's death are missing, one destroyed by Hughes.) Nevertheless the *Journals,* written for Plath herself, offer an invaluable insight into Plath's struggle to clear the way for her poetry.
4. Plath felt a strong sense of rivalry with other women poets, particularly contemporaries: "Who rivals? Well, in history Sappho, Elizabeth Barrett Browning, Christina Rossetti, Amy Lowell, Emily Dickinson, Edna St. Vincent Millay—all dead. Now: Edith Sitwell and Marianne Moore, the aging giantesses, and poetic godmother Phyllis McGinley is out—light verse: she's sold herself. Rather: May Swenson, Isabella Gardner, and most close, Adrienne Cecile Rich—who will soon be eclipsed by these eight poems." *Journals* (March 28, 1958), 211. Later Plath was more accepting, possibly even influenced by Rich's example: "Read A. C. Rich today, finished her book of poems in half an hour: they stimulate me: they are easy, yet professional, full of infelicities and numb gesturings at something, but instinct with 'philosophy,' what I need." *Journals* (January 28, 1959), 293. Plath did have female mentors: her patroness, the popular novelist Olive Higgins Prouty, who endowed Plath's scholarship at Smith, her Smith professor Mary Ellen Chase, and Dorothea Krook at Cambridge. In *The Bell Jar,* however, Prouty is satirized as the absurdly genteel Philomena Guinea; also, "the famous woman poet at my college," a lesbian, "stared at me in horror" (232) when Esther says she wants to marry and have children. The one female figure to escape sabotage is Dr. Ruth Buescher, Plath's analyst in 1953 and again in 1957–59; she is the Dr. B of *The Journals* and the original for the wise Dr. Nolan in *The Bell Jar,* the psychiatrist who gives Esther permission to hate her mother.
5. Put simply, Plath put the man on a pedestal and then sought his approval, daughter-style. Plath "managed" Hughes, typing and retyping his poems, suggesting possible publication outlets and preparing the manuscript of *Hawk in the Rain* for the YMHA Poetry Center First Publication prize; she then wrote to her mother: "I am so happy *his* book is accepted *first.* It will make it so much easier when mine is accepted—if not by the Yale Series, then by some other place. I can rejoice then, much more, knowing Ted is ahead of me." *Letters* (Feb. 24, 1957), 297. This is one of several similar journal entries and letters; Plath's devastation when Hughes left her must have owed much to this huge but fixed role she had allotted him in her psychic economy.
6. Judith Kroll's *Chapters in a Mythology: The Poetry of Sylvia Plath* (New York: Harper & Row, 1976) offers a thorough and informed examination of Plath's use of the White Goddess imagery.
7. See C. S. Butler, "Poetry and the Computer: Some Quantitative Aspects of the Style of Sylvia Plath," *Proceedings of the British Academy,* Vol. 65 (1979), 291–312.
8. A. Alvarez has described Plath's dramatic reading aloud of "Daddy" and other poems in his memoir of her final days, *The Savage God* (London: Weidenfeld and Nicholson, 1971), 5–34. Elizabeth Hardwick's "On Sylvia Plath," in *Ariel Ascending: Writings about Sylvia Plath,* ed. Paul Alexander (New York: Harper & Row, 1985), 100–15, offers a pragmatic estimate of how differently these same phrases might sound today if Plath had not reinforced their drama by her death.
9. Margaret Dickie Uroff, *Sylvia Plath and Ted Hughes* (Urbana, Illinois: Univ. of Illinois Press, 1979), discusses Plath and Hughes's mutual influencing. However, the comparison she makes between Plath's "Wuthering Heights" and Hughes's "Wind" points to more differences than similarities.

10. Frances McCullough, "Editor's Note," *The Journals of Sylvia Plath* (New York: Ballantine, 1982), xi.
11. M. L. Rosenthal, *The New Poets: American and British Poetry Since World War II* (New York: Oxford Univ. Press, 1967); Rosenthal first used the term "confessional" in a 1959 review of Lowell's *Life Studies*, "Poetry as Confession," *The Nation* 190 (1959): 154–55.
12. "Read Freud's *Mourning and Melancholia* this morning after Ted left for the library. An almost exact description of my feelings and reasons for suicide: a transferred murderous impulse from my mother onto myself: the 'vampire' metaphor Freud uses, 'draining the ego': that is exactly the feeling I have getting in the way of my writing: Mother's clutch." *Journals*, 279.
13. See William Rubin, "De Chirico and Modernism," *De Chirico* (New York: Museum of Modern Art, 1982), 55–80, for a linking of Chirico with *depaysment* and with Rousseau's light and composition. Plath's "On the Decline of Oracles" (1957), which also alludes to the Swiss Romantic painter Arnold Böcklin, derives from Chirico's "The Enigma of the Oracle." Plath may have consulted James Thrall Soby's *Giorgio de Chirico* (New York: Museum of Modern Art, 1955) which points out that Böcklin's mythological images were a major formative influence on Chirico, or she may have sensed the connection on her own. "Snakecharmer" (1957) and "The Dream" derive from Rousseau paintings of the same titles. "Virgin in a Tree" and "Perseus: The Triumph of Wit over Suffering" derive from Klee etchings with the same titles; "The Ghost's Leavetaking" (1958) was originally "after Paul Klee"; "Battle-Scene: From the Comic-Operatic Fantasy 'The Seafarer' " derives not from the Old English poem but from a Klee painting. "Yadwigha, on a Red Couch, among Lilies" (1958) derives from Rousseau's painting.
14. Gilles Deleuze and Félix Guattari, *Anti-Oedipus: Capitalism and Schizophrenia* (Minneapolis: Univ. of Minnesota Press, 1983).

SUGGESTIONS FOR FURTHER READING

EMILY DICKINSON

Anderson, Charles R. *Emily Dickinson's Poetry: Stairway of Surprise.* New York: Holt, Rinehart and Winston, 1960.

Benfey, Christopher E. G. *Emily Dickinson and the Problem of Others.* Amherst: University of Massachusetts Press, 1984.

Cameron, Sharon. *Lyric Time: Dickinson and the Limits of Genre.* Baltimore: Johns Hopkins University Press, 1979.

Cody, John. *After Great Pain: The Inner Life of Emily Dickinson.* Cambridge, Mass: Harvard University Press, 1971.

Kazin, Alfred. *An American Procession.* New York: Alfred A. Knopf, 1984.

Keller, Karl. *The Only Kangaroo among the Beauty: Emily Dickinson and America.* Baltimore: Johns Hopkins University Press, 1979.

Kher, Inder Nath. *The Landscape of Absence: Emily Dickinson's Poetry.* New Haven: Yale University Press, 1974.

Leyda, Jay. *The Years and Hours of Emily Dickinson.* New Haven: Yale University Press, 1960.

McNeil, Helen. *Emily Dickinson.* New York: Pantheon, 1986.

Miller, Ruth. *The Poetry of Emily Dickinson.* Middletown, Conn.: Wesleyan University Press, 1968.

Porter, David. *Dickinson: The Modern Idiom.* Cambridge, Mass.: Harvard University Press, 1981.

Weisbuch, Robert. *Emily Dickinson's Poetry.* Chicago: University of Chicago Press, 1972.

Wells, Henry W. *Introduction to Emily Dickinson.* New York: Hendricks House, 1947.

Whicher, George. *This Was a Poet: A Critical Biography of Emily Dickinson.* New York: Scribner's, 1938.

Wolff, Cynthia Griffin. *Emily Dickinson.* New York: Alfred A. Knopf, 1986.

ROBERT FROST

In addition to the works cited in this essay:

Criticism and Biography

Brower, Reuben. *The Poetry of Robert Frost.* New York: Oxford University Press, 1963.

Poirier, Richard. *Robert Frost: The Work of Knowing.* New York: Oxford University Press, 1974.

Pritchard, William. *Frost: A Literary Life Reconsidered.* New York: Oxford University Press, 1984.

Other Materials

Kemp, John. *Robert Frost and New England: The Poet as Regionalist.* Princeton: Princeton University Press, 1979.

Mertins, Louis. *Robert Frost: Life and Talks-Walking.* Norman: University of Oklahoma Press, 1965.

Poirier, Richard. *A World Elsewhere.* New York: Oxford University Press, 1967.

WALLACE STEVENS

Bates, Milton, *Wallace Stevens: A Mythology of Self*. Berkeley: University of California Press, 1985.
Bloom, Harold. *Wallace Stevens.* Ithaca, N.Y.: Cornell University Press, 1977.
Brazeau, Peter. *Parts of a World: Wallace Stevens Remembered.* New York: Random House, 1983.
Doggett, Frank and Robert Buttel. *Wallace Stevens: A Celebration.* Princeton: Princeton University Press, 1979.
Stevens, Holly. *Souvenirs and Prophecies: The Young Wallace Stevens.* New York: Alfred A. Knopf, 1976.
Vendler, Helen. *Wallace Stevens: Words Chosen Out of Desire.* Nashville: University of Tennessee Press, 1984.

EZRA POUND

Kenner, Hugh. *The Pound Era.* Berkeley: University of California Press, 1971.
Pound, Ezra. *ABC of Reading.* New Haven: Yale University Press, 1934, and New York: New Directions, 1960.
———. *The Confucian Odes: The Classic Anthology Defined by Confucius.* Tr. E. Pound. New York: New Directions, 1954.
———. *Literary Essays of Ezra Pound.* Edited and with an introduction by T. S. Eliot. Norfolk, Conn.: New Directions, 1954.
———. *Selected Prose,* 1909–1965. Edited and with an introduction by William Cookson. London: Faber and Faber, 1973.

MARIANNE MOORE

In addition to the works cited in the essay:
Costello, Bonnie. *Marianne Moore: Imaginary Possessions.* Cambridge, Mass., and London: Harvard University Press, 1981.
Jarrell, Randall. *Poetry and the Age.* New York: Farrar, Straus and Giroux, 1953.
Kenner, Hugh. *A Homemade World: The American Modernist Writers.* New York: Alfred A. Knopf, 1975.
Marianne Moore Issue. *Twentieth-Century Literature.* 30 (Summer/Fall 1984).
Sargeant, Winthrop. "Humility, Concentration, and Gusto." *New Yorker* 32 (February 16, 1957), 38–73.
Slatin, John M. *The Savage's Romance: The Poetry of Marianne Moore.* University Park, Pa.: Pennsylvania State University Press, 1985.
———. "American Beauty: William Carlos Williams and Marianne Moore." In Oliphant, Dave, and Thomas Zigal, eds. *WCW & Others.* Austin, Texas: Harry Ransom Humanities Research Center, 1985, 49–73.
———. "Scarecrows and Curios." *Marianne Moore Newsletter* 1 (1977): 13–15.
Stapleton, Laurence. *Marianne Moore: The Poet's Advance.* Princeton: Princeton University Press, 1978.
Vendler, Helen. "Marianne Moore." In *Part of Nature, Part of Us: Modern American Poets.* Cambridge, Mass., and London: Harvard University Press, 1980, 59–76.
Willis, Patricia C., ed. *The Complete Prose of Marianne Moore*. New York: Elizabeth Sifton Books/Viking, 1986.

T. S. ELIOT

Works by T. S. Eliot

To Criticize the Critic, and Other Writings. New York: Farrar, Straus & Giroux, 1965.
Notes Towards a Definition of Culture. New York: Harcourt, Brace, 1949.

Works About T. S. Eliot

Ackroyd, Peter. *T. S. Eliot: A Life.* New York: Simon and Schuster, 1984.

Bush, Ronald. *T. S. Eliot: A Study in Character and Style.* New York: Oxford University Press, 1983.

Chace, William M. *The Political Identities of Ezra Pound and T. S. Eliot.* Stanford: Stanford University Press, 1973.

Gardner, Helen. *The Composition of the Four Quartets.* New York: Oxford University Press, 1978.

———, *The Art of T. S. Eliot.* New York: Dutton, 1950.

Gordon, Lyndall. *T. S. Eliot's Early Years.* New York: Oxford University Press, 1978.

Kenner, Hugh. *The Invisible Poet: T. S. Eliot.* New York: Harcourt Brace and World, 1968.

Litz, Walton. *Eliot in His Time.* Princeton: Princeton University Press, 1973.

Margolis, John D. *T. S. Eliot's Intellectual Development 1922–1939.* Chicago: University of Chicago Press, 1972.

Matthiessen, Francis Otto. *The Achievement of T. S. Eliot.* 3d ed. New York: Oxford University Press, 1959.

Smith, Grover Cleveland. *T. S. Eliot's Poetry and Plays: A Study in Sources and Meaning.* Chicago: University of Chicago Press, 1962.

Stead, C. K. *The New Poetic.* London: Hutchinson University Library, 1964.

HART CRANE

Blackmur, R. P. *Form and Value in Modern Poetry.* New York: Doubleday, 1957.

Dembo, L. S. *Hart Crane's Sanskrit Charge.* Ithaca: Cornell University Press, 1960.

Grossman, Allen. "Hart Crane and Poetry: A Consideration of Crane's Intense Poetics with Reference to 'The Return.' " *ELH* 48 (1981).

Horton, Philip. *Hart Crane: The Life of an American Poet.* New York: Viking, 1957.

Irwin, John T. "Naming Names: Hart Crane's 'Logic of Metaphor.' " *Southern Review* 11 (1975).

Leibowitz, Herbert. *Hart Crane.* New York: Columbia University Press, 1968.

Nietzsche, Friedrich. *The Birth of Tragedy and The Genealogy of Morals.* trans. Francis Golffing. New York: Doubleday, 1956.

Paul, Sherman. *Hart's Bridge.* Urbana: University of Illinois Press, 1972.

Tate, Allen. *The Man of Letters in the Modern World.* New York: Meridian Books, 1955.

Trachtenberg, Alan. *Brooklyn Bridge: Fact and Symbol.* Chicago: University of Chicago Press, 1979.

Unterecker, John. *Voyager: A Life of Hart Crane.* New York: Farrar, Straus & Giroux, 1969.

Weber, Brom. *Hart Crane.* New York: The Bodley Press, 1948.

Winters, Yvor. *In Defense of Reason.* New York: Swallow and Morrow, 1947.

LANGSTON HUGHES

Works by Langston Hughes

I Wonder As I Wander. New York: Holt, Rinehart and Winston, 1956. Autobiography.

Not Without Laughter. New York: Alfred A. Knopf, 1930. Novel.

The Ways of White Folks. New York: Alfred A. Knopf, 1934. Short stories.

The Best of Simple. New York: Hill and Wang, 1961. Short stories.

Good Morning Revolution: Uncollected Social Protest Writings by Langston Hughes, Edited by Faith Berry. New York: Lawrence Hill, 1973.

Works About Langston Hughes

Berry, Faith. *Langston Hughes: Before and Beyond Harlem.* Westport, Conn.; Lawrence Hill, 1983. Biography.

ELIZABETH BISHOP

Books by Elizabeth Bishop

Elizabeth Bishop, *The Complete Poems,* New York: Farrar, Straus & Giroux, and London: Chatto and Windus, 1983.

———. *The Collected Prose.* New York: Farrar, Straus & Giroux, and London: Chatto and Windus, 1984.

———. (ed. and tr.) *The Diary of "Helena Morley."* New York: Farrar, Straus and Cudahy, 1957, and London: Victor Gollancz, 1958, reprinted Virago Press, 1981.

——— and Emanuel Brasil, eds., *An Anthology of Twentieth-Century Brazilian Poetry.* Middletown, Conn.: Wesleyan University Press, 1972.

Works About Elizabeth Bishop

Costello, Bonnie. "Marianne Moore and Elizabeth Bishop: Friendship and Influence." *Twentieth Century Literature* 30 (Summer/Fall 1984), 30–149.

Kalstone, David. *Five Temperaments.* New York: Oxford University Press, 1977, 12–40.

Keller, Lynn. "Words Worth a Thousand Postcards: The Bishop/Moore Correspondence," *American Literature* 55 (Fall 1983), 405–29.

MacMahon, Candace W. *Elizabeth Bishop: A Bibliography.* Charlottesville: University Press of Virginia, 1980.

Motion, Andrew. *Elizabeth Bishop.* London: British Academy/Longwood Publications Group, 1986.

Mullen, Richard. "Elizabeth Bishop's Surrealist Inheritance." *American Literature* 54 (March 1982), 63–80.

Schwartz, Lloyd and Estess, Sybil P., eds. *Elizabeth Bishop and Her Art.* Ann Arbor: University of Michigan Press, 1983.

Stevenson, Anne. *Elizabeth Bishop.* New York: Twayne, 1966.

Vendler, Helen. "Domestication, Domesticity, and the Otherworldly." *Part of Nature, Part of Us.* Cambridge: Harvard University Press, 1980, 97–110.

World Literature Today 51 (Winter 1977), special issue devoted to Bishop with Bishop's own chronology and several critical articles and homages.

ROBERT LOWELL

Alvarez, A. "A Talk with Robert Lowell." *Encounter* 24 (February 1965): 39–43.

Axelrod, Steven Gould. *Robert Lowell: Life and Art.* Princeton: Princeton University Press, 1978.

Bell, Vereen M. *Robert Lowell: Nihilist as Hero.* Cambridge Mass.: Harvard University Press, 1982.

Thomas Parkinson, ed. *Robert Lowell: A Collection of Critical Essays.* Englewood Cliffs, N. J.: Prentice-Hall, 1968.

Staples, Hugh B. *Robert Lowell: The First Twenty Years.* New York: Farrar, Straus & Cudahy, 1962.

the chapters on Lowell in Helen Vendler's *Part of Nature, Part of Us: Modern American Poets.* Cambridge: Harvard University Press, 1980.

Williamson, Alan. *Pity The Monsters.* New Haven: Yale University Press, 1974.

Yenser, Stephen. *Circle to Circle: The Poetry of Robert Lowell.* Berkeley: University of California Press, 1975.

SYLVIA PLATH

Books by Sylvia Plath

The Bed Book. London: Faber and Faber, 1966, and New York: Harper & Row, 1966. Poetry for children.

The Bell Jar. London: Heinemann, 1963, and Faber and Faber, 1966, and New York: Harper & Row, 1971.

Collected Poems. Edited by Ted Hughes. London: Faber and Faber, 1981, and New York: Harper & Row, 1982. This volume contains the complete contents of *The Colossus, Crossing the Water, Winter Trees,* and *Ariel,* and also uncollected poems, juvenilia, and notes by Hughes.

Johnny Panic and the Bible of Dreams. Edited by Ted Hughes. London: Faber and Faber, 1977, and New York: Harper & Row, 1978.

The Journals of Sylvia Plath. Edited by Frances McCullough (Ted Hughes, consulting ed.) New York: The Dial Press, 1982.

Letters Home: Correspondence 1950–1963. Edited by Aurelia Schober Plath. New York: Harper & Row, 1975, and London: Faber and Faber, 1976.

Books About Sylvia Plath

Aird, Eileen. *Sylvia Plath.* New York: Harper & Row, 1973.

Alexander, Paul, ed. *Ariel Ascending.* New York: Harper & Row Colophon Books, 1985.

Kroll, Judith. *Chapters in a Mythology: The Poetry of Sylvia Plath.* New York: Harper & Row, 1976.

———. "Sylvia Plath." In *Notable American Women: The Modern Period,* edited by Barbara Sicherman and Carol Hurd Green. Cambridge: Harvard University Press, 1979, 548–51.

Lane, Gary, ed. *Sylvia Plath: New Views on the Poetry.* Baltimore and London: Johns Hopkins University Press, 1979.

——— and Maria Stevens. *Sylvia Plath: A Bibliography* Metuchen, N.J. and London: Scarecrow Press, 1978.

Newman, Charles, ed. *The Art of Sylvia Plath: A Symposium.* London: Faber and Faber, 1970.

Orr, Peter, ed. *The Poet Speaks.* London: Routledge & Kegan Paul, 1966, 167–72. Interview.

Rosenthal, M. L. *The New Poets: American and British Poetry since World War II.* New York: Oxford University Press, 1967.

Uroff, Margaret Dickie. *Sylvia Plath and Ted Hughes.* Urbana: University of Illinois Press, 1979.

Williamson, Alan. *Introspection and Contemporary American Literature.* Cambridge: Harvard University Press, 1984.

NOTES ON THE CONTRIBUTORS

CALVIN BEDIENT is professor of English at the University of California, Los Angeles. His books include *Eight Contemporary Poets* (Oxford University Press) and *In the Heart's Last Kingdom: Robert Penn Warren's Major Poetry* (Harvard University Press). His book-length study of T. S. Eliot's *The Waste Land* was published in 1986 by the University of Chicago Press.

ROBERT B. SEWALL was born in Albany, New York. He was graduated from Williams College and received a Ph.D. in English in 1933 from Yale University, where he taught from 1934–76. He is the author of *The Life of Emily Dickinson* (1974), for which he won the National Book Award for biography, and *The Lyman Letters: New Light on Emily Dickinson and Her Family* (1965); and also editor of *Emily Dickinson: A Collection of Critical Essays* (1963).

RICHARD POIRIER teaches English at Rutgers University and is the author of several books of literary and cultural criticism, including *Robert Frost: The Work of Knowing, The Performing Self,* and *A World Elsewhere.* He is editor of *Raritan Quarterly* and vice-president of The Library of America.

HELEN VENDLER is Kenan Professor of English literature at Harvard University, and poetry critic of *The New Yorker.* She is the author of books on Yeats, Stevens, Herbert, and Keats (all published by Harvard University Press). Her essays on modern American poets have been collected in *Part of Nature, Part of Us: Modern American Poets,* which won the National Book Critics Circle Prize in 1980. Her most recent book is *Wallace Stevens: Words Chosen Out of Desire* (University of Tennessee Press, 1985, rpt. Harvard University Press, 1986). She reviews contemporary poetry for many journals, and has edited *The Harvard Book of Contemporary American Poetry* (1986).

MARJORIE PERLOFF is Professor of English and Comparative Literature at Stanford University. Her books include *The Poetic Art of Robert Lowell* (1973), *Frank O'Hara: Poet among Painters* (1977), *The Poetics of Indeterminacy: Rimbaud to Cage* (1981), and *The Futurist Moment: Avant-Garde, Avant Guerre and the Language of Rupture* (1986). She is also editor of a collection of essays entitled *The Dance of the Intellect: Studies in the Pound Tradition* (1985).

HUGH KENNER is professor of English literature at The Johns Hopkins University. He has written many books on modern literature, including two on Ezra Pound, three on Joyce, two on Beckett, and one on T. S. Eliot. Among his other books is a study of Buckminster Fuller's mathematical equations.

JOHN M. SLATIN is associate professor of English at the University of Texas at Austin. His articles on Marianne Moore have appeared in various journals, and he is the author of *The Savage's Romance: The Poetry of Marianne Moore* (Pennsylvania State University Press, 1986). He is currently working on a cultural history of blindness entitled *The Imagination of Blindness.*

FRANK KERMODE, formerly professor at London and Cambridge universities, was recently at Columbia University. He is the author of several books, including *Romantic Image* (1957), *The Sense of an Ending* (1967), and *The Genesis of Secrecy* (1979). He was the editor of Eliot's *Selected Prose* (1975).

ALAN WILLIAMSON is professor of English at the University of California, Davis. He is the author of *Pity the Monsters: The Political Vision of Robert Lowell, Introspection and Contemporary Poetry,* and a book of poems, *Presence.*

ARNOLD RAMPERSAD is professor of English and American literature at Rutgers University. He is the author of *The Art and Imagination of W.E.B. DuBois* and many essays and reviews on Afro-American writing. The first volume of his two-part biography of Langston Hughes was published in 1986 by Oxford University Press.

VEREEN BELL is associate professor and chairman of the Department of English at Vanderbilt University. He is the author of *Robert Lowell: Nihilist as Hero* (Harvard University Press) and *The Achievement of Cormac McCarthy* (forthcoming).

HELEN MCNEIL is lecturer in American literature and film at the University of East Anglia, Norwich, England. She writes on American literature and broadcasts regularly on BBC Three. Her critical study *Emily Dickinson* was published by Virago Press (Britain) and Pantheon Books in 1986.

INDEX

LIST OF ILLUSTRATIONS

The New York Center for Visual History and Helen Vendler would like to thank those who kindly supplied photographs for reproduction in this book.

p. viii Walt Whitman in his later years. Library of Congress: Prints and Photographs Division. p. xi The New York Armory Show, 1913. Walt Kuhn Papers, Archives of American Art, Smithsonian Institution. p. xiv The Others, April 1916. Reproduced with the permission of the Poetry/Rare Books Collection, University Libraries, State University of New York at Buffalo. p. xv The Others, April 1916. Reproduced with the permission of the Poetry/Rare Books Collection, University Libraries, State University of New York at Buffalo. p. xvii W.E.B. DuBois. Schomburg Center for Research in Black Culture, The New York Public Library, Astor, Lenox and Tilden Foundations. p. xviii Countee Cullen. Schomburg Center for Research in Black Culture, The New York Public Library, Astor, Lenox and Tilden Foundations. p. xxi Zora Neale Hurston. Collection of American Literature, The Beinecke Rare Book and Manuscript Library, Yale University. p. xxii Sylvia Plath and Marianne Moore, 1955. Photographer: Gordon N. Converse. Courtesy of the *Christian Science Monitor;* from the collection of The Rosenbach Museum and Library. p. xxv William Carlos Williams and Ezra Pound. Photograph by Richard Avedon. Copyright © 1958 by Richard Avedon Inc. All rights reserved. p. xxvi Elizabeth Bishop and Robert Lowell, Rio de Janeiro, 1962. Photograph by Paulo Muñiz. Courtesy Vassar College Library. p. xxvii John Keats. Picture Collection, The New York Public Library, Astor, Lenox and Tilden Foundations. p. xxviii William Shakespeare. Picture Collection, The New York Public Library, Astor, Lenox and Tilden Foundations. p. xxix Elizabeth Barrett Browning. By permission of the Houghton Library. p. xxix Robert Browning. Library of Congress: Prints and Photographs Division.

p. 2 Holograph page by Walt Whitman. Notes for poem "Crossing Brooklyn Ferry." Library of Congress: Prints and Photograph Division. p. 3 Walt Whitman from the frontispiece of the first edition of *Leaves of Grass,* 1855. Rare Books and Manuscripts Division, The New York Public Library, Astor, Lenox and Tilden Foundations. p. 4 Ralph Waldo Emerson. Library of Congress: Prints and Photographs Division. p. 11 Walt Whitman, 1854. Rare Books and Manuscripts Division, The New York Public Library, Astor, Lenox and Tilden Foundations. p. 14 "Spirit of the Frontier, 1872" also known as "Westward Ho" or "Manifest Destiny." Artist: John Gast. Library of Congress: Prints and Photographs Division. From *American Heritage* Picture Collection. p. 19 *New York Sunday Dispatch,* 25 November 1849. Library of Congress: Prints and Photographs Division. p. 21 Interior view of Niblo's Garden Theatre. Picture Collection, The New York Public Library, Astor, Lenox and Tilden Foundations. p. 23 Frederic Edwin Church: *Niagra.* In the collection of The Corcoran Gallery of Art, Museum Purchase. p. 26 Walt Whitman, ca. 1849. Library of Congress: Prints and Photographs Division. pp. 30, 31 Illustrations from the *Aurora,* Paterson Free Public Library. p. 32 "Nude Model Before Curtain," by Thomas Eakins. Philadelphia Museum of Art: Bequest of Mark Lutz. p. 35 Bierstadt, Albert: *Among the Sierra Nevada Mountains, California,* 1868, oil on canvas, 72 × 120 in. (183.0 × 305.0 CM), 1977.107.1; National Museum of American Art, Smithsonian Institution; bequest of Helen Huntington Hull. p. 38 Dead Civil War soldier. Library of Congress: Prints and Photographs Division. p. 41 Army hospital during the Civil War. Library of Congress: Prints and Photographs Division. p. 43 Abraham Lincoln. Library of Congress: Prints and Photographs Division. p. 46 Walt Whitman's birthplace. Library of Congress: Prints and Photographs Division. p. 48 Walt Whitman in Camden. Photograph by William Reeder. Hirshhorn Museum and Sculpture Garden, Smithsonian Institution, transferred from HMSG Archives, 1983.

p. 50 Holograph page of "My life had stood . . ." from *The Complete Poems of Emily Dickinson,* edited by Thomas H. Johnson. Copyright 1914, 1929, 1935, 1942 by Martha Dickinson Bianchi; copyright © renewed 1957, 1963 by Mary L. Hampson. Reprinted by permission of Little, Brown and Company. From the collection of the Houghton Library. p. 52 Emily Dickinson's signature. From *Years and Hours of Emily Dickinson,* by Jay Leyda. p. 52 Daguerreotype of Emily Dickinson. By permission of the Trustees of Amherst College. p. 53 The Dickinson homestead. Courtesy of the Jones Library, Inc., Amherst, Massachusetts. p. 58 First Congregational Church, Amherst. Courtesy of the Jones Library, Inc., Amherst, Massachusetts. p. 63 Holograph page of "The soul selects . . ." reprinted by permission of the publishers and the Trustees of Amherst College from *The Poems of Emily Dickinson,* Thomas H. Johnson, ed., Cambridge, Mass.: The Belknap Press of Harvard University Press, copyright 1951, © 1955, 1979, 1983 by the President and Fellows of Harvard College. From the collection of the Houghton Library. p. 66 Susan Gilbert Dickinson. By permission of the Houghton Library. p. 66 Holograph pages of "Safe in their Alabaster Chambers . . ." Reprinted by permission of the Houghton Library. p. 68 T. W. Higginson. From *Years and Hours of Emily Dickinson,* by Jay Leyda. p. 74 Holograph page of "I'm ceded—I've stopped . . ." reprinted by permission of the publishers and the Trustees of Amherst College from *The Poems of Emily Dickinson,* Thomas H. Johnson, ed., Cambridge, Mass.: The Belknap Press of Harvard University Press, copyright 1951, © 1955, 1979, 1983 by the President and Fellows of Harvard College. p. 80 Nineteenth-century interior. Courtesy of the Jones Library, Inc., Amherst, Massachusetts. p. 84 Props used in the *Voices & Visions* film *Emily Dickinson* from the collection of The New York Center for Visual History. p. 88 Footpath between Dickinson homestead and the Evergreens. By permission of the Houghton Library.

p. 90 Excerpt of letter from Robert Frost to John Bartlett. Courtesy of the Estate of Robert Frost. From the Robert Frost Collection, University of Virginia Library, Manuscripts Department. p. 92 Elinor Miriam White, 1895. Courtesy of the Estate of Robert Frost. Robert Frost Collection, University of Virginia Library, Manuscripts Department. p. 92 Robert Lee Frost, 1895. George H. Browne, Robert Frost Collection, Plymouth State College and Dartmouth College Library. p. 96 William James. Library of Congress: Prints and Photographs Division. p. 98 A scene from the *Voices & Visions* film *Robert Frost.* p. 103 Stone wall. The Bettmann Archive. p. 106 Edward Thomas. Mysanwy Thomas. p. 109 Robert Frost, ca. 1915. Dartmouth College Library. p. 112 Postcard of Lake Willoughby, Vermont. From the collection of Robert Carnevale. p. 117 Frost family. George H. Browne, Robert Frost Collection, Plymouth State College. p. 118 Photograph "At Biarritz" by Alfred Stieglitz, 1890. The Alfred Stieglitz Collection, the National Gallery of Art, Washington, D.C. p. 120 Robert Frost at podium. Dartmouth College Library.

p. 122 Typescript page "From the Journal of Crispin" from *The Collected Poems of Wallace Stevens.* Copyright 1954 by Wallace Stevens. Reprinted by permission of Alfred A. Knopf, Inc. From the collection of American Literature, The Beinecke Rare Book and Manuscript Library, Yale University. p. 124 Wallace Stevens, 1900. Reproduced courtesy of the Henry E. Huntington Library, San Marino, California. p. 127 Florida swamp. The Bettmann Archive. p. 130 Wallace Stevens, 1916. Courtesy of Holly Stevens. p. 135 Wallace Stevens, 1922. Reproduced courtesy of the Henry E. Huntington Library, San Marino, California. p. 139 "Village Carnival" by Paul Klee. Philadelphia Museum of Art: The Louise and Walter Arensberg Collection. p. 142 Wallace Stevens at Hartford Accident and Indemnity Company, 1938. Courtesy of Hartford Insurance Group. p. 146 "Still Life" by Pierre Tal Coat. Watkinson Library, Trinity College Library. p. 150 George Santayana. The Bettmann Archive. p. 153 Wallace Stevens, 1951. Reproduced courtesy of the Henry E. Huntington Library, San Marino, California.

p. 156 Typescript page "Between Walls." William Eric Williams and Paul H. Williams. Reprinted by permission of New Directions Publishing Corporation, Agents. From the Poetry/Rare Books Collection, University Libraries, State University of New York at Buffalo. p. 158 William Carlos Williams. William E. and Paul H. Williams. p. 162 Elena Hoheb Williams. Collection of American Literature, The Beinecke Rare Book and Manuscript Library, Yale University. pp. 168, 169 *291,* 1915. Collection of American Literature, The Beinecke Rare Book and Manuscript Library, Yale University. p. 171 "Nude Descending a Staircase #2" by Marcel Duchamp. Philadelphia Museum of Art: The Louise and Walter Arensberg Collection. p. 176 *Kora in Hell Improvisations* book cover. William E. and Paul H. Williams. p. 178 William Carlos Williams outside his office. William E. and Paul H. Williams. p. 179 Prescription pad. Reproduced with the permission of the Poetry/Rare Books Collection, University Libraries, State University of New York at Buffalo. p. 183 John Marin. *Region of Brooklyn Bridge Fantasy.* Watercolor on paper, 18¾ × 22¼ inches. Collection of Whitney Museum of American Art. Purchase. Acq.#49.8. p. 187 William Carlos Williams with patient. Eve Arnold/Magnum Photos. p. 195 "Lackawanna Station, Paterson NJ, 1968." Photograph by George Tice, courtesy of The Witkin Gallery, Inc. p. 197 Passaic Falls. Paterson Museum, Paterson, New Jersey. p. 202 William Carlos Williams. Eve Arnold/Magnum Photos.

p. 204 Typescript page. Ezra Pound, "Pull Down the Vanity." Copyright © 1987 by the Trustees of the Ezra Pound Literary Trust. Reprinted by permission of New Directions Publishing Corporation, Agents. From the Collection of American Literature, The Beinecke Rare Book and Manuscript Library, Yale University. p. 206 Ezra Pound. Collection of American Literature, The Beinecke Rare Book and Manuscript Library, Yale University. p. 209 Ezra Pound, 1913. Photograph by Alvin Langdon Coburn. International Museum of Photography at George Eastman House. p. 213 Announcement for *Blast,* 1914. p. 214 Henri Gaudier-Brzeska working on *Hieratic Head,* ca. 1914. p. 218 Castle at Altaforte from the *Voices & Visions* film *Ezra Pound/American Odyssey.* p. 220 "Summer

Mountains" by Ch'u Ting. The Metropolitan Museum of Art, Gift of the Dillon Fund, 1973 (1973.120.1). p. 225 George Antheil and Olga Rudge, 1920. Courtesy of Olga Rudge. p. 228 Lady playing the cithara. The Metropolitan Museum of Art, Rogers Fund, 1903 (03.13.5). p. 230 American Disciplinary Training Center, Pisa. U.S. Army photograph MM-46-25163. p. 231 Fresco from Schifanoia Palace, Ferrara. Courtesy of Comune Di Ferrara, Musei Civici D'Arte Antica, Ferrara, Italy. p. 236 Ezra Pound in the medical compound of the American Disciplinary Training Center, Pisa. U.S. Army photograph. p. 238 Ezra Pound in an art gallery, Venice, ca. 1967. Photograph by Horst Tappe. p. 240 Ezra Pound in a *tragherio*, Venice, 1963. Photograph by Horst Tappe.

p. 242 Holograph page of "An Octopus" used by permission of Clive E. Driver, Literary Executor of the Estate of Marianne C. Moore. From the collection of The Rosenbach Museum and Library. p. 244 Marianne Moore, 1924. The Rosenbach Museum and Library. p. 250 Female argonaut. Miami Seaquarium. p. 254 "Study of Gneiss Rock at Glenfinlas" by John Ruskin. Ashmolean Museum, Oxford. p. 259 BIRD, BEAST OR FISH? Photograph reproduced in the *New York Herald Tribune*, January 26, 1930. p. 262 Egyptian bottle in the shape of a fish. Courtesy of the Trustees of the British Museum. p. 265 Marianne Moore with her mother, 1938. The Rosenbach Museum and Library. p. 268 Lucas Cranach the Elder, German 1472–1553, "Adam and Eve," 1528. Oil on panel, h: 22⅝; w: 13¾. Acc# 62.279. Copyright © 1987 The Detroit Institute of Arts, gift of Mr. and Mrs. Henry Ford II. p. 278 La Fontaine, 1668. Picture Collection, The New York Public Library, Astor, Lenox and Tilden Foundations. p. 274 Watercolor of Marianne Moore's desk. Robert Andrew Parker.

p. 276 Typescript page of "Words for an Old Man" reprinted by permission of Mrs. Valerie Eliot and Faber and Faber Ltd. Copyright © 1987 by Valerie Eliot. From the collection of the Houghton Library. p. 278 T. S. Eliot. Courtesy of Mrs. Valerie Eliot. From the collection of the Houghton Library. p. 281 Charlotte Champe Eliot. Courtesy of Mrs. Valerie Eliot. From the collection of the Houghton Library. p. 284 The Eliots' St. Louis parlor. Courtesy of Mrs. Valerie Eliot. From the collection of the Houghton Library. p. 287 Gloucester, Massachusetts. The Bettmann Archive p. 289 Charles Baudelaire. Photograph by Carjat. International Museum of Photography at George Eastman House. p. 294 T. S. Eliot at his desk at Faber and Faber. Courtesy of Mrs. Valerie Eliot. From the collection of the Houghton Library. p. 301 T. S. Eliot with actors, 1951. BBC-HPL/The Bettmann Archive. p. 304 T. S. Eliot and others, 1960. Mark Gerson, photographer. p. 307 Anglican church at Little Gidding. Photo Precision Ltd., Huntington. p. 310 Western *campanile* of St. Paul's after bombing raid. Cecil Beaton photograph, courtesy of Sotheby's, London.

p. 312 Typescript page "Voyages II." Hart Crane Papers, Rare Book and Manuscript Library, Columbia University. p. 314 Hart Crane, 1916. Hart Crane Papers, Rare Book and Manuscript Library, Columbia University. p. 314 Hart Crane, 1931. William H. Wright and Margaret Aikin Wright. p. 318 Hart Crane's home in Cleveland. Courtesy of the Ohio State University Libraries. p. 322 Hart Crane, Allen Tate and William Slater Brown, 1925. Hart Crane Papers, Rare Book and Manuscript Library, Columbia University. p. 325 Film still from *The Kid*. The Bettmann Archive. p. 328 Hart Crane's notebook. Hart Crane Papers, Rare Book and Manuscript Library, Columbia University. p. 331 Emil Opffer. A thanks to Peter Kraft-Lund and family. p. 334 Hart Crane. Hart Crane Papers, Rare Book and Manuscript Library, Columbia University. p. 337 Charles Sheeler, American, 1883–1965. *Rolling Power*, 1939. Oil on canvas, 15 × 30 in. (38.1 × 76.2 cm.). Smith College Museum of Art, Northampton, Massachusetts. Purchased 1940. p. 340 Joseph Stella. *The Brooklyn Bridge: Variation on an Old Theme* (1939). Oil, 70 × 42 inches. Collection of Whitney Museum of American Art. Purchase. Acq. #42.15. pp. 344, 345 Postcard of Taxco Cathedral with verso. From Hart Crane to Solomon M. Grunberg 1931 (?). Hart Crane Papers, Rare Book and Manuscript Library, Columbia University. p. 346 Hart Crane. Photograph by Walker Evans. Hart Crane Papers, Rare Book and Manuscript Library, Columbia University. p. 350 Herman Melville, 1868. Mrs. Eleanor Melville Metcalf.

p. 352 Holograph page of "The Weary Blues" from *Selected Poems of Langston Hughes*. Copyright © 1959 by Langston Hughes. Reprinted by permission of Alfred A. Knopf, Inc. From the collection of the Schomburg Center for Research in Black Culture, The New York Public Library, Astor, Lenox and Tilden Foundations. p. 354 Langston Hughes, 1920. Collection of American Literature, The Beinecke Rare Book and Manuscript Library, Yale University. p. 356 Sheridan Leary. Library of Congress: Prints and Photographs Division. p. 361 Carl Sandburg. Library of Congress: Prints and Photographs Division. p. 365 Jacket cover for *The Weary Blues* by Langston Hughes. Copyright 1926 by Alfred A. Knopf, Inc., and renewed 1954 by Langston Hughes. Reprinted by permission of the publisher. From the Collection of American Literature, The Beinecke Rare Book and Manuscript Library, Yale University. p. 368 Revue Nègre poster, 1925. The Bettmann Archive. p. 368 Bessie Smith. The Bettmann Archive. p. 369 Fats Waller. Schomburg Center for Research in Black Culture, The New York Public Library, Astor, Lenox and Tilden Foundations. p. 373 Harlem belles, 1920s. Schomburg Center for Research in Black Culture, The New York Public Library, Astor, Lenox and Tilden Foundations. p. 377 Langston Hughes, 1930. Milton Meltzer. Schomburg Center for Research in Black Culture, The New York Public Library, Astor, Lenox and Tilden Foundations. p. 378 "Summer Magic" by Ellis Wilson. 200S-HN-WIL(E)-41, National Archives. p. 380 Billie Holiday. Photograph by Robin Carson. Ole Brask Collection. p. 383 The wife of an evicted sharecropper, 1939. Photograph by Rothstein. Library of Congress: Prints and Photographs Division. p. 385 Revival meeting. Library of Congress: Prints and Photographs Division. p. 386 Musicians in the back of a car. Library of Congress: Prints and Photographs Division. p. 391 "Red Jackson—Harlem Gang Leader." Photograph by Gordon Parks. p. 392 Langston Hughes signing autographs. Moorland-Spingarn Research Center, Howard University.

p. 394 Holograph page of "Arrival at Santos" by Elizabeth Bishop courtesy Vassar College Library. Copyright the Estate of Elizabeth Bishop. By permission of the Estate of Elizabeth Bishop, Executrix Alice Methfessel. p. 396 Elizabeth Bishop, age twelve. Courtesy Vassar College Library. By permission of the Estate of Elizabeth Bishop, Executrix Alice Methfessel. p. 399 Great Village, Nova Scotia. Courtesy Vassar College Library. By permission of the Estate of Elizabeth Bishop, Executrix Alice Methfessel. p. 402 Illustration from *Vassarion* (yearbook), 1934. Courtesy Vassar College Library. p. 404 Postcard of mountains of Therezopolis, Brazil. Courtesy Vassar College Library. By permission of the Estate of Elizabeth Bishop, Executrix Alice Methfessel. p. 408 Amazon River port, 1961. Photograph by Elizabeth Bishop. By permission of the Estate of Elizabeth Bishop, Executrix Alice Methfessel. p. 413 *Robinson Crusoe*, frontispiece, 1719. Picture Collection, The New York Public Library, Astor, Lenox and Tilden Foundations. p. 416 Elizabeth Bishop. Photo by J. L. Castel, Brazil, 1954. Used by arrangement with Farrar, Strauss and Giroux, Inc. p. 418 1924 map of Nova Scotia. Map Division, The New York Public Library, Astor, Lenox and Tilden Foundations. p. 423 Untitled construction by Joseph Cornell. Mr. and Mrs. Joseph R. Shapiro. p. 424 Watercolor by Elizabeth Bishop. By permission of the Estate of Elizabeth Bishop, Executrix Alice Methfessel.

p. 426 Typescript page of "Skunk Hour" by Robert Lowell reproduced with permission of the Estate of Robert Lowell. From the collection of the Houghton Library. p. 428 Robert Lowell. By permission of the Houghton Library. p. 430 John Lowell. With the permission of the President and Fellows of Harvard College. p. 430 James Russell Lowell. Picture Collection, The New York Public Library, Astor, Lenox and Tilden Foundations. p. 431 Percival Lowell. Lowell Observatory photograph. p. 434 Jonathan Edwards. Picture Collection, The New York Public Library, Astor, Lenox and Tilden Foundations. p. 437 Charlotte Winslow, 1915. Courtesy of Christina Lowell Brazelton. p. 438 Robert Traill Spence Lowell, Sr., and Jr., ca. 1920. Courtesy of Christina Lowell Brazelton. p. 442 The Winslow family graveyard. By permission of the Houghton Library. p. 447 Robert Lowell and Elizabeth Hardwick, 1949. Courtesy of Elizabeth Hardwick. p. 451 Randall Jarrell, Robert Lowell and Peter Taylor, 1948. University Archives, University of North Carolina at Greensboro, Randall Jarrell Collection. p. 458 Saint Gauden's monument. From *Lay This Laurel*, copyright © 1973 by The Eakins Press Foundation. Photographs by Richard Benson. p. 462 Robert Lowell, 1967. Photo copyright © 1967 by Jill Krementz. p. 465 Vermeer: Artist in His Studio. Bildarchiv Foto Marburg/Art Resource, New York.

p. 468 Holograph page of "Ariel." Reproduced from the Sylvia Plath Collection in the Smith College Library, Rare Book Room. Copyright © 1987 by Ted Hughes. p. 470 Sylvia Plath, 1950. Courtesy of Mrs. Aurelia S. Plath. p. 474 Page from *Mademoiselle* magazine, 1953. Courtesy *Mademoiselle*. Copyright 1953 (© renewed in 1981) by The Condé Nast Publications, Inc. From the collection of Lilly Library, Indiana University. p. 475 Sylvia Plath's "Jobiography." Courtesy *Mademoiselle*. Copyright 1953 (© renewed in 1981) by The Condé Nast Publications, Inc. From the collection of Lilly Library, Indiana University. p. 478 Glascock Poetry Award, 1955. Courtesy of the *Christian Science Monitor*. From the Collection of Smith College Library, Rare Book Room. p. 481 D. H. Lawrence. The Bettmann Archive. p. 481 Virginia Woolf. The Bettmann Archive. p. 484 Title page and illustration from "Bumblebees and Their Ways." Used with permission of Macmillan Publishing Company from *Bumblebees and Their Ways* by Otto Emil Plath. Copyright 1934 by Macmillan Publishing Company, © renewed 1962 by Aurelia S. Plath. From the collection of New York University, Elmer Holmes Bobst Library. p. 485 Holograph page of "Stings." Reproduced from the Sylvia Plath Collection in the Smith College Library, Rare Book Room. Copyright © 1987 by Ted Hughes. p. 488 Ted Hughes and Sylvia Plath, 1959. Courtesy *Mademoiselle*. Copyright © 1959 by The Condé Nast Publications, Inc. p. 491 Sylvia Plath with her children. Courtesy of Mrs. Aurelia S. Plath. p. 494 Sylvia Plath. Courtesy of Mrs. Aurelia S. Plath.